Bilingual Dict

English-Pashto
Pashto-English
Dictionary

Compiled by
Amir Khan

STAR Foreign Language BOOKS

© Publishers

ISBN : 978 1 908357 67 0

This Edition : 2023

Published by

STAR Foreign Language BOOKS

a unit of
Star Books
56, Langland Crescent
Stanmore HA7 1NG, U.K.
info@starbooksuk.com
www.bilingualbooks.co.uk

Printed in India at
Star Print-O-Bind, New Delhi-110 020

About this Dictionary

Developments in science and technology today have narrowed down distances between countries, and have made the world a small place. A person living thousands of miles away can learn and understand the culture and lifestyle of another country with ease and without travelling to that country. Languages play an important role as facilitators of communication in this respect.

To promote such an understanding, **STAR Foreign Language BOOKS** has planned to bring out a series of bilingual dictionaries in which important English words have been translated into other languages, with Roman transliteration in case of languages that have different scripts. This is a humble attempt to bring people of the word closer through the medium of language, thus making communication easy and convenient.

Under this series of *one-to-one dictionaries*, we have published almost 57 languages, the list of which has been given in the opening pages. These have all been compiled and edited by teachers and scholars of the relative languages.

Publishers

Bilingual Dictionaries in this Series

English-Afrikaans / Afrikaans-English	Abraham Venter
English-Albanian / Albanian-English	Theodhora Blushi
English-Amharic / Amharic-English	Girun Asanke
English-Arabic / Arabic-English	Rania-al-Qass
English-Bengali / Bengali-English	Amit Majumdar
English-Bosnian / Bosnian-English	Boris Kazanegra
English-Bulgarian / Bulgarian-English	Vladka Kocheshkova
English-Burmese (Myanmar) / Burmese (Myanmar)-English	Kyaw Swar Aung
English-Cambodian / Cambodian-English	Engly Sok
English-Cantonese / Cantonese-English	Nisa Yang
English-Chinese (Mandarin) / Chinese (Mandarin)-Eng	Y. Shang & R. Yao
English-Croatian / Croatain-English	Vesna Kazanegra
English-Czech / Czech-English	Jindriska Poulova
English-Danish / Danish-English	Rikke Wend Hartung
English-Dari / Dari-English	Amir Khan
English-Dutch / Dutch-English	Lisanne Vogel
English-Estonian / Estonian-English	Lana Haleta
English-Farsi / Farsi-English	Maryam Zaman Khani
English-French / French-English	Aurélie Colin
English-Georgian / Georgina-English	Eka Goderdzishvili
English-Gujarati / Gujarati-English	Sujata Basaria
English-German / German-English	Bicskei Hedwig
English-Greek / Greek-English	Lina Stergiou
English-Hindi / Hindi-English	Sudhakar Chaturvedi
English-Hungarian / Hungarian-English	Lucy Mallows
English-Italian / Italian-English	Eni Lamllari
English-Japanese / Japanese-English	Miruka Arai & Hiroko Nishimura
English-Korean / Korean-English	Mihee Song
English-Latvian / Latvian-English	Julija Baranovska
English-Levantine Arabic / Levantine Arabic-English	Ayman Khalaf
English-Lithuanian / Lithuanian-English	Regina Kazakeviciute
English-Malay / Malay-English	Azimah Husna
English-Nepali / Nepali-English	Anil Mandal
English-Norwegian / Norwegian-English	Samuele Narcisi
English-Pashto / Pashto-English	Amir Khan
English-Polish / Polish-English	Magdalena Herok
English-Portuguese / Portuguese-English	Dina Teresa
English-Punjabi / Punjabi-English	Teja Singh Chatwal
English-Romanian / Romanian-English	Georgeta Laura Dutulescu
English-Russian / Russian-English	Katerina Volobuyeva
English-Serbian / Serbian-English	Vesna Kazanegra
English-Sinhalese / Sinhalese-English	Naseer Salahudeen
English-Slovak / Slovak-English	Zuzana Horvathova
English-Slovenian / Slovenian-English	Tanja Turk
English-Somali / Somali-English	Ali Mohamud Omer
English-Spanish / Spanish-English	Cristina Rodriguez
English-Swahili / Swahili-English	Abdul Rauf Hassan Kinga
English-Swedish / Swedish-English	Madelene Axelsson
English-Tagalog / Tagalog-English	Jefferson Bantayan
English-Tamil / Tamil-English	Sandhya Mahadevan
English-Thai / Thai-English	Suwan Kaewkongpan
English-Tigrigna / Tigrigna-English	Tsegazeab Haiiegebriel
English-Turkish / Turkish-English	Nagme Yazgin
English-Ukrainian / Ukrainian-English	Katerina Volobuyeva
English-Urdu / Urdu-English	S. A. Rahman
English-Vietnamese / Vietnamese-English	Hoa Hoang
English-Yoruba / Yoruba-English	O. A. Temitope

STAR Foreign Language BOOKS

ENGLISH-PASHTO

A

a *a.* يو yaw
aback *adv.* برته beyrta
abaction *n* په pa sat
abactor *n* تلونکی pa sat tloonkay
abandon *v.t.* پريوول preykhowal
abase *v.t.* يول teetawal
abasement *n* سپکوالی spakwalay
abash *v.t.* شرمول sharmawal
abate *v.t.* لول lagawal
abatement *n.* لونه lagawana
abbey *n.* خانقا khanqa
abbreviate *v.t.* لنول landawal
abbreviation *n* لنيز landeez
abdicate *v.t,* پريودل preykhodal
abdication *n* کيدل وه gokha keydal
abdomen *n* خه kheyta
abdominal *a.* يیز ه geyda yeez
abduct *v.t.* تتول takhtawal
abduction *n* تتونه takhtawana
abed *adv.* کی بستر په pa bistar ki
aberrance *n.* بلارتوب bey laritob
abet *v.t.* لمسول lamsawal
abetment *n.* لمسون lamsoon
abeyance *n.* ال tal
abhor *v.t.* کرکهکول kraka kawal
abhorrence *n.* کرکه kraka
abide *v.i* اوسدل oseydal
abiding *a* پايدار paydar

ability *n* قابليت qabileeyat
abject *a.* خوار khwar
ablaze *adv.* زلاند zaland
ablactate *v. t* کوچنیلهشدوبلول koochnay la sheydo beylawal
ablactation *n* لهشدوبلدا la sheydo beyleyda
able *a* و war
ablush *adv* شرمنده sharminda
ablution *n* اودس awdas
abnegate *v. t* انکارکول inkar kawal
abnegation *n* انکار inkar
abnormal *a* ناسم na sam
aboard *adv* پهکتی pa kakhtay ki
abode *n* مسکن maskan
abolish *v.t* لهمنهول la manza wral
abolition *v* لهمنهونه la manza wrana
abominable *a* کرکجن krakjan
aboral *adj* لهخولیخهليری la kholi sakha leyri
aborigines *n. pl* پخوانیاوسيدونکی pakhwanay useydoonkay
abort *v.i* زيانول zyanawal
abortion *n* بوختهزدنه bey wakhta zeygeydana
abortive *adv* بثمره be samara
abound *v.i.* زياتدل zyateydal
about *adv* تقريباً taqreeban
about *prep* شاوخوا shaw khwa
above *adv* پهلوه pa lwara
above *prep.* پورته porta
abreast *adv* نپرن sang par sang
abridge *v.t* لنول landawal
abridgement *n* لنيز landeez
abroad *adv* بهر bahar
abrogate *v. t.* لغوکول lugho kawal

abrupt *a* ناپایه nasapa

abruption *n* ناپی nasapee

abscess *n* دانه dana

abscond *v.i* تتدل takhteydal

absence *n* غرحاضري ghayr haziree

absent *a* غرحاضر ghayr hazir

absolute *a* پوره poora

absolutely *adv* بیخي beykhee

absolve *v.t* بخل bakhal

absorb *v.t* جذبول jazbawal

abstain *v.i.* ه کول dada kawal

abstract *a* مختصر mukhtasar

abstract *n* خلاصه khulasa

abstract *adj* مجرد mujarrad

abstraction *n.* بلدنه beyleydana

absurd *a* بمعنى bey mana

absurdity *n* پوچتوب poochtob

abundance *n* پریماني preymanee

abundant *a* زیات zyat

abuse *v.t.* کنل khkanzal

abuse *n* کنا khkanza

abusive *a* ناوه nawara

abut *v* تکیه کول takya kawal

abyss *n* ژورند zhawar dand

academic *a* تحصیلي tahseelee

academy *n* اکادیمي akademee

accede *v.t.* اتفاق ته رسدل etifaq ta raseydal

accelerate *v.t* ندی کول garanday kawal

acceleration *n* ندیتوب garandeetob

accent *n* خج khaj

accentuate *v.t* اچول زور zor achawal

accept & منل manal

acceptable *a* دمنلو و da manalo war

acceptance *n* قبلول qablawal

access *n* لاس رسدنه las raseydana

accession *n* افتخارته رسدنه iftikhar ta raseydana

accessory *n* زیات zyat

accident *n* په peykha

accidental *a* تصادفي tasadufee

acclaim *v.t* چکچکه کول chakckahi kawal

acclaim *n* چکچک chakchaki

acclamation *n* دشاباسي نار da shabasee narey

acclimatise *v.t* موسم سره مان عادتول mosam sara zan adatawal

accommodate *v.t* ایول zayawal

accommodation *n.* استونه astoganzay

accompaniment *n* ملتا maltya

accompany *v.t.* مل کیدل mal keydal

accomplice *n* ملری malgaray

accomplish *v.t.* بشپکول bashpar kawal

accomplished *a* بشپ bashpar

accomplishment *n.* بشپتیا bashpartya

accord *v.t.* موافق کیدل muwafiq keydal

accord *n.* جوجای jor jaray

accordingly *adv.* له دامله la dey amala

account *n.* حساب heesab

account *v.t.* انیرل angeyral

accountable *a* مسؤل masool

accountancy *n.* حسابداري hisabdaree

accountant *n.* محاسب muhasib

accredit *v.t.* اعتمادكول aytimad kawal

accredited *adj* داعتمادنامهخاوند da aytimad namey khawand

accumulate *v.t.* غونول ghondawal

accumulation *n* غونيدنه ghondeydana

accuracy *n.* درستوالی drustwalay

accurate *a.* درست drust

accursed *a.* لعنتي lanatee

accusation *n* تورلونه tor lagawana

accuse *v.t.* تورلول tor lagawal

accused *n.* تورن toran

accustom *v.t.* رودول rogdawal

accustomed *a.* رودی rogday

ace *n* ٹ takay

acerb *adj* ترش torsh

acerbate *v.t* پارول parawal

acescent *adj* تريو treew

acetify *v.* سركهكدل sarka keydal

ache *n.* درد dard

ache *v.i.* خويدل khoogeydal

achieve *v.t.* لاستهراوستل las ta rawastal

achievement *n.* برياليتوب baryaleetob

achromatic *adj* بيرنه beyranga

acid *a* تيزابي tayzabee

acid *n* تيزاب tayzab

acidity *n.* تيزابيت tayzabeeyat

acknowledge *v.* تصديق tasdeeq

acknowledgement *n.* اعتراف aytiraf

acne *n* وانكه zwanaka

acorn *n.* دخرويدانی da kharwee daney

acoustic *a* اوازپوهنه awaz pohana

acquaint *v.t.* اشناكول ashna kawal

acquaintance *n.* پژندلوي peyzhandgalwee

acquest *n* لاستهراوستل las ta rawastal

acquiesce *v.i.* غاهايودل ghara eekhodal

acquiescence *n.* غاهايودنه ghara eekhodana

acquire *v.t.* تحصيلول tahseelawal

acquirement *n.* تحصيل tahseel

acquisition *n.* لاستهراوستنه las ta rawastana

acquit *v.t.* ازادول azadawal

acquittal *n.* خلاصون khlasoon

acre *n.* جريب jeereb

acreage *n.* جريبانه jeerebana

acrimony *n* تريخوالی treekhwalay

acrobat *n.* الباز dalbaz

across *adv.* پور pori

across *prep.* پهلنو pa lando

act *n.* عملكول amal kawal

act *v.i.* اغيزهاچول agheyza achawal

acting *n.* عمل amal

action *n.* كنه krana

activate *v.t.* فعالول faalawal

active *a.* فعال faal

activity *n.* فعاليت faaleeyat

actor *n.* فنكار fankar

actress *n.* كارهفن fankara

actual *a.* رتينه rakhteenay

actually *adv.* پەریتیاسره pa reekhtya sara

acumen *n.* تروال teyrawalay

acute *a.* تیز teyz

adage *n.* متل matal

adamant *a.* کلک klak

adamant *n.* نەماتدونکی na mateydoonkay

adapt *v.t.* سمول samawal

adaptation *n.* توافق tawafuq

adays *adv* ورځ wrazanay

add *v.t.* زیاتول zyatawal

addict *v.t.* رودول rogdawal

addict *n.* عادت adat

addiction *n.* رودوال rogdwalay

addition *n.* زیاتونه zyatwalay

additional *a.* اضافي izafee

addle *adj* وروست wrost

address *v.t.* خطاب کول khitab kawal

addressee *n.* مخاطب mukhatib

adduce *v.t.* راول rawral

adept *n.* ماهر mahir

adept *a.* تکه takra

adequacy *n.* برابروال barabarwalay

adequate *a.* مناسب munasib

adhere *v.i.* لول lagawal

adherence *n.* طرفداری tarafdaree

adhesion *n.* لاس نیوی las neeway

adhesive *n.* سری sareykh

adhesive *a.* سریناک sreykhnak

adhibit *v.t.* قبلول qablawal

adieu *n.* خدای دی مل شه khuday di mal sha

adieu *interj.* خدای په اماني khuday pa amanee

adjacent *a.* متصل mutasil

adjective *n.* صفت sifat

adjoin *v.t.* متصل کول mutasil kawal

adjourn *v.t.* بل وخت ته زندول bal wakht ta zandawal

adjournment *n.* لنمهالی ـ land mahalay zand

adjudge *v.t.* قضاوت کول qazawat kawal

adjunct *n.* ځانسره مرسته sangi sara mrasta

adjuration *n* پرانیستنه pranistana

adjust *v.t.* سمول samawal

adjustment *n.* تعدیل tadeel

administer *v.t.* اداره کول idara kawal

administration *n.* اداره idara

administrative *a.* اداري idaree

administrator *n.* مدیر mudeer

admirable *a.* دخوونو da khwakhay war

admiral *n.* امیرالبحر ameerul bahar

admiration *n.* تحسین tehseen

admire *v.t.* قدر کول qadar kawal

admissible *a.* روا rawa

admission *n.* داخله dakhila

admit *v.t.* اقرارول iqrarawal

admittance *n.* ننوتنه nanawatana

admonish *v.t.* اخطارورکول akhtar warkawal

admonition *n.* تنبه tambeeya

adnascent *adj.*

ado *n.* شورماشور shormashor

adobe *n.* خته khakhta

adolescence *n.* بلوغ balogh

adolescent *a.* بالغ baligh

adopt *v.t.* خپلول khpalawal
adoption *n* خپلونه khpalawana
adorable *a.* مينه‌ناک meenanak
adoration *n.* پرستش parastish
adore *v.t.* قدر کول qadar kawal
adorn *v.t.* سينارول seengarawal
adscititious *adj* اضافي izafee
adscript *adj.* لمنليک lamanleek
adulation *n* چاپلوسی chaplosee
adult *a* بالغ baligh
adult *n.* بالغ‌کس baligh kas
adulterate *v.t.* زناکول zana kawal
adulteration *n.* زنا zana
adultery *n.* زناکاري zana karee
advance *v.t.* مخکی‌کیدل makhki keydal
advance *n.* ترقي‌یافته taraqee yafta
advancement *n.* ترقي taraqee
advantage *n.* فایده fayda
advantage *v.t.* ګاته‌اخیستل gata akheystal
advantageous *a.* فایده‌مند fayda mand
advent *n.* دمخه‌دکرسمس‌ورځ da makha da krismas wraz
adventure *n* مهم muhim
adventurous *a.* مهماتي muhimatee
adverb *n.* فعل‌ته‌اوند،قد fayl ta arwand; qayd
adverbial *a.* دقیدپه‌اوند da qayd pa arwand
adversary *n.* حریف hareef
adverse *a* بدبخت badbakht
adversity *n.* بدمرغی badmarghay
advert *v.* متوجه‌کول mutawajo kawal

advertise *v.t.* اعلانول aylanawal
advertisement *n* اعلان aylan
advice *n* نصیحت naseehat
advisable *a.* مقتضي muqtazee
advisability *n* مصلحت maslihat
advise *v.t.* نصیحت‌کول naseehat kawal
advocacy *n.* قضاوت qazawat
advocate *n* مدافع‌وکیل mudafay wakeel
advocate *v.t.* طرفداری‌کول tarafdaree kawal
aerial *a.* هوایي hawayee
aerial *n.* هوا د da hawa
aeriform *adj.* دهوا‌په‌شان da hawa pa shan
aerify *v.t.* په‌هوا‌اول pa hawa arawal
aerodrome *n* پروازګاه parwazgah
aeronautics *n.pl.* هوا‌بازي hawabazee
aeroplane *n.* الوتکه alwataka
aesthetic *a.* ښکلا‌پالونکی khkula palonkay
aesthetics *n.pl.* ښکلا‌پژندنه khkula peyzhandana
aestival *adj* اوني ornay
afar *adv.* له‌ورا la wara
affable *a.* خوش‌خلقه khosh khalqa
affair *n.* امر amar
affect *v.t.* اغیزندل agheyz khandal
affectation *n* تصنع tasano
affection *n.* مینتوب mayantob
affectionate *a.* مينه‌ناک meenanak
affidavit *n* اعتبارلیک aytibar leek
affiliation *n.* تون taroon
affinity *n* قرابت qarabat
affirm *v.t.* ادعاکول ida kawal

affirmation *n* خاطرجمعي khatir jamee

affirmative *a* مثبت musbat

affix *v.t.* لول lagawal

afflict *v.t.* لتاول latarawal

affliction *n.* بدمرغی bad marghay

affluence *n.* وړدنه wareydana

affluent *a.* جاري jaree

afford *v.t.* زغمل zghamal

afforest *v.t.* نل جول zangal jorawal

affray *n* جنجال janjal

affront *v.t.* سپکاوی spakaway

affront *n* سپکول spakawal

afield *adv.* په بدیا کي pa beydya ki

aflame *adv.* په شغلو pa shoghlo

afloat *adv.* لاهو lahoo

afoot *adv.* پیاده pyada

afore *prep.* واندینی warandeenay

afraid *a.* ویریدل weyreydal

afresh *adv.* سره له la sara

after *prep.* پسې pasey

after *adv* وروسته wrosta

after *conj.* ورپسې warpasey

afterwards *adv.* پس pasey

again *adv.* بیا bya

against *prep.* مخالف mukhalif

agamist *n* یووللبوی؛پرته لهجفتیرزدل yaw dawl bootay; parta la juftgeeray zeygeydalay

agape *adv.,* وته په غا gota pa ghakh

agaze *adv* اندمن andeykhman

age *n.* عمر oomar

aged *a.* زو zor

agency *n.* اژانس azhans

agenda *n.* دغوندبحثمواد da ghondi da behes mawad

agent *n* اجنٺ ajant

aggravate *v.t.* په غصه کول pa ghosa kawal

aggravation *n.* غصه کوونه ghosa kawona

aggregate *v.t.* مجموعهجوړول majmooa jorawal

aggression *n* تری teyray

aggressive *a.* تیری کوونکی teyray kawoonkay

aggressor *n.* یرغلر yarghal gar

aggrieve *v.t.* غمجنول ghamjanawal

aghast *a.* حیران hayran

agile *a.* تکه takra

agility *n.* تکهتوب takratob

agitate *v.t.* خوول khotawal

agitation *n* لمسونه lamsawona

agist *v.t.* دمزدپهبدل کرول da mazd pa badal ki sarawal

aglow *adv.* په شغلوروان pa shoghlo rokhan

agnus *n*

ago *adv.* مخک makhki

agog *adj.* بقرار bey qarar

agonist *n* په اضطراب اخته pa iztirab akhta

agonize *v.t.* په عذابول pa azabawal

agony *n.* درد dard

agronomy *n.* کرنپوهنه karanpohana

agoraphobia *n.* ومشتیتوب gotmeyshtaytob

agrarian *a.* زراعتي zaratee

agree *v.i.* موافقت کول muwafiqat kawal

agreeable *a.* موافق muwafiq

agreement *n.* تون taroon

agricultural *a* کرنیز karaneez

agriculture *n* کرنه karana

agriculturist *n.* ماهر دکرنز da karani mahir

ague *n* لزندهتبه larzanda taba

ahead *adv.* مخکی makhki

aheap *adv*

aid *n* مرسته mrasta

aid *v.t* مرستهکول mrasta kawal

aigrette *n* جوغه jogha

ail *v.t.* ناروغدل narogheydal

ailment *n.* ناروغي naroghee

aim *n.* موخه mokha

aim *v.i.* مرام moram

air *n* هوا hawa

aircraft *n.* الوتکه alwataka

airy *a.* هوايي hawayee

ajar *adv.* نيمکه neem kakha

akin *a.* شباهتلرل shabahat laral

alacrious *adj* چابک chabak

alacrity *n.* چمتووالی chamtoowalay

alarm *n* دخطرزنگ da khatar zang

alarm *v.t* لهخطرخهخبروول la khatar sakha khabrawal

alas *interj.* ایهی ay hay

albeit *conj.* کهسهم ka sa ham

album *n.* البوم albom

albumen *n* دهگیسپین da hagay speen

alchemy *n.* کیمیاگري keemyagaree

alcohol *n* شراب sharab

ale *n* انلیسیآبجو eengleesee abjoo

alert *a.* وړ weekh

alertness *n.* ویوالی weekhwalay

algebra *n.* الجبر aljabar

alias *n.* فرضيیادروغينوم farzee ya daroghee noom

alias *adv.* پهبلنامه pa bal nama

alibi *n.* دجرمپدوپهمهالبهانهکول da juram peykheydo pa mahal bahana kawal

alien *a.* پردی praday

alienate *v.t.* دانمخالفجوول da zan mukhalif jorawal

alight *v.i.* روخانوال rokhanawal

align *v.t.* پهیوهکرهکدرول pa yawa karkha ki darawal

alignment *n.* یوهکرهیالیکهکدرونه yawa karkha ya lika ki darawana

alike *a.* یوول؛ورته yaw dawal; warta

alike *adv* یوشان yaw shan

aliment *n.* خواه؛غذا khwara; ghaza

alimony *n.* خر khars

aliquot *n.* عادکوونکیعدد ad kawoonkay adad

alive *a* ژوندی؛سرشار zhwanday; sarshar

all *a.* ټول؛بشپر tol; bashpar

all *n* ټول tol

all *adv* لهیوهسره؛هروول la yawa sara; har dawal

all *pron* هروک؛هرچا har sok; har cha

allay *v.t.* آرامول aramawal

allegation *n.* الزام؛ادعا ilzam; adaa

allege *v.t.* الزاملول؛ادعاکول ilzam lagawal; adaa kawal

allegiance *n.* تابعیت tabieeyat

allegorical *a.* مجازي؛كنايوي majazee; kanayawee

allegory *n.* كنايه؛حكايت kanaya; hikayat

allergy *n.* حساسيت لرنه hasaseeyat larana

alleviate *v.t.* آرامول؛كمول aramawal; kamawal

alleviation *n.* آرام؛كموالى aram; kam walay

alley *n.* كوه؛لاره koosa; lara

alliance *n.* پوستون peywastoon

alligator *n* نهنگ nahang

alliterate *v.* يوورته غلرونكي تورې سره دپرله پسې كلمو پيلدل yaw warta ghag laroonkee toree sara da parla pasi kalmo peyleydal

alliteration *n.* ورته غلرونكي تورې سره دپرله پسې كلمو پيلدنه warta ghag laroonkee toree sara da parla pasey kalmo peyleydana

allocate *v.t.* ځانى كول zangaray kawal

allocation *n.* ځاننه؛ځاكنه zangarana; takana

allot *v.t.* ځانى كول zangaray kawal

allotment *n.* وش؛تخصيص weysh; takhsees

allow *v.t.* اجازه وركول ijaza warkawal

allowance *n.* مزد؛زيره mazd; zeyra

alloy *n.* چارج؛الياژ charj

allude *v.i.* نغوته كول nghota kawal

allure *v.t.* په طمع كول pa tama kawal

allurement *n* تطميع؛برامتا tatmee; bramta

allusion *n* نغوته؛اشاره nghota; ishara

allusive *a.* كنايوي؛رمزي kinayawee; ramzee

ally *v.t.* نخلول nkhalawal

ally *n.* هم تونى؛ژمن ham taroonay; zhman

almanac *n.* كليزه kaleeza

almighty *a.* قادرمطلق qadari mutlaq

almond *n.* بادام badam

almost *adv.* تقريبا taqreeban

alms *n.* خرات kheyrat

aloft *adv.* پورته؛بر سره porta; bar seyra

alone *a.* يواز yawazey

along *adv.* ملرى؛مل؛ور سره malgaray; mal; warsara

along *prep.* د...په اودو ك؛د..په امتداد ك da ... pa oogdo ki; da ... pa imtidad ki

aloof *adv.* لرى؛په موه ك leyri; pa gokha ki

aloud *adv.* په لوغ pa lwar ghag

alp *n.* لوغر lwar ghag

alpha *n* ديونانى ابلومى تورى da yoonanee abeysey loomray toray

alphabet *n.* ابى abeysey

alphabetical *a.* دابى په اوند da abeysey pa arwand

alpinist *n* غرختونكى ghar khatoonkay

already *adv.* مخكله ده؛قبلا makhki la dey; qablan

also *adv.* همداشان؛همداول hamda shan; hamda dawl

altar *n.* قربانځاى qorban zay

alter *v.t.* بدلول badlawal

alteration *n* بدلون badloon

altercation *n.* شخه،مباحثه shkhara; mobahisa

alternate *a.* يوپهمنځکې،متناوب yaw pa manz ki; motanawab

alternate *v.t.* يوپهبل‌پسراتلل yaw pa bal pasey ratlal

alternative *n.* متناوب،تردوه‌برخوپور نازی motanawab; tar dwa barkho pori zangaray

alternative *a.* پرله‌پسواندیز parla pasey wrandeyz

although *conj.* که‌هم ka sa ham

altimeter *n* لووالی‌معلوموونکی lwar walay maloomowoonkay

altitude *n.* لووالی lwar walay

alto *n* ترولولوغ tar tolo lwar ghag

altogether *adv.* په‌بشپول pa bashpar dawl

aluminium *n.* دالومینیوم‌فلز da alomeeneeyom filiz

always *adv* تل،همشه tal; hameysha

alveary *n* دشاتولوی da shato lokhay

am یم(لومی‌کس؛لکه:زه‌یم) yam (loomray kas; laka: za yam)

amalgam *n* دسیمابویوالیاژچدغلونو کولولپاره‌په‌کاري da seemabo yaw alyazh chi da ghakhoonu dakawalo lapara pakareygee

amalgamate *v.t.* دسیمابوپه‌دغه‌الیاژ غلونه‌کول da seemabo pa dagha alyazh ghakhoona dakawal

amalgamation *n* ونه،یوای‌کونه gadawana; yaw zay kawana

amass *v.t.* راغونول raghondawal

amateur *n.* مینه‌وال،شوقین meenawal; shoqeen

amatory *adj* له‌مینک la meeni dak

amaze *v.t.* حرانول heyranawal

amazement *n.* حرانتیا heyrantya

ambassador *n.* سفیر،سیاسي‌وری safeer; seeyasee zaray

ambiguity *n.* ابهام،وونتوب ibham; goongtob

ambiguous *a.* مبهم،شکمن mubhim; shakman

ambition *n.* هیله،آرزو heela; arzoo

ambitious *a.* دلوهمت‌خاوند da lwar himat khawand

ambulance *n.* امبولانس ambolans

ambulant *adj* رنده،متحرک garzanda; mutaharik

ambulate *v.t* تگ‌کول tag kawal

ambush *n.* کمین‌ورته‌نیول kameen warta neewal

ameliorate *v.t.* سمول samawal

amelioration *n.* سمونه،جوت samawana; jorakht

amen *interj.* آمین،خدای‌دوکي ameen; khuday di wakree

amenable *a* مسؤلانه masoolana

amend *v.t.* رغول،سمول raghawal; samawal

amendment *n.* سمون،اصلاح samoon; islah

amends *n.pl.* تلافي،جبران talafee; jibran

amiability *n.* لوريني،مهرباني loreenee; mehrabanee

amiable *a.* لوراند،مهربان lorand; mehraban

amicable *adj.* دوستانه dostana

amid *prep.* په‌منځ pa manz ki

amiss *adv.* ناوه،ناسم nawara; nasam

amity *n.* ملرتیا،آشنایي malgartya; ashnayee

ammunition *n.* مهمات،اسلحه muhamat; aslaha

amnesia *n* نسیان،هرونه nasyan; heyrawana

amnesty *n.* عمومي بخنه amoomee bakhana

among *prep.* په ـ ـ ـ ک،په ـ ـ ـ منځ ک pa ... ki; pa ... manz ki

amongst *prep.* په ـ ـ ـ منځ ک،له ـ ـ ـ لخه pa ... manz ki; la ... dali sakha

amoral *a.* غیر اخلاقي ghayr akhlaqee

amount *n* کچ،مقدار kach; miqdar

amount *v.i* صعود کول،مقدار لرل، زیاتدل saood kawal; miqdar laral; zyateydal

amount *v.* په مقدار یا پیمائش کبرابرېدل pa miqdar ya peymayish ki barabareydal

amorous *a.* عاشقانه ashiqana

amour *n* مینه،عشق meena; ishq

ampere *n* دبرناجریان یاشدت ناپ کوونکپمانه da breykhna jaryan ya shidat nap kawoonki peymana

amphibious *adj* دوه‌اخیز dwa arkheeza

amphitheatre *n* دننداتون بیضوي سالون da nandartoon beyzwee salon

ample *a.* پرمانه،مفصل preymana; mufsal

amplification *n* پراختیا،پیاوتیا parakhtya; pyawartya

amplifier *n* پیاوی کوونکی، واکمنوونکی pyawaray kawoonkay; zwakmanawoonkay

amplify *v.t.* پراخول parakhawal

amulet *n.* کو،دم دُرها kodi; dam durha

amuse *v.t.* مشغولول mashghulawal

amusement *n* مشغولتیا،تفریح mashghultya; tafreeh

an *art* یو (لکه یو کس،یو کتاب) yaw (laka yaw kas; yaw keetab)

anabaptism *n* دتعمید دغسل نه ور کونه da tameed da ghusal na warkawana

anachronism *n* له زو عصر سره‌اه لرونکی la zor asar sara ara laroonkay

anadem *n* غاکی gharakay

anaemia *n* وینه‌لي weena lagay

anaesthesia *n* بې هوي bey hokhee

anaesthetic *n.* بهوه bey hokha

anal *adj.* دکو ندمقعدپه اوند da koni da maqad pa arwand

analogous *a.* دپرتلنو war da partalani war

analogy *n.* قیاس،پرتلنه qayas; partalana

analyse *v.t.* تجزیه کول tajzeeya kawal

analysis *n.* تجزیه،شننه tajzeeya; shanana

analyst *n* تجزیه‌نار،پروونکی tajzeeya nigar; zeyrowoonkay

analytical *a* شننوونکی،تجزیاتي shanawoonkay; tajzeeyatee

anamnesis *n* يادآوري yadawaree

anarchism *n.* وي پالنه gadwadee palana

anarchist *n* بلواگر balwagar

anarchy *n* وي؛بغاوت gadwadee; baghawat

anatomy *n.* كالبدپژندنه kalbad peyzhandana

ancestor *n.* پلارنيكونه plar neekoona

ancestral *a.* نيكانه؛دپلارنيكه په اوند neekana; da plar neeka pa arwand

ancestry *n.* پلرن؛كورز plaranay; koranay

anchor *n.* دكتلنر da kakhtay langar

anchorage *n* دكتلنرای da kakhtay langarzay

ancient *a.* لرغونی larghonay

ancon *n* نل sangal

and *conj.* او aw

anecdote *n.* لنه كيسه landa keesa

anemometer *n* بادمچ bad meych

anew *adv.* له سره؛دوباره la sara; dobara

anfractuous *adj* خم دار khamdar

angel *n* فرته farikhta

anger *n.* غصه ghusa

angina *n* دزه دشريانونو درد da zra da sharyanoonu dard

angle *n.* زاويه zaweeya

angle *n* كونج؛گوه konj; gokha

angry *a.* غصه؛په قهر ghusa; pa qahar

anguish *n.* غمجني ghamjanee

angular *a.* زاويه لرونكی zaweeya laroonkay

anigh *adv.* نژد nazhdey

animal *n.* ناور zanawar

animate *v.t.* ژوندوركول؛ژوندوربخل zhwand warkawal; zhwand warbakhal

animate *a.* ژوندی zhwanday

animation *n* احيا؛پارونه ahya; parawana

animosity *n* دمني dukhmanee

animus *n* اراده؛نيت irada; nyat

aniseed *n* تخم بادیان tukhmi badyan

ankle *n.* بجلكه؛بنری bajlaka; khangaray

anklet *n* زولانی zolanay

annalist *n.* تاریخ ليكونكی tareekh leekoonkay

annals *n.pl.* پل؛تاریخچه peykh lar; tareekhcha

annex *v.t.* ضميمه كول؛نلول zameema kawal; nakhlawal

annexation *n* انضمام؛ضميمه كونه inzimam; zameema kawana

annihilate *v.t.* له منه ول la manza waral

annihilation *n* ويجاونه weejarawana

anniversary *n.* كليزه؛هركال kaleeza; har kal

announce *v.t.* اعلانول aylanawal

announcement *n.* خبرتیا؛اعلان khabartya; aylan

annoy *v.t.* ورول zorawal

annoyance *n.* ورونه zorawana

annual *a.* كلنی kalanay

annuitant *n* معاش اخستونكی moash akheystoonkay

annuity *n.* كلنىمعاش kalanay moash

annul *v.t.* لغوه كول lughwa kawal

anoint *v.t.* پەتلوغوول pa teylu ghwarawal

anomalous *a* لەدودەبهر la dooda bahar

anomaly *n* بترتيبه bey tarteeba

anon *adv.* رژر deyr zhar

anonymity *n.* بنومتيا bey noomtya

anonymity *n.* نوموركي noom warakay

anonymous *a.* بنومه،نارندده beynooma; na sarganda

another *a* يوبل yaw bal

answer *n* واب zawab

answer *v.t* وابوركول zawab warkawal

answerable *a.* پەواب مسؤول،وابده pa zawab masool; zawabday

ant *n* مى meygay

antacid *adj.* ضدحموضت ziddi hamoozat

antagonism *n* مخالفت،دمني mukhalifat; dukhmanee

antagonist *n.* مخالف،دمن mukhalif; dukhman

antagonize *v.t.* مخالفت كول mukhalifat kawal

antarctic *a.* پەسولي قطب پوراوند pa sweylee qotab pori arwand

antecede *v.t.* كدل تروادد tri warandi keydal

antecedent *n.* مخكنى،وادد makhkanay; warandi

antecedent *a.* پخوانى،مخكنى pakhwanay; makhkanay

antedate *n* لەريتنيتاريخخمخكي تاريخويل la reekhtanee tareekh sakha makhki tareekh wayal

antelope *n.* غره gharsa

antenatal *adj.* لەزدونوادندي la zeygeydoon warandi

antennae *n.* آنن antan

antenuptial *adj.* لەوادەواند la wada warandi

anthem *n* ملي سرود milee sarood

anthology *n.* ادبيغورچا adabee ghorchanr

anthropoid *adj.* دانسانولەبيزو da insan dawla beezo

anti *pref.* مخالف،پرضد mukhalif; par zid

anti-aircraft *a.* هواضدوسله hawa zid wasla

antic *n* بانوله bey andwala

anticardium *n*

anticipate *v.t.* واندوينه كول warandwayana kawal

anticipation *n.* واندوينه warandwayana

antidote *n.* زهرضد zeher zid

antipathy *n.* مخالفانهاحساس mukhalifana ihsas

antiphony *n.* تهليلوينه tahleel wayana

antipodes *n.* مقابلكي muqabil takee

antiquarian *a.* لرغونى larghonay

antiquarian *n* لرغونپژندونكي larghon peyzhandoonkay

antiquary *n.* لرغونپژندونكي larghon peyzhandoonkay

antiquated *a.* منسوخشوى mansookh shaway

antique a. لرغونی larghonay

antiquity n. لرغونزمانه larghoni zamana

antiseptic n. عفونت‌ضد afoonat zid

antiseptic a. انتان‌ضددرمل antanzid durmal

antithesis n. تضاد tazad

antitheist n. تضادخوی tazad khwakhay

antonym n. ضداونقیض zid aw naqeez

anus n. مقعد maqad

anvil n. سندان sandan

anxiety a اضطراب aztirab

anxious a. مضطرب muztarib

any a. هیڅ،هر hees; har

any adv. هیڅ hees

anyhow adv. په‌هرحال pa har hal

apace adv. په‌چکسره pa chatkay sara

apart adv. برسره bar seyra

apartment n. اپارتمان apartman

apathy n. بحسی bey hisee

ape n شادو shado

ape v.t. تقلیدکول taqleed kawal

aperture n. سوری sooray

apex n. و که؛دزاویري‌راس sooka; da zaweeyi ras

aphorism n لنډه‌وینا landa weyna

apiary n. دشاتودمچیوای da shato da machyo zay

apiculture n. دشاتودمچیوروزنه da shato da machyo rozana

apish a. ناپوه napoh

apologize v.i. بخنه‌غوتل bakhkhana ghokhtal

apologue n اخلاقي‌کیسه ikhlaqee keesa

apology n. بخنه bakhkhana

apostle n. استازی،رسول astazay; rasool

apotheosis n. له‌حدخه‌زیاته‌ستاینه la had sakha zyata stayana

apparatus n. اسباب،لوازم asbab; lawazim

apparel n. اسباب،کالي asbab; kalee

apparent a. رنډ sargand

appeal n. التماس،زاري iltimas; zaree

appeal v.t. التماس‌کول،مراجعه‌کول iltimas kawal; murajia kawal

appear v.i. رنډیدل sargandeydal

appearance n به،ظهور zahoor; banra

appease v.t. تسکینول،خاموشول taskeenawal; khamoshawal

appellant n. مبارزه‌غوتونکی mobariza ghokhtoonkay

append v.t. تاولرل،زیاتول taraw laral; zyatawal

appendage n. پایسور paysoor

appendicitis n. داپانیکس‌پسوب da apandeeks parsob

appendix n. پایو paysoor

appendix n. ضمیمه zameema

appetence n. هیله،اشتیاق heela; ishteeyaq

appetent adj. هیله‌من؛آرزومن heela man; arzoo man

appetite n. غذایي‌اشتها ghazayee ishtiha

appetite n. ذاتي‌لوالتیا zatee leywaltya

appetizer *n.* لهخوردمخهاشتها کنکیستوراو la khwaro da makha ishtiha rawastoonkay skhak

applaud *v.t.* آفرینویل afreen wayal

applause *n.* تحسین؛ستاینه tehseen; stayana

apple *n.* مه manra

appliance *n.* آله؛وسایل ala; wasayal

applicable *a.* مناسب؛دإجراو munasib; da ijra war

applicant *n.* غوتونکی؛غوتنلیک ورکوونکی ghokhtoonkay; ghokhtan leek warkawoonkay

application *n.* غوتنلیک ghokhtanleek

apply *v.t.* عملیکول؛عریضهکول amalee kawal; areeza kawal

appoint *v.t.* ماکل؛مارل takal; gomaral

appointment *n.* ماکنه؛دملاقاتژمنه takana; da mulaqat zhmana

apportion *v.t.* وشل weyshal

apposite *adj* مناسب munasib

apposite *a.* پرای par zay

appositely *adv* پهمناسبول pa munasib dawl

approbate *v.t* تصوییول tasweebawal

appraise *v.t.* تخمینول؛ارزول takhmeenawal; arzawal

appreciable *a.* دقدردانو da qadardanay war

appreciate *v.t.* قدردانیکول qadardanee kawal

appreciation *n.* قدردانی qadardanee

apprehend *v.t.* پوهدل؛دَرَکول poheydal; darakawal

apprehension *n.* پوهاوی؛درک pohaway; darak

apprehensive *a.* پوهنیز؛اندمن pohaneez; andeykhman

apprentice *n.* شاردي shagardee

apprise *v.t.* خبرول khabrawal

approach *v.t.* نژدکدل nazhdey keydal

approach *n.* نژدوالی؛لاسرسدا nazhdeywalay; las raseyda

approbation *n.* تصویب tasweeb

appropriate *v.t.* مناسبول؛زانیکول munasibawal; zangaray kawal

appropriate *a.* مناسب munasib

appropriation *n.* مناسبت؛وتیا munasibat; wartya

approval *n.* تجویز؛تصویب tajweez; tasweeb

approve *v.t.* تصوییول؛موافقتکول tasweebawal; muwafiqat kawal

approximate *a.* نژد nazhdey

apricot *n.* زردآلو zard aloo

appurtenance *n* جز؛وسایل juz; wasayil

apron *n.* پشبند peysh band

apt *a.* لوال؛مناسب leywal; munasib

aptitude *n.* ذهنیتوجه zehnee tawajo

aquarium *n.* دیبکسهچدریائيمخلوق پکنندارلپارهساتلیشي da kheekhey baksa chi daryayee makhlooq paki nandarey lapara satalay shee

aqueduct *n* داوبوبهنز da obo bahanz

arable *adj* کرنیزهمکه karaneeza zmaka

arbiter *n.* قاضي qazee

arbitrary *a.* قضائي؛ثالثانه qazayee; salisana

arbitrate *v.t.* قضاوت کول؛منتوب کول qazawat kawal; manzgartob

arbitration *n.* منتوب manzgartob

arbitrator *n.* منی manzgaray

arc *n.* قوس qos

arcade *n.* کماني لاره kamanee lara

arch *n.* کمان kaman

arch *v.t.* دکمان په به اول da kaman pa banra arawal

arch *a* رئیس؛اصلی rayees; aslee

archaic *a.* لرغونی؛زو larghonay; zor

archangel *n* مقربه فرته moqarraba farikhta

archbishop *n.* لوی اسقف loy asqaf

archer *n* لیندوالا؛خت کاری leenday wala; khakht karay

architect *n.* معمار maymar

architecture *n.* معماري maymaree

archives *n.pl.* دلاسوندونو اوپاوضبط da laswandoono aw panro zabat

Arctic *n* په شمالي قطب پوراوند pa shumalee qotab pori arwand

ardent *a.* شوقین؛لوال shawqeen; leywal

ardour *n.* ولوله؛لوالتیا walwala; leywaltya

arduous *a.* له کاوه ک la karawa dak

area *n* مساحت masahat

arena *n* دلوبور da lobo dagar

argue *v.t.* بحث کول behes kawal

argument *n.* مباحثه؛دلیل mubahisa; daleel

arid *adj.* وچ wach

aright *adv* مستقیم mostaqeem

aright *adv.* مستقیما mostaqeeman

arise *v.i.* پورته کدل porta keydal

aristocracy *n.* اشراف واکي ashraf wakee

aristocrat *n.* داشراف واکپلوی da ashraf wakay palaway

arithmetic *n.* شمرپوهنه shmeyr pohana

arithmetical *a.* شمرپوهنیز shmeyr pohaneez

ark *n* کت kakhtay

arm *n.* م mat

arm *v.t.* وسله وال کول wasla wal kawal

armada *n.* بحری واک behree zwak

armament *n.* وسله wasla

armature *n.* زغره؛وسله zghara; wasla

armistice *n.* زبندي daz bandee

armlet *a* م بند mat band

armour *n.* زغره zghara

armoury *n.* وسله تون wasla toon

army *n.* پو؛لکر poz; lakhkar

around *prep.* ردچاپره gard chapeyra

around *adv* په شاو خوا ک pa shaw khwa ki

arouse *v.t.* ویول weekhawal

arraign *v.* محکمته حاضرول mahkamey ta hazirawal

arrange *v.t.* اول odal

arrangement *n.* اوون odoon

arrant *n.* بدنامه badnama

array *v.t.* اول odal

array *n.* ترتيب tarteeb

arrears *n.pl.* ندلي‌پورونه zandeydalee poroona

arrest *v.t.* نيول neewal

arrest *n.* نيونه؛توقيف neewana; tawqeef

arrival *n.* رارسدنه raraseydana

arrive *v.i.* رارسدل raraseydal

arrogance *n.* ان‌ليدنه zan leedana

arrogant *a.* كبرجن kabarjan

arrow *n* غشی ghashay

arsenal *n.* وسله‌تون waslatoon

arson *n* په‌قصدي‌ول‌اوربلوونه pa qasdee dawl orbalawona

art *n.* فن fan

artery *n.* سورر soor rag

artful *a.* چلباز chalbaz

article *n* مقاله maqala

articulate *a.* ژبور zhabawar

artifice *n.* أستادي ustadee

artificial *a.* مصنوعي masnooee

artillery *n.* توپخانه topkhana

artisan *n.* صنعتر sanatgar

artist *n.* هنرمند honarmand

artistic *a.* هنري honaree

artless *a.* بهنره bey honara

as *adv.* هغه‌كچ؛كله‌چ؛رنه‌چ hagha kach; kala chi; saranga chi

as *conj.* رنه‌چ saranga chi

as *pron.* لكه؛غوند laka; ghondi

ascend *v.t.* پورته‌تلل porta tlal

ascent *n.* عروج arooj

ascertain *v.t.* معلوم‌ول maloomawal

ascetic *n.* رياضت‌كوونكی reeyazat kawoonkay

ascetic *a.* زاهد zahid

ascribe *v.t.* منسوب‌ول mansoobawal

ash *n.* اير eerey

ashamed *a.* شرم‌دلی sharmeydalay

ashore *adv.* په‌ساحل‌باند pa sahil bandi

aside *adv.* په‌يوه‌لوري‌ك pa yawa lori ki

aside *n.* جداانه judagana

asinine *adj.* خروله khar dawla

ask *v.t.* پوتل pokhtal

asleep *adv.* ويده weeda

aspect *n.* ره seyra

asperse *v.* بدنام‌ول badnamawal

aspirant *n.* هيله‌من heelaman

aspiration *n.* اخستنه‌ساه sa akheystana

aspire *v.t.* زه‌كدل zra keydal

ass *n.* خر khar

assail *v.* بريدكول breed kawal

assassin *n.* قاتل qatil

assassinate *v.t.* قتل‌ول qatlawal

assassination *n* قتل؛وژنه qatal; wazhana

assault *n.* بريد breed

assault *v.t.* بريدكول breed kawal

assemble *v.t.* چمتوكول chamtoo kawal

assembly *n.* جره jarga

assent *v.i.* جوجاي‌كول jor jaree kawal

assent *n.* جوجاي jor jaree

assert *v.t.* پركنده‌اظهاركول preykanda izhar kawal

assess v.t. تشخيصول tashkheesawal

assessment n. مالياتي وضعيت،اكل malyatee wazeeyat; atkal

asset n. پانه panga

assign v.t. سپارل sparal

assignee n. ماړلشوی gomaral shaway

assimilate v. يوشان كول،جذب كول yaw shan kawal; jazab kawal

assimilation n دخوو جذب اوتركيب da khwaro jazab aw tarkeeb

assist v.t. مرسته كول mrasta kawal

assistance n. مرسته mrasta

assistant n. مرستيال mrastyal

associate v.t. ارتباط لرل irtibat laral

associate a. شريك،مرستندوى shareek; mrastandoy

associate n. ونهوال،شريك wanda wal; shareek

association n. پوستون peywastoon

assoil v.t. رخصتول rukhsatawal

assort v.t. لبندي كول dalbandee kawal

assuage v.t. كمول kamawal

assume v.t. ومان كول gooman kawal

assumption n. ومان،هو gooman; hod

assurance n. ١ dad

assure v.t. دادوركول dad warkawal

asterisk n. (*دانه) ستورى storgay (da nakha *)

asthma n.ساهلنى salanday

astonish v.t. حرانول heyranawal

astonishment n. حرانتيا heyrantya

astound v.t نوسول gangosawal

astray adv., منحرف munharif

astrologer n. ستورپوهاند stor pohand

astrology n. ستورپوهنه stor pohana

astronaut n. ستوريونى stor yoonay

astronomer n. ستورپژاند stor peyzhand

astronomy n. ستوروين پوه stor ween poh

asunder adv. پرته parta

asylum n پناهاى panahzay

at prep. كبد__پهلور ki; da ... pa lori

atheism n ملحدتوب mulhidtob

atheist n لهخدايهمنكر la khudaya monkar

athirst adj. تى tagay

athlete n. ورزش كار warzish kar

athletic a. چست chust

athletics n. دورزش كارعلم da warzish karay ilam

athwart prep. لهدخواهغهخواته la dey khwa hagha khwa ta

atlas n. دهوادونودنخچوكتاب da heywadoono da nakhcho keetab

atmosphere n. فضا faza

atoll n. داپوهانوﻝ da tapoogano lar

atom n. ام،ترولوكوچنىبركى atam; tar tolo koochnay basarkay

atomic a. اومى atomee

atone v.i. كفارهوركوﻝ kafara warkawal

atonement n. كفاره kafara

atrocious a. برحمه bey rehma

atrocity n برحمي bey rehmee

attach v.t. نلول nakhlawal

attache *n.* سفیرسره‌اوندچاروا‌کی safeer sara arwand charwakay

attachment *n.* تاو taraw

attack *n.* برید؛یرغل breed; yarghal

attack *v.t.* یرغل‌راول yarghal rawral

attain *v.t.* برلاسی‌کدل barlasay keydal

attainment *n.* بریالیتوب baryaleetob

attempt *v.t.* هه‌کول hasa kawal

attempt *n.* هه hasa

attend *v.t.* حاضردل؛پام‌کول hazireydal; pam kawal

attendance *n.* حاضري؛بار haziree; sar

attendant *n.* خدمتار khidmatgar

attention *n.* توجه tawajo

attentive *a.* متوجه mutawajo

attest *v.t.* واهي‌ورکول؛تصدیقول gawahee warkawal; tasqeekawal

attire *n.* لباس libas

attire *v.t.* سینا018رول seengarawal

attitude *n.* دچلندول da chaland dawl

attorney *n.* وکیل wakeel

attract *v.t.* زه‌راکل zra rakkhal

attraction *n.* زه‌راکنه zra rakkhana

attractive *a.* زه‌راکوونکی؛جلبوونکی zra rakkhowoonkay; jalabowoonkay

attribute *v.t.* تخصیص‌ورکول؛په‌اوند لل takhsees warkawal; pa arwand ganral

attribute *n.* زانی‌صفت zangaray sifat

auction *n.* لیلام leelam

auction *v.t.* لیلامول leelamawal

audible *a.* داوریدوو da awreydo war

audience *n.* اوریدونکي awreydoonkee

audit *n.* پلنه palatana

audit *v.t.* پلل‌اوارل palatal aw saral

auditor *n.* دحسابدارارونکی da hisabdaray saroonkay

auditorium *n.* دکانفرانس‌تالار da kanfarans talar

auger *n.* برمه barma

aught *n.* هرشی؛په‌هیول har shay; pa hees dawl

augment *v.t.* زیاتول zyatawal

augmentation *n.* زیادت zyadakht

August *n.* دانرزي‌کال‌اتمه‌میاشت da angreyzee kal atama myasht

august *n* عظیم؛ستر azeem; star

aunt *n.* ترور tror

aurilave *n.* غوپاکوونکی ghwag pakowoonkay

aurora *n* سپده‌داغ speyda dagh

auspicate *v.t.* پرانستنه‌کول pranistana kawal

auspice *n.* فال fal

auspicious *a.* مبارک mubarak

austere *a.* سخت؛تریخ sakht; treekh

authentic *a.* صحیح sahee

author *n.* لیکوال leekwal

authoritative *a.* واکمن wakman

authority *n.* واک؛پرله wak; preykhla

authorize *v.t.* واک‌ورکول wak warkawal

autobiography *n.* خپل‌لاسی‌ژوند‌لیک khpal lasay zhwand leek

autocracy *n* خپلواکه‌حکومت khpalwaka hookoomat

autocrat *n* بشپواکمن bashpar wakman

autocratic *a* زورواکه zorwaka

autograph *n.* دليکوال‌خپله‌ليکلی لاسليک da leekwal khpala leekalay lasleek

automatic *a* حپل کاری khpal karay

automobile *n.* موټر motar

autonomous *a* خپلواک‌حکومت khpalwak hukoomat

autumn *n.* منی؛خزان manay; khazan

auxiliary *a.* مرستندويه mrastandoya

auxiliary *n.* مرستندوی mrastandoy

avail *v.t.* تری‌ه‌اخستل tri gata akheystal

available *a* موجود mawjood

avarice *n.* حرص hiras

avenge *v.t.* کسات‌اخستل kasat akheystal

avenue *n.* لوی‌وا loy wat

average *n.* حد مننی manzanay had

average *a.* متوسط mutawasit

average *v.t.* اوسطاکل awsat takal

averse *a.* بزار beyzar

aversion *n.* بزاري beyzaree

avert *v.t.* دفع‌کول؛برته‌رول dafa kawal; beyrta garzawal

aviary *n.* دالوتونکواله da alwatoonko zala

aviation *n.* هوايون hawayoon

aviator *n.* هوايونی hawayoonee

avid *adj.* هيله‌من heelaman

avidity *adv.* حرص hiras

avidly *adv* په‌هيله‌منه‌توه pa heela mana toga

avoid *v.t.* دده‌کول dada kawal

avoidance *n.* دده؛اجتناب dada; ijtinab

avow *v.t.* منته‌کول manakhta kawal

await *v.t.* انتظاراستل intizar eystal

awake *v.t.* ويدل؛ويول weekheydal; weekhawal

awake *a* ويخ weekh

award *v.t.* فتواورکول fitwa warkawal

award *n.* فتوا؛بنه fitwa; bakhana

aware *a.* باخبر ba khabar

away *adv.* لری؛يولورته leyri; yaw lori ta

awe *n.* ار dar

awful *a.* داروونکی darowoonakay

awhile *adv.* يوه‌موده yaw sa mooda

awkward *a.* بی‌خونده bey khwanda

axe *n.* تبر tabar

axis *n.* چورلۍ choorleez

axle *n.* رخ sarkh

B

babble *n.* اپلتوينه apalti wayana

babble *v.i.* اپلتويل apalti wayal

babe *n.* کوچنی koochnay

babel *n* نامفهومه‌شوراوزو namafhooma shor aw zwag

baboon *n.* بيزو beezo

baby *n.* کوچنی koochnay

bachelor *n.* بی bey khazi

back *n.* شا؛ملا sha; mla

back *adv.* ترشا tar sha

backbite *v.t.* غيبت كول ghaybat kawal

backbone *n.* دملاتير da mla teer

background *n.* الرليد lar leed

backhand *n.* دلاس پهوزار da las pa sat goozar

backslide *v.i.* په كونا ويدل pa konato khwayeydal

backward *a.* په pa sat

backward *adv.* مخ پهوه makh pa zwara

bacon *n.* دخو دغو لاندى da khoog da ghwakhi landay

bacteria *n.* يو لرنباتي او حواني مكروبونه yaw lar nabatee aw heywanee meykroboona

bad *a.* ناوه nawara

badge *n.* علامه،نه alama; nakha

badger *n.* گرزندپلوروونكى garzand plorowoonkey

badly *adv.* په ناوه ول pa nawara dawl

badminton *n.* دنس لوبه چپه يوسالون كي تر سره كي da tayna loba chi pa yaw salon ki ta sara keygee

baffle *v.t* گرانه جوډل،بپايلپريودل. grana joreydal; bey payle preykhodal

bag *n.* كوه kasora

bag *v. i.* كوه كاچول kasora ki achawal

baggage *n.* دسفرتوه da safar tokha

bagpipe *n.* دموسيقي يو ل بادي آله da moseeqay yaw dawl badee ala

bail *n.* ضمانت zamanat

bail *v. t.* په ضمانت خلاصول pa zamanat khlasawal

bailable *a.* قابل ضمانت qabili zamanat

bailiff *n.* دجرماندمواد وسركاري ناظر da jormaney da mawado sarkaree nazir

bait *n* زناوريا كبان نيولو لپاره په دام كد خوو مواد zanawar ya kaban neewalo lapara pa dam ki da khwaro mawad

bait *v.t.* كارته دام كد خوو مواد ايودل khkar ta dam ki da khwaro mawad eekhodal

bake *v.t.* په سكروو پخول pa skarwato pakhawal

baker *n.* په سكروو پخوونكى،نانواى pa skarwato pakhowoonkey; nanway

bakery *n* دو ډوى پخواني او خوگو جوولو نانوايي da doday pakhawani aw khwago jorawalo nanwayee

balance *n.* تله،حساب tala; heesab

balance *v.t.* برابرول barabarawal

balcony *n.* دبالاخاني بالكن da balakhani balkun

bald *a.* پك،گنجى pak; ganjay

bale *n.* بلا bala

bale *v.t.* لاندى كول landi kawal

baleful *a.* ضررناك zararnak

ball *n.* غونسكه ghondaska

ballad *n.* يو ول قصيده yaw dawl qaseeda

ballet *sn.* دله ييزه هنري ورزشي نا dala yeeza honaree warzishee nasa

balloon *n.* بوغ boghay

ballot *n* درايپله da rayi panra

ballot *v.i.* پەپلەرای‌ورکول pa panra ray warkawal

balm *n.* ملهم malham

balsam *n.* اوبەملهم oba malham

bamboo *n.* باس banras

ban *n.* بندز bandeyz

ban *n* دابندزپرکه da bandeyz preykra

banal *a.* بېخوندە bey khwanda

banana *n.* کله kayla

band *n.* پټی، کړ patay; karay

bandage ~*n.* دەپ‌تڼی da tap tarani patay

bandage *v.t* تپ‌ای‌پەپټل tap zay pa patay taral

bandit *n.* داهامار dara mar

bang *v.t.* دربوول drabowal

bang *n.* دربوونه drabowana

bangle *n.* بنی bangree

banish *v.t.* اله‌وطنه‌شل la watana sharal

banishment *n.* اله‌وطنه‌شنه la watana sharana

banjo *n.* دموسیقی‌یوچدایروی‌دهلري da moseeqay yaw geetar chi dayrawee geyda laree

bank *n.* بانک،ک bank; kas

bank *v.t.* بانک‌کپسای‌ودل bank ki peysey eekhodal

banker *n.* بانکوال bankwal

bankrupt *n.* بې‌ارزتوب؛دواليه bey arzakhtob; deywaleeya

bankruptcy *n.* دواليه‌کدز deywaleeya keydang

banner *n.* برغ beyragh

banquet *n.* تشریفاتي‌ملمستیا tashreefatee meylmastaya

banquet *v.t.* دتشریفاتي‌ملمستیا da tashreefatee meylmastya bandobast kawal

bantam *n.* کوچني‌کورنی‌چر koochnay koranay charg

banter *v.t.* پري‌توکي‌کول pri toki kawal

banter *n.* ټوکمار tokmar

bantling *n.* مسخره maskhara

baptism *n.* په‌عیسائیت‌کدتعمیدغسل pa eesaeeyat ki da tameed ghosal

baptize +*v.t.* دتعمیدغسل‌ورکول da tameed ghosal warkawal

bar *n.* پټه،کاره pata; katara

bar *v.t* ټل،ممنوع‌رول taral; mamnoo garzawal

barb *n.* دغشي‌شاتنه da ghashee shatanay sanda

barbarian *a.* وحشیانه wehsheeyana

barbarian *n.* وحشي‌انسان wehshee insan

barbarism *n.* وحشیتوب wehsheetob

barbarity *n* وحشیانه‌عمل wehsheeyana amal

barbarous *a.* وحشي wehshee

barber *n.* دم،نايي dam; nayee

bard *n.* شاعر shair

bare *a.* لوس؛بربند los; barband

bare *v.t.* بربنول barbandawal

barely *adv.* ایله eela

bargain *n.* راکورکه rakra warkra

bargain *v.t.* راکورکه‌کول rakra warkra kawal

barge *n.* دمال‌دولوکت da mal leygdawalo kakhtay

bark n. دسپي کونجدنه da spee kuranjeydana

bark v.t. غپل؛کونجدل ghapal; kuranjeydal

barley n. وربشي warbashi

barn n. دغلزرمتون da ghaley zeyrmatoon

barnacles n یوول کب چد کتیخ پورنلي yaw dawl kab chi da kakhtay beykh pori nakhalee

barometer n هوامچ hawa meych

barouche n. یووللوراربابیزه دب yaq dol salor araba beza bagai

barrack n. دفواستونای da foz astoganzay

barrage n. داوبوبند da obo band

barrel n. بئشکه؛تیوب boshka; tyoob

barren n شا shar

barricade n. دخنونوپه مرسته بندیز da khandoono pa mrasta bandeyz

barrier n. بندیزلول bandeyz lagawal

barrister n. وکیل wakeel

barter1 v.t. دمال دادلون بدلون تجارت کول da mal da adloon badloon tijarat kawal

barter2 n. دونجون تجارت da wanjoon tijarat

base n. بنسا bansat

base a. سپک؛ناکس spak; nakas

base v.t. بنسايودل bansat eekhodal

baseless a. بے بنیاده bey boonyada

basement n. لاندینی پور landeenay por

bashful a. شرمندوکی sharmandookay

basic a. بنسیز bansateez

basil n. کشمالی kashmalay

basin n. تشت tasht

basis n. زمینه zameena

bask v.i. پیتاوي ته کناستل peytawee ta kkheynastal

basket n. وکر tokray

bass n. دیوکب نوم da yaw kab noom

bastard n. ارمونی armoonay

bastard a. کم اصله kam asla

bat n پرک khaparak

bat n دغونسکوهلونه da ghondaski wahalo danda

bat v. i په نه دغونسکوهلولوبه کول pa danda da ghondaski wahalo loba kawal

batch n ل dalgay

bath n لمبا lamba

bathe v. t لمبدل lambeydal

baton n دصاحب منصبانولته da sahib mansabano lakhta

batsman n. په نه غونسکه وهونکی پا لوبغای pa danda ghondaska wahoonkay lobgharay

battalion n کنک kandak

battery n بر batray

battle n جہ jang

battle v. i. جندل jangeydal

bawd n بوا barwa

bawl n.i. په چغوفریادکول pa cheygho faryad kawal

bawn n.

bay n کوچنی خلیج koochnay khaleej

bayonet n نزه neyza

be v.t. کدل(دشتون رابطه فعل) keydal (da shtoon rabita fayl) be *pref.* دانرزژبیومختای توری da angreyzay zhabi yaw makhtaray toray

beach *n* دردریابنه da daryab sanda

beacon *n* سمندري راغ samandaree sragh

bead *n* دتسبیح دانه da tasbeeh dana

beadle *n.* دکلیسا ناظم da kaleesa nazim

beak *n* موکه makhooka

beaker *n* کوری katoray

beam *n* تیر teer

beam *v. i* واراناچول،تیر اچول warang achawal; teer achawal

bean *n.* لوبیا lobya

bear *n* یږ yag

bear *v.t* زول،زدل، غالل galal; zeygeydal; zeygawal

beard *n* یره geera

bearing *n* برداري bordbaree

beast *n* حیوان heywan

beastly *a* حیوانوله heywan dawla

beat *v. t.* وهل wahal

beat *n* ضرب،وهنه zarb; wahana

beautiful *a* ښکلی khkulay

beautify *v. t* ښکلی کول khkulay kawal

beauty *n* ښکلا khkula

beaver *n* بحري سپی bahree spay

because *conj.* ځکه zaka

beck *n.* په اشاره سره هر کار ته چمتو کدل pa ishara sara har kar ta chamtoo keydal

beckon *v.t.* اشاره ورکول ishara warkawal

become *v. i* کدل keydal

bed *n* پالنگ palang

bedevil *v. t* زورول zorawal

bedding *n.* دویده کدو کالي da weeda keydo kalee

bed-time *n.* دخوب وخت da khob wakht

bee *n.* مچ machay

beech *n.* دترو پاو او در کونجه زي لرونکي یوه ونه da teyro panro aw drey konja zaree laroonki yawa wana

beef *n* دغوایي غوه da ghwayee ghwakha

beehive *n.* بین gabeen

beer *n* بیر،یونالکولي یاک beer; yaw nalkawalay skhak

beet *n* چغندر chughandar

beetle *n* خزدکه khazdaka

befall *v. t* پدل peykheydal

before *prep* له ... ـخه واند la … sakha warandi

before *adv.* دواند da warandi

before *conj* مخکله دچ makhki la dey chi

beforehand *adv.* له واند،دمخه la warandi; da makha

befriend *v. t.* ورسره ملرتیا کول warsara malgartya kawal

beg *v. t.* گدایي کول gadayee kawal

beget *v. t* تولیدول tawleedawal

beggar *n* گدا،دروزر gada; darweyzgar

begin *n* پیل کول payl kawal

beginning *n.* پیل،سر payl; sar

beguile *v. t* غولول gholawal

behalf *n* خاطر،لوری khatir; loray

behave *v. i.* چلند کول chaland kawal

behaviour *n* چلند،اخلاقchaland; akhlaq

behead *v. t.* سرغوولsar ghosawal

behind *adv* پهشاpa sha

behind *prep* ...له _خهشاتهla ... sakha sha ta

behold *v. t* مشاهدهکولmoshahida kawal

being *n* شتون؛وجودshtoon; wajood

belabour *v. t* پهسويوهلpa sotee wahal

belated *adj.* ندلیzandeydalay

belch *v. t* سابندولsabandaval

belief *n* عقیده aqeeda

believe *v. t* عقیدهلرلaqeeda laral

bell *n* زنگzang

belle *n* کلنجلkhkuli najlay

bellicose *a* جاوو jagrawoo

belligerency *n* جهماريjagramaree

belligerent *a* جهییز؛جاووjagrayeez; jagrawoo

belligerent *n* جهکونکیjagra kawoonkay

bellow *v. i* رمباوهلrambari wahal

bellows *n.* دپبن؛سیda pakh banay; sagay

belly *n* ه geyda

belong *v. i* ارهلرلara laral

belongings *n.* کالياوسامانkalee aw saman

beloved *a* محبوب mahboob

beloved *n* معشوق mashooq

below *adv* تر___لاندtar ... landi

below *prep* لاند landi

belt *n* کمربند kamar band

belvedere *n* المرخولlmar khwalay

bemuse *v. t* مستول mastawal

bench *n* اودهوکoogda sawkay

bend *n* کووالی kogwalay

bend *v. t* کدل،کولkageydal; kagawal

beneath *adv* تر___لاندtri ... landi

beneath *prep* لاندیlandi; teet

benefaction *n.* ه kheygara

benefice *n* صوفیانهاوزاهدانهژوندsofiana au zahidana jwand

beneficial *a* ور gatawar

benefit *n* ه،فایدهgata; fayda

benefit *v. t.* هرسولgata rasawal

benevolence *n* سخاوت sakhawat

benevolent *a* سخي sakhee

benevolent *v. t* سخاوتکولsakhawat kawal

benign *adj* مهربان mehraban

benignly *adv* پهمهربانۍسرهpa mehrabanay sara

bent *n* کووالی kogwalay

bequeath *v. t.* میراثکپرودلmeeras ki preykhodal

bereave *v. t.* محرومولmahroomawal

bereavement *n* محرومیتmahroomeeyat

berth *n* داورايّاوکتخوبخانهda orgadee aw kakhtay khob khana

beside *prep.* له پرته parta la

besides *prep* برسرهbar seyra

besides *adv* پر___برسرهpar ... bar seyra

besiege *v. t* محاصرهکولmuhasira kawal

bestow *v. t* بسپنهورکول baspana warkawal

bestrew *v. t* پورل؛شنل pokhal; shanal

bet *v.i* شرط‌تل shart taral

bet *n* شرط shart

betray *v.t.* خيانت کول khayanat kawal

betrayal *n* خيانت؛غداري khayanat; ghadaree

betroth *v. t* پهنامهکول pa nama kawal

betrothal *n.* نامزدي namzadgee

better *a* غوره ghwara

better *adv.* پهغورهول pa ghwara dawl

better *v. t* غورهکدل؛غورهکول ghwara keydal; ghwara kawal

betterment *n* بهتري behtaree

between *prep* پهمنزک pa manz ki

beverage *n* اک skhak

bewail *v. t* ماتم کول matam kawal

beware *v.i.* متوجهاوسدل mutawajo oseydal

bewilder *v. t* ګنس کول gangas kawal

bewitch *v.t* جادوکول jadoo kawal

beyond *prep.* هغهخوالري hagha khwa leyri

beyond *adv.* الله...پورته la ... porta

bi *pref* دانرزژبيومختاتوری da angreyzay zhabi yaw makhtaray toray

biangular *adj.* دوهزاويلرونکي dwa zaweeyi laroonkay

bias *n* تعصب tasob

bias *v. t* تعصبکول tasob kawal

bible *n* انجيل injeel

bibliography *+n* کتابپژندنه kitab peyzhandana

bibliographer *n* کتابپژاند kitab peyzhand

bicentenary *adj* دوهسوهکلن dwa sawa kalan

bicker *v.t* شخهکول shkhara kawal

bicycle *n.* بايسکل baysakal

bid *v.t* پهمزايدهکواندزورکول pa muzayda ki warandeyz warkawal

bid *n* پهمزايدهکواندز pa muzayda ki warandeyz

bidder *n* پهمزايدهکواندزکوونکی pa muzayda ki warandey kawoonkay

bide *v. t* کاميابپارهسختانتظارکول kamyabay lapara sakht intizar kawal

biennial *adj* دوهکلنوار dwa kalan war

bier *n* دتابوتدايودوای da taboot da eekheydo zay

big *a* لوی loy

bigamy *n* دوهخزلرنه dwa khazi larana

bight *n* کوراکو kog rakog

bigot *n* متعصبکس motasib kas

bigotry *n* تعصب tasob

bile *n* صفرا safra

bilingual *a* دوهژبيز dwa zhabeez

bill *n* قانونيلايحه؛بل qanoonee layha; bil

billion *n* بيليون؛دپسويوشمره beelyoon; da peyso yaw shmeyra

billow *n* لويهسپه loya sapa

billow *v.i* پوهل sapey wahal

bilk *v. t* غولول gholawal

bimonthly *adj.* دوه‌میاشتنی dwa myashtanay

binary *adj* له‌دوه‌هندسوجو la dwa hindso jor

bind *v.t* تل taral

binding *a* پایدار paydar

binocular *n.* دوه‌ستریزدوربین dwa stargeez doorbeen

biographer *n* ژوندلیک‌لیکونکی zhwand leek leekoonkay

biography *n* ژوندلیک zhwand leek

biologist *n* ژوندپوهاند zhwand pohand

biology *n* ژوندپوهنه zhwand pohana

bioscope *n* دفلم‌ودلوپروجکور da filam khodalo projektor

biped *n* دوه‌پلرونکی‌جاندار dwa pkhey laroonkay jandar

birch *n.* یوول‌ونه yaw dawl wana

bird *n* الوتونکی alwatoonkay

birth *n.* زدنه zeygeydana

biscuit *n* بسکو biskot

bisect *v.t* نیمول neemawal

bisexual *adj.* دوه‌رګه،دوه‌جنسه dwa raga; dwa jinsa

bishop *n* اسقف په‌عیسائیت‌کی pa eesaeeyat ki asqaf

bison *n* یوول‌غرنی‌اووحشی‌بکام لرونکی‌غوایی yaw dawl gharanay aw wehshee bakam laroonkay ghwayay

bit *n* یوه‌توته،له‌برخه yawa tota; laga barkha

bitch *n* سپ spay

bite *v.t.* چیچل cheechal

bite *n* چک؛چیچ chak; cheech

bitter *a* تریخ treekh

bi-weekly *adj* دوه‌اونیزه dwa ooneeza

bizarre *adj* عجیب ajeeb

blab *v.t. & i* بپتی‌کول bey patee kawal

black *a* تور tor

blacken *v.t.* تورول torawal

blackmail *n* په‌زورونودپسووصولتیا pa darawano da peyso wasooltya

blackmail *v.t* دبدنامه‌په‌ارله‌چاخه‌پس اخستل da badnamay pa dar la cha sakha peysey akheystal

blacksmith *n* پ pakh

bladder *n* مثانه masana

blade *n.* تغ teygh

blain *n* التهابی‌پسوب iltihabee parsob

blame *v.t* ملامتمل malamat ganral

blame *n* ملامتیا،الزام malamatya; ilzam

blanch *v.t. & i* پوستول postawal

bland *adj.* آرامه arama

blank *a* ساده،پاک sada; pak

blank *n* تش‌ای،نالیکلپاه tash zay; naleekali panra

blanket *n* ش sharay

blare *v.t* جارووهل jar wahal

blast *n* چاودنه chawdana

blast *v.i* چول؛چاودل chowal; chawdal

blaze *n* شوغله shoghla

blaze *v.i* لمبه‌کدل؛زوراخستل lamba keydal; zor akheystal

bleach *v.t* سپینول؛وینل speenawal; weenzal

blear *v.t* تاریکول tareekawal

bleat *n* بعبع ba ba

bleat *v. i* بعبع کول،امبامباکول ba ba kawal; amba amba kawal

bleed *v. i* وینه کدل weeni keydal

blemish *n* داغ dagh

blend *v. t* مخلوطول makhlootawal

blend *n* مخلوط،وله makhloot; gadola

bless *v. t* برکت ورکول barakat warkawal

blether *v. i* ناوه غدل nawara ghageydal

blight *n* بادوهنه bad wahana

blind *a* وند roond

blindfold *v. t* سترتل stargi taral

blindness *n* نه لیدا na leeda

blink *v. t. & i* سترک وهل stargak wahal

bliss *n* کامله خوي kamila khwakhee

blister *n* تاکه tanraka

blizzard *n* دواورتوپان da wawri toopan

bloc *n* کونده konda

block *n* بند،خه band; khand

block *v.t* خنکدل،بندول khand keydal; bandawal

blockade *n* بندیز bandeyz

blockhead *n* احمق سی ahmaq saray

blood *n* وینه weena

bloodshed *n* وینه توینه toyawana weena

bloody *a* په وینو للی pa weeno laralay

bloom *n* غو ghotay

bloom *v.i.* غوکول ghotay kawal

blossom *n* غو ghotay

blossom *v.i* غوکول ghotay kawal

blot *n.* داغ dagh

blot *v. t* داغ لول dagh lagawal

blouse *n* جاکوله کمیس jakat dawla kamees

blow *v.i.* بادچلدل bad chaleydal

blow *n* بادچلدنه bad chaleydana

blue *n* نیل neel

blue *a* آبی رنز abee rang

bluff *v. t* تراستل teyr eystal

bluff *n* تراستنه teyr eystana

blunder *n* لویه تروتنه loya teyrwatana

blunder *v.i* ناوه تروتنه کول nawara teyrwatana kawal

blunt *a* پ pas

blur *n* تتدنه tateydana

blurt *v. t* بی پامه غدل bey pama ghageydal

blush *n* دمخ سوروالی da makh soorwalay

blush *v.i* لهشرمدومخ سوریدل la sharmeydo makh sooreydal

boar *n* وحشی خو wahshee khoog

board *n* دبتخته da beyray takhta

board *v. t.* بکسپردل beyray ki spareydal

boast *v.i* لافوهل lafi wahal

boast *n* لاف lafi

boat *n* کوچنکه koochnay kakhtay

boat *v.i* کتچلول kakhtay chalawal

bodice *n* سینه بند seena band

bodily *a* بدني badanee

bodily *adv.* جسما،یوای jisman; yaw zay

body *n* بدن badan

bodyguard *n.* ساتندوی satandoy

bog *n* جبه jaba

bog *v.i* جبه کوبدل jaba ki doobeydal

bogus *a* درواغ darwagh

boil *n* جوش josh

boil *v.i.* اشول eyshawal

boiler *n* جوشوونکی joshawoonkay

bold *a.* زهور zra war

boldness *n* ورتیا زه zra wartya

bolt *n* دکولپزبانچه da kolp zabancha

bolt *v. t* کولپبندول kolp bandawal

bomb *n* بم bam

bomb *v. t* بمباريکول bambaree kawal

bombard *v. t* بمباريکول bambaree kawal

bombardment *n* بمباري bambaree

bomber *n* بماچوونکالواتکه bam achowoonki alwataka

bonafide *adv* ببهان bey bahaney

bonafide *a* سماوجدي sam aw jadee

bond *n* بند،لاسوند band; laswand

bondage *n* مریيتوب mrayeetob

bone *n.* هوکی hadookay

bonfire *n* لویاور loy or

bonnet *n* یوولخول yaw dawl khwali

bonus *n* انعام eenam

book *n* لیکی leekay

book *v. t.* درجکول darj kawal

book-keeper *n* الیکیساتونکی leekay satoonkay

book-mark *n.* دلیکينان da leekee nakhan

book-seller *n* لیکيپلوروونکی leekee plorowoonkay

book-worm *n* دلیکيچینجی da leekee cheenjay

bookish *n.* کتابي keetab

booklet *n* کتابوی keetabgotay

boon *n* نعمت naymat

boor *n* شلسی shadal saray

boost *n* پرمخورنه par makh warana

boost *v. t* پرمخول par makh waral

boot *n* بو،فایده boot; fayda

booth *n* پره sapara

booty *n* ولجه walja

booze *v. i* مستول mastawal

border *n* پوله poola

border *v.t* پولهلرل poola laral

bore *v. t* سوریکول sooray kawal

bore *n* دیوهپایپداخليسوری da yawa payp dakhilee sooray

born *v.* زیيدل zeygeydal

borne *adj.* زمدلی zeygeydalay

borrow *v. t* پوراخستل por akheystal

bosom *n* سینه seena

boss *n* رئیس rayees

botany *n* بوپوهنه bootpohana

botch *v. t* ناماهرانهپوندول namahirana peywandawal

both *a* دواه dwara

both *pron* دواه،هم۔۔۔هم dwara; ham … ham

both *conj* نهیواز na yawazi

bother *v. t* زحمتول zehmatawal

botheration *n* جنجال janjal

bottle *n* بوتل botal

bottom *n* تل،بخ tal; beykh

bough *n* انه sanga

boulder *n* لويمول‌بره loya gol dabara

bouncer *n* باو batoo

bound *n.* وپ top

boundary *n* پوله poola

bountiful *a* لورينه lawreena

bounty *n* انعام eenam

bouquet *n* للدسته guldasta

bout *n* نوبت؛حالت nobat; halat

bow *v. t* بيدل teeteydal

bow *n* بت؛کو teet; kog

bow *n* کمان kaman

bowel *n.* ددنه‌برخه da geydi dananay barkha

bower *n* پره sapara

bowl *n* کاسه kasa

bowl *v.i* دغونسکپه‌شان‌ارغدل da ghondaski pa shan eyrghareydal

box *n* صندوق sandooq

boxing *n* دسوک‌وهڼلوبه da sook wahani loba

boy *n* هلک halak

boycott *v. t.* سره‌ايکختمول sara areeki khatmawal

boycott *n* دايکوبندز da areeko bandeyz

boyhood *n* هلکتوب halaktob

brace *n* تانه taranga

bracelet *n* وى wakhay

brag *v. i* نازيدل nazeydal

brag *n* ناز؛با naz; bati

braille *n* دندولپارماني‌ليک da rando lapara zangaray leek

brain *n* دماغ dimagh

brake *n* دموربرک da motar brayk

brake *v. t* برک‌لول brayk lagawal

branch *n* انه sanga

brand *n* تجارتي‌نه tijaratee nakha

brandy *n* يوول‌شراب yaw dawl sharab

brass *n.* برنج؛ژ birinj; zhar

brave *a* توريالى tooryalay

bravery *n* مانه meyrana

brawl *v. i. & n* ناندروهل؛ناندر nandaray wahal; nandaray

bray *n* دخره‌رمبا da khra rambari

bray *v. i* هندل hangeydal

breach *n* نقض nuqz

bread *n* و doday

breadth *n* پراخوالى parakhwalay

break *v. t* ماتدل؛ماتول mateydal; matawal

break *n* ماتوالى؛زۀ matwalay; zand

breakage *n* ماتدنه mateydana

breakdown *n* ناپه‌خرابتيا nasapa kharabtya

breakfast *n* سهارنۍ saharanay

breakneck *n* ترهوونکى tarhowoonkay

breast *n* تي tee

breath *n* ساه sa

breathe *v. i.* ساه‌اخستل sa akheystal

breeches *n.* ترزنانه‌پورلپټلون tar zangana pori land patloon

breed *v.t* رزل rozal

breed *n* تخم؛روزنه tokham; rozana

breeze *n* ومه wagma

breviary *n.* غورچاشوى‌کتاب ghorchanr shaway keetab

brevity *n* لنون landoon

brew *v. t.* ماک‌جوول skhak jorawal

brewery *n* ماک‌جوونه skhak jorawana

bribe *n* بډ badi

bribe *v. t.* بوهل/ورکول badi wahal / warkawal

brick *n* ختہ khakhta

bride *n* ناو nawi

bridegroom *n.* شالملی shazalmay

bridge *n* پل pol

bridle *n* پزوان peyzwan

brief *a.* مختصر mukhtasar

brigade *n.* غوه ghond

bright *a* لاند zaland

brighten *v. t* روانول rokhanawal

brilliant *a* نامتو namtoo

brim *n* ه sanda

brine *n* اوبه ترو trawey oba

bring *v. t* راول rawral

brinjal *n* بانجان banjan

brink *n.* ژ zhay

brisk *adj* چک chatak

bristle *n* وژغونه wazhghona

british *adj* بریتانوي breetanawee

brittle *a.* کسن krasan

broad *a* پراخ prakh

broadcast *n* خپرونه khparawana

broadcast *v. t* خپرول khparawal

brocade *n* کمخاب kimkhab

broccoli *n.* یو دول‌گوپی yaw dawl gopee

brochure *n* کتابگوتی kitabgotay

brochure *n* رساله risala

broker *n* سمسار samsar

brood *n* دجاندارو پہ یوای زیدلي ماشومان da jandaro pa yaw zay zeygeydalee mashooman

brook *n.* ویاله wyala

broom *n* جارو jaroo

bronze *n. & adj* برونز;برونزي رن bronz; bronzee rang

broth *n* وروا khorwa

brothel *n* فاحشہ خانه fahisha khana

brother *n* ورور wror

brotherhood *n* ورورولي wrorwalee

brow *n* وریز wreez

brown *a* نصواري naswaree

brown *n* نصواري رن naswaree rang

browse *n* پہ لوستنہ پلل pa lostana palatal

bruise *n* میدیدنه meydeydana

bruit *n* ونوسی gongosay

brush *n* برش brash

brutal *a* برحمه bey rehma

brute *n* وحشي ناور wahshee zanawar

bubble *n* پوکاره pookanra

bucket *n* ولچه dolcha

buckle *n* سک sagak

bud *n* غنچه ghoncha

budget *n* بوډجه،لخت انولتیا bodija; lagakht andwaltya

buff *n* پیکہ زیر رن peeka zyar rang

buffalo *n.* مه meykha

buffoon *n* مسخره maskhara

bug *n.* خزنده khazanda

bugle *n* شپل shpeylay

build *v. t* تعمیرول tameerawal

build *n* جوت jorakht

building *n* وداۓ wadanay

bulb *n.* برنايي‌راغ breykhnayee sragh

bulk *n* حجم hojam

bulky *a* وزن‌لرونکی wazan laroonkay

bull n غوايی ghwayay

bulldog *n* يوول‌سپی yaw dawl spay

bullet *n* مرم marmay

bulletin *n* خبرپانه khabar panra

bully *n* دپهلوان da pkhey palawan

bully *v. t.* تهديدول tahdeedawal

bulwark *n* دبنددوال da band deywal

bumper *n.* فنر،بمپر finar; bampar

bunch *n* وی wagay

bundle *n* keyday

bungalow *n* ما manray

bungle *v. t* خرابول kharabawal

bungle *n* خرابونه kharabawana

bunk *n* هرول‌راکته‌کدونکی‌چپرکيا بستره har dawl rakakhta keydoonkay chaparkat ya bistara

bunker *n* تحويلخانه tahweelkhana

buoy *n* لامبوزن‌توکی lambozan tokay

buoyancy *n* لامبووهنه lambowahana

burden *n* بار bar

burden *v. t* بارول barawal

burdensome *a* سخت،ناوه sakht; nawara

bureau *n.* دفتر daftar

Bureacuracy *n.* اداري‌تأسيسات idaree taseesat

bureaucrat *n* اداري‌مأمور idaree mamoor

burglar *n* غل ghal

burglary *n* غلا ghla

burial *n* خوونه khakhowana

burn *v. t* سوزول swazawal

burn *n* سون soon

burrow *n* ترمکلاندسوه tar zmakay landi soora

burst *v. i.* چاوددل chawdeydal

burst *n* چاودنه chawdana

bury *v. t.* خول khakhawal

bus *n* اتوبوس atoboos

bush *n* بوی bootay

business *n* راکه‌ورکه،دنده rakra warkra; danda

businessman *n* تاجر tajir

bustle *v. t* په‌جنجال‌اودل pa janjal oreydal

busy *a* بوخت bokht

but *prep* مرداچ magar da chi

but *conj.* خو،ول kho; wali

butcher *n* قصاب qasab

butcher *v. t* په‌ظلم‌وژل pa zolam wazhal

butter *n* کوچ kuch

butter *v. t* چاپلوسي‌کول chaplosee kawal

butterfly *n* پتنگ patang

buttermilk *n* پروی peyrawee

buttock *n* کونای konatay

button *n* ز tanray

button *v. t.* تبندول tanray bandawal

buy *v. t.* خريداري‌کول khareedaree kawal

buyer *n.* پرودونکی peyrodoonkay

buzz *v. i* بندل bangeydal

buzz *n.* بنار bangar

by *prep* دـ...پهوسيله da ... pa waseela

by *adv* لهاخه la arakha

bye-bye *interj.* خدای دمل شه khuday di mal sha

bylaw, bye-law *n* ضمني قانون;سیمه ییزقانون zimnee qanoon; seemayeez qanoon

bypass *n* فرعي لار faree lar

by-product *n* فرعي محصول faree mahsool

byre *n* غوجله ghojala

byword *n* متل matal

C

cab *n.* دکرایموټر da karayi motar

cabaret *n.* موسیقي واله ملمستون moseeqee wala meylmastoon

cabbage *n.* ویپي gopee

cabin *n.* کوچنۍ خونه koochnay khoona

cabinet *n.* دوزیرانودلخونه da wazeerano da dalgay khoona

cable *n.* سیمي پۍ seemee paray

cable *v. t.* په سیمي پۍ تل pa seemee paree taral

cache *n* ساتنای satanzay

cachet *n* ټاپه tapa

cackle *v. i* ککوهل kakari wahal

cactus *n.* زاقوم zaqoom

cad *n* سپک اوبي تربیسی spak aw bey tarbeeyey saray

cadge *v. i* دایي کول gadayee kawal

cafe *n.* قهوه خانه qahwa khana

cage *n.* زندان zandan

cake *n.* کک kayk

calamity *n.* آفت afat

calcium *n* دفلز کلسیم da kilseeyum filiz

calculate *v. t.* شمرل shmeyral

calculator *n* شمرونکي ماشین shmeyroonkay masheen

calculation *n.* شمر shmeyr

calendar *n.* کالهنداره kalhindara

calf *n.* خوسکی khuskay

call *v. t.* رابلل rabalal

call *n.* بلنه balana

caller *n* رابلوونکي rabalowoonkay

calligraphy *n* لیکنۍ بنره leekanay banra

calling *n.* بلنه;چغه balana; cheygha

callow *adj* بتجرب bey tajrubey

callous *a.* سخت زی sakht zaray

calm *n.* آرامت aramakht

calm *n.* خاموشي khamoshee

calm *v. t.* خاموشول khamoshawal

calmative *adj* آراموونکي aramowoonkay

calorie *n.* دتودوخدمعلومو ندرجه da tawdokhey da maloomawani daraja

calumniate *v. t.* تورلول tor lagawal

camel *n.* او ookh

camera *n.* دعکاس کامره da akasay kamra

camp *n.* پنغالی pandghalay

camp *v. i.* خمدرول kheymey darawal

campaign *n.* مبارزه mubariza

camphor *n.* كافور kafoor

can *n.* لوى حلبى halbee lokhay

can *v. t.* په حلبى لوى کاچول pa halbee lokhee ki achawal

can *v.* تواندل twaneydal

canal *n.* وياله wyala

canard *n* دروغجن خبر daroghjan khabar

cancel *v. t.* باطلول،حذفول batilawal; hazafawal

cancellation *n* حذف،فسخ hazaf; faskh

cancer *n.* ناسور؛چنا nasoor; changakh

candid *a.* لاند zaland

candidate *n.* نوماند noomand

candle *n.* شمع shama

candour *n.* سپين ويي speen goyee

candy *n.* پتاسه patasa

candy *v. t.* شيريني رانيول sheereenee raneewal

cane *n.* لکه،مسافرخانه lakara; musafir khana

cane *v. t.* په لکه وهل pa lakara wahal

canister *n.* دمزري کوچنو کر da meyzaree koochnay tokray

cannon *n.* يوسترو پيک yaw star topak

canon *n* مذهبي قانون mazhabee qanoon

canopy *n.* پر sapray

canteen *n.* يوول خونای yaw dawl khwaranzay

canter *n* تفريحي چکر tafreehee chakar

canton *n* برخه barkha

cantonment *n.* دنظامي لتمهای da nizamee dalgay tamzay

canvas *n.* تت tat

canvass *v. t.* رایغوتل rayi ghokhtal

cap *n.* خولۍ khwalay

cap *v. t.* په سرخولای ودل pa sar khwali eekhodal

capability *n.* وتيا wartya

capable *a.* و war

capacious *a.* پراخ prakh

capacity *n.* پراختيا prakhtya

cape *n.* سر sar

capital *n.* پلازمنه،پانه plazmeyna; panga

capital *a.* توری لوی loy toray

capitalist *n.* پانوال pangawal

capitulate *v. t* تسليميدل tasleemeydal

caprice *n.* وسواس waswas

capricious *a.* وسواسي waswasee

Capricorn *n* دجدي مياشت da jadee myasht

capsize *v. i.* سرچپه کول sar chapa kawal

capsular *adj* د کپسول په شکل da kipsool pa shakal

captain *n.* جتورن؛مشر jagtooran; mashar

captaincy *n.* مشري masharee

caption *n.* د پرکه نيوز د da neewani preykra

captivate *v. t.* مسحورول mashoorawal

captive *n.* بندي bandee

captive *a.* مسحور mashoor

captivity *n.* زندانيتوب zandaneetob

capture *v. t.* نيول؛تسخيرول neewal; taskheerawal

capture *n.* نيونه neewana

car *n.* موږ motar

carat *n.* قيراط qeerat

caravan *n.* قافله qafila

carbon *n.* دكاربن فلزياس da karban filiz ya geys

card *n.* كارت؛پله kart; panra

cardamom *n.* هل heyl

cardboard *n.* لهسخت كاغذه جوه شوي نري تته la sakht kaghaza jora shawi naray gata

cardiacal *adjs* پهزړه پوراوند pa zra pori arwand

cardinal *a.* بنسيز bansateez

cardinal *n.* پهعيسائيت كيومذهبيمشر pa eesaeeyat ki yaw mazhabee mashar

care *n.* پام pam

care *v. i.* پام كول pam kawal

career *n.* دژوندكنلاره da zhwand kranlar

careful *a* ړ zeyr

careless *a.* بفكره bey fikra

caress *v. t.* نازول nazawal

caricature *n.* لهٹوكواومسخروكداكانور la toko aw maskharo dak anzor

carious *adj* بوسيده boseeda

carnage *n* ول وژنه tol wazhana

carnival *n* جشن jashn

carol *n* سرود؛نغمه sarood; naghma

carpenter *n.* تركاڼ tarkanr

carpentry *n.* تركاڼي tarkanree

carpet *n.* غالۍ ghalay

carriage *n.* لدونه leygdawana

carrier *n.* لدوونكى leygdawoonkay

carrot *n.* ګازره gazara

carry *v. t.* وړل؛بارول waral; bar waral

cart *n.* كراچى krachay

carton *n* پ peytay

cartoon *n.* كاريكاتور kareekatoor

cartridge *n.* كارتوس؛مرم kartoos; marmay

carve *v. t.* تول؛تراشل togal; trashal

cascade *n.* وبى zarobay

case *n.* بكس baks

cash *n.* نغدپسـ naghdi peysey

cash *v. t.* پسنغدول peysey naghdawal

cashier *n.* خزانهدار khazana dar

casing *n.* پو pokhakh

cask *n* دمايعاتولپارهپايپ da mayato lapara payp

casket *n* كوچنىبكس koochnay baks

cast *v. t.* اچول؛طرحهكول achawal; tarha kawal

cast *n.* اچونه؛وضعيت achawana; wozeeyat

caste *n* نژاد nazhad

castigate *v. t.* نيوكهكول neewaka kawal

casting *n* ريختهري؛قالبكاچونه reykhta garee; qalib ki achawana

cast-iron *n* چدن chadan

castle *n.* كلا kala

castor oil *n.* تل ول يو yaw dawl teyl

casual *a.* تصادفي tasadofee

casualty *n.* په؛مينه peykha; mreena

cat *n.* پيشو peesho

catalogue *n.* الیک lar leek

cataract *n.* دستری‌ل da stargi gol

catch *v. t.* نیول neewa

catch *n.* نیونه neewana

categorical *a.* پرکنده preykanda

category *n.* له،طبقه dala; tabqa

cater *v. i* خواہ‌چمتوکول khwara chamtoo kawal

caterpillar *n* دورمو‌چینجی da wreykhmo cheenjay

cathedral *n.* عمومی‌کلیسا amoomee kaleesa

catholic *a.* کاتولیک‌عیسائ katoleek eesayee

cattle *n.* دغواموله da ghwameykho gala

cauliflower *n.* ل‌وپی gol gopee

causal *adj.* سببی sababee

causality *n* دعلت‌او‌معلول‌ترمنایکه da ilat aw malool tar manz areeka

cause *n.* سبب sabab

cause *v.t* لامل‌رلدل lamal garzeydal

causeway *n* وچه‌پخه‌لاره wacha pakha lara

caustic *a.* سوزوونکی sozawoonkay

caution *n.* خبرداری khabardaray

caution *v. t.* خبرداری‌ورکول khabardaray warkawal

cautious *a.* بدار baydar

cavalry *n.* سپاره‌عسکر spara askar

cave *n.* سمه smas

cavern *n.* لوی‌سم loy askar

cavil *v. t* عبونه‌پلل ayboona palatal

cavity *n.* کنده kanda

caw *n.* کاغ‌کاغ kragh kragh

caw *v. i.* کاغ‌کاغ‌کول kagh kagh kawal

cease *v. i.* لاس‌اخستل las akheystal

ceaseless ~*a.* پرله‌پس parla pasi

cedar *n.* سرو sarwa

ceiling *n.* چت chat

celebrate *v. t. & i.* لمانل lmanzal

celebration *n.* لماننه lmanzana

celebrity *n* نوموی noomawaray

celestial *adj* آسمانی asmanee

celibacy *n.* یوازیتوب yawazitob

celibacy *n.* تنهایی tanhayee

cell *n.* سلول؛کوچنی‌زندان؛حجره siloel; koochnay zandan; hajra

cellar *n* زرخانه zeyr khana

cellular *adj* سلولی siloolee

cement *n.* سمنه simant

cement *v. t.* په‌سمنوجورول pa simanto jorawal

cemetery *n.* میستون mreestoon

cense *v. t* عطرواوخوشبویوسره‌عبادات کول atro aw khushbooyo sara ibadat kawal

censer *n* عطردان atardan

censor *n.* دمطبوعاتواوچلندونوارونکی da matbooato aw chalandoono saroonkay

censor *v. t.* دمطبوعاتواوچلندونوارنه کول da matbooato aw chalandoono sarana kawal

censorious *adj* عب‌پلونکی ayb palatoonkay

censorship *n.* دسانسورجره da sansor jargagay

censure *n.* سخته‌نیوکه sakhta neewaka

censure *v. t.* سخته نيوكه كول sakhta neewaka kawal

census *n.* سرشمرنه sar shmeyrana

cent *n* سلمه salama

centenarian *n* سلمه كليزه salama kaleeza

centenary *n.* دسلم كليزجشن da salami kaleezi jashan

centennial *adj.* سل كليزه sal kaleeza

center *n* مركز markaz

centigrade *a.* دتودوخيوپيمائش da tawdokhay yaw paymayish

centipede *n.* زنزه zanza

central *a.* مركزي markazee

centre *n* مركز markaz

centrifugal *adj.* الهمركزخهراكونك la markaz sakha rakhkoonkay

century *n.* پهـسليزه peyray; saleeza

ceramics *n* دكودويلوي da kawdoree lokhee

cereal *n.* غَلَه ghala

cereal *a* غَلَهييز ghalayeez

cerebral *adj* دكوچنيدماغپهاوند da koochnee dimagh pa arwand

ceremonial *a.* تشريفاتي tashreefatee

ceremonious *a.* دتشريفاتوپابند da tashreefato paband

ceremony *n.* جشن jashan

certain *a* يقيني yaqeenee

certainly *adv.* يقينا yaqeenan

certainty *n.* پوخباور pokh bawar

certificate *n.* شهادتنامه shahadat nama

certify *v. t.* تصديقول tasdeeqawal

cerumen *n* دغوزوه da ghwag zawa

cesspool *n.* دپخلنيدلوووينلواى da pakhlanzee da lokho weenzalo zay

chain *n* زنير zanzeer

chair *n.* كرسـ kursay

chairman *n* رئيس rayees

challenge *n.* مبارزه mubariza

challenge *v. t.* مبارزتهبلل mubarizey ta tlal

chamber *n.* خونه khoona

chamberlain *n* ناظر،پرهدار nazir; peyra dar

champion *n.* اتل atal

champion *v. t.* اتلولىكول atlawali kawal

chance *n.* موقع،فرصت moqa; fursat

chancellor *n.* لوىمنشي،لومرىوزير loy munshee; loomray wazeer

chancery *n* دلوىمنشييالوميوزير دندهيامقام da loy munshee ya loomree wazeer danda ya maqam

change *v. t.* بدلول badlawal

change *n.* بدلون badloon

channel *n* بهن،وسيله bahanz; waseela

chant *n* سندره sandara

chaos *n.* وي gadwadee

chaotic *adv.* پهوسره pa gadwaday sara

chapel *n.* دعبادتكوچنىاى da ibadat koochnay zay

chapter *n.* باب،درس،پركى bab; dars; saparkay

character *n.* سيرت seerat

charge *v. t.* دندهسپارل،تهمتلول danda sparal; tohmat lagawal

charge *n.* سپارنه،تهمت sparana; tohmat

chariot *n* جني کراچ jangee krachay

charitable *a.* خراتي kheyratee

charity *n.* خرات kheyrat

charm1 *n.* سحر،ښکلا seher; khkula

charm2 *v. t.* په سحر مجذوبول pa seher majzoobawal

chart *n.* د نقشې جوړولو کاغذ da naqshey jorawalo kaghaz

charter *n* اجازه لیک،قرارداد eejaza leek; qarardad

chase1 *v. t.* ارل saral

chase2 *n.* ارنه،تعقیب sarana; taqeeb

chaste *a.* پاک pak

chastity *n.* پاکبازي pakbazee

chat1 *n.* اټر خبر khabari atari

chat2 *v. i.* خبراتر کول khabari atari kawal

chatter *v. t.* کټپتکول krati prati kawal

chauffeur *n.* موروان motarwan

cheap *a* ارزان arzan

cheapen *v. t.* ارزانول arzanawal

cheat *v. t.* غولول gholawal

cheat *n.* دوکه doka

check *v. t.* معاینه کول moayna kawal

check *n* معاینه moayna

checkmate *n* د شطرنج په لوبه کې کشت او مات da shatranj pa loba ki kasht aw mat

cheek *n* اننی anangay

cheep *v. i* چونریدل choonreydal

cheer *n.* د خوچغه da khwakhay cheygha

cheer *v. t.* په خوچغه وهل pa khwakhay cheygha wahal

cheerful *a.* خندان khandan

cheerless *a* خواشینی khwasheenee

cheese *n.* پنر paneer

chemical *a.* کیمیایی keymyayee

chemical *n.* مواد کیمیایی keymyayee mawad

chemise *n* ترجامو لانداچوونکی کمیس tar jamo landi achowoonkay kamees

chemist *n.* کیمیاپوه keymya poh

chemistry *n.* کیمیاپوهنه keymya pohana

cheque *n.* چک cheyk

cherish *v. t.* نازول nazawal

chess *n.* شطرنج shatranj

chest *n* ر tatar

chestnut *n.* بلوط balot

chew *v. t* ژوول zhowal

chevalier *n* زه ورسرتری zrawar sarteyray

chicken *n.* چرګوری chargooray

chide *v. t.* ملامتول malamatawal

chief *a.* مهم muhim

chieftain *n.* سردار sardar

child *n* ماشوم mashoom

childhood *n.* ماشومتوب mashoomtob

childish *a.* ماشومانه mashoomana

chill *n.* سوخه sarokha

chilli *n.* مرچ mrich

chilly *a* یخ yakh

chimney *n.* پرناه parnara

chimpanzee *n.* هغه لوی بدنه بیزو چپه ونو کژوندکوي hagha loybadana beezo chi pa wano ki zhwand kawee

chin *n.* زنه zana

china n. چینيلوی cheenee lokhee

chirp v.i. چرچر کول charchari kawal

chirp n چرچر charchari

chisel n سکنه sakana

chisel v. t. پهسکنسرهپرکول pa sakani sara prey kawal

chit n. وانکه zwanaka

chivalrous a. زهور zrawar

chivalry n. زهورتوب zrawartob

chlorine n یوولکمیايیماده yaw dawl keymyayee mada

chloroform n دبهوکمیايیماده da bey hokhay keymyayee mada

choice n. غوراوی ghoraway

choir n په کلیساکسروديل pa kaleesa ki saroodee dalgay

choke v. t. زندکول zanday kawal

cholera n. دهضوبا da hayzey waba

chocolate n چاکل chaklayt

choose v. t. غورهکول ghwara kawal

chop v. t وهکول tota kawal

chord n. دسرونوجوت da suroonw jorakht

chorus n. دسندرغاول da sandar gharo dalgay

Christ n. حضرتعیسیٰعلیهالسلام hazrat eesa alayhissalam

Christendom n. زمسیحي maseehee naray

Christian n عیسائي eesayee

Christian a. عیسوي eesawee

Christianity n. عیسائیت eesaeeyat

Christmas n کرسمس(دعیسائیانو اختر) krismis (da eesayano akhtar)

chronic a. اودمهاله oogad mahala

chronicle n. دتاریخاوزنلهمخدپرالیک da tareekh aw neytey la makhi da peykho lar leek

chronology n. پلیکنه peykh leekana

chronograph n دوختسنجوزنآله da wakht sanjawani ala

chuckle v. i لهانسرهخندل la zan sara khandal

chum n خوملری khog malgaray

church n. کلیسا kaleesa

churchyard n. دکلیسااودهغبهرني دوالونومنکچاپرهمکه da kaleesa aw da haghi baharanee deywaloono manz ki chapeyra zmaka

churl n سپکشخص spak shakhs

churn v. t. & i. شاربل؛کوچجوول sharbal; kuch jorawal

churn n. منداو mandaroo

cigar n. سر sigrat

cigarette n. کوچنیسیار koochnay seegar

cinema n. سینما seenama

cinnabar n دسیمابوکان da seemabo kan

cinnamon n دارچینئ darcheenee

cipher, cipher n. رمزيتوری ramzee toray

circle n. دایره dayra

circuit n. دوره؛چاپریال dawra; chapeyryal

circumspect adj. محتاط muhtat

circular a دایروي dayrawee

circular n. مجله mujala

circulate v. i. چاپربدل chapeyr garzeydal

circulation *n* جریان jaryan

circumference *n.* ددایرمحیط da dayrey muheet

circumstance *n* حال؛صورت؛برنوالی hal; soorat; sarangwalay

circus *n.* سرکس sarkas

cist *n* جعبه jaba

citadel *n.* بالاحصار balahisar

cite *v. t* تذکره کول tazkira kawal

citizen *n* اصلي استوګن aslee astogan

citizenship *n* تابعیت؛مدني حقونه او دند tabieeyat; madanee haqoona aw dandi

city *n* بار khar

civic *a* مدني madanee

civics *n* مدني علوم madanee oloom

civil *a* مدني؛اولسي madanee; oolasee

civilian *n* ملکي وى malkee wagaray

civilization *n.* ولنیز پرمختہ tolaneez parmakhtag

civilize *v. t* متمدنرول motamadin garzawal

clack *n. & v. i* ناندر؛ناندروهل nandarey; nandarey wahal

claim *n* ادعا adaa

claim *v. t* ادعاکول adaa kawal

claimant *n* مدعي modaee

clamber *v. i* پهلاسواوپورتهتلل pa laso aw pkho porta tlal

clamour *n* و zwag

clamour *v. i.* وجوول zwag jorawal

clamp *n* لغته laghata

clandestine *adj.* مخفي makhfee

clap *v. i.* لاسونهپکول lasoona parkawal

clap *n* دلاسونوپکار da lasoono parkar

clarify *v. t* وضاحت کول wazahat kawal

clarification *n* وضاحت wazahat

clarity *n* لاندتوب zalandtob

clash *n.* کر takar

clash *v. t.* کروهل takar wahal

clasp *n* تسمه؛چنګک tasma; chingak

class *n* درجه؛ولی daraja; tolgay

classic *a* غوره او اعلی ghwara aw ala

classic *n* لرغوني علوم larghonee oloom

classical *a* لرغوني larghonee

classification *n* لبندي dalbandee

classify *v. t* لبندي کول dalbandee kawal

clause *n* عبارت ibarat

claw *n* لمنګو mangoley

clay *n* دکلالخه da kulalay khata

clean *a* پاک pak

clean *v. t* پاکول pakawal

cleanliness *n* صفائي safayee

cleanse *v. t* وینل weenzal

clear *a* لانده zalanda

clear *v. t* روښانول؛پاکول rokhanawal; pakawal

clearance *n* پاکوالی؛چاونه pakwalay; chanrawana

clearly *adv* پهسرندول pa sargand dawl

cleft *n* درز darz

clergy *n* روحانیون rohaneeyoon

clerical *a* پا اوند پهروحانیونوپور pa rohaneeyoono pori arwand

clerk *n* دفتري؛منشي daftaree monshee

clever *a.* هوښیار hookhyar

clew *n.* رخی sarkhay

click *n.* کپ krap

client *n..* پرودونکی peyrodoonkay

cliff *n.* ز garang

climate *n.* موسم mosam

climax *n.* اوج oj

climb1 *n.* ورختنه warkhatana

climb *v.i* ورختل warkhatal

cling *v. i.* پوستدل peywasteydal

clinic *n.* طبی کتنای tibee katanzay

clink *n.* شرنا shranga

cloak *n.* یوول چوغه yaw dawl chogha

clock *n.* garay

clod *n.* لوه loota

cloister *n.* خانقا khanqa

close *n.* تلی ای taralay zay

close *a.* بند band

close *v.t* تل taral

closet *n.* الماری almaray

closure *n.* محصورای mahsoor zay

clot *n.* دوینپرشووه da weeni pran shawi tota

clot *v. t* پرندل praneydal

cloth *n* وکر tokar

clothe *v. t* جاماغوستل jami aghostal

clothes *n.* جام jami

clothing *n* کالی kalee

cloud *n.* ورﻩ wareez

cloudy *a* ورین wareezan

clove *n* لونگ lawang

clown *n* مسخره maskhara

club *n* انجمن anjuman

clue *n* اثر،اشاره asar; ishara

clumsy *a* بی هنره bey honara

cluster *n* geyday

cluster *v. i.* کول geyday kawal

clutch *n* دموترکلچ da motar klach

clutter *v. t* شیانتیت اوپرک ایوول shayan teet aw park eekhowal

coach *n* اتوبوس،أستاد atoboos; ustad

coachman *n* موروان motarwan

coal *n* دبروسکاره da dabaro skara

coalition *n* یوکدنه yaw keydana

coarse *a* شل shalag

coast *n* ساحل sahil

coat *n* کو kot

coating *n* پو pokhakh

coax *v. t* غوهمالی کول ghora malee kawal

cobalt *n* دکوبالکمیایي عنصر da kobalt keymyayee onsar

cobbler *n* موچي mochee

cobra *n* کبرامار kubra mar

cobweb *n* دغاله da ghanrey zala

cocaine *n* دمخدرومواد یوقسم da mukhadira mawado yaw qisam

cock *n* چر charg

cocker *v. t* ویادل wyareydal

cockle *n* واه wakha

cockroach *n* سورندی soor garanday

coconut *n* کوپره kopra

code *n* کو،رمزي شمره kod; ramzee shmeyra

co-education *n.* مخلوطتعلیم makhloot taleem

coefficient *n.* مشترک عامل mushtarik amil

co-exist *v. i* ژوندسره‌کول gad zhwand sara kawal

co-existence *n* ژوندون gad zhwandoon

coffee *n* قهوه qahwa

coffin *n* تابوت taboot

cog *n* دندانه dandana

cogent *adj.* دواک‌اوزورتن da zwak aw zor sakhtan

cognate *adj* هم‌آره ham ara

cognizance *n* خبرتیا khabartya

cohabit *v. t* په‌ژوندکول pa gada zhwand kawal

coherent *a* منطقي mantaqee

cohesive *adj* سرناکه sreykhnaka

coif *n* رخچینه rakhchina

coin *n* سکه sika

coinage *n* سکه‌جوول sika jorawal

coincide *v. i* توافق‌سره‌پدل tawafuq sara peykheydal

coke *v. t* تکلیس‌کول taklees kawal

cold *a* سو sor

cold *n* ساه sara

collaborate *v. i* په‌ه‌کارکول pa gada kar kawal

collaboration *n* ه gadey hasi

collapse *v. i* له‌منه‌تلل la manza tlal

collar *n* غاه ghara

colleague *n* همکار hamkar

collect *v. t* راغونول raghondawal

collection *n* راغونونه raghondawana

collective *a* ولنیز tolaneez

collector *n* راغونونکی raghondawoonkay

college *n* پوهنی pohanzay

collide *v. i.* ټکرکول takar kawal

collision *n* ټکر takar

collusion *n* دناوه‌دپاره‌جوجای‌کول da nawara gato da para jorjaray kawal

colon *n* دلویوکولمولاندینی‌برخه da loyo koolmo landeenay barkha

colonial *a* کلاکي khkeylakee

colony *n* کلاکي‌سیمه khkeylakee seema

colour *n* رن rang

colour *v. t* رنول rangawal

column *n* لیکه leeka

coma *n.* هوی‌ب bey hokha

comb *n* منه gmanz

combat1 *n* جه jagra

combat *v. t.* جندل jangeydal

combatant1 *n* جه‌مار jagra mar

combatant *a.* جه‌ماری jagra maree

combination *n* والی gadwalay

combine *v. t* سره‌ول sara gadawal

come *v. i.* راتلل ratlal

comedian *n.* دخندوونکوننداره‌مو هنرمندda khandawoonko nandaro honar mand

comedy *n.* خندوونکننداره khandawoonki nandara

comet *n* لکای‌ستوری lakay wal storay

comfit *n.* یوول‌خواه yaw dawl khwaga

comfort1 *n.* آرام aram

comfort *v. t* آرامورکول aram warkawal

comfortable *a* آرامورکوونکی aram warkawoonkay

comic *a* خندوونکی khandawoonkay

comic *n* کارون kartoon

comical *a* خندوونکی khandawoonkay

command *n* فرمان؛مشري farman; masharee

command *v. t* فرمان ورکول؛مشري کول farman warkawal; masharee kawal

commandant *n* قومندان qomandan

commander *n* سرلښکر sar lakhkar

commemorate *v. t.* دیادونغونهجوول da yadawani ghonda jorawal

commemoration *n.* یادغونه yad ghonda

commence *v. t* پیلېدل payleydal

commencement *n* پیل payl

commend *v. t* ستایل stayal

commendable *a.* ستایلی stayalay

commendation *n* ستاینه stayana

comment *v. i* رایورکول ray warkawal

comment *n* رای؛انتقاد ray; intiqad

commentary *n* تفسیر tafseer

commentator *n* مفسر mufassir

commerce *n* تجارت tijarat

commercial *a* تجارتي tijaratee

commiserate *v. t* زهسوی کول zra saway kawal

commission *n.* مأموریت mamooreeyat

commissioner *n.* مأمور mamoor

commissure *n.* دای پوند da peywand zay

commit *v. t.* مرتکب کدل murtakib keydal

committee *n* پلاوی plaway

commodity *n.* سوداریزمال sodagareez mal

common *a.* عام am

commoner *n.* عاديوی adee wagaray

commonplace *a.* عادي adee

commonwealth *n.* ولنیزهخره tolaneeza khayr kheygara

commotion *n* غورځ ghorzang

commove *v. t* پرېشانهکول preyshana kawal

communal *a* دلهییز dalaeez

commune *v. t* دزهخوالهکول da zra khwala kawal

communicate *v. t* خبراترکول khabari atari kawal

communication *n.* رابطه rabita

communiqué *n.* دولتياعلان dawlatee aylan

communism *n* کمونیزم kamooneezam

community *n.* ولنه tolana

commute *v. t* داستوناودکارايترمنځ سفرکول da astogni aw da kar zay tr manz safar kawal

compact *a.* خلاصهشوی khulasa shaway

compact *n.* ژمنه؛معاهده zhmana; moahida

companion *n.* ملری malgary

company *n.* شرکت shirkat

comparative *a* پرتلهییز partalaeez

compare *v. t* سرهسنجول sara sanjawal

comparison *n* سنجونه sanjawona

compartment *n.* اپارتمان apartman

compass *n* محيط،پرکار moheet; parkar

compassion *n* زه‌سواندي zra swanday

compel *v. t* مجبورول majboorawal

compensate *v.t* جبرانول jibranawal

compensation *n* جبران jibran

compete *v. i* سيالي کول syalee kawal

competence *n* سيالي syalee

competent *a.* دوتياخاوند da wartya khawand

competition *n.* مسابقه musabiqa

competitive *a* مسابقانه musabiqana

compile *v. t* تدوينول tadweenawal

complacent *adj.* راضي razee

complain *v. i* يله‌کول geela kawal

complaint *n* يله geela

complaisance *n.* مهرباني mehrabanee

complaisant *adj.* مهربان mehraban

complement *n* تشريفات tashreefat

complementary *a* بشپړونکى bashparawoonkay

complete *a* بشپړ bashpar

complete *v. t* بشپړول bashparawal

completion *n* پاى‌ته‌رسونه pay ta rasawal

complex *a* پېچلى peychalay

complex *n* فکري‌تمايل fikree tamayal

complexion *n* دسيري‌رنگ da seyri rang

compliance *n.* فرمانبرداري farmanbardaree

compliant *adj.* فرمانبردار farmanbardar

complicate *v. t* پېچلى‌کول peychalay kawal

complication *n.* پېچلتيا peychaltya

compliment *n.* احترام ehtiram

compliment *v. t* احترام‌اودرناوى‌کول ehtiram aw dranaway kawal

comply *v.i* غاه‌ايودل ghara eekhodal

component *adj.* اهم‌جز aham juz

compose *v.t* په‌کمپيوټرتصنيفول pa campyootar tasneefawal

composition *n* ترکيب tarkeeb

compositor *n* تصنيفوونکى tasneefawoonkay

compost *n* ترکيب tarkeeb

composure *n.* آرامت aramakht

compound *n* مرکب‌جسم murakab jisam

compound *a* مرکب murakab

compound *n* اڼ angar

compound *v.i* ترکيبول tarkeebawal

comprehend *v.t* پوهدل poheydal

comprehension *n* پوهه poha

comprehensive *a* پرفهم purfehem

compress *v. t.* تخته‌کول takhta kawal

compromise *n* روغه‌جوه rogha jora

compromise *v.t.* روغه‌جوه‌کول rogha jora kawal

compulsion *n* زور zor

compulsory *a* لازمي lazmee

compunction *n.* افسوس afsos

computation *n.* ڼه ghanra

compute *v.t.* ڼه‌کول ghanra kawal

comrade *n.* ملګرى malgaray

conation *n.* هه hasa

concave *adj.* مقعر maqar

conceal *v. t.* پول patawal

concede *v.t.* تسليمول tasleemawal

conceit *n* غرورلرل gharoor laral

conceive *v. t* تصوركول tasawor kawal

concentrate *v.t* توجهساتل tawajo satal

concentration *n.* توجه tawajo

concept *n* عقیده aqeeda

conception *n* ادراک idrak

concern *v. t* تشویشلرل tashweesh laral

concern *n* تشویش tashweesh

concert *n.* دموسیقاناسته da moseeqay nasta

concert2 *v. t* مرتبکول muratab kawal

concession *n* بخنه bakhkhana

conch *n.* حلزونیصدف hilzonee sadaf

conciliate *v.t.* پخلاکول pukhla kawal

concise *a* مختصر mukhtasar

conclude *v. t* پایلهرسدل payli ta raseydal

conclusion *n.* نتیجه nateeja

conclusive *a* فصلهکن faysala kun

concoct *v. t* اختراعکول ikhtira kawal

concoction *n.* اختراع ikhtira

concord *n.* توافق tawafuq

concrete *n* دکانکریوماده da kankreeto mada

concrete *a* کلک klak

concrete *v. t* دکانکریوجوول da kankreeto jorawal

concubinage *n.* نامشروعژوند na mashroo gad zhwand

concubine *n* بشرعدوادهژوندترول bey shari da wada zhwand teyrawal

condemn *v.t.* ملامتول malamatawal

condemnation *n* ملامتیا malamatya

condense *v. t* منقبضکول munqabiz kawal

condition *n* حالت،شرط halat; shart

conditional *a* شرطیه sharteeya

condole *v.i* همدردیکول. hamdardee kawal

condolence *n* خواخوي khwakhoogee

condonation *n.* ترناهوورتردنده tar goona warteyridana

conduct *n* خوی khooy

conduct *v. t* چلندکول chaland kawal

conductor *n* چلوونکی chalowoonkay

cone *n.* مخروط makhroot

confectioner *n* خواهجووونکی khwaga jorowoonkay

confectionery *n* دخواوپلورنی da khwago ploranzay

confer *v.i* اعطاکول ata kawal

conference *n* غونه ghonda

confess *v. t.* اقرارکول iqrar kawal

confession *n* اقرار iqrar

confidant *n* رازدار razdar

confide *v. i* رازسپارل raz sparal

confidence *n* اطمینان itminan

confident *a.* مطمئن mutmain

confidential *a.* محرمانه mahramana

confine *v. t* محدودول mahdoodawal

confinement *n.* دپولواکنه da poolo takana

confirm *v. t* تائیدول tayeedawal

confirmation *n* تصدیق tasdeeq

confiscate *v. t* مصادرهکول musadira kawal

confiscation *n* مصادره musadira

conflict *n.* اختلاف ikhtilaf

conflict *v. i* اختلافپداکدل ikhtilaf peyda keydal

confluence *n* جریان gad jaryan

conformity *n.* ورتهوالی warta walay

conformity *n.* رعایت riayat

confraternity *n.* دوورولولنه da wrorwalay tolana

confrontation *n.* مقابله muqabila

confuse *v. t* نسول gangasawal

confusion *n* وارخطایی war khatayee

confute *v.t.* ردول radawal

conge *n.* اجازهلیک eejaza leek

congenial *a* همخویه ham khooya

congratulate *v.t* مبارکیویل mubarakee wayal

congratulation *n* مبارکی mubarakee

congress *n* مجلس majlis

conjecture *n* اکل atkal

conjecture *v. t* ومانکول gooman kawal

conjugal *a* دوادهپهاه da wada pa ara

conjugate *v.t. & i.* صرفکول sarf kawal

conjunct *adj.* متصل mutasil

conjure *v.t.* پهکووحاضرول pa kodo hazirawal

conjure *v.i.* کوکول kodi kawal

connect *v. t.* وصلکول wasl kawal

connection *n* تاو taraw

connivance *n.* پهاجازه pata eejaza

conquer *v. t* غلبهکول ghalaba kawal

conquest *n* غلبه ghalaba

conscience *n* شعور shaoor

conscious *a* باشعوره ba shaoora

consecrate *v.t.* تقدیسول taqdeesawal

consecutive *adj.* متواتر mutawatir

consecutively *adv* پرلهپس parla pasey

consensus *n.* عمومیخوه amoomee khwakha

consent *n.* کدنه راضي razee keydana

consent *v. i* راضيکدل razee keydal

consent3 *v.t.* راضيکول razee kawal

consequence *n* پایله payla

consequent *a* منتج mantaj

conservative *a* محافظهکار muhafiza kar

conservative *n* محافظهکاري muhafiza karee خووونکی khokhawoonkay

conserve *v. t* ژوندیساتل zhwanday satal

consider *v. t* پهپامکنیول pa pam ki neewal

aconsiderable *a* دپامنهو war da pam na war

considerate *a.* احترام‌ساتوونکی ehtiram satowoonkay

consideration *n* پام pam

considering *prep.* په‌پام‌وکچ pa pam war kach

consign *v.t.* امانت‌سپارل amanat sparal

consign *v. t.* تائیدول tayeedawal

consignment *n.* امانت‌پلورنه amanat plorana

consist *v. i* شاملدل shamileydal

consistence,-cy *n.* دوام dawam

consistent *a* محکم muhkam

consolation *n* اینه dadeena

console *v. t* ۱ورکول dad warkawal

consolidate *v. t.* ینول teengawal

consolidation *n* ینوالی teengwalay

consonance *n.* هم‌آهني ham agangee

consort *n.* همسفر hamsafar

conspectus *n.* زمینه zameena

conspicuous *a.* مالوم maloom

conspiracy *n.* دسیسه daseesa

conspirator *n.* خاین khayin

conspire *v. i.* خیانت‌کول khyanat kawal

constable *n* دپولس‌ارندوی da poolas sarandoy

constant *a* مستقل mustaqil

constellation *n.* دستورومجمع da storo majma\

constipation *n.* قبض qabz

constituency *n* انتخاباتي‌حوزه intikhabatee hoza

constitute *v. t* انتخابول intikhabawal

constitution *n* اساسي‌قانون asasee qanoon

constrict *v.t.* تنول tangawal

construct *v. t.* جورول jorawal

construction *n* وداني‌جوول wadanee jorawal

consult *v. t* مشوره‌کول mashwara kawal

consultation *n* مشوره mashwara

consume *v. t* مصرف‌کدل masraf keydal

consumption *n* مصرف masraf

consumption *n* لت lagakht

contact *n.* رابطه rabita

contact *v. t* رابطه‌کول rabita kawal

contain *v.t.* نیول ای zay neewal

contaminate *v.t.* خرابول kharabawal

contemplate *v. t* دایمي‌پام‌کول daymee pam kawal

contemplation *n* تفکر tafakur

contemporary *a* هم‌مهاله ham mahala

contempt *n* حقارت haqarat

contend *v. i* سیالي‌کول syalee kawal

content *a.* راضي razee

content *v. t* راضي‌کول razee kawal

content *n* ظرفیت zarfeeyat

content *n.* مفاد mafad

contention *n* مباحثه mubahisa

contentment *n* رضایت reeyazat

contest *v. t* مقابله‌کول muqabila kawal

contest *n.* مسابقه musabiqa

context *n* زمینه zameena

continent *n* براعظم baryazam

continental *a* براعظم پوراوند baryazam pori arwand

contingency *n.* احتمال ehtimal

continual *adj.* مداوم madawam

continuation *n.* بهیر baheer

continue *v. i.* لرل دوام dawam laral

continuity *n* تسلسل tasalsul

continuous *a* جاري jaree

contour *n* خاکه khaka

contraception *n.* لهبلاربتخه مخنیوی la blarbakht sakha makhneeway

contract *n* عقد aqd

contract *v. t* قراردادکول qarardad kawal

contrapose *v.t.* مخالف مفهوم ورکول mukhalif mafhoom warkawal

contractor *n* تون کوونکی taroon kawoonkay

contradict *v. t* ماتول matawal

contradiction *n* تکذیب takzeeb

contrary *a* مخالف mukhalif

contrast *v. t* رندتوپیرلرل sargand topeer larl

contrast *n* رندتوپیر sargand topeer

contribute *v. t* ونهورکول wanda warkawal

contribution *n* ونه wanda

control *n* مخنیوی makhneeway

control *v. t* مخنیوی کول makhneeway kawal

controller *n.* ناظر nazir

controversy *n* مباحثه mubahisa

contuse *v.t.* وکل tokal

conundrum *n.* معما moama

convene *v. t* غوندل ghondeydal

convener *n* دجرغی غرای da jargey gharay

convenience *n.* راحت rahat

convenient *a* باآرام ba aram

convent *n* صومعه somia

convention *n.* کانفرانس kanfarans

conversant *a* دخبروسی da khabaro saray

conversant *adj.* باخبر ba khabar

conversation *n* مکالمه mukalima

converse *v.t.* خبراترکول khabari atari kawal

conversion *n* سرچپه کونه sar chapa kawana

convert *v. t* سرچپه کول sar chapa kawal

convert *n* اونه arawana

convey *v. t.* ورسول warrasawal

conveyance *n* دای سهولت da gadee sahoolat

convict *v.t.* ملامتول malamatawal

convict *n* مجرم mujrim

conviction *n* مجرمیت mujrimeeyat

convince *v. t* قانع کول qanay kawal

convivial *adj.* خندان khandan

convocation *n.* راغونونه raghondawana

convoke *v.t.* پهدعوت رابلل pa dawat rabalal

convolve *v.t.* تاوول tawowal

coo *n* غومبر ghombar

coo *v. i* غومبرکول ghombar kawal

cook *v. t* پخول pakhawal

cook *n* پخلی pakhlay

cooker *n* ر پخلي pakhleegar

cool *a* سو sor

cool *v. i.* سول sarawal

cooler *n* سوونکی sarowoonkay

coolie *n* پني pandee

co-operate *v. i* همکاري کول hamkaree kawal

co-operation *n* همکاري hamkaree

co-operative *a* مرستندویه mrastandoya

co-ordinate *a.* هم رتبه ham rotba

co-ordinate *v. t* موزونول mawzoonawal

co-ordination *n* همکاري hamkaree

co-partner *n* ونه وال wanda wal

cope *v. i* ورسره مخامخ کیدل warsara makhamakheydal

coper *n.* معامله ر moamilagar

copper *n* مس mis

coppice *n.* وڼ ganri wani

copulate *v.i.* پوستدل peywasteydal

copy *n* نقل naqal

copy *v. t* نقل جوول naqal jorawal

coral *n* مرجان marjan

cord *n* رسۍ rasay

cordial *a* قلبي qalbee

corbel *n.* د ونانی د تیر راواتلي برخه da wananay da teer rawatali barkha

core *n.* تخمدان tukhamdan

coriander *n.* دڼیا danrya

cork *n.* د بلوط د کوړنی د یوي وني پوستکی da balot da koranay d yawi wani postakay

corn *n* جواری joowaray

corner *n* و gut

coronation *n* تاج اوډنه taj eekhodana

coronet *n.* تاج کوچنی koochnay taj

corporal *a* بدني badanee

corporate *adj.* یو شوی yaw shaway

corporation *n* اتحادیه شرکت etihadeeya shirkat

corps *n* پلاوی plaway

corpse *n* مړی maray

correct *a* درست drost

correct *v. t* درستول drostawal

correction *n* سموونه samawona

correlate *v.t.* ارتباط ورکول irtibat warkawal

correlation *n.* ارتباط irtibat

correspond *v. i* مکاتبه کول makatiba kawal

correspondence *n.* مکاتبه makatiba

correspondent *n.* خبریال khabaryal

corridor *n.* دهلیز dehleez

corroborate *v.t.* غتلی کول ghakhtalay kawal

corrosive *adj.* استحصالي isteyhsalee

corrupt *v. t.* فاسدول fasidawal

corrupt *a.* فاسد fasid

corruption *n.* بدي badi

cosmetic *a.* سینروونکی seengarowoonkay

cosmetic *n.* سینار seengar

cosmic *adj.* د کائناتو په اوند da kaynato pa arwand

cost *v.t.* بیه لرل baya laral

cost *n.* لګت lagakht

costal *adj.* ساحلي sahilee

cote *n.* د مرغانو ځاله da marghano zala

costly *a.* قیمتي qeematee

costume *n.* لباس libas

cosy *a.* گرم او نرم؛هوسا garm aw naram; hosa

cot *n.* ږاله؛پره zala; sapara

cottage *n* کوټ kotangay

cotton *n.* پنبه poonba

couch *n.* تخت؛استراحتای takht; istirahat zay

cough *n.* وخی tokhay

cough *v. i.* وخدل tokheydal

council *n.* شورا shoora

councillor *n.* دشوراغی da shoora gharay

counsel *n.* سلاکاري؛سلاکار salakaree; salakar

counsel *v. t.* سلاکاري کول salakaree kawal

counsellor *n.* سلاکار salakar

count *n.* شمره shmeyra

count *v. t.* شمره کول shmeyra kawal

countenance *n.* ره؛قیافه seyra; qeeyafa

counter *n.* په دفترو کداستقبال او دمز pa daftaro ki da istiqbal oogad meyz

counter *v. t* مخالفت کول؛واب ور کول mukhalifat kawal; zawab warkawal

counteract *v.t.* باطلول batilawal

countercharge *n.* وابی تهمت zawabee tuhmat

counterfeit *a.* مصنوعي masnooee

counterfeiter *n.* جعل ساز jal saz

countermand *v.t.* لغوه کول lughwa kawal

counterpart *n.* نژدملری nazhdey malgaray

countersign *v.t.* امضاکول imza kawal

countess *n.* دنواب مرمن da nawab meyrman

countless *a.* بشمره bey shmeyra

country *n.* هواد heywad

county *n.* علاقه ilaqa

coup *n.* سرچپه پرحکومت باند sar chapa par hookoomat bandi

couple *n* جوه jora

couple *v. t* جوه کول jora kawal

couplet *n.* بت چیوه قافیه ولري beyt chi yawa qafeeya walaree

coupon *n.* دکاغذیوه رسید da kaghaz yawa raseed

courage *n.* زه ورتوب zra wartob

courageous *a.* زه ور zra war

courier *n.* قاصد qasid

course *n.* دزده کو دوره da zdakro dawra

court *n.* عدالت؛محکمه adalat; mahkama

court *v. t.* غوه مالي کول ghwaramalee kawal

courteous *a.* مهربان mehraban

courtesan *n.* درباري فاحشه darbaree fahisha

courtesy *n.* احترام ehtiram

courtier *n.* درباري darbaree

courtship *n.* واده نه مخکدهلک او نجل ترمزمینه ناکخبر wada na makhki da halak aw najlay tar manz meena naki khabari

courtyard *n.* غولی gholay

cousin *n.* دتره,ماما,یاترورزوی‌یالور da tra, mama, ya tror zoy ya loor

covenant *n.* ژمنه,تون zhmna; taroon

cover *v.t.* پوښل pokhal

cover *n.* پوښ;جلد pokh; jild

coverlet *n.* بستن brastan

covet *v.t.* آرزوکول arzoo kawal

cow *n.* غوا ghwa

cow *v. t.* ارول;برول darawal; beyrawal

coward *n.* بزه bey zra

cowardice *n.* ارنتوب darantoob

cower *v.i.* ارخه‌زه‌چاودل dar.sakha zra chawdal

cozy ساده;آسانه sada; asana

crab *n* چنا changakh

crack *n* درز darz

crack *v. i* درزمو‌ندل;ماتدل darz moondal; mateydal

cracker *n* ماتدونکی mateydoonkay

crackle *v.t.* تکدل trakeydal

cradle *n* زانو zango

craft *n* هنر honar

craftsman *n* هنرمند honar mand

crafty *a* ماهر;چلباز mahir; chalbaz

cram *v. t* زبانی‌یادول zubanee yadawal

crambo *n.* شاعرکی‌هغه‌کلیمه‌چقافیه‌ید بلاهغله‌قافیسره‌جوه‌وي shairay ki hagha kaleema chi qafeeya yi da bali haghi qafeeyi sara jora wee

crane *n* کلنگ,زاله kalang; zanra

crankle *v.t.* زاویه‌دارکول zaweeyadar kawal

crash *v. i* وهوه‌کدل tota tota keydal

crash *n* نساپه‌تکر nasapa takar

crass *adj.* احمق‌او‌لوده ahmaq aw lawda

crate *n.* دخوراکی‌موادوصندوق da khorakee mawado sandooq

crave *v.t.* غوتل ghokhtal

craw *n.* جحوره jajoora

crawl *v. t* خاپورکول khapori kawal

crawl *n* خاپو khapori

craze *n* شوق shawq

crazy *a* لونی leywanay

creak *v. i* کنجدل kranjeydal

creak *n* کنجی kranjay

cream *n* پروی peyraway

crease *n* دجامو‌نجکدووالادرز da jamo gonji keydo wala darz

create *v. t* تولیدول tawleedawal

creation *n* پدایت peydayakht

creative *adj.* پنوونکی panzowoonkay

creator *n* خالق khaliq

creature *n* مخلوق makhlooq

credible *a* باوري bawaree

credit *n* ارزت;باور arzakht; bawar

creditable *a* معتبر motabar

creditor *n* پوراخستونکی por akhistoonkay

credulity *adj.* زرباوره zar bawara

creed *n.* باورلیک bawar leek

creed *n* اعتقاد aytiqad

creek *n.* کوچنی‌خلیج koochnay khaleej

creep *v.i* پرسینه‌ویدل par seena khwayeydal

creeper *n* خزنده khazanda

cremate *v. t* سوزول او ايرکول sozawal aw eerey kawal

cremation *n* ايرکوونه eerey kawona

crest *n* تاج؛جوغه taj; jogha

crew *n.* دکتکارمندان da kakhtay karmandan

crib *n.* آخور akhor

cricket *n* کری karray

crime *n* جنايت janayat

crimp *n* دوتانوتاواوکلوته da weykhtano taw aw klokhta

crimple *v.t.* ونورکول gonzi warkawal

criminal *n* جنايتکار janayat kar

criminal *a* جنايي janayee

crimson *n* سورلدنه sooreydana

cringe *v. i.* زانراغونول zan raghondawal

cripple *n* شلشو shal shoot

crisis *n* بحران buhran

crisp *a* تاوراتاو taw rataw

criterion *n* کچ؛مقياس kach; miqyas

critic *n* دانتقادهنر da intiqad hunar

critical *a* حساس hasas

criticism *n* انتقاد intiqad

criticize *v. t* نيوکهکول neewaka kawal

croak *n.* قرقرکول qar qar kawal

crockery *n.* خاورنلوي khawran lokhay

crocodile *n* نهنگ nahang

crook *a* بدشکله bad shakla

crop *n* غله؛فصل ghala; fasal

cross *v. t* پوروتل؛غوول pori watal; ghosawal

cross *n* دضربنه؛شخه da zarab nakha; shkhara

cross *a* دوهره،مخالف dwa raga; mukhalif

crossing *n.* تربدنه،دوتلولار،مخالفت teyreydana; da watalo lar; mukhalifat

crotchet *n.* چارتاپينو chartapee not

crouch *v. i.* درناوىورکول dranaway warkawal

crow *n* کاغه،کارغه kragha; kargha

crow *v. i* چغوهل cheyghi wahal

crowd *n* هوه ganra gonra

crown *n* تاج taj

crown *v. t* تاجپوشيکول taj poshee kawal

crucial *adj.* رسخت deyr sakht

crude *a* خام kham

cruel *a* ظالم zalim

cruelty *n* ظلم zulm

cruise *v.i.* پهکتکتفريحتهتلل pa kakhtay ki tafree ta tlal

cruiser *n* لويهمسافريکت loya musafiree kakhtay

crumb *n* دوپارچه da doday parcha

crumble *v. t* مدول maydawal

crump *adj.* کو kog

crusade *n* صليبيجهاد saleebee jihad

crush *v. t* ماتورکول matey warkawal

crust *n.* خزهسطحه khayza satha

crutch *n* دمعذورولک da mazooro lakray

cry *n* چغه cheygha

cry *v. i* چغوهل cheyghi wahal

cryptography *n.* داکدلیکنمزيدر da ramzee leekani ilam

crystal *n* بلور balor

cub *n* داوربچیناوحشي da wahshee zanawar bachay

cube *n* مكعب makab

cubical *a* مكعبي makabee

cubiform *adj.* مكعبوله makab dawla

cuckold *n.* فاحشه fahisha

cuckoo *n* دکوکومرغ da kookoo marghay

cucumber *n* بادرنگ badrang

cudgel *n* سوی sotay

cue *n* لاروونکیخبره lar khowoonki khabara

cuff *n* لستوخوله lastonr khula

cuff *v.t* لستوخولهوراچول lastonr khula warchawal

cuisine *n.* دپخلیلارود da pakhlee lar khod

culminate *v.i.* اوجتهرسدل oj ta raseydal

culprit *n* تورن؛غل toran; ghal

cult *n* عبادت ibadat

cultivate *v.t* کرل karal

cultural *a* فرهني farhangee

culture *n* کلتور kaltoor

culvert *n.* کوتره kawtara

cunning *a* چالاک chalak

cunning *n* چالاکي chalakee

cup *n.* پیاله pyala

cupboard *n* المار almaray

cupidity *n* شهوت shahwat

curable *a* رغدونکی ragheydoonkay

curative *a* داوندپهرغدو da ragheydo pa arwand

curb *n* توقیف tawqeef

curb *v.t* محدودول mahdoodawal

curd *n* مسته mastey

cure *n* درملنه darmalana

cure *v.t.* درملنهیکول darmalana yi kawal

curfew *n* وربندي garz bandee

curiosity *n* ظرافت؛دکنجکاوحس zarafat; da kanjkaway his

curious *a* کنجکاو؛دقیق kanjkaw; daqeeq

curl *n.* ک karay

currant *n.* ممیزدانبي bey daney mameez

currency *n* دهوادرسميسکه da heywad rasmee sika

current *n* سل؛جریان sayl; jaryan

current *a* موجوده mawjooda

curriculum *n* درسينصاب darsee nisab

curse *n* لعنت lanat

curse *v.t* لعنتورکول lanat warkawal

cursory *a* پهسرسريول pa sarsaree dawl

curt *a* لنډ land

curtain *n* پرده parda

curve *n* کووالی kog walay

curve *v.t* کووالیورکول kog walay warkawal

cushion *n* بالت balakht

cushion *v.t* پوورکول pokh warkawal

custodian *n* ساتونکی satoonkay

custody *v* ساتنه کاخستل satana ki akheystal

custom *n*. دود dood

customary *a* رواجي riwajee

customer *n* پرودونکی peyrodoonkay

cut *v. t* پرکول prey kawal

cut *n* چاک،درز chak; darz

cycle *n* بایسکل،چکر baysakal; chakar

cyclic *a* چکري،دوروي chakaree

cyclist *n* بایسکل سوار baysakal sawar

cyclone *n*. بادوباراني توپان badobaranee toopan

cylinder *n* تیوب tyoob

cynic *n* بدومانه انسان badgoomana insan

D

dabble *v. i.* لمدول lamdawal

dacoit *n*. داهاچوونکی dara achowoonkay

dacoity *n*. داه dara

dad, daddy *n* ابا aba

daffodil *n*. دزینرسل da zyar nargas gul

daft *adj.* ملایم mulayam

dagger *n*. خنجر khanjar

daily *a* روزانه rozana

daily *adv.* هرهور hara waraz

daily *n*. ورپاه warazpanra

dainty *a*. لطیف lateef

dainty *n*. دلطیف ذوق ستن da lateef zoq sakhtan

dairy *n* دشدواوندشیان da sheydo arwand shayan

dais *n*. دناستانی مز da nasti zangaray meyz

daisy *n* داودي گل dawoodee gul

dale *n* کوچنی دره koochnay dara

dam *n* داوبوبند da obo band

damage *n*. نقصان nuqsan

damage *v. t*. تاوانورکول tawan warkawal

dame *n*. مرمن meyrman

damn *v. t.* لعنت ویل lanat wayal

damnation *n*. غندنه ghandana

damp *a* نم nam

damp *n* لمدوالی lamdwalay

damp *v. t.* لمدول lamdawal

damsel *n*. پغله peyghla

dance *n* ابا gada; nasa

dance *v. t.* ډل gadeydal

dandelion *n*. یوول یاچزیلان لري yaw dawl gaya chi zyar gulan laree

dandle *v.t.* له ماشوم سره لوبکول la mashoom sara lobi kawal

dandruff *n* دسرپخه da sar pakha

dandy *n* لالی gulalay

danger *n*. خطر khatar

dangerous *a* خطرناک khatarnak

dangle *v. t* وندول zorandawal

dank *adj.* نمناک namnak

dap *v.i.*

dare *v. i.* همت کول himat kawal

daring *n*. جرأت،همت jorat; himat

daring *a* باهمته bahimata

dark *a* تت؛نارند tat; nasargand

dark *n* تیاره tyara

darkle *v.i.* تیاره کېدل tyara ki pateydal

darling *n* محبوب mehboob

darling *a* زه ته نژد zra ta nazhdey

dart *n.* برغز barghaz

dash *v. i.* په شدت وهل pa shidat wahal

dash *n* برید breed

date *n* خرما؛نه khorma; neyta

date *v. t* حسابول،تاریخ معلوم ول hisabawal; tareekh maloomawal

daub *n.* تپنه tapana

daub *v. t.* خېرنول kheyranawal

daughter *n* لور loor

daunt *v. t* ناهیلی کول naheelay kawal

dauntless *a* بی باکه bey baka

dawdle *v.i.* بېهوده وخت تېرول bayhooda wakht teyrawal

dawn *n* لمر راختنه lmar rakhatana

dawn *v. i.* د لمرراختل da lmar rakhatana

day *n* ورز waraz

daze *n* حرانتیا heyrantya

daze *v. t* حرانول heyranawal

dazzle *n* برېدنه breykheydana

dazzle *v. t.* ستربرېدل stargi breykheydal

dead *a* مه mar

deadlock *n* بنلست bandakht

deadly *a* ناوه؛وژونک nawara; wazhoonkay

deaf *a* کونر konr

deal *n* معامله moamila

deal *v. i* معامله کول moamila kawal

dealer *n* معامله کوونکی moamila kawoonkay

dealing *n.* سوداریزه راکه ورکه sawdagareeza rakra warkra

dean *n.* د پوهنيرئیس da pohanzee rayees

dear *a* محترم mohtaram

dearth *n* کمت kamakht

death *n* مینه mreena

debar *v. t.* منع کول mana kawal

debase *v. t.* سپکول spakawal

debate *n.* بحث behes

debate *v. t.* بحث کول behes kawal

debauch *v. t.* خرابول kharabawal

debauch *n* خرابونه kharabawana

debauchee *n* فاسق fasiq

debauchery *n* فسق fasq

debility *n* کمزورتیا kamzortya

debit *n* پور por

debit *v. t* پور کول por kawal

debris *n* د بااستعمال او خرابو یزونوری da bey istimala aw kharabo seezoono deyray

debt *n* پور por

debtor *n* پوروری por waray

decade *n* لسیزه laseeza

decadent *a* فسادي fasadee

decamp *v. i* که کول kada kawal

decay زوال zawal

decay *v. i* خرابېدل kharabeydal

decease *n* مینه mreena

decease *v. i* مه کېدل mar keydal

deceit *n* دوکه doka

deceive *v. t* دوکه کول doka kawal

december *n* دانرزي کال دولسمه da angreyzee kal dolasama myasht میاشت

decency *n* نزاکت nazakat

decent *a* مؤدب moadab

deception *n* چل chal

decide *v. t* پرېکه کول preykra kawal

decimal *a* اعشاري aysharee

decimate *v.t.* دلسو کسانو له منخه ديوه هغه وژل da laso kasano la manz sakha da yawa hagha wazhal

decision *n* پرېکه preykra

decisive *a* فصله کن faysala kon

deck *n* د کختی عرشه da kakhtay arsha

deck *v. t* عرشه جوړول arsha jorawal

declaration *n* اعلاميه aylameeya

declare *v. t.* اعلانول aylanawal

decline *n* زوال zawal

decline *v. t.* زوال موندل zawal moondal

decompose *v. t.* تجزیه کول tajzeeya kawal

decomposition *n.* تجزیه tajzeeya

decontrol *v.t.* نیونخه ایستل neewani sakha eystal

decorate *v. t* سینارول seengarawal

decoration *n* سینار seengar

decorum *n* پرای چلند par zay chaland

decrease *v. t* کمول kamawal

decrease *n* کمت kamakht

decree *n* فرمان farman

decree *v. i* فرمان صادرول farman sadirawal

decrement *n.* نقصان nuqsan

dedicate *v. t.* الکول dalay kawal

dedication *n* وقف waqaf

deduct *v.t.* کمول kamawl

deed *n* چلند؛ عمل chaland; amal

deem *v.i.* فرض کول farz kawal

deep *a.* ژور zhawar

deer *n* غره gharsa

defamation *n* تهمت tuhmat

defame *v. t.* تهمت لول tuhmat lagawal

default *n.* قصور؛ دوالیه qasoor; deywaleeya

defeat *n* ماتۍ mati

defeat *v. t.* ماتور کول mati warkawal

defect *n* نقص nuqs

defence *n* دفاع difa

defend *v. t* دفاع کول difa kawal

defendant *n* دفاع کوونکی difa kawoonkay

defensive *adv.* په دفاعي توه pa difaee toga

deference *n* تواضع tawazo

defiance *n* سرکشي sar kashee

deficit *n* نیمتیا neemgartya

deficient *adj.* نقضي nuqzee

defile *n.* خرنتیا kheyrantya

define *v. t* تعریفول tareefawal

definite *a* معین moeen

definition *n* تعریف tareef

deflation *n.* بادوستنه bad weystana

deflect *v.t. & i.* اوډل؛ اول awreydal; arawal

deft *adj.* غتلی ghakhtalay

degrade *v. t* عزت کمول eezat kamawal

degree *n* سند؛ درجه sanad; daraja

deist *n.* دخدای‌په‌وجودبباور da khuday pa wajood bawar

deity *n.* خدای khuday

deject *v. t* مايوسول mayoosawal

dejection *n* مايوسي mayoosee

delay *v.t. & i.* ندل،زول zandawal; zandeydal

deligate1 *n* له dala

delegate *v. t* په‌دله‌تلل pa dala tlal

delegation *n* غونه ghonda

delete *v. t* حذفول hazafawal

deliberate *v. i* قصدي‌كول qasdee kawal

deliberate *a* ارادي iradee

deliberation *n* سنجوونه،چرت sanjawana; churt

delicate *a* لطيف lateef

delicious *a* خوندور khwandawar

delight *n* خوشالي khoshalee

delight *v. t.* خوشالول khoshalawal

deliver *v. t* رسول rasawal

delivery *n* رسونه rasawana

delude *n.t.* دوکه،دوکهورکول doka; doka warkawal

delusion *n.* فريب fareyb

demand *n* غوتنه ghokhtana

demand *v. t* غوتنه‌کول ghokhtana kawal

demarcation *n.* دپولوايودنه da poolo eekhodana

dement *v.t* لوني‌کول leywanay kawal

demerit *n* ناوتيا nawartya

democracy *n* ولسواکي woolaswakee

democratic *a* جمهوري jamhooree

demolish *v. t.* نول rangawal

demon *n.* دو dew

demonetize *v.t.* بارزته‌کول bey arzakhta kawal

demonstrate *v. t* توضيح‌ورکول tawzee warkawal

demonstration *n.* توضيح tawzee

demoralize *v. t.* بداخلاقه‌کول bad akhlaqa kawal

demur *n* اعتراض،شک aytiraz; shak

demur *v.t* اعتراض‌کول aytiraz kawal

den *n* غار ghar

denial *n* مننه نه na manana

denote *v. i* نه‌ايودل nakha eekhodal

denounce *v. t* تورنول toranawal

dense *a* لوده، lawda; ganr

density *n* ه ganra

dentist *n* دغاونواکر da ghakhoono daktar

denude *v.t.* لوول loosawal

denunciation *n.* اخطار،تهديد akhtar; tahdeed

deny *v. t.* انکارکول inkar kawal

depart *v. i.* جلاکدل jala keydal

department *n* اداريانه idaree sanga

departure *n* جلاکدنه jala keydana

depauperate *v.t.* ضعيف‌کول zaeef kawal

depend *v. i.* انحصارلرل inhisar laral

dependant *n* انحصارلرونکی inhisar laroonkay

dependence *n* تابعيت،انحصار tabayeeyat; inhisar

dependent *a* تابع tabay

depict *v. t.* رسمول rasmawal

deplorable *a* خواشينوونکی khwasheenawoonkay

deploy *v.t.* پهليکهکشاملول pa leeka ki shamilawal

deponent *n.* شاهديليکونکی shahidee leekoonkay

deport *v.t.* لهوطنهشل la watana sharal

depose *v.t* وهکول gokha kawal

deposit *n.* بانکيحساب bankee hisab

deposit *v.t* بانککحساباپودل bank ki hisab eekhodal

depot *n* تحويلخانه tahweelkhana

depreciate *v.t.i.* بقدرهکدل/کول bey qadra keydal / kawal

depredate *v.t.* لول lootal

depress *v. t* فشارلاندراوستل fishar landi rawastal

depression *n* فشار fishar

deprive *v. t* محرومول mehroomawal

depth *n* ژورتيا zhawartya

deputation *n* استازيتوب astazeetob

depute *v. t* استازيتوبورکول astazeetob warkawal

deputy *n* نمائنده numayinda

derail *v. t.* بلارکول bey lari kawal

derive *v. t.* اخذکول akhaz kawal

descend *v. i.* کتهکدل kkhata keydal

descendant *n* اولاد awlad

descent *n.* کتهکدنه؛نسل kkhata keydana; nasal

describe *v.t* بيانول bayanawal

description *n* بيان؛توضيح bayan; tawzee

descriptive *a* بيانيه bayaneeya

desert *v. t.* بوفاييکول bey wafayee kawal

desert *n* بديا؛بوفايي beydya; bey wafayee

deserve *v. t.* حقدارومدل haqdar garzeydal

design *v. t.* طرحکول tarah kawal

design *n.* طرح؛خاکه tarah; khaka

desirable *a* پهزرهپور pa zra pori

desire *n* غوتنه ghokhtana

desire *v.t* آرزولرل arzoo laral

desirous *a* هيلهمن heela man

desk *n* دليکنمز da leekani meyz

despair *n* ناهيلي na heelee

despair *v. i* ناهيلیکدل na heelay keydal

desperate *a* نااميده na oomeeda

despicable *a* خوار khwar

despise *v. t* کرکهکول kraka kawal

despot *n* واکمن؛حاکم wakman; hakim

destination *n* منزل manzil

destiny *n* تقدير taqdeer

destroy *v. t* ويجاول weejarawal

destruction *n* ويجاي weejaree

detach *v. t* زانتهکول zanta kawal

detachment *n* بلتون beyltoon

detail *n* تفصيل tafseel

detail *v. t* تفصيلورکول tafseel warkawal

detain *v. t* ايسارول؛بنول eesarawal; zandawal

detect *v. t* معلومول maloomawal

detective *a* تفتيشي tafteeshee

detective *n.* کارپوه karpoh

determination *n.* قصد qasad

determine *v. t* تصميمول tasmeemawal

dethrone *v. t* ببرخوکول bey barkhi kawal

develop *v. t.* ترقيورکول taraqee warkawal

development *n.* پرمختگ par makhtag

deviate *v. i* منحرفکدل munharif keydal

deviation *n* سرغونه sar gharawana

device *n* آله،وسيله ala; waseela

devil *n* شطان sheytan

devise *v. t* اختراعکول ikhtira kawal

devoid *a* تش،خالي tash; khalee

devote *v. t* وقفکول waqaf kawal

devotee *n* وقفکوونکی waqaf kawoonkay

devotion *n* اخلاص ikhlas

devour *v. t* جذبول jazbawal

dew *n.* پرخه parkha

diabetes *n* دشکرناروغی da shakari naroghee

diagnose *v. t* معلومول maloomawal

diagnosis *n* تشخيص tashkhees

diagram *n* خاکه khaka

dial *n.* ساعت،دزنآواز saat; da zang awaz

dialect *n* دژبلهجه da zhabi lahja

dialogue *n* مرکه maraka

diameter *n* دقطرداير da dayri qutar

diamond *n* الماس almas

diarrhoea *n* اسهال ishal

diary *n* ديادتونوکتابگوتی da yadakhtoono kitabgotay

dice *n.* چکهپاو

dictate *v. t* حکمچلول hokam chalawal

dictation *n* حکم،حاکميت hokam; hakimeeyat

dictator *n* حاکم hakim

diction *n* دوييوغورهکونه da wayyo ghwara kawana

dictionary *n* قاموس qamoos

dictum *n* قضاييوينا qazayee wayna

didactic *a* تعليمي taleemee

die *v. i* مدل mreydal

die *n* مهر،پايه muhar; tapa

diet *n* غذا ghaza

differ *v. i* توپيرلرل tawpeer laral

difference *n* توپير tawpeer

different *a* مختلف mukhtalif

difficult *a* مشکل mushkil

difficulty *n* ستونزه stoonza

dig *n* کيندنه keendana

dig *v.t.* کنستل kanastal

digest *v. t.* هضمول hazmawal

digest *n.* مجله هضم، hazam; mujalla

digestion *n* هاضمه hazima

digit *n* عدد adad

dignify *v.t* احترامورکول ehtiram warkawal

dignity *n* عزت eezat

dilemma *n* وينهستونزه goonga stoonza

diligence *n* هههاوهاند hasa aw hand

diligent *a* کزيار zeeyar kakh

dilute *v. t* اوبلنکول oblan kawal

dilute *a* اوبلن oblan

dim *a* تت tat

dim *v. t* تتول tatawal

dimension *n* اندازه،حجم andaza; hujam

diminish *v. t* کوچنی کول koochnay kawal

din *n* غوغا ghawgha

dine *v. t.* وخول doday khwaral

dinner *n* مامنو makhamanay doday

dip *n.* غوه،غوپه ghota; ghopa

dip *v. t* غوپه کول ghopa kawal

diploma *n* تعليمی سند taleemee sanad

diplomacy *n* سفارت کاري safarat karee

diplomat *n* سفارت کار safarat kar

diplomatic *a* سفارتي safaratee

dire *a* ضروري deyr zarooree

direct *a* نغه په نغه neygh pa neygha

direct *v. t* امر کول amar kawal

direction *n* امر،لارو دنه amar; lar khodana

director *n.* مدير mudeer

directory *n* لارود کتابوی larkhod keetabgotay

dirt *n* چرک chark

dirty *a* چل chatal

disability *n* ناتواني natwanee

disable *v. t* ناتوانه کول natwana kawal

disabled *a* ناتوان natwan

disadvantage *n* تاوان،ضرر tawan; zarar

disagree *v. i* اختلاف لرل ikhtilaf laral

disagreeable *a.* ناخو nakhwakh

disagreement *n.* ناخوي nakhwakhee

disappear *v. i* ورکدل wrakeydal

disappearance *n* ورکتوب wraktob

disappoint *v. t.* مأيوسول mayoosawal

disapproval *n* ناخوي nakhwakhee

disapprove *v. t* ردول radawal

disarm *v. t* بوسلکول bey wasley kawal

disarmament *n.* بوسلکوونه bey wasley kawona

disaster *n* بدمرغي bad marghee

disastrous *a* تباه کن taba kun

disc *n.* يکلی،سک teekalay; disc

discard *v. t* پرودل preykhodal

discharge *v. t* رخصتول rukhsatawal

discharge *n.* رخصت rukhsat

disciple *n* مريد،شارد mureed; shagard

discipline *n* نظم،قاعده nazm; qayda

disclose *v. t* کاره کول khkara kawal

discomfort *n* ناآرامي naaramee

disconnect *v. t* ايکغوول areeki ghosawal

discontent n ناآرامه naarama

discontinue *v. t* ادامه درول idama darawal

discord *n* اختلاف ikhtilaf

discount *n* تخفيف takhfeef

discourage *v. t.* بجرأته کول bey jurata kawal

discourse *n* موضوع؛ونا mawzoo; wayna

discourteous *a* بادبه bey adaba

discover *v. t* افشا کول afsha kawal

discovery *n.* موندنه moondana

discretion *n* واک

discriminate *v. t.* توپيرول tawpeerawal

discrimination *n* توپيرموندنه tawpeer moondana

discuss *v. t.* مركه کول maraka kawal

disdain *n* توهين tawheen

disdain *v. t.* توهين کول tawheen kawal

disease *n* رنز ranz

disguise *n* چماوچل cham aw chal

disguise *v. t* بهبدلول banra badlawal

dish *n* لوی lokhay

dishearten *v. t* زهماتول zra matawal

dishonest *a* خاين khayin

dishonesty *n.* خيانت khyanat

dishonour *v. t* بعزتي کول bey eezatee kawal

dishonour *n* بعزتي bey eezatee

dislike *v. t* کرکه کول kraka kawal

dislike *n* کرکه؛ناخوي kraka; na khwakhee

disloyal *a* نمک حرام namak haram

dismiss *v. t.* لهدندرخصتول la dandi rukhsatawal

dismissal *n* برطرفي bartarfee

disobey *v. t* سرغونه کول sargharawana kawal

disorder *n* بنظمي bey nazmee

disparity *n* ناورتهوالی nawarta walay

dispensary *n* درملتون darmaltoon

disperse *v. t* تجزيه کول tajzeeya kawal

displace *v. t* بهر کول bahar kawal

display *v. t* ننداره ظاهرول nandarey ta zahirawal

display *n* نمايش numayish

displease *v. t* خپه کول khapa kawal

displeasure *n* خپان khapgan

disposal *n* لر کوونه leyri kawona

dispose *v. t* لر کول؛غورول leyri kawal; ghorzawal

disprove *v. t* باطلول batilawal

dispute *n* شخه shkhara

dispute *v. t* شخه کول shkhara kawal

disqualification *n* ناوتوب nawartob

disqualify *v. t.* نابريالی بلل nabaryalay balal

disquiet *n* نارامه na arama

disregard *n* باعتنائي bey aytinayee

disregard *v. t* باعتنائي کول bey aytinayee kawal

disrepute *n* سپک تيا spak tia

disrespect *n* بی ادبی be adabi

disrupt *v. t* منقطع کول munqata kawal

dissatisfaction *n* باطميناني bey itminanee

dissatisfy *v. t.* نارضايت کول na razayat kawal

dissect *v. t* وموه کول tota tota kawal

dissection *n* غوونه ghosawana

dissimilar *a* ناورته nawarta

dissolve *v. t* حل کول hal kawal

dissuade *v. t* منع کول mana kawal

distance *n* وان watan

distant *a* لر leyri

distil *v. t* عرقاستل arq eystal

distillery *n* تقطير taqteer

distinct *a* ممتاز mumtaz

distinction *n* امتیاز eemtiyaz

distinguish *v. i* رتبهورکول rutba warkawal

distort *v. t* بدشکلهکول bad shakla kawal

distress *n* اضطراب iztirab

distress *v. t* مضطربکول muztarib kawal

distribute *v. t* ونهونهکول wanda wanda kawal

distribution *n* وش weysh

district *n* ولسوالي woolaswalee

distrust *n* ناباوري nabawaree

distrust *v. t.* ناباورهکول nabawara kawal

disturb *v. t* پرشانهکول parayshana kawal

ditch *n* کنده kanda

dive *v. i* غوپهوهل ghopa wahal

dive *n* غوپه ghopa

diverse *a* رنارنگ rangarang

divert *v. t* منصرفکول munsarif kawal

divide *v. t* جلاکول jala kawal

divine *a* روحاني roohanee

divinity *n* الهي؛خدای ilahee; khuday

division *n* وش weysh

divorce *n* طلاق talaq

divorce *v. t* طلاقول talaqawal

divulge *v. t* افشاکول afsha kawal

do *v. t* کول kawal

docile *a* فرمانبردار farmanbardar

dock *n.* لنرای langar zay

doctor *n* طبیب،ډاکر tabeed; daktar

doctorate *n* ډاکردرجه da daktaray daraja

doctrine *n* شعائر shaayar

document *n* دستاوز dastawayz

dodge *n* دوکه doka

dodge *v. t* تراستل teyr eystal

dog *n* سپی spay

dog *v. t* تعقیبول taqeebawal

dogma *n* عقیده دیني deenee aqeeda

dogmatic *a* پردینيعقیداوند par deenee aqeedi arwand

doll *n* لانکه lanzaka

dollar *n* دامریکارسميسکه da amreeka rasmee sika

domain *n* قلمرو qalamraw

dome *n* ومبت goombat

domestic *a* کورني،اصلي koranay; aslee

domestic *n* کورنيیز koranay seez

domicile *n* استونه astogna

dominant *a* غالب ghalib

dominate *v. t* غلبهلرل ghalaba laral

domination *n* برلاسی barlasay

dominion *n* واکمني wakmanee

donate *v. t* هدیهورکول hadeeya warkawal

donation *n.* بسپنه baspana

donkey *n* خر khar

donor *n* اهداکوونکی ahdaa kawoonkay

doom *n* قیامت qyamat

doom *v. t.* سپارلتهمر marg ta sparal

door *n* ور war

dose *n* ددرملويوخوراک da darmalo yaw khorak

dot *n* ټکی takay

dot *v. t* ټکيلول takay lagawal

double *a* غبر ghbarg

double *v. t.* غبرګول ghbargawal

double *n* دوهاخیز dwa arkheez

doubt *v. i* شکلرل shak laral

doubt *n* شک shak

dough *n* لمدهکياوه lamda karee ora

dove *n* کوتره kawtara

down *adv* کته kkhata

down *prep* مخپزو makh pa zwar

down *v. t* کتهکول؛راپرول kkhata kawal; raparzawal

downfall *n* رالوېدنه ralwaydana

downpour *n* زياتورت zyat warakht

downright *adv* کاملا kamilan

downright *a* صادق sadiq

downward *a* کتنی kakhtay

downward *adv* مخپهکته makh pa kkhata

downwards *adv* لاندخواته landi khwa ta

dowry *n* جهز jahayz

doze *n.* چرتوهنه churut wahana

doze *v. i* سپکخوبکول spak khob kawal

dozen *n* درجن darjan

draft *v. t* طرحهکول tarha kawal

draft *n* مسوده musawida

draftsman *a* مسودهچمتوکوونکي musawida chamtoo kawoonkay

drag *n* راکشونه rakashawana

drag *v. t* راکشول rakashawal

dragon *n* اامار khamar

drain *n* لت lakhtay

drain *v. t* وچول wachawal

drainage *n* وچونه wachawana

dram *n* دوزنيومقياس da wazan yaw miqyas

drama *n* رامه؛ننداره drama; nandara

dramatic *a* ناپي nasapee

dramatist *n* ننداره‌جووونکي nandara jorawoonkay

draper *n* وکرپلورونکي tokar ploroonkay

drastic *a* غتلی ghakhtalay

draught *n* وچتيا wachtya

draw *v. t* انزورول anzorawal

draw *n* پچهاچوونه pacha achowana

drawback *n* بتوب bey gatitob

drawer *n* دراز daraz

drawing *n* انور anzor

drawing-room *n* دهرکليخونه da harkalee kota

dread *n* وره weyra

dread *v. t* ورول weyrawal

dread *a* ترهوونکی tarhowoonkay

dream *n* خوب khob

dream *v. i.* خوبليدل khob leedal

drench *v. t* اوبهکول oba kawal

dress *n* جامه jami

dress *v. t* جامهاغوستل jami aghostal

dressing *n* کالي؛مرهم kalee; marham

drill *n* برمه barma

drill *v. t.* برمه سره سوری کول barma sara sooray kawal

drink *n* ښاک skhak

drink *v. t* څکل skhal

drip *n* څاڅه saseydana

drip *v. i* څڅل saseydal

drive *v. t* ځای چلول gaday chalawal

drive *n* موټرواني motor wanee

driver *n* موټروان motor wan

drizzle *n* نری ورت naray warakht

drizzle *v. i* نری ورت وریدل naray warakht wareydal

drop *n* څاکی saskay

drop *v. i* څڅل،له لاسه غورزیدل saseydal; la lasa ghorzeydal

drought *n* وچتیا wachtya

drown *v.i* اوبو کلاهو کیدل obo ki lahoo keydal

drug *n* درمل darmal

druggist *n* درمل پلورونکی darmal ploroonkay

drum *n* ول dol

drum *v.i.* ول وهل dol wahal

drunkard *n* نشه یی nasha saray

dry *a* وچ wach

dry *v. i.* وچدل wacheydal

dual *a* غبر؛دوه کسی ghbarg; dwa kasee

duck *n.* هیله heelay

duck *v.i.* اوبو کغوپه کیدل obo ki ghopa keydal

due *a* مناسب munasib

due *n* داداینی وړ da adayani war

due *adv* بالکل bilkul

duel *n* جه تن په تن jagara tan pa tan

duel *v. i* تن په تن جنډل tan pa tan jangeydal

duke *n* انلستان کتر شاهزاده لاندلقب inglastan ki tar shahzada landi laqab

dull *a* غبی ghabee

dull *v. t.* غبی کول ghabee kawal

duly *adv* پهخپل ای pa khpal zay

dumb *a* ونی goongay

dunce *n* پاو غبی سی pas aw ghabee saray

dung *n* خوشایه khooshaya

duplicate *a* نقلی جوه؛ jora; naqlee

duplicate *n* دویمه نسخه dwayma nuskha

duplicate *v. t* نقل جوول naqal jorawal

duplicity *n* دوه مخي dwa makhee

durable *a* پایدار paydar

duration *n* موده mooda

during *prep* ددوران ک dey dawran ki

dusk *n* درنااوتیارترمندوخت da ranra aw tyarey tar manz wakht

dust *n* دو doori

dust *v.t.* دوپاکول doori pakawal

duster *n* دوپاکوونکی doori pakawoonkay

dutiful *a* مطیع mutee

duty *n* وجیبه؛دنده wajeeba; danda

dwarf *n* لوشتکی lweyshtakay

dwell *v. i* ژوندکول zhwand kawal

dwelling *n* مشتای meysht zay

dwindle *v. t* کمول kamawal

dye *v. t* رنول rangawal

dye *n* رنورکونه rang warkowana

dynamic *a* داینامک dainamik

dynamics *n.* دجسمونودحرکت مبحث da jismoonu da harkat mubhis

dynamite *n* منفجره مواد د munfajira mawad

dynamo *n* هغه ماشین چپه حرکت کولو تری نه برناپداکي hagha masheen chi pa harakat kawalo trina breykhna payda keygee

dynasty *n* دپاچايانوکورنۍ da pachayano koranay

dysentery *n* خوني پچش khoonee peychash

E

each *a* هريو har yaw

each *pron.* هرکس har kas

eager *a* لوال leywal

eagle *n* عقاب oqab

ear *n* غو ghwag

early *adv* په چکې pa chatakay

early *a* زر؛بيني zar; beeranay

earn *v. t* په لاس راول pa las rawral

earnest *a* مهم muhim

earth *n* ځمکه zmaka

earthen *a* خاورين khawreen

earthly *a* دنياوي doonyawee

earthquake *n* زلزله zalzala

ease *n* آساني asanee

ease *v. t* آسانول asanawal

east *n* ختيز khateez

east *adv* دختيزپه لور da khateez pa lor

east *a* ختيوال khateezwal

easter *n* دمسيحانواختر da maseehano akhtar

eastern *a* ختيوال khateezwal

easy *a* آسان asan

eat *v.t* خول khwaral

eatable *n.* دخوروزونه da khwaro seezoona

eatable *a* دخوو war

ebb *n* کمېدنه kameydana

ebb *v. i* کمول kamawal

ebony *n* دآبنوس بوټی da abnoos bootay

echo *n* دآوازانعکاس da awaz inikas

echo *v. t* غته انعکاس ورکول ghag ta inikas warkawal

eclipse *n* دسپومتندرنيونه da spogmay tandar neewana

economic *a* اقتصادي iqtisadee

economical *a* کم ارزته kam arzakhta

economics *n.* اقتصادپوهنه iqtisad pohana

economy *n* اقتصاد iqtisad

edge *n* پيکه peeska

edible *a* د خولو و da khwaralo war

edifice *n* ما manray

edit *v. t* چاپ ته چمتوکول chap ta chamtoo kawal

edition *n* چاپ chap

editor *n* دمجلې پروونکی da mujaley khparowoonkay

editorial *a* مديري mudeeree

editorial *n* دمجلس رمقاله da mujaley sar maqala

educate *v. t* تربيه ورکول tarbeeya warkawal

education *n* وونه;تربیه khowana; tarbeeya

efface *v. t* پاکول pakawal

effect *n* اغز agheyz

effect *v. t* اغزکول;اجراءکول agheyz kawal; ijra kawal

effective *a* اغزمن agheyz man

effeminate *a* ینه khazeena

efficacy *n* اغزناکتوب agheyznaktob

efficiency *n* فعالیت;ورتوب faaleeyat; gatawartob

efficient *a* فعال;ور faal; gatawar

effigy *n* تمثال timsal

effort *n* هه hasa

egg *n* هـ hagay

ego *n* خپلذات khpal zat

egotism *n* ان‌غوتنه zan ghokhtana

eight *n* اته ata

eighteen *a* اتلس atalas

eighty *n* اتیا atya

either *a.,* لهدومخهیو la dwa sakha yaw

either *adv.* هریو har yaw

eject *v. t.* بهرتهغورول bahar ta ghorzawal

elaborate *v. t* پهمهارتبشپول pa maharat bashparawal

elaborate *a* ماهرانه mahirana

elapse *v. t* لهوختهاوتل la wakhta awookhtal

elastic *a* ژاولن zhawlan

elbow *n* نل sangal

elder *a* مشر mashar

elder *n* سپین‌یری speen geeray

elderly *a* مشری masharee

elect *v. t* اکل takal

election *n* ول‌اکنه tol takana

electorate *n* انتخابي‌پلاوی intikhabee plaway

electric *a* برنایي breykhnayee

electricity *n* برنا breykhna

electrify *v. t* برناورکول breykhna warkawal

elegance *n* ظرافت zarafat

elegant *adj* باذوقه ba zawqa

elegy *n* مرثیه marseeya

element *n* عنصر unsar

elementary *a* ابتدائي ibtidayee

elephant *n* فیل feel

elevate *v. t* لوول lwarawal

elevation *n* لوورونه lwarawana

eleven *n* یوولس yawolas

elf *n* پری peyray

eligible *a* حق‌دار haqdar

eliminate *v. t* لهمنهول la manza wral

elimination *n* وستنه weystana

elope *v. i* لهشهسرهیوای‌تدل la shahay sara yaw zay takhteydal

eloquence *n* فصاحتاوبلاغت fasahat aw balaghat

eloquent *a* فصیح fasee

else *a* بل bal

else *adv* پرتهلهدی prata la dey

elucidate *v. t* روانهکول rokhana kawal

elude *v. t* باطلول batilawal

elusion *n* سترپوونه stargi patawana

elusive *a* غولونکی ghawalaunkay

emancipation *n.* نجات nijat

embalm *v. t* خوشبویه کول khoshbooya kawal

embankment *n* پشته poshta

embark *v. t* په کښتۍ کې pa kakhtay ki wral

embarrass *v. t* شرمول sharmawal

embassy *n* سفارت safarat

embitter *v. t* تریخول treekhawal

emblem *n* علامه،نان alama; nakhan

embodiment *n* تجسم tajasum

embody *v. t.* جسم ورکول jisam warkawal

embolden *v. t.* زه ورتیاورکول zra wartya warkawal

embrace *v. t.* غاه ورکول ghara warkawal

embrace *n* غه،غاه gheyga; ghara

embroidery *n* ګلدوزي guldozee

embryo *n* جنین janeen

emerald *n* زمرد zamrod

emerge *v. i.* راختل،راکاردل rakhatal; rakhkareydal

emergency *n* بېنیحالت beeranay halat

eminance *n* پوی لو lwar poray

eminent *a* نامتو،عالاجنابه namtoo; alee janaba

emissary *n* جاسوس jasoos

emit *v. t* خارجول kharijawal

emolument *n* د پسـ اجور da ajoorey peysey

emotion *n* جذبه jazba

emotional *a* جذباتي jazbatee

emperor *n* ولواک tolwak

emphasis *n* ینار teengar

emphasize *v. t* ینارکول teengar kawal

emphatic *a* زوردار zordar

empire *n* سلطنت saltanat

employ *v. t* کارتهول kar ta hasawal

employee *n* کارمند karmand

employer *n* استخداموونکی istikhdamowoonkay

employment *n* دنده شغل، shoghal; danda

empower *v. t* واک ورکول wak warkawal

empress *n* ملکه malika

empty *a* تش tash

empty *v* تشول tashawal

emulate *v. t* تقلیدکول taqleed kawal

enable *v. t* ورول war garzawal

enact *v. t* وضع کول،رول لوبول waza kawal; rol lobawal

enamel *n* میناکاري meenakaree

enamour *v. t* په مینه مجذوبول pa meena majzoobawal

encase *v. t* په پوکاچول pa pokh ki achawal

enchant *v. t* زه ترول zra tri wral

encircle *v. t.* راورول rageyrawal

enclose *v. t* بندول bandawal

enclosure *n.* حصار hisar

encompass *v. t* احاطه کول ihata kawal

encounter *n.* شخه shkhara

encounter *v. t* شخه کول shkhara kawal

encourage *v. t* اوهورکول ooga warkawal

encroach *v. i* ناومهپورته کول nawara gata porta kawal

encumber *v. t.* په کاواخته کول pa karaw akhta kawal

encyclopaedia *n.* پوهنغونه pohanghond

end *v. t* پای ته رسول pay ta rasawal

end *n.* پای pay

endanger *v. t.* له خطر سره مخامخ کول la khatar sara makahmakhawal

endear *v.t* مینه ورکول meena warkawal

endearment *n.* نازوونه nazowana

endeavour *n* زیار zeeyar

endeavour *v.i* زیار باسل zeeyar basal

endorse *v. t.* تصویبول tasweebawal

endow *v. t* وقف کول waqaf kawal

endurable *a* بردبار burdbar

endurance *n.* بردباري brudbaree

endure *v.t.* زغمل zhghamal

enemy *n* دمن dukhman

energetic *a* قوي qawee

energy *n.* توان twan

enfeeble *v. t.* ناتوانه کول natwana kawal

enforce *v. t.* اجرا کول ijra kawal

enfranchise *v.t.* د تابعیت حق ورکول da tabieeyat haq warqawal

engage *v. t* استخدامول istikhdamawal

engagement *n.* تماس tamas

engine *n* ماشین masheen

engineer *n* مهندس muhandis

English *n* انرزي angreyzee

engrave *v. t* حکاکي کول hakakee kawal

engross *v.t* لوی لوی لیکل loy loy leekal

engulf *v.t* راچاپیرول rachapeyrawal

enigma *n* ونبیان goong bayan

enjoy *v. t* خونداخستل khwand akheystal

enjoyment *n* لذت lazat

enlarge *v. t* پراختیاورکول parakhtya warkawal

enlighten *v. t.* روان فکره کول rokhan fikra kawal

enlist *v. t* نوم لیکنه کول noom leekana kawal

enliven *v. t.* ژوندوربل zhwand warbakhal

enmity *n* دمني dukhmanee

ennoble *v. t.* رتبه ورکول rutba warkawal

enormous *a* ولوی deyr loy

enough *a* کافي kafee

enough *adv* د کفایت ترکچ da kifayat tar kachi

enrage *v.t* په غصه کول pa ghosa kawal

enrapture *v. t* په وجدراوستل pa wajad rawastal

enrich *v. t* شتمن کول shtaman kawal

enrol *v. t* نوم لیکنه کول noom leekana kawal

enshrine *v. t* په زیارت کایودل pa zyarat ki eekhodal

enslave *v.t.* غلام جورول ghulam jorawal

ensue *v.i* په پایله کواقع کدل pa payla ki waqay keydal

ensure *v. t* اینه ورکول dadeena warkawal

entangle *v.t* پراخته کول pri akhta kawal

enter *v. t* ننوتل،داخلدل nanawatal; dakhileydal

enterprise *n* لویه‌سوداري loya sawdagaree

entertain *v. t* خاطرداري‌كول khatirdaree kawal

entertainment *n.* خاطرداري؛هركلی khatirdaree; har kalay

enthrone *v. t* پاچاكول pacha kawal

enthusiasm *n* جوش‌اوخروش josh aw kharosh

enthusiastic *a* له‌جوشه‌ک la josha dak

entice *v. t.* پارول parawal

entire *a* پوره poora

entirely *adv* په‌كامله‌توه pa kamila toga

entitle *v. t.* په‌نوم‌كول pa noom kawal

entity *n* هستي hastee

entomology *n.* دحشراتوعلم da hashrato ilam

entrance *n* ننوتنه nanawatana

entrap *v.t.* په‌لومه‌كې‌رول pa looma ki geyrawal

entreat *v. t.* زاري‌كول zaree kawal

entreaty *n.* معامله moamila

entrust *v. t* امانت‌ورسپارل amanat warsparal

entry *n* ننوتنه nanawatana

enumerate *v. t.* حسابول heesabawal

envelop *v. t* په‌لفافه‌كاچول pa lifafa ki achwal

envelope *n* لفافه lifafa

enviable *a* دكينه‌كو da keena kakhay war

envious *a* كينه‌كښ keena kakh

environment *n.* چاپريال chapeyryal

envy *v* سيالي‌كول syalee kawal

envy *v. t* كينه‌ساتل keena satal

epic *n* رزمي‌شاعریاشاعري razmee shair ya shairee

epidemic *n* وبايي wabayee

epigram *n* خوكلام khog kalam

epilepsy *n* مري meyrgee

epilogue *n* دشعروروستبرخه da shayr warostay barkha

episode *n* ټوک tok

epitaph *n* دقبربرليک da qabar dabarleek

epoch *n* دوره؛دنوي‌موسم‌پيل dawra; da nawee mosam payl

equal *a* برابر barabar

equal *v. t* برابرول barabarawal

equal *n* هم‌پور ham por

equality *n* برابری barabaree

equalize *v. t.* مساوي‌كول masawee kawal

equate *v. t* مساوي‌ګڼل masawee ganral

equation *n* تساوي tasawee

equator *n* داستواكره da istiwa karkha

equilateral *a* متساوی‌الاضلاع mutasavi ul azla

equip *v. t* آماده‌كول amada kawal

equipment *n* وسايل wasayil

equitable *a* يوشان yaw shan

equivalent *a* مساوي masawee

equivocal *a* دوه‌اخيز dwa arkheez

era *n* دوران dawran

eradicate v. t لهمنهول la manza wral

erase v. t محوهكول mahwa kawal

erect v. t نصبول nasbawal

erect a لك،نغ lak; neygh

erection n درءلا dareyda

erode v. t خوساكول،سولول khoosa kawal; soolawal

erosion n سولدنه sooleydana

erotic a عشقيه،جنسي ishqeeya; jinsee

err v. i غلطيكول ghalatee kawal

errand n پغام paygham

erroneous a لارورکی lar wrakay

error n غلطي ghalatee

erupt v. i لرزدل larzeydal

eruption n لرزدنه larzeydana

escape n تخته teykhta

escape v.i تتدل takhteydal

escort n بدره،دسفرملری badraga; da safar malgaray

escort v. t پهبدرهملرتياكول pa badraga malgartya kawal

especial a خصوصي khusoosee

essay n. مقاله،نمونه maqala; namoona

essay v. t. مقالهليکل maqala leekal

essayist n مقالهليکونکی maqala leekoonkay

essence n روح،اصل rooh; asal

essential a ضروري zarooree

establish v. t. تأسيسول taseesawal

establishment n تأسيس tasees

estate n جايداد jaydad

esteem n درناوی dranaway

esteem v. t درناویورکول dranaway warkawal

estimate n. اندازه andaza

estimate v. t اكلول atkalawal

estimation n قدر qadar

etcetera n اونور،وغره aw nor; waghayra

eternal adj ابدي abadee

eternity n ابديت abadeeyat

ether n ايتر،شينآسمان eetar; sheen asman

ethical a اخلاقي akhlaqee

ethics n. اخلاقپوهنه akhlaq pohana

etiquette n دمعاشرتدآدابوعلم da moashirat da adabo ilam

etymology n رهپيزدنه .eykha peyzhandana

eunuch n نری nar khazay

evacuate v. t تشول tashawal

evacuation n تشونه tashawana

evade v. t سترگیپریپول stargi pri patawal

evaluate v. t ارزول arzawal

evaporate v. i پهبخارالوتل pa bukhar alwatal

evasion n هكوونه dada kawona

even a جفت،جوره juft; jora

even v. t هوارول hawarawal

even adv كاملا،همدارنه kamilan; hamda ranga

evening n ماښام makham

event n په،واقعه peykha; waqia

eventually adv. کپهپای pa pay ki

ever adv تل،هيکله tal; heeskala

evergreen a بادوامه ba dawama

evergreen n تلشين tal sheen

everlasting *a.* تل پاتی tal pati

every *a* هر يو har yaw

evict *v. t* له قانوني لارای خه وستل la qanoonee lari zay sakha weystal

eviction *n* ایستنه eystana

evidence *n* ثبوت saboot

evident *a.* رنده sarganda

evil *n* بدروح؛شطان bad rooh; shaytan

evil *a* ناوه،خراب na wara; kharab

evoke *v. t* حافظته راوستل hafizey ta rawastal

evolution *n* بدلون؛ارتقا badloon; irtiqa

evolve *v.t* ظاهرېدل zahireydal

ewe *n* مه meyga

exact *a* کره kara

exaggerate *v. t.* مبالغه کول mubaligha kawal

exaggeration *n.* مبالغه mubaligha

exalt *v. t* دنول dangawal

examination *n.* معاينه،امتحان moayina; imtihan

examine *v. t* امتحان اخستل imtihan akheystal

examinee *n* امتحان ورکوونکی imtihan warkowoonkay

examiner *n* امتحان اخستوونکی imtihan akheystoonkay

example *n* ساری saray

excavate *v. t.* کيندول keendawal

excavation *n.* کيندنه keendana

exceed *v.t* زياتی کول zyatee kawal

excel *v.i* تر واندکدل tri wrandi keydal

excellence *n.* برتري bartaree

excellency *n* جناب janab

excellent *a.* اعلی ala

except *v. t* مستثنی کول mustasna kawal

except *prep* مر،پرته له magar; prata la

exception *n* استثناء istisna

excess *n* افراط afrat

excess *a* زيات zyat

exchange *n* مبادله؛صرافي mubadila; safaree

exchange *v. t* مبادله کول mubadila kawal

excise *n* غر مستقيم ماليات geyr mustaqeem maleeyat

excite *v. t* تحريک کول tehreekawal

exclaim *v.i* چغه وهل cheygha wahal

exclamation *n* چغه cheygha

exclude *v. t* مستثنی وول mustasna garzawal

exclusive *a* يوازی،تنها yawazi; tanha

excommunicate *v. t.ه* ايکور سره شو کول areeki warsara shookawal

excursion *n.* پوهنيز سر pohaneez sayr

excuse *v.t* معافول maafawal

excuse *n* معافيت؛بخنه maafeeyat; bakhana

execute *v. t* تعميلول tameelawal

execution *n* تعميل tameel

executioner *n.* جلاد،تعميلوونکی jalad; tameelawoonkay

exempt *v. t.* مستثنی کول mustasna kawal

exempt *adj* معاف،خوندي maaf; khwandee

exercise *n.* ورزش warzish

exercise *v. t* ورزش کول warzish kawal

exhaust *v. t.* ستومانه کول stomana kawal

exhibit *n.* ننداره nandara

exhibit *v. t* نندارته واند کول nandari ta wrandi kawal

exhibition *n.* نندارتون nandartoon

exile *n.* جلاوطني jalawatnee

exile *v. t* جلاوطن کول jalawatan kawal

exist *v.i* وجودلرل wajood laral

existence *n* وجود،شتون wajood

exit *n.* دوتدلاره،اخراج da watani lar; ikhraj

expand *v.t.* پراختیاورکول parakhtya warkawal

expansion *n.* پراختیا parakhtya

ex-parte *a* یواخیز yaw arkheez

ex-parte *adv* دیولوریهه da yaw lori pa gata

expect *v. t* هیله کول heela kawal

expectation *n.* هیله،طمع heela; tama

expedient *a* مصلحتي ور maslihatee gatawar

expedite *v. t.* کول ندی garanday kawal

expedition *n* ندیتوب garandeetob

expel *v. t.* اخراجول ikhrajawal

expend *v. t* مصرفول masrafawal

expenditure *n* خر khars

expense *n.* مصرف،لت masraf; lagakht

expensive *a* گران gran

experience *n* تجربه tajroba

experience *v. t.* تجربه کول tajroba kawal

experiment *n* آزموینه azmoyana

expert *a* تجربه کار tajroba kar

expert *n* کارپوه kar poh

expire *v.i.* وخت یپوره کدل wakht yi poora keydal

expiry *n* خاتمه khatima

explain *v. t.* توضیح کول tawzee kawal

explanation *n* توضیح،دلیل tawzee; daleel

explicit *a.* ساده،واضح sada; wazeh

explode *v. t.* چاودول chawdal

exploit *n* کار ستر star kar

exploit *v. t* لوی کار کول loy kar kawal

exploration *n* اکتشاف iktishaf

explore *v.t* اکتشافي سفر کول iktishafee safar kawal

explosion *n.* چاودنه chawdana

explosive *n.* بم،دچاودنمواد bam; da chawdani mawad

explosive *a* انفجاري infijaree

export *n* صادرات sadirat

export *v. t.* بل هوادته لدول bal haywad ta leygdawal

expose *v. t* رابرسره کول rabarseyra kawal

express *v. t.* بیانول bayanawal

express *a* چک chatak

express *n* بیان bayan

expression *n.* اظهار izhar

expressive *a.* اخباري،رسا akhbaree; rasa

expulsion *n.* استنه eystana
extend *v. t* اودول oogdawal
extent *n.* حد had
external *a* بهرنی baharanay
extinct *a* نایاب nayab
extinguish *v.t* اوروژل or wazhal
extol *v. t.* زیاتهستاینهکول zyata stayana kawal
extra *a* اضافي izafee
extra *adv* لهحدهزیات la hada zyat
extract *n* خلاصه،اقتباس khulasa; iqtibas
extract *v. t* اقتباسکول iktibas kawal
extraordinary *a.* مخصوص makhsoos
extravagance *n* اسراف israf
extravagant *a* اسرافکوونکی israf kawoonkay
extreme *a* بحده bey hada
extreme *n* پای،آخر pay; akhar
extremist *n* افراطيشخص afratee shakhs
exult *v. i* ویارهدل weeyareydal
eye *n* ستره starga
eyeball *n* دسترگی da stargi gatay
eyelash *n* دسترگوبله da stargo banra
eyewash *n* دسترووینلودرمل da stargo weenzalo doormal

F

fable *n.* افسانه afsana
fabric *n* وکر،کالبد tokar; kalbad

fabricate *v.t* ورتهاومشابهکول warta aw mushabay kawal
fabrication *n* جوونه،ساخت jorawana; sakht
fabulous *a* افسانوي afsanawee
facade *n* دودانهمخ da wadanay makh
face *n* مخ makh
face *v.t* مخامخکدل makhamakh keydal
facet *n* دمعاشرتدآدابوکتاب da moashirat da adabo keetab
facial *a* دمخسینارکول da makh seengar kawal
facile *a* آسانه asana
facilitate *v.t* آسانول asanawal
facility *n* سهولت sahoolat
fac-simile *n* فاکسماشین faks masheen
fact *n* حقیقت haqeeqat
faction *n* وند gond
factious *a* لهییز dala yeez
factor *n* عامل amil
factory *n* کارخانه karkhana
faculty *n* پوهنیزهانه pohaneeza sanga
fad *n* ذوقيکار zawqee kar
fade *v.i* ماوىکدل mraway keydal
faggot *n* دلریوی da lagyo geyday
fail *v.i* پاتراتلل pati ratlal
failure *n* ناکامي nakamee
faint *a* کمزوری،بزه kamzoray; bey zra
faint *v.i* کمزوریکدل kamzoray keydal
fair *a* لالی،صفا golalay; safa
fair *n.* ملا mayla

fairly *adv.* په‌مناسب‌ول pa munasib dawl

fairy *n* اپر khapeyray

faith *n* ایمان eeman

faithful *a* باایمان،وفادار ba eeman; wafadar

falcon *n* باز baz

fall *v.i.* راغورِدل raghorzeydal

fall *n* غورِدنه،انحطاط ghorzeydana

fallacy *n* عب ayb

fallow *n* ییوشومکه yeywi shawi zmaka

false *a* غلط ghalat

falter *v.i* تمبِدل tambeydal

fame *n* آوازه،شهرت awaza; shohrat

familiar *a* بلد balad

family *n* کورنی koranay

famine *n* وچکالي wachkalee

famous *a* نومیالی noomyalay

fan *n* ببوزی babozay

fanatic *a* متعصب،متشدد mutaasib; mutashadad

fanatic *n* متعصب‌شخص mutaasib shakhs

fancy *n* وهم،خیال wehem; khyal

fancy *v.t* ‌زان‌ته‌راکل،متاثره‌کول zan ta rakkhal; mutasira kawal

fantastic *a* شاندار،وسواسي shandar; waswasee

far *adv.* له___لر la … leyri

far *a* لر leyri

far *n* لروالی leyri walay

farce *n* خندوونکنداره khandowoonki nandara

fare *n* کرایه karaya

farewell *n* مخه‌ه makha kha

farewell *interj.* په‌مخه‌ده pa makha di kha

farm *n* دکرمکه da kar zmaka

farmer *n* کروندر karwandagar

fascinate *v.t* زه‌ول zra wral

fascination *n.* زه‌وِنه zra wrana

fashion *n* ول،سینار dol; seengar

fashionable *a* سینارپال seengarpal

fast *a* ندی،تز garanday; teyz

fast *adv* په‌چکسره pa chatakay sara

fast *n* روژه rozha

fast *v.i* روژه‌نیول rozha neewal

fasten *v.t* تل taral

fat *a* چاغ chagh

fat *n* وربسی sorb saray

fatal *a* مري margee

fate *n* برخلیک barkhleek

father *n* پلار plar

fathom *v.t* حل‌کول hal kaval

fathom *n* وازه(قلاچ) waaza (qalach)

fatigue *n* ستوالی stariwalay

fatigue *v.t* ستی‌کول staray kawal

fault *n* غلطي ghalatee

faulty *a* عبجن aybjan

fauna *n* ديوسيم‌دناوروااوبووقسمونه da yaw seemi da zanawaro aw booto qismoona

favour1 *n* ه kheygara

favour *v.t* ه‌کول kheygara kawal

favourable *a* واره‌من wara man

favourite *a* ترولوخو tar tolo khwakh

favourite *n* په‌زه‌پوری pa zra pory

fear *n* وره weyra

fear *v.i* ورِدل weyreydal

fearful *a.* وروونکی weyrowoonkay

feasible *a* کیدونکی kedonkay

feast *n* ملمستیا؛جشن meylmastya; jashan

feast *v.i* پهملمستیارابللل pa meylmastya rabalal

feat *n* لویهکارنامه loya karnama

feather *n* وزر؛بکه wazar; banraka

feature *n* ره،شکل seyra; shakal

February *n* دانرزيکالدویمهمیاشت da angreyzee kal dwayama myasht

federal *a* ایتلافي aytilafee

federation *n* ایالت ayalat

fee *n* مزد،فیس mazd; fees

feeble *a* کمزوری kamzoray

feed *v.t* خواهورکول khwara warkawal

feed *n* خواه khwara

feel *v.t* لمسول؛درککول lamsawal; darak kawal

feeling *n* لمس،احساس lams; ehsas

feign *v.t* ریاکول reeya kawal

felicitate *v.t* شاباسیورکول shabasay warkawal

felicity *n* شاباسی؛نکمرغي shabasay; neykmarghee

fell *v.t* پرزول parzawal

fellow *n* مل mal

female *a* ینه khazeena

female *n* خزه khaza

feminine *a* مؤنث moannas

fence *n* کاره katara

fence *v.t* کارهپرراول katar pri ragarzawal

fend *v.t* دفاعکول difa kawal

ferment *n* تومنه tomna

ferment *v.t* تخمرکول tokhmar kawal

fermentation *n* تخمر،هجان tokhmar; hayjan

ferocious *a* غضبناک ghazabnak

ferry *n* دمسافروکته da musafiro kakhtay

ferry *v.t* تراتکول tag ratag kawal

fertile *a* رازه khayraza

fertility *n* رازي khayrazee

fertilize *v.t* رازهکول khayraza kawal

fertilizer *n* سره sara

fervent *a* پُرجوش purjosh

fervour *n* لیوالتیا levaltia

festival *n* مله mayla

festive *a* دجشنو da jashan war

festivity *n* دخاصموقعپهاهجشن da khas moqey pa ara jashan

festoon *n* هغهاملچدکپهري hagha ameyl chi da karay pa seyr zareygee

fetch *v.t* راول rawral

fetter *n* زولنه zolana

fetter *v.t* زولانوراچول zolanay warachawal

feud *n.* دنمي dookhmanee

feudal *a* لواکي dalwakee

fever *n* تبه taba

few *a* یوو yaw so

fiasco *n* ناکامي nakamee

fibre *n* تار tar

fickle *a* ناپایدار napaydar

fiction *n* افسانه afsana

fictitious *a* مصنوعي masnooee

fiddle *n* وایلون waylon

fiddle *v.i* واىلونغول،اپلتوىل waylon ghagawal; apalti wayal

fidelity *n* ريختينولي reekhteenwalee

fie *interj* اوشرمه washarmeyga !

field *n* ر،ـمكه dagar; zmaka

fiend *n* دو deyo

fierce *a* غضبناک ghazabnak

fiery *a* سوزنده؛خوني sozanda; khoonee

fifteen *n* پنلس peenzalas

fifty *n.* پنوس panzos

fig *n* اينر eenzar

fight *n* شخه shkhara

fight *v.t* شخهكول shkhara kawal

figment *n* وهم؛خيال wehem; khyal

figurative *a*

figure *n* نقش؛به naqsh; banra

figure *v.t* بهلرل،ليدلكدل banra laral; keedal keydal

file *n* دوته؛دوسيه dotanay; doseeya

file *v.t* ثبتول؛پهترتيبسرهايودل sabtawal; pa tarteeb sara eekhodal

file *n* سوهان sohan

file *v.t* سوهانول sohanawal

file *v.i.* پهليكهتلل pa leeka tlal

fill *v.t* دكول dakawal

film *n* دسينمافيلم da sinayma filam

film *v.t* فيلمچمتوكول filam chamtoo kawal

filter *n* چا chanr

filter *v.t* چاول chanrawal

filth *n* خيرى kheeray

filthy *a* خرن kheyran

final *a* پركنده؛آخري preykanda; akheyree

finance *n* ماليات maleeyat

financial *a* ماليتي maleeyatee

financier *n* پانوال pangawal

find *v.t* موندل moondal

fine *n* جريمه jareema

fine *v.t* جريمهكول jareema kawal

fine *a* شاندار shandar

finger *n* وته gota

finger *v.t* وتهوروول gota warwral

finish *v.t* پاىتهرسول pay ta rasawal

finish *n* انتها پاى؛ pay; intiha

finite *a* محدود mahdood

fir *n* نتر nakhtar

fire *n* اور or

fire *v.t* اورلول or lagawal

firm *a* كلک klak

firm *n.* سوداريزهمؤسسه sawdagareeza moassisa

first *a* لومى loomray

first *n* ور لوم loomray wraz

first *adv* ترهرهدمخه tar har sa da makha

fiscal *a* مالي malee

fish *n* كب kab

fish *v.i* كبنيول kab neewal

fisherman *n* كبنيوونكى kab neewoonkay

fissure *n* درز darz

fist *n* موى؛سوک mootay; sook

fistula *n* نل؛نيچه nal; necha

fit *v.t* متناسبكول mutanasib kawal

fit *a* مناسب munasib

fit *n* برابر barabar

fitful *a* ناكراره nakarara

fitter *n* نصبوونكى nasbawoonkay

five *n* پنه peenza

fix *v.t* نصبول nasbawal

fix *n* ورراتلنه geyr ratlana

flabby *a* شول‌پول shool pool

flag *n* برغ beyragh

flagrant *a* بدنام badnam

flame *n* لمبه lamba

flame *v.i* لمبه‌ورته‌کول lamba warta kawal

flannel *n* دفلالین‌وکر da flaleen tokar

flare *v.i* نساپه‌لمبه‌لدل nasapa lambey lageydal

flare *n* تیزه‌اوسترو‌ونکی‌را teyza aw stargi wroonki ranra

flash *n* لمدنه zaleydana

flash *v.t* پک‌وهل park wahal

flask *n* یو بوتل‌چپه‌لابراتوار‌ککاری yaw botal chi pa labratwar ki kareygee

flat *a* پلن plan

flat *n* اپارتمان apartman

flatter *v.t* چاپلوسی‌کول chaplosee

flattery *n* چاپلوسی chaplosee

flavour *n* خونداوبوی khwand aw booy

flaw *n* چاود،عیب chawd; ayb

flea *n.* ورغه wraga

flee *v.i* تختدل takhteydal

fleece *n* و waray

fleece *v.t* وشوکول waray shookawal

fleet *n* بجنی jangee beyray

flesh *n* غوه ghwakha

flexible *a* کمیدونکی kamedonkay

flicker *n* دشمالی‌امریکایومارغه‌چپه‌سر da shomalee amreeka yaw margha chi pa sar soor takay laree

flicker *v.t* لزدل larzeydal

flight *n* الوتنه alwatana

flimsy *a* بدوامه bey dawama

fling *v.t* ارتاوول artawol

flippancy *n* ستاخی gustakhee

flirt *n* نخره،مکز nakhrey; makeyz

flirt *v.i* دعشق‌نازنخرکول da ishq naz nakhrey kawal

float *v.i* داوبوپه‌سرلامبووهل da obo pa sar lambo wahal

flock *n* رمه،گله rama; gala

flock *v.i* غوندیدل ghondeydal

flog *v.t* په‌تزسره‌حرکت‌کول pa teyzay sara harakat kawal

flood *n* خوب،سل kharob; seyl

flood *v.t* داوبوسل‌راتلل da obo seyl ratlal

floor *n* دزمکی‌مخ،پو da zmaki makh; por

floor *v.t* په‌مکه‌وهل pa zmaka wahal

flora *n* دیوسیمه‌دنباتاتوقسمونه da yaw seemi da nabatato qismoona

florist *n* گل‌پلورونکی gul ploroonkay

flour *n* اوه ora

flourish *v.i* وده‌کول wada kawal

flow *n* بهدن baheydang

flow *v.i* بهدل baheydal

flower *n* ل gol

fluent *a* روان rawan

fluid *a* سیال،مایع syal; maya

fluid *n* بهاند bahand

flush *v.i* نساپی‌پرکدل‌یابهدل nasapee parkeydal ya baheydal

flush *n* نلاپی،پک،یابهیر nasapee park ya baheer

flute *n* شپل shpeylay

flute *v.i* شپلوهل shpeylay wahal

flutter *n* لزدنه larzeydana

flutter *v.t* لزدل larzeydal

fly *n* مچ mach

fly *v.i* الوتل alwatal

foam *n* کف، زگ zag; kaf

foam *v.t* زگ کول zag kawal

focal *a* مرکزی markazi

focus *n* توجه tawajo

focus *v.t* توجه کول tawajo kawal

fodder *n* بوس،پروه parora; boos

foe *n* حریف،دمن hareef; dukhman

fog *n* بخار،لوی bokhar; loogay

foil *v.t* جلوه ورکول jalwa warkawal

fold *n* راماتوونه،راکونه ramatowana; rakagawana

fold *v.t* راتاوول،راماتول ratawowal; ramatawal

foliage *n* دونوپا da wano panri

follow *v.t* متابعت کول mutabiat kawal

follower *n* مرید mureed

folly *n* ناپوهي napohee

foment *v.t* پەتودواوبووینل pa tawdo obo weenzal

fond *a* شوقین shawqeen

fondle *v.t* نازول nazawal

food *n* خواه khwara

fool *n* ناپوه napoh

foolish *a* احمق ahmaq

foolscap *n* لوبەپاه loba panra

foot *n* په poomba

for *prep* لپاره lapara

for *conj.* پمای pa zay

forbid *v.t* منع کول mana kawal

force *n* توان؛زور twan; zor

force *v.t* زورکارول zor karawal

forceful *a* قوی qavi

forcible *a* اجباری ajbari

forearm *n* لجه leycha

forearm *v.t* مخکلهمخکچمتوکول makhki la makhki chamtoo kawal

forecast *n* واندوینه warandwayana

forecast *v.t* واندوینەکول warandwayana kawal

forefather *n* پلارنیکه plarneeka

forefinger *n* دشهادتوته da shahadat gota

forehead *n* تندی tanday

foreign *a* خارجي kharijee

foreigner *n* خارجيهوادوال kharijee heywadwal

foreknowledge *n.* غبپوهنه ghayb pohana

foreleg *n* دحواناتومخکپ da haywanato makhki pkhey

forelock *n* اوربل orbal

foreman *n* جمعدار jamadar

foremost *a* ترولوغوره tar tolo ghwara

forenoon *n* لەغرمەمخک la gharmey makhki

forerunner *n* لارود larkhod

foresee *v.t* واندوینەکول warandwayana kawal

foresight *n* واندوینه warandwayana

forest *n* نل zangal

forestall *v.t* دمخەاخستل da makha akheystal

forester n نل وان zangal wan

forestry n نل پوهه zangal poha

foretell v.t واندوینه کول warandwayana kawal

forethought n دراتلونکیغمخونه da ratlonke gham khwarana

forever adv دتللپاره da tal lapara

forewarn v.t خبرداریورکول khabardaray warkawal

foreword n سریزه sareeza

forfeit v.t جریمهورکول jareema warkawal

forfeit n تاوان؛جریمه tawan; jareema

forfeiture n ضبطونه zabtawana

forge n دآهنرکوره da ahangaray kora

forge v.t پهسندانباندکول pa sandan bandi takawal

forgery n جعلکاری jal kari

forget v.t هرول heyrawal

forgetful a بیتوجه be tawaja

forgive v.t بخل bakhal

forgo v.t تیریدل teredal

forlorn a ناوهسی nawara saray

form n ریخت؛ترکیب reykht; tarkeeb

form v.t. ترکیبول؛برهورکول tarkeebawal; seyra warkawal

formal a رسمی rasmee

format n ظاهريبه zahiree banra

formation n جوت jorakht

former a پخوانی

formerly adv پخوا؛دمخه pakhwa; da makha

formidable a اروونکی darowoonkey

formula n قاعده،فارمول qayda; farmool

formulate v.t داصولوپهشکلرندول da usoolo pa shakal sargandawal

forsake v.t. ترککول tark kawal

forswear v.t. توبهکول toba kawal

fort n. کلا kala

forte n. هنر honar

forth adv. لهکورسخهلري la kor sakha leyri

forthcoming a. راتلونکی ratloonkey

forthwith adv. نابه nasapa

fortify v.t. سنرونهجوول sangaroona jorawal

fortitude n. جسميتوان jismee twan

fort-night n. دواوونز dwey oonay

fortress n. سنر؛مورچل sangar; morchal

fortunate a. نکمرغه neykmargha

fortune n. قسمت qismat

forty n. لوت salweykht

forum n. هجره hujra

forward a. پرمختللی par makh tlalay

forward adv دمخخواته da makh khwa ta

forward v.t پرمختلل؛رسول par makh tlal; rasawal

fossil n. فوسیل fosil

foster v.t. شدورکول sheydey warkawal

foul a. ناول؛خرن nawalay; kheyran

found v.t. بنسایودل bansat eekhodal

foundation *n.* بنياد boonyad

founder *n.* بنسايودونکی bansat eekhodoonkay

foundry *n.* هغمای چه ويلی شوی فلز په قالبو کی اچوی hagha zai che weele shavi falz pa qalabo ke achavi

fountain *n.* فواره fawara

four *n.* څلور salor

fourteen *n.* څوارلس swarlas

fowl *n.* چره charga

fowler *n.* وحشی مارغانوکاری wahshee marghano khkari

fox *n.* ګيده gedara

fraction *n.* کسر،ماتدنه kasar; mateydana

fracture *n.* ماتوالی matwalay

fracture *v.t* ماتول matawal

fragile *a.* نازک nazuk

fragment *n.* وه،برخه tota; barkha

fragrance *n.* بوی booy

fragrant *a.* خوشبويه khooshbooya

frail *a.* نازک nazak

frame *v.t.* قالبول qalibawal

frame *n* قالب؛چوکا qalib; chawkat

franchise *n.* قانونی حق qanoni haq

frank *a.* ويه سپين speen goya

frantic *a.* هذيانی hazyanee

fraternal *a.* دوستانه dostana

fraternity *n.* اخوت akhoowat

fratricide *n.* وروروژنه wror wazhana

fraud *n.* دوکه doka

fraudulent *a.* دوکباز dokey baz

fraught *a.* ک،شتمن dak; shtaman

fray *n* زت zarakht

free *a.* آزاد azad

free *v.t* آزادول azadawal

freedom *n.* آزادي azadee

freeze *v.i.* کنګل کدل kangal keydal

freight *n.* دبارونکرايه da barwrani karaya

french *a.* فرانسوي faransawee

French *n* فراسوي ويا ژبه faransawee wagaray ya zhaba

frenzy *n.* شداتوب sheydatob

frequency *n.* فريکوينسی frekvency

frequent *n.* مکرر mukarrar

fresh *a.* تازه taza

fret *n.* زري دوزي zaree dozee

fret *v.t.* زري دوزي کول zaree dozee kawal

friction *n.* مونه mokhana

Friday *n.* جمعه jooma

fridge *n.* يخچال yakhchal

friend *n.* ملری malgaray

fright *n.* ناپير nasapee dar

frighten *v.t.* ناپی ارول nasapee darawal

frigid *a.* سو deyr sor

frill *n.* دزلفانو چتر da zulfano chatar

fringe *n.* حاشيه،چرمه hasheeya; charma

fringe *v.t* حاشيه ورکول hasheeya warkawal

frivolous *a.* بهووده bayhooda

frock *n.* فراک frak

frog *n.* چنه changakha

frolic *n.* خوشالي khoshalee

frolic *v.i.* خوشاي کول khoshalee kawal

from *prep.* له...خه la … sakha

front *n.* مخه makha

front *a* دمخ،مخامخ da makhi; makhamakh

front *v.t* ورته‌مخ‌کول warta makh kawal

frontier *n.* برید،پوله breed; poola

frost *n.* پرخه parkha

frown *n.* توندخویي،مخالفت tond khooyee; mukhalifat

frown *v.i* مخالفت‌کاره‌کول mukhalifat khkara kawal

frugal *a.* ساده sada

fruit *n.* موه meywa

fruitful *a.* ور gatavar

frustrate *v.t.* کون مأیوسه mayoosa kawal

frustration *n.* مأیوسي mayoosee

fry *v.t.* وریتول wreetawal

fry *n* سره‌کغوه sra kari ghwakha

fuel *n.* دسوخت‌تل da sokht teyl

fugitive *a.* ژرترئدونکی zhar teyreydoonkay

fugitive *n.* تتدونکی takhteydoonkay

fulfil *v.t.* ترسره‌کول tar sara kawal

fulfilment *n.* ترسره‌کوونه tar sara kawona

full *a.* کامل kamil

full *adv.* خورار khora deyr

fullness *n.* تکمیل takmeel

fully *adv.* په‌بشپول pa bashpar dawl

fumble *v.i.* اشتباه‌کول ishtiba kawal

fun *n.* وکی toki

function *n.* کار kar

function *v.i* کارکول kar kawal

functionary *n.* مأمور،عامل mamoor; amil

fund *n.* سرمایه sarmaya

fundamental *a.* بنیادي boonyadee

funeral *n.* دجنازمراسم da janazey marasim

fungus *n.* فنجی funji

funny *n.* خندوونکی khandowoonkay

fur *n.* دنناوروپوست‌وتان da zanawaro post weykhtan

furious *a.* غضبناک ghazabnak

furl *v.t.* غونول،تاوول ghondawal; tawowal

furlong *n.* داودوالی‌یوه‌میچه da ogad wali yawa mecha

furnace *n.* تنور tanoor

furnish *v.t.* آرایش arayish

furniture *n.* دکوراسباب da kor asbab

furrow *n.* یبوشوهمکه yeywi shawi zmaka

further *adv.* برسره‌پرد bar seyra par dey

further *a* ترولور tar tolo deyr

further *v.t* پرمخ‌ورل par makh wral

fury *n.* غصه ghosa

fuse *v.t.* ترکیبول،ویله‌کول tarkeebawal; weeli kawal

fuse *n* فیوز fyooz

fusion *n.* ویله‌کدنه weeli keydana

fuss *n.* شورماشور shor mashor

fuss *v.i* شورماشورجوول shor mashor jorawal

futile *a.* بفاید bey faydey

futility *n.* بفایدتوب bey faydeytob

future *a.* راتلونکی ratloonkay

future *n* مستقبل mustaqbil

G

gabble *v.i.* بک بک کول bak bak kawal

gadfly *n.* خرمچ khar mach

gag *v.t.* پوزبندتل pozband taral

gag *n.* پوزبند pozband

gaiety *n.* ادي boonyadee

gain *v.t.* ترلاسه کول tar lasa kawal

gain *n* استفاده istifada

gainsay *v.t.* انکار inkar

gait *n.* ز tak

galaxy *n.* کهکشان kahkashan

gale *n.* سيل selai

gallant *a.* شجاع shoja

gallant *n* مؤدب;ساتندوی moadab; satandoy

gallantry *n.* بهادري bahadaree

gallery *n.* لوژ lozh

gallon *n.* د پمايش لن da gaylan paymayish

gallop *n.* چکــغل chatak zghal

gallop *v.t.* چکــغلول chatak zghalawal

gallows *n.* په دارونه. pa dar zarawona

galore *adv.* په پريمانا pa preymanay

galvanize *v.t.* فلزته اوبه ورکول filiz ta oba warkawal

gamble *v.i.* قمارکول qomar kawal

gamble *n* قماربازي qomar bazee

gambler *n.* قمارباز qomar baz

game *n.* لوبه;مسابقه loba; musabiqa

game *v.i* مسابقه کول musabiqa kawal

gander *n.* (نر) قاز qaz (nar)

gang *n.* له dala

gangster *n.* بدماش badmash

gap *n* رخنه rakhna

gape *v.i.* رخنه پداکول rakhna payda kawal

garage *n.* دموررغونيادروناى da motar raghawani ya darawani zay

garb *n.* کالي kalee

garb *v.t* کالىپه اغوستل kali pa aghostal

garbage *n.* کثافت kasafat

garden *n.* باغ bagh

gardener *n.* باغوان baghwan

gargle *v.i.* غغه کول ghar ghara kawal

garland *n.* امل ameyl

garland *v.t.* اميل ameyl

garlic *n.* اوه ooga

garter *n.* دجورابوبند da jorabo band

gas *n.* ګاز gaz

gasp *n.* تزه ساه اخستنه teyza sa akheystana

gasp *v.i* تزه ساه اخستل teyza sa akheystal

gastric *a.* دمعدى da maide

gate *n.* لويه دروازه loya darwaza

gather *v.t.* راولول ratolawal

gaudy *a.* نمايشي numayishee

gauge *n.* اندازه;درجه andaza; daraja

gauntlet *n.* اوددستکش oogad dastkash

gay *a.* خوشاله khoshala

gaze *v.t*

کيدل پر zer kedal

gaze *n* یریر کتنه zer zer katana

gazette *n.* مجله mujala

gear *n.* وار،ابزار gararay; abzar

geld *v.t.* خصي کول khasee kawal

gem *n* غمی ghamay

gender *n.* تذکیراوتأنیث tazkeer aw tanees

general *a.* عمومي amoomee

generally *adv.* پهولیزول pa toleez dawl

generate *v.t.* تولیدول tawleedawal

generation *n.* نسل nasal

generator *n.* تولیدوونکی tawleedawoonkay

generosity *n.* سخاوت sakhawat

generous *a.* سخي sakhee

genius *n.* قابل qabil

gentle *a.* باشرفه ba sharfa

gentleman *n.* محترم mohtaram

gentry *n.* تعلیم یافته خلك او د تربیتنان talim yafta khalak au da tarbiye sakhtanan

genuine *a.* اصلي aslee

geographer *n.* مکپوه zmakpoh

geographical *a.* د مکپوهني په اروند da zmakpohani pa arwand

geography *n.* مکپوهنه zmakpohana

geological *a.* د مکپژندني په اروند da zmakpeyzhandani pa arwand

geologist *n.* مکپژاند zmakpeyzhand

geology *n.* مکپژندنه zmakpeyzhandana

geometrical *a.* هندسی hindsi

geometry *n.* جیومیری geometry

germ *n.* جراثیم jaraseem

germicide *n.* جراثیموژونکی jaraseem wazhoonkay

germinate *v.i.* وده کول wada kawal

germination *n.* وده wada

gesture *n.* اشاره ishara

get *v.t.* لاس ته راول las ta rawral

ghastly *a.* ویروونکی werawonki

ghost *n.* اروا arwa

giant *n.* دو deyw

gibbon *n.* کیبون gebon

gibe *v.i.* ملنوهل malandi wahal

gibe *n* ملد malandi

giddy *a.* سربداله sar badala

gift *n.* لا dalay

gifted *a.* مستعد mustaid

gigantic *a.* بدذ لوی loy badanay

giggle *v.i.* بواکه خنددل bey waka khandeydal

gild *v.t.* د سرو زرو اوبه ورکول da sro zaro oba warkawal

gilt *a.* د سرو زرو اوبه ورکشوی da sro zaro oba warkray shaway

ginger *n.* سوز sond

giraffe *n.* زرافه zarafa

gird *v.t.* پترنه چاپره کول patay trina chapeyra kawal

girder *n.* شاهتیر shateer

girdle *n.* ملا وستنی mla wastanay

girdle *v.t* کمربندتل kamarband taral

girl *n.* نجل najlay

girlish *a.* نجلغوند najlay ghonde

gist *n.* د کلامنچو da kalam nachor

give *v.t.* ورکول warkawal

glacier *n.* یخچال yakhchal

glad *a.* خوشال khoshal

gladden *v.t.* خوشاله‌کول khoshala kawal

glamour *n.* طلسم،زراکنه talasum; zra rakkhana

glance *n.* غلندنظر zghaland nazar

glance *v.i.* غلندنظرکول zghaland nazar kawal

gland *n.* مرغی margharay

glare *n.* لا zala

glare *v.i* لدل zaleydal

glass *n.* دپیاله،یه da kheekhey pyala; kheekha

glaze *v.t.* لول zalaval

glazier *n.* یه‌غووونکی kheekha ghosowoonkay

glee *n.* سرور suroor

glide *v.t.* ویدل khwayeydal

glider *n.* بماشینه‌کوچنالوتکه‌چددهوایه بی‌ماشینه koochnay alwataka chi da hawa pa waseela aloozee وسیله‌الوزي

glimpse *n.* غلندنظر zghaland nazar

glitter *v.i.* یقدل parqeydal

glitter *n* یقدنه parqeydana

global *a.* نیوال nareewal

globe *n.* ردی garday

gloom *n.* سیوری ganr syoray

gloomy *a.* تیاره tyara

glorification *n.* تجلیل tajleel

glorify *v.t.* تجلیلول tajleelawal

glorious *a.* پرتمین purtameen

glory *n.* عظمت azmat

gloss *n.* توضیح tawzee

glossary *n.* دلغاتونوملیک da lughato noomleek

glossy *a.* لاند zaland

glove *n.* لاس‌ماغو las magho

glow *v.i.* برېدل breykheydal

glow *n* برې breykh

glucose *n.* لوکوز gulucose

glue *n.* سر sareykh

glut *v.t.* مول marawal

glut *n* زیات‌خوراک،مت zyat khorak; marakht

glutton *n.* پرخوراک‌مین par khorak mayan

gluttony *n.* زیات‌خوراک‌خونه zyat khorak khwarana

glycerine *n.* لیسرین glicrine

go *v.i.* تلل tlal

goad *n.* مچک machak

goad *v.t* سکونل skoondal

goal *n.* مقصد maqsad

goat *n.* وزه wza

gobble *n.* کریه‌کول krega kawal

goblet *n.* جام jam

god *n.* خدای khuday

goddess *n.* الهه ilaha

godhead *n.* خدایي khuday

godly *a.* دیندار dendar

godown *n.* زرمتون zeyrmatoon

godsend *n.* خدای‌ورکی‌شی khuday warkaray shay

goggles *n.* دسترورغورندویه‌عنک da stargo zhghorandoya aynaki

gold *n.* سره‌زر sra zar

golden *a.* طلایي tilayee

goldsmith *n.* زرر zargar

golf *n.* دلف‌لوبه da gulf loba

gong *n.* جآوازه‌زنگ jag awaza zang

good *a.* ه kha

good *n* نکی neykee

good-bye *interj.* دخدای‌پامان da khuday paman

goodness *n.* هوالی kha walay

goodwill *n.* هنیت kha nyat

goose *n.* بته bata

gooseberry *n.* ازغن‌توت azghan toot

gorgeous *a.* برمناک baramnak

gorilla *n.* وریلابیزو goreela beezo

gospel *n.* انجیل injeel

gossip *n.* بی‌اساسهخبری be asasa khabary

gourd *n.* دنسواروکدو da naswaro kadoo

gout *n.* نقرس naqras

govern *v.t.* حکمرانی‌کول hukamranee kawal

governance *n.* حکمرانی hukamranee

governess *n.* وونکی khowoonkay

government *n.* حکومت hukoomat

governor *n.* والي walee

gown *n.* دواودجامه da khazo oogdey jamey

grab *v.t.* په‌لاس‌کتتول pa las ki takhtawal

grace *n.* عفوه تایید، tayeed; afwa

grace *v.t.* کلاوربل khkula warbakhal

gracious *a.* مهربانه mehrabana

gradation *n.* درجه‌بندي darja bandee

grade *n.* مرتبه martaba

grade *v.t* درجه‌بندي‌کول darja bandee kawal

gradual *a.* گام‌په‌گام gam pa gam

graduate *v.i.* لیسانسه‌سرته‌رسول leesansa sar ta rasawal

graduate *n* زدکوتی،لیسانسه zdakrotay; leesansa

graft *n.* پوند peywand

graft *v.t* پوندلول peywand lagawal

grain *n.* غَله ghala

grammar *n.* ژبدود zhabdood

grammarian *n.* ژبود zhabkhod

gramophone *n.* دراموفون‌دموسیقآله da gramofon da mawseeqay ala

granary *n.* دغَلودام da ghaley godam

grand *a.* ستر star

grandeur *n.* لویی loyee

grant *v.t.* وربل warbakhal

grant *n* اهداء ihda

grape *n.* انور angoor

graph *n.* هندسی‌نمایش hindsee mumayish

graphic *a.* دهندسواونخچوپه‌اوند da hindso aw nakhcho pa arwand

grapple *n.* لاس‌اوروان‌کدنه las aw greywan keydana

grapple *v.i.* لاس‌اوروان‌کدل las aw greywan keydal

grasp *v.t.* پوهول pohawal

grasp *n* پوهاوی pohaway

grass *n* واه wakha

grate *n.* رنده randa

grate *v.t* رنده‌کول randa kawal

grateful *a.* مننندوی manandoy

gratification *n.* مسرت musarat

gratis *adv.* ویا warya

gratitude *n.* حق پیژندنه haq peyzhandana

gratuity *n.* اجر ajar

grave *n.* قبر qabar

grave *a.* سخت،خطرناک sakht; khatarnak

gravitate *v.i.* دجاذبدقوپهوسیله دحرکت کول da jazibey da qawey pa waseela harakat kawal

gravitation *n.* کشش kashish

gravity *n.* وزن wazan

graze *v.i.* رول sarawal

graze *n.* روونه sarawana

grease *n.* ریس grees

grease *v.t* ریس ورکول grees warkawal

greasy *a.* ریس ورکی شوی grees warkray shaway

great *a* عظیم azeem

greed *n.* حرص hiras

greedy *a.* حرصی hirasee

greek *n.* یونانی وی یاژبه yoonanee wagaray ya zhaba

Greek *a* یونانی yoonanee

green *a.* زرغون،تازه zarghon; taza

green *n.* شین رنز sheen rang

greenery *n.* شینکی sheenkay

greet *v.t.* سلام کول salam kawal

grenade *n.* لاسی بم lasee bam

grey *a.* خ khard

greyhound *n.* تازی سپی tazee spay

grief *n.* غم gham

grievance *n.* له،شکایت geela; shikayat

grieve *v.t.* غمجنول ghamjanawal

grievous *a.* غمجن ghamjan

grind *v.i.* مده کدل mayda keydal

grinder *n.* دژرندماشین da zhrandi masheen

grip *v.t.* پهلاس کنیول pa las ki neewal

grip *n* پهلاس کنیونه pa las ki neewana

groan *v.i.* زروي کول zgeyrwee kawal

groan *n* زروی zheyrwee

grocer *n.* سبزي پلورونکی sabzee ploroonkay

grocery *n.* سبزي پلورنای sabzee ploranzay

groom *n.* شالمی shazalmay

groom *v.t* کلاوربل khkula warbakhal

groove *n.* ناوه،کانال nawa; kanal

grope *v.t.* لاس پول las tapawal

gross *n.* اصلي برخه،دباریوپمائش aslee barkha; da bar yaw paymayish

gross *a* ناخالص،برجسته nakhalis; barjasta

grotesque *a.* عجیب اوغریب ajeeb aw ghareeb

ground *n.* ر dagar

group *n.* له dala

group *v.t.* پهلووشل pa dalo weyshal

grow *v.t.* وده کول wada kawal

grower *n.* ودهورکوونکی،پالونکی wada warkawoonkay; paloonkay

growl *v.i.* غمبدل ghrambeydal

growl *n* غمبار ghrambar

growth *n.* وده،کرهه wada; karhanra

grudge *v.t.* بخيلي‌كول bakheelee kawal

grudge *n* بخل bukhal

grumble *v.i.* وندل doongeydal

grunt *n.* غورغور ghor ghor

grunt *v.i.* غورغوركول ghor ghor kawal

guarantee *n.* ضمانت zamanat

guarantee *v.t* ضمانت‌وركول zamanat warkawal

guard *v.i.* ژغورل zhghoral

guard *n* ژغورونكى،ساتونكى zhghoroonkay; satoonkay

guardian *n.* ولي walee

guava *n.* امرود amrood

guerilla *n.* نارسمي‌جنيالى narasmee jangyalay

guess *n.* اكل atkal

guess *v.i* اكل‌كول atkal kawal

guest *n.* ملمه meylma

guidance *n.* لاروونه lar khowana

guide *v.t.* لاروونه‌كول lar khowana kawal

guide *n.* لار ود lar khod

guild *n.* صنف،ولى sanf; tolay

guile *n.* مكر،حيله makar; heela

guilt *n.* جرم juram

guilty *a.* مجرم mujrim

guise *n.* ظاهر،شكل zahir; shakal

guitar *n.* دارموسيقةآله da geetar da mawseeqay ala

gulf *n.* خليج khaleej

gull *n.* ساده saada

gull *v.t* غولول ghwalaval

gulp *n.* لويه‌نم loya namray

gum *n.* اور،سر ooray; sareykh

gun *n.* توپک topak

gust *n.* سيله seelay

gutter *n.* لتى lakhtay

guttural *a.* ستونيز stoonez

gymnasium *n.* لوبغالى lobghalay

gymnast *n.* دجمناسک‌دلوبوماهر da jamnastic da lobo mahir

gymnastic *a.* دجمناسک‌په اوند؛چست da jamnastic pa arwand; chust

gymnastics *n.* دجمناسک‌لوب da jamnastic lobi

H

habit *n.* عادت adat

habitable *a.* داستوڼو da astogni war

habitat *n.* دناوروواومارغانوداوسدوای da zanawaro aw marghano da oseydo zay

habitation *n.* استوڼای astoganzay

habituate *v. t.* رودی‌کول rogday kawal

hack *v.t.* ‌پ‌جوول،غوول tap jorawal; ghosawal

hag *n.* غوروی ghoravy

haggard *a.* نر dangar

haggle *v.i.* اصراركول israr kawal

hail *n.* ‌ل galay

hail *v.i* اورل galay wareydal

hail *v.t* سلام‌اچول salam achawal

hair *n* وته weykhta

hale *a.* لالى gulalay

half *n.* نيماپي neemayee

half *a* نیم neem

hall *n.* دالان؛تالار dalan; talar

hallmark *n.* دطلااوسپینوزروباندجو نان da tila aw speeno zaro bandi jor nakhan

hallow *v.t.* تقدیسول taqdeesawal

halt *v. t.* دردل dareydal

halt *n* دردنه dareydana

halve *v.t.* نیماییکول neemayee kawal

hamlet *n.* کوچنیکلی koochnay kalay

hammer *n.* ک satak

hand *n* لاس laas

hand *v.t* مرستهکول mrasta kawal

handbill *n.* لاسپهلاسخپروونکخبرتیا laas pa las khparowoonki khabartya

handbook *n.* لاسیکتاب laasi kitab

handcuff *n.* اتک atkaray

handcuff *v.t* اتکاچول atkaray achawal

handful *n.* لشان lag shan

handicap *v.t.* کمزوریکول kamzoray

handicap *n* معذور mazoor

handicraft *n.* لاسیصنعت laasee sanat

handiwork *n.* لاسیکار laasee kaar

handkerchief *n.* دستمال dastmal

handle *n.* لاستی lastay

handle *v.t* پهلاسسمول pa las samawal

handsome *a.* لالی gulalay

handy *a.* آسانه asana

hang *v.t.* وندول zwarandawal

hanker *v.i.* هوسکول hawas kawal

haphazard *a.* ناپی nasapi

happen *v.t.* پدل peykheydal

happening *n.* پدنه peykheydana

happiness *n.* خوی khwakhee

happy *a.* خو khwakh

harass *v.t.* اذیتول azeeyatawal

harassment *n.* اذیت azeeyat

harbour *n.* لنرای langarzay

harbour *v.t* پناهورکول pana warkawal

hard *a.* سخت sakht

harden *v.t.* سختول sakhtawal

hardihood *n.* بباکی bey bakee

hardly *adv.* پهسختسره pa sakhtay sara

hardship *n.* ربه rabra

hardy *adj.* جسور jasoor

hare *n.* سویه soya

harm *n.* تاوان tawan

harm *v.t* تاوانرسول tawan rasawal

harmonious *a.* همغای hamghardi

harmonium *n.* دهارمونیومدموسیقآله da harmoneeyom da mawseeqay ala

harmony *n.* جوجای jor jaray

harness *n.* پزوان peyzwan

harness *v.t* رامول ramawal

harp *n.* چن chang

harsh *a.* شدید shadeed

harvest *n.* دفصلونولو da fasloono law

haverster *n.* دلوماشین؛لوری da law masheen; law garay

haste *n.* بیه beera

hasten *v.i.* بیهکول beera kawal

hasty *a.* بیهناک beeranak

hat *n.* خولۍ khwalay

hatchet *n.* تشه،كور teysha; kawdar

hate *n.* كركه kraka

hate *v.t.* كركه كول kraka kawal

haughty *a.* كبرجن kabarjan

haunt *v.t.* تراتكول tag ratag kawal

haunt *n* تراټ tag ratag

have *v.t.* درلودل darlodal

haven *n.* پناهای panazay

havoc *n.* چپاول chapawal

hawk *n* شاهين shaheen

hawker *n* رندپلورونكی garzand ploroonkay

hay *n.* پروه prora

hazard *n.* خطر khatar

hazard *v.t* خطرسره مخامخاخول khata sara makhamakhawal

haze *n.* غبار ghobar

hazy *a.* ردجن gardjan

he *pron.* هغه hagha

head *n.* سر sar

head *v.t* رهبري كول rahbaree kawal

headache *n.* دسرخوږدنه da sar khoogeydana

heading *n.* سرليک sarleek

headlong *adv.* بهناك bera naak

headstrong *a.* خپلسری khpal saray

heal *v.i.* رغول raghawal

health *n.* روغتيا roghtya

healthy *a.* سلامت salamat

heap *n.* زيات مقدار zyat

heap *v.t* زيات مقدارورکول zyat miqdar warkawal

hear *v.t.* اورول awrawal

hearsay *n.* آوازه،بنوسی awaza; gangosay

heart *n.* زه zra

hearth *n.* منقل،نغری munqal; nagharay

heartily *adv.* په زه ورتوب pa zarawartob

heat *n.* تودوخه tawdokha

heat *v.t* تودول tawdawal

heave *v.i.* هسكول hasakaval

heaven *n.* جنت janat

heavenly *a.* آسماني asmanee

hedge *n.* خنډ،کاره khand; katara

hedge *v.t* خنياکاره راتاوول khand ya katara ratawowal

heed *v.t.* توجه كول tawajo kawal

heed *n* توجه tawajo

heel *n.* پونده poonda

hefty *a.* دروند droond

height *n.* لووالی lwarwalay

heighten *v.t.* لوول lwarawal

heinous *a.* ناوه nawara

heir *n.* وارث waris

hell *a.* دوزخ dozakh

helm *n.* دكتسرۍ da kakhtay stayring

helmet *n.* فلزي خولۍ filizee khwalay

help *v.t.* مرسته كول mrasta kawal

help *n* مرسته mrasta

helpful *a.* كومكي komakee

helpless *a.* بياره،بمدداره bey yara; bey madadgara

helpmate *n.* دژوندملری da zhwand malgaray

hemisphere *n.* ژ jai

hemp *n.* بن bang

hen *n.* چرگه charga

hence *adv.* له دلامله la dey lamala

henceforth *adv.* پس له د pas la dey

henceforward *adv.* پس له د pas la dey

henchman *n.* باوري لاروی bawaree laraway

henpeck *a.* پرميه بچوهل pa merda barach wahal

her *pron.* دهغ،هغته da haghey; haghey ta

her *a* دهغ da haghey

herald *n.* جارچي،الچي jarchee; aylchee

herald *v.t* زوی ورکول zeyray warkawal

herb *n.* طبي بوی tibee botay

herculean *a.* ران gran

herd *n.* رمه rama

herdsman *n.* شپون shpoon

here *adv.* دخوا،دلته deykhwa; dalta

hereabouts *adv.* په دشاوخوا ک pa dey shawkhwa ki

hereafter *adv.* تر دورو سته tar dey wrosta

hereditary *n.* موروثي mawroosee

heredity *n.* ميراث meeras

heritage *n.* ميراث meeras

hermit *n.* وشه نشين زاهد gosha nasheen zahid

hermitage *n.* دانزو اای da anzwa zay

hernia *n.* چوره،فتق choora; fataq

hero *n.* اتل،قهرمان atal; qaharman

heroic *a.* قهرماني qaharmanee

heroine *n.* تله،قهرمانه tala; qaharmana

heroism *n.* اتلوي،قهرماني atlawee; qaharmanee

herring *n.* یوول کب yaw dol kab

hesitant *a.* دشمالي امریکا یوول کب da shomalee amreeka yaw dawl kab

hesitate *v.i.* زه نازه کدل zra na zra keydal

hesitation *n.* زه نازه توب zra na zratob

hew *v.t.* قطع کول،غووـل qata kawal; ghosawal

heyday *n.* دنکمر غاوج da naykmarghay oj

hibernation *n.* دژمي موسم په خوب تر وونه da zhamee mosam pa khob teyrowana

hiccup *n.* سل salgay

hide *n.* پونه patawana

hide *v.t* پول patawal

hideous *a.* ربدشکله deyr bad shakla

hierarchy *n.* مذهبي حکومت mazhabee hukoomat

high *a.* عالي،لو alee; lwar

highly *adv.* په لوی کچ pa loy kach

Highness *n.* عزت مأب eezat mab

highway *n.* لوی لاز loya lar

hilarious *a.* رخندو ونکی deyr khandowoonkay

hilarity *n.* خوشالي khoshalee

hill *n.* غوز ghonday

hillock *n.* کوچنغوز koochnay ghonday

him *pron.* هغته hagha ta

hinder *v.t.* نارامه کول narama kawal

hindrance *n.* خن؛مزاحمت khand; muzahimat

hint *n.* اشاره ishara

hint *v.i* اشاره کول ishara kawal

hip *n* کونای konatay

hire *n.* کرایه؛اجاره karaya; eejara

hire *v.t* کرایه کول karaya kawal

hireling *n.* مزدور mazdoor

his *pron.* دهغه da hagha

hiss *n* سوبدنه sonreydana

hiss *v.i* سوبدل sonreydal

historian *n.* تاریخ لیکونکی tareekh leekoonkay

historic *a.* تاريخي tareekhee

historical *a.* تاريخي tareekhee

history *n.* تاریخ؛پل tareekh; peykh lar

hit *v.t.* کر کول takar kawal

hit *n* کر؛تصادف takar; tasadof

hitch *n.* کان؛جکه takan; jatka

hither *adv.* دغهای ته dagha zay ta

hitherto *adv.* تر اوسه tar osa

hive *n.* دمچیو کور da muchyo kor

hoarse *a.* زِه zeg

hoax *n.* وکه toka

hoax *v.t* وکه کول toka kawal

hobby *n.* مشغولا mashghola

hockey *n.* دهاکولوبه da hakay loba

hoist *v.t.* پورته کول porta kawal

hold *n.* پورته کوونه porta kawona

hold *v.t* پهواک کلرل pa wak ki laral

hole *n* سوری sooray

hole *v.t* سوری کول sooray kawal

holiday *n.* دآرامور da aram wraz

hollow *a.* خالي؛پوده khalee; pooda

hollow *n.* سوری sooray

hollow *v.t* تشول؛خالي کول tashawal; khalee kawal

holocaust *n.* عاموژنه am wazhna

holy *a.* مقدس muqadas

homage *n.* احترام ehtiram

home *n.* کور kor

homicide *n.* وژنه wazhana

homogeneous *a.* همجنسه hamjinsa

honest *a.* امين ameen

honesty *n.* ديانت deeyanat

honey *n.* شهد shehed

honeycomb *n.* دشاتوبین da shato gabeen

honeymoon *n.* دوادهلومنیماشت da wada loomranay myasht

honorarium *i.* حق الوکاله haqul wakala

honorary *a.* اعزازي ayzazee

honour *n.* احترام ehtiram

honour *v.t* درناوی ورته کول dranaway warta kawal

honourable *a.* محترم mohtaram

hood *n.* پوني؛اوباش paroonay; obash

hoodwink *v.t.* دوکه کول doka kawal

hoof *n.* سوه؛کومه swa; korma

hook *n.* چنک changak

hooligan *n.* لوچک او کوه بی وان loochak aw koosa dabay zwan

hoot *n.* دتحقیرچغه da tehqeer cheygha

hoot *v.i* دتحقیرچغهوهل da tehqeer cheygha wahal

hop *v.i* وپونهوهل topoona wahal

hop *n* بير،افين،غوریپری beer; afeen; ghorzay parzay

hope *v.t.* ورتههيلهلرل warta heela laral

hope *n* اميد omeed

hopeful *a.* هيلهمن heelaman

hopeless *a.* نااميده na omeeda

horde *n.* قبيله qabeela

horizon *n.* افقیکره ofqee karkha

horn *n.* كر khkar

hornet *n.* يوولسترهغومبسه yaw dawl stara ghombasa

horrible *a.* هيبتناک haybatnak

horrify *v.t.* ترهول tarhawal

horror *n.* ترهه tarha

horse *n.* آس as

horticulture *n.* پوهنيزهباغواني pohaneeza baghwanee

hose *n.* داوبوشيندنانیپلاستيكینل da obo sheendani zangaray plasteekee nal

hosiery *n.* دجورابواوبنينونوجوونهيا دا jorabo aw پلورنی banaynoono jorawona ya ploranzay

hospitable *a.* ملمهپال meylma pal

hospital *n.* روغتون roghtoon

hospitality *n.* ملمستيا meylmastya

host *n.* كوربه korba

hostage *n.* يرغمل yarghmal

hostel *n.* دپوهنتونياووني‌ليله da pohantoon ya khowonzee laylya

hostile *a.* مخالف mukhalif

hostility *n.* مخالفت mukhalifat

hot *a.* گرماوتود garam aw tod

hotchpotch *n.* گوآش gadwad ash

hotel *n.* ملمستون meylmastoon

hound *n.* كاریسپی khkaree spay

hour *n.* يوساعت yaw saat

house *n* كور،سرای kor; sray

house *v.t* مشتکول meysht kawal

how *adv.* پهول،نه pa sa dawl; sanga

however *adv.* خوبياهم kho bya ham

however *conj* كههم ka sa ham

howl *v.t.* كوكول،چغوهل kooki kawal; cheyghi wahal

howl *n* كوکی kooki

hub *n.* دفعاليتمركز da faaleeyat markaz

hubbub *n.* غرو،هياهو ghreew; hya hoo

huge *a.* پياوی،لوی pyawaray; loy

hum *v. i* بندل bangeydal

hum *n* بندنه bangeydana

human *a.* انساني insanee

humane *a.* مهربان mehraban

humanitarian *a* بشرپال bashar pal

humanity *n.* بشريت bashareeyat

humanize *v.t.* انسانول،سیکول insanawal; saray kawal

humble *a.* خاكسار khaksar

humdrum *a.* بیخونده bey khwanda

humid *a.* نمجن،لوند namjan; loond

humidity *n.* رطوبت ratoobat

humiliate *v.t.* توهينول tawheenawal

humiliation *n.* توهين tawheen

humility *n.* خاكساري khaksaree

humorist *n.* وكمار tokmar

humorous *a.* توكی toki

humour *n.* خوش طبعي khush tabee

hunch *n.* بوکام؛راوتلتیا bokam; rawataltya

hundred *n.* سل sal

hunger *n* لوه loga

hungry *a.* وی wagay

hunt *v.t.* ښکارکول khkar kawal

hunt *n* ښکار khkar

hunter *n.* ښکاري khkaree

huntsman *n.* ښکاریسی khkaree saray

hurdle1 *n.* خنډ؛کاره تاوونه khand; katara tawowan

hurdle2 *v.t* خنډرول؛کاره ترتاوول khand darawal; katara tri tawowal

hurl *v.t.* شل؛استل sharal; eystal

hurrah *interj.* شاباش؛دخوشالیوآواز shabash; da khoshalay yaw awaz

hurricane *n.* توند اوتزباد tond aw teyz awaz

hurry *v.t.* توندي کول tondee kawal

hurry *n* توندي tondee

hurt *v.t.* ژوبلول zhoblawal

hurt *n* شوبل shobal

husband *n* مه meyra

husbandry *n.* کرهه؛باغباني karhanra; baghbanee

hush *n* چوپتیا choptya

hush *v.i* خاموشول khamoshawal

husk *n.* پوستکی postakay

husky *a.* وچ؛آواز wach; dad awaz

hut *n.* کوله koodala

hyaena, hyena *n.* کو؛دسپي په ریوناور kog; da spee pa seyr yaw zanawar

hybrid *a.* پوندي،دوهري peywandee; dwa ragay

hybrid *n* پوندي بوی یافصل peywandee bootay ya fasal

hydrogen *n.* دهایروجن ګاز da haydrojan gaz

hygiene *n.* روغتیاپوهنه roghtya pohana

hygienic *a.* په روغتیاپوراوند pa roghtya pori arwand

hymn *n.* مذهبي ترانه mazhabee tarana

hyperbole *n.* مبالغه وینا mubaligha wayna

hypnotism *n.* په مصنوعي ول دویده کولوعمل اوعلم pa masnooee dawl da weeda kawalo amal aw ilam

hypnotize *v.t.* په مصنوعي ول ویده کول pa masnooee dawl weeda kawal

hypocrisy *n.* په ریاکاران بریالی کونه pa reeyakaray zan baryalay kawona

hypocrite *n.* ریاکارسی reeyakar saray

hypocritical *a.* ریاکارانه او دوه مخي reeyakarana aw dwa makhee

hypothesis *n.* مفروضه؛یوخیال mafrooza; yaw khyal

hypothetical *a.* خیالي؛مفروضي khyalee; mafroozee

hysteria *n.* دتشنج رنز da tashannuj ranz

hysterical *a.* تشنج وهلی شخص tashannuj wahalay shakhs

I

I *pron.* زه za

ice *n.* واوره wawra

iceberg *n.* دواوریووکی‌غر da wawri warookay ghar

icicle *n.* وندهکنل‌شوی‌واوره zwaranda kangal shawi wawra

icy *a.* واورين wawreen

idea *n.* خيال،فكر khyal; fikar

ideal *a.* خيالي،تصوري khyalee; tasawwuree

ideal *n.* مكمل‌اوبشپان‌سان mukamal aw bashbar insan

idealism *n.* خيال‌پالنه khyal palana

idealist *n.* خيالي‌انسان khyalee insan

idealistic *a.* انريال،تصوري angeyryal; tasawwuree

idealize *v.t.* خيالي‌به‌ورکول khyalee banra warkawal

identical *a.* مشابه mushabay

indentification *n.* پژندلوي،شناخت peyzhandgalwee; shanakht

identify *v.t.* شناخت‌كول shanakht kawal

identity *n.* شناخت shanakht

idiom *n.* لهجه،نه lehja; garana

idiomatic *a.* لهجوي lehjawee

idiot *n.* لوده lawda

idiotic *a.* بعقله bey aqla

idle *a.* بكاره bey kara

idleness *n.* بكاري bey karee

idler *n.* بكاره bey kara

idol *n.* بت boot

idolater *n.* بت‌پرست boot parast

if *conj.* كاش اى كه، ka; ay kash

ignoble *a.* كم‌اصل kam asal

ignorance *n.* ناپوهي napohee

ignorant *a.* ناپوه napoh

ignore *v.t.* سترپرپول stargey pri patawal

ill *a.* رنور ranzoor

ill *adv.* ناسم،ناجو nasam; najor

ill *n* بده‌چاره bada chara

illegal *a.* غرقانوني gheyr qanoonee

illegibility *n.* نه‌لوستل‌کدل na lostal keydal

illegible *a.* نه‌لوستل‌کدونکی na lostal keydoonkay

illegitimate *a.* ناروا،ارموني narawa; armoonay

illicit *a.* ارموني،غرقانوني armoonay; gheyr qanoonee

illiteracy *n.* ناپوهي،کم‌تعليمي napohee; kam taleemee

illiterate *a.* بتعليمه bey taleema

illness *n.* بيماري beemaree

illogical *a.* نامعقول namaqool

illuminate *v.t.* لاندهکول zalanda kawal

illumination *n.* روانتيا rokhantya

illusion *n.* فريب،وهم farayb; wehem

illustrate *v.t.* شرحهکول sharha kawal

illustration *n.* شرحه،توضيح sharha; tawzee

image *n.* تصوير،شكل tasweer; shakal

imagery *n.* تصور،خيال tasawwur; khyal

imaginary *a.* خيالي khyalee

imagination *n.* تصور،ګومان tasawwur; gooman

imaginative *a.* تصوري tasawwuree

imagine *v.t.* ګومان واکل کول gooman aw atkal kawal

imitate *v.t.* پروي کول،نقل کول peyrawee kawal; naqal kawal

imitation *n.* پروي،تقليد peyrawee; taqleed

imitator *n.* تقليد کوونکی taqleed kawoonkay

immaterial *a.* غير مادي gheyr madee

immature *a.* ناپخته napukhta

immaturity *n.* ناپختي napukhtagee

immeasurable *a.* لامحدود lamehdood

immediate *a* فوري fawree

immemorial *a.* ديرپخواني deyr pakhwanay

immense *a.* خورا ډير khora deyr

immensity *n.* ډيررت deyrakht

immerse *v.t.* جذبول،غرقول jazbawal; gharqawal

immersion *n.* غوپه کونه ghopa kawona

immigrant *n.* کوال kadwal

immigrate *v.i.* کوچيدل koocheydal

immigration *n.* کوالتوب kadwaltob

imminent *a.* خطرناک،نژد khatarnak; nazhdey

immodest *a.* بحيا bey haya

immodesty *n.* بحيايي bey hayayee

immoral *a.* بداخلاق bad akhlaq

immorality *n.* بداخلاقي bad akhlaqee

immortal *a.* تلژوندی tal zhwanday

immortality *n.* تلپاتوب talpatitob

immortalize *v.t.* تلپاتوکول talpati kawal

immovable *a.* بحرکت bey harakat

immune *a.* محفوظ mehfooz

immunity *n.* حفاظت،مصئونتيا heefazat; masuntya

immunize *v.t.* درنپرضدواکسين ورکول da ranz pr zid wakseen warkawal

impact *n.* اثر،فشار asar; fishar

impart *v.t.* ونهورکول،پهبرخهکول wanda warkawal; gata pa barkha kawal

impartial *a.* بطرفه bey tarafa

impartiality *n.* بطرفي bey tarafee

impassable *a.* ناشوني nashoonay

impasse *n.* بلاريای be lari zai

impatience *n.* بصبري bey sabree

impatient *a.* بصبره bey sabra

impeach *v.t.* تورنول toranawal

impeachment *n.* تورونه،تعقيب torawona; taqeeb

impede *v.t.* مانع کدل manay keydal

impediment *n.* خنکدنه khand keydana

impenetrable *a.* راسخ او کلک klak aw rasikh

imperative *a.* امري،لازمي amaree; lazimee

imperfect *a.* ناقص naqis

imperfection *n.* نيمتيا neemgartya

imperial *a.* پاچاهي pachahee

imperialism *n.* امپراطوري ampratooree

imperil *v.t.* په‌خطر کاچول pa khatar ke achaval

imperishable *a.* تلپات talpati

impersonal *a.* غرشخصي gheyr shakhsee

impersonate *v.t.* شخصيت نه‌ورکول shakhseeyat na warkawal

impersonation *n.* ان‌دبل شخصيت په رمل zan da bal shakhseeyat pa seyra ganral

impertinence *n.* بادبي bey adabee

impertinent *a.* بادبه bey adaba

impetuosity *n.* سختي او شدت sakhtee aw shiddat

impetuous *a.* سخت او شديد sakht aw shadeed

implement *n.* کارونه karawona

implement *v.t.* کارول؛عمل کراوستل karawal; amal ki rawastal

implicate *v.t.* په‌جنايت کلاس لرل pa jinayat ki las laral

implication *n.* په‌جنايت ککتيا pa jinayat kakartya

implicit *a.* کامل؛مکمل kamil; mukamal

implore *v.t.* زار کول zaray kawal

imply *v.t.* ضمن مفهوم zaman mafhoom

impolite *a.* بادبه bey adaba

import *v.t.* واردول waridawal

import *n.* واردات waridat

importance *n.* اهميت ahmeeyat

important *a.* اهم aham

impose *v.t.* مسلطول musallatawal

imposing *a.* مسلط musallat

imposition *n.* لازمي کوونه lazimee kawona

impossibility *n.* ناشونتيا nashoontya

impossible *a.* ناشونی nashoonay

impostor *n.* چلباز chalbaz

imposture *n.* چلبازي chalbazee

impotence *n.* جنسي کمزورتيا jinsee kamzortya

impotent *a.* په‌جنسي توه کمزوری pa jinsee toga kamzoray

impoverish *v.t.* ناتوان کول natwan kawal

impracticability *n.* ناعملي توب na amaleetob

impracticable *a.* ناعملي na amalee

impress *v.t.* متاثرول mutasirawal

impression *n.* اثر؛خيال asar; khyal

impressive *a.* مؤثر moassar

imprint *v.t.* په‌فشار سره‌جوول pa fishar sara jorawal

imprint *n.* چاپ شوی‌شی chap shaway shay

imprison *v.t.* زنداني کول zandanee kawal

improper *a.* نامناسب na munasib

impropriety *n.* ناوتوب nawartob

improve *v.t.* سمول؛سمسورول samawa ; samsorawal

improvement *n.* سمسورتيا samsortya

imprudence *n.* بپامي bey pamee

imprudent *a.* بپامه bey pama

impulse *n.* انزه angeyza

impulsive *a.* انزوي angeyzwee

impunity *n.* له‌سزا خه‌بنه la saza sakha bakhana

impure *a.* ناولی nawalay

impurity *n.* ناپاکی napakee

impute *v.t.* ملامتول malamatawal

in *prep.* په که pa ki

inability *n.* ناتواني natwanee

inaccurate *a.* ناسم nasam

inaction *n.* بېکاري bey karee

inactive *a.* بېکاره bey kara

inadmissible *a.* ناروا narawa

inanimate *a.* بېروحه،جامد bey rooha; jamid

inapplicable *a.* نا جو na jor

inattentive *a.* بېپامه bey pama

inaudible *a.* نه اورېدونکی na awreydoonkay

inaugural *a.* په پرانستنی پوراوند pa pranistani pori arwand

inauguration *n.* پرانستنه pranistana

inauspicious *a.* بدمرغه badmargha

inborn *a.* فطري fitree

incalculable *a.* بېشماره bey shmara

incapable *a.* ناتوان natwan

incapacity *n.* کمزورتيا kamzortia

incarnate *a.* مجسم mujassam

incarnate *v.t.* مجسم کول mujassam kawal

incarnation *n.* وجودورکوونه wajood warkowana

incense *v.t.* فتنه اچول fitna achawal

incense *n.* فتنه fitna

incentive *n.* محرک mohrik

inception *n.* آغاز aghaz

inch *n.* د وطن يو پمائش da watan yaw paymayish

incident *n.* حادثه hadisa

incidental *a.* حادثاتی hadisatee

incite *v.t.* لمسول lamsawal

inclination *n.* آمادي،ميلان amadagee; meelan

incline *v.i.* هول،کوپول hasawal; kropawal

include *v.t.* شاملول shamilawal

inclusion *n.* شمولتيا shamooltya

inclusive *a.* شامل shamil

incoherent *a.* نااروند na arwand

income *n.* ګه،حاصل gata; hasil

incomparable *a.* بېجو bey jorey

incompetent *a.* نالائق nalayiq

incomplete *a.* ناتکميل natakmeel

inconsiderate *a.* بېاحتياطه bey ehteeyata

inconvenient *a.* ناراحه narama

incorporate *v.t.* يوکول yaw kawal

incorporate *a.* يوشوی yaw shaway

incorporation *n.* پوستون،يوکدا peywastoon; yaw keyda

incorrect *a.* غلط ghalat

incorrigible *a.* نه رغدونکی nā ragheydoonkay

incorruptible *a.* نه خرابدونکی na kharabeydoonkay

increase *v.t.* زياتول zyatawal

increase *n* زياښت zyadakht

incredible *a.* د نه مننو da na manani war

increment *n.* رت deyrakht

incriminate *v.t.* تورنول toranawal

incubate *v.i.* چروي استل chargooree eystal

inculcate *v.t.* تلقين کول talqeen kawal

incur *v.t.* خواشينى‌كول khwasheenee kawal

incurable *a.* لاعلاج la ilaj

indebted *a.* قرضدار qarzdar

indecency *n.* بى‌نزاكتي bey nazakatee

indecent *a.* بى‌نزاكته bey nazakata

indecision *n.* بى‌عزمى be azami

indeed *adv.* په‌ريتينى‌ول pa reekhteenee dawl

indefensible *a.* نه‌ژغورونكى na zhghoroonkay

indefinite *a.* غرمحدود gheyr mehdood

indemnity *n.* تاوان؛جبران tawan; jibran

independence *n.* خپلواكي khpalwakee

independent *a.* خپلواكه khpalwaka

indescribable *a.* نه‌شرحه‌كدونكى na sharha keydoonkay

index *n.* لارودليك lar khod lar leek

Indian *a.* هندي؛هندوستاني hindee; hindoostanee

indicate *v.t.* رندول؛دلالت‌كول sargandawal; dalalat kawal

indication *n.* دلالت؛اشاره dalalat; ishara

indicative *a.* اشاره‌كوونكى ishara kawoonkay

indicator *n.* اشاره‌كوونكى ishara kawoonkay

indict *v.t.* دادعاليك‌له‌مختورنول da ida leek la makhi toranawal

indictment *n.* په‌ادعاليك‌سره‌مخ تورنونه pa ida leek sara makh torawona

indifference *n.* بتفاوتي bey tafawatee

indifferent *a.* بى‌تفاوت bey tafawat

indigenous *a.* سوچه‌اصلي؛ aslee; soocha

indigestible *a.* نه‌هضمدونكى na hazmeydoonkay

indigestion *n.* نه‌هضمدنه na hazmeydana

indignant *a.* قهردلى qahreydalay

indignation *n.* قهر qahar

indigo *n.* تزآسماني‌رنگ teyz asmanee rang

indirect *a.* نامستقيم na mustaqeem

indiscipline *n.* بى‌نظمي bey nazmee

indiscriminate *a.* لوده؛بعقل lawda; bey aqla

indispensable *a.* ضروري zarooree

indisposed *a.* ناساز nasaz

indisputable *a.* مسلم musallam

indistinct *a.* نامشخص na mushakhkhas

individual *a.* زاني؛يوازان zanee; yawazi zan

individualism *n.* يوازتوب yawazitob

individuality *n.* زاناني؛فردي zan zanee; fardee

indolent *a.* كاهل kahil

indoor *a.* دننى؛داخلي danananay; dakhilee

indoors *adv.* په‌كوردننه pa kor danana

induce *v.t.* مجبورول majboorawal

inducement *n.* سبب sabab

induct *v.t.* داخلول؛درك‌كول dakhilawal; darak kawal

induction *n.* داخلدا dakhileyda

indulge *v.t.* خپلواکهپرودل khpalwaka preykhodal

indulgence *n.* اجازهورکونه eejaza warkawona

indulgent *a.* خپلواکهپرودلیشوی khpalwaka preykhodalay shaway

industrial *a.* صنعتي sanatee

industrious *a.* زیارکه zeeyar kakh

industry *n.* صنعت sanat

ineffective *a.* غرمؤثر ghayr moassar

inertia *n.* عطالت italat

inevitable *a.* ناچار nachar

inexact *a.* نادرست nadrust

inexorable *a.* برحم bey rehem

inexpensive *a.* کمخره kam kharsa

inexperience *n.* ناتجربهکار na tajroba kar

inexplicable *a.* ستونزمن stoonzman

infallible *a.* نهغولدونکی na gholeydoonkay

infamous *a.* بدنام badnam

infamy *n.* بدنامي badnamee

infancy *n.* کوچنیتوب koochneetob

infant *n.* کوچنی koochnay

infanticide *n.* دکوچنووژنه da koochno wazhana

infantile *a.* دکوچنوپهاوند da koochno pa arwand

infantry *n.* پوپیاده pyada pawz

infatuate *v.t.* حماقتکول himaqat kawal

infatuation *n.* حماقت himaqat

infect *v.t.* ککول kakarawal

infection *n.* ککتیا kakartya

infectious *a.* ککر kakar

inference *n.* استنباط istimbat

inferior *a.* کمتر kamtar

inferiority *n.* کمتري kamtaree

infernal *a.* دوزخي dozakhee

infinite *a.* لامحدود la mehdood

infinity *n.* لامحدودیت la mehdoodeeyat

infirm *a.* ضعیف zaeef

infirmity *n.* ضعف zof

inflame *v.t.* پارول parawal

inflammable *a.* اوراخیستونکی or akheystoonkay

inflammation *n.* التهاب،سودنه iltihab; sozeydana

inflammatory *a.* التهابي iltihabee

inflation *n.* اقتصاديپسوب iqtisadee parsob

inflexible *a.* نهبدلدونکی؛نهکدونکی na badleydoonkay; na kageydoonkay

inflict *v.t.* سزاورکول saza warkawal

influence *n.* اغز agheyz

influence *v.t.* اغزلرل agheyz laral

influential *a.* اغزناک agheyznak

influenza *n.* زکام zukam

influx *n.* بهیر؛جریان baheer; jaryan

inform *v.t.* خبرول khabrawal

informal *a.* غررسمي ghayr rasmee

information *n.* معلومات maloomat

informative *a.* باخبر ba khabar

informer *n.* خبروونکی khabrawoonkay

infringe *v.t.* لاساچول laas achawal

infuriate *v.t.* قهرول qahrawal

infuse *v.t.* دمول damaval

ingrained *a.* پوخ pokh

ingratitude *n.* ناشكري na shukree

ingredient *n.* ترکیبی‌جز tarkeebee joz

inhabit *v.t.* استونه‌کول astogna kawal

inhabitable *a.* داستونو da astogni war

inhabitant *n.* استون astogan

inhale *v.i.* بویول booyawal

inherent *a.* میراثي meerasee

inherit *v.t.* په‌میراث‌راول pa meeras rawral

inheritance *n.* میراث meeras

inhibit *v.t.* مخنیوی‌کول makhneeway kawal

inhibition *n.* مخنیوی makhneeway

inhospitable *a.* نامهربان na mehraban

inhuman *a.* غرانساني ghayr insanee

inimical *a.* زیانمن zeeyanman

inimitable *a.* بساریتوب beysareetob

initial *a.* بنیادي،ابتدایي boonyadee; ibtidayee

initial *n.* آغاز;شروع aghaz; shoro

initial *v.t* شروع‌کول shoro kawal

initiate *v.t.* لومړی‌ګام‌پورته‌کول loomray gam porta kawal

initiative *n.* آغاز aghaz

inject *v.t.* ستنه‌وهل stana wahal

injection *n.* اماله،تزریق imala; tazreeq

injudicious *a.* بانصافه bey insafa

injunction *n.* دنیوزحکم da neewani hokam

injure *v.t.* پی‌کول tapee kawal

injurious *a.* وروونکی zorowoonkay

injury *n.* زخم zakham

injustice *n.* بانصافي bey insafee

ink *n.* سیاهي seeyahee

inkling *n.* راپور rapor

inland *a.* دمکبریدونو‌کدننه da zmaki breedoono ki danana

inland *adv.* دهوادخواته da haywad khwa ta

in-laws *n.* د‌کورودانرونه‌اوخوند da korwadani ronra aw khwayndi

inmate *n.* استون astogan

inmost *a.* په‌منځکی pa manz ke

inn *n.* مسافرخانه moosafar khana

innate *a.* طبیي tibbee

inner *a.* داخلي dakhilee

innermost *a.* مننبرخه manzanay barkha

innocence *n.* بناهتوب bey goonahtob

innocent *a.* بناه bey goona

innovate *v.t.* بدلون‌راوستل badloon rawastal

innovation *n.* بدلون،نوی‌شی badloon; naway shay

innovator *n.* بدلون‌راوستونکی badloon rawastoonkay

innumerable *a.* بشمره bey shmeyra

inoculate *v.t.* خال‌وهل khal wahal

inoculation *n.* خال‌وهنه khal wahana

inoperative *a.* غرفعال ghayr faal

inopportune *a.* بوخته،بموقع bey wakhta; bey moqa

input *n.* ونه،بولتونه wanda; tol lagakhtoona

inquest *n.* رونه garweygna

inquire *v.t.* پوښتل pokhtal

inquiry *n.* تحقيق tehqeeq

inquisition *n.* پوښتنه pokhtana

inquisitive *a.* تحقيقي،تفتيشي tehqeeqee; tafteeshee

insane *a.* ګنده ganda

insanity *n.* خچنتوب khachantob

insatiable *a.* نه راضه کدونکی na razee keydoonkay

inscribe *v.t.* نقش کول naqsh kawal

inscription *n.* کتیبه kateeba

insect *n.* حشره hashra

insecticide *n.* حشره وژونکی hashra wazhoonkay

insecure *a.* غرمحفوظ ghayr mehfooz

insecurity *n.* بی اطمیناني bey itmaynanee

insensibility *n.* بی حسي bey hisee

insensible *a.* بی حس bey his

inseparable *a.* نه بلدونکی beyleydoonkay

insert *v.t.* ننوستل،بایول nanaweystal; zayawal

insertion *n.* ننوستنه nanaweystana

inside *n.* کولمه او احشاء koolmey aw ahsha

inside *prep.* دننه danana

inside *a* دننی؛داخلي danananay; dakhilee

inside *adv.* په داخل پوراوند pa dakhil pori arwand

insight *n.* بصیرت baseerat

insignificance *n.* بی ماناتوب bey manatob

insignificant *a.* بی مانا bey mana

insincere *a.* ریاکار،بی مخلص reeyakar; bey mukhlis

insincerity *n.* دوه مخي؛ریا dwa makhay; reeya

insinuate *v.t.* چاپلوسي کول chaplosee kawal

insinuation *n.* چاپلوسي chaplosee

insipid *a.* بی خونده bey khwanda

insipidity *n.* بی خوندي bey khwandee

insist *v.t.* اصرار کول israr kawal

insistence *n.* اصرار israr

insistent *a.* اصرار کوونکی israr kawoonkay

insolence *n.* اهانت ihanat

insolent *a.* ګستاخ gostakh

insoluble *n.* نه ویلا کدونکی na waylay keydoonkay

insolvency *n.* نه ویلا کدنه na wayla keydana

insolvent *a.* نا بسیا؛پاتراغلی na basya; pati raghalay

inspect *v.t.* پلنه کول palatana kawal

inspection *n.* پلنه palatana

inspector *n.* پلوونکی palatoonkay

inspiration *n.* اثر asar

inspire *v.t.* متاثرول mutasirawal

instability *n.* نایکاوتوب nateekawtob

install *v.t.* په کاراچول pa kar achawal

installation *n.* په‌کاراچونه pa kar achawona

instalment *n.* قسط qist

instance *n.* نمونه،بله namoona; beylga

instant *n.* جاري jaree

instant *a.* این areen

instantly *adv.* ژرترژره zhar tar zhara

instigate *v.t.* لمسول lamsawal

instigation *n.* لمسون lamsoon

instil *v.t.* تدریجي‌تلقین‌کول tadreejee talqeen kawal

instinct *n.* حواني‌شعور haywanee shaoor

instinctive *a.* حواني‌شعورلرونکی haywanee shaoor laroonkay

institute *n.* مؤسسه moassisa

institution *n.* مرکز،سازمان markaz; sazman

instruct *v.t.* وونه‌کول khowana kawal

instruction *n.* درس،هدایت dars; hidayat

instructor *n.* درس‌ورکوونکی dars warkowoonkay

instrument *n.* آله،وسیله ala; waseela

instrumental *a.* آلاتي alatee

instrumentalist *n.* دموسیقه‌دآلاتو ماهر da mawseeqay da alato mahir

insubordinate *a.* نافرمان nafarman

insubordination *n.* نافرماني nafarmanee

insufficient *a.* ناکافي nakafee

insular *a.* لنفکرى land fikray

insularity *n.* لنفکري land fikree

insulate *v.t.* جلاکول jala kawal

insulation *n.* بلتون beyltoon

insulator *n.* جلاکوونکی jala kawoonkay

insult *n.* سپکاوی spakaway

insult *v.t.* بدردویل badi radi wayal

insurance *n.* بیمه beema

insure *v.t.* بیمه‌کول beema kawal

insurgent *a.* باغیانه baghyana

insurgent *n.* باغ baghee

insurrection *n.* بلواري balwagaree

intact *a.* سالم salim

intangible *a.* نامحسوس na mehsoos

integral *a.* ضروري zarooree

integrity *n.* ایمانداري eemandaree

intellect *n.* فهم fehem

intellectual *a.* فکري fikree

intellectual *n.* مفکر mufakkir

intelligence *n.* استخبارات istikhbarat

intelligent *a.* هویار hookhyar

intelligentsia *n.* قابل‌خلک qabil khalk

intelligible *a.* واضح wazeh

intend *v.t.* اراده‌کول irada kawal

intense *a.* شدید shadeed

intensify *v.t.* شدت‌زیاتول shiddat zyatawal

intensity *n.* تزي،شدت teyzee; shiddat

intensive *a.* شدید shadeed

intent *n.* هو hod

intent *a.* منظور manzoor

intention *n.* قصد qasad

intentional *a.* قصدي qasdee

intercept *v.t.* رابطه‌شنول rabita shandawal

interception *n.* مخنيوی makhneeway

interchange *n.* مبادل mubadil

interchange *v.* مبادله‌كول mubadila kawal

intercourse *n.* مقاربت،معامله muqaribat; moamila

interdependence *n.* يوپه‌بل‌باندتكيه yaw pa bal bandi takia

interdependent *a.* يوپه‌بل‌باندتكيه yaw pa bal bandi takia

interest *n.* جالبيت jalibeeyat

interested *a.* جالب jalib

interesting *a.* په‌زه‌پور pa zra pori

interfere *v.i.* دخالت‌كول dakhalat kawal

interference *n.* دخالت dakhalat

interim *n.* عارضي‌مدت arzee mudat

interior *a.* داخلي dakhilee

interior *n.* دننه danana

interjection *n.* حرف‌ندا،دخالت harfi nida; dakhalat

interlock *v.t.* په‌قلف‌بندول pa qulf bandawal

interlude *n.* كوونكی‌وان dakowoonkay watan

intermediary *n.* مصالحت‌كوونكی musalihat kawoonkay

intermediate *a.* منی manzgaray

interminable *a.* پايدار paydar

intermingle *v.t.* ول gadaval

intern *v.t.* توقيف‌كول tawqeef kawal

internal *a.* داخلي dakhilee

international *a.* نيوال nareewal

interplay *n.* دوه‌اخيزاغز dwa arkheez agheyz

interpret *v.t.* ژبانه‌كول zhbarana kawal

interpreter *n.* ژبان zhbaran

interrogate *v.t.* تفتيش‌كول tafteesh kawal

interrogation *n.* رونه garweygna

interrogative *a.* پوتونکی pokhtoonkay

interrogative *n* دپوتنه da pokhtani nakha

interrupt *v.t.* قطع‌كول qata kawal

interruption *n.* پركون preykoon

intersect *v.t.* قطع‌كول qata kawal

intersection *n.* تقاطع taqato

interval *n.* موده،دمه mooda; dama

intervene *v.i.* مداخله‌كول mudakhila kawal

intervention *n.* مداخله mudakhila

interview *n.* مركه maraka

interview *v.t.* مركه‌كول maraka kaval

intestinal *a.* دكولمو‌په‌اوند da koolmo pa arwand

intestine *n.* كولمه koolmey

intimacy *n.* نژداشناتوب nazhdey ashnatob

intimate *a.* اشنا،نژد ashna; nazhdey

intimate *v.t.* مطلب‌رسول matlab rasawal

intimation *n.* اشاره،خبرتيا ishara; khabartya

intimidate *v.t.* ترهول tarhawal

intimidation *n.* ترهه tarha

into *prep.* ک‍_‍_په،دننه danana; pa ... ki

intolerable *a.* نه‌زغموونکی na zghamowoonkay

intolerance *n.* نه‌زغمنه na zghamana

intolerant *a.* نه‌زغموونکی na zghamowoonkay

intoxicant *n.* نشه‌یاک nashayee skhak

intoxicate *v.t.* نشه‌کول nasha kawal

intoxication *n.* نشه‌کوونه nasha kawona

intransitive *a. verb* لازمي‌فعل lazimee fayl

intrepid *a.* بوړ bey weyri

intrepidity *n.* نه‌ارنه na darana

intricate *a.* پچلی peychalay

intrigue *v.t.* پچلی‌کول peychalay kawal

intrigue *n* پچلتیا peychaltya

intrinsic *a.* حقیقی haqiki

introduce *v.t.* معرفي‌کول marifee kawal

introduction *n.* پژندلوي peyzhandgalwee

introductory *a.* سریزه،ابتدایي sareeza; ibtidayee

introspect *v.i.* زان‌ل zan seyral

introspection *n.* زان‌نه zan seyrana

intrude *v.t.* تری‌کول teyray kawal

intrusion *n.* تری teyray

intuition *n.* فراست firasat

intuitive *a.* بصیرت‌لرونکی baseerat laroonkay

invade *v.t.* بریدکول breed kawal

invalid *a.* بی‌بنیاده bey boonyada

invalid *a.* غرقانوني ghayr qanoonee

invalid *n* بیمار beemar

invalidate *v.t.* باطلول batilawal

invaluable *a* بارزته bay arzakhta

invasion *n.* حمله hamla

invective *n.* بده‌ژبه bada zhaba

invent *v.t.* اختراع‌کول ikhtira kawal

invention *n.* نوت nawakht

inventive *a.* اختراعي ikhtiraee

inventor *n.* نوتر nawakhtgar

invert *v.t.* تحریفول tehreefawal

invest *v.t.* پانسمانول pansmanawal

investigate *v.t.* تحقیق‌کول tehqeeq kawal

investigation *n.* تحقیق tehqeeq

investment *n.* پانه‌اچوونه panga achowana

invigilate *v.t.* ارل saral

invigilation *n.* ارنه sarana

invigilator *n.* ارن saran

invincible *a.* نه‌لیدونکی na leedoonkay

inviolable *a.* منزه،محفوظ munazza; mehfooz

invisible *a.* نالیدلی naleedalay

invitation *v.* بلنه balana

invite *v.t.* بلنه‌ورکول balana warkawal

invocation *n.* دم،دعا dam; doa

invoice *n.* بجک beyjak

invoke *v.t.* مرسته‌غوشتل mrasta ghoshtal

involve *v.t.* ونه‌ورکول wanda warkawal

inward *a.* دننه danana

inwards *adv.* دننه‌خواته danana khwa ta

irate *a.* قارشوی qarshavi

ire *n.* غضب ghazab

Irish *a.* ايرليني eerlayndee

Irish *n.* ايرليني‌وی‌یاژبه eerlayndee wagaray ya zhaba

irksome *a.* ستومانه‌کوونکی stomana kawoonkay

iron *n.* اوسپنه ospana

iron *v.t.* اوتوکول oto kawal

ironical *a.* پغور peghor

irony *n.* پغور peghor

irradiate *v.i.* وانه‌اچول waranga achawal

irrational *a.* نامعقوله namaqoola

irreconcilable *a.* ته‌پخلا‌کیدونکی ta pakhula kedonkay

irrefutable *a.* نه‌ردیدونکی na radeydoonkay

irregular *a.* بقاعد bey qaydey

irregularity *n.* بقاعلی bey qaydagee

irrelevant *a.* نامناسب namunasib

irrespective *a.* باعتنا bey aytina

irresponsible *a.* بپروا bey parwa

irrigate *v.t.* اوبول obawal

irrigation *n.* اوبوونه obawana

irritable *a.* عصبانی asbanee

irritant *a.* فسخ‌کوونکی fasakh kawoonkay

irritant *n.* پاروونکی parowoonkay

irritate *v.t.* په‌قاروال pa qaraval

irritation *n.* پاروونه parawana

irruption *n.* هجوم hajoom

island *n.* ټاپو tapoo

isle *n.* ټاپووزمه tapoo wazma

isolate *v.t.* وه gokha

isolation *n.* یوازیتوب yawazitob

issue *v.i.* صادرول sadirawal

issue *n.* معامله maamila

it *pron.* دا،هغه da; hagha

Italian *a.* ايالوی eetalwee

Italian *n.* ايالوی‌وی‌یاژبه eetalwee wagaray ya zhaba

italic *a.* په‌لرغونوايالويانوپوراوند pa larghono eetalweeyano pori arwand

italics *n.* رنده‌کاه‌توري reykhanda kaga toree

itch *n.* خار kharakh

itch *v.i.* خارلرل kharakh laral

item *n.* شی shay

ivory *n.* دفيل‌غا da feel ghakh

ivy *n* یوول‌بوی‌چه‌تل‌شین‌وی yaw dol botay che tal sheen we

J

jab *v.t.* ننه‌ایستنه nana estana

jabber *v.t.* ناشمرخبرکول na shmeyri khabari kawal

jack *n.* دموټرجک da motar jak

jack *v.t.* په‌جک‌سره‌پورته‌کول pa jak sara

jackal *n.* شغال shaghal

jacket *n.* جاکټ jakat

jade *n.* یوقیمتی‌کانی yaw qeematee kanray

jail *n.* بندیخانه bandeekhana

jailer *n.* دبنديخانمسؤل da bandeekhaney masool

jam *n.* مربا muraba

jam *v.t.* چيتول؛بندول cheetawal; bandawal

jar *n.* يوول دبوتل yaw dawl da kheekhey botal

jargon *n.* زانرهنرۍژبه zangari honaree zhaba

jasmine, jessamine *n.* دياسمين ل da yasmeen gul

jaundice *n.* دزيي رنز da zyaree ranz

jaundice *v.t.* پهزيي اخته کول pa zyaree akhta kawal

javelin *n.* نزه لاسي سپکه spaka lasee nayza

jaw *n.* ژامه zhama

jay *n.* لهکاغدکورنیومارغه la kraghi da koranay yaw margha

jealous *a.* نیت بدی nyat baday

jealousy *n.* نیت بدي nyat badee

jean *n.* يوول پتلون yaw dawl patloon

jeer *v.i.* پغوروركول peyghor warkawal

jelly *n.* يوول خواه خواه yaw dawl khwaga khwara

jeopardize *v.t.* خطرسرهمخامخاخول khatar sara makhamakhawal

jeopardy *n.* خطر khatar

jerk *n.* جکه jaka

jerkin *n.* چرمي واسک charmee waskat

jerky *a.* ککدلی takeydalay

jersey *n.* اوبدلشویبینهجاک obdal shaway khazeena jakat

jest *n.* پغور peyghor

jest *v.i.* پغوروركول peyghor warkawal

jet *n.* توره کهربا tora kahruba

Jew *n.* يهودي yahoodee

jewel *n.* قیمتي کانی qeematee kanray

jewel *v.t.* پهغمیوکلی کول pa ghamyo khkulay kawal

jeweller *n.* زرر zargar

jewellery *n.* جواهراتپلورنی jawahirat ploranzay

jingle *n.* شرنهار shranghar

jingle *v.i.* شرندل shrangeydal

job *n.* دنده danda

jobber *n.* قاچاقچي qachaqchee

jobbery *n.* دقاچاق دنده da qachaq danda

jocular *a.* خندونکی khandoonkay

jog *v.t.* وورول khorawal

join *v.t.* پوندول peywandawal

joiner *n.* ترکا tarkanr

joint *n.* مفصل mafsal

jointly *adv.* پهگدهسره pa gada sara

joke *n.* وکه toka

joke *v.i.* وککول toki kawal

joker *n.* مسخره maskhara

jollity *n.* عش aysh

jolly *a.* مست mast

jolt *n.* ناپهمکان nasapa takan

jolt *v.t.* چدل racheydal

jostle *n.* وبدا khwayeyda

jostle *v.t.* خوت وركول khozakht warkawal

jot *n.* برکی basarkay

jot *v.t.* مختصرلیکل mukhtasar leekal

journal *n.* جریده jareeda

journalism *n.* پلیکنه peykh leekana

journalist *n.* پلیکونکی peykh leekoonkay

journey *n.* سفر safar

journey *v.i.* سفرکول safar kawal

jovial *a.* عشاوعشرت کول aysh aw ishrat kawal

joviality *n.* عشاوعشرت aysh aw ishrat

joy *n.* لذت lazat

joyful, joyous *n.* خوندور khwandawar

jubilant *a.* خوشاله khoshala

jubilation *n.* خوي khwakhee

jubilee *n.* یوخاص کلیزه yaw khas kaleeza

judge *n.* قضایي حکم qazayee hukam

judge *v.i.* قضایي فصله کول qazayee faysala kawal

judgement *n.* قضاوت qazawat

judicature *n.* دقاضیانوپلاوی da qazyano plaway

judicial *a.* قضایﺉ qazayee

judiciary *n.* قضایﺉواک qazayee zwak

judicious *a.* قضاپوراوند qaza pori arwand

jug *n.* لاستي لویه پیاله lastee loya pyala

juggle *v.t.* شعبده بازي کول shobda bazee kawal

juggler *n.* شعبده باز shobda baz

juice *n* دمواوبه da meywey oba

juicy *a.* دمواوبه لرونکی da meywey oba laroonkay

jumble *v.t.* وکول gadwad kawal

jump *n.* وپ top

jump *v.i* وپ وهل top wahal

junction *n.* دپوستونﺂی da peywastoon zay

juncture *n.* اتصال itisal

jungle *n.* ځل zangal

junior *a.* ناتجربه کار na tajruba kar

junior *n.* کشر kashar

junk *n.* دره darga

jupiter *n.* مشتري mushtree

jurisdiction *n.* قانونﺉواک qanoonee wak

jurisprudence *n.* قانون پوهنه qanoon pohana

jurist *n.* قانونپوه qanoonpoh

juror *n.* دمنصفه پلاوي غی da munsifa plawee gharay

jury *n.* قضایﺉ dalgay qazayee dalgay

juryman *n.* دمنصفه پلاوي غی da munsifa plawee gharay

just *a.* نیاوگر nyawgar

just *adv.* سمدلاسه samdalasa

justice *n.* نیاو nyaw

justifiable *a.* دسپینونو da speenawani war

justification *n.* سپینونه speenawana

justify *v.t.* سپینول speenawal

justly *adv.* په عادلانه توه pa adilana toga

jute *n.* سن sand

juvenile *a.* دوانو da zwanay war

K

keen *a.* حاد had

keenness *n.* فراست firasat

keep *v.t.* ساتل satal

keeper *n.* ساتونکی satoonkay

keepsake *n.* يادار yadgar

kennel *n.* دسپي‌خونه da spee khoona

kerchief *n.* دسمال dasmal

kernel *n.* هسته hasta

kerosene *n.* دخاوروتل da khawro teyl

ketchup *n.* دپيازماراومسالوروب da pyaz tamatar aw masalo roob

kettle *n.* جوشه چای chay josha

key *n.* کلي kalee

key *v.t* په کلي‌سره‌خلاصول pa kalee sara khlasawal

kick *n.* لغته laghata

kick *v.t.* لغته‌وهل laghata wahal

kid *n.* ماشوم mashoom

kidnap *v.t.* تتول takhtawal

kidney *n.* پوتوری pokhtawargay

kill *v.t.* وژل wazhal

kill *n.* وژنه wazhana

kiln *n.* بټ batai

kin *n.* خپلوان khpalwan

kind *n.* قسم qisam

kind *a* مهربان mehraban

kindergarten *n.* وکتون waraktoon

kindle *v.t.* اوربلول or balawal

kindly *adv.* په‌مهربانسره pa mehrabanay sara

king *n.* پاچا pacha

kingdom *n.* پاچاهي pachahee

kinship *n.* خپلولي khpalwalee

kiss *n.* مچو macho

kiss *v.t.* مچوکول macho kawal

kit *n.* تغاره taghara

kitchen *n.* پخلناى pakhlanzay

kite *n.* کاغذباد kaghaz bad

kith *n.* اونيان gawandyan

kitten *n.* دپيشوبچی da peesho bachay

knave *n.* بدماش badmash

knavery *n.* بدماشي badmashee

knee *n.* ونه gonda

kneel *v.i.* ونه‌کيدل gonda kedal

knife *n.* چاقو chaqoo

knight *n.* قهرمان qahraman

knight *v.t.* قهرماني کول qahramanee kawal

knit *v.t.* اوبدل obdal

knock *v.t.* ټکول takawal

knot *n.* غوه ghota

knot *v.t.* کول غوه ghota kawal

know *v.t.* پوهدل poheydal

knowledge *n.* پوهه poha

L

label *n.* ټپه tapa

label *v.t.* ټپه‌لول tapa lagawal

laboratory *n.* آزموينتون azmoyantoon

laborious *a.* خواري‌کی khwaree ke

labour *n.* کاو؛مزدوري karaw; mazdooree

labour *v.i.* مزدوري کول mazdooree kawal

labourer *n.* مزدور mazdoor

labyrinth *n.* کلچ kagleych

lac, lakh *n* لاک lak

lace *n.* دبوبند da boot band

lace *v.t.* دبوبندتل da boot band taral

lacerate *v.t.* شکېدل shkeydal

lack *n.* کمت kamakht

lack *v.t.* کمول kamawal

lackey *n.* نوکر nawkar

lacklustre *a.* دروښتيانشتوالی da rokhantya nashtwalay

laconic *a.* پهخبرواتروکله pa khabaro ataro ki land

lactate *v.i.* شدورکول sheydey warkawal

lactose *n.* دشدوقند da sheydo qand

lad *n.* ځوانهلک zwan halak

ladder *n.* پوړ poray

lade *v.t.* چارجورکول charge warkawal

ladle *n.* مه samsa

lady *n.* مرمن meyrman

lag *v.i.* شاتهپاتکدل shata pati keydal

laggard *n.* شاتهپاتشخص shata pati shakhs

lagoon *n.* ډنډ dand

lair *n.* دوحشيناورهله da wahshee zanawar zala

lake *n.* جیل jeel

lama *n.* دتبتاومنولیاهوادونوبوداييملا da tibat aw mangoleeya haywanoono boodayee mula

lamb *n.* ورى wray

lambaste *v.t.* پهمترو کهوهل pa matrooka wahal

lame *a.* ووزنوهلی goozan wahalay

lame *v.t.* ووزنوهل goozan wahal

lament *v.i.* وير کول weer kawal

lament *n* وير weer

lamentable *a.* غمجن ghamjan

lamentation *n.* ماتم matam

lambkin *n.* تندیورى tandi wari

laminate *v.t.* پهمختلفوطبقوباندجلا کول pa mukhtalifo tabqo bandi jala kawal

lamp *n.* څراغ sragh

lampoon *n.* ملنده malande

lampoon *v.t.* ملنکول malande kawal

lance *n.* نزه neyza

lance *v.t.* پهنزهوهل pa neyza wahal

lancer *n.* نزهوهونکی neyza wahoonkay

lancet *n.* نتر neykhtar

land *n.* ځمکه zmaka

land *v.i.* پهځمکهکناستل pa zmaka kkheynastal

landing *n.* وچهتهوتنه wachi ta watana

landscape *n.* لرليد larleed

lane *n.* کوڅه koosa

language *n.* ژبه zhaba

languish *v.i.* ماوىکدل mraway keydal

lank *a.* اوډاونر oogad aw dangar

lantern *n.* ديوه deewa

lap *n.* غ gheyg

lapse *v.i.* دوختتروتل da wakht teyr watal

lapse *n* انحراف inhiraf

lard *n.* دخووازده da khoog wazda
large *a.* پراخ parakh
largesse *n.* الا dalay
lark *n.* دسندربولومارغانویوهله da sandar bolo marghano yawa dala
lascivious *a.* شهواني shahwanee
lash *a.* شلاخه shlakha
lash *n* باه banra
lass *n.* وانهنجل zwana najlay
last1 *a.* وروستی wrostay
last *adv.* پهپایله کی pa payla ki
last *v.i.* ادامهلرل idama laral
last *n* وروستنی wrostanay
lastly *adv.* ترولوآخر tar tolo akheyr
lasting *a.* دوامدار dawamdar
latch *n.* قفلچلهدواوخواوخهپرانستل شي qufal chi la dwaro khwaw sakha pranistal shee
late *a.* ندلی zandeydalay
late *adv.* ترنروروسته tar zand wrosta
lately *adv.* پهوروستیووختونوک pa wrostyo wakhtoono ki
latent *a.* مکنون maknoon
lath *n.* دلرينرپ da largee naray patay
lathe *n.* دخراطمشین da kharatay masheen
lathe *n.* دغلودانوزرمه da ghalo dano zeyrma
lather *n.* دصابون da saboon zag
latitude *n.* عرضالبلد arzul balad
latrine *n.* بیتالخلا baytul khala
latter *a.* آخري akheyree
lattice *n.* شبکه shabaka
laud *v.t.* دستاینسندرهویل da stayani sandara wayal

laud *n* دستاینسندره da stayani sandara
laudable *a.* دستاینو da stayani war
laugh *n.* خندا khanda
laugh *v.i* خندل khandal
laughable *a.* خندونکی khandoonkay
laughter *n.* دخندیدوغ da khandeydo ghag
launch *v.t.* توغول toghawal
launch *n.* توغوونه toghawana
launder *v.t.* وینل weenzal
laundress *n.* کالیوینوونکه kalee weenzoonki khaza
laundry *n.* دوبیخانه dobee khana
laurel *n.* یوهتلشنهونه yawa tal shna wana
laureate *a.* دلارلدونبهپاوپسولللشوی da laril da wani pa panro psolal shaway
laureate *n* ملکالشعرا malakush shoara
lava *n.* داورشینديغرهویلیمواد da or sheendee ghra weelee mawad
lavatory *n.* دمخلاسوینلوخونه da makh las weenzalo khoona
lavish *a.* اسرافي israfee
lavish *v.t.* اسرافکول israf kawal
law *n.* قانون qanoon
lawful *a.* روا rawa
lawless *a.* بقانونه bey qanoona
lawn *n.* چمن chaman
lawyer *n.* قانونپوه qanoonpoh
lax *a.* شل shal
laxative *n.* قبضنرموونکی qabz narmowoonkay
laxative *a* قبضیتضد qabzeeyat zid

laxity *n.* نرمي narmee

lay *v.t.* سملاستل samlastal

layer *n.* لايه laya

layman *n.* بمهارته کس bey maharata kas

laze *v.i.* تمبلي کول tambalee kawal

laziness *n.* ستوماني stomanee

lazy *n.* تمبل tambal

lea *n.* چمنزار chamanzar

leach *v.t.* مينل meenzal

lead *n.* لاروونه lar khowana

lead *v.t.* رهبري کول rehbaree kawal

lead *n.* سيم هادي hadee seem

leaden *a.* سربي sarpee

leader *n.* لارود larkhod

leadership *n.* لاروونه larkhowana

leaf *n.* پله panra

leaflet *n.* پله کوچنی koochnay panra

league *n.* اتحاديه itehadeeya

leak *n.* رخنه rakhna

leak *v.i.* دل saseydal

leakage *n.* رخنه rakhna

lean *n.* تکيه کوونه takeeya kawona

lean *v.i.* تکيه کول takeeya kawal

leap *v.i.* وپ top

leap *n* وپ وهل top wahal

learn *v.i.* زده کول zda kawal

learned *a.* عالم alim

learner *n.* زده کوونکی zda kawoonkay

learning *n.* زده که zdakra

lease *n.* اجاره eejara

lease *v.t.* اجاره کول eejara kawal

least *a.* کوچنی koochnay

leather *n.* رمن sarman

leave *n.* رخصت rukhsat

leave *v.t.* پرودل preykhodal

lecture *n.* درس dars

lecture *v* درس ورکول dars warkawal

lecturer *n.* مدرس mudarris

ledger *n.* د حسابونو ثبت کتاب da heesaboono sabt keetab

lee *n.* لهبادخه خوندي ای la bad sakha khwandee zay

leech *n.* جراثيم jaraseem

leek *n.* پهپياز پوري ارواند يو دول سبزي pa pyaz pori arwand yaw dawl sabzee

left *a.* کې keenr

left *n.* دهرشي کيه خوا da har shee keenra khwa

leftist *n* پهسياست کآزادخوی شخص pa seeyasat ki azad khwakhay shakhs

leg *n.* په pkha

legacy *n.* ميراث meeras

legal *a.* قانوني qanoonee

legality *n.* قانونيت qanooneeyat

legalize *v.t.* قانوني کول qanoonee kawal

legend *n.* افسانه afsana

legendary *a.* افسانوي afsanawee

leghorn *n.* يو دول مارغه yaw dawl margha

legible *a.* خوانا khwana

legion *n.* دپوي لکريه طبقه da pawzee lakhkar yawa tabqa

legionary *n.* طبقة يو د لکر پوي د تشکيل da pawzee lakhkar da yaw tabqey tashkeel

legislate *v.i.* قانون وضع کول qanoon waza kawal

legislation *n.* قانون وضع كوونه qanoon waza kawona

legislative *a.* قانوني qanoonee

legislator *n.* قانون‌ساز qanoonsaz

legislature *n.* مقننه‌پلاوى muqannana plaway

legitimacy *n.* قانونيتوب qanooneetob

legitimate *a.* روا rawa

leisure *n.* آرامت aramakht

leisure *a* فارغ farigh

leisurely *a.* آرامه arama

leisurely *adv.* په‌آرام‌سره pa aram sara

lemon *n.* ليمو leemoo

lemonade *n.* دليموشربت da leemoo sharbat

lend *v.t.* پوروركول por warkawal

length *n.* اودوالى oogadwalay

lengthen *v.t.* اودول oogdawal

lengthy *a.* اود oogad

lenience, leniency *n.* نرمت narmakht

lenient *a.* نرم naram

lens *n.* عدسه adsa

lentil *n.* دمسوردال da masoor dal

Leo *n.* دزمري‌برج da zmaree burj

leopard *n.* پان prang

leper *n.* جذامي jazamee

leprosy *n.* جذام jazam

leprous *a.* جذامي jazamee

less *a.* ل lag

less *n* يوكم‌مقدار yaw kam miqdar

less *adv.* په‌كم‌مقدار pa kam miqdar

less *prep.* ترلگ‌مقدار tar lag miqdar

lessee *n.* اجاره‌كوونكى ijara kaonke

lessen *v.t* كمول kamawal

lesser *a.* كم kam

lesson *n.* لوست lost

lest *conj.* داسنه‌چ dasi na chi

let *v.t.* اجازه‌وركول eejaza warkawal

lethal *a.* وژونكى wazhoonkay

lethargic *a.* ستومانه stomana

lethargy *n.* ستوماني stomanee

letter *n* ليك leek

level *n.* سطح sata

level *a* اوار awar

level *v.t.* اوارول awarawal

lever *n.* ام aram

lever *v.t.* پورته‌كول porta kawal

leverage *n.* دام‌كار da aram kar

levity *n.* سپكوالى spakwalay

levy *v.t.* ماليات‌لول maleeyat lagawal

levy *n.* ماليات maleeyat

lewd *a.* شهوت‌پرست shahwat parast

lexicography *n.* سيندكنه seend kakhana

lexicon *n.* قاموس qamoos

liability *n.* مسؤليت masooleeyat

liable *a.* مسؤل masool

liaison *n.* رابطه rabita

liar *n.* دروغجن daroghjan

libel *n.* تهمت tuhmat

libel *v.t.* تهمت‌لول tuhmat lagawal

liberal *a.* روآندى roonr anday

liberalism *n.* روبان‌فكري rokhan fikray

liberality *n.* آزادپالنه azad palana

liberate *v.t.* آزادول azadawal

liberation *n.* آزادي azadee

liberator *n.* آزادي‌بخوونكى azadee bakhkhoonkay

libertine *n.* عياش ayash

liberty *n.* اختيار ikhtyar

librarian *n.* دكتابتون‌چارواكى da keetabtoon charwakay

library *n.* كتابتون keetabtoon

licence *n.* دكاراجازه‌ليك da kar eejaza leek

license *v.t.* اجازه‌ليك‌وركول eejaza leek warkawal

licensee *n.* اجازه‌ليك‌اخستونكى eejaza leek akheystoonkay

licentious *a.* شهوتى shahwatee

lick *v.t.* په‌ژبل pa zhaba satal

lick *n* نه satana

lid *n.* سرپو sar pokh

lie *v.i.* دروغ‌ويل darogh wayal

lie *v.i* غدل ghazeydal

lie *n* دروغ darogh

lien *n.* دنيونحق da neewani haq

lieu *n.* ای؛عوض zay; iwaz

lieutenant *n.* دويم‌بريدمن dwayam breedman

life *n* ژوند zhwand

lifeless *a.* بى‌ژونده bey zhwanda

lifelong *a.* ول‌عمرى tol umree

lift *n.* پورته‌كوونه porta kawona

lift *v.t.* پورته‌كول porta kawal

light *n.* رڼا ranra

light *a* برنډوى breykhandoy

light *v.t.* رڼول ranrawal

lighten *v.i.* بلدل baleydal

lighter *n.* اورك ortak

lightening *n.* پكدنه parkeydana

lignite *n.* يوول‌دبروسكاره yaw dawl da dabaro skara

like *a.* ورته warta

like *n.* ورته‌والى warta walay

like *v.t.* خوول khwakhawal

like *prep* په‌ورته‌ول pa warta dawl

likelihood *n.* شونتيا shoontya

likely *a.* كدونى keydoonay

liken *v.t.* ورته‌كول warta kawal

likeness *n.* ورته‌توب wartatob

likewise *adv.* همداشان hamda shan

liking *n.* مل meyl

lilac *n.* پيكه‌بنفش‌رنز peeka banafsh rang

lily *n.* دسپين‌سوسن‌ل da speen sosan gul

limb *n.* دبدنغى da badan gharay

limber *v.t.* ورزش‌تمان‌چمتوكول warzash ta zan chamtoo kawal

lime *n.* آهك ahak

lime *v.t* آهك‌كول ahak kawal

lime *n.* ماله malta

limelight *n.* دپام‌ولامل da pam war lamal

limit *n.* حد had

limit *v.t.* محدودول mahdoodawal

limitation *n.* محدوديت mahdoodeeyat

limited *a.* محدود mahdood

limitless *a.* لامحدود la mehdood

line *n.* كره karkha

line *v.t.* په‌ليكه‌درول pa leeka darawal

line *v.t.* ليكه‌پركل leeka pri kakhal

lineage *n.* پت pakht

linen *n.* كتانۍوكر katanee tokar

linger *v.i.* وختنول wakht zandawal

lingo *n.* ژبه زا zangari zhaba

lingua franca *n.* دعامكارونژبه da am karawani zhaba

lingual *a.* ژبنى zhabanay

linguist *n.* ژبپوه zhabpoh

linguistic *a.* ژبپوهنيز zhabpohaneez

linguistics *n.* ژبپوهنه zhabpohan

lining *n* خطكشي khat kashee

link *n.* ک karay

link *v.t* يوكول yaw kawal

linseed *n.* دكتانتخم da katan tukham

lintel *n.* ددروازدسرتير da darwazey da sar teer

lion *n* زمرى zmaray

lioness *n.* زمر zmaray

lip *n.* شونه shoonda

liquefy *v.t.* مايعكول maya kawal

liquid *a.* سيالشى syal shay

liquid *n* مايع maya

liquidate *v.t.* مايعكول maya kawal

liquidation *n.* دحسابونوتصفيه da heesaboono tasfeeya

liquor *n.* مشروب mashroob

lisp *v.t.* دژبپهوكهخبركول da zhabi pa sooka khabari kawal

lisp *n* دژبپهوكهخبركونه da zhabi pa sooka khabari kawona

list *n.* نوملیک noomleek

list *v.t.* نومونهلیکل noomoona leekal

listen *v.i.* اوردل awreydal

listener *n.* اوريدونکى awreydoonkay

listless *a.* بیمیله be mela

literacy *n.* لیکلوست leek lost

literal *a.* لفظي lafzee

literary *a.* ادبي adabee

literate *a.* لوستى lostay

literature *n.* دادبياتوعلم da adabeeyato ilam

litigant *n.* مرافعهكوونكى murafia kawoonkay

litigate *v.t.* مرافعهكول murafia kawal

litigation *n.* مرافعه murafia

litre *n.* دمايعشيدپمائشيوهپمانه da maya shee da paymayish yawa paymana

litter *n.* دناروغانودولودپارهيوولک da naroghano da wralo dapara yaw dol kat

litter *v.t.* پهفاضلهشيانوديوايلل pa fuzla shayano da yaw zai laral

litterateur *n.* اديب adeeb

little *a.* لگ lag

little *adv.* لگ سه lag sa

little *n.* لمقدار lag miqdar

littoral *a.* تانه taranga

liturgical *a.* عبادتي ibadatee

live *v.i.* ژوندكول zhwand kawal

live *a.* ژوندى zhwanday

livelihood *n.* معاش muash

lively *a.* چكاوچابك chatak aw chabak

liver *n.* ينه yana

livery *n.* جامهزا zangari jamey

living *a.* ژوندى zhwanday

living *n* ژوندون zhwandoon

lizard *n.* سمساره samsara

load *n.* بار bar

load *v.t.* بارول barawal

loadstar *n.* قطبی‌ستوری qutbee storay

loadstone *n.* آهن‌ربا ahan ruba

loaf *n.* ټيکله teekala

loaf *v.i.* وخت‌ضائع‌کول wakht zaya kawal

loafer *n.* کوه‌بی‌سی koosa dabay saray

loan *n.* پور por

loan *v.t.* پورکول por kawal

loath *a.* غصه‌ناک ghusanak

loathe *v.t.* غصه‌کدل ghusa keydal

loathsome *a.* زه‌تروونکی zra torowoonkay

lobby *n.* دالان dalan

lobe *n.* پرده parda

lobster *n.* سمندری‌چنا samandaree changakh

local *a.* سیمه‌ییز seemayeez

locale *n.* سیمه seema

locality *n.* محل mahal

localize *v.t.* سیمه‌ییزکول seemayeez kawal

locate *v.t.* ای‌کل zay takal

location *n.* موقعیت moqeeyat

lock *n.* کولپ kolp

lock *v.t* کولپول kolpawal

lock *n* کو kawsay

locker *n.* کولپ‌لرونکالمار kolp laroonki almaray

locket *n.* امل ameyl

locomotive *n.* محرک mahrak

locus *n.* هندسی‌ای hindsee zay

locust *n.* ملخ moolakh

locution *n.* وينا wayna

lodge *n.* کوچنی‌استوگنای koochnay astoganzay

lodge *v.t.* لنمهاله‌استوگنه‌کول land mahala astogna kawal

lodging *n.* مشتای meysht zay

loft *n.* ترچت‌لاندای tar chat landi zay

lofty *a.* مغرورانه maghroorana

log *n.* کونده konda

logarithim *n.* لوگاریتم logareetam

loggerhead *n.* احمق‌سی ahmaq saray

logic *n.* منطق mantaq

logical *a.* منطقي mantaqee

logician *n.* منطق‌پوه mantaq poh

loin *n.* صلب salb

loiter *v.i.* وزاروخت‌ترول wazgar wakht teyrawal

loll *v.i.* غدل ghazeydal

lollipop *n.* خوه‌پتاسه khwaga patasa

lone *a.* تنها tanha

loneliness *n.* تنهايي tanhayee

lonely *a.* يواز yawazi

lonesome *a.* بیاره bey yara

long *a.* اود oogda

long *adv* په‌اودوالي pa oogadwalee

long *v.i* هيله‌لرل heela laral

longevity *n.* اودژوند oogad zhwand

longing *n.* هوس hawas

longitude *n.* طول‌البلد toolul balad

look *v.i* کتل katal

look *a* کتنه katana

loom *n* داوبدماشين da obdani masheen

loom v.i. معلومدل maloomeydal
loop n. وَل wal
loop-hole n. روندان rokhandan
loose a. سست sast
loose v.t. سستول sastawal
loosen v.t. پرانستل pranistal
loot n. چپاول chapawal
loot v.i. چپاوکول chapaw kawal
lop v.t. دسرانغوول da sar sangi ghosawal
lop n. دسمندرنرمپ da samandar narmi sapey
lord n. ارباب arbab
lordship n. اربابتوب arbabtob
lore n. ووناهاوروزنه khowana aw rozana
lorry n. لار laray
lose v.t. لهلاسهورکول la lasa wrakawal
loss n. زیان zyan
lot n. ونه wanda
lot n پچه pacha
lotion n. پاکوونه pakowana
lottery n. پچهاچونه pacha ahowana
loud a. لواوازی lwar awazay
lounge v.i. مبدل zambeydal
lounge n. دراحتخونه da rahat khoona
louse n. سپه spaga
lovable a. محبوب mehboob
love n مینه meena
love v.t. مینهکول meena kawal
lovely a. وران gran
lover n. مین mayan
loving a. مینهناک meenanak
low a. کته kkhata

low v.i. خرابدل kharabeydal
low n. ماوی mraway
lower v.t. کتهکول kkhata kawal
lowliness n. کتهوالی kkhata walay
lowly a. دتواضعلهمخ da tawazo la makhi
loyal a. باوفا bawafa
loyalist n. وفادار wafadar
loyalty n. وفاداري wafadaree
lubricant n. غووونکیمواد ghwarowoonkay mawad
lubricate v.t. غوول ghwarawal
lubrication n. غوونه ghwarowana
lucent a. شفاف shafaf
lucerne n.
lucidity n. روتیا roonrtya
luck n. بخت bakht
luckily adv. خوشبختهسره khoshbakhtee
luckless a. بدقسمته bad qismata
lucky a. نکمرغه neykmargha
lucrative a. ور gatavar
lucre n. مال mal
luggage n. سامان saman
lukewarm a. تمن tarman
lull v.t. خاموشول khamoshawal
lull n. آرامت aramakht
lullaby n. للو للو lalo lalo
luminary n. روانهجسم rukhana jisam
luminous a. روانه rokhana
lump n. لویهلوه loya tota
lump v.t. لویدل loyidal
lunacy n. لونتوب leywantob
lunar a. سپومیز spogmeez
lunatic n. لونیکس leywanay kas

lunatic *a.* لوني leywanay

lunch *n.* دغرمو da gharmey doday

lunch *v.i.* دغرموخول da gharmey doday khwaral

lung *n* سی sagay

lunge *n.* نناپتوغونه nasapee toghawona

lunge *v.i* بریدکول breed kawal

lurch *n.* چل chal

lurch *v.i.* رخدل sarkheydal

lure *n.* غولونه gholowona

lure *v.t.* دوکهکول doka kawal

lurk *v.i.* چاتهپدل cha ta pateydal

luscious *a.* شیرین sheereen

lush *a.* شاداب shadab

lust *n.* شهوت shahwat

lustful *a.* شهواني shahwanee

lustre *n.* روواڼی rond walay

lustrous *a.* ځلاند zaland

lusty *a.* شهوتپاروونکی shahwat parowoonkay

lute *n.* دختوددرزونودنیوڼلپارازنگریخته da khakhto da darzoono da neewani lapara zangari khata

luxuriance *n.* عظمت azmat

luxuriant *a.* عظیم azeem

luxurious *a.* تجمل tajamulee

luxury *n.* تجمل tajamul

lynch *v.t.* بیدمحاکمیلهحکمهدچاوژل be da muhakimy la hukma da cha wajal

lyre *n.* دبربطدربابپخواڼهآله da barbat da rabab pakhwanay ala

lyric *a.* غنايي ghanayee

lyric *n.* غوونه ghagowona

lyrical *a.* احساساتياوغنايي ehsasatee aw ghinayee

lyricist *n.* غزلليکونکی ghazal leekoonkay

M

magical *a.* جادويي jadooyee

magician *n.* رکو kodgar

magisterial *a.* آمرانه amirana

magistracy *n.* دناحیدمحکمریاست da naheeyey da mahkamey reeyasat

magistrate *n.* قاضي qazee

magnanimity *n.* لويي loyee

magnanimous *a.* عظیم azeem

magnate *n.* نجیبزاده najeeb zada

magnet *n.* مقناطیس miqnatees

magnetic *a.* مقناطیسي miqnatees

magnetism *n.* مقناطیسیت miqnateeseeyat

magnificent *a.* عظیم azeem

magnify *v.t.* عظمتوربل azmat warbakhal

magnitude *n.* پراختیا parakhtya

magpie *n.* یوولکورنتورهاوسپینهکوتره yaw dawl koranay toora aw speena kawtara

mahogany *n.* سوربخنقهوهييرنگ soorbakhan qahwayee rang

mahout *n.* فيلوان feelwan

maid *n.* ناودهشوه na wada shawi khaza

maiden *n.* پغله peyghla

maiden *a* رمروغ rogh ramat

mail *n.* پست pust

mail *v.t.* پست لل pust leygal

mail *n* زغره zghara

main *a* اصلي او ضروري aslee aw zarooree

main *n* توان twan

mainly *adv.* په اصل کې pa asal ki

mainstay *n.* اصلي تابعيت aslee tabieeyat

maintain *v.t.* ادامه ور کول idama warkawal

maintenance *n.* ساتنه satana

maize *n.* جوار joowar

majestic *a.* شاهانه shahana

majesty *n.* اعليحضرت aleehazrat

major *a.* ضروري zarooree

major *n* جن jagran

majority *n.* ډيرکی deyrkay

make *v.t.* جوول jorawal

make *n* جو jor

maker *n.* جووونکی jorowoonkay

mal adjustment *n.* ناسمي nasamee

mal administration *n.* ناتنظيمي natanzeemee

malady *n.* خرابتيا kharabtya

malaria *n.* تبه نوبتي nobatee taba

maladroit *a.* خام او ناوه kham aw nawara

malafide *a.* ناوه نيت na wara nyat

malafide *adv* په ناوه توه pa nawara toga

malaise *n.* ناقراري na qararee

malcontent *a.* ناراضه na raza

malcontent *n* ناراض na raz

male *a.* نارينه nareena

male *n* سی saray

malediction *n.* بدوينه bad wayana

malefactor *n.* بدکار bad kar

maleficent *a.* تباه کار tabah kar

malice *n.* کرکه kraka

malicious *a.* کرکجن krakjan

malign *v.t.* بدغوتل bad ghokhtal

malign *a.* پليد paleed

malignancy *n.* پليدي paleedgee

malignant *a.* خبيث khabees

malignity *n.* خباثت khabasat

malleable *a.* سوک خوونکی sotak khwaroonkay

malmsey *n.* قبرسي خواه شراب qabrasee khwaga sharab

malnutrition *n.* کم خوراکي kam khorakee

malpractice *n.* ناوه کار کوونه na wara kar kawona

malt *n.* مالت لرونکي اک جوول malt laroonkay skhak jorawal

mal-treatment *n.* بدچلند bad chaland

mamma *n.* تی tay

mammal *n.* تی لرونکی tay laroonkay

mammon *n.* شتمني shtamanee

mammoth *n.* له تاريخ خه د مخه دوري لوی فيل la tareekh sakha da makha dawri loy feel

mammoth *a* ډير لوی deyr loy

man *n.* انسان insan

man *v.t.* د انسان په وسيله په کاروول da insan pa waseela pa karowal

manage *v.t.* انتظام کول intizam kawal

manageable *a.* د چلونقابل da chalowani qabil

management *n.* مديريت mudeereeyat

manager *n.* مدير mudeer

managerial *a.* مديري mudeeree

mandate *n.* امريه amreeya

mandatory *a.* امر amree

mane *n.* دسيوتان da saree weykhtan

manes *n.* دمواروماز da maro arwagani

manful *a.* دمازخاوند da meyrani khawand

manganese *n.* يوعنصر yaw unsar

manger *n.* آخور akhor

mangle *v.t.* اوتوكول oto kawal

mango *n* ام am

manhandle *v.t.* پهزورسرهادارهكول pa zor sara idara kawal

manhole *n.* دنكاسياوبوسورى da nikasee obo sooray

manhood *n.* نارينتوب nareentob

mania *n* لونتوب leywantob

maniac *n.* لونى leywanay

manicure *n.* لاسونهاونوكانسينارول lasoona aw nookan seengarawal

manifest *a.* رند sargand

manifest *v.t.* حاضرول hazirawal

manifestation *n.* نمايش numayish

manifesto *n.* اعلاميه aylameeya

manifold *a.* چنده و so chanda

manipulate *v.t.* پهلاسسرهسمول pa las sara samawal

manipulation *n.* مهارت maharat

mankind *n.* انسانينژاد insanee nizhad

manlike *a.* انساني insanee

manliness *n* نارينتوب nareentob

manly *a.* پهنارينتوبسره pa nareentob sara

manna *n.* منواوسلوا man aw salwa

mannequin *n.* دنندارفنكارهنجل da nandarey fankara najlay

manner *n.* طريقه tareeqa

mannerism *n.* ادب adab

mannerly *a.* پهادبسره pa adab sara

manoeuvre *n.* پهتدبيرسرهكاراخستنه pa tadbeer sara kar akheystana

manoeuvre *v.i.* پهتدبيرسرهكار اخستل pa tadbeer sara kar akheystal

manor *n.* لوىجاير loy jageer

manorial *a.* جايردارانه jageerdarana

mansion *n.* قصر qasar

mantel *n.* سادر sadar

mantle *n* چوغه chogha

mantle *v.t* چوغهاغوستل chogha aghostal

manual *a.* لاسي lasee

manual *n* لاسكنه las kakhana

manufacture *v.t.* توليدول tawleedawal

manufacture *n* توليدوونه tawleedawana

manufacturer *n* توليدوونكى tawleedawoonkay

manumission *n.* آزادي azadee

manumit *v.t.* غلامآزادول gholam azadawal

manure *n.* پارو paro

manure *v.t.* كودوركول kod warkawal

manuscript *n.* خطي khatee

many *a.* متعدد mutaadad

map *n* نخچه nakhcha

map *v.t.* نخچهجوول nakhcha jorawal

mar *v.t.* مانعكول manay kawal

marathon *n.* يوغاستيسيالي yaw zghastee syalee

maraud *v.i.* لوبل lootal

marauder *n.* لومار lootmar

marble *n.* دمرمركانى da marmar kanray

march *n* لاريون laryoon

march *n.* منظمحركت munazzam harakat

march *v.i* پهموزونقدمتلل pa mawzoon qadam tlal

mare *n.* دخرهينه da khra khazeena

margarine *n.* نباتيكوچ nabatee koch

margin *n.* حاشیه hasheeya

marginal *a.* حاشیوي hasheeyawee

marigold *n.* همشهبهارل hamaysha bahar gul

marine *a.* سمندري samandaree

mariner *n.* مالو manroo

marionette *n.* يووله‌هيل yaw dawl heelay

marital *a.* ازدواجي azdawajee

maritime *a.* سمندري samandaree

mark *n.* نان nakhan

mark *v.t* ناناول nakhan lagawal

marker *n.* نه‌ايودونكى nakha eekhoodoonkay

market *n* بازار bazar

market *v.t* سوداريكول sawdagaree kawal

marketable *a.* دسودارو da sawdagaray war

marksman *n.* نه‌ويشتونكى nakha weeshtoonkay

marl *n.* طنابااوپى‌غل tanab aw paray gharal

marmalade *n.* دنارنجمربا da naranj murabba

maroon *n.* تورپوستى‌غلام tor postay ghulam

maroon *a* سوربخنخرمايي‌رنگ soorbakhan khurmayee rang

maroon *v.t* بايه‌ردل bey zaya garzeydal

marriage *n.* واده wada

marriageable *a.* دوادهو da wada war

marry *v.t.* وادهكول wada kawal

Mars *n* دمريخسياره da mareekh seeyara

marsh *n.* لجنزار lajanzar

marshal *n* سرلكر sar lakhkar

marshal *v.t* تنظيمول tanzeemawal

marshy *a.* لجنزاره lajanzara

marsupial *n.* كوه‌لرونكى kasora laroonkay

mart *n.* سودا sawda

marten *n.* موشخرما mosh khurma

martial *a.* جني jangee

martinet *n.* سختير sakhtgeer

martyr *n.* شهید shaheed

martyrdom *n.* شهادت shahadat

marvel *n.* حرانوونكى heyranawoonkay

marvel *v.i* حراندل heyraneydal

marvellous *a.* حرانوونکی hayranawoonkay

mascot *n.* ښه شگون kha shagoon

masculine *a.* نرینه nareena

mash *n.* اوبلن خوراک oblan khorak

mash *v.t* مدول maydawal

mask *n.* نقاب naqab

mask *v.t.* نقاب اچول naqab achowal

mason *n.* خر khatgar

masonry *n.* خري khatgaree

masquerade *n.* یو ول وین کالی yaw dawl wareen kalee

mass *n.* ولی tolay

mass *v.i* ونه اخستل wanda akheystal

massacre *n.* تل وژنه tol wazhana

massacre *v.t.* قتلول qatlawal

massage *n.* موښنه mokhana

massage *v.t.* موښل mokhal

masseur *n.* موښوونکی mokhowoonkay

massive *a.* لوی او عظیم loy aw azeem

massy *a.* لوی بدنی loy badanay

mast *n.* د بیړی خاده da beyray khada

master *n.* استاد ustad

master *v.t.* استادي کول ustadee kawal

masterly *a.* استادانه ustadana

masterpiece *n.* شاهکار shahkar

mastery *n.* مهارت maharat

masticate *v.t.* نرمول narmawal

masturbate *v.i.* موی وهل mootay wahal

mat *n.* پوز poozay

matador *n.* غویی سره لوبه کوونکی ghwayee sara loba kawoonkay

match *n.* اورلیت orlageet

match *v.i.* اورلیت بلول orlageet balowal

match *n* مسابقه musabiqa

matchless *a.* بی ساری bey saray

mate *n.* ملری malgaray

mate *v.t.* وول gadwadawal

mate *n* جوه jora

mate *v.t.* جوه کول jora kawal

material *a.* مادي madee

material *n* ماده mada

materialism *n.* ماده پرستي mada parastee

materialize *v.t.* مجسم کول mujassam kawal

maternal *a.* مورنی moranay

maternity *n.* زنتون zeygantoon

mathematical *a.* د ریاضي په اوند da reeyazii pa arwand

mathematician *n.* reeyazee poh

mathematics *n* ریاضي reeyazee

matinee *n.* مازدیر ملمستیا mazdeegaray meylmastya

matriarch *n.* د تبر مشره da tabar mashra

matricidal *a.* مور وژونکی mor wazhoonkay

matricide *n.* مور وژنه mor wazhana

matriculate *v.t.* وونی تر سره کول khowanzay tar sara kawal

matriculation *n.* د وونی پوری زدکه da khowanzee pori zdakri

matrimonial *a.* ازدواجي azdawajee

matrimony *n.* واده wada

127

matrix *n.* تخمدان tukhamdan

matron *n.* دكوره ka kor khaza

matter *n.* ماده mada

matter *v.i.* اهميت لرل ahmeeyat laral

mattock *n.* دوه سرى كلذ dwa saray kalang

mattress *n.* توشكه toshaka

mature *a.* پوخ شوى pokh shaway

mature *v.i* پخدل pakheydal

maturity *n.* بلوغ bulogh

maudlin *a* ينهانى نوم khazeena zangaray noom

maul *n.* لرين سك largeen satak

maul *v.t* په سك وهل pa satak wahal

maulstick *n.* دلاس تكيه da las takya

maunder *v.t.* كول ډايى gadayee kawal

mausoleum *n.* مقبره maqbara

mawkish *a.* ستومانه كوونكى stomana kawoonkay

maxilla *n.* پورتنزامه portanay zama

maxim *n.* نصيحت naseehat

maximize *v.t.* اخرى حد پورى رسول akhiree had pori rasawal

maximum *a.* اخرى حد akhiree had

maximum *n* زيات نه زيات zyat na zyat

May *n.* دانرزي كال درېمه مياشت da angreyzee kal dreyma myasht

may *v* تواندل twaneydal

mayor *n.* دار ناظم da khar nazim

maze *n.* تاوراتاو زينه taw rataw zeena

me *pron.* ماله ma la

mead *n.* دمالت او خمرى ياك da malt aw khumree skhak

meadow *n.* لوى چمنزار loy chamanzar

meal *n.* خوراك khorak

mealy *a.* اوه وله ora dawla

mean *a.* معمولى mamoli

mean *n.* مننى كى manzani takay

mean *v.t* مانا اخستل mana akheystal

meander *v.i.* چكروهل chakar wahal

meaning *n.* مانا mana

meaningful *a.* پُرمانا pur mana

meaningless *a.* بمانا bey maney

meanness *n.* كمينه توب kameenatob

means *n* وسايل wasayil

meanwhile *adv.* په دې دوران pa dey dawran

measles *n* شرى sharay

measurable *a.* د سنجونو da sanjawani war

measure *n.* پمائش paymayish

measure *v.t* پمائش كول paymayish kawal

measureless *a.* بى پمانا bey paymani

measurement *n.* پمائش paymayish

meat *n.* غوه ghwakha

mechanic *n.* ماشين پوه masheen poh

mechanic *a* ميخانيكى meykhanikee

mechanical *a.* ميخانيكى meykhanikee

mechanics *n.* دماشينو علم da masheeno ilam

mechanism *n.* طريقه كار tareeqa kar

medal *n.* مال midal

medallist *n.* دمال‌خاوند da midal khawand

meddle *v.i.* مداخله‌کوونکی mudakhila kawoonkay

medieval *a.* دمننیوپیوتاریخپوراوند da manzanyo peyryo tareekh pori arwand

medieval *a.* دمننیوپیوتاریخپوراوند da manzanyo peyryo tareekh pori arwand

median *a.* وسطي wastee

mediate *v.i.* جوه‌کول jora kawal

mediation *n.* جوه jora

mediator *n.* منی manzgaray

medical *a.* طبي tibee

medicament *n.* درملنه darmalana

medicinal *a.* ددرمل‌په‌اوند da darmal pa arwand

medicine *n.* درمل darmal

medico *n.* طبیب tabeeb

mediocre *a.* معتدل motadil

mediocrity *n.* اعتدال aytidal

meditate *v.t.* ذکرکول zikar kawal

mediation *n.* ذکر zikar

meditative *a.* تفکري tafakurree

medium *n* ذریعه zareeya

medium *a* دمنندرجه da manzanay darajey

meek *a.* حلیم haleem

meet *n.* ملاقات mulaqat

meet *v.t.* ملاوول milawawal

meeting *n.* لیدنه‌کتنه leedana katana

megalith *n.* یادگاري‌بره yadgaree dabara

megaphone *n.* غږساند ghag rasand

melancholia *n.* وسواس waswas

melancholic *a.* وسواسي waswasee

melancholy *n.* وسواس waswas

melancholy *adj* وسواسي waswasee

melee *n.* تن‌په‌تن‌جه tan pa tan jagara

meliorate *v.t.* تروۀکول taraqee kawal

mellow *a.* نرم naram

melodious *a.* پرآهن pur ahang

melodrama *n.* بریالمینه baryalay meena

melodramatic *a.* عاشقانه ashiqana

melody *n.* خوه‌سندره khwaga sandara

melon *n.* هندوانه hindwana

melt *v.i.* ویلکدل weeli keydal

member *n.* غی gharay

membership *n.* غیتوب ghareetob

membrane *n.* غشا ghasha

memento *n.* دموۀعا da maro dua

memoir *n.* یادښت yadakht

memorable *a.* یادگاري yadgaree

memorandum *n* یادښت yadakht

memorial *n.* یادگار yadgar

memorial *a* یادگاري‌برلیک yadgaree dabar leek

memory *n.* حافظه hafiza

menace *n* تهدید tahdeed

menace *v.t* تهدیدول tanhdeedawal

mend *v.t.* رغول raghawal

menial *a.* پست past

menial *n* نوکر nawkar

meningitis *n.* دمغزوالتهاب da maghzo iltihab

menopause *n.* دحض‌بندیدا da hayz bandeyda

menses *n.* حض hayz

menstrual *a.* دحض‌په‌اوند da hayz pa arwand

menstruation *n.* دحض‌جریان da hayz jaryan

mental *a.* ذهني zehnee

mentality *n.* فكري‌توان fikree twan

mention *n.* یادوونه yadowana

mention *v.t.* ذكركول zikar kawal

mentor *n.* قابل‌سلاكار qabil salakar

menu *n.* دخواونیولیک da khwaro naywleek

mercantile *a.* تجارتي tijaratee

mercenary *a.* دبهرهوادمزدور da bahar haywad mazdoor

merchandise *n.* سوداري‌سامان sawdagaree saman

merchant *n.* سودار sawdagar

merciful *a.* لوراند lorand

merciless *adj.* برحمه bey rehma

mercurial *a.* سیمابي seemabee

mercury *n.* سیماب seemab

mercy *n.* زه‌سوى؛رحم zra saway; rehem

mere *a.* ایله؛بس‌هم‌دومره eela; bas ham domra

merge *v.t.* شاملول shamilawal

merger *n.* شاملوونکی shamilawoonkay

meridian *a.* دنصف‌النهار‌کره؛غرمه da nisfun nihar karkha; gharma

merit *n.* لیاقت leeyaqat

merit *v.t* لیاقت‌لرل leeyaqat laral

mermaid *n.* سمندري‌حوره samandaree hoora

merman *n.* سمندري‌نارینه‌مخلوق samandaree nareena makhlooq

merriment *n.* خوشالي khoshalee

merry *a* خوشاله khoshala

mesh *n.* جال،لومه jal; looma

mesh *v.t* په‌لومه‌سره‌نیول pa loomi sara neewal

mesmerism *n.* مصنوعي‌خوبونه masnooee khobawana

mesmerize *v.t.* په‌مقناطیسي‌خوب‌ویدول pa miqnateesee khob weedawal

mess *n.* ناولشی nawalay shay

mess *v.i* ککول kakarawal

message *n.* پغام paygham

messenger *n.* پغام‌وونکی paygham wroonkay

messiah *n.* مسیح‌علیه‌السلام masee alayhis salam

Messrs *n.* اغلي khaghalay

metabolism *n.* حیاتي‌اوتون hayatee awakhtoon

metal *n.* فلز filiz

metallic *a.* فلزي filizee

metallurgy *n.* دفلزاتو‌داستناو‌ویلاکوزي‌پوهه da filizato da eystani aw weeli kawoni poha

metamorphosis *n.* دشکل‌او‌بدلوونه da shakal aw banri badlawona

metaphor *n.* استعاره istiara

metaphysical *a.* ماورایي‌طبیعت‌پور‌اوند mawarayee tabeeyat pori arwand

metaphysics *n.* دماورایي‌طبیعت‌علم da mawarayee tabeeyat ilam

mete *v.t* اندازه‌کول andaza kawal

meteor *n.* لکوال‌ستوری lakay wal storay

meteoric *a.* دستورو‌په‌اوند da storo pa arwand

meteorologist *n.* هواپژاند hawa peyzhand

meteorology *n.* هواپژندنه hawa peyzhandana

meter *n.* مقياس miqyas

method *n.* طريقه tareeqa

methodical *a.* طريقهلرونکی tareeqa laroonkay

metre *n.* دوايوپيمائش da wat yaw paymayish

metric *a.* دشعردبحراووزنعلم da shayr da bahar aw wazan ilam

metrical *a.* دوزناوکچپهاوند da wazan aw kach pa arwand

metropolis *n.* پلازمينه plazmayna

metropolitan *a.* لویهارپوراوند loy khar pori arwand

metropolitan *n.* اصلیهاوبی aslee tatobay

mettle *n.* فطرت fitrat

mettlesome *a.* سرکخ sar kakh

mew *v.i.* دپيشوغکول da peesho ghag kawal

mew *n.* دپيشوغ da peesho ghag

mezzanine *n.* دلومنياودويمپورترمننيمپو da loomranee aw dwayam por tar manz neem por

mica *n.* کانيهه kanee kheekha

microfilm *n.* دعکسونولپارهيوکوچنیفيلم da aksoono lapara yaw koochnay filam

micrology *n.* دکوچنيوشيانوعلم da koochnyo shayano ilam

micrometer *n.* دکوچنيوشيانوداندازآله da koochnyo shayano da andazey ala

microphone *n.* دغلوولوآله da ghag lwarawalo ala

microscope *n.* دکوچنيوشيانودوربين da koochnyo shayano doorbeen

microscopic *a.* دوربينی doorbeenee

microwave *n.* کوچنمقناطيسيپه koochnay miqnateesee sapa

mid *a.* منز manz

midday *n.* نيمايیور neemayee wraz

middle *a.* منز manz

middle *n* مرکز markaz

middleman *n.* دلال dalal

middling *a.* وسط wast

midget *n.* لويشتکیسی lweyshtakay saray

midland *n.* دهواددننبرخه da haywad dananay barkha

midnight *n.* نيمهشپه neema shpa

mid-off *n.* دمرکزیلاسته da markaz khee las ta

mid-on *n.* دمرکزکيلاسته da markaz keenr las ta

midriff *n.* بلوونی beylowanay

midst *n.* مرکزيبرخه markazee barkha

midwife *n.* دايی dayee

might *n.* توان twan

mighty *adj.* زورور zorawar

migraine *n.* سرخوی sar khoogay

migrant *n.* کوال kadwal

migrate *v.i.* کهکول kada kawal

migration *n.* کوالی kadwalee

milch *a.* شدورکوونکی sheydey warkowoonkay

mild *a.* نرم naram

mildew *n.* چاس chanrasay

mile *n.* داودوالي‌يوپمائش da oogadwalee yaw paymayish

mileage *n.* دميل‌له‌مخسنجوونه da meel la makhi sanjawana

milestone *n.* دژوندمهمه‌دوره da zhwand muhima dawra

milieu *n.* محيط muheet

militant *a.* جهمار jagra mar

militant *n* جهماری jagra maree

military *a.* پو pawz

military *n* پوي pawzee

militate *v.i.* جندل jangeydal

militia *n.* نظامي‌واک nizamee zwak

milk *n.* شد sheydey

milk *v.t.* شدورکول sheydey warkawal

milky *a.* له‌شدوک la sheydo dak

mill *n.* ژرنده zhranda

mill *v.t.* ژرنده‌کول zhranda kawal

millennium *n.* زرکاله zar kala

miller *n.* ژرندی zhrandagaray

millet *n.* دن،باجره gdan; bajra

milliner *n.* ينه‌خواجوونکي khazeena khwali jorawoonkay

millinery *n.* ينه‌خواپلورونه khazeena khwali plorawana

million *n.* لس‌لکه las laka

millionaire *n.* مالداره،شتمن maldara; shtaman

millipede *n.* نه zanza

mime *n.* خندوونکننداره khandowoonkay

mime *v.i* وککول toki kawal

mimesis *n.* پکوونه peykhi kawona

mimic *a.* تقليدي taqleedee

mimic *n* وکمار tokmar

mimic *v.t* پکول peykhi kawal

mimicry *n* وکماري tokmaree

minaret *n.* مناره munara

mince *v.t.* مده‌مده‌کول meyda meyda kawal

mind *n.* ذهن،خيال zehen; khyal

mind *v.t.* پام‌کول،فکرکول pam kawal; fikar kawal

mindful *a.* فکرمند fikarmand

mindless *a.* بپروا bey parwa

mine *pron.* زما zama

mine *n* کان،معدن kan; madan

miner *n.* کان‌کيندونکی kan keendoonkay

mineral *n.* کاني‌بر kanee dabar

mineral *a* کاني،معدني kanee; madanee

mineralogist *n.* کان‌پژندونکی kan peyzhandoonkay

mineralogy *n.* کان‌پژندنه kan peyzhandana

mingle *v.t.* ترکيبول tarkeebawal

miniature *n.* کوچني‌برليک koochnay dabarleek

miniature *a.* ميناتوري meena toree

minim *n.* ترولوکوچنی tar tolo koochnay

minimal *a.* ترولول tar tolo lag

minimize *v.t.* ترولوکم‌کچ‌ته‌رسول tar tolo kam kach ta rasawal

minimum *n.* ترولوکم‌مقدار tar tolo kam miqdar

minimum *a* کم‌نه‌کم‌حد kam na kam had

minion *n.* غوه‌مال ghwara mal

minister *n.* وزير wazeer

minister *v.i.* سمبالول sambalawal

ministrant *a.* خادم khadim

ministry *n.* وزارت wazarat

mink *n.* يوولغموشخرما yaw dawl ghat mosh khurma

minor *a.* کم،ل kam; lag

minor *n* کوچنی koochnay

minority *n.* لکی lagkay

minster *n.* دراهبانونمزدک da rahibanu namazdak

mint *n.* ضرابخانه zarabkhana

mint *n* پودينه podeena

mint *v.t.* سکهجوول sika jorawal

minus *prep.* ترصفرکم tar sifar kam

minus *a* منفي manfee

minus *n* نشتون،دمنفيعلامه nashtoon; da manfee alama

minuscule *a.* کوچنی،ووکی koochnay; warookay

minute *a.* رکوچنی deyr koochnay

minute *n.* شيبه sheyba

minutely *adv.* پهدقيقهتوه pa daqeeqa toga

minx *n.* ستاخسیيابه gustakh saray ya khaza

miracle *n.* معجزه mojiza

miraculous *a.* معجزاتي mojizatee

mirage *n.* سراب sarab

mire *n.* چيک cheekar

mire *v.t.* پهچيکرونونستل pa cheekaro nanawistal

mirror *n* ه کهخ kheekha

mirror *v.t.* منعکسول munakisawal

mirth *n.* عيش aysh

mirthful *a.* پُرعيش puraysh

misadventure *n.* ناوهپه nawara peykha

misalliance *n.* ناوهيووالی nawara yawwalay

misanthrope *n.* لهانسانانواوبشريوله خهبزارانسان la insanano aw basharee tolani sakha beyzara insan

misapplication *n.* ناوهاستعمال nawara istimal

misapprehend *v.t.* ناسمدرککول nasam darak kawal

misapprehension *n* تروتنه teyr watana

misappropriate *v.t.* بخول badi khwaral

misappropriation *n.* بدي،رشوت badi; rishwat

misbehave *v.i.* ناسمچلندکول nasam chaland kawal

misbehaviour *n.* ناوهچلند nawara chaland

misbelief *n.* ناوهباور nawara bawar

miscalculate *v.t.* ناسمشمرل nasam shmeyral

miscalculation *n.* ناسمهشمره nasama shmeyra

miscall *v.t.* پهغلطهغکول pa ghalata ghag kawal

miscarriage *n.* ناوهچلند nawara chaland

miscarry *v.i.* دماشومدزوناميدشنول da mashoom da zeygoon omeed shandawal

miscellaneous *a.* متنوع mutanaway

miscellany *n.* درنارنشيانوله da rangarang shayano gadola

mischance *n.* بدبختي bad bakhtee

mischief *n* ضرر zarar

mischievous *a.* شریر shareer

misconceive *v.t.* ناسمپوهدل nasam poheydal

misconception *n.* غلطوهان ghalat goomat

misconduct *n.* بداخلاقيكول bad akhlaqee kawal

misconstrue *v.t.* ناسمتعبيرول nasam tabeerawal

miscreant *n.* بوجدانه bey wajdana

misdeed *n.* بدچلند bad chaland

misdemeanour *n.* ناہ goona

misdirect *v.t.* غلطهلاروونهكول ghalata larkhowana kawal

misdirection *n.* ناسمهلاروونه nasama larkhowana

miser *n.* كنجوس kanjoos

miserable *a.* بختهبد bad bakhta

miserly *a.* خسيس؛كنجوس khasees; kanjoos

misery *n.* بدبختي badbakhtee

misfire *v.i.* سمكارنهكول sam kar na kawal

misfit *n.* ناسمشى nasam shay

misfortune *n.* بدمرغي bad marghee

misgive *v.t.* غلطخبرورکول ghalat khabar warkawal

misgiving *n.* بدلوماني bad goomanee

misguide *v.t.* بلاركول bey lari kawal

mishap *n.* بدهپه bada peykha

misjudge *v.t.* غلطقضاوتكول ghalat qazawat kawal

mislead *v.t.* ہمراهكول gomra kawal

mismanagement *n.* ناواهچلوونه nawara chalowana

mismatch *v.t.* سرهنهجوړل sara na joreydal

misnomer *n.* غلطنوم ghalat noom

misplace *v.t.* پهناسمهایککارول pa nasam zay ki karawal

misprint *n.* غلطچاپ ghalat chap

misprint *v.t.* غلطچاپول ghalat chapawal

misrepresent *v.t.* ناسمودل nasam khodal

misrule *n.* بېنظمي bey nazmee

miss *n.* پېغله peyghla

miss *v.t.* لهلاسهورکول la lasa warkawal

missile *n.* توغوندى toghanday

mission *n.* استوونه؛داستازوپنغالى astawana; da astazo pandghalay

missionary *n.* تبليغاتيپلاوى tableeghatee plaway

missis, missus *n..* ترخپلاغزلاند tar khpal agheyz landi seemo ta da pacha garzand astazay سيموتهدپاچارندداستازى

missive *n.* پغاملرونکليکنه paygham laroonki leekana

mist *n.* ګرد gard

mistake *n.* تروتنه teyr watara

mistake *v.t.* تروتل teyr watal

mister *n.* اغلى khaghalay

mistletoe *n.* يوولبوى yaw dawl bootay

mistreat *v.t.* بدسلوککول bad salook kawal

mistress *n.* مرمن meyrman

mistrust *n.* بباوري bey bawaree

mistrust *v.t.* پربارورنه کول pri bawar na kawal

misty *a.* لمر ده ک la garda dak

misunderstand *v.t.* ناسم پوهدل nasam poheydal

misunderstanding *n.* غلط تعبیر ghalat tabeer

misuse *n.* کارونه ناسم nasam karowana

misuse *v.t.* ناسم کارول nasam karawal

mite *n.* د کوچنی چینجی deyr koochnay cheenjay

mite *n* ذره zara

mithridate *n.* زهرضد zahar zad

mitigate *v.t.* تخفیفول takhfeefawal

mitigation *n.* کمت kamakht

mitre *n.*

mitten *n.* یوول دستکش yaw dawl dastkash

mix *v.i* وول gadwadawal

mixture *n.* مرکب؛وله murakab; gadola

moan *v.i.* زیروی کول zgeyrwee kawal

moan *n.* زیروی؛فریاد zgeyrway; faryad

moat *n.* کنده kanda

moat *v.t.* کنده کیندل kanda keendal

mob *n.* وه ه ganra goonra

mob *v.t.* هوه کول ganra goonra kawal

mobile *a.* رند؛متحرک garzand; mutaharik

mobility *n.* ردنه garzeydana

mobilize *v.t.* په جریان راوستل pa jaryan rawastal

mock *v.i.* ملنپرکول malandi pri kawal

mock *adj* ملن؛پغور malandi; peyghor

mockery *n.* پخ کول peykhey kawal

modality *n.* کفیت kayfeeyat

mode *n.* طرز؛دود tarz; dood

mode *n.* ول؛بان سمبالونه dol; zan sambalawana

model *v.t.* تنظیم کول tanzeem kawal

moderate *a.* معتدل motadil

moderate *v.t.* معتدل کول motadil kawal

moderation *n.* اعتدال aytidal

modern *a.* تازه؛نوی taza; naway

modernity *n.* تجدد؛تازه توب tajaddud; tazatob

modernize *v.t.* نوبه ورکول nawi banra warkawal

modest *a.* حیاناک hayanak

modesty *n* حیا haya

modicum *n.* ذره zara

modification *n.* اصلاح isla

modify *v.t.* اصلاح کول isla kawal

modulate *v.t.* تعدیلول tadeelawal

moil *v.i.* ستومانه کدل stomana keydal

moist *a.* نمجن namjan

moisten *v.t.* نم پداکول nam payda kawal

moisture *n.* نم nam

molar *a* مدوونکی meydawoonkay

molasses *n* شات؛شیره shat; sheera

mole *n.* خال khal

molecular *a.* ذروی zarawee

molecule *n.* ذره zara

molest *v.t.* ظلم کول zulam kawal

molestation *n.* ظلم زیاتی zulam zyatay

molten *a.* ویلی شوی weeli shaway

moment *n.* شېبه sheyba

momentary *a.* ژر ترډونکی zhar teyreydoonkay

momentous *a.* دآني حرکت په قوی پوری اوند da anee harakat pa qawey pori arwand

momentum *n.* دآني حرکت قوه da anee harakat qawa

monarch *n.* ولواک tolwak

monarchy *n.* ولواکي tolwakee

monastery *n.* خانقا khanqa

monasticism *n* رهبانیت rehbaneeyat

Monday *n.* دوشنبه doshamba

monetary *a.* پولي polee

money *n.* پسے peysey

monger *n.* دلال dalal

mongoose *n.* موش خرما mosh khurma

mongrel *a* دوه رهحوان dwa raga haywan

monitor *n.* وونکی khowoonkay

monitory *a.* ارنه کوونکی sarana kawoonkay

monk *n.* راهب rahib

monkey *n.* بیزو beezo

monochromatic *a.* ابوالی ککیچنوالی abwalay karkeychanwalay

monocle *n.* یو سترېزه عینک yaw stargeeza aynak

monocular *a.* یو سترېز yaw stargeez

monody *n.* مرثیه marseeya

monogamy *n.* دیو لرنه da yawey khazi larana

monogram *n.* طغرا taghara

monograph *n.* هنري لاسلیک honaree lasleek

monogynous *a.* یو مه لرونکی yawa khaza laroonkay

monolatry *n.* دیو خدای عبادت da yaw khuday ibadat

monolith *n.* یو موه yawa tota

monologue *n.* یو کسیزونا yaw kaseez wayna

monopolist *n.* دامتیاز خاوند da eemteeyaz khawand

monopolize *v.t.* انحصاري امتیاز اخستل inhisaree eemteeyaz akheystal

monopoly *n.* اجاره داري eejara daree

monosyllable *n.* یو هجا yaw hija

monosyllabic *a.* یو هجايي کلمه yaw hijayee kalma

monotheism *n.* توحید tawheed

monotheist *n.* مؤمن momin

monotonous *a.* یو آوازی yaw awazay

monotony *n* یو آواز لرنه yaw awaz larana

monsoon *n.* نوبتي بادوباران nobatee bad wa baran

monster *n.* بلا bala

monstrous *a.* بلايي balayee

month *n.* میاشت myasht

monthly *a.* میاشتنی myashtanay

monthly *adv* هره میاشت hara myasht

monthly *n* میاشتنۍ مجله myashtanay mujala

monument *n.* تاریخی‌یادار tareekhee yadgar

monumental *a.* یادار‌ي yadgaree

mouse *v.i* غرﻪ یوول‌امریکایي yaw dawl amreekayee gharsanay

mood *n.* مزاج mizaj

moody *a.* پرشانه parayshana

moon *n.* سپوږﻣ spogmay

moor *n.* ۱ dag

moor *v.t* پزوانول peyzwanawal

moot *n.* مناظرﻩ munazira

mop *n.* صفاکوونکی‌وکر safa kawoonkay tokar

mop *v.t.* صفاکول safa kawal

mope *v.i.* پرشانه‌کدل parayshana keydal

moral *a.* اخلاقي akhlaqee

moral *n.* پند pand

morale *n.* اخلاقیات akhlaqeeyat

moralist *n.* اخلاق‌وونکی akhlaq khowoonkay

morality *n.* اخلاقي‌چلند akhlaqee chaland

moralize *v.t.* اخلاقي‌فکرورکول akhlaqee fikar warkawal

morbid *a.* خوسا khosa

morbidity *n* ناروغوالی na roghwalay

more *a.* نور nor

more *adv* په‌زیادتر‌مقدارسره pa zyadtar miqdar sara

moreover *adv.* برسره‌پردی barseyra par dey

morganatic *a.* له‌ناسیال‌سره‌واده‌کوونکی la nasyal sara wada kawoonkay

morgue *n.* میستون mreestoon

moribund *a.* مري‌حال margee hal

morning *n.* ﻬﻪ gaheez

moron *n.* ساده sada

morose *a.* بدخویه bad khooya

morrow *n.* بلهور bala wraz

morsel *n.* ﻪ maray

mortal *a.* فاني fanee

mortal *n* فاني‌بشر fanee bashar

mortality *n.* میﻨﻪ mreena

mortar *v.t.* لنرﻩ،هاون langaree; hawan

mortgage *n.* رهن rehen

mortgage *v.t.* رهن‌کول rehen kawal

mortagagee *n.* مرتهن murtahin

mortify *v.t.* تباه‌کول taba kawal

mortuary *n.* مرده‌خانه murda khana

mosaic *n.* دموزائیک‌انور da mozayeek anzor

mosque *n.* جومات joomat

mosquito *n.* میاشی myashay

moss *n.* سنﺪل gul sang

most *a.* زیات‌تر zyat tar

most *adv.* زیاتره zyattara

most *n* ترولولوی‌مقدار tar tolo loy miqdar

mote *n.* خاشه khasha

motel *n.* دسرک‌دغامل‌مستون da sarak da ghari meylmastoon

moth *n.* حشرﻩ hashra

mother *n* مور mor

mother *v.t.* پالل؛روزل palal; rozal

motherhood *n.* موروالی morwalay

motherlike *a.* دمورپه‌شان da mor pa shan

motherly *a.* مورﻧ moranay

motif *n.* اصليبه aslee banra
motion *n.* حركت harakat
motion *v.i.* حركت كول harakat kawal
motionless *a.* بحركته bey harakata
motivate *v* پاروول parawal
motivation *n.* پاروونه parowana
motive *n.* محرك muhrak
motley *a.* رنارز rangarang
motor *n.* خوندهوسيله khozanda waseela
motor *v.i.* حركت وركول harakat warkawal
motorist *n.* موټرچلوونكى motar chalowoonkay
mottle *n.* خال خال khal khal
motto *n.* شعار shaar
mould *n.* قالب qalib
mould *v.t.* قالبول qalibawal
mould *n* تركيب tarkeeb
mould *n* نمونه namoona
moult *v.i.* پوستكى اچول postakay achawal
mound *n.* خاكرز khakrayz
mount *n.* غوز ghonday
mount *v.t.* پرختل pri khatal
mount *n* صعود saood
mountain *n.* غر ghar
mountaineer *n.* غرختونكى ghar khatoonkay
mountainous *a.* غرهييز gharayeez
mourn *v.i.* ماتم كول matam kawal
mourner *n.* ماتم كوونكى matam kawoonkay
mournful *n.* ماتمي matamee
mourning *n.* ماتم matam

mouse *n.* موك mogak
moustache *n.* برت breyt
mouth *n.* خوله khola
mouth *v.t.* پس پس كول pas pas kawal
mouthful *n.* لقمه luqma
movable *a.* خوت منونكى khozakht manoonkay
movables *n.* دكورمالونهاولوازم da kor maloona aw lawazim
move *n.* حركت،بكان harakat; takan
move *v.t.* ځاىبدلول zay badlawal
movement *n.* حركت harakat
mover *n.* خوونكى khozawoonkay
movies *n.* سينما sinama
mow *v.t.* كوټه كول koota kawal
much *a* زيات zyat
much *adv* زياتره zyattara
mucilage *n.* لعاب loab
muck *n.* تورهخاوره tora khawra
mucus *n.* دغوخيرى da ghwag kheeray
mud *n.* خه khata
muddle *n.* وي gadwadee
muddle *v.t.* ككول kakarawal
muffle *v.t.* پچل peychal
muffler *n.* دغادسمال da ghari dasmal
mug *n.* غهپياله ghata pyala
muggy *a.* خپهكوونكى khapa kawoonkay
mulberry *n.* توت toot
mule *n.* كچر kachar
mulish *a.* دوهره dwa raga
mull *n.* ململ malmal
mull *v.t.* غوركول ghor kawal

mullah *n.* دمسلمانانو ديني عالم da moosalmanano deenee alim

mullion *n.* دچوکاعمودي برخه da chawkat amoodee barkha

multifarious *a.* رنارنگ rangarang

multiform *n.* وشکلی so shaklay

multilateral *a.* واخيز so arkheez

multiparous *a.* پهيوای ربچيان زونکی pa yaw zay deyr bachyan zeygoonkay

multiple *a.* وونی so goonay

multiple *n* مرکب murakab

multiplicand *n.* مضروب mazroob

multiplication *n.* ضرب zarab

multiplicity *n.* زيات شمر zyat shmeyr

multiply *v.t.* ضرب کول zarab kawal

multitude *n.* يوزيات مقدار yaw zyat miqdar

mum *a.* خاموش khamosh

mum *n* مور mor

mumble *v.i.* ژولاخبر کول zhowali khabari kawal

mummer *n.* ماسک اغوستی لوبغای mask aghostay lobgharay

mummy *n.* موميايی شوی می momyayee shaway maray

mummy *n* مور mor

mumps *n.* دغومبری رنز da sat dad ghmbaray ranz

munch *v.t.* دغوايی په شان شخوندوهل da ghwayee pa shan shkhwand wahal

mundane *a.* دنيوي doonyawee

municipal *a.* ماري kharee

municipality *n.* ماروالي kharwalee

munificent *a.* بونکی bakhoonkay

muniment *n.* سند sanad

munitions *n.* وسلي wasley

mural *a.* ديوالي deywalee

mural *n.* ديوال deywal

murder *n.* وژنه wazhana

murder *v.t.* وژل wazhal

murderer *n.* وژونکی wazhoonkay

murderous *a.* قاتلانه qatilana

murmur *n.* بزهار bazhar

murmur *v.t.* وگ کول zwag kawal

muscle *n.* دبدن په da badan pata

muscovite *n.* دماسکوارا وسدونکی da masko khar oseydoonkee

muscular *a.* عضلاتی uzlatee

muse *v.i.* فکر کول fikar kawal

muse *n* فکر؛غور fikar; ghor

museum *n.* دلرغونو شيانو نندارای da larghono shayano nandarzay

mush *n.* پهاوبوياشدوکاشدلی دجوارو اوه pa obo ya sheydo ki eysheydalee da joowaro ora

mushroom *n.* مرخی markheyray

music *n.* موسيقي mawseeqee

musical *a.* دموسيقی په اوند da mawseeqay pa arwand

musician *n.* موسيقي جوونکی mawseeqee jorawoonkay

musk *n.* مشک mushk

musket *n.* داودميل توپک da oogad meel topak

musketeer *n.* وپکوال topak wal

muslin *n.* سان san

must *v.* بايد bayad

must *n.* دانورو شيره da angooro sheera

must *n* لزوم lazoom

mustache *n.* برتونه breytoona

mustang *n.* يووحشي‌آس yaw wahshee as

mustard *n.* خردل khardal

muster *v.t.* راغوختل raghokhtal

muster n راغوندوونه raghondawana

musty *a.* پوپنک‌وهلی popanak wahalay

mutation *n.* اوتون awakhtoon

mutative *a.*

mute *a.* خاموش khamosh

mute *n.* بغه‌توری bey ghaga toray

mutilate *v.t.* فلجول faljawal

mutilation *n.* فالج falij

mutinous *a.* باغيانه baghyana

mutiny *n.* بغاوت baghawat

mutiny *v. i* بغاوت‌کول baghawat kawal

mutter *v.i.* ژوولخبر zhowali khabari

mutton *n.* دپسه‌غوه da psa ghwakha

mutual *a.* شریک shareek

muzzle *n.* پوزبند pozband

muzzle *v.t* پوزبندوراچول pozband warachawal

my *a.* زما zama

myalgia *n.* دعضلاوماهیچدرد da uzley aw maheechey dard

myopia *n.* نژدلیدنه nazhdey leedana

myopic *a.* نژدلیدی nazhdey leeday

myosis *n.*

myriad *n.* لس‌زره las zara

myriad *a* لس‌زریز las zareez

myrrh *n.* یوه‌سرناکه‌خوشبویه‌ماده yawa sreykhnaka khoshbooya mada

myrtle *n.* نکریز nakreezi

myself *pron.* ماخپله ma khpala

mysterious *a.* پُراسرار purasrar

mystery *n.* راز raz

mystic *a.* صوفیانه soofyana

mystic *n* صوفي soofee

mysticism *n.* تصوف tasawwuf

mystify *v.t.* حرانول hayranawal

myth *n.* خیالي‌کیسه khyalee keesa

mythical *a.* افسانوي afsanawee

mythological *a.* افسانوي afsanawee

mythology *n.* افسانه‌پژندنه afsana peyzhandana

N

nab *v.t.* نیول neewal

nabob *n.* نواب nawab

nadir *n.* ډه‌کته‌برخه deyra kkhata barkha

nag *n.* ورډلیشخص zoreydalay shakhs

nag *v.t.* مسلسل‌دردلرل musalsal dard laral

nail *n.* نوک nook

nail *v.t.* په‌نوکانونلول pa nookano nakhlawal

naive *a.* ساده sada

naivete *n.* ساده‌توب sadatob

naivety *n.* ناتجربه‌کاري natajruba karee

naked *a.* برند barband

name *n.* نوم noom

name *v.t.* نومورکول noom warkawal

namely *adv.* دسارپهتوه da sari pa toga

namesake *n.* همنومه ham nooma

nap *v.i.* سترهپول starga patawal

nap *n.* سترهپوونه starga patawana

nap *n* ویناستر wareen astar

nape *n.* ورم wurmeyg

napkin *n.* دسمال dasmal

narcissism *n.* زانستاینه zan stayana

narcissus *n* دنرسگل da nargas gul

narcosis *n.* نشهییمواد nashayee mawad

narcotic *n.* نشهییمواد nashayee mawad

narrate *v.t.* کیسهکول keesa kawal

narration *n.* کیسه،بیان keesa; bayan

narrative *n.* داستان dastan

narrative *a.* داستانی dastanee

narrator *n.* بیانوونکی bayanawoonkay

narrow *a.* تنگ tang

narrow *v.t.* تنول tangawal

nasal *a.* پهپوزهپوراوند pa poza pori arwand

nasal *n* دپوزدننه da pozi danana

nascent *a.* پندلی panzeydalay

nasty *a.* ککر kakar

natal *a.* پدایشي paydayshee

nation *n.* قام qam

national *a.* قام qamee

nationalism *n.* پالنهقام qam palana

nationalist *n.* قامپال qam pal

nationality *n.* ملیت mileeyat

nationalization *n.* ملیکدنه milee keydana

nationalize *v.t.* ملیکول milee kawal

native *a.* اصلي aslee

native *n* وطني watanee

nativity *n.* زیدنه zeygeydana

natural *a.* فطري fitree

naturalist *n.* پنونپال panzoon pal

naturalize *v.t.* طبیعيکول tabiee kawal

naturally *adv.* پهطبیعيول pa tabiee dawl

nature *n.* قدرت qudrat

naughty *a.* شریر shareer

nausea *n.* زهراهسکدنه zra rahaskeydana

nautical *a.* سمندري samandaree

naval *a.* سمندري samandaree

nave *n.* دکلیسامرکز da kaleesa markaz

navigable *a.* دکتچلوونو da kakhtay chalowani war

navigate *v.i.* کتچلول kakhtay chalawal

navigation *n.* سمندریون samandaryoon

navigator *n.* ماو manroo

navy *n.* سمندريواک samandaree zwak

nay *adv.* دانکارتوریئنه da inkar toray na

neap *a.* دسمندریهپه da samandar teeta sapa

near *a.* نژد nazhdey

near *prep.* رورته deyr warta
near *adv.* تقریبا taqreeban
near *v.i.* نژدکدل nazhdey keydal
nearly *adv.* تقریبا taqreeban
neat *a.* پاک pak
nebula *n.* دشپیهاسمانکتتردد da shpey pa asman ki tat gard
necessary *n.* ضروريشی zarooree shay
necessary *a* ضروري zarooree
necessitate *v.t.* اکول ar kawal
necessity *n.* محتاجي muhtajee
neck *n.* غاه، ghara; sat
necklace *n.* امل ameyl
necromancer *n.* دموپهمرستهغبوینه da maro pa mrasta ghayb wayana
necropolis *n.* هدیره hadeera
nectar *n.* خوندورشراب khwandawar sharab
need *n.* اتیا artya
need *v.t.* اتیالرل artya laral
needful *a.* مجبور majboor
needle *n.* ستن stan
needless *a.* غرضروري ghayr zarooree
needs *adv.* لهناچارخه la nacharay sakha
needy *a.* محتاج muhtaj
nefarious *a.* بدکاره badkara
negation *n.* نفي nafee
negative *a.* منفي manfee
negative *n.* عدد منفي manfee adad
negative *v.t.* ردول radawal
neglect *v.t.* غفلتکول ghaflat kawal

neglect *n.* غفلت ghaflat
negligence *n.* بیپروایي bey parwayee
negligent *a.* بیپروا bey parwa
negligible *a.* ناچیز na cheez
negotiable *a.* دخبرواترورو da khabaro ataro war
negotiate *v.t.* مذاکرهکول muzakira kawal
nagotiation *n.* مذاکره muzakira
negotiator *n.* جوجایکوونکی jor jaray kawoonkay
negress *n.* تورپوسته tor posti khaza
negro *n.* تورپوستیسی tor postay saray
neigh *v.i.* داسشیشنل da as sheeshneydal
neigh *n.* داسشیشنه da as sheeshney
neighbour *n.* ګاوني gawandee
neighbourhood *n.* ګاوند gawand
neighbourly *a.* داوندپهاروند da gawand pa arwand
neither *conj.* نهخو na khu
neolithic *a.* دانسانانودژوندندنوبری دوره da insanano da zhwand da nawi dabareeney dawra
neon *n.* یوعنصر yaw unsar
nephew *n.* ورارہ wrara
nepotism *n.* خپلپالنه khpal palana
Neptune *n.* دنپونسیاره da niptoon seeyara
Nerve *n.* عصب asb
nerveless *a.* بعصبه bey asba
nervous *a.* عصبي asbee
nescience *n.* جهالت jahalat
nest *n.* ھله zala
nest *v.t.* ھلهجوول zala jorawal

nether *a.* لاندينى landeenay

nestle *v.i.* ﻧﺎﻟﻪﺟﻮﻝ zala jorawal

nestling *n.* ﺩﻣﺮﻏﺒﭽﻰ da marghay bachay

net *n.* ﺟﺎﻝ jal

net *v.t.* ﺟﺎﻝﻏﻮﻭﻝ jal ghorawal

net *a* ﺧﺎﻟﺺ khalis

net *v.t.* ﺳﻮﭼﻤﻪﻻﺱﺗﻪﺭﺍﻭﻝ soocha gata las ta rawral

nettle *n.* ﻟﻪ laramay

nettle *v.t.* ﺍﺫﺍﺭﻭﻝ azarawal

network *n.* ﺟﺎﻝ jal

neurologist *n.* ﻋﺼﺐﭘﮋﺍﻧﺪ asb peyzhandana

neurology *n.* ﻋﺼﺐﭘﮋﻧﺪﻧﻪ asb peyzhandana

neurosis *n.* ﺍﺭﻭﺍﻳﻴﺰﻩﻧﺎﺭﻭﻏﻲ arwayeeza naroghee

neuter *a.* ﺑﻐﺮﺿﻪ bey gharaza

neuter *n* ﺑﺠﻨﺴﻪﻧﻮﻡ bey jinsa noom

neutral *a.* ﺑﻄﺮﻓﻪ bey tarafa

neutralize *v.t.* ﺑﻄﺮﻓﻪﻛﻮﻝ bey tarafa kawal

neutron *n.* ﺩﺍﻟﻮﻡﻳﻮﻩﻣﻨﺬﺭﻩ da atom yawa manzanay zara

never *adv.* ﻫﻴﻜﻠﻪﻫﻴﻮﺧﺖ heeskala; hees wakht

nevertheless *conj.* ﻛﻤﻪﻫﻢ ka sa ham

new *a.* ﻧﻮﻯ naway

news *n.* ﺧﺒﺮﻭﻧﻪ khabrawona

next *a.* ﺭﺍﺗﻠﻮﻧﻜﻰ ratloonkay

next *adv.* ﻭﺭﻭﺳﺘﻪﻟﻪ wrosta la

nib *n.* ﺗﺮﻣﻮﻛﻪ teyra sooka

nibble *v.t.* ﭘﻪﻏﺎﻭﺷﻜﻮﻝ pa ghakho shkawal

nibble *n* ﻭﻣﻮﻩ wara tota

nice *a.* ﻭﺭﻳﻦ wreen

nicety *n.* ﻭﺭﻳﻨﺘﻮﺏ wreentob

niche *n.* ﺗﺎﺧﭽﻪ takhcha

nick *n.* ﺩﭼﺎﻭﺩﻭﻧﻪ da chawdo nakha

nickel *n.* ﺩﻧﻜﻞﻋﻨﺼﺮ da nikal unsar

nickname *n.* ﻛﻮﺭﻧﻰﻧﻮﻡ koranay noom

nickname *v.t.* ﻛﻮﺭﻧﻰﻧﻮﻡﺍﻳﻮﺩﻝ koranay noom eekhodal

nicotine *n.* ﻳﻮﺯﻫﺮﺟﻨﻪﻣﺎﺩﻩ yaw zaharjana mada

niece *n.* ﻭﺭﺭﻩ wreyra

niggard *n.* ﺑﺨﻴﻞ bakheel

niggardly *a.* ﭘﻪﺑﺪﻧﻴﺘﺴﺮﻩ pa badnyatay sara

nigger *n.* ﺗﻮﺭﭘﻮﺳﺘﻜﻰ tor postakay

nigh *adv.* ﺗﻘﺮﻳﺒﺎ taqreeban

nigh *prep.* ﻧﮋﺩ nazhdey

night *n.* ﺷﭙﻪ shpa

nightingale *n.* ﺑﻠﺒﻞ bulbul

nightly *adv.* ﺩﺷﭙﻰ da shpey

nightmare *n.* ﺍﺭﻭﻭﻧﻜﻰﺧﻮﺏ darowoonkay khob

nightie *n.* ﺩﺧﻮﺏﻛﺎﻟﻰ da khob kalee

nihilism *n.* ﺩﻣﺎﺩﺍﻭﻧﺪﺷﺘﻮﻥﻧﻪﻣﻨﻪ da madey aw naray da shtoon na manana

nil *n.* ﻧﺸﺖ nasht

nimble *a.* ﭼﻚ chatak

nimbus *n.* ﻧﻮﺭﺍﻧﻰﺷﭙﻮﻝ nooranee shpol

nine *n.* ﻧﻬﻪ naha

nineteen *n.* ﻧﻮﻟﺲ noolas

nineteenth *a.* ﻧﻮﻟﺴﻢ noolasam

ninetieth *a.* ﻧﻮﻳﻢ nawyam

ninth *a.* ﻧﻬﻢ naham

ninety *n.* نوي nawee

nip *v.t* نتل nakhteyzal

nipple *n.* دتيوكه da tee sooka

nitrogen *n.* دنايتروجنباز da naytrojan gaz

no *a.* منفي manfee

no *adv.* نه na

no *n* هي،نفي hees; nafee

nobility *n.* نجابت najabat

noble *a.* شريف shareef

noble *n.* شريفسى shareef saray

nobleman *n.* شريفسى shareef saray

nobody *pron.* هيوک heesok

nocturnal *a.* دشپ da shpey

nod *v.i.* سرخوول sar khozawal

node *n.* سرخوونه sar khozawana

noise *n.* و zwag

noisy *a.* غالمغالي ghalmaghalee

nomad *n.* كوچى kochay

nomadic *a.* كوچيانه kochyana

nomenclature *n.* نوملر noom lar

nominal *a.* نوميز noomeez

nominate *v.t.* نوماندكول noomand kawal

nomination *n.* نومونه noomawana

nominee *n* نوماند noomand

non-alignment *n.* نهپيوستون na peywastoon

nonchalance *n.* بېپروايي bey parwayee

nonchalant *a.* بېپروا bey parwa

none *pron.* هييو hees yaw

none *adv.* هيكله heeskala

nonetheless *adv.* لهدسرهسره la dey sara sara

nonpareil *a.* غرمساوي ghayr masawee

nonpareil *n.* يوولمه yaw dawl manra

nonplus *v.t.* پرېشانهكول pareyshana kawal

nonsense *n.* چي chatee

nonsensical *a.* بايه bey zaya

nook *n.* دمستطيليشكلكونج da mustateelee shakal konj

noon *n.* غرمه gharma

noose *n.* لومه looma

noose *v.t.* پهلومهكرول pa looma ki geyrawal

nor *conj* خو نه na khu

norm *n.* جوتاوتركيب jorakht aw tarkeeb

norm *n.* اخلاقيمعيار akhlaqee mayar

normal *a.* عادي adee

normalcy *n.* عاديحالت adee halat

normalize *v.t.* قانونلاندراوستل qanoon landi rawastal

north *n.* شمال shomal

north *a* شمالي shomalee

north *adv.* مخپهشمال makh pa shomal

northerly *a.* پهشمالک pa shomal ki

northerly *adv.* دشمالپهلور da shomal pa lor

northern *a.* شمالي shomalee

nose *n.* پوزه poza

nose *v.t* پوزهمول poza mokhal

nosegay *n.* لسانه gul sanga

nosy *a.* بدبويه bad booya

nostalgia *n.* دپرديتوباحساس da pradeetob ehsas

nostril *n.* دپوزسوری da pozi sooray

nostrum *n.* دهردرددوااومعالجدرمل da har dard dwa aw moalij darmal

not *adv.* دنهمنفي كلمه da na manfee kalma

notability *n.* اهميت ahmeeyat

notable *a.* ديادونو da yadawani war

notary *n.* ليكونكى leekoonkay

notation *n.* يادت yadakht

notch *n.* چوله chola

note *n.* چوله كول chola kawal

note *v.t.* يادتول yadakhtawal

noteworthy *a.* دتوجهو da tawajo war

nothing *n.* بارزتهشى bey arzakhta shay

nothing *adv.* هيكله heeskala

notice *a.* خبرتيا khabartya

notice *v.t.* خبرول khabrawal

notification *n.* خبروونه khabrawana

notify *v.t.* اعلانول aylanawal

notion *n.* فكر،آند fikar; and

notional *a.* فكرى fikree

notoriety *n.* بدنامتوب badnamtob

notorious *a.* بدنام badnam

notwithstanding *prep.* چ ار agar chay

notwithstanding *adv.* لهدىسرهسره la dey sara sara

notwithstanding *conj.* كهدهم ka sa ham

nought *n.* نشت،صفر nasht; sifar

noun *n.* اسم،نوم isam; noom

nourish *v.t.* خواهوركول khwara warkawal

nourishment *n.* روزنه rozana

novel *a.* نوى naway

novel *n* ژمان،عشقيه كيسه ruman; ishqeeya keesa

novelette *n.* لنه كيسه landa keesa

novelist *n.* كيسهليكونكى keesa leekoonkay

novelty *n.* نوت nawakht

november *n.* دانرزيكالىيولسمه ميات da angreyzee kal yawolasama myasht

novice *n.* نوى كار naway kar

now *adv.* اوس os

now *conj.* داچ da chi

nowhere *adv.* هيچرته hees cheyrta

noxious *a.* تاواناوونكى tawan arowoonkay

nozzle *n.* نل nalay

nuance *n.* جزيي juzee

nubile *a.* دوادهو da wada war

nuclear *a.* هستوي hastawee

nucleus *n.* مركزيهسته markazee hasta

nude *a.* لغ laghar

nude` *n* لغهمجسمه laghara mujasima

nudity *n.* لغتوب laghartob

nudge *v.t.* پهنلوهل pa sangal wahal

nugget *n.* قطعه qita

nuisance *n.* ور،خوابدوونه zor; khwa badowana

null *a.* باطل batil

nullification *n.* باطلوونه batilawona

nullify *v.t.* باطلول batilawal

numb *a.* بحسه bey hisa
number *n.* شمېر shmeyr
number *v.t.* شمېرل shmeyral
numberless *a.* بشمېره bey shmeyra
numeral *a.* عددي adadee
numerator *n.* شمرونکى shmeyroonkay
numerical *a.* عددي adadee
numerous *a.* بشمېره bey shmeyra
nun *n.* راهبه rahiba khaza
nunnery *n.* ينهصومعه khazeena somia
nuptial *a.* پهنکاحپوراوند pa nika pori arwand
nuptials *n.* دوادهرسم da wada rasam
nurse *n.* رنورپال ranzoor pal
nurse *v.t* خدمتکول khidmat kawal
nursery *n.* روزنتون rozantoon
nurture *n.* پالنه palana
nurture *v.t.* پالل palal
nut *n* چارمغز char maghaz
nutrition *n.* غذا ghaza
nutritious *a.* غذايي ghazayee
nutritive *a.* دغذاپهاوند da ghaza pa arwand
nuzzle *v.* پهخاورهباندپوزهمول pa khawra bandi poza mokhal
nylon *n.* نايلون naylon
nymph *n.* سمندريهپر samandaree khapeyray

O

oak *n.* ونه seyray wuna
oar *n.* دکتراشپل da kakhtay rashpeyl
oarsman *n.* راشپلوهونکى rashpeyl wahoonkay
oasis *n.* رغياه raghyanra
oat *n.* سارايياوربشه sarayee orbasha
oath *n.* لوه lora
obduracy *n.* سرتمبهي sartambagee
obdurate *a.* برزى dabar zaray
obedience *n.* اطاعت itaat
obedient *a.* تابع tabay
obeisance *n.* احترام ehtiram
obesity *n.* چاغت chaghakht
obey *v.t.* غاهايودل ghara eekhodal
obituary *a.* دميناعلان da mreeni aylan
object *n.* شى shay
object *v.t.* اعتراضکول aytiraz kawal
objection *n.* نيوکه neewaka
objectionable *a.* داعتراضو da aytiraz war
objective *n.* هدف hadaf
objective *a.* واقعي waqiee
oblation *n.* نذر nazar
obligation *n.* احسان؛ژمنه ehsan; zhmana
obligatory *a.* واجب wajib
oblige *v.t.* ناچارکول nachar kawal
oblique *a.* ريبند reyband
obliterate *v.t.* محوهکول mahwa kawal
obliteration *n.* پاکوونه pakowana
oblivion *n.* هروونه heyrawana
oblivious *a.* بخبره bey khabara

oblong *a.* اود oogda

oblong *n.* مستطيل mustateel

obnoxious *a.* كرغن kargheyran

obscene *a.* فاحش fahish

obscenity *n.* فحشتوب fahashtob

obscure *a.* مبهم mubhim

obscure *v.t.* تتول tatawal

obscurity *n.* ابهام ibham

observance *n.* رسمپالنه rasam palana

observant *a.* اوار awsar

observation *n.* پاملرنه pam larana

observatory *n.* ساراى sar zay

observe *v.t.* معاينهكول muayna kawal

obsess *v.t.* نارامهكول narama kawal

obsession *n.* سودا sawda

obsolete *a.* لهكارهلوىدلى la kara lweydalay

obstacle *n.* مانع manay

obstinacy *n.* سرغاوى sar gharaway

obstinate *a.* سرتمبه sar tamba

obstruct *v.t.* مانعكدل manay keydal

obstruction *n.* بنلت bandakht

obstructive *a.* مخنيوىكوونكى makhneeway kawoonkay

obtain *v.t.* لاستهراول las ta rawral

obtainable *a.* شونى shoonay

obtuse *a.* كرخت karakht

obvious *a.* واضح wazay

occasion *n.* موقع moqa

occasion *v.t* موقعراپدل moqa rapeykheydal

occasional *a.* اتفاقي itifaqee

occasionally *adv.* اتفاقاً itifaqan

occident *n.* لوىديز lweydeez

occidental *a.* لوىديزه naray lweydeeza naray

occult *a.* مخفي makhfee

occupancy *n.* خپلونه khpalawana

occupant *n.* نيوونكى neewoonkay

occupation *n.* دنده danda

occupier *n.* نيوونكى neewoonkay

occupy *v.t.* كول ليا lagya kawal

occur *v.i.* پدل peykheydal

occurrence *n.* په peykha

ocean *n.* لوىسمندر loy samandar

oceanic *a.* سمندري samandaree

octagon *n.* اتهمخيز ata makheez

octangular *a.* اتهويز ata guteez

octave *n.* اتهسطريشعر ata satree shayr

October *n.* دانزيكاللسمهمياشت da angreyzee kal lasama myasht

octogenarian *a.* اتياكلن atya kalan

octogenarian *a* اتياكلنانسان atya kalan insan

octroi *n.* بخشش bakhshish

ocular *a.* بصري basree

oculist *n.* دستروۀاكر da stargo dakdar

odd *a.* طاق taq

oddity *n.* عجيباوغريبشى ajeeb aw ghareeb shay

odds *n.* ناانولتوب na andwaltob

ode *n.* قصيده qaseeda

odious *a.* خوابدوونكى khwa badoonkay

odium *n.* عداوت adawat

odorous *a.* خوشبويه khoshbooya

odour *n.* خوشبو khoshbooya

offence *n.* جرم juram

offend *v.t.* ګناه کول goona kawal

offender *n.* ګناهار goona gar

offensive *a.* کرغن kargheyran

offensive *n* يرغلګر yarghalgar

offer *v.t.* واندز کول warandeyz kawal

offer *n* پشنهاد payshnihad

offering *n.* هديه hadeeya

office *n.* کارای،دفتر karzay; daftar

officer *n.* ددفترچارواکی da daftar charwakay

official *a.* دفتري daftaree

official *n* اداري چارواکی idaree charwakay

officially *adv.* پهرسمي توه pa rasmee toga

officiate *v.i.* رسمي مقام نيول rasmee maqam neewal

officious *a.* اداري،مسؤولي idaree; masoolee

offing *n.* ساحلي اوبه sahilee oba

offset *v.t.* ورسره برابري کول warsara barabaray kawal

offset *n* برابري،نيالی barabaree; nyalgee

offshoot *n.* بچګی bachgay

offspring *n.* بچګی bachgay

oft *adv.* ډله deyr zala

often *adv.* ډله deyr zala

ogle *v.t.* پهنخرو کتل pa nakhro katal

ogle *n* نازنخره naz nakhra

oil *n.* تل teyl

oil *v.t* پهتلوغوول pa teylo ghwarawal

oily *a.* غو ghwar

ointment *n.* ملهم malham

old *a.* عمرخولی oomar khwaralay

oligarchy *n.* دشتمنوواکمني da shtamano wakmanee

olive *n.* زتون zaytoon

olympiad *n.* دالمپيک دنيوالوسيالو لوبغای da ulampeek da nareewalo syalo lobgharay

omega *n.* ديوناني ابآخري توری da yoonanee abeysey akhiree toray

omelette *n.* خاينه khageena

omen *n.* پال pal

ominous *a.* بدمرغه bad margha

omission *n.* حذفوونه hazafawana

omit *v.t.* حذفول hazafawal

omnipotence *n.* بشپواکمني bashpar wakmanee

omnipotent *a.* بشپواکمن bashpar wakman

omnipresence *n.* هرای موجودي har zay mawjoodgee

omnipresent *a.* هرای ته حاضر har zay ta hazir

omniscience *n.* لاپايه پوهنه lapaya pohana

omniscient *a.* پهرهپوه pa har sa poh

on *prep.* پر،باند par; bandi

on *adv.* سربره sar beyra

once *adv.* پخوا pakhwa

one *a.* يو yaw

one *pron.* وک،يوکس sok; yaw kas

oneness *n.* يوتوب yawtob

onerous *a.* سخت sakht

onion *n.* پياز pyaz

on-looker *n.* کتونکی katoonkay

only *a.* یواز yawazi

only *adv.* په‌یواز pa yawazi

only *conj.* صرف siraf

onrush *n.* غیزه‌نوموونه ghageeza noomawana

onset *n.* حمله hamla

onslaught *n.* سخته‌حمله sakhta hamla

onus *n.* ژمنه zhmana

onward *a.* مخ‌خواته makh khwa ta

onwards *adv.* دمخ‌پلوه‌ته da makh palwa ta

ooze *n.* نرمه‌خه narma khata

ooze *v.i.* نندل naneydal

opacity *n.* تتوالی tatwalay

opal *n.* یوررنگی‌رنونه‌لرونکماده‌چ غمی‌ترجوی yaw rangarang khkulee rangoona laroonki mada chi ghamee tri joreygee

opaque *a.* تت tat

open *a.* پرانستی pranistay

open *v.t.* پرانستل pranistal

opening *n.* پرانستنه؛سوری pranistana; sooray

openly *adv.* په‌مکاره‌ول pa khkara dawl

opera *n.* موزیکاله‌رامه mozeekala drama

operate *v.t.* په‌کاراچول pa kar achowana

operation *n.* عملیات amaleeyat

operative *a.* عملی amalee

operator *n.* اداره‌کوونکی idara kawoonkay

opine *v.t.* رسمی‌بیان‌ورکول rasmee bayan warkawal

opinion *n.* رایه raya

opium *n.* افیون afyoon

opponent *n.* مخالف mukhalif

opportune *a.* پرای par zay

opportunism *n.* مصلحت maslihat

opportunity *n.* موقع moqa

oppose *v.t.* مخالفت‌کول mukhalifat kawal

opposite a. مخالف mukhalif

opposition *n.* مقاومت muqawmat

oppress *v.t.* ظلم‌کول zulam kawal

oppression *n.* ظلم zulam

oppressive *a.* ظالمانه zalimana

oppressor *n.* ظالم zalim

opt *v.i.* اکل takal

optic *a.* په‌لیدپوراوند pa leed pori arwand

optician *n.* عینک‌جووونکی aynak jorawoonkay

optimism *n.* امید‌پُر pur omeed

optimist *n.* باوري bawaree

optimistic *a.* امیدلرونکی omeed laroonkay

optimum *n.* این‌کچ areen kach

optimum *a* مناسب munasib

option *n.* غوراوی ghoraway

optional *a.* اختیاري ikhtyaree

opulence *n.* بایتوب badaytob

opulent *a.* شتمن shtaman

oracle *n.* الهام ilham

oracular *a.* الهامی ilhamee

oral *a.* ژبنی zhabanay

orally *adv.* په‌ژبني‌ول pa zhabanee dawl

orange *n.* نارنج naranj

orange *a* نارنجي naranjee

oration *n.* ونا wayna

orator *n.* وناوال waynawal

oratorical *a.* ادیبانه adeebana

oratory *n.* دوﻧﺎﻓﻦ da wayna fan

orb *n.* ﻛﺮه kura

orbit *n.* ﺗﻠﻮری،ﻣﺪار tag loray; madar

orchard *n.* دﻣﻮهﺑﺎ غ da meywa bagh

orchestra *n.* دﻣﻮﺳﻴﻘﻠﻪ da mawseeqay dala

orchestral *a.* ﻟﻪﻳﻴﺰهﻣﻮﺳﻴﻘﻲ dala yeeza mawseeqee

ordeal *n.* ﻟﻪﻛﺎوهﻛﻪآزﻣﻮﻳﻨﻪ la karawa daka azmoyana

order *n.* ﻓﺮﻣﺎن farman

order *v.t* ﻓﺮﻣﺎنورﻛﻮل farman warkawal

orderly *a.* ﭘﻪﻣﻨﻈﻤﻪﺗﻮه pa munazzama toga

orderly *n.* ﺗﻨﻈﻴﻢ tanzeem

ordinance *n.* ﺣﻜﻢ hukam

ordinarily *adv.* ﭘﻪﻋﺎدتﺳﺮه pa adat sara

ordinary *a.* ﻣﻌﻤﻮﻟﻲ mamoolee

ordnance *n.* ﺗﻮﭘﺨﺎﻧﻪ topkhana

ore *n.* ﻛﺎﻧﻲﺑﺮه kanee dabara

organ *n.* ﻏﻲ،ﻩ gharay; had

organic *a.* ﻋﻀﻮي uzwee

organism *n.* ژوﻧﺪیوﺟﻮد zhwanday wajood

organization *n.* اداره idara

organize *v.t.* ﺗﺮﺗﻴﺒﻮل tarteebawal

orient *n.* ﺧﺘﻴﺰ khateez

orient *v.t.* ﺧﺘﻴﺰﺗﻪﺗﻠﻞ khateez ta tlal

oriental *a.* ﺧﺘﻴﺰوال khateezwal

oriental *n* آﺳﻴﺎ aseeya

orientate *v.t.* ﻻرﻣﻮﻧﺪل lar moondal

origin *n.* اﺻﻞ،آر asal; ar

original *a.* اﺻﻠﻲ aslee

original *n* اﺻﻞاوﺳﻴﺪوﻧﻜﻰ asal oseydoonkay

originality *n.* اﺻﺎﻟﺖ asalat

originate *v.t.* ﺳﺮﭼﻴﻨﻪﻛﺪل sar cheena keydal

originator *n.* ﺳﺮﭼﻴﻨﻪ sar cheena

ornament *n.* زور zaywar

ornament *v.t.* ﺳﻴﻨﺎرول seengarawal

ornamental *a.* ﺳﻴﻨﺎرﭘﻮراوﻧﺪ seengar pori arwand

ornamentation *n.* زﺑﺎﺋﺶ zaybayish

orphan *n.* ﻳﺘﻴﻢ yateem

orphan *v.t* ﻳﺘﻴﻢﻛﻮل،ﻳﺘﻴﻢﻛﺪل yateem kawal; yateem keydal

orphanage *n.* ﻳﺘﻴﻤﺎﻧﻮداﺳﺘﻮﻧﺎی yateemano da astogni zay

orthodox *a.* ﭘﻪدودﻳﺰدﻳﻦﺑﺎوري pa doodeez deen bawaree

orthodoxy *n.* ﭘﻪدودﻳﺰدﻳﻦﺑﺎورﻟﺮوﻧﻜﻰ pa doodeez deen bawar laroonkay

oscillate *v.i.* ردﻛﺪل reygdeydal

oscillation *n.* ردﻛﺪﻧﻪ reygdeydana

ossify *v.t.* هوﻛﻴﺰﻛﻮل hadokeez kawal

ostracize *v.t.* ﭘﻪﻋﻤﻮﻣﻲراﻳﻮﺳﺮهﺷﻞ pa amoomee rayo sara sharal

ostrich *n.* ﺷﺘﺮﻣﺮغ shutar murgh

other *a.* ﺑﻞ،ﺟﺪا bal; juda

other *pron.* ﺑﻞ،ﻧﻮر bal; nor

otherwise *adv.* ﻟﻪدﭘﺮﺗﻪ la dey parta

otherwise *conj.* اوﻛﻪﻧﻪ aw ka na

otter *n.* دﺣﺸﺮاﺗﻮﻻروا da hashrato larwa

ottoman *n.* عثماني ترکیه usmanee turkeeya

ounce *n.* دوزنیوپیمانه da wazan yaw paymana

our *pron.* زموږ zamoong

oust *v.t.* بهرکول bahar kawal

out adv. دباند da bandi

out-balance *v.t.* پردرندل pri draneydal

outbid *v.t.* لونرخواندکول lwar narkh warandi kawal

outbreak *n.* پیلدنه payleydana

outburst *n.* پاونواوبلوا pasoon aw balwa

outcast *n.* شلشوی sharal shaway

outcast *a* بیکوره bey kora

outcome *n.* پایله payla

outcry *a.* نارسور narey soorey

outdated *a.* منسوخ mansookh

outdo *v.t.* زیاتکارکول zyat kar kawal

outdoor *a.* دباند da bandi

outer *a.* باندینی bandeenay

outfit *n.* اسباب،لوازم asbab; lawazim

outfit *v.t* وسایلپهلاسورکول wasayil pa las warkawal

outgrow *v.t.* زیاتهپراختیاموندل zyata parakhtya moondal

outhouse *n.* اڼ angar

outing *n.* تفریحيچکر tafreehee chakar

outlandish *a.* پردی praday

outlaw *n.* شلشویکس sharal shaway kas

outlaw *v.t* لهحقوقمحرومول la haqooqo mahroomawal

outline *n.* شکلبندي shakal bandee

outline *v.t.* طرحکول tarha kawal

outlive *v.i.* وعمرلرل deyr oomar laral

outlook *n.* لرلید larleed

outmoded *a.* نادوده nadooda

outnumber *v.t.* لهشمرهاو،دل la shmeyra awreydal

outpatient *n.* دروغتونسرپايينارو غ da roghtoon sarpayee narogh

outpost *n.* سرحديویکی sarhadee sawkay

output *n.* حاصل hasil

outrage *n.* غضب ghazab

outrage *v.t.* پهغضبکول pa ghazab kawal

outright *adv.* مستقیماً mustaqeeman

outright *a* پهیوهدم pa yawa dam

outrun *v.t.* پهمنهواندکدل pa manda warandi keydal

outset *n.* شروع shuro

outshine *v.t.* زیاتلدل zyat zaleydal

outside *a.* بهرنی baharanay

outside *n* دبهر da bahar

outside adv بهرته bahar ta

outside prep دباند da bandi

outsider *n.* پردی praday

outsize *a.* غیرمعمولي ghayr mamoolee

outskirts *n.pl.* داربانذنبرخ da khar bandanay barkhi

outspoken *a.* سپینهونـاکووِنکی speena wayna kawoonkay

outstanding *a.* هسک،وتلی hask; watalay

outward *a.* بهرنی baharanay

outward *adv* بهرلورته bahar lor ta

outwards *adv* بهرته bahar ta

outwardly *adv.* بهرلورته bahar lor ta

outweigh *v.t.* ورخهدرندل warsakha draneydal

outwit *v.t.* ترچادمخهكدل tar cha da makha keydal

oval *a.* هوله hagay dawla

oval *n* بضوي‌جسم bayzwee jisam

ovary *n.* تخمدان tukhamdan

ovation *n.* عمومي‌هركلی amoomee har kalay

oven *n.* تنور tanoor

over *prep.* سربربيرهپردې sar beyra par dey

over *adv* پهدبرخه‌كي pa dey barkha ki

over *n* هسک hask

overact *v.t.* زيات‌كاركول zyat kar kawal

overall *n.* سرجمع sar jama

overall *a* جامع jamay

overboard *adv.* دسيندپهلوري da seend pa lori

overburden *v.t.* زيات‌بارول zyat barawal

overcast *a.* ترسيوري‌لاند tar syooree landi

overcharge *v.t.* زيات‌لت‌راوستل zyat lagakht rawastal

overcharge *n* زيات‌لت zyat lagakht

overcoat *n.* بالاپوش balaposh

overcome *v.t.* برلاسی‌كدل barlasay keydal

overdo *v.t.* زيات‌كاركول zyat kar kawal

overdose *n.* زيات‌درمل‌خول zyat darmal khwaral

overdose *v.t.* زيات‌درمل‌خول zyat darmal khwaral

overdraft *n.* لهاعتبارخهزيات‌ترلاسه la aytibar sakha zyat tar lasa shaway

overdraw *v.t.* لهشته‌پانخهراخستل la shta pangi sakha deyr akheystal

overdue *a.* ندل zandeydaly

overhaul *v.t.* ولوبرخوكبدلونونه tolo barkho ki badloonoona rawastal

overhaul *n.* لهسره‌بياسنجونه la sara bya sanjawana

overhear *v.t.* ترآخره‌اورلدل tar akhira awreydal

overjoyed *a* زيات‌خوشاله zyat khoshala

overlap *v.t.* زيات‌پچل zyat peychal

overlap *n* زيات‌سره‌ندلی zyat sara nakhleydalay

overleaf *adv.* پهبله‌پاه pa bala panra

overload *v.t.* زيات‌بارول zyat barawal

overload *n* زيات‌بار zyat bar

overlook *v.t.* متوجه‌كدل mutawajo keydal

overnight *adv.* دشپله‌مخ da shpey la makhi

overnight *a* دشپ da shpey

overpower *v.t.* فتح‌كول fata kawal

overrate *v.t.* لوه‌بيه‌وركول lwara baya warkawal

overrule *v.t.* پرمسلط کول pri musallat kawal

overrun *v.t* پربریدکول pri breed kawal

oversee *v.t.* ارل saral

overseer *n.* سرپرست sar parast

overshadow *v.t.* تیاره کول tyara kawal

oversight *n.* تروتنه نظري nazaree teyrwatana

overt *a.* معلوم maloom

overtake *v.t.* لاندکول landi kawal

overthrow *v.t.* له پواچول la pkho achawal

overthrow *n* غورونه ghorzawana

overtime *adv.* تراکلي وخت زیات tar takalee wakht zyat

overtime *n* اضافي کار izafee kar

overture *n.* پیلامه،سریزه peelama; sareeza

overwhelm *v.t.* بشپرغوپه کول bashpar ghopa kawal

overwork *v.i.* اضافي کارکول izafee kar kawal

overwork *n.* زیات کار zyat kar

owe *v.t* پوروی کدل por waray keydal

owl *n.* ونه goong

own *a.* خپل،ہاني khpal; zanee

own *v.t.* لرل laral

owner *n.* لرونکی،مالک laroonkay; malik

ownership *n.* ملکیت milkeeyat

ox *n.* غویی ghwyay

oxygen *n.* دآکسیجن ہاز da akseejan gaz

---

oyster *n.* یوسمندري صدف yaw samandaree sadaf

pace *n* دتلورفتار da tlo raftar

pace *v.i.* په یوخاص اندازه تلل pa yaw khas andaza tlal

pacific *a.* آرامسمندر aram samandar

pacify *v.t.* خاموشول khamoshawal

pack *n.* بنل bandal

pack *v.t.* بنل کول bandal kawal

package *n.* ی geyday

packet *n.* کوچنی بی koochnay dabay

packing *n.* باربندي barbandee

pact *n.* معاهده muahida

pad *n.* توشکچه toshakcha

pad *v.t.* پلی سفرکول pali safar kawal

padding *n.* دنالیدجوونچاره da naleegay da jorawani chara

paddle *v.i.* راشپل وهل rashpeyl wahal

paddle *n* پلنه تخته plana takhta

paddy *n.* نه ژرنده شووریج na zhranda shawi wareeji

page *n.* پله panra

page *v.t.* په لوغمعلومات ورکول pa lwar ghag maloomat warkawal

pageant *n.* ودنه khodana

pageantry *n.* پرتمینه ننداره purtameena nandara

pagoda *n.* دبودايانوبتخانه da boodayano butkhana

pail *n.* ولچه dolcha

pain *n.* درد dard

pain *v.t.* دردول dardawal

painful *a.* دردناک dardnak

painstaking *a.* محتاط muhtat

paint *n.* رنگ rang

paint *v.t.* رنول rangawal

painter *n.* رنوونکی rangawoonkay

painting *n.* نقاشي؛انورري naqashee; anzorgaree

pair *n.* جوه jora

pair *v.t.* جوه کدل jora keydal

pal *n.* يار،شريک yar; shareek

palace *n.* ما manray

palanquin *n.* ول dolay

palatable *a.* مزه ناک mazanak

palatal *a.* په تالوپوراوند pa taloo pori arwand

palate *n.* تالو taloo

palatial *a.* هوادارستراى hawadar star zay

pale *n.* زيړ zyar

pale *a* پيکه peeka

pale *v.i.* پيکه کدل peeka keydal

palette *n.* دنقاشدرنونوخه کاراخستنه da naqashay da rangoono sakha kar akheystana

palm *n.* کجوره kajoora

palm *v.t.* لاس ورکول las warkawal

palm *n.* دلاس ورغوى da las warghaway

palmist *n.* ورغوى کتونکی warghaway katoonkay

palmistry *n.* ورغوى کتنه warghaway katana

palpable *a.* دلمسو da lams war

palpitate *v.i.* درزيدل drazeydal

palpitation *n.* دزه درزا da zra draza

palsy *n.* وز goozanr

paltry *a.* کثافات او چل kasafat aw chatalay

pamper *v.t.* پهنازپالل pa naz palal

pamphlet *n.* رساله risala

pamphleteer *n.* رساله ليکونکی risala leekoonkay

panacea *n.* د هر مرض دوا da har maraz dawa

pandemonium *n.* دشطانما da shaytan manray

pane *n.* يوه ملورکونجموه yawa salor konja tota

panegyric *n.* مدحه madha

panel *n.* چوکاپلورکونجه ده chawkat; salor konja dara

panel *v.t.* کته پرايودل kata pri eekhodal

pang *n.* يکه sreeka

panic *n.* اضطراب iztirab

panorama *n.* هراخيزه منظره har arkheeza manzara

pant *v.i.* لنداوتزه ساه اخستل landa aw teyza sa akheystal

pantaloon *n.* پتلون patloon

pantheism *n.* دخداى دولوپواووا کونو مجموعه بلل da khuday da tolo peykho aw zwakoono majmoo ganral

pantheist *n.* دخداى په قدرت باوري da khuday pa qudrat bawaree

panther *n.* پانگ prang

pantomime *n.* ماسکونه اغوستي لوبغاي maskoona aghostee lobgharee

pantry *n.* دلوخونه da lokho khoona

papacy *n.* دكليسادپاپمقام da kaleesa da pap maqam

papal *a.* دكليسادپاپپوراوند da kaleesa da pap pori arwand

paper *n.* كاغذ kaghaz

par *n.* يوشانوالى yawshanwalay

parable *n.* نمونه namoona

parachute *n.* دژغورنچتر da zhghorani chatray

parachutist *n.* چترباز chatarbaz

parade *n.* رسمهشت rasam gasht

parade *v.t.* رسمهشت كول rasam gasht kawal

paradise *n.* جنت janat

paradox *n.* متقابلواندز mutaqabil warandeyz

paradoxical *a.* متضاد mutazad

paraffin *n.* يوهمومولهماده yawa mom dawla mada

paragon *n.* نمونه،معيار namoona; mayar

paragraph *n.* دليكنيوهبرخه da leekani yawa barkha

parallel *a.* برابر barabar

parallel *v.t.* برابرول barabarawal

parallelism *n.* يوشانتوب yawshantob

parallelogram *n.* متوازيالاضلاع mutawazeeul azla

paralyse *v.t.* وزوهل goozanr wahal

paralysis *n.* وز goozanr

paralytic *a.* وزوهلى goozanr wahalay

paramount *n.* لوپوىحاكم lwar poray hakim

paramour *n.* شه shahay

paraphernalia *n. pl* جهز jahayz

paraphrase *n.* آزادهليكنه azada leekana

paraphrase *v.t.* شرحهكول،آزادليكل sharha kawal; azada leekal

parasite *n.* جراثيم jaraseem

parcel *n.* پنكى pandukay

parcel *v.t.* پهووشل pa toto weyshal

parch *v.t.* وريتول wreetawal

pardon *v.t.* بنهكول bakhana kawal

pardon *n.* مغفرت maghfirat

pardonable *a.* دمغفرتو da maghfirat war

parent *n.* مورپلار mor plar

parentage *n.* نسب nasab

parental *a.* دمورپلارپهاوند da mor plar pa arwand

parenthesis *n.* ليندكۍ leendakay

parish *n.* ناحيه،علاقه naheeya; ilaqa

parity *n.* مساويتوب masaweetob

park *n.* دعمومىتفريحاى da amoomee tafree zay

park *v.t.* پهيواىكدرول pa yaw zay ki darawal

parlance *n.* وناءبيان wayna; bayan

parley *n.* مكالمه makalima

parley *v.i* مذاكرهكول muzakira kawal

parliament *n.* ملىشورا milee shoora

parliamentarian *n.* دملىشوراغاى da milee shoora gharay

parliamentary *a.* شورايي shoorayee

parlour *n.* دسينارخونه da seengar khoona

parody *n.* دنوردودسبک‌تقليد da noro da subak taqleed

parody *v.t.* خندوونکهنري‌ننداره‌واند کول khandawoonki hunaree nandara warandi kawal

parole *n.* ضمانت zamanat

parole *v.t.* په‌ضمانت‌پرول pa zamanat preykhwal

parricide *n.* دمورپلاروژنه da mor plar wazhana

parrot *n.* طوطي totee

parry *v.t.* اوسپکول oogey spakawal

parry *n.* دفاعي‌خوت difaee khozakht

parson *n.* سيمه‌ييزپادري seemayeez padree

part *n.* برخه barkha

part *v.t.* برخه‌اخستل barkha akheystal

partake *v.i.* شريکدل shareekeydal

partial *a.* برخيز؛جزيي barkheez; juzayee

partiality *n.* پلويتوب palaweetob

participate *v.i.* شرکت‌لرل shirkat laral

participant *n.* شرکت‌کوونکى shirkat kawoonkay

participation *n.* شرکت shirkat

particle *a.* ذره zara

particular *a.* خاص khas

particular *n.* خاص‌سى khas saray

partisan *n.* پلوى palaway

partisan *a.* طرفدار tarafdar

partition *n.* وش weysh

partition *v.t.* وشل weyshal

partner *n.* ونه‌وال wandawal

partnership *n.* شراکت shirakat

party *n.* ونډ gond

pass *v.i.* پوروتل pori watal

pass *n* پوروتنه pori watana

passage *n.* دوتولاره da wato lara

passenger *n.* لاروى laraway

passion *n.* جذبه jazba

passionate *a.* جذباتي jazbatee

passive *a.* غرفعال ghayr faal

passport *n.* پژندپله peyzhandana

past *a.* تر teyr

past *n.* ترمهال teyr mahal

past *prep.* دمخه da makha

paste *n.* خميره khameera

paste *v.t.* سريخوال sreykhawal

pastel *n.* رنه‌انور ranga anzor

pastime *n.* بوختيا bokhtya

pastoral *a.* روحاني‌لارود roohanee larkhod

pasture *n.* ساى sar zay

pasture *v.t.* رول sarawal

pat *v.t.* نازول nazawal

pat *n* نازوونه nazawana

pat *adv* په‌مناسبه‌توه pa munasiba toga

patch *v.t.* پوندلول peywand lagawal

patch *n* وه،؛پينه tota; peena

patent *a.* واضح wazeh

patent *n* دکارحق da kar haq

patent *v.t.* انحصاري‌حق‌ورکول inhisaree haq warkawal

paternal *a.* پلرنى plaranay

path *n.* تلورى،؛لار tagloray; lar

pathetic *a.* غروراوستونکی ghreew rawastoonkay

pathos *n.* شفقت shafqat

patience *n.* صبر sabar

patient *a.* صبرکوونکی sabar kawoonkay

patient *n* مریض mareez

patricide *n.* دپلاروژنه da plar wazhana

patrimony *n.* پلرنیمیراث plaranay meeras

patriot *n.* هوادوال haywad wal

patriotic *a.* هوادپال haywad pal

partiotism *n.* هوادپالنه haywad palana

patrol *v.i.* شتکول gasht kawal

patrol *n* شت gasht

patron *n.* ساتندوی satandoy

patronage *n.* پالنه palana

patronize *v.t.* ساتل،پالل satal; palal

pattern *n.* طرحه،نمونه tarha; namoona

paucity *n.* لتوب lagtob

pauper *n.* تشلاسی tash lasay

pause *n.* وقفه waqfa

pause *v.i.* وقفهکول waqfa kawal

pave *v.t.* پهبروپول pa dabaro pokhal

pavement *n.* سنفرشي sangfarshee

pavilion *n.* لویهکد loya keygday

paw *n.* خپه khapara

paw *v.t.* منولپرخول mangoli prey khakhawal

pay *v.t.* اداکول ada kawal

pay *n* اداینه،جبران adayana; jibran

payable *a.* داداینو da adayani war

payee *n.* پسترلاسهکوونکی peysey tar lasa kawoonkay

payment *n.* دپسواداینه da peyso adayana

pea *n.* یوولچ yaw dawl chanrey

peace *n.* پخلاینه،سوله pukhlayana; sola

peaceable *a.* دسولو da soli war

peaceful *a.* سولهییز solayeez

peach *n.* شفتالو shaftaloo

peacock *n.* طاوس tawas

peahen *n.* ینهطاوس khazeena tawas

peak *n.* وکه،موکه sooka; makhooka

pear *n.* ناک nak

pearl *n.* ملغلره malghalara

peasant *n.* کلیوال kaleewal

peasantry *n.* کلیوالهخوی kaleewala khooy

pebble *n.* شه shaga

peck *n.* سطلتهورتهلوی satal ta warta lokhay

peck *v.i.* پهموکهوهل pa makhooka wahal

peculiar *a.* خاص khas

peculiarity *n.* خاصیت khaseeyat

pecuniary *a.* نغدي naghdey

pedagogue *n.* وونکی khowoonkay

pedagogy *n.* وونهاوروزنه khowana aw rozana

pedal *n.* رکاب rakab

pedal *v.t.* دبایسکلرکابپهپووهل da baysakal rakab pa pkho wahal

pedant *n.* کورنیوونکی koranay khowoonkay

pedantry *n.* دخپلپوهبهیهوودنه da khpali pohi bey zaya khodana

pedestal *n.* پايه،ستون paya; satoon

pedestrian *n.* پلاره pali lara

pedigree *n.* نسب‌نامه nasabnama

peel *v.t.* پوستکی‌اچول postakay achawal

peel *n.* پوستکی postakay

peep *v.i.* په‌غلاغلاکتل pa ghla ghla katal

peep *n* په‌غلاکتنه pa ghla katana

peer *n.* سيال؛جوه syal; jora

peerless *a.* بجو bey jorey

peg *n.* موی؛سنجاق magaway; sanjaq

peg *v.t.* په‌موي‌راوندول pa magwee razwarandawal

pelf *n.* دنيايي‌مال doonyayee mal

pell-mell *adv.* په‌وول pa gadwad dawl

pen *n.* قلم qalam

pen *v.t.* ليکل؛په‌بندکاچول leekal; pa band ki achawal

penal *a.* جزايي jazayee

penalize *v.t.* جريمه‌کول jareema kawal

penalty *n.* جريمه jareema

pencil *n.* پنسل؛دنقاشبرس pensal; da naqashay burs

pencil *v.t.* په‌پنسل‌جوول‌ياليکل pa pensal jorawal ya leekal

pending *prep.* معلق moallaq

pending *a* نااجرا na ijra

pendulum *n.* بنول bandol

penetrate *v.t.* پکنفوذکول paki nafooz kawal

penetration *n.* نفوذ؛ننوتنه nafooz; nanawatana

penis *n.* دنارينه‌جنسي‌آله da nareena jinsee ala

penniless *a.* تش‌لاسی tash lasay

penny *n.* يوه‌پسه؛دامريکاسکه yawa paysa; da amreeka sika

pension *n.* دتقاعدتنخوا da taqaid tankha

pension *v.t.* دتقاعدتنخوااخستل da taqaid tankha akheystal

pensioner *n.* متقاعد mutaqaid

pensive *a.* پرشان parayshan

pentagon *n.* پنځوی peenza gotay

peon *n.* ددفترقاصد da daftar qasid

people *n.* خلک khalq

people *v.t.* آبادول؛مشت‌کول abadawal; meysht kawal

pepper *n.* مرچ mrich

pepper *v.t.* تريخول treekhawal

per *prep.* په‌وسيله pa waseela

perambulator *n.* دماشومانوانه da mashoomano tanga

perceive *v.t.* درک‌کول؛موندل darak kawal; moondal

perceptible *adj* ددرک‌و da darak war

per cent *adv.* سلنه؛فيصدي salana; feesadee

percentage *n.* دسلوله‌مخ da salo la makhi

perception *n.* درک؛احساس darak; ehsas

perceptive *a.* ادراکي idrakee

perch *n.* دلري‌تير da largee teer

perch *v.i.* په‌يوخوندي‌ياي‌کنستل pa yaw khwandee zay kkheynastal

perennial *a.* پایتلرونکی payakht laroonkay

perennial *n.* دوامدارشی dawamdar shay

perfect *a.* زبردست، پوره؛ poora; zabardast

perfect *v.t.* پوره‌کول؛بشپول poora kawal; bashparawal

perfection *n.* پوره‌والی؛کمال poora walay; kamal

perfidy *n.* بی وفایي bey wafayee

perforate *v.t.* سوری‌کول sooray kawal

perforce *adv.* لەناکامخه la nakamay sakha

perform *v.t.* اجراکول ijra kawal

performance *n.* سرته‌رسونه؛اجرا sar ta rasawana; ijra

performer *n.* اجراکوونکی ijra kawoonkay

perfume *n.* عطر atar

perfume *v.t.* دعطروبوی‌ورکول da atro booy warkawal

perhaps *adv.* کدای‌شي؛شاید keyday shee; shayad

peril *n.* خطر khatar

peril *v.t.* په‌خطر کاچول pa khatar ki achawal

perilous *a.* خطرناک khatarnak

period *n.* وخت؛دوران wakht; dawran

periodical *n.* مهالیز mahaleez

periodical *a.* نوبتي nawbatee

periphery *n.* چاپریال chapeyryal

perish *v.i.* تلف‌کول talf kawal

perishable *a.* لەمنه‌تلونکی la manza tloonkay

perjure *v.i.* ژمنه‌ماتول zhmana matawal

perjury *n.* ژمنه‌ماتونه zhmana matawana

permanence *n.* دوام dawam

permanent *a.* دایمي daymee

permissible *a.* داجازو da eejazey war

permission *n.* اجازه eejaza

permit *v.t.* اجازه‌ورکول eejaza warkawal

permit *n.* اجازه eejaza

permutation *n.* اوتوناوونجون awakhtoon aw wanjoon

pernicious *a.* زیاناوونکی zyan arowoonkay

perpendicular *a.* ولا walar

perpendicular *n.* شاقول shaqol

perpetual *a.* دایمي daymee

perpetuate *v.t.* بقاوربل baqa warbakhal

perplex *v.t.* حرانول hayranawal

perplexity *n.* پچلتیا peychaltya

persecute *v.t.* شکنجه‌کول shkanja kawal

persecution *n.* شکنجه shkanja

perseverance *n.* یکاو teekaw

persevere *v.i.* استقامت‌لرل istiqamat laral

persist *v.i.* اصرارکول israr kawal

persistence *n.* اصرار israr

persistent *a.* یندونکی teengeydoonkay

person *n.* نفر؛شخص nafar; shakhs

personage *n.* مهم‌شخصیت muhim shakhseeyat

personal *a.* شخصي shakhsee

personality *n.* هويت؛شخصيت haweeyat; shakhseeyat

personification *n.* دشخصيت‌تجسم da shakhseeyat tajassum

personify *v.t.* ورته‌شخصيت‌ورکول wartashakhseeyat warkawal

personnel *n.* کارمندان karmandan

perspective *n.* ليد؛منظره leed; manzara

perspiration *n.* سخت‌کار sakht kar

perspire *v.i.* سخت‌کارکول sakht kar kawal

persuade *v.t.* هول hasawal

persuasion *n.* هوونه؛تحريک hasawana; tahreek

pertain *v.i.* اهلرل ara laral

pertinent *a.* مربوط marboot

perturb *v.t.* ناراموه‌کول narama kawal

perusal *n.* کره‌کتنه kara katana

peruse *v.t.* کتل‌اوپلل katal aw palatal

pervade *v.t.* نفوذکول nafooz kawal

perverse *a.* خپل‌سری khpal saray

perversion *n.* خپل‌سري khpal saree

perversity *n.* خپل‌سري؛فساد khpal saree; fasad

pervert *v.t.* له‌سملاراول la sami lari arawal

pessimism *n.* بدبيني bad beenee

pessimist *n.* بدبين‌کس bad been kas

pessimistic *a.* بدبين bad been

pest *n.* وبا waba

pesticide *n.* طاعون‌ضدعامل taoon zad amil

pestilence *n.* دطاعون‌ناروغي da taoon naroghee

pet *n.* نازولی؛ران nazawalay; gran

pet *v.t.* نازول nazawal

petal *n.* دگل‌پاه da gul panra

petition *n.* غوتنليک ghokhtanleek

petition *v.t.* تقاضاکول taqaza kawal

petitioner *n.* عرض‌کوونکی arz kawoonkay

petrol *n.* بنزين؛نفت benzeen; naft

petroleum *n.* نفتي‌مواد naftee mawad

petticoat *n.* کميس‌لانداغوستل‌کدونک‌ينه‌لمن kamees landi aghostal keydoonkay khazeena laman

petty *a.* ناچيز nacheez

petulance *n.* ستاخي gustakhee

petulant *a.* ستاخ gustakh

phantom *n.* تصور؛غولوونکی‌ظاهر tasawwur; gholawoonkay zahir

pharmacy *n.* درملتون darmaltoon

phase *n.* مرحله marhala

phenomenal *a.* حرانوونکی heyranawoonkay

phenomenon *n.* کفيت kayfeeyat

phial *n.* ووکی‌يه‌يي‌بوتل warookay kheekhayee botal

philanthropic *a.* انسان‌پاله insan pala

philanthropist *n.* انسان‌پال insan pal

philanthropy *n.* بشردوسته bashar dosta

philological *a.* ژبپوهنپوراوند zhabpohani pori arwand

philologist *n.* ژبپوهاند zhabpohand

philology *n.* ژبپوهنه zhabpohana

philosopher *n.* فيلسوف feelasof

philosophical *a.* فيلسوفيانه feelasofyana

philosophy *n.* فلسفه falsafa

phone *n.* تلفون taylafoon

phonetic *a.* غيز ghageez

phonetics *n.* دغونودترکيباوحرفونود وينعلم da ghagoono da tarkeeb aw harfoono da wayang ilam

phosphate *n.* دفسفريک اسيدماله da fasfureek aseed malga

phosphorus *n.* فاسفرس لرونکی fasfuras laroonkay

photo *n* تصوير tasweer

photograph *v.t.* عکس اخستل aks akheystal

photograph *n* عکس aks

photographer *n.* عکس جوونکی aks jorawoonkay

photographic *a.* عکسي aksee

photography *n.* عکاسي akasee

phrase *n.* نه؛عبارت garana; ibarat

phrase *v.t.* کلمه بندي کول kalma bandee kawal

phraseology *n.* عبارت کاروونه؛کلمه بندي ibarat karawana; kalma bandee

physic *n.* طب؛فزيک tib; fizeek

physic *v.t.* ورته درمل ورکول warta darmal warkawal

physical *a.* بدني badanee

physician *n.* اکر daktar

physicist *n.* حکيم؛درمل جوونکی hakeem;darmal jorawoonkay

physics *n.* فزيک fizeek

physiognomy *n.* رو پژندنه seyra peyzhandana

physique *n.* دبدن جوت da badan jorakht

pianist *n.* دپيانو دموسيقآله غوونکی da pyano da mawseeqay ala ghagoonkay

piano *n.* دپيانو دموسيقآله da pyano da mawseeqay ala

pick *v.t.* غونول؛جلاکول ghondawal; jala kawal

pick *n.* جلاکونه jala kawana

picket *n.* دستک؛موی dastak; magaway

picket *v.t.* پزوانول peyzwanawal

pickle *n.* اچار achar

pickle *v.t* په سرکه کايودل pa sarka ki eekhodal

picnic *n.* لهييزچکر dalayeez chakar

picnic *v.i.* لهييزچکرته تلل dalayeez chakar ta tlal

pictorical *a.* انوريز anzoreez

picture *n.* انور anzor

picture *v.t.* انوراخستل anzor akheystal

picturesque *a.* دانوراخستنو da anzor akheystanai war

piece *n.* وه tota

piece *v.t.* ودانول wadanawal

pierce *v.t.* په ترده شي سوری کول pa teyra shee sooray kawal

piety *n.* رحم؛تقوا rehem; taqwa

pig *n.* خو koog

pigeon *n.* کوتره kawtara

pigmy *n.* يکی teetakay

pile *n.* کوه kwata

pile *v.t.* کوه کول kwata kawal

piles *n.* بواسير bawaseer

pilfer *v.t.* دكمشيغلاكول da kam shee ghla kawal

pilgrim *n.* زيارت؛حج zyarat; haj

pilgrimage *n.* زيارت؛حج zyarat; haj

pill *n.* دانه dana

pillar *n.* ستنه؛پايه stana; paya

pillow *n* بالت balakht

pillow *v.t.* پهبالتسرايودل pa balakht sar eekhodal

pilot *n.* پيلو؛جالهوان paylot; jalawan

pilot *v.t.* پيلويكول؛رهنماييكول paylotee kawal; rehnumayee kawal

pimple *n.* رمكه؛دانه garmaka; dana

pin *n.* كوچنيمخ koochnay meykh

pin *v.t.* مخومبل meykh toombal

pinch *v.t.* چيچل cheechal

pinch *v.* غلاكول ghla kawal

pine *n.* دصنوبرونه da sanobar wana

pine *v.i.* كول karawal

pineapple *n.* اناناس ananas

pink *n.* رنلابي gulabee rang

pink *a* لابي gulabee

pinkish *a.* لابيرنتهمايل gulabee rang ta mayil

pinnacle *n.* اوج؛ترهوكه oj; teyra sooka

pioneer *n.* مخك makhkakh

pioneer *v.t.* رهبريكول rehbaree kawal

pious *a.* پرهزار parhayzgar

pipe *n.* نل؛سوري nal; soornray

pipe *v.i* نلونوكاوبهرسول naloono ki oba rasawal

piquant *a.* تريخاوخوندور treekh aw khwandawar

piracy *n.* دحقغلا da haq ghla

pirate *n.* غل ghal

pirate *v.t* غلاكول ghla kawal

pistol *n.* تمانچه tamancha

piston *n.* خوندهميله khozanda meela

pit *n.* كنده kanda

pit *v.t.* پهكندهكاچول pa kanda ki achawal

pitch *n.* نصبشويای nasab shaway zay

pitch *v.t.* نصبكول؛توغول nasab kawal; toghawal

pitcher *n.* كوزه kooza

piteous *a.* زاهد zahid

pitfall *n.* دام dam

pitiable *a.* درحمو da rehem war

pitiful *a.* زهسواندی zra swanday

pitiless *a.* برحمه bey rehma

pitman *n.* كيندونكی keendoonkay

pittance *n.* پهميپسخرات pa maree pasi khayrat

pity *n.* خويزه zra khoogee

pity *v.t.* سزلزه zra seyzal

pivot *n.* چورليز choorleez

pivot *v.t.* پهمحورتاودل pa mehwar taweydal

place *n.* ربای dagar; zay

place *v.t.* پمایكول pa zay kawal

placid *a.* امن dadman

plague *a.* وبا؛طاعون waba; taoon

plague *v.t.* پهبلااختهكول pa bala akhta kawal

plain *a.* دگ dag

plain *n.* هوار hawar

plaintiff *n.* دعواكوونکی dawa kawoonkay

plan *n.* تدبیر tadbeer

plan *v.t.* تدبیرکول tadbeer kawal

plane *n.* الوتکه alwataka

plane *v.t.* الوتل؛رنده کول alwatal; randa kawal

plane *a.* هواره سطح hawara sata

plane *n* دترکارنده da tarkanray randa

planet *n.* سیاره seeyara

planetary *a.* سیاروي seeyarawee

plank *n.* دلريهواره تخته da largee hawara takhta

plank *v.t.* په دودوویشل pa daro daro weyshal

plant *n.* بوی bootay

plant *v.t.* کرل؛نیالول karal; nyalawal

plantain *n.* کله kayla

plantation *n.* کرونده karwanda

plaster *n.* پلستر؛لو palistar; leyw

plaster *v.t.* پلسترول palistarawal

plate *n.* لوی lokhay

plate *v.t.* فلزيپورکول filizee pokh warkawal

plateau *n.* لوه سطح lwara sata

platform *n.* کنلاره؛منبر kranlara; mimbar

platonic *a.* دافلاطوندلارلاروی da aflatoon da lari laraway

platoon *n.* بلوک؛يوه له همکاراشخاص blok; yawa dala hamkar ashkhas

play *n.* لوبه loba

play *v.i.* لوبکول lobi kawal

player *n.* لوبغای lobgharay

plea *n.* حقوقي دعوا haqooqee dawa

plead *v.i.* دفاع کول difa kawal

pleader *n.* مدافع وکیل mudafay wakeel

pleasant *a.* په زه پوري pa zra pori

pleasantry *n.* خوطبعي khwakh tabee

please *v.t.* خوندورکول khwand warkawal

pleasure *n.* لذت lazat

plebiscite *n.* دعام وورایه da am wagaro raya

pledge *n.* تعهد؛ژمنه taahud; zhmana

pledge *v.t.* تعهدکول taahud kawal

plenty *n.* زیات کچ zyat kach

plight *n.* تون؛بیعت taroon; beyt

plod *v.i.* نوېدل nagokheydal

plot *n.* زمینه؛دمکيوموه zameena; da zmaki yawa tota

plot *v.t.* پلان جوول plan jorawal

plough *n.* يیو yeywi

plough *v.i* مکه يیوکول zmaka yeywi kawal

ploughman *n.* کروندسر karwandagar

pluck *v.t.* شکول؛ولول shukawal; tolawal

pluck *n* ولونه tolawana

plug *n.* خولپوی؛پل kholpotay; plag

plug *v.t.* خولپويپکايودل kholpotay paki eekhodal

plum *n.* آلوچه aloocha

plumber *n.* نلدوان؛سرپکار naldawan; sarp kar

plunder *v.t.* لول lootal

plunder *n* ولجه،غنيمت walja; ghaneemat

plunge *v.t.* غوه كول ghota kawal

plunge *n* غوه،غوپه ghota; ghopa

plural *a.* جمع jama

plurality *n.* په جمع پوراوند pa jama pori arwand

plus *a.* مثبت musbat

plus *n* دجمعنه،مثبت da jama nakha; musbat

ply *v.t.* اوزارپه كارول،پماكلارسفركول awzar pa karawal; pa takali lar safar kawal

ply *n* دلريوپه da largee yaw pata

pneumonia *n* دسوالتهاب da sago iltihab

pocket *n.* جب jeyb

pocket *v.t.* جب كايودل jeyb ki eekhodal

pod *n.* پو،تكى pokh; teykay

poem *n.* شعر shayr

poesy *n.* شاعري،ديوان shairee; deewan

poet *n.* شاعر shair

poetaster *n.* شاعروى shair gotay

poetess *n.* شاعرمه shaira khaza

poetic *a.* شاعرانه shairana

poetics *n.* شاعرانكلا shairana khkula

poetry *n.* شاعري shairee

poignacy *n.* توندي tondee

poignant *a.* توند tond

point *n.* كى،بوكه takay; sooka

point *v.t.* كى لول،اشاره كول takay lagawal; ishara kawal

poise *v.t.* ثابت قدمساتل sabit qadam satal

poise *n* وضعيت،وقار wuzeeyat; waqar

poison *n.* زهر zahar

poison *v.t.* زهرور كول zahar warkawal

poisonous *a.* زهرجن zaharjan

poke *v.t.* بايه پلنه كول bey zaya palatana kawal

poke *n.* چوخوونه chokhawana

polar *n.* شمالي ياسولمي قطب shumalee ya sweylee qutab

pole *n.* قطب،ستن qutab; stan

police *n.* امنيتيوواك،پوليس amneeyatee zwak; polees

policeman *n.* امنيتيمامور amneeyatee mamoor

policy *n.* كنلاره kranlara

polish *v.t.* صقلي كول sayqalee kawal

polish *n* رنب،صقل rang; sayqal

polite *a.* نرم naram

politeness *n.* نرمي narmee

politic *a.* مهذب muhazzab

political *a.* سياسي seeyasee

politician *n.* سياستوال seeyasatwal

politics *n.* سياست پوهنه seeyasat pohana

polity *n.* سياستداري seeyasatdaree

poll *n.* رايه raya

poll *v.t.* رايهور كول raya warkawal

pollen *n.* نباتي كوچني سپورونه nabatee koochnee sporawan

pollute *v.t.* ناولى كول nawalay kawal

pollution *n.* ناوليتوب nawaleetob

polo *n.* دهاکيوهلوبه da hagay yawa loba

polygamous *a.* شمرلرونکی ganr shmeyr khazi laroonkay

polygamy *n.* شمرلرنه ganr shmeyr khazi larana

polyglot1 *n.* پهوژبوپوه pa so zhabo poh

polyglot2 *a.* پهوژبوپوهدنه pa so zhabo poheydana

polytechnic *a.* راخيزفنونوپوراوند deyr arkheez fanoono pori arwand

polytechnic *n.* راخيزفنياوتخنيکي پوهنتون deyr arkheez fanee aw takhneekee pohantoon

polytheism *n.* پهوخدايانوباور pa ganro khudayano bawar

polytheist *n.* پهوخدايانوباورلرونکي pa ganro khudayano bawar laroonkay

polytheistic *a.* پهوخدايانوپوراوند pa ganro khudayano pori arwand

pomp *n.* دبدبه dabdaba

pomposity *n.* شان؛شوکت shan; shawkat

pompous *a.* شاندار shandar

pond *n.* ډند dand

ponder *v.t.* غورکول ghor kawal

pony *n.* کوچنیاس koochnay as

poor *a.* مسکين miskeen

pop *v.i.* پهزورهتپول pa zora trapawal

pop *n* پهزورهدرزونه pa zora drazawana

pope *n.* دکاتوليکيعيسائيانورهبر da katoleekee eesayano rehbar

poplar *n.* سپدار sapeedar

poplin *n.* دپوپلينوکر da poplayn tokar

populace *n.* عاموی am wagaray

popular *a.* عمومي؛نوموی amoomee; noomawaray

popularity *n.* شهرت shuhrat

popularize *v.t.* مشهورول mashhoorawal

populate *v.t.* مشتکول meysht kawal

population *n.* نفوس nafoos

populous *a.* ganr nafoosa نفوسه

porcelain *n.* چينيلوي cheenee lokhee

porch *n.* دالان dalan

pore *n.* کوچنیسوری koochnay sooray

pork *n.* دخوغوه da khoog ghwakha

porridge *n.* مخلوطشوشوربا makhloot shaway shorba

port *n.* بندر bandar

portable *a.* دلادونو da leygdawani war

portage *n.* لادونه leygdawana

portal *n.* ور؛کماندلرونکیور war; kaman laroonkay war

portend *v.t.* ورخهخبرول warsakha khabrawal

porter *n.* پنی pandee

portfolio *n.* داسنادواوکاغذوبکس؛د وزارتدندهاومقام da asnado aw kaghazo bakas; da wazarat danda aw maqam

portico *n.* برنه baranda

portion *n* جز juz

portion *v.t.* پهبرخووشل pa barkho weyshal

portrait *n.* دمخ‌عکس da makh aks

portraiture *n.* دمخ‌دبرخنقاشي da makh da barkhi naqashee

portray *v.t.* دمخ‌انوراستل da makh anzor eystal

portrayal *n.* مجسم‌کونه mujassam kawana

pose *v.i.* په‌یومانی‌وضعیت‌کانوراستل pa yawa zangaree wuzeeyat ki anzor eystal

pose *n.* اقامه،یومانی‌وضعیت iqama; yawa zangaray wuzeeyat

position *n.* مقام،حالت maqam; halat

position *v.t.* ایودل eekhodal

positive *a.* مثبت musbat

possess *v.t.* په‌واک‌کلرل pa wak ki laral

possession *n.* لرنه،نیونه larana; neewana

possibility *n.* کېدون keydoon

possible *a.* کېدونی keydoonay

post *n.* پست،دپست‌اداره pust; da pust idara

post *v.t.* لیک‌یاسامان‌په‌پست‌لدول leek ya saman pa pust leygdawal

post *n* مسؤلیت masooleeyat

post *v.t.* په‌مسؤلیت‌اکل pa masooleeyat takal

post *adv.* وروسته،بعد wrusta; badan

postage *n.* پستی‌ک pustee tikat

postal *a.* پستي pustee

post-date *v.t.* دپدتاریخ‌په‌زندلیکل da peykhi da tareekh pa zand leekal

poster *n.* اعلان aylan

posterity *n.* نسل nasal

posthumous *a.* دپلارمینوروسته‌زندلی da plar mreeni wrusta zeygeydalay

postman *n.* پست‌رسان pust rasan

postmaster *n.* دپست‌رئیس da pust rayees

post-mortem *a.* تر‌مینوروسته tar mreeni wrusta

post-mortem *n.* دتر‌مینوروسته‌معاینه tar mreeni wrusta moayna

post-office *n.* دپست‌اداره da pust idara

postpone *v.t.* زندول zandawal

postponement *n.* تاخیر takheer

postscript *n.* دکتاب‌پایو da keetab paysoor

posture *n.* حالت،کفیت halat; keyfeeyat

pot *n.* لوی lokhay

pot *v.t.* په‌لوی‌کاچول pa lokhee ki achawal

potash *n.* دپاس‌فلز da putas filiz

potassium *n.* دپسیم‌عنصر da putasyum unsar

potato *n.* الو aloo

potency *n.* لیاقت،توان leeyaqat; twan

potent *a.* پیاوی pyawaray

potential *a.* پیاوی،زورلرونکی pyawaray; zorlaroonkay

potential *n.* زور،استعداد zor; istaydad

pontentiality *n.* پیاوتیا pyawartya

potter *n.* کلال kulal

pottery *n.* کلالي kulalee

pouch *n.* کوه kasora

poultry *n.* چرګان،ساتنه chargan satana

pounce *v.i.* پهيوشيورغورځدل pa yaw shee warghorzeydal

pounce *n* ناپهبريد nasapa breed

pound *n.* درونډوزار droond goozar

pound *v.t.* پرلهپسوزارونهوركول parla pasi goozaroona warkawal

pour *v.i.* وريدل wareydal

poverty *n.* تنسه tangsa

powder *n.* دوه doora

powder *v.t.* دوهاچول،شيندل doora achawal; sheendal

power *n.* طاقت taqat

powerful *a.* طاقتور taqatwar

practicability *n.* عمليتوب amaleetob

practicable *a.* كارډونكى kareydoonkay

practical *a.* عملي amalee

practice *n.* مشق،تجربه mashq; tajruba

practise *v.t.* مشق كول mashq kawal

practitioner *n.* وكالت كوونكى،ماهر wakalat kawoonkay; mahir

pragmatic *a.* د عملي فلسفه پهاوند da amalee falsafey pa arwand

pragmatism *n.* عملي فلسفه amalee falsafa

praise *n.* تحسين tehseen

praise *v.t.* ارزول arzawal

praiseworthy *a.* د و ستايﻪ da stayani war

prank *n.* شرارت shararat

prattle *v.i.* زيات غدل zyat ghageydal

prattle *n.* بايه خبر bey zaya khabari

pray *v.i.* لمونځ كول lmoonz kawal

prayer *n.* لموﻨﺞ lmoonz

preach *v.i.* وعظ كول waaz kawal

preacher *n.* واعظ waiz

preamble *n.* د كتاب سريزه da keetab sareeza

precaution *n.* احتياط ehteeyat

precautionary *a.* احتياطي ehteeyatee

precede *v.* مخكك كدل makhki keydal

precedence *n.* واندتوب wranditob

precedent *n.* واند wrandi

precept *n.* حكم hukam

precepter *n.* لارود larkhod

precious *a.* قيمتي qeematee

precis *n.* لنون،غورچا landoon; ghorchanr

precise *n.* جامع jamay

precision *n.* كرهوالى karawalay

precursor *n.* منادي manadee

predecessor *n.* نيكونهاوپلرونه neekoona aw plaroona

predestination *n.* سرنوﺖ sarnawakht

predetermine *v.t.* دمخهبرخليک ﺎكل da makha barkhleek takal

predicament *n.* ناﻣﺴﺎﻋﺪﺣﺎﻟﺖ namasaid halat

predicate *n.* مسند masnad

predict *v.t.* اكل كول atkal kawal

prediction *n.* اكل atkal

predominance *n.* برتري bartaree

predominant *a.* برتر bartar

predominate *v.i.* برلاسى كدل barlasay keydal

pre-eminence *n.* غوراوی ghoraway

pre-eminent *a.* ترولوغوره tar tolo ghwara

preface *n.* سريزه sareeza

preface *v.t.* سريزهليكل sareeza leekal

prefect *n.* قوماندان qomandan

prefer *v.t.* ترجيحوركول tarjee warkawal

preference *n.* غوراوی ghoraway

preferential *a.* امتيازي imteeyazee

prefix *n.* مختای makhtaray

prefix *v.t.* پرمختایزياتول pri makhtaray zyatawal

pregnancy *n.* بلاربت blarbakht

pregnant *a.* اميدواره umeedwara

prehistoric *a.* تاريخخهمخكيني tareekh sakha makhkeenay

prejudice *n.* لهپلنيپرتهقضاوتكول la palatani parta qazawat kawal

prelate *n.* خليفه khaleefa

preliminary *a.* ابتدايي ibtidayee

preliminary *n* لومی loomray

prelude *n.* مقدمه muqadima

prelude *v.t.* مقدمهچمتوكول muqadima chamtoo kawal

premarital *a.* لهودادهمخكيني la wada makhkeenay

premature *a.* نابالغ nabaligh

premeditate *v.t.* دمخهسنجول da makha sanjawal

premeditation *n.* دمخهسوچ da makha soch

premier *a.* لومنی loomranay

premier *n* مشر،رهبر mashar; rahbar

premiere *n.* مشره،رهبره mashra; rahbara

premium *n.* دبيمپسے da beemey peysey

premonition *n.* خبرداري khabardaree

preoccupation *n.* تصرف،دلومريتوب حق tasarruf; da loomreetob haq

preoccupy *v.t.* تصرفكول tasarruf kawal

preparation *n.* تياری tayaray

preparatory *a.* ابتدايي ibtidayee

prepare *v.t.* تيارول tayarawal

preponderance *n.* زياتوالی zyatwalay

preponderate *v.i.* زياتدل zyateydal

preposition *n.* داضافتتوری da izafat toray

prerequisite *a.* اين،شرطيه areen; sharteeya

prerequisite *n* شرط اين areen shart

prerogative *n.* رسميحق rasmee haq

prescience *n.* دغبوعلم da ghaybo ilam

prescribe *v.t.* نسخهوركول nuskha warkawal

prescription *n.* نسخه nuskha

presence *n.* موجودي mawjoodgee

present *a.* موجود mawjood

present *n.* ال dalay

present *v.t.* رسماوراندكول rasman warandi kawal

presentation *n.* پژندنه peyzhandana

presently *adv.* اوسمهال os mahal

preservation n. خوندينه khwandeeyeena

preservative n. خوندي كوونكی khwandee kawoonkay

preservative a. دخرابدومخنيوونكی da kharabeydo makhneewoonkay

preserve v.t. خوندي ساتل khwandee satal

preserve n. مُربا،بانانحصاري سيمه muraba; zangari inhisaree seema

preside v.i. مشري كول masharee kawal

president n. ولس مشر woolas mashr

presidential a. رياستي reeyasatee

press v.t. زورور كول؛تخته كول zor warkawal; takhta kawal

press n. زور،مطبوعات zor; matbooat

pressure n. فشار fishar

pressurize v.t. فشار اچول fishar achawal

prestige n. آبرو abroo

prestigious a. دعزت په اوند da eezat pa arwand

presume v.t. مُسَلمل؛صحيح ومان كول musallam ganral; sahee gooman kawal

presumption n. احتمال؛صحيح ومان ehtimal; sahee gooman

presuppose v.t. واندخه ومان كول wrandi sakha gooman kawal

presupposition n. واندخه ومان wrandi sakha gooman

pretence n. ودنه ان zan khodana

prtend v.t. تظاهر كول tazahar kawal

pretension n. تظاهر،بهانه tazahar; bahana

pretentious a. ان ودنپوراوند zan khodani pori arwand

pretext n بهانه bahana

prettiness n. ككلا khkula

pretty a لالی gulalay

pretty adv. په انداز pa kha andaz

prevail v.i. دودل doodeydal

prevalance n. خپراوی khparaway

prevalent a. دودشوی dood shaway

prevent v.t. مخنيوی كول makhneeway kawal

prevention n. مخنيوی makhneeway

preventive a. مخنيوونكی makhneewoonkay

previous a. پخوانی pakhwanay

prey n. ككار khkar

prey v.i. ككاركول khkar kawal

price n. بيه baya

price v.t. بيه موندل baya moondal

prick n. دسكونلويارډلونه da skoondalo ya gareydalo nakha

prick v.t. سكونل؛چوخول skoondal; chokhawal

pride n. كبر kabar

pride v.t. كبر كول kabar kawal

priest n. پادري padree

priestess n. ينه پادري khazeena padree

priesthood n. كاهنتوب،ملاتوب kahintob; mulatob

prima facie adv. په يوه نظر pa yawa nazar

primarily *adv.* په‌ابتدايی‌توه pa ibtidayee toga

primary *a.* ابتدايی ibtidayee

prime *a.* لومنی؛مهم loomranay; muhim

prime *n.* اوج؛غوره‌وخت oj; ghwara wakht

primer *n.* دابكتاب da abisi keetab

primeval *a.* دابتدايی‌بشريت‌دور da ibtidayee bashareeyat dawr

primitive *a.* لرغونی‌تمدن‌پوراوند larghonee tamaddun pori arwand

prince *n.* شاهزاده shahzada

princely *a.* دشاهزاده‌په‌شان da shahzada pa shan

princess *n.* شاهزاد shahzadgay

principal *n.* دووني‌رئيس da khowanzee rayees

principal *a* مهم muhim

principle *n.* اصول usool

print *v.t.* چاپول chapawal

print *n* چاپ؛خپرونه chap; khparawana

printer *n.* چاپوونكی chapawoonkay

prior *a.* واندينی wrandeenay

prior *n* لوپوی‌راهب lwar poray rahib

prioress *n.* لوپوراهبه lwar pori rahiba

priority *n.* ترجيح tarjee

prison *n.* بنديخانه bandeekhana

prisoner *n.* بندي bandee

privacy *n.* خلوت khilwat

private *a.* خصوصي؛خپل‌ذاتي khasoosee; khpal zatee

privation *n.* بی‌برخوالی bey barkhiwalay

privilege *n.* امتياز eemteeyaz

prize *n.* انعام eenam

prize *v.t.* انعام‌وركول eenam warkawal

probability *n.* احتمال ehtimal

probable *a.* شونی shoonay

probably *adv.* احتمالاً ehtimalan

probation *n.* آزمايخت azmayakht

probationer *n.* ترآزمايت‌لاندكارمنديا tar azmayakht landi karmand ya zandanee زنداني

probe *v.t.* آزمويل azmoyal

probe *n* دجراحميله da jarahay meela

problem *n.* ستونزه stoonza

problematic *a.* ستونزمن stoonzman

procedure *n.* طريقه tareeqa

proceed *v.i.* پرمخ‌تلل par makh tlal

proceeding *n.* كاري‌بهير karee baheer

proceeds *n.* عايداتي‌محصول ayidatee mahsool

process *n.* كاري‌دوره karee dawra

procession *n.* لهييزخوت dalayeez khozakht

proclaim *v.t.* اعلانول aylanawal

proclamation *n.* بيانيه bayaneeya

proclivity *n.* په‌ذات‌بندخبيستوب pa zat bandi khabeestob

procrastinate *v.i.* ال‌دل taleydal

procrastination *n.* ال tal

proctor *n.* ناظر؛قانوني‌وكيل nazir; qanoonee wakeel

procure *v.t.* موندل moondal

procurement *n.* موندنه moondana

prodigal *a.* مُسرف musraf

prodigality *n.* بدخرهسی bad kharsa saray

produce *v.t.* تولیدول tawleedawal

produce *n.* تولید؛حاصل tawleed; hasil

product *n.* حاصل hasil

production *n.* تولیدشوی‌مواد tawleed shaway mawad

productive *a.* تولیدي tawleedee

productivity *n.* سرشاري؛تولیدي‌وتیا sar sharee; tawleedee wartya

profane *a.* بعزته؛کفریه bey eezata; kufreeya

profane *v.t.* کفرکول kufar kawal

profession *n.* کسب؛دنده kasab; danda

professional *a.* کسبي؛ماهر kasabee; mahir

professor *n.* پوهاند pohand

proficiency *n.* مهارت maharat

proficient *a.* ماهر mahir

profile *n.* د کردارکتنه؛نیمرخ‌انور da kirdar katana; neemrukh anzor

profile *v.t.* پهمقطعي‌ول‌ودل pa maqtaee dawl khodal

profit *n.* ګټ gata

profit *v.t.* ګټ‌کول gata kawal

profitable *a.* ګټندویه gatandoya

profiteer *n.* ګټندویی gatandoyay

profiteer *v.i.* زیاتهګټکول zyata gata kawal

profligacy *n.* لوچکی loochkay

profligate *a.* لوچک loochak

profound *a.* ژورفکره؛روآنده zhawar fikra; roonr anda

profundity *n.* معرفت؛فکري‌ژوروالی marifat; fikree zhawarwalay

profuse *a.* سرشار sarshar

profusion *n.* سخاوت sakhawat

progeny *n.* اولاد؛بای‌ناستی awlad; zay nastay

programme *n.* کاري‌پلان karee plan

programme *v.t.* کاري‌پلان‌جوول karee plan jorawal

progress *n.* جریان jaryan

progress *v.i.* جریان‌لرل jaryan laral

progressive *a.* پرمختیایي parmakhtyayee

prohibit *v.t.* بندزلول bandeyz lagawal

prohibition *n.* بندز bandeyz

prohibitive *a.* ممنوعه mamnooa

prohibitory *a.* ممنوعه mamnooa

project *n.* پروژه parozha

project *v.t.* پروژهجوول parozha jorawal

projectile *n.* توغول‌کدونکي‌جسم toghawal keydoonkay jisam

projectile *a* توغول‌شوی toghawal shaway

projection *n.* طرحهجوونه tarha jorawana

projector *n.* دسینماماشین da seenama masheen

proliferate *v.i.* زیاتدل zyateydal

proliferation *n.* زیاتدا zyateyda

prolific *a.* حاصل‌ورکوونکي hasil warkawoonkay

prologue *n.* سریزه sareeza

prolong *v.t.* اودول oogdawal

prolongation *n.* اودوالى oogadwalay

prominence *n.* نومياليتوب noomyaleetob

prominent *a.* وتلىاوبرجسته watalay aw barjasta

promise *n* وعده wada

promise *v.t* وعده‌كول wada kawal

promising *a.* اميدبونكى umeed bakhoonkay

promissory *a.* د اقرار da iqrar

promote *v.t.* پرمخ‌بيول par makh beywal

promotion *n.* وده wada

prompt *a.* فورى fawree

prompt *v.t.* په‌فعاليت‌راوستل pa faaleeyat rawastal

prompter *n.* پراختياوركوونكى parakhtya warkawoonkay

prone *a.* مستعد mustaid

pronoun *n.* نومړى noomzaray

pronounce *v.t.* تلفظ‌كول talaffuz kawal

pronunciation *n.* تلفظ talaffuz

proof *n.* دليل daleel

proof *a* له‌زيان‌خه‌خوندى la zyan sakha khwandee

prop *n.* ستنه،ملاتړى stana; mlataray

prop *v.t.* ملاتړكول mlatar kawal

propaganda *n.* تبليغات tableeghat

propagandist *n.* آوازخپروونكى awazey khparawoonkay

propagate *v.t.* تبليغول tableeghawal

propagation *n.* انتشار،تبليغ intishar; tableegh

propel *v.t.* په‌حركت‌راوستل pa harakat rawastal

proper *a.* مناسب munasib

property *n.* جايداد jaydad

prophecy *n.* نبوت naboowat

prophesy *v.t.* پغمبري‌كول peyghambaree kawal

prophet *n.* نبي nabee

prophetic *a.* نبوي nabawee

proportion *n.* تناسب tanasub

proportion *v.t.* متناسب‌كول mutanasib kawal

proportional *a.* متناسب mutanasib

proportionate *a.* متناسب mutanasib

proposal *n.* تجويز tajweez

propose *v.t.* تجويزوركول tajweez warkawal

proposition *n.* سكاله،پشنهاد skala; payshnihad

propound *v.t.* مطرح‌كول matrah kawal

proprietary *a.* اختصاصي،ملكيتي ikhtisasee; malkeeyatee

proprietor *n.* مالک malik

propriety *n.* خصوصي‌مالكيت khasoosee malkeeyat

prorogue *v.t.* نول zandawal

prosaic *a.* بي‌خونده bey khwanda

prose *n.* نثر nasar

prosecute *v.t.* په‌قانوني‌پلوه‌تعقيبول pa qanoonee palwa taqeebawal

prosecution *n.* تعقيب قانوني qanoonee taqeeb

prosecutor *n.* قانوني‌وكيل qanoonee wakeel

prosody *n.* دعروضوعلم da aroozo ilam

prospect *n.* لرليد،قيافه larleed; qyafa

prospective *a.* پهراتلونكيپوراوند pa ratloonkee pori arwand

prospectus *n.* خبرپله khabar panra

prosper *v.i.* كاميابدل kamyabeydal

prosperity *n.* خوشحالي khoshhalee

prosperous *a.* موفق،خوشحاله muwafaq; khoshhala

prostitute *n.* فاحشانسان fahish insan

prostitute *v.t.* پسولپارهزناكول peyso lapara zana kawal

prostitution *n.* بدلمني bad lamanee

prostrate *a.* پهمكهپروت pa zmaka prot

prostrate *v.t.* سجدهكول sajeeda kawal

prostration *n.* سجده،فرمانبرداري sajeeda; farmanbardaree

protagonist *n.* سردنه sar danga

protect *v.t.* ژغورل zhghoral

protection *n.* ژغورنه zhghorana

protective *a.* ژغورندوى zhghorandoy

protector *n.* ژغورونكى zhghoroonkay

protein *n.* پروتين proteen

protest *n.* شكايت shikayat

protest *v.i.* شكايتكول shikayat kawal

protestation *n.* شكايت،برندهناخوي shikayat; sarganda nakhwakhee

prototype *n.* اصلينمونه aslee namoona

proud *a.* زانوذى zankhoday

prove *v.t.* ثابتول sabitawal

proverb *n.* متل،زرينهونا matal; zareena wayna

proverbial *a.* دمتلپهاوند da matal pa arwand

provide *v.i.* ورتهبرابرول warta barabarawal

providence *n.* دخدايقدرت da khuday qudrat

province *n.* ولايت wilayat

provincial *a.* ولايتي wilayatee

provincialism *n.* پهولايتاوونه pa wilayat arawana

provision *n.* تياري،مقرراتاكل tayaree; muqarrarat takal

provisional *a.* لنمهاليبندوبست land mahalee bandobast

proviso *n.* شرط shart

provocation *n.* لمسوونه lamsawana

provocative *a.* لمسوونكي lamsawoonkay

provoke *v.t.* تحريكول tahreekawal

prowess *n.* لياقت leeyaqat

proximate *a.* نژدى nazhdey

proximity *n.* نژدوالى nazhdeywalay

proxy *n.* نماينده numayinda

prude *n.* محتاطانسان muhtat insan

prudence *n.* احتياط ehteeyat

prudent *a.* محتاط muhtat

prudential *a.* محتاط muhtat

prune *v.t.* سينارول seengarawal

pry *v.i.* پدقتسرهپلل pa diqat sara palatal

psalm *n.* زبور zaboor

pseudonym *n.* تخلص takhallus

psyche *n.* فكر،ارو fikar; arwa

psychiatrist *n.* داروايیزونناروغیواكر da arwayeezo naroghyo daktar

psychiatry *n.* ارواييزطبابت arwayeez tababat

psychic *a.* روحي roohee

psychological *a.* ارواپوهنیز arwa pohaneez

psychologist *n.* پوه ارو arwa poh

psychology *n.* ارواپوهنه arwa pohana

psychopath *n.* ارواييزنارو غ arwayeez narogh

psychosis *n.* لونتوب leywantob

psychotherapy *n.* روحيتداوي roohee tadawee

puberty *n.* بلوغت baloghat

public *a.* ملي؛عمومي milee; amoomee

public *n.* ولس woolas

publication *n.* نشر؛خپراوى nashar; khparaway

publicity *n.* تبلیغات tableeghat

publicize *v.t.* عامخلکپرخبرول am khalk pri khabrawal

publish *v.t.* نشرول nashrawal

publisher *n.* خپرندوى khparandoy

pudding *n.* یوولغوینساس yaw dawl ghwakheen sas

puddle *n.* دبدرفتاه da badraft sah

puddle *v.t.* خوكلودل khato ki lweydal

puerile *a.* ماشومانه mashoomana

puff *n.* پف،دخولدهوااواز paf; da khuley da hawa awaz

puff *v.i.* دپفاوازخولنهوتل da paf awaz khuley na watal

pull *v.t.* كول

pull *n.* كوونه

pulley *n.* رخ sarkh

pullover *n.* یوولجاک yaw dawl jakat

Shankar *n.* دموغونهبرخه da meywey ghwakhana barkha

pulp *v.t.* غونكدل ghwakhan keydal

pulpit *a.* دریپمنبر dareez; mimbar

pulpy *a.* غون ghwakhan

pulsate *v.i.* لزدل larzeydal

pulsation *n.* ردہا reygdeyda

pulse *n.* نبض nabaz

pulse *v.i.* درزدل drazeydal

pulse *n* ردہا reygdeyda

pump *n.* داوبوراالستنماشین da obo raeystani masheen

pump *v.t.* دپمپپہوسیلہراالستل da pamp pa waseela raeystal

pumpkin *n.* كدو kadoo

pun *n.* دلفظونولوب da lafzoono lobey

pun *v.i.* دلفظونولوبكول da lafzoono lobey kawal

punch *n.* دسوكـوزار da sook goozar

punch *v.t.* پہسوكـوهل pa sook wahal

punctual *a.* پروخت؛دوختپابند par wakht; da wakht paband

punctuality *n.* وخت پژندنه wakht peyzhandana

punctuate *v.t.* کی او نقطی ودل takee aw nuqtey eekhodal

punctuation *n.* نقطی ودنه nuqtey eekhodana

puncture *n.* سوری،شلدلی sooray; shleydalay

puncture *v.t.* سوری کدل،شلدل sooray keydal; shleydal

pungency *n.* تریخوالی treekhwalay

pungent *a.* تریخ treekh

punish *v.t.* سزاورکول saza warkawal

punishment *n.* سزا saza

punitive *a.* سزایي sazayee

puny *a.* لنی یا کوچنی landay ya koochnay

pupil *n.* زده کوونکی zda kawoonkay

puppet *n.* لاسپوی،ای lasposay; goodagay

puppy *n.* دسپی بچی da spee bachay

purblind *n.* کاملاوند kamilan roond

purchase *n.* پرودنه peyrodana

purchase *v.t.* پرودل peyrodal

pure *a.* سوچه soocha

purgation *n.* چاوونه،سپینوونه chanrowana; speenawana

purgative *n.* دامالدرمل da imaley darmal

purgative *a.* مُسهل،پاکوونکی mushal; pakowoonkay

purgatory *n.* ن برزخي barzakhee naray

purge *v.t.* پاکول،اماله کول pakawal; imala kawal

purification *n.* ویننه weenzana

purify *v.t.* پاکول pakawal

purist *n.* سوچه والی غوتونکی soochawalay ghokhtoonkay

puritan *n.* اخلاقي اصیلوالی غوتونکی شخص akhlaqee aseelwalay ghokhtoonkay shakhs

purity *n.* سوچه والی soochawalay

purple *adj./n.* ارغواني،ارغواني رن arghawanee; arghawanee rang

purport *n.* مفهوم،مانا mafhoom; mana

purport *v.t.* مفهومي کول mafhoomee kawal

purpose *n.* موخه،هدف mokha; hadaf

purpose *v.t.* هولرل hod laral

purposely *adv.* په هومن ول pa hodman dawl

purr *n.* دپیشو غرغر da peesho ghur ghur

purr *v.i.* دپیشو غرل da peesho ghureydal

purse *n.* دپسو کوه da peyso kasora

purse *v.t.* راول،جب وهل rageyrawal; jeyb wahal

pursuance *n.* پس کدنه pasi keydana

pursue *v.t.* پس کدل pasi keydal

pursuit *n.* پس کدنه pasi keydana

purview *n.* بریدونه او حدود breedoona aw hadood

pus *n.* چرک،زوه chark; zoh

push *v.t.* له کول teyla kawal

push *n.* له،کو teyla; kokhakh

put *v.t.* ایو دل eekhodal

puzzle *n.* نستوب gangastob

puzzle *v.t.* نس كول gangas kawal

pygmy *n.* لوشتينک انسان lweyshteenak insan

pyorrhoea *n.* دغاچرک da ghakh chark

pyramid *n.* مصري هرم misree haram

pyre *n.* دمي سوو نلپاره دلريو از گوه da maree sozawani lapara da largyo zangari kota

python *n.* لوی مار loy khamar

Q

quack *v.i.* دهياغدل da heelay ghageydal

quack *n* دهياغ da heelay ghag

quackery *n.* چلبازي chalbazee

quadrangle *n.* وی لور salor gotay

quadrangular *a.* لورويز salor goteez

quadrilateral *a. & n.* پلورويپور پا salor gotee pori arwand

quadruped *n.* ساروی،پلورپلرونكی sarway; salor pkhey laroonkay

quadruple *a.* لوربرخيز salor barkheez

quadruple *v.t.* لورغبره كول salor ghbarga kawal

quail *n.* مز؛كرک maraz; krak

quaint *a.* پوه،عاقل poh; aqil

quake *v.i.* لزدل larzeydal

quake *n* لزدنه larzeydana

qualification *n.* صلاحيت؛تعليم salaheeyat; taleem

qualify *v.i.* ورمدل؛رتبه موندل war garzeydal; rutba moondal

qualitative *a.* رنيز srangeez

quality *n.* رنوالی؛معيار srangwalay; mayar

quandary *n.* سرردانی sargardanee

quantitative *a.* ومرهييز somrayeez

quantity *n.* ومرهوالی somrawalay

quantum *n.* كچ؛مقدار kach; miqdar

quarrel *n.* شخه shkhara

quarrel *v.i.* جنجال كول janjal kawai

quarrelsome *a.* جنجالي janjalee

quarry *n.* كارشوی ناور يا انسان khkar shaway zanawar ya insan

quarry *v.i.* كانيبررااستل kanree dabari raistal

quarter *n.* لورمه salorama

quarter *v.t.* پلوروبرخووشل pa saloro barkho weyshal

quarterly *a.* لورمياشتنی salor myashtanay

queen *n.* ملكه malika

queer *a.* عجيب ajeeb

quell *v.t.* آرامول aramawal

quench *v.t.* آرامول؛مول aramawal; marawal

query *n.* پوتنروز pokhtani garweygni

query *v.t* تر پوتلاندنيول tar pokhtani landi neewal

quest *n.* كو kokhakh

quest *v.t.* كوكول kokhakh kawal

question *n.* پوښتنه،سوال sawal; pokhtana

question *v.t.* پوښتل pokhtal

questionable *a.* د پوښتنه و da pokhtani war

questionnaire *n.* پوښتنليک pokhtanleek

queue *n.* ليکه،کتار katar; leeka

quibble *n.* کنايه kinaya

quibble *v.i.* ابهامويل ibham wayal

quick *a.* چک chatak

quick *n* هاند hasand

quicksand *n.* خوندهاوويندهشه khozanda aw khwayanda shaga

quicksilver *n.* سيماب seemab

quiet *a.* غلی،ساکن ghalay; sakin

quiet *n.* چوپتيا choptya

quiet *v.t.* آرامول aramawal

quilt *n.* بالاپو balapokh

quinine *n.* دکونينبوی da koneen bootay

quintessence *n.* دوجودپنمعنصر da wajood peenzam unsar

quit *v.t.* اخستل ورخه لاس las warsakha akheystal

quite *adv.* پهرتينیول pa rakhteenee dawl

quiver *n.* لزه larza

quiver *v.i.* لزدل larzeydal

quixotic *a.* خيالپرسته khyal parasta

quiz *n.* لنهآزموينه landa azmoyana

quiz *v.t.* آزموينهکول azmoyana kawal

quorum *n.* نصاب nisab

quota *n.* برخه barkha

quotation *n.* اقتباس،بيان iqtibas; bayan

quote *v.t.* رانقلول ranaqlawal

quotient *n.* خارجقسمت kharij qismat

R

rabbit *n.* سويه soya

rabies *n.* دلونيسپينناروغي da leywanee spee naroghee

race *n.* سيالی،دمنمسابقه syalee; da mandi musabiqa

race *v.i* دمنمسابقهکول da mandi musabiqa kawal

racial *a.* توکميز،نژادي tokmeez; nazhadee

racialism *n.* توکمپالنه tokampalana

rack *v.t.* شکنجهکول shkanja kawal

rack *n.* طاقچه taqcha

racket *n.* نس teynas

radiance *n.* نورانيت nooraneeyat

radiant *a.* نوراني nooranee

radiate *v.t.* زليدل zaleydal

radiation *n.* زلا zala

radical *a.* بنسيزسمونپال bansateez samoonpal

radio *n.* رايو radeeyo

radio *v.t.* پهرايوخپرول pa radeeyo khparawal

radish *n.* مولۍ moolay

radium *n.* يورايواکتيفاوتشعشعي عنصر yaw radyoekteef aw tashashee unsar

radius *n.* دقطرنيمايي da qutar neemayee

rag *n.* دزوركروه da zor tokar tota

rag *v.t.* زوركرپوندول zor tokar peywandawal

rage *n.* غصه ghusa

rage *v.i.* غصهناک‌کدل ghusanak keydal

raid *n.* يرغل yarghal

raid *v.t.* يرغل‌کول yarghal kawal

rail *n.* اورای orgaday

rail *v.t.* داوسپنپلغول da ospani patlay ghazawal

railing *n.* کاره katara

raillery *n.* مسخر maskharey

railway *n.* داورای‌کره da orgadee karkha

rain *v.i.* اورت‌وربدل orakht wareydal

rain *n* اورت orakht

rainy *a.* باراني baranee

raise *v.t.* پورته‌کول porta kawal

raisin *n.* مويز maweez

rally *v.t.* لهييزه‌غونه‌راولول dalayeeza ghonda ratolawal

rally *n* لهييزه‌غونه dalayeeza ghonda

ram *n.* م،وری mag; wray

ram *v.t.* په‌سختسره‌وهل pa sakhtay sara wahal

ramble *v.t.* سردان‌کول sargardan kawal

ramble *n* سردانی sargardanee

rampage *v.i.* لونتوب‌کول leywantob

rampage *n.* غالمغالي ghalmaghalee

rampant *a.* خپورشوی،پراخ khpor shaway; parakh

rampart *n.* دخاورواوشوحفاظتي‌دوال da khawro aw shago hifazatee deywal

rancour *n.* کينه keena

random *a.* بترتيبه bey tarteeba

range *v.t.* ترتيبول tarteebawal

range *n.* لړ،ترتيب laray; tarteeb

ranger *n.* ترتيبوونکی،ساتندوی tarteebawoonkay; satandoy

rank *n.* مقام،پو maqam; poray

rank *v.t.* مقام‌لرل maqam laral

rank *a* ژرسترد‌ونکی zhar stareydoonkay

ransack *v.t.* مالونه‌لول maloona lootal

ransom *n.* دتاوان‌پيس da tawan peysey

ransom *v.t.* تاوان‌اخستل tawan akheystal

rape *n.* دزورزياتي‌زنا da zor zyatee zana

rape *v.t.* په‌زورزنا‌کول pa zor zana kawal

rapid *a.* تز teyz

rapidity *n.* چکتيا chataktya

rapier *n.* يوول‌نرسپکه‌توره yaw dawl naray spaka toora

rapport *n.* موافقايک mawafiqi areeki

rapt *a.* غلاشوی ghla shaway

rapture *n.* وجد wajad

rare *a.* ناياب nayab

rascal *n.* دوکه‌مار‌وبحيا dokamar aw bey haya

rash *a.* بپامه bey pama

rat *n.* موک mogak

rate *v.t.* بيه‌ايودل baya eekhodal

rate *n.* نرخ،شرح narkh; sharah

rather *adv.* مخكله،البته makhki la; albata

ratify *v.t.* تصويبول tasweebawal

ratio *n.* نسبت،شرح nisbat; sharah

ration *n.* دخواوكلونه da khwaro takali wanda

rational *a.* پهدلايلولا pa dalayalo walar

rationale *n.* آراوبنس ar aw bansat

rationality *n.* اصوليت،عقلانيت usooleeyat; aqlaneeyat

rationalize *v.t.* منطقيبهوركول mantaqee banra warkawal

rattle *v.i.* پهلوغويل pa lwar ghag wayal

rattle *n* دتقتقغ da traq traq ghag

ravage *n.* لوتالان loot talan

ravage *v.t.* لول،تالاكول lootal; tala kawal

rave *v.i.* پهغصهكدل pa ghusa keydal

raven *n.* توركارغه tor kargha

ravine *n.* اودهژورهدره oogda zhawara dara

raw *a.* خام kham

ray *n.* وانه waranga

raze *v.t.* ويجاول weejarawal

razor *n.* پل،نرچاه pal; naray chara

reach *v.t.* رسدل raseydal

react *v.i.* غبرونول ghbargoon khowal

reaction *n.* غبرون ghbargoon

reactionary *a.* پرشاتی،مخالف par sha tagay; mukhalif

read *v.t.* لوستل lostal

reader *n.* لوستونکی lostoonkay

readily *adv.* پهآسانتياسره pa asantya sara

readiness *n.* چمتووالی chamtoowalay

ready *a.* چمتو chamtoo

real *a.* حقيقي haqeeqee

realism *n.* رختياپاله rakhtyapala

realist *n.* رختياپال rakhtyapal

realistic *a.* حقيقي haqeeqee

reality *n.* حقيقت haqeeqat

realization *n.* ادراک idrak

realize *v.t.* درککول darak kawal

really *adv.* پهرختينيول pa rakhteenee dawl

realm *a.* سلطنت saltanat

ream *n.* د۵۰۰کاغذونوبنل da peenzo sawo kaghazoonu bandal

reap *v.t.* ربل reybal

reaper *n.* لوری،دلوماشين lawgaree; da law masheen

rear *n.* وروستبرخه wrostanay barkha

rear *v.t.* روزل،تربيهوركول rozal; tarbeeya warkawal

reason *n.* سبب،دليل sabab; daleel

reason *v.i.* دليلواندکول daleel wrandi kawal

reasonable *a.* معقول maqool

reassure *v.t.* بياتسلوركول bya tasal warkawal

rabate *n.* کمت kamakht

rebel *v.i.* سرغاویکول sar gharaway kawal

rebel *n.* سرغاوی sar gharaway

rebellion *n.* بغاوت baghawat

rebellious *a.* باغيانه baghyana

rebirth *n.* بیازون bya zeygoon

rebound *v.i.* برتهراستندل beyrta rastaneydal

rebound *n.* پرشاتؤ،برتهمړدنه par shatag; beyrta garzeydana

rebuff *n.* منعؤ،ردونه mana; radawana

rebuff *v.t.* منع کول mana kawal

rebuke *v.t.* ملامتول malamatawal

rebuke *n.* ملامتيا malamatya

recall *v.t.* برتهراغوتل beyrta raghokhtal

recall *n.* پهيادراوستنه pa yad rawastana

recede *v.i.* پهشاکدل pa sha keydal

receipt *n.* رسيد raseed

receive *v.t.* ترلاسه کول tar lasa kawal

receiver *n.* ترلاسه کوونکی tar lasa kawoonkay

recent *a.* تازه،نوی taza; naway

recently *adv.* لوختمخک lag wakht makhki

reception *n.* هراغلی،هر کلی kha raghalay; har kalay

receptive *a.* منونکی؛درک کوونکی manoonkay; darak kawoonkay

recess *n.* وقفه waqfa

recession *n.* پهشاتلنه pa sha tlana

recipe *n.* نسخه،فورمول nuskha; formool

recipient *n.* اخستونکی akheystoonkay

reciprocal *a.* متقابل،متناوب mutaqabal; mutanawab

reciprocate *v.t.* متقابلعمل کول mutaqabal amal kawal

recital *n.* راپور،مفصلبيان rapor; mufassil bayan

recitation *n.* لهيادهولستل la yada lostal

recite *v.t.* لهيادهويل la yada wayal

reckless *a.* بېپروا bey parwa

reckon *v.t.* شمرل،اندازهلول shmeyral; andaza lagawal

reclaim *v.t.* بیاراستندل bya rastaneydal

reclamation *n* بیاراستندنه؛زمکسمون bya rastaneydana; zmaksamoon

recluse *n.* يوازانسان yawazi insan

recognition *n.* پژندنه peyzhandana

recognize *v.t.* تصديق کول tasdeeq kawal

recoil *v.i.* پهشاتلل؛منعکس کدل pa sha tlal; munakkis keydal

recoil *adv.* پهشاتگ pa shatag

recollect *v.t.* دوباره راغوندول dobara raghondawal

recollection *n.* پهيادراوستنه pa yad rawastana

recommend *v.t.* سپارتنهورته کول sparakhtana warta kawal

recommendation *n.* سپارتنه،توصيه sparakhtana; tawseeya

recompense *v.t.* حسابسپينول heesab speenawal

recompense *n.* تاوان،عوض tawan; awaz

reconcile *v.t.* سره پخلا کول sara pukhla kawal

reconciliation *n.* پخلاينه pukhlayana

record *v.t.* ثبتول،پهيادراوستل sabtawal; pa yad rawastal record *n.* ثبت،يادت sabt; yadakht

recorder *n.* ثبتوونکى sabtawoonkay

recount *v.t.* لهسرهشمرل la sara shmeyral

recoup *v.t.* جبرانول jibranawal

recourse *n.* مراجعه murajia

recover *v.t.* برتهترلاسهکول beyrta tar lasa kawal

recovery *n.* تلافي talafee

recreation *n.* تفريح tafree

recruit *n.* نوىعسکر naway askar

recruit *v.t.* تازهانتخابول taza intikhabawal

rectangle *n.* مستطيل mustateel

rectangular *a.* مستطيلشکللرونکى mustateel shakal laroonkay

rectification *n.* اصلاح؛سموونکى isla; samowoonkay

rectify *v.i.* اصلاحکول isla kawal

rectum *n.* دکولماخريبرخه da koolmey akhiree barkha

recur *v.i.* ستندل staneydal

recurrence *n.* ستندنه staneydana

recurrent *a.* ستندونکى staneydoonkay

red *a.* سور soor

red *n.* رنسور soor rang

redden *v.t.* سورکول soor kawal

reddish *a.* سوربخن soorbakhan

redeem *v.t.* لهروخهخلاصول la garway sakha khlasawal

redemption *n.* لهروخهخلاصون la garway sakha khlasoon

redouble *v.t.* دوهچندهکول dwa chanda kawal

redress *v.t.* تداويکول tadawee kawal

redress *n* تداوي،تلافي tadawee; talafee

reduce *v.t.* کمول kamawal

reduction *n.* کمى kamay

redundance *n.* نهاستعمالدا na istimaleyda

redundant *a.* بکاره bey kara

reel *n.* رخ؛دعکاسدفيلمهرخ sarkh; da akasay da feelam sarkh

reel *v.i.* رخدل sarkheydal

refer *v.t.* مراجعهکول،برتهکتنهکول murajia kawal; beyrta katana kawal

referee *n.* لوبارى lobsaray

reference *n.* ورتلنه wartlana

referendum *n.* ولپوتنه tolpokhtana

refine *v.t.* تزکيهکول tazkeeya kawal

refinement *n.* تزکيه tazkeeya

refinery *n.* چلاى chanrzay

reflect *v.t.* منعکسکول munakis kawal

reflection *n.* انعکاس inikas

reflective *a.* انعکاسي inikasee

reflector *n.* منعکسجسم munakis jisam

reflex *n.* انعکاس inikas

reflex *a* منعکسشوى munakis shaway

reflexive *a* معکوس،معکوسفعل makoos; makoos fayl

reform *v.t.* سموئتيارامنتهکول samoontya ramanz ta kawal

reform *n.* سموئتيا samoontya

reformation *n.* اصلاح isla

reformatory *n.* اصلاح كوونكى۰isla kawoonkay

reformatory *a* اصلاح كوونكى isla kawoonkay

reformer *n.* سمونپال samoonpal

refrain *v.i.* اجتناب كول ijtinab kawal

refrain *n* اجتناب ijtinab

refresh *v.t.* تازه كول taza kawal

refreshment *n.* تازه كوونه taza kawana

refrigerate *v.t.* ساتل يخ yakh satal

refrigeration *n.* يخاوتازه ساتنه yakh aw taza satana

refrigerator *n.* يخچال yakhchal

refuge *n.* پناه؛ كوالتوب pana; kadwaltob

refugee *n.* پناه غوتونكى pana ghokhtoonkay

refulgence *n.* بریدنه breykheydana

refulgent *a.* پركند parkand

refund *v.t.* حساب برته وركول heesab beyrta warkawal

refund *n.* برته اداشوی حساب beyrta ada shaway heesab

refusal *n.* مننه نه na manana

refuse *v.t.* ردول radawal

refuse *n.* رد؛انكار rad; inkar

refutation *n.* نه مننه na manana

refute *v.t.* ردول radawal

regal *a.* پاچاهي pachahee

regard *v.t.* رعايت كول؛احترام كول riayat kawal; ehtiram kawal

regard *n.* رعايت؛احترام riayat; ehtiram

regenerate *v.t.* بياتوليدول؛بيازدل bya tawleedawal; bya zeygeydal

regeneration *n.* نوی توليد naway tawleed

regicide *n.* پاچاوژونكى pacha wazhoonkay

regime *n.* حكومتي نظام hukoomatee nizam

regiment *n.* غند؛دحكومت واكمني ghwand; da hukoomat wakmanee

regiment *v.t.* اداره كول؛پسوغنونو وشل idara kawal; pa so ghwandoono weyshal

region *n.* ناحيه naheeya

regional *a.* سيمه ييز seemayeez

register *n.* دثبت دفتر da sabt daftar

register *v.t.* په دفتر كښتول pa daftar ki sabtawal

registrar *n.* ثبتوونكى sabtawoonkay

registration *n.* نوم ليكنه noom leekana

registry *n.* دلاسوندونودثبت اداره da laswandoono da sabt idara

regret *v.i.* خپان كول khapgan kawal

regret *n* خپان؛پماني khapgan; pkheymanee

regular *a.* منظم munazzam

regularity *n.* قاعده؛تنظيم qayda; tanzeem

regulate *v.t.* له قانون سره برابرول la qanoon sara barabarawal

regulation *n.* تنظيم tanzeem

regulator *n.* برابروونكى barabarawoonkay

rehabilitate *v.t.* بیاودانول bya wadanawal

rehabilitation *n.* بیاودانتیا bya wadantya

rehearsal *n.* تکرار،تمرین takrar; tamreen

rehearse *v.t.* تمرین کول tamreen kawal

reign *v.i.* حکومت کول hukoomat kawal

reign *n* پاچاهي دوره pachahee dawra

reimburse *v.t.* برته ورکول beyrta warkawal

rein *n.* وا wagi

rein *v.t.* مخه یراول makha yi ragarzawal

reinforce *v.t.* واک وربل zwak warbakhal

reinforcement *n.* وربنه واک zwak warbakhana

reinstate *v.t.* لومني مقام ته ستنول loomranee maqam ta stanawal

reinstatement *n.* بحالي،برته ګمارنه bahalee; beyrta gumarana

reiterate *v.t.* یو کار تکرارول yaw kar takrarawal

reiteration *n.* د کار تکرار da kar takrar

reject *v.t.* ردول radawal

rejection *n.* ردونه radawana

rejoice *v.i.* خوشالیدل khoshaleydal

rejoin *v.t.* دوباره یو کدل dobara yaw keydal

rejoinder *n.* دفاعي واب difaee zawab

rejuvenate *v.t.* دوباره ژوانول dobara zwanawal

rejuvenation *n.* نوواني nawi zwanee

relapse *v.i.* زو حالت ته ستندل zor halat ta staneydal

relapse *n.* برته ستندنه beyrta staneydana

relate *v.t.* ارتباط لرل irtibat laral

relation *n.* ارتباط،نسبت irtibat; nisbat

relative *a.* مربوط marboot

relative *n.* خپلوان khpalwan

relax *v.t.* دمه کول dama kawal

relaxation *n.* دمه،ارام dama; aram

relay *n.* دمه کوونکی dama kawoonkay

relay *v.t.* پ ه اکلي وخت دمه کول pa takalee wakht dama kawal

release *v.t.* پرودل preykhodal

release *n* پرودنه preykhodana

relent *v.i.* نرمدل narmeydal

relentless *a.* سخت زی sakht zaray

relevance *n.* مناسبت munasibat

relevant *a.* مطابق،اوند mutabiq; arwand

reliable *a.* باوري bawaree

reliance *n.* توکل tawkal

relic *n.* لرغوني آثار larghonee asar

relief *n.* آرام aram

relieve *v.t.* آرام وربل aram warbakhal

religion *n.* دین deen

religious *a.* ديني deenee

relinquish *v.t.* خوشی کول khoshay kawal

relish *v.t.* خونداخستل khwand akheystal

relish *n* ذوق؛خوند zoq; khwand

reluctance *n.* ناخوي nakhwakhee

reluctant *a.* زتورى zratoray

rely *v.i.* لرل ا dad laral

remain *v.i.* پاته‌کدل pata keydal

remainder *n.* پاته‌شوى pata shaway

remains *n.* پاته‌شوي؛مي pata shawee; maree

remand *v.t.* دوباره‌زندانته‌استول dobara zandan ta astawal

remand *n* بیانیوونه bya neewana

remark *n.* پام؛یادوونه pam; yadawana

remark *v.t.* پامورته‌کول؛نظرورکول pam warta kawal; nazar warkawal

remarkable *a.* په‌زه‌پور pa zra pori

remedial *a.* درملنه‌کوونکی darmalana kawoonkay

remedy *n.* علاج ilaj

remedy *v.t* شفاوربل shafa warbakhal

remember *v.t.* په‌یادراوستل pa yad rawastal

remembrance *n.* حافظه hafiza

remind *v.t.* ورپه‌یادول warpayadawal

reminder *n.* په‌یادراوستونکی pa yad rawastoonkay

reminiscence *n.* خاطره؛یادار khatira; yadgar

reminiscent *a.* تذکري tazkiree

remission *n.* معافیت maafeeyat

remit *v.t.* معافول؛تخفیفول maafawal; takhfeefawal

remittance *n.* پسساستوونه peysey astawana

remorse *n.* افسوس afsos

remote *a.* لری leyri

removable *a.* دلرکدنو da leyri keydani war

removal *n.* له‌منه‌ونه la manza wrana

remove *v.t.* لمایه‌پورته‌کول la zaya porta kawal

remunerate *v.t.* تاوانورکول tawan warkawal

remuneration *n.* تاوانورکوونه tawan warkawana

remunerative *a.* په‌جبرانپوراوند pa jibran pori arwand

renaissance *n.* ادبي‌اوفرهني‌نوت adabee aw farhangee nawakht

render *v.t.* سهولت‌ورکول؛تحویلول sahoolat warkawal; tahweelawal

rendezvous *n.* ملاقات‌اوخبراتر mulaqat aw khabari atari

renew *v.t.* تازه‌کوال taza kawal

renewal *n.* تازه‌کوونه taza kawana

renounce *v.t.* انکارکول inkar kawal

renovate *v.t.* له‌نوي‌سره‌رغول la nawee sara raghawal

renovation *n.* سموونه samawana

renown *n.* شهرت shohrat

renowned *a.* مشهور mashahoor

rent *n.* کرایه karaya

rent *v.t.* کرایه‌کول karaya kawal

renunciation *n.* پروونه؛لاس‌تراخستنه preykhowana; las tri akheystana

repair *v.t.* تعمیرول tameerawal

repair *n.* رغوونه raghawana

raparable *a.* دتعميريدوو da tameereydo war

repartee *n.* حاضروابي hazir zawabee

repatriate *v.t.* خپل هوادته برته رارلدل khpal haywad ta beyrta ragarzeydal

repatriate *n* خپل هوادته برته ستندونکی khpal haywad ta staneydoonkay

repatriation *n.* خپل هوادته برته ستندنه khpal haywad ta beyrta staneydana

repay *v.t.* لهسره ادا كول la sara ada kawal

repayment *n.* لهسره ادايي la sara adaygee

repeal *v.t.* نه منل،لغوه كول na manal; lughwa kawal

repeal *n* نه مننه na manana

rcpeat *v.t.* خبره يا لوست تكرارول khabara ya lost takrarawal

repel *v.t.* پهشاتمبول pa sha tambawal

repellent *a.* مخنيوونکی makhneewoonkay

repellent *n* شونکی sharoonkay

repent *v.i.* پماندل pkheymaneydal

repentance *n.* پماني pkheymanee

repentant *a.* ار توبه tobagar

repercussion *n.* مخنيوی او وقايه makhneeway aw waqaya

repetition *n.* تكرار takrar

replace *v.t.* ای نيول zay neewal

replacement *n.* ای نيوونه،تعويض zay neewana; taweez

replenish *v.t.* لهسره زرمه كول la sara zeyrma kawal

replete *a.* ترزرموک tar zeyrmo dak

replica *n.* نسخه،نقل nuskha; naqal

reply *v.i.* واب ورکول zawab warkawal

reply *n* واب،دفاع zawab; difa

report *v.t.* راپرور كول rapor warkawal

report *n.* راپور،خبر rapor; khabar

reporter *n.* خبريال khabaryal

repose *n.* استراحت istirahat

repose *v.i.* استراحت كول istirahat kawal

repository *n.* زرمتون zeyramtoon

represent *v.t.* بيانول bayanawal

representation *n.* معرفي كوونه marifee kawana

representative *n.* نماينده numayanda

representative *a.* نماينلي کوونکی numayindagee kawoonkay

repress *v.t.* پهشاتمبول pa sha tambawal

repression *n.* جلويري jilogeeree

reprimand *n.* رنه ratana

reprimand *v.t.* رل ratal

reprint *v.t.* بياچاپول bya chapawal

reprint *n.* دوباره چاپ dobara chap

reproach *v.t.* شرمول،رسواكول sharmawal; ruswa kawal

reproach *n.* ملامتي malamatee

reproduce *v.t.* بياتوليدول bya tawleedawal

reproduction *n* بياتوليدوونه bya tawleedawana

reproductive *a.* زوونکی zeygowoonkay

reproof *n.* غندنه ghandana

reptile *n.* رمک sarmakhkay

republic *n.* جمهوري jamhooree

republican *a.* ولسپاله woolaspala

republican *n.* ولسپال woolaspal

repudiate *v.t.* انکارکول inkar kawal

repudiation *n.* انکار inkar

repugnance *n.* نفرت nafrat

repugnant *a.* مخالف mukhalif

repulse *v.t.* دفع کول dafa kawal

repulse *n.* تمبوونه tambawana

repulsion *n.* تمبوونه tambawana

repulsive *a.* تمبوونکی tambawoonkay

reputation *n.* هنوم،اعتبار kha noom; aytibar

repute *v.t.* هنوملرل kha noom laral

repute *n.* آبرو abroo

request *v.t.* تقاضاکول taqaza kawal

request *n.* تقاضا taqaza

requiem *n.* دجنازلمونز da janazey lmoonz

require *v.t.* اتیاورتهلرل artya warta laral

requirement *n.* شرط،اتیا shart; artya

requisite *a.* اینشرط areen shart

requiste *n.* احتیاج ehteeyaj

requisition *n.* مصادره masadira

requisition *v.t.* مصادره کول masadira kawal

requite *v.t.* بدلهورکول badla warkawal

rescue *v.t.* نجات،ورکول nijat warkawal

rescue *n.* نجات،خلاصون nijat; khlasoon

research *v.i.* شنلاوسپل shanal aw sparal

research *n.* شننهاوسپنه shanana aw sparana

resemblance *n.* یورنوالی yawrangwalay

resemble *v.t.* یورنوالیلرل yawrangwalay laral

resent *v.t.* ناخويهکارهکول na khwakhee khkara kawal

resentment *n.* خوابدي khwabadee

reservation *n.* زانسرهخونديساتنه zan sara khwandee satana

reserve *v.t.* زانسرهخونديساتل،زرمه کول zan sara khwandee satal; zeyrga kawal

rservoir *n.* داوبوزرمه da obo zeyrma

reside *v.i.* استونهلرل astogna laral

residence *n.* مشتای meysht zay

resident *a.* استونيپوراوند astogni pori arwand

resident *n.* اوسدونکی oseydoonkay

residual *a.* پاتهشوی pata shaway

residue *n.* پاتهشوبرخه pata shaway barkha

resign *v.t.* زانشاتهکول zan sha ta kawal

resignation *n.* استعفا istifa

resist *v.t.* مخهپکول makha dap kawal

resistance *n.* مقاومت maqawmat

resistant *a.* مقاوم،پایند maqawam; payand

resolute *a.* ينعزمه؛سرپه‌لاس teeng azama; sar pa las

resolution *n.* عزمرندوونه؛قرارداد azam sargandawana; qarardad

resolve *v.t.* حل‌کول hal kawal

resonance *n.* دغانازه da ghag angaza

resonant *a.* انازه‌کوونکی angaza kawoonkay

resort *v.i.* پناه‌ورول pana warwaral

resort *n* دتفریح‌ای da tafree zay

resound *v.i.* منعکس‌کدل munakkis keydal

resource *n.* وسیله waseela

resourceful *a.* چاره‌ساز chara saz

respect *v.t.* درناوی‌کول dranaway kawal

respect *n.* احترام ehtiram

respectful *a.* محترم muhtaram

respective *a.* خصوصي khasoosee

respiration *n.* کنه‌ساه sa kakhana

respire *v.i.* ساه‌اخستل sa akeystal

resplendent *a.* لاند zaland

respond *v.i.* واب‌ورکول zawab warkawal

respondent *n.* واب‌ورکوونکی zawab warkawoonkay

response *n.* واب zawab

responsibility *n.* ذمه‌واري zima waree

responsible *a.* ذمه‌وار zima war

rest *v.i.* سملاستل samlastal

rest *n* آرام aram

restaurant *n.* خونای khwaranzay

restive *a.* نارامه narama

restoration *n.* بیارغاوونه bya raghawana

restore *v.t.* اصلاح‌کول isla kawal

restrain *v.t.* مخه‌پ‌کول makha dap kawal

restrict *v.t.* محدودول mahdoodawal

restriction *n.* ب‌نلت bandakht

restrictive *a.* محدودوونکی mahdoodawoonkay

result *v.i.* نتیجه‌ورکول nateeja warkawal

result *n.* نتیجه nateeja

resume *v.t.* بیاپیلول bya paylawal

resume *n.* ادامه idama

resumption *n.* بیاپیلوونه bya paylawana

resurgence *n.* بیاراژوندی‌کدنه bya razhwanday keydana

resurgent *a.* بیاراژوندی‌شوی bya razhwanday shaway

retail *v.t.* په‌پرچون‌ل‌پلورل pa parchoon dawl ploral

retail *n.* پرچون‌پلورنه parchoon plorana

retail *adv.* په‌وومله pa so so zala

retail *a* پرچون‌پلورونکی parchoon ploroonkay

retailer *n.* دپرچون‌سودار da parchoon sawdagar

retain *v.t.* ان‌سره‌ساتل zan sara satal

retaliate *v.i.* تاوان‌ورکول tawan warkawal

retaliation *n.* تاوان‌ورکوونه tawan warkawana

retard *v.t.* سوکه‌کول sawka kawal

retardation *n.* سوکه؛پوونه sawka; pasawana

retention *n.* ساتنه satana

retentive *a.* ساتونکی satoonkay

reticence *n.* خاموشي khamoshee

reticent *a.* خاموش khamosh

retina *n.* دسترشبکیه da stargey shabkeeya

retinue *n.* ملازم؛نوکر mulazim; nawkar

retire *v.i.* وناستیکدل got nastay keydal

retirement *n.* پهوناستی pa got nastay

retort *v.t.* متقابلوابورکول mutaqabil zawab warkawal

retort *n.* متقابلواب mutaqabil zawab

retouch *v.t.* لاسپکوهل las paki wahal

retrace *v.t.* وربرباندبرتهتلل warbandi beyrta tlal

retread *v.t.* زانشاتهکول zan sha ta kawal

retread *n.* زشا shatag

retreat *v.i.* پرشاتلل par sha tlal

retrench *v.t.* لتونهکمول lagakhtoona kamawal

retrenchment *n.* کمت؛سپما kamakht; sapma

retrieve *v.t.* برتهاخستل beyrta akheystal

retrospect *n.* ترمهالتهستندا teyr mahal ta staneyda

retrospection *n.* ترمهالتهنظراچوونه teyr mahal ta nazar achawana

retrospective *a.* تروپوپوراوند teyro peykho pori arwand

return *v.i.* ستندل staneydaı

return *n.* راړدنه؛بدله ragarzeydana; badla

revel *v.i.* عیاشيکول ayashee kawal

revel *n.* عیاشي ayashee

revelation *n.* مکاشفه makashifa

reveller *n.* عیاش ayash

revelry *n.* خوی khwakhee

revenge *v.t.* کساتاخیستل kasat akheystal

revenge *n.* کسات؛غچ kasat; ghach

revengeful *a.* کرکجن krakjan

revenue *n.* ماليه maleeya

revere *v.t.* احترامکول ehtiram kawal

reverence *n.* لواوی lwaraway

reverend *a.* داحترامو da ehtiram war

reverent *a.* پاسلرونکی pas laronki

reverential *a.* درناوی dranaway

reverie *n.* دورخوب da wrazi khob

reversal *n.* معکوسوونه makoosawana

reverse *a.* ضد؛معکوس zid; makoos

reverse *n* پهکدنه؛شکست pa sat keydana; shakast

reverse *v.t.* پهکدل pa sat keydana

reversible *a.* پهکدونکی pa sat keydoonkay

revert *v.i.* رجوعکول rujoo kawal

review *v.t.* بیاکتل bya katal

review *n* بیاکتنه bya katana

revise *v.t.* اصلاحکول isla kawal

revision *n.* اصلاح؛نوینظر isla; naway nazar

revival *n.* بیاراژوندیکدنه bya razhwanday keydana

revive *v.i.* بیاراژوندیکدل bya razhwanday keydal

revocable *a.* دفسخ کوونو war da faskh kawoni war

revocation *n.* فسخ کوونه faskh kawana

revoke *v.t.* فسخ کول faskh kawal

revolt *v.i.* پاون کول pasoon kawal

revolt *n.* پاون pasoon

revolution *n.* پاون pasoon

revolutionary *a.* انقلابي inqilabee

revolutionary *n* انقلابي وی inqilabee wagaray

revolve *v.i.* چورلدل choorleydal

revolver *n.* رخندوی sarkhandoy

reward *n.* اجر؛جزا ajar; jaza

reward *v.t.* اجرورکول ajar warkawal

rhetoric *n.* دبدیع علم da badee ilam

rhetorical *a.* فصاحت او بلاغت fasahat aw balaghat

rheumatic *a.* دبندونو په درداخته کس da bandoono pa dard akhta kas

rheumatism *n.* دبندونو ددردرنز da bandoono da dard ranz

rhinoceros *n.* کرګدن kargadan

rhyme *n.* قافیه qafeeya

rhyme *v.i.* قافیه جوول qafeeya jorawal

rhymester *n.* قافیه سازي qafeeya sazee

rhythm b. وزني هم ham waznee

rhythmic *a.* موزون؛هموزن mawzoon; ham wazan

rib *n.* پوة pokhtay

ribbon *n.* پټانه patay; taranga

rice *n.* وریژ wareezhi

rich *a.* بای baday

riches *n.* شتمني shtamanee

richness *a.* شتمني shtamanee

rick *n.* دخش خش غ da khash khash ghag

rickets *n.* دهوکي دپوستوالي رنز da hadookee da postwalee ranz

rickety *a.* نرمت narmakht

rickshaw *n.* کوچنی درپایلرونکي ای koochnay drey payey laroonkay gaday

rid *v.t.* آزادول azadawal

riddle *n.* غلبل ghalbeyl

riddle *v.i.* غلبیلول ghalbeylawal

ride *v.t.* سپردل spareydal

ride *n* سپرل sparlay

rider *n.* چلوونکي؛سپور chalowoonkay; spor

ridge *n.* دغونیو یاغرونو ل da ghondyo ya ghroono laray

ridicule *v.t.* ورپورخندل warpori khandal

ridicule *n.* مسخر maskharey

ridiculous *a.* لەمسخروک la maskharo dak

rifle *v.t.* پەتوندپل pa tonday palatal

rifle *n* ټوپک topak

rift *n.* غووالی ghoswalay

right *a.* نغ؛سم neygh; sam

right *adv* پەسمەتوه pa sama toga

right *n* خی لاس؛سم کار khay las; sam kar

right *v.t.* سمدل sameydal

righteous *a.* پرهزار parhayzgar

rigid *a.* سخت sakht

rigorous *a.* سخت sakht

rigour *n.* شخوالی shakhwalay

rim *n.* ژ zhay

ring *n.* ک karay

ring *v.t.* زنوهل zang wahal

ringlet *n.* کيزهنه kareeza nakha

ringworm *n.* دپوستکييوهچاسيساري
ناروغي da postakee yawa
chanrasee saree naroghee

rinse *v.t.* پهاوبووينل pa obo
weenzal

riot *n.* بلوا balwa

riot *v.t.* بلواکول balwa kawal

rip *v.t.* غوول ghosawal

ripe *a* پوخ pokh

ripen *v.i.* پخدل pakheydal

ripple *n.* په sapa

ripple *v.t.* پهپداکول sapa payda
kawal

rise *v.* راختل rakhatal

rise *n.* راختنه rakhatana

risk *v.t.* خطرسرهمخامخول khatar
sara makhamakhawal

risk *n.* خطر khatar

risky *a.* خطرناک khatarnak

rite *n.* مذهبيتشريفات mazhabee
tashreefat

ritual *n.* دعبادتمراسم da ibadat
marasim

ritual *a.* دعبادتمراسموپوراوند da
ibadat marasimo pori arwand

rival *n.* رقيب raqeeb

rival *v.t.* رقابتکول raqabat kawal

rivalry *n.* رقابت raqabat

river *n.* سيند seend

rivet *n.* رپ reypat

rivet *v.t.* نلسره sara gandal

rivulet *n.* وياله wyala

road *n.* سکک sarak

roam *v.i.* ـشتکول gasht kawal

roar *n.* غوریدنه ghoreydana

roar *v.i.* غوریدل ghoreydal

roast *v.t.* وریتول wreetawal

roast *a* وریتشوی wreet shaway

roast *n* وریتهشوغوه wreeta shawi
ghwakha

rob *v.t.* لوبل lootal

robber *n.* شوکمار shookmar

robbery *n.* شوکه shooka

robe *n.* اوداواوزادکميس oogad aw
azad kamees

robe *v.t.* اوداوازادکميساغوستل
oogad aw azad kamees
aghostal

robot *n.* ماشينيسی masheenee
saray

robust *a.* صحتمن؛قوي sayhat
man; qawee

rock *v.t.* هغهخواـخواخوـدل hagha
khwa deykhwa khozeydal

rock *n.* کانئ kanray

rocket *n.* توغندی toghanday

rod *n.* ميله؛لکه meela; lakara

rodent *n.* شخوندوهونکی shkhwand
wahoonkay

roe *n.* يواروپايیکوچنغره yaw
aroopayee koochnay gharsa

rogue *n.* رذيلسی razeel saray

roguery *n.* رذالت razalat

roguish *a.* چلباز chalbaz

role n. وظيفه؛رول wazeefa; rol

roll *n.* تاوشویيز taw shaway seez

roll *v.i.* چورلدل choorleydal

roll-call *n.* حاضريـاخستنه haziree
akheystana

roller *n.* ويندوی khwayandoy

romance *n.* رومان؛دمينکيسه roman; da meeni keesa

romantic *a.* افسانهوله afsana dawla

romp *v.i.* پهمينهاوشورماشورسرهلوبدل pa meena aw shor mashor sara lobeydal

romp *n.* غالمغالغلدنه ghalmaghal zghaleydana

rood *n.* صليب saleeb

roof *n.* چت chat

roof *v.t.* چتجوول chat jorawal

rook *n.* تورکارغه tor kargha

rook *v.t.* دوکهکول doka kawal

room *n.* خونه khoona

roomy *a.* ځایلرونکی؛هوادار zay laroonkay; hawadar

roost *n.* دمرغانوﺎله da marghano zala

roost *v.i.* شپهترول؛ځایورکول shpa teyrawal; zay warkawal

root *n.* ريه reykha

root *v.i.* ريغول reykhi ghazawal

rope *n.* پی paray

rope *v.t.* پهپۍتل pa paree taral

rosary *n.* تسبيح tasbee

rose *n.* ﻻب gulab

roseate *a.* ﻟورين؛ﻟوزمه gulwareen; gulwazma

rostrum *n.* ممبر؛درﯦ mimbar; dareez

rosy *a.* ﻟورين gulwareen

rot *n.* خرابدا kharabeyda

rot *v.i.* خرابدل؛ورستدل kharabeydal; wrusteydal

rotary *a.* چورلدونکی choorleydoonkay

rotate *v.i.* چورلدل choorleydal

rotation *n.* چورلدنه choorleydana

rote *n.* رودتیا rogdtya

rouble *n.* دروسيسکه da rooseeyi sika

rough *a.* الوژور lwar zhawar

round *a.* ردبول gard; golay

round *adv.* هرلورته har lori ta

round *n.* ک؛دوره karay; dawra

round *v.t.* ردول؛راغونول gardawal; raghondawal

rouse *v.i.* پههجانراپاﻟدل pa hayjan rapaseydal

rout *v.t.* بشپهماتورکول bashpara mati warkawal

rout *n* کامﻟهماﺕ kamila mati

route *n.* تلوری tagloray

routine *n.* ورﺰنهچار wrazanay chari

routine *a* رودﯦز rogdeez

rove *v.i.* سرهتاوول sara tawawal

rover *n.* رﻧد garzand

row *n.* ليکه leeka

row *v.t.* دکتراشپلوهل da kakhtay rashpeyl wahal

row *n* لفظیشخه lafzee shkhara

row *n.* دکتراشپل da kakhtay rashpeyl

rowdy *a.* فريادي faryadee

royal *a.* شاهي shahee

royalist *n.* ولواکپال tolwakpal

royalty *n.* پاچاهي pachahee

rub *v.t.* سولول soolawal

rub *n* سولوونه soolawana

rubber *n.* وچکپاک wachkakhpak

rubbish *n.* ناولی nawalay

rubble *n.* دكانوبرويوغوذ da kanro dabaro yaw ghond

ruby *n.* ياقوت yaqoot

rude *a.* بتربيه bey tarbeeyey

rudiment *n.* سرچينه sar cheena

rudimentary *a.* بنسيز bansateez

rue *v.t.* كول افسوس afsos kawal

rueful *a.* غمجن ghamjan

ruffian *n.* بشرفه bey sharafa

ruffle *v.t.* ناهوارول nahawarawal

rug *n.* غالٱ ghalay

rugged *a.* ناهوار nahawar

ruin *n.* ويجاي weejaree

ruin *v.t.* ويجاول weejarawal

rule *n.* واك;حكومت wak; hookoomat

rule *v.t.* حكومتكول hookoomat kawal

ruler *n.* واكمن wakman

ruling *n.* حكم hukam

rum *n.* اداريچاروٱكى idaree charwakay

rum *a* منظم munazzam

rumble *v.i.* غومبدل ghroombeydal

rumble *n.* غمبهار ghrambahar

ruminant *a.* شخوندوهونكى shkhwand wahoonkay

ruminant *n.* شخوندوهونكىٱروى shkhwand wahoonkay sarway

ruminate *v.i.* شخوندوهل shkhwand wahal

rumination *n.* شخوندوهنه shkhwand wahana

rummage *v.i.* لٱوسپل seyral aw sparal

rummage *n* نٱوسپنه seyrana aw sparana

rummy *n.* دپتويوللوبه da pato yaw dawl loba

rumour *n.* اوازه awaza

rumour *v.t.* اوٱزخپرول awazey khparawal

run *v.i.* منډهوهل manda wahal

run *n.* منډه manda

rung *n.* دپودستكي da poray dastakee

runner *n.* غاستونكى zghastoonkay

rupee *n.* دهنداوپاكستانسكه da hind aw pakistan sika

rupture *n.* يروٱلى seeriwalay

rupture *v.t.* يركول seeri kawal

rural *a.* كليوٱل kaleewal

ruse *n.* چل;چلباز chal; chalbaz

rush *n.* نٱپىاووحركت nasapee aw gadwad harakat

rush *v.t.* جنجالجوډل;تصادمكول janjal joreydal; tasadum kawal

rush *n* يوولونه yaw dawl wana

rust *n.* زنگ zang

rust *v.i* زنگوهل zang wahal

rustic *a.* ساده;خندونى sada; khandoonay

rustic *n* كليوٱلسى kaleewal saray

rusticate *v.t.* كليوٱلژوندكول kaleewal zhwand kawal

rustication *n.* كليوٱليبهوركوونه kaleewalee banra warkawana

rusticity *n.* زنوهنه zang wahana

rusty *a.* زنوهلى zang wahalay

rut *n.* پهمكهدرخنه pa zmaka da sarkh nakha

ruthless *a.* برحمه bey rahma

rye *n.* جودر؛تورغنم joodar; tor ghanam

S

sabbath *n.* دشنبور da shambey wraz

sabotage *n.* تخریب takhreeb

sabotage *v.t.* تخریبول takhreebawal

sabre *n.* درنه‌توره drana toora

sabre *v.t.* په‌توره‌وهل pa toora wahal

saccharin *n.* یوه‌قندی‌ماده yawa qandee mada

saccharine *a.* قندلرونکی qand laroonkay

sack *n.* بوجه bojay

sack *v.t.* له‌دندخه‌خارجول la dandi sakha kharijawal

sacrament *n.* دینی‌او‌مذهبی‌دود deenee aw mazhabee dood

sacred *a.* مقدس muqaddas

sacrifice *n.* قربانی qurbanee

sacrifice *v.t.* قربانول qurbanawal

sacrificial *a.* فداکارانه fidakarana

sacrilege *n.* دمقدسویزونوغلا da muqadaso seezoonu ghla

sacrilegious *a.* دمقدسویزونوغلا کوونکی da muqadaso seezoonu ghla kawoonkay

sacrosanct *a.* مقدس؛نابدلدونکی muqaddas; na badleydoonkay

sad *a.* خپه khapa

sadden *v.t.* خپه‌کول khapa kawal

saddle *n.* زین zeen

saddle *v.t.* زین‌یاکته‌ایودل zeen ya kata eekhodal

sadism *n.* دبرحم‌جنسي‌مینه da bey rahmay jinsee meena

sadist *n.* په‌بی‌رحم‌سره‌جنسي‌خوند اخستونکی pa bey rahmay sara jinsee khwand akheystoonkay

safe *a.* محفوظ mahfooz

safe *n.* تجر tajaray

safeguard *n.* ساتندوی satandoy

safety *n.* امنیت amneeyat

saffron *n.* زعفران zafran

saffron *a* دزعفران‌په‌شان da zafran pa shan

sagacious *a.* هوښیار hookhyar

sagacity *n.* فراست firasat

sage *n.* یوول‌بوی yaw dawl bootay

sage *a.* هوښیار hookhyar

sail *n.* په‌کښ‌سفر pa kakhtay ki safar

sail *v.i.* کښ‌کتلل kakhtay ki tlal

sailor *n.* کښ‌چلوونکی kakhtay chalawoonkay

saint *n.* ولي؛بزر walee; buzurg

saintly *a.* دیندار deendar

sake *n.* لپاره؛حق lapara; haq

salable *a.* دلیلام‌و da leelam war

salad *n.* سلاته salata

salary *n.* تنخوا؛اجوره tankha; ajoora

sale *n.* پلورنه plorana

salesman *n.* پلورونکی ploroonkay

salient *a.* مهم‌ر deyr muhim

saline *a.* مالین malgeen

salinity *n.* تریووالی treewwalay

saliva *n.* لا lari

sally *n.* نالپاوچکفعاليت nasapee aw chatak faaleeyat

sally *v.i.* غورځكول ghorzang kawal

saloon *n.* لويه‌خونه loya khoona

salt *n.* ماله malga

salt *v.t* ماله‌پرموډل malga pri mokhal

salty *a.* مالين malgeen

salutary *a.* مثبت‌اغزلرونکی musbat agheyz laroonkay

salutation *n.* سلام‌دعا salam dua

salute *v.t.* سلام‌اچول salam achawal

salute *n* سلام،درناوی salam; dranaway

salvage *n.* دکتیادمال‌یادان‌ژغورنه da kakhtay ya da mal ya da zan zhghorana

salvage *v.t.* دکتاومال‌اوان‌ژغورل da kakhtay aw mal aw zan zhghoral

salvation *n.* خلاصون khlasoon

same *a.* شان یو yaw shan

sample *n.* نمونه namoona

sample *v.t.* بله‌آزمویل beylga azmoyal

sanatorium *n.* دنري‌رنددرملنای da naree ranz da darmalani zay

sanctification *n.* تقدیس taqdees

sanctify *v.t.* تقدیسول taqdeesawal

sanction *n.* بندیز bandeyz

sanction *v.t.* بندزلول bandeyz lagawal

sanctity *n.* پرهزاري parheyzgaree

sanctuary *n.* عبادتای ibadatzay

sand *n.* شه shaga

sandal *n.* سپکپل spaki saplay

sandalwood *n.* سپین‌صندل speen sandal

sandwich *n.* دکوچ‌سلاتواوخوراکي مواډوخه‌جوه‌وه da koch salatoaw khorakee mawado sakha jora doday

sandwich *v.t.* ددوه‌شیانومن‌کایوډل da dwa shayano manz ki eekhodal

sandy *a.* شلنه shaglana

sane *a.* رم‌روغ rogh ramat

sanguine *a.* وینه‌ییز weenayeez

sanitary *a.* روغتیاي roghtyayee

sanity *n.* روغتیا roghtya

sap *n.* نباتي‌شیره nabatee sheera

sap *v.t.* شیره‌تراستل sheera tri eystal

sapling *n.* نیال،قلمه nyal; qalma

sapphire *n.* شین‌یاقوت sheen yaqoot

sarcasm *n.* پغور peyghor

sarcastic *a.* کنایي kinayee

sardonic *a.* پغوروزمه peyghor wazma

satan *n.* شطان shaytan

satchel *n.* دووني‌دکتابونوکوه da khowanzee da keetabono kasora

satellite *n.* سپومک،پلیوني spogmakay; pleewanay

satiable *a.* قانع‌کدونکی qanay keydoonkay

satiate *v.t.* قانع‌کول qanay kawal

satiety *n.* قناعت،مت qanaat; marakht

satire *n.* غندنلیک ghandanleek

satirical *a.* طنزیه tanzeeya

satirist *n.* هجولیکونکی hijoleekoonkay

satirize *v.t.* مسخره‌كول maskhara kawal

satisfaction *n.* رضايت rizayat

satisfactory *a.* قانع؛رضايي qanay; rizayee

satisfy *v.t.* راضي‌كول razee kawal

saturate *v.t.* مشبوع‌كول mashboo kawal

saturation *n.* اشباع ashba

Saturday *n.* دشنبور da shambey wraz

sauce *n.* ساس sas

saucer *n.* نالبكى nalbakay

saunter *v.t.* چكروهل chakar wahal

savage *a.* وحشي wahshee

savage *n* وحشي‌ناورياانسان wahshee zanawar ya insan

savagery *n.* وحشت wahshat

save *v.t.* ژغورل zghoral

save *prep* چ دا مر magar da chi

saviour *n.* ژغورندوى zghorandoy

savour *n.* ذايقه zayqa

savour *v.t.* مزه‌اخستل maza akheystal

saw *n.* اره ara

saw *v.t.* په‌اره‌ريبل pa ara reybal

say *v.t.* ويل wayal

say *n.* وينا؛خبره wayna; khabara

scabbard *n.* دتورپو da toori pokh

scabies *n.* دخارت‌رنز da kharakht ranz

scaffold *n.* دغلودساز‌اچوبندي da ghlo da saza chawbandee

scale *n.* تله؛پيمانه tala; paymana

scale *v.t.* ناپول؛وزن‌كول napawal; wazan kawal

scalp *n* كوپر kopray

scamper *v.i* په‌بيسره‌ته‌دل pa beeri sara takhteydal

scamper *n* چكه‌تته chataka teykhta

scan *v.t.* گام‌په‌گام gam pa gam seyral

scandal *n* رسوايي ruswayee

scandalize *v.t.* رسواكول ruswa kawal

scant *a.* لږكم lag; kam

scanty *a.* ناكافي nakafee

scapegoat *n.* فديه feedeeya

scar *n* دتپ‌ى‌ادا غ da tap zay ya dagh

scar *v.t.* داغ‌لول dagh lagawal

scarce *a.* كمياب kamyab

scarcely *adv.* په‌مشكل‌سره pa mushkil sara

scarcity *n.* قلت qilat

scare *n.* ترهه tarha

scare *v.t.* ترهول tarhawal

scarf *n.* دوتانوپولودسمال da weykhtano patawalo dasmal

scatter *v.t.* وشنل‌باى‌پماى‌كول weyshnal; zay pa zay kawal

scavenger *n.* لاشخورناورياامارغه lashkhor zanawar ya margha

scene *n.* منظره manzara

scenery *n.* منظر manzar

scenic *a.* كلامنظره‌لرونكى khkuli manzara laroonkay

scent *n.* عطر atar

scent *v.t.* معطركول moattar kawal

sceptic *n.* دبدويندفلسفپليوني da badwayani da falsafey pleewanay

sceptical *a.* شكمن shakman

scepticism *n.* شكمني shakmanee

schedule *n.* مهالوېش mahalweysh

schedule *v.t.* مهالوېش کوخت ورکول mahalweysh ki wakht warkawal

scheme *n.* تدبیر؛طرحه tadbeer; tarha

scheme *v.i.* تدبیرجوړول tadbeer jorawal

schism *n.* باتفاقي bey itifaqee

scholar *n.* ادیب؛محقق adeeb; muhaqqiq

scholarly *a.* عالمانه alimana

scholarship *n.* زده کولپاره مالي مرسته؛ تحصیل zdakro lapara malee mrasta; tehseel

scholastic *a.* استادانه ustadana

school *n.* ووني khowanzay

science *n.* دساینس علم da sayins ilam

scientific *a.* ساینسي sayinsee

scientist *n.* ساینس پوه sayins poh

scintillate *v.i.* سپرغبادول sparghay badawal

scintillation *n.* برېدنه breykheydana

scissors *n.* قیچي qeechee

scoff *n.* طنز tanz

scoff *v.i.* طنزکول tanz kawal

scold *v.t.* کنل کول kanzal kawal

scooter *n.* ددوه پایو موړسایکل da dwa payo motarsaykal

scope *n.* مفاداوه mafad aw gata

scorch *v.t.* په سطح سوول pa sata swazawal

score *n.* شمېره؛کرخه shmeyra; karkha

score *v.t.* شمرل shmeyral

scorer *n.* شمرونکی shmeyroonkay

scorn *n.* تحقیر tehqeer

scorn *v.t.* سپک ل spak ganral

scorpion *n.* لم laram

Scot *n.* اسکالنډيوی skatlandee wagaray

scotch *a.* دمخنیويوسیله da makhneewee waseela

scotch *n.* درز؛چاود darz; chawd

scot-free *a.* له مالیخه معاف la maleeyey sakha maf

scoundrel *n.* لوچك lochak

scourge *n.* متروکه matrooka

scourge *v.t.* وېجاول weejarawal

scout *n* ساروی sargaray

scout *v.i* ساروي کول sargaree kawal

scowl *v.i.* تروه ننیول trawa tanda neewal

scowl *n.* ننه تروه trawa tanda

scramble *v.i.* پەزحمت سره پر مخ تلل pa zehmat sara par makh tlal

scramble *n* په لاسو او پوتلنه pa laso aw pkho tlana

scrap *n.* خوزاوخوشایه khasozey aw khoshaya

scratch *n.* ړدنه؛نشت gareydana; nasht

scratch *v.t.* ړدل؛ړول gareydal; garawal

scrawl *v.t.* په بیه لیکل pa beera leekal

scrawl *n* ناوړه لیکنه nawara leekana

scream *v.i.* چغه هل cheyghey wahal

scream *n* چغه سوره cheygha soora

screen *n.* دسینمایاتلویزیون پرده da seenama ya talweezyon parda

screen *v.t.* پهپردسرهپول pa pardey sara pokhal

screw *n.* پچ peych

screw *v.t.* پهپچنلول pa peych nakhlawal

scribble *v.t.* پهبیهلیکل pa beera leekal

scribble *n.* بداونوهلیکنه bad aw nawara leekana

script *n.* مسوده musawwida

scripture *n.* اسمانيکتاب asmanee keetab

scroll *n.* طوماريحرکت toomaree harakat

scrutinize *v.t.* کرهکتنهکول kara katana kawal

scrutiny *n.* کرهکتنه kara katana

scuffle *n.* مزاحمت؛شورماشور muzahimat; shormashor

scuffle *v.i.* مزاحمتکول muzahimat kawal

sculptor *n.* مجسمهجووونکی mujassima jorawoonkay

sculptural *a.* مجسمهوله mujassima dawla

sculpture *n.* مجسمه mujassima

scythe *n.* لور lor

scythe *v.t.* پهلورسرهریبل pa lor sara reybal

sea *n.* سمندر samandar

seal *n.* سمندريخو samandaree khoog

seal *n.* مهربابه muhur; tapa

seal *v.t.* تلبندول taral; bandawal

seam *n.* دجامودرز da jamo darz

seam *v.t.* درزونهبندول darzoona bandawal

seamy *a.*

search *n.* تفتیش؛پلنه tafteesh; palatana

search *v.t.* پلل palatal

season *n.* موسم mosam

season *v.t.* مالهپرمول malga pri mokhal

seasonable *a.* دموسمسرهسم da mosam sara sam

seasonal *a.* موسمي mosamee

seat *n.* چوک chawkay

seat *v.t.* چوکورکول chawkay warkawal

secede *v.i.* ورخموهکدل warsakha gokha keydal

secession *n.* بیلدا byaleyda

secessionist *n.* بلتونپال beyltoonpal

seclude *v.t.* جلاکول jala kawal

secluded *a.* جلاشوی jala shaway

seclusion *n.* جلاتوب jalatob

second *a.* دویم dwayam

second *n* ثانیه saneeya

second *v.t.* یودندخهعارضيبلدندتهاول yaw dandi sakha arzee bali dandi ta arawal

secondary *a.* ثانوي؛ددویمدرجه sanwee; da dwayami darajey

secrecy n. رازساتنه raz satana

secret *a.* خفیه khoofeeya

secret *n.* راز raz

secretariat *e* n. ددفتريکارمندانو پلاویيااداریهای da daftaree karmandano plaway ya idaree zay

secretary *n.* منشي munshee

secrete *v.t.* رازساتل raz satal

secretion *n.* رازساتنه raz satana

secretive *a.* خفيه khoofeeya

sect *n.* مسلک maslak

sectarian *a.* مسلكي maslakee

section *n.* برخه barkha

sector *n.* ناحيه naheeya

secure *a.* محفوظ mehfooz

secure *v.t.* حفاظت كول heefazat kawal

security *n.* امنيت amneeyat

sedan *n.* كجاوه kajawa

sedate *a.* نرماوينه naram aw teeng

sedate *v.t.* دتسكين درمل وركول da taskeen darmal warkawal

sedative *a.* آرامبونكى aram bakhoonkay

sedative *n* مسكن درمل musakkan darmal

sedentary *a.* كورناستى kornastay

sediment *n.* شنشوب shanshob

sedition *n.* بلوا balwa

seditious *a.* بلواګرانه balwagarana

seduce *n.* بدكار badkar

seduction *n.* بدكاري badkaree

seductive *a* بدكارانه badkarana

see *v.t.* كتل،ليدل katal; leedal

seed *n.* زى zaray

seed *v.t.* زي شيندل zaree sheendal

seek *v.t.* پناه ورول pana warwral

seem *v.i.* پەنظرراتلل pa nazar ratlal

seemly *a.* پەمناسب ول pa munasib dawl

seep *v.i.* رالدل rasaseydal

seer *n.* ليدونكى leedoonkay

seethe *v.i.* اشلدل eysheydal

segment *n.* برخه barkha

segment *v.t.* پەبرخوويشل pa barkho weyshal

segregate *v.t.* نوروخهجلاكول noro sakha jala kawal

segregation *n.* جلاتوب jalatob

seismic *a.* لزاند larzand

seize *v.t.* لاستەراول las ta rawral

seizure *n.* نيوونه neewana

seldom *adv.* كم ر deyr kam

select *v.t.* غوره كول ghwara kawal

select *a* غوره ghwara

selection *n.* انتخاب intikhab

selective *a.* انتخابي intikhabee

self *n.* ان،نفس zan; nafas

selfish *a.* ځانغواى zanghwaray

selfless *a.* بغرضه bey gharaza

sell *v.t.* خرول kharsawal

seller *n.* پلورونكى ploroonkay

semblance *n.* قيافه qeeyafa

semen *n.* نطفه،تخم nutfa; tukham

semester *n.* دزده كدوره da zdakri dawra

seminal *a.* نطفوي nutfawee

seminar *n.* دغونه بحث da behes ghonda

senate *n.* دسپين يروجرجه da speengeero jarga

senator *n.* دسپين يرودجرغى da speengeero da jargey gharay

senatorial *a.* سناتوري sanatoree

senatorial *a* دمشرانوجرپوراوند da masharano jargey pori arwand

send *v.t.* لدول leygdawal

senile *a.* عمرخولىانسان oomar khwaralay insan

senility *n.* زت zarakht

senior *a.* مشر،زو mashar; zor

senior *n.* مشر سی mashar saray

seniority *n.* مشرتوب mashartob

sensation *n.* هجان hayjan

sensational *a.* هجاني hayjanee

sense *n.* حس his

sense *v.t.* محسوسول mehsoosawal

senseless *a.* حسه بې bey hisa

sensibility *n.* حساسيت hasaseeyat

sensible *a.* باخبر،حساس bakhabar; hasas

sensitive *a.* حساس،نازک hasas; nazak

sensual *a.* شهواني shahwanee

sensualist *n.* شهوتپرست shahwat parast

sensuality *n.* شهوتپرستي shahwat parastee

sensuous *a.* شهواني shahwanee

sentence *n.* غونله،سزا ghondla; saza

sentence *v.t.* غونلهجوول،سزاورکول ghondla jorawal; saza warkawal

sentience *n.* ادراک idrak

sentient *a.* ادراکي idrakee

sentiment *n.* احساس ehsas

sentimental *a.* احساسي،جذباتي ehsasee; jazbatee

sentinel *n.* سارندویسرتری sarandoy sarteyray

sentry *n.* وکیدار sawkeedar

separable *a.* جلاکدونکی jala keydoonkay

separate *v.t.* جلاکول jala kawal

separate *a.* جلاشوی jala shaway

separation *n.* جلاتوب jalatob

sepsis *n.* وینتهننوتلیچرک weeney ta nanawatalay chark

September *n.* دانرزيکالنهمهمیاشت da angreyzee kal nahama myasht

septic *a.* انتانياوعفونيجسم antanee aw afoonee jisam

sepulchre *n.* مقبره maqbara

sepulture *n.* مقبره maqbara

sequel *n.* راتلونکپ،افسانه ratloonki peykhey; afsana

sequence *n.* لړ،تسلسل laray; tasalsul

sequester *v.t.* جلاکول jala kawal

serene *a.* خاموش khamosh

serenity *n.* آرامت aramakht

serf *n.* مریی mrayay

serge *n.* وینوکر wareen tokar

sergeant *n.* اجرایويچارواکی ijraywee charwakay

serial *a.* دورهیی،مسلسل dawrayee; musalsal

serial *n.* سلسله،وبرخیزهفیلمیاکیسه silsila; so barkheeza feelam ya keesa

series *n.* لړ laray

serious *a* خطرناک khatarnak

sermon *n.* وعظ waaz

sermonize *v.i.* وعظکول waaz kawal

serpent *n.* مار mar

serpentine *n.* دمارغوندهتاوراتاو da mar ghonda tawrataw

servant *n.* خدمتار khidmatgar

serve *v.t.* خدمتکول khidmat kawal

serve *n.* دنسلوبهکدغونسکوهنه da taynas loba ki da ghondaski wahana

service *n.* خدمت khidmat

service *v.t* چوپورتهکول chopar warta kawal

serviceable *a.* چوپتهچمتو chopar ta chamtoo

servile *a.* خدمتګارانه khidmatgarana

servility *n.* نوکرصفتي nawkar sifatee

session *n.* مجلس majlis

set *v.t* جوول،ودانول jorawal; wadanawal

set *a* لهواندچمتوشوی،معین la wrandi chamtoo shaway; muayyan

set *n* ټوله tolga

settle *v.i.* آبادول،تصفیهکول abadawal; tasfeeya kawal

settlement *n.* جوجای،استوګنه jorjaray; astogna

settler *n.* نوىکوال naway kadwal

seven *n.* اووه owa

seven *a* اوومه owama

seventeen *n.,* a اولس owallas

seventeenth *a.* اوولسم owallasam

seventh *a.* اووم owam

seventieth *a.* اويايم awyayam

seventy *n.,* a اویا awya

sever *v.t.* پرانستل pranistal

several *a* و،وونه so; so goonay

severance *n.* جلاکوونه jala kawal

severe *a.* شدید shadeed

severity *n.* شدت shidat

sew *v.t.* ګنل gandal

sewage *n.* ناولاوچلاوبه nawali aw chatali oba

sewer *n* دناولواوبوبهنوونه da nawalo obo bahanzoona

sewerage *n.* دناولواوبودمکلاندبهنوونه da nawalo obo da zmaki landi bahanzoona

sex *n.* جنس،شهوت jins; shahwat

sexual *a.* شهواني shahwanee

sexuality *n.* شهوانیت shahwaneeyat

sexy *n.* شهوتپارى shahwat paray

shabby *a.* بشرم bey sharam

shackle *n.* اتک،زولانا atkaray; zolanay

shackle *v.t.* اتکاچول atkaray achawal

shade *n.* سیورى syoray

shade *v.t.* پهسیوريکساتل pa syoree ki satal

shadow *n.* سیورى syoray

shadow *v.t* سیورىپراچول syoray pri achawal

shadowy *a.* سیورىلرونکى syoray laroonkay

shaft *n.* استوانه astawana

shake *v.i.* لزدل larzeydal

shake *n* لزه larza

shaky *a.* لزدونکى larzeydoonkay

shallow *a.* سرسري،کمژور sarsaree; kam zhawar

sham *v.i.* تظاهرکول tazahur kawal

sham *n* دروغ،پلمه darogh; palma

sham *a* ناریتونى nareekhtoonay

shame *n.* شرم sharam

shame *v.t.* شرمول sharmawal

shameful *a.* شرمناک sharamnak

shameless *a.* بشرمه bey sharma

shampoo *n.* دوتووينلومايع مركب da weykhto weenzalo maya murakkab

shampoo *v.t.* په‌شامپووته‌وينل pa shampoo weykhta weenzal

shanty *a.* جونه jongara

shape *n.* شكل shakal

shape *v.t* شكلوركول shakal warkawal

shapely *a.* دكلبخاوند da khkuli banri khawand

share *n.* ونږ‌سكت wand; skakht

share *v.t.* له‌نوروسره‌وشل la noro sara weyshal

share *n* دشرمای‌هوكی da sharamzay hadookay

shark *n.* يولوی‌سمندری‌کب yaw loy samandaree kab

sharp *a.* تره teyra

sharp *adv.* له‌کمت‌اوزيادت‌پرته la kamakht aw zyadakht parta

sharpen *v.t.* تره‌کول teyra kawal

sharpener *n.* تره‌کوونكی teyra kawoonkay

sharper *n.* پنسل‌تراشی pensal tarashay

shatter *v.t.* مدول maydawal

shave *v.t.* تراشل،حجامت‌جوول trashal; hajamat jorawal

shave *n* يره‌خرينه geera khrayna

shawl *n.* شال shal

she *pron.* هغه،هاghagha khaza

sheaf *n.* دسته،بنل dasta; bandal

shear *v.t.* بياتی‌كول،سكولل byatee kawal; skwalal

shears *n. pl.* ستربياتي stari byatee

shed *v.t.* بهول،باشل bahawal; pashal

shed *n* بهدنه،پره baheydana; sapara

sheep *n.* پسه psa

sheepish *a.* ساده sada

sheer *a.* نازک،ورږمين nazak; wreykhmeen

sheet *n.* پلنه‌پاه plana panra

sheet *v.t.* پول،هادرپرغوول pokhal; sadar pri ghwarawal

shelf *n.* تاخچه takhcha

shell *n.* قشر،پوستكی qashar; postakay

shell *v.t.* قشرترسپينول qashar tri speenawal

shelter *n.* پناهای panazay

shelter *v.t.* پناهوركول pana warkawal

shelve *v.t.* تاخچه‌جوول takhcha jorawal

shepherd *n.* شپون shpoon

shield *n.* ال dal

shield *v.t.* په‌ال‌سره‌زغورل pa dal sara zhghoral

shift *v.t.* ای‌بدلول zay badlawal

shift *n* دای‌بدلون da zay badloon

shifty *a.* چلباز chalbaz

shilling *n.* دبريتانيدسكشلمه‌برخه da breetaneeyey da sikey shalama barkha

shilly-shally *v.i.* زه‌نازه‌توب‌كول zra nazratob kawal

shilly-shally *n.* دوهزی dwa zaray

shin *n.* لينی leengay

shine *v.i.* پكدل parkeydal

shine *n* پک،بلدنه park; zaleydana

shiny *a.* لمرين lmareen

ship *n.* کټ kakhtay

ship *v.t.* په کټ کالدول pa kakhtay ki leygdawal

shipment *n.* د کتبار،محموله da kakhtay bar; mahmoola

shire *n.* ایالت ayalat

shirk *v.t.* ناغيي کول nagheeree kawal

shirker *n.* ناغي کوونکی nagheeree kawoonkay

shirt *n.* کمیس kamees

shiver *v.i.* ارتعاش irtiash

shoal *n.* لژور lag zhawar

shoal *n* له dala

shock *n.* صدمه،بوزار sadma; goozar

shock *v.t.* سخت بوزارخول sakht goozar khwaral

shoe *n.* بو boot

shoe *v.t.* بوانپه بوکول bootan pa pkho kawal

shoot *v.t.* توغول،ویشتل toghawal; weeshtal

shoot *n* ویشتنه،دبوو راوتلتیا weeshtana; da booto rawataltya

shop *n.* پلورنی ploranzay

shop *v.i.* پلورل ploral

shore *n.* ساحل sahil

short *a.* لنډ land

short *adv.* په لنډه توه pa landa toga

shortage *n.* کمت kamakht

shortcoming *n.* کمراتلنه kam ratlana

shorten *v.t.* لنول landawal

shortly *adv.* په لنډه توه pa landa toga

shorts *n. pl.* جانی،ترزنونانولډپتلون jangay; tar zangoonano land patloon

shot *n.* مرمه،دنویشتنه marmay; da nakhi weeshtana

shoulder *n.* اوه،ولی ooga; walay

shoulder *v.t.* په اوسره زورکول pa oogey sara zor kawal

shout *n.* کریکه،فریاد kreeka; faryad

shout *v.i.* کریکه وهل kreeka wahal

shove *v.t.* په زورسره پرمخ بیول pa zor sara par makh beywal

shove *n.* غلوونه zghalawana

shovel *n.* بلچه beylcha

shovel *v.t.* بلچه سره لری کول beylchey sara leyri kawal

show *v.t.* وول khowal

show *n.* وونه khowana

shower *n.* سخت باران sakht baran

shower *v.t.* باران ورل baran wareydal

shrew *n.* حشره خوری موک hashara khoray mogak

shrewd *a.* پلمه ر palmagar

shriek *n.* چغاو کریک cheyghey aw kreeki

shriek *v.i.* چغاو کریکوهل cheyghey aw kreeki wah⌐l

shrill *a.* تزر،فریادي teرz; faryadee

shrine *n.* زیارتای zyaratzay

shrink *v.i* وزکدل gonzi keydal

shrinkage *n.* وزکوونه gonzi kawana

shroud *n.* کفن،پو kafan; pokh

shroud *v.t.* کفن وراغوستل kafan waraghostal

shrub *n.* لهسرکاومیوجواک la sarkey aw meywey jor skhak

shrug *v.t.* اوپورتهخوول oogey porta khozawal

shrug *n* داوویورتهحرکت da oogo porta harakat

shudder *v.i.* لپیدل lapreydal

shudder *n* لپیدنه lapreydana

shuffle *v.i.* هخوادهخواحرکت کول hakhwa deykhwa harakat kawal

shuffle *n.* مبدنه،نولدنه zambeydana; ngokheydana

shun *v.t.* زانترساتل zan tri satal

shunt *v.t.* منحرف کول munharif kawal

shut *v.t.* بندول،راکته کول bandawal; rakkhata kawal

shutter *n.* راکتهکدونکیاوسپنیزهور rakkhata keydoonkay aw ospaneeza war

shuttle *n.* ماکو makoo

shuttle *v.t.* دماکوسفرکول da makoo safar kawal

shuttlecock *n.* دبمنوندلوبپرلرونک da baydminton da lobey parey laroonki ghondaska غونسکه

shy *n.* شرمندوکی sharmindookay

shy *v.i.* شرمدل sharmeydal

sick *a.* ناروغه narogha

sickle *n.* لور lor

sickly *a.* کمزوریانسان kamzoray insan

sickness *n.* کمزورتیا kamzortya

side *n.* خوا،اخ khwa; arkh

side *v.i.* یوخواتهتلل yawey khwa ta tlal

siege *n.* محاصره،کلابند muhasira; kalabandee

siesta *n.* غرمنیخوب gharmanay khob

sieve *n.* غلبل ghalbeyl

sieve *v.t.* غلبلول ghalbeylawal

sift *v.t.* شیندل sheendal

sigh *n.* آهکنه ah kkhana

sigh *v.i.* افسوسکول،آهکل afsos kawal; ah kkhal

sight *n.* لیدنه leedana

sight *v.t.* لیدل leedal

sightly *a.* لیدلکدونی،ترپاملاند leedal keydoonay; tar pam landi

sign *n.* علامه،نه alama; nakha

sign *v.t.* پهنونانوسرهپوهول pa nakho nakhano sara pohawal

signal *n.* علامه،لارود alama; larkhod

signal *a.* وتلی،رمزي watalay; ramzee

signal *v.t.* پهاشاروپوهول pa isharo pohawal

signatory *n.* لاسلیکونکی lasleekoonkay

signature *n.* لاسلیک lasleek

significance *n.* قدر،مفهوم،اهمیت qadar; mafhoom; ahmeeyat

significant *a.* مهم muhim

signification *n.* مانا،لویت mana; loyakht

signify *v.t.* ماناورکول mana warkawal

silence *n.* چوپتیا choptya

silence *v.t.* غلیکول ghalay kawal

silencer *n.* غلى‌كوونكى ghalay kawoonkay

silent *a.* بغه bey ghaga

silhouette *n.* دهرهنيم‌مخ da har sa neem makh

silk *n.* ورم wreykham

silken *a.* ورمين wreykhmeen

silky *a.* ورمين wreykhmeen

silly *a.* بعقل bey aqal

silt *n.* خه،لهه khata; laha

silt *v.t.* په‌خولل pa khato laral

silver *n.* سپين‌زر speen zar

silver *a* نقرهيي naqrayee

silver *v.t.* په‌سپينوزروپول pa speeno zaro pokhal

similar *a.* په‌ر،يوشان pa seyr; yaw shan

similarity *n.* ورته‌والى wartawalay

simile *n.* تشبيه tashbee

similitude *n.* دبيورنوالى da banri yaw rangwalay

simmer *v.i.* له‌غصه‌خولدل la ghusey khoteydal

simple *a.* ساده،آسان sada; asan

simpleton *n.* احمق ahmaq

simplicity *n.* ساده‌توب sadatob

simplification *n.* ساده‌كو ن sada kawang

simplify *v.t.* ساده‌كول sada kawal

simultaneous *a.* په‌يوه‌وخت pa yawa wakht

sin *n.* ناه goona

sin *v.i.* ناه‌كول goona kawal

since *prep.* وروسته‌له wrusta la

since *conj.* چ دا da chi

since *adv.* له‌هغه‌وخته‌چ la hagha wakhta chi

sincere *a.* مخلص mukhlis

sincerity *n.* خلوص khuloos

sinful *a.* ناهار goonagar

sing *v.i.* سندره‌ويل sandara wayal

singe *v.t.* سوزول sozawal

singe *n* سوزيدنه sozeydana

singer *n.* سندرغاى sandargharay

single *a.* يواز؛يوكسيز yawazi; yaw kaseez

single *n.* يو،تنها yaw; tanha

single *v.t.* يوازتلل،يوكدل yawazi tlal; yaw keydal

singular *a.* مفرد،يو mufrad; yaw

singularity *n.* يوازتوب yawazeytob

singularly *adv.* په‌يوازسره pa yawazi sara

sinister *a.* كيلاسى keenr lasay

sink *v.i.* غرقدل،تنزل‌كول gharqeydal; tanazzul kawal

sink *n* وبدنه doobeydana

sinner *n.* ناهار goonagar

sinuous *a.* په‌ييز؛دموجونوپه‌اوند sapayeez; da mawjoono pa arwand

sip *v.t.* په‌غپ‌غپ‌ل pa ghrap ghrap skhal

sip *n.* غپ ghrap

sir *n.* اغلى،حضرت khaghalay; hazrat

siren *n.* هارن haran

sister *n.* خور khor

sisterhood *n.* خورولى khorwalee

sisterly *a.* دخورپه‌شان da khor pa shan

sit *v.i.* كناستل kkheynastal

site *n.* مكان،ترودازلاندمكه makan; tar wadanay landi zmaka

situation *n.* حالت halat

six *n., a* شپ,شپم shpag; shpagam

sixteen *n., a.* شپاس,شپاسم shparas; shparasam

sixteenth *a.* شپاسم shparasam

sixth *a.* شپم shpagam

sixtieth *a.* شپيتم shpeytam

sixty *n., a.* شپيته shpeyta

sizable *a.* نسبتاًلوی nisbatan loy

size *n.* اندازه,کچ andaza; kach

size *v.t.* اندازهکول andaza kawal

sizzle *v.i.* غدل zghageydal

sizzle *n.* غ غ zagh zagh

skate *n.* ناوهاوپستسی nawara aw past saray

skate *v.t.* پهيخويدل pa yakh khwayeydal

skein *n.* لاستی,کلاوه lastay; kalawa

skeleton *n.* کالبد,جوت kalbad; jorakht

sketch *n.* سادهنخچه,طرحه sada nakhcha; tarha

sketch *v.t.* سادهنخچهجووَل sada nakhcha jorawal

sketchy *a.* نيمی neemgaray

skid *v.i.* پايورکول payey warkawal

skid *n* دپايتير da payey teer

skilful *a.* کارپوه karpoh

skill *n.* هنر hunar

skin *n.* رمن sarman

skin *v.t* پوکیتراول patokay tri arawal

skip *v.i.* وپونهوهل toopoona wahal

skip *n* کتهاوپورتهتوپ kkhata aw porta top

skipper *n.* وپوهونکی top wahoonkay

skirmish *n.* جزيیجه juzyee jagara

skirmish *v.t.* سرسریجندل sarsaree jangeydal

skirt *n.* دپرانستلمنزنانهکو da pranasti lamani zanana kot

skirt *v.t.* لمنوراچول laman warachawal

skit *n.* پغور peyghor

skull *n.* کوپ kopray

sky *n.* اسمان asman

sky *v.t.* رپورتهکول deyr porta kawal

slab *n.* برينهتخته dabareena takhta

slack *a.* سستي sastee

slacken *v.t.* سوکهکول,سستول sawka kawal; sastawal

slacks *n.* چکربانددتلوپتلون chakar bandi da tlo patloon

slake *v.t.* خاموشول khamoshawal

slam *v.t.* پهزوراولوغسرهبندول pa zor aw lwar ghag sara bandawal

slam *n* دسختاوتزغاواز da sakht aw teyz ghag awaz

slander *n.* بدنامي badnamee

slander *v.t.* بدناموَل badnamawal

slanderous *a.* تومتي tomatee

slang *n.* عامهژبه ama zhaba

slant *v.t.* رېبندکول,کواوپههتلل reyband kawal; kog aw pa dada tlal

slant *n* کهکره kaga karkha

slap *n.* هپ sapeyra

slap *v.t.* پهپورتهکول sapeyra porta kawal

slash *v.t.* پهمکانسرهغوول pa takan sara ghosawal

slash *n* چکــوزار chatak goozar

slate *n.* يوه‌برينه‌پله yawa dabareena panra

slattern *n.* تمبل‌سى tambal saray

slatternly *a.* په‌تمبل‌سره pa tambal sara

slaughter *n.* تول وژنه tol wazhna

slaughter *v.t.* په‌تول‌وژنه‌لاس‌پوركول pa tol wazhna las pori kawal

slave *n.* مريى mrayay

slave *v.i.* مريتوب‌ته‌ورل mrayeetob ta wral

slavery *n.* مريتوب mrayeetob

slavish *a.* مريى‌وله mrayay dawla

slay *v.t.* له‌منه‌ول la manza wral

sleek *a.* نرم؛صيقلى naram; sayqalee

sleep *v.i.* ويده‌كدل weeda keydal

sleep *n.* خوب khob

sleeper *n.* دويده‌كدنواون da weeda keydani wagon

sleepy *a.* خوبولى khobawalay

sleeve *n* لستوى lastonray

sleight *n.* مهارت maharat

slender *n.* نر dangar

slice *n.* قاش qash

slice *v.t.* پركول preykawal

slick *a* ساده؛مطلق sada; mutlaq

slide *v.i.* رغدل raghreydal

slide *n* ويدنه khwayeydana

slight *a.* كم؛نايز kam; naseez

slight *n.* پست؛ل past; lag

slight *v.t.* سپك‌نظركول spak nazar kawal

slim *a.* نازك nazuk

slim *v.i.* نركدل dangar keydal

slime *n.* چكه؛لعاب chakara; luab

slimy *a.* سرناك sreykhnak

sling *n.* مچنوغزه machnoghza

slip *v.i.* ويدل؛خوشى‌كول khwayeydal; khoshay kawal

slip *n.* رغدنه؛بلارتوب raghreydana; bey laritob

slipper *n.* دكورداستعمال‌سپكپل da kor da istimal spaki saplay

slippery *a.* ويند khwayand

slipshod *a.* پروت؛بېروا prot; bey parwa

slit *n.* چاود؛غووالى chawd; ghoswalay

slit *v.t.* سورى‌كول sooray kawal

slogan *n.* ناره؛شعار nara; shuar

slope *n.* ربنده‌همكه reybanda zmaka

slope *v.i.* ربندتوب‌پداكول reybandtob payda kawal

sloth *n.* كاهلى kahilee

slothful *n.* كاهل kahil

slough *n.* له‌خواولهوكـاى la khato aw laho dak zay

slough *n.* اخلاقي‌فساد akhlaqee fasad

slough *v.t.* مپوستكى‌غورول mar postakay ghorzawal

slovenly *a.* ونزو gonzi gonzi

slow *a* ورو؛سست wro; sast

slow *v.i.* په‌ورووروتلل pa wro wro tlal

slowly *adv.* په‌قراره pa qarara

slowness *n.* سستي sastee

sluggard *n.* لسى lat saray

sluggish *a.* ناكار؛ل nakar; lat

sluice *n.* ورخ؛پم warkh; patam

slum *n.* چله‌ياجونه chatala ya jongara

slumber *v.i.* سپک‌خوب‌کول spak khob kawal

slumber *n.* سپک‌خوب spak khob

slump *n.* دپام‌ومقدار da pam war miqdar

slump *v.i.* په‌یوه‌دمندل pa yawa dam nareydal

slur *n.* اشاره؛پیوند ishara; peywand

slush *n.* احمقانه‌احساسات ahmaqana ehsasat

slushy *a.*

slut *n.* بدلمنه bad lamana khaza

sly *a.* مکار؛موذي makar; mozee

smack *n.* کلونه‌او‌مچکه khkulawana aw machaka

smack *v.i.* غنه‌مچوتراخستل ghagana macho tri akheystal

smack *n* خوند khwand

smack *n.* سطحي‌مالومات sathee maloomat

smack *v.t.* په‌چپ‌چپ‌سره‌خول pa chrap chrap sara khwaral

small *a.* کوچنی koochnay

small *n* ووکی‌شی‌یاانسان warookay shay ya insan

smallness *adv.* ووکتیا warooktya

smallpox *n.* دچیچک‌ناروغي da cheechak naroghee

smart *a.* توند؛تز؛چالاک tond; teyz; chalak

smart *v.i* خوگیدل khoogeydal

smart *n* لالی‌انسان gulalay insan

smash *v.t.* دوکول dari wari kawal

smash *n* ټکر؛مده‌شووه takar; mayda shawi tota

smear *v.t.* داغي‌کول daghee kawal

smear *n.* داغ؛ککتیا dagh; kakartya

smell *n.* بوی booy

smell *v.t.* بویول؛بوی‌ورکول booyawal; booy warkawal

smelt *v.t.* یوول‌کوچنی‌خوراکي‌کب yaw dawl koochnay khorakee kab

smile *n.* خندا khanda

smile *v.i.* موسکاکول moska kawal

smith *n.* مسر misgar

smock *n.* ینه‌زرپراهني khazeena zayr parahanee

smog *n.* غلیظه‌او‌تته‌له ghaleeza aw tata lara

smoke *n.* لوی loogay

smoke *v.i.* لوی‌کدل loogay keydal

smoky *a.* لوی‌وهلی loogay wahalay

smooth *a.* سلیس؛هوار salees; hawar

smooth *v.t.* نرمول narmawal

smother *v.t.* دلوی‌له‌کبله‌ساه‌بنددل da loogee la kabala sa bandeydal

smoulder *v.i.* سوزدل‌او‌لوی‌کول sozeydal aw loogay kawal

smug *a.* پرهزپارسی parheyzgar saray

smuggle *v.t.* قاچاقول qachaqawal

smuggler *n.* قاچاق‌کوونکی qachaq kawoonkay

snack *n.* له‌خواه lag sa khwara

snag *n.* دغابخ da ghakh beykh

snail *n.* ژوره zhawara

snake *n.* مار mar

snake *v.i.* په‌مارپیچي‌ول‌حرکت‌کول pa marpeychee dawl harakat kawal

snap *v.t.* له‌ترکهار‌سره‌ماتول la trakahar sara matawal

snap *n* دتک‌ تک اواز da trak trak awaz

snap *a* لنمهالی؛نابی land mahalay; nasapee

snare *n*. لومه looma

snare *v.t.* پهلومه‌کرارول pa looma ki rageyrawal

snarl *n*. دام dam

snarl *v.i.* ستونزمنول stoonzmanawal

snatch *v.t.* برمته‌کول barmata kawal

snatch *n*. شوکونه؛تتوونه shookawana; takhtawana

sneak *v.i.* پهغلاغلاتلل pa ghla ghla tlal

sneak *n* پحرکت pat harakat

sneer *v.i* پهمسخروسره‌غدل pa maskharo sara ghageydal

sneer *n* مسخره؛ملنه maskhara; malanda

sneeze *v.i.* پرنجدل pranjeydal

sneeze *n* پرنج pranj

sniff *v.i.* بویول booyawal

sniff *n* پهپوزه‌کش‌کوونه pa poza kash kawana

snob *n*. غراشرافی‌شخص ghayr ashrafee shakhs

snobbery *n*. عام‌وګی am wagaray

snobbish *v* کبرجن؛عادي kabarjan; adee

snore *v.i.* خرهارکول kharhar kawal

snore *n* خرخر khar khar

snort *v.i.* غوریدل ghoreydal

snort *n*. خرهار kharhar

snout *n*. شونډک؛پوز shoondak; poz

snow *n*. واوره wawra

snow *v.i.* واوره‌ورېدل wawra wareydal

snowy *a*. واورین wawreen

snub *v.t.* رټل؛ردول ratal; radawal

snub *n*. رتنه؛ردوونه ratana; radawana

snuff *n*. نسوار naswar

snug *n*. کوچنی‌خونه koochnay khoona

so *adv*. لهدکبله؛پرد�اساس la dey kabala; par dey asas

so *conj*. که zaka

soak *v.t.* لمدول lamdawal

soak *n*. غوپه‌کوونه ghopa kawana

soap *n*. صابون saboon

soap *v.t.* صابون‌پرمول saboon pri mokhal

soapy *a*. صابوني saboonee

soar *v.i.* لوه‌الوتنه‌کول lwara alwatana kawal

sob *v.i.* لمدیدل lamdeydal

sob *n* سل salgay

sober *a*. عاقل aqil

sobriety *n*. معقولیت؛هویاري maqooleeyat; hookhyaree

sociability *n*. دژوندوتیا da gad zhwand wartya

sociable *a*. مینه‌ناک meenanak

social *n*. ولنیز tolaneez

socialism *n* پرنپالي parganpalee

socialist *n,a* پرنپال parganpal

society *n*. ولنه tolana

sociology *n*. ولنپوهنه tolanpohana

sock *n*. جوراب jorabey

socket *n*. ژورغالی؛کاسه zhawarghalay; kasa

sod *n*. چمن chaman

sodomite *n.* بچهباز؛کوني bachabaz; koonee

sodomy *n.* بچهبازي؛کونيتوب bachabazee; kooneetob

sofa *n.* نرمهاودهوﻙ narma oogda sawkay

soft *n.* لطيف نرم؛ naram; lateef

soften *v.t.* نرمول؛ملايمکدل narmawal; mulayim keydal

soil *n.* خاوره khawra

soil *v.t.* خرندل kheyraneydal

sojourn *v.i.* ناستیکول zay nastay kawal

sojourn *n* مهالياستونه land mahalee astogna

solace *v.t.* تسکينول taskeenawal

solace *n.* تسکين taskeen

solar *a.* لمرين lmareen

solder *n.* کوشر kawsheyr

solder *v.t.* کوشرول kawsheyrawal

soldier *n.* سپايي spayee

soldier *v.i.* سپايجودل spayee joreydal

sole *n.* دپیابوتلی da pkhey ya boot talay

sole *v.t* بوتهتلیاچول boot ta talay achawal

sole *a* تنها tanha

solemn *a.* سنین؛جدي sangeen; jiddee

solemnity *n.* وقار؛تشريفات waqar; tashreefat

solemnize *v.t.* لهتشريفاتوسرهترسره کول la tashreefato sara tar sara kawal

solicit *v.t.* تقاضاکول؛زارکول taqaza kawal; zaray kawal

solicitation *n.* غوتنه؛زار ghokhtana; zaray

solicitor *n.* حقوقيسلاکار haqooqee salakar

solicitious *a.* هيلهمن؛نارامه heelaman; narama

solicitude *n.* پرشاني؛زياتدقت parayshanee; zyat diqat

solid *a.* جامد jamid

solid *n* سختشی sakht shay

solidarity *n.* غمرازي؛مسؤليت ghamrazee; gad masooleeyat

soliloquy *n.* لمانسرهغدنه la zan sara ghageydana

solitary *a.* تنها tanha

solitude *n.* خلوت khilwat

solo *n* يوکسيزهسندره yaw kaseeza sandara

solo *a.* يوازيني؛انفرادي yawazeenay; infiradee

solo *adv.* پهانفراديتوه pa infiradee toga

soloist *n.*

solubility *n.* دويلکدنووتيا da weeli keydano wartya

soluble *a.* دويلکدنوو da weeli keydano war

solution *n.* حللاره hal lara

solve *v.t.* حللارهورتهموندل hal lara warta moondal

solvency *n.* حلدنه haleydana

solvent *a.* ويلکدونکی؛حلوونکی weelikeydoonkay; halawoonkay

solvent *n* محلل muhlal

sombre *a.* سيوریلرونکی syoray laroonkay

some *a.* ينشمر;يو zeeni; yaw shmeyr

some *pron.* وک;کوميو sok; kom yaw

somebody *pron.* کومکس kom kas

somebody *n.* يووک yaw sok

somehow *adv.* پهيوهول pa yaw dawl

someone *pron.* کومکس;يووک kom kas; yaw sok

somersault *n.* سرکوز sarkondai

something *pron.* يوسيز;يوشى yaw seez; yaw shay

something *adv.* ترياوانداز tar yawey andazey

sometime *adv.* کلهناکله kala na kala

sometimes *adv.* ينيوختونه zeeni wakhtoona

somewhat *adv.* ترياوهحده tar yawa hada

somewhere *adv.* يوچر;پهکومهاىک yaw cheyri; pa kom zay ki

somnambulism *n.* پهخوبکردنه pa khob ki garzeydana

somnambulist *n.* کخوبپه ردونکى pa khob ki garzeydoonkay

somnolence *n.* خوبولىحالت khobawalay halat

somnolent *n.* خوبولى khobawalay

son *n.* زوى zoy

song *n.* سندره sandara

songster *n.* سندربول sandarbol

sonic *a.* اورديېز awreydyeez

sonnet n. غزل ghazal

sonority *n.* غنتوب ghagantob

soon *adv.* ژر deyr zhar

soot *n.* لوى loogay

soot *v.t.* دبخاردنللوى da bukharay da nal loogay

soothe *v.t.* آرامول aramawal

sophism *n.* ترياستنه teyr eystana

sophist *n.* فسطايي fastayee

sophisticate *v.t.* ترياستل teyr eystal

sophisticated *a.* غولوونکى gholawoonkay

sophistication *n.* تحريف;غولوونه tahreef; gholawana

sorcerer *n.* کودر kodgar

sorcery *n.* کوري kodgaree

sordid *a.* خسيس;بدلارى khasees; badlaray

sore *a.* دردناک;پي dardnak; tapee

sore *n* زخم zakham

sorrow *n.* خپان khapgan

sorrow *v.i.* غمجندل ghamjaneydal

sorry *a.* خواشيني khwasheenee

sort *n.* جنس;قسم jins; qisam

sort *v.t* پهقسمونوکوشل pa qismoono ki weyshal

soul *n.* روح rooh

sound *a.* روغ rogh

sound *v.i.* غخپردل ghag khpareydal

sound *n* غ ghag

soup *n.* وروا khorwa

sour *a.* تريو treew

sour *v.t.* تروشول;ناراضهکول troshawal; naraza kawal

source *n.* سرچينه sar cheena

south *n.* سول swayl

south *n.* سولي swaylee

south *adv* دسولۍلورته da swayl lor ta

southerly *a.* پهسولۍکپروت pa swayl ki prot

southern *a.* سولۍ swaylee

souvenir *n.* یادار yadgar

sovereign *n.* پاچا pacha

sovereign *a* واکمن zwakman

sovereignty *n.* پاچاهي pachahee

sow *v.t.* تخمشنل tukham shanal

sow *n.* خوینه khazeena khoog

space *n.* دهواچاپریال da hawa chapeyryal

space *v.t.* فضاکردل،بایورکول faza ki garzeydal; zay warkawal

spacious *a.* زایلرونکی zay laroonkay

spade *n.* بلچه beylcha

spade *v.t.* پهبلچسرهاول pa beylchey sara arawal

span *n.* مدت،باکلشویوخت mudat; takal shaway wakht

span *v.t.* پراختیاورکول parakhtya warkawal

Spaniard *n.* اسپانوي aspanawee

spaniel *n.* زواروغوىببرسپی zwar ghwagay babar spay

Spanish *a.* اسپانوي aspanawee

Spanish *n.* اسپانويوىیاژبه aspanawee wagaray ya zhaba

spanner *n.* پچکش peych kash

spare *v.t.* وربل warbakhal

spare *a* اضافي izafee

spare *n.* پرهز parheyz

spark *n.* سکروه skarwata

spark *v.i.* ورکول srak kawal

spark *n.* برکی basarkay

sparkle *v.i.* ورکدل srakeydal

sparkle *n.* ورکدنه srakeydana

sparrow *n.* کورنمرغ koranay marghay

sparse *a.* تیتپرک teet park

spasm *n.* داضطرابحالت da iztirab halat

spasmodic *a.* تشنجي tashannujee

spate *n.* سل seyl

spatial *a.* هوايي hawayee

spawn *n.* دکبه da kab hagay

spawn *v.i.* دکبهاچول da kab hagay achawal

speak *v.i.* غدل ghageydal

speaker *n.* غدونکی ghageydoonkay

spear *n.* نزه neyza

spear *v.t.* پهنزهغوول pa neyza ghosawal

spearhead *n.* دنزوکه da neyzey sooka

spearhead *v.t.* بریدکول breed kawal

special *a.* خاص khas

specialist *n.* کارپوه karpoh

speciality *n.* مهارت maharat

specialization *n.* اختصاص ikhtisas

specialize *v.i.* متخصصکدل mutakhassas keydal

species *n.* دساهلرونکودنوقسمونه da sa laroonko da noogi qismoona

specific *a.* مخصوص makhsoos

specification *n.* تعیین taayyun

specify *v.t.* تعیینکول taayyun kawal

specimen *n.* بله beylga

speck *n.* پای tapay

spectacle *n.* منظره،تماشا manzara; tamasha

spectacular *a.* دلیدومنظره da leed war manzara

spectator *n.* لیدونکی leedoonkay

spectre *n.* اروا،پری arwa; peyray

speculate *v.i.* اندسه کول andeykhna kawal

speculation *n.* احتکار ehtikar

speech *n.* وناکونه wayna kawana

speed *n.* رفتار raftar

speed *v.i.* په چکسرمغلدل pa chatakay sara zghaleydal

speedily *adv.* په چکسره pa chatakay sara

speedy *a.* چابک chabak

spell *n.* اب abeysey

spell *v.t.* ابکول،املاکول abeysey kawal; imla kawal

spell *n* دوره،دوران dawra; dawran

spend *v.t.* مصرفول masrafawal

spendthrift *n.* زیات لت کوونکی zyat lagakht kawoonkay

sperm *n.* نطفه nutfa

sphere *n.* دایره dayra

spherical *a.* دایروي dayrawee

spice *n.* مساله masala

spice *v.t.* مساله پردوول masala pri doorawal

spicy *a.* مسالدار،خوندور masaleydar; khwandawar

spider *n.* غه ghanra

spike *n.* دغنمویاجواروی da ghanamo ya joowaro wagay

spike *v.t.* په نزه غوول pa neyza ghosawal

spill *v.i.* توپول،نول toyawal; narawal

spill *n* توی شوی بیز toy shaway seez

spin *v.i.* رخول،تاوول sarkhawal; tawawal

spin *n.* تاوخونه taw khwarana

spinach *n.* سابه saba

spinal *a.* دملاتیرپوراوند da mla teer pori arwand

spindle *n.* دوک dok

spine *n.* دملاتیر da mla teer

spinner *n.* سڼغونکی،تاوورکوونکی sanay gharoonkay; taw warkawoonkay

spinster *n.* ناواده کنجل nawada kari najlay

spiral *n.* مارپیچ،بنول mar peych; bandol

spiral *a.* تاوراتاو taw rataw

spirit n. روا،جذبه /arwa; jazba

spirited *a.* فکري،جذباتي fikree; jazbatee

spiritual *a.* روحاني roohanee

spiritualism *n.* داروانوپهنباور da arwagano pa naray bawar

spiritualist *n.* روحاني پال roohanee pal

spirituality *n.* روحایت roohaneeyat

spit *v.i.* توکاتوکل tookanri tookal

spit *n* توکا،لا tookanri; lari

spite *n.* کینه keena

spittle *n* توکا tookanri

spittoon *n.* توکا tookanri

splash *v.i.* افرازول،چپ چپ کول afrazawal; chrap chrap kawal

splash *n* افراز؛چپ‌چپ afraz; chrap chrap

spleen *n.* توری،طحال toray; tahal

splendid *a.* باعظمت ba azmat

splendour *n.* عظمت azmat

splinter *n.* دلری‌ده da largee dara

splinter *v.t.* وموه‌کول tota tota kawal

split *v.i.* ماتول؛بلول matawal; beylawal

split *n* درز؛نفاق darz; nifaq

spoil *v.t.* ورستول،خرابول wrustawal; kharabawal

spoil *n* خرابي kharabee

spoke *n.* درخ‌پره‌یامیله da sarkh para ya meela

spokesman *n.* ویاند wayand

sponge *n.* سفنج sfanj

sponge *v.t.* په‌سفنج‌پاکول pa sfanj pakawal

sponsor *n.* ژمن‌پلاریامور zhman plar ya mor

sponsor *v.t.* مسؤلیت‌ورکول masooleeyat warkawal

spontaneity *n.* ناپی‌توب nasapeetob

spontaneous *a.* په‌مانی‌توه،باختیاره pa zanee toga; bey ikhtyara

spoon *n.* کاشوغه kashogha

spoon *v.t.* په‌کاشوغه‌سره‌خول pa kashoga sara khwaral

spoonful *n.* دیو کاشوغ‌په‌اندازه da yaw kashoghi pa andaza

sporadic *a.* انفرادي infiradee

sport *n.* لوبه loba

sport *v.i.* لوبه‌کول loba kawal

sportive *a.* ورزشي warzashee

sportsman *n.* لوبغای lobgharay

spot *n.* کی،بای takay; zay

spot *v.t.* په‌نه‌کول،داغي‌کول pa nakha kawal; daghee kawal

spotless *a.* داغه بی bey dagha

spousal *n.* واده wada

spouse *n.* دژوندملری da zhwand malgaray

spout *n.* نل،ناوه،فواره nal; nawa; fawara

spout *v.i.* دچینه‌په‌شکل‌وردل da cheeney pa shakal wareydal

sprain *n.* دررد da rag dard

sprain *v.t.* په‌دردراوستل،راوتل pa dard rawastal; rag awakhtal

spray *n.* نندنه،شیندنه naneydana; sheendana

spray *n* دحشراتوزهرجن‌درمل da hasharato zaharjan darmal

spray *v.t.* شیندل،دحشراتوزهرجن درمل‌پاشل sheendal; da hasharato zaharjan darmal pashal

spread *v.i.* ویول،غوول weerawal; ghwarawal

spread *n.* پراختیا،انتشار parakhtya; intishar

spree *n.* مستي mastee

sprig *n.* دبوي‌کوچنانه da bootee koochnay sanga

sprightly *a.* تراوتازه tar aw taza

spring *v.i.* سرچینه‌اخستل،وپ‌وهل sar cheena akheysta; top wahal

spring *n* چینه،پسرلی cheena; pasarlay

sprinkle *v. t.* نندل،تیتول naneydal; teetawal

sprint v.i. چک‌غلدل chatak zghaleydal

sprint n چکي‌غاستي‌سيالي chatakee zghastee syalee

sprout v.i. و کدل؛نوتکه‌کول tookeydal; notaki kawal

sprout n نوتکه؛نيال؛بوکه notaka; nyal; sooka

spur n. سيخک؛تره‌راوتلتيا seekhak; teyra rawataltya

spur v.t.

spurious a. ناريتوني؛ارموني nareekhtoonay; armoonay

spurn v.t. ردول؛په‌لغته‌وهل radawal; pa laghata wahal

spurt v.i. ناپه‌سرعت‌زياتول nasapa surat zyatawal

spurt n ناپي‌هه nasapee hasa

sputnik n. سپومکه spogmakay

sputum n. خراشکی kharashkay

spy n. ارر sargar

spy v.i. ارري‌کول sargaree kawal

squad n. لنظامي nizamee dalgay

squadron n. دنظامي‌مشرانويوهل da nizamee masharano yawa dalgay

squalid a. خيرن kheeran

squalor n. مرداري murdaree

squander v.t. کول تلف talf kawal

square n. وی‌لمور salor gotay

square a لمورويز salor goteez

square v.t. لمورويزه‌بهورکول؛جوجای salor gooteeza banra warkawal; jor jaray kawal

squash v.t. خچ‌پچ‌کول khach pach kawal

squash n خچ‌پچ‌شوی khach pach shaway

squat v.i. دپوپه‌پنجوکناستل da pkho pa panjo kkheynastal

squeak v.i. چغسوروهل cheyghi soorey wahal

squeak n چغن‌غ؛فرياد chaghan ghag; faryad

squeeze v.t. چيتول cheetawal

squint v.i. کوستری‌کدل kog stargay keydal

squint n کوسترتوب kog stargtob

squire n. ملک؛خان malak; khan

squirrel n. موش‌خرما mosh khurma

stab v.t. په‌خنجروهل pa khanjar wahal

stab n. دحمله‌هه da hamley hasa

stability n. ‌يکاو teekaw

stabilization n. ‌ينت teengakht

stabilize v.t. ‌يکاووربل teekaw warbakhal

stable a. تثبيت‌شوی tasbeet shaway

stable n غوجل؛پنغالی ghojal; pand ghalay

stable v.t. ‌يناوورکول teengar warkawal

stadium n. لوبغالی lobghalay

staff n. کارمندان karmandan

staff v.t. مرسته‌وسره‌کول mrasta warsara kawal

stag n. نارينه‌سرهوزه nareena sra gowaza

stage n. دننداره‌صحنه da nandarey sahna

stage v.t. دريورته‌ايودل dareez warta eekhodal

stagger *v.i.* للنتل،ببدل zambeydal; rang rang tlal

stagger *n.* ببدنه zambeydana

stagnant *a.* بحركته،ولا bey harakata; walar

stagnate *v.i.* راكدكدل؛بحركته‌كدل rakad keydal; bey harakata keydal

stagnation *n.* كساد،ركود kasad; rakood

staid *a.* دروند،ثابت droond; sabit

stain *n.* داغ dagh

stain *v.t.* خيرنول kheyranawal

stainless *a.* زنگ‌نه‌اخستونکی zang na akheystoonkay

stair *n.* پوړی‌،مرتبه poŗay; martaba

stake *n* لرگینه‌لکه largeena lakara

stake *v.t.* په‌لرۍیالکيپورتل pa largee ya lakari pori taral

stale *a.* زوړ؛پاته‌شوی zor; pata shaway

stale *v.t.* زوړل،له‌موډه‌لوېدل zarawal; la moda lweydal

stalemate *n.* په‌شطرنج‌کمات‌او‌مبهوت pa shatranj ki mat aw mabhoot

stalk *n.* داانستن da adaney stan

stalk *v.i.* ناز‌نخرو‌تلل،پا‌saral; pa naz nakhro tlal

stalk *n* دشرابوجام da sharabo jam

stall *n.* کوچنۍ‌رینه‌خونه koochnay largeena khoona

stall *v.t.* له‌حرکته‌غوروول la harakata ghorzawal

stallion *n.* نارینه‌اس nareena as

stalwart *a.* غتلی،هومن ghakhtalay; hodman

stalwart *n* زور،ټرم zrawar; garam

stamina *n.* توان،ژوندواک twan; zhwand zwak

stammer *v.i.* توتله‌کدل totla keydal

stammer *n* توتله‌توب totlatob

stamp *n.* نقش،مهر naqsh; muhar

stamp *v.i.* مهرلول muhar lagawal

stampede *n.* ناپی‌لیېزحرکت nasapee dalayeez harakat

stampede *v.i* له‌یيزحرکت‌کول dalayeez harakat kawal

stand *v.i.* دریدل dareydal

stand *n.* دریدنه،ددریدوای dareydana; da dareydo zay

standard *n.* معيار mayar

standard *a* معياري mayaree

standardization *n.* دمعيارلبندي da mayar dalbandee

standardize *v.t.* معياري‌کول mayaree kawal

standing *n.* حالت halat

standpoint *n.* ثابت‌تماى sabit tamzay

standstill *n.* سکون،دریدنه sakoon; dareydana

stanza *n.* شعري‌بند shayree band

staple *n.* پایه،اوسپنیزه‌را paya; ospaneeza geera

staple *a* اهم،اصلي aham; aslee

star *n.* ستوری storay

star *v.t.* لمدل،شهرت‌پداکول zaleydal; shuhrat payda kawal

starch *n.* نشاسته nishasta

starch *v.t.* په‌نشاسته‌کلکول pa nishasta klakawal

stare *v.i.* یریر‌کتل zeyr zeyr katal

stare *n.* ركتنه،وانه rad rad katana; waranga

stark *n.* وچ کلک،تنها wach klak; tanha

stark *adv.* په‌بشپول pa bashpar dawl

starry *a.* له‌ستوروک la storo dak

start *v.t.* پیل‌کول payl kawal

start *n* پیل payl

startle *v.t.* لامایه‌وپوهل la zaya top wahal

starvation *n.* لوه،قحطي lwaga; qahtee

starve *v.i.* له‌لومدل la lwagi mreydal

state *n.* حالت،ریاست،دولت halat; reeyasat; dawlat

state *v.t* بیانول bayanawal

stately *a.* عالي alee

statement *n.* بیان bayan

statesman *n.* سیاستوال seeyasatwal

static *n.* ساکن sakin

statics *n.* دساکنوجسمونونیزمانه da sakino jismoono seyraneeza sanga

station *n.* تمای،مرکز tamzay; markaz

station *v.t.* مستقرکول،تمای‌کپرول mustaqar kawal; tamzay ki preykhwal

stationary *a.* ساکن sakin

stationer *n.* کتابپلوری keetabploray

stationery *n.* دلیکنیزووسایلو پلورونکی da leekaneezo wasayalo plooroonkay

statistical *a.* سرشمرنه sar shmeyrana

statistician *n.* دسرشمرنکارپوه da sar shmeyrani karpoh

statistics *n.* دشمرنعلم da shmeyrani ilam

statue *n.* مجسمه mujassima

stature *n.* قد،بدني‌به qad; badanee banra

status *n.* حالت،مرتبه halat; martaba

statute *n.* قانون qanoon

statutory *a.* له‌قانون‌سره‌سم la qanoon sara sam

staunch *a.* وفادار،ثابت‌قدم wafadar; sabit qadam

stay *v.i.* پاتکدل،مشت‌کدل pati keydal; meysht keydal

stay *n* درډنه،قیام dareydana; qayam

steadfast *a.* ثابت‌قدم sabit qadam

steadiness *n.* پیاوی‌عظم pyawaray azam

steady *a.* یونواخت،امن yaw nawakht; dadman

steady *v.t.* ثابت‌قدم‌ساتل sabit qadam satal

steal *v.i.* غلاکول ghla kawal

stealthily *adv.* په‌په‌سره pa pata sara

steam *n* بخار،له bukhar; lara

steam *v.i.* بخارکول bukhar kawal

steamer *n.* بخارکوونکی bukhar kawoonkay

steed *n.* اس as

steel *n.* پولاد pawlad

steep *a.* ژور zhawar

steep *v.t.* لمدول lamdawal

steeple *n.* برج،مناره burj; munara

steer *v.t.* چلول chalawal

stellar *a.* پایاوستنته‌ورته payey aw stani ta warta

stem *n.* ‫رﻩ،تنﻩ‬ reekha; tana

stem *v.i.* ‫تنﻩپداکول‬ tana payda kawal

stench *n.* ‫بدبویی‬ bad booyee

stencil *n.* ‫دتوروﺍوشکلونودمنقوشپاﻩ‬ da toro aw shakloono da manqooshay panra

stencil *v.i.* ‫دتوروﺍوشکلونودمنقوشپاپﻩ‬ ‫مرستﻩنقشجوول‬ da toro aw shakloono da manqooshay panri pa mrasta naqsh jorawal

stenographer *n.* ‫چکلیکونکی‬ chatak leekoonkay

stenography *n.* ‫چکلیکنﻩ‬ chatak leekana

step *n.* ‫پل،ﮔام‬ pal; gam

step *v.i.* ‫پلیردل،ﮔاماخستل‬ palee garzeydal; gam akheystal

steppe *n.* ‫بونوﺍوپراخﻩﺍوزمﻩجلﻩ‬ bey wano aw parakha dag wazma jalga

stereotype *n.* ‫کلیشﻩ،دکلیشﻩجوونفن‬ kaleesha; da kaleeshey jorawani fan

stereotype *v.t.* ‫کلیشﻩﺍوفیلمبرﺍبرول‬ kaleesha aw feelam barabarawal

stereotyped *a.* ‫تقلیدشوی‬ taqleed shaway

sterile *a.* ‫شنﻩ،بحاصلﻩ‬ shand; bey hasila

sterility *n.* ‫شنتوب‬ shandtob

sterilization *n.* ‫لﻩکارﻩغورونﻩ‬ la kara ghorzawana

sterilize *v.t.* ‫بحاصلﻩکول‬ bey hasila kawal

sterling *a.* ‫دقانوني معیارخاوند‬ da qanoonee mayar khawand

sterling *n.* ‫دبریتانیرسمی سکﻩ‬ da breetaneeyey rasmee sika

stern *a.* ‫سختیر‬ sakhtgeer

stern *n.* ‫سختیرﺍنسان‬ sakhtgeer insan

stethoscope *n.* ‫طبيغو‬ tibee ghwagay

stew *n.* ‫وروﺍپخوونکی‬ khorwa pakhowoonkay

stew *v.t.* ‫وروورواشول‬ wro wro eyshawal

steward *n.* ‫خادم‬ khadim

stick *n.* ‫لکﻩ،ﺍمسا‬ lakara; amsa

stick *v.t.* ‫نلدل،پﻩلکوهل‬ nakhleydal; pa lakari wahal

sticker *n.* ‫سردونکی کاغذ‬ sreykheydoonkay kaghaz

stickler *n.* ‫ﺍصرﺍرکوونکی شخص‬ israr kawoonkay shakhs

sticky *n.* ‫سرناک‬ sreykhnak

stiff *n.* ‫شخ،نغ‬ shakh; neygh

stiffen *v.t.* ‫کلکول‬ klakawal

stifle *v.t.* ‫زندکول،خاموشول‬ zanday kawal; khamoshawal

stigma *n.* ‫دشرمدﺍغ‬ da sharam dagh

still *a.* ‫غلی،ساکت‬ ghalay; sakit

still *adv.* ‫همشﻩ،تردچ‬ hamaysha; tar dey chi

still *v.t.* ‫آرﺍمول‬ aramawal

still *n.* ‫چوپتیا‬ choptya

stillness *n.* ‫خاموشي‬ khamoshee

stilt *n.* ‫یوﺍودپلرونکی مارغﻩ‬ yaw oogdey pkhey laroonkay margha

stimulant *n.* ‫پاروونکی‬ parawoonkay

stimulate *v.t.* ‫پارول‬ parawal

stimulus *n.* دپاردنوسیله da pareydani waseela

sting *v.t.* چیچل cheechal

sting *n.* چیچ cheech

stingy *a.* نـ لرونکی neykh laroonkay

stink *v.i.* بدبویلرل bad booy laral

stink *n* بدبویي bad booyee

stipend *n.* تنخوا tankha

stipulate *v.t.* تونلاسلیکول taroon lasleekawal

stipulation *n.* دتونماده da taroon mada

stir *v.i.* حرکتورکول harakat warkawal

stirrup *n.* رکاب rakab

stitch *n.* ننه gandana

stitch *v.t.* پوندول،ننل peywandawal; gandal

stock *n.* ذخیره zakheera

stock *v.t.* ذخیرهکول zakheera kawal

stock *a.* موجود،زرمهشوی mawjood; zeyrma shaway

stocking *n.* اودینهجوراب oogdey khazeena jorabey

stoic *n.* خاموشاوجنجالخهلرپروت انسان khamosh aw janjal sakha leyri prot insan

stoke *v.t.* پهاورتلاچول pa or teyl achawal

stoker *n.* دسوزولومواد da sozawalo mawad

stomach *n.* خه kheyta

stomach *v.t.* زغمل zghamal

stone *n.* بره،کانی dabara; kanray

stone *v.t.* پهبرووویشتلیامول pa dabaro weeshtal ya mokhal

stony *a.* برین dabareen

stool *n.* لوموک lwara sawkay

stoop *v.i.* کدل kageydal

stoop *n* کونه kagawana

stop *v.t.* درول darawal

stop *n* درـدنه dareydana

stoppage *n* توقف tawaquf

storage *n.* وـدام godam

store *n.* سترپلورنی star ploranzay

store *v.t.* وـدامکساتل godam ki satal

storey *n.* طبقه،پور tabqa; por

stork *n.* ل لگ lag lag

storm *n.* توپان،سوران toopan; sooran

storm *v.i.* ناپبریدکول nasapaee breed kawal

stormy *a.* توپانی،هجاني toopanee; hayjanee

story *n.* کیسه keesa

stout *a.* شجاع shuja

stove *n.* بخار bukharay

stow *v.t.* مخفيکول،پول makhfee kawal; patawal

straggle *v.i.* بایهودهکول،بترتیبهوده کول bey zaya wada kawal; bey tarteeba wada kawal

straggler *n.* کوهبی،وروستوپاتشوی koosa dabay; wrusto pati shaway

straight *a.* نغ neygh

straight *adv.* پهمستقیمول pa mustaqeem dawl

straighten *v.t.* تنظیمول tanzeemawal

straightforward *a.* پهانپیلی pa dang peyalee

straightway *adv.* مستقیما mustaqeeman

strain *v.t.* فشارلاندراوستل fishar landi rawastal

strain *n* فشار;زور fishar; zor

strait *n.* دمکنرتانه da zmaki naray taranga

straiten *v.t.* پهتنسهکاچول pa tangsa ki achawal

strand *v.i.* یوازپرودل yawazi preykhodal

strand *n* دسیندغاہ da seend ghara

strange *a.* ناآشنا naashna

stranger *n.* پردی praday

strangle *v.t.* دچاغاہتختهکول da cha ghara takhta kawal

strangulation *n.* زندکوونه zanday kawana

strap *n.* ریتاہ;تسمه reetara; tasma

strap *v.t.* پهتسمیهتل pa tasmey sara taral

stratagem *n.* جنيچال jangee chal

strategic *a.* تدبیري tadbeeree

strategist *n.* دجنيتدبیرونوماہر da jangee tadbeeroono mahir

strategy *n.* دجنيتدبیرونوفن da jangee tadbeeroono fan

stratum *n.* طبقه;قشر tabqa; qashar

straw *n.* پوزی;مزری pozay; meyzaray

strawberry *n.*

stray *v.i.* دربهدربدل dar pa dar garzeydal

stray *a* سرودان;کوهبی sargardan; koosa dabay

stray *n* سردانی sargardanee

stream *n.* ویاله wyala

stream *v.i.* بهدل;جاريکدل baheydal; jaree keydal

streamer *n.* دجامودلبووپ da jamo da gul booto patay

streamlet *n.* کوچنویاله koochnay wyala

street *n.* کوه koosa

strength *n.* قوت;پایت qoowat; payakht

strengthen *v.t.* قويکدل;قويکول qawee keydal; qawee kawal

strenuous *a.* فعال faal

stress *n.* کو;فشار kokhakh; fishar

stress *v.t* ترفشارلاندراوستل tar fishar landi rawastal

stretch *v.t.* غول;پراختیاورکول ghazawal; parakhtya warkawal

stretch *n* غوونه ghazawana

stretcher *n.* درنوردولودلاسيوسیله da ranzoor da wralo lasee waseela

strew *v.t.* تیتول;شنل teetawal; shanal

strict *a.* سخت sakht

stricture *n.* زورزیاتی zor zyatay

stride *v.i.* لويلویهامونهاخستل loy loy gamoona akheystal

stride *n* پهامونوسرهاندازهنیونه pa gamoono sara andaza neewana

strident *a.* کوکوونکيغ koonr kawoonkay ghag

strife *n.* جنجال;ههاوهاند janjal; hasa aw hand

strike *v.t.* کاربندزکول;ویشتل kar bandeyz kawal; weeshtal

strike *n* وهل بول؛کاربدنز wahal dabawal; kar bandeyz

striker *n.* وهونکی wahoonkay

string *n.* مزی؛تار mazay; tar

string *v.t.* سیم یامزی وراچول؛کش کول seem ya mazay warachawal; kash kawal

stringency *n.* سختیري sakhtgeeree

stringent *a.* سخت؛کنجوس sakht; kanjoos

strip *n.* پ؛نرتسمه patay; naray tasma

strip *v.t.* بربنول barbandawal

stripe *n.* اوده مختلف رنونه لرونکپ oogda mukhtalif rangoona laroonki patay

stripe *v.t.* لیکه لیکه کول leeka leeka kawal

strive *v.i.* زیار کل zyar kakhal

stroke *n.* ضربه؛ٻوزار zarba; goozar

stroke *v.t.* ٻوزار کول؛لاس پرراکل goozar kawal; las pri rakakhal

stroke *n* حمله؛دزنغ hamla; da zang ghag

stroll *v.i.* وروورو چکروهل wro wro chakar wahal

stroll *n* چکروهنه chakar wahana

strong *a.* زورور zorawar

stronghold *n.* پناي؛مورچل patanzay; morchal

structural *a.* جوتیز jorakhtaneez

structure *n.* جوت jorakht

struggle *v.i.* زیار کل zyar kakhal

struggle *n* زیار zyar

strumpet *n.* فاحشه fahisha

strut *v.i.* په نازنخروتلل pa naz nakhro tlal

strut *n* د ناز نخروتٻ da naz nakhro tag

stub *n.* کونده؛ريه koonda; reekha

stubble *n.* بربره گيرہ babara geera

stubborn *a.* خپل سرى khpal saray

stud *n.* مخل gul meykhay

stud *v.t.* په مل مخو سيناروٻ pa gul meykho seengarawal

student *n.* زدکيال zdakryal

studio *n.* کاري خونه karee khoona

studious *a.* کتاب لوستى keetab lostay

study *v.i.* زدکه کول؛لوستل zdakra kawal; lostal

study *n.* مطالعه؛لوست mutalia; lost

stuff *n.* ماده؛بیز mada; seez

stuff 2 *v.t.* په زوره کوٻ pa zora dakawal

stuffy *a.* زندشوی zanday shaway

stumble *v.i.* تروتل teyr watal

stumble *n.* پرشانی parayshanee

stump *n.* دوني کونده da wani koonda

stump *v.t* په لوغسره راولدٻ pa lwar ghag sara ralwaydal

stun *v.t.* حرانول hayranawal

stunt *v.t.* حرانوونکی ورزشي کرتٻ کوٻ hayranawoonkay warzashee kartab kawal

stunt *n* شهکارکرتٻ shahkar kartab

stupefy *v.t.* حرانول hayranawal

stupendous *a.* حرانوونکی؛عجیب hayranawoonkay; ajeeb

stupid *a* لوده lawda

stupidity *n.* لودہ توٻ lawdatob

sturdy *a.* سرتمبه sar tamba

sty *n.* دخواستونای astoganzay da khoog

stye *n.* دخواستونای da khoog astoganzay

style *n.* طرز tarz

subdue *v.t.* مطيع‌كول mutee kawal

subject *n.* تبعه،وى،ماده،جسم taba; wagaray; mada; jisam

subject *a* مسند،مطيع masnad; mutee

subject *v.t.* پهواك‌كراوستل pa wak ki rawastal

subjection *n.* اطاعت itaat

subjective *a.* موضوعي،فاعلي mawzooee; failee

subjudice *a.* لهقضايي‌پركاوهوپرته la qazayee preykri aw hod parta

subjugate *v.t.* رام‌كول ram kawal

subjugation *n.* اطاعت itaat

sublet *v.t.* فرعي‌مستاجرته‌دااجارحق ورکول faree mustajar ta da eejarey haq warkawal

sublimate *v.t.* تصفيه‌كول tasfeeya kawal

sublime *a.* تصفيه‌كونكى tasfeeya kawoonkay

sublime *n* چاونه chanrawana

sublimity *n.* رفعت rifat

submarine *n.* سمندرلاندپوى samandar landi pawzee beyray

submarine *a* ترسمندرلاند tar samandar landi

submerge *v.i.* پهاوبوكغوپهكدل pa obo ki ghopa keydal

submission *n.* غاهايودنه ghara eekhodana

submissive *a.* مطيع mutee

submit *v.t.* تسليم‌كدل tasleem keydal

subordinate *a.* تابع tabay

subordinate *n* اطاعت‌كونكى itaat kawoonkay

subordinate *v.t.* اطاعت‌كول itaat kawal

subordination *n.* اطاعت itaat

subscribe *v.t.* تصويبول tasweebawal

subscription *n.* دورپاونبيه،نسخه ليكنه da warzpanri gadoonbaya; nuskha leekana

subsequent *a.* ورپسې warpasey

subservience *n.* پهدردخونه pa dard khwarana

subservient *a.* مفيد mufeed

subside *v.i.* خاموش‌شدل khamosheydal

subsidiary *a.* كومكي komakee

subsidize *v.t.* مالي‌مرسته‌كول malee mrasta kawal

subsidy *n.* مالي‌مرسته malee mrasta

subsist *v.i.* ژوندكول zhwand kawal

subsistence *n.* ژوند zhwand

substance *n.* ماده،ذات mada; zat

substantial *a.* واقعي،موثق waqiee; muwassaq

substantially *adv.* پهحقيقت‌كې pa haqeeqat ki

substantiate *v.t.* مادي‌بهورکول madee banra warkawal

substantiation *n.* تجسم tajassum

substitute *n.* ايناستى zaynastay

substitute *v.t.* دبل‌پراى‌ايودل da bal par zay eekhodal

substitution *n.* تبديل tabdeel

subterranean *a.* پاوغلى pat aw ghalay

subtle *n.* دقيق،پلمه‌ر palmagar; daqeeq

subtlety *n.* زيات‌دقت zyat diqat

subtract *v.t.* تفريق‌قول tafreeqawal

subtraction *n.* تفريق tafreeq

suburb *n.* دارد‌شاوخواسيمه da khar da shawkhwa seema

suburban *a.* دارد‌شاوخواسيماستون da khar da shawkhwa seemi astogan

subversion *n.* انهدام inhidam

subversive *a.* نه‌دلى nareydalay

subvert *v.t.* نول narawal

succeed *v.i.* بريالى‌كدل baryalay keydal

success *n.* بريا barya

successful *a* بريالى baryalay

succession *n.* پرله‌پستوب parla pasitob

successive *a.* پرله‌پس parla pasi

successor *n.* ‌ايناستى zaynastay

succumb *v.i.* له‌پولويدل la pkho lweydal

such *a.* همداشان،دارنه hamda shan; da ranga

such *pron.* دداول‌خلك،داول‌شيان da dawl khalk; da dawl shayan

suck *v.t.* رودل،تى‌رودل rodal; tay rodal

suck *n.* رودنه rodana

suckle *v.t.* شدوركول sheydey warkawal

sudden *n.* ناپى‌په nasapee peykha

suddenly *adv.* په‌ندى‌ول؛ناپه pa garandee dawl; nasapa

sue *v.t.* تعقيبول taqeebawal

suffer *v.t.* وړدل،زغمل zoreydal; zghamal

suffice *v.i.* كافى‌كدل kafee keydal

sufficiency *n.* كفايت،كافى‌مقدار kifayat; kafee miqdar

sufficient *a.* كافى،پوره kafee; poora

suffix *n.* روستاى rostaray

suffix *v.t.* روستاى‌جوول rostaray jorawal

suffocate *v.t* ساه‌يوربندول sa yi warbandawal

suffocation *n.* ساه‌وربندوونه sa warbandawana

suffrage *n.* په‌ول‌اكنوكدراى‌وركولو په‌تل‌تاكنو كى د راى warkawalo haq حق pa tol takano ki da ray warkawalo haq

sugar *n.* بوره،قند boora; qand

sugar *v.t.* بوره‌وركول boora warkawal

suggest *v.t.* خپله‌روهمكاره‌كول khpala groha khkara kawal

suggestion *n.* روهه‌رندوونه groha sargandawana

suggestive *a.* نغوته‌كوونكى naghota kawoonkay

suicidal *a.* ‌ان‌وژني zan wazhnee

suicide *n.* وژنه‌ان zan wazhna

suit *n.* مرافعه،يوه‌جوجامه murafia; yawa jor jamey

suit *v.t.* راضي‌كول razee kawal

suitability *n.* موافقت muwafiqat

suitable *a.* موافق muwafiq

suite *n.* اپارتمان‌او‌دهغلوازم apartman aw da haghey lawazim

suitor *n.* مدعي mudaee

sullen *a.* تون‌دخويه tond khooya

sulphur *n.* دسلفرگاز da salfar gaz

sulphuric *a.* سلفرلرونکی salfar laroonkay

sultry *a.* رماونمجن garam aw namjan

sum *n.* ولپس،مجموعه toley peysey; majmooa

sum *v.t.* جمع کول jama kawal

summarily *adv.* په‌لنه‌توه pa landa toga

summarize *v.t.* په‌لنه‌توه‌بیانول pa landa toga bayanawal

summary *n.* لنون landoon

summary *a* لند land

summer *n.* درمموسم da garmay mosam

summit *n.* دلویدرجغونه da loyi darajey ghonda

summon *v.t.* غایودلوته‌رابلل ghari eekhodalo ta rabalal

summons *n.* دقانونی‌رابلنچی da qanoonee rabalani cheetay

sumptuous *a.* عیاش،مسرفي ayash; masrafee

sun *n.* لمر lmar

sun *v.t.* لمرته‌ایودل lmar ta eekhodal

Sunday *n.* یک‌شنبه،یوز yak shamba; yoonay

sunder *v.t.* بلول beylawal

sundry *a.* رنار،بلابل ranga rang; beyla beyl

sunny *a.* لمرین lmareen

sup *v.i.* غوپغوپل ghorap ghorap skhal

superabundance *n.* رت deyrakht

superabundant *a.* خورار khora deyr

superb *a.* درونداوپتمن droond aw patman

superficial *a.* برسرن،سطحي barseyran; sathee

superficiality *n.* برسرنتوب barseyrantob

superfine *a.* غوره‌اوممتاز ghwara aw mumtaz

superfluity *n.* زیادت zyadakht

superfluous *a.* اضافي izafee

superhuman *a.* فوق‌بشر foq bashar

superintend *v.t.* سرپرستي‌کول sarparastee kawal

superintendence *n.* مدیریت mudeereeyat

superintendent *n.* سرپرست sarparast

superior *a.* پورتني،غوره portanay; ghwara

superiority *n.* پورته‌والی portawalay

superlative *a.* ترولوه tar tolo kha

superlative *n.* تفضیلي tafzeelee

superman *n.* فوق‌بشرخصوصیات لرونکی‌انسان foq bashar khusooseeyat laroonkay insan

supernatural *a.* فوق‌العاده foqul ada

supersede *v.t.* دبل‌پای‌نیول da bal seez zay neewal

supersonic *a.* له‌غږپرته la ghag porta

superstition *n.* موهوم‌پرستي mawhoom parastee

superstitious *a.* موهوم‌پرست mawhoom parast

supertax *n.* پراضافي‌عایداتومالیه par izafee aydato maleeya

supervise *v.t.* نظارت كول nazarat kawal

supervision *n.* نظارت nazarat

supervisor *n.* ناظر nazir

supper *n.* ملام makham

supple *a.* غوژخوونكى ghozh khwaroonkay

supplement *n.* تكميل،ضميمه takmeel; zameema

supplement *v.t.* تكميل كول takmeel kawal

supplementary *a.* اضافي izafee

supplier *n.* رسوونكى،دتداركاتومسؤل rasawoonkay; da tadarikato masool

supply *v.t.* رسول rasawal

supply *n* تداركات،جنس tadarikat; jins

support *v.t.* ملاتركول mlatar kawal

support *n.* ملاتى mlataray

suppose *v.t.* تصوركول tasawwur kawal

supposition *n.* تصور،فرض،خيال tasawwur; farz; khyal

suppress *v.t.* پايمالول paymalawal

suppression *n.* پايمالوونه paymalawana

supremacy *n.* لواوى lwaraway

supreme *a.* متعال،ترولولو mutaal; tar tolo lwar

surcharge *n.* اضافي ماليه izafee maleeya

surcharge *v.t.* اضافي ماليهلول izafee maleeya lagawal

sure *a.* امن،يقيني dadman; yaqeenee

surely *adv.* پهامنول pa dadman dawl

surety *n.* اطمينان itmaynan

surf *n.* سپه sapa

surface *n.* برسرنمخ؛سطح barseyran makh; sata

surface *v.i* باندنىمخوركول bandinay makh warkawal

surfeit *n.* بزارهكول،مول beyzara kawal; marawal

surge *n.* لوهپه lwara sapa

surge *v.i.* پجوول،پاندكدل sapey jorawal; sapand keydal

surgeon *n.* دجراحاكر da jarahay daktar

surgery *n.* جراحي jarahee

surmise *n.* اكل atkal

surmise *v.t.* اكلكول atkal kawal

surmount *v.t.* پرزياتدل pri zyateydal

surname *n.* كورنىنوم koranay noom

surpass *v.t.* ورخهمخككدل warsakha makhki keydal

surplus *n.* پاتهشونى،اضافي pata shoonay; izafee

surprise *n.* حرانتيا hayrantya

surprise *v.t.* حرانول hayranawal

surrender *v.t.* تسليمدل tasleemeydal

surrender *n* سپارنه sparana

surround *v.t.* احاطهكول ihata kawal

surroundings *n.* چاپريال chapeyryal

surtax *n.* مالياتيجريمه maleeyatee jareema

surveillance *n.* نظارت nazarat

survey *n.* اندازهيري،درجهبندي
andaza geyree; daraja bandee

survey *v.t.* اندازهيري کول andaza
geyree kawal

survival *n.* بقا baqa

survive *v.i.* ژوندىپاتكدل
zhwanday pati keydal

suspect *v.t.* بدګومانه کدل
badgoomana keydal

suspect *a.* مشکوک mashkook

suspect *n* شکمن shakman

suspend *v.t.* معلق کول،بنول muallaq
kawal; zandawal

suspense *n.* معلق muallaq

suspension *n.* تعليق،درونه taleeq;
darawana

suspicion *n.* شک shak

suspicious *a.* شکمن shakman

sustain *v.t.* ادامهور کول،خونديساتل
idama warkawal; khwandee
satal

sustenance *n.* خوندينه،ساتنه
khwandeyana; satana

swagger *v.i.* پهتکبرتلل pa takabbur
tlal

swagger *n* مغرور maghroor

swallow *v.t.* دچچپهشاناوازونه کول
da chanrchanri pa shan
awazoona kawal

swallow *n.* چچه chanrchanra

swallow *n.* دچچاوازونه da
chanrchanri awazoona

swamp *n.* دناولواوبو da nawalo
obo dand

swamp *v.t.* وبدل doobeydal

swan *n.* يومارغه yaw margha

swarm *n.* وه ه ganra goonra

swarm *v.i.* هوهجوول ganra goonra
jorawal

swarthy *a.* توررنی tor rangay

sway *v.i.* هخوادخوامبدل hakhwa
deykhwa zambeydal

sway *n* موجيحرکت mojee harakat

swear *v.t.* قسمخول qasam khwaral

sweat *n.* خول khwaley

sweat *v.i.* خولاکدل khwaley keydal

sweater *n.* هغه کس چخولاکوي،
رموونکیجاک hagha kas chi
khwaley kawee;
garmowoonkay jakat

sweep *v.i.* ربول reybazawal

sweep *n.* رب reybaz

sweeper *n.* ربوهونکی reybaz
wahoonkay

sweet *a.* خو khog

sweet *n* محبوب mahboob

sweeten *v.t.* خوول khwagawal

sweetmeat *n.* حلويات halweeyat

sweetness *n.* خووالی khogwalay

swell *v.i.* تسپودپداکدل taspod
payda keydal

swell *n* پسوب parsob

swift *a.* چک chatak

swim *v.i.* لامبووهل lambo wahal

swim *n* لامبووهنه lambo wahana

swimmer *n.* لامبووهنونکی lambo
wahoonkay

swindle *v.t.* غولول gholawal

swindle *n.* فرب farayb

swindler *n.* غولوونکی
gholawoonkay

swine *n.* سرکوزی sar koozay

swing *v.i.* تاوخول taw khwaral

swing *n* تاو، دفعاليت دوره taw; da faaleeyat dawra

swiss *n.* سويسي وى باژبه sweesee wagaray ya zhaba

swiss *a* سويسي sweesee

switch *n.* سوچ، ټ swich; tanray

switch *v.t.* بدلول، دبريناتكتهپورته كول badlawal; da breykhna tanray kkhata porta kawal

swoon *n.* كمزورتيا kamzortya

swoon *v.i* بهوه كدل bey hokha keydal

swoop *v.i.* نيول لاند بريد ناپه nasapa breed landi neewal

swoop *n* ناپي بريد nasapee breed

sword *n.* توره toora

sycamore *n.* يو مصرياينر yaw misree eenzar

sycophancy *n.* چاپلوسي chaplosee

sycophant *n.* چاپلوسه سى chaplosa saray

syllabic *n.* هجايي، ديوپاستازى hijayee; da yawey sapey astazay

syllable *n.* هجا،په hija; sapa

syllabus *n.* دزدكددورمضامين da zdakri da dawrey mazameen

sylph *n.* حوره hoora

sylvan *a.* نل مشتى zangal meyshtay

symbol *n.* علامه alama

symbolic *a.* نه لرونكى nakha laroonkay

symbolism *n.* په نوعلاموكاره كوونه pa nakho alamo khkara kawana

symbolize *v.t.* تركيبول tarkeebawal

symmetrical *a.* متناسب mutanasib

symmetry *n.* تطابق tatabuq

sympathetic *a.* زرسواند zraswand

sympathize *v.i.* خواخوي كاره كول khwakhoogee khkara kawal

sympathy *n.* هم اندتوب ham andtob

symphony *n.* له ييزساز dalayeez saz

symposium *n.* دوستانه مجلس dostana majlis

symptom *n.* علامه alama

symptomatic *a.* د ناروغنهاوعرض da naroghay nakha aw arz

synonym *n.* هم مانيزويي ham maneez wayay

synonymous *a.* هم مانا ham mana

synopsis *n.* اجمال، لنون ajmal; landoon

syntax *n.* غونله پوهه، دنحوعلم ghondla poha; da nahwi ilam

synthesis *n.* ترکيب، يوايت tarkeeb; yaw zayakht

synthetic *a.* مصنوعي masnooee

synthetic *n* مصنوعيز masnooee seez

syringe *n.* سرنج sirinj

syringe *v.t.* سرنج وهل sirinj wahal

syrup *n.* درمليزمحلول darmaleez mahlool

system *n.* قاعده، نظام qayda; nizam

systematic *a.* له نظام سره سم la nizam sara sam

systematize *v.t.* كنلارهورته جوول kranlara warta jorawal

T

table *n.* مز meyz

table *v.t.* سره‌نلول sara nakhlawal

tablet *n.* ‌ولۍ golay

taboo *n.* پرهز؛تقديس parheyz; taqdees

taboo *a.* حرام haram

taboo *v.t.* حرام لۍ haram ganral

tabular *a.* جدولي jadwalee

tabulate *v.t.* په‌نوم‌اكايول pa noom lar ki zayawal

tabulation *n.* لتليک‌جوړونه lakhtleek jorawana

tabulator *n.* لتليک‌جوړوونکی lakhtleek jorawoonkay

tacit *a.* ضمني؛اخيز zimnee; arkheez

taciturn *a.* خاموش khamosh

tackle *n.* مخه‌نيونه،کاري‌وسايل makha neewana; karee wasayal

tackle *v.t.* مخه‌نيول makha neewal

tact *n.* مهارت maharat

tactful *a.* ماهرانه mahirana

tactician *n.* کارپوه‌شخص karpoh shakhs

tactics *n.* مهارتونه‌او‌تدبيرونه maharatoona aw tadbeeroona

tactile *a.* دلمس‌حس‌پوراوند da lams his pori arwand

tag *n.* ريتاه؛پ reetara; patay

tag *v.t.* پپرلول patay pri lagawal

tail *n.* لکۍ lakay

tailor *n.* ‌ګنډونکی gandoonkay

tailor *v.t.* خياطي‌کول khayatee kawal

taint *n.* داغ؛ککتيا dagh; kakartya

taint *v.t.* ملوث‌کول mulawwis kawal

take *v.t* اخستل؛نيول akheystal; neewal

tale *n.* کيسه keesa

talent *n.* وتيا wartya

talisman *n.* کوي kodi

talk *v.i.* غدل؛خبرکول ghageydal; khabari kawal

talk *n* خبر khabari

talkative *a.* ژبغاند zhabgharand

tall *a.* هسک؛ج hask; jag

tallow *n.* وازده‌ويلاکوونه‌او‌غوروونه wazda weeli kawana aw ghwarawana

tally *n.* چوبخط؛شمره chobkhat; shmeyra

tally *v.t.* تطبيقول tatbeeqawal

tamarind *n.* هندي‌املي hindee imlee

tame *a.* کورنی؛اهلي koranay; ahlee

tame *v.t.* اهلي‌کول ahlee kawal

tamper *v.i.* جوجای‌کول jor jaray kawal

tan *v.i.* دلمرراکبدن‌خدل da lmar ranra ki badan khareydal

tan *n., a.* قهويي؛قهويي‌رن qahwayee; qahwayee rang

tangent *n.* مماس mamas

tangible *a.* دلمس‌ويز؛محسوس da lams seez; mahsoos

tangle *n.* اخته‌او‌مبتلا؛تاوراتاو akhta aw mubtila; tawrataw

tangle *v.t.* په‌جال‌کرارول،اخته‌کول pa jal ki rageyrawal; akhta kawal tank *n.* داوبوزرمتون،بانک da obo zeyramtoon; tank

tanker *n.* دتلولدونكلار da teylo leygdawoonki laray

tanner *n.* دباغ dabagh

tannery *n.* درمنوآش کوونه da sarmano ash kawana

tantalize *v.t.* چاتهلاسوراچول cha ta law warachawal

tantamount *a.* انول،معادل andwal; muadil

tap *n.* شیردان،سوری،نلکه sheerdan; sooray; nalka

tap *v.t.* ول،وروروووهل sasawal; wro wro wahal

tape *n.* په،تار patay; tar

tape *v.t* پهپسرهتل pa patay sara taral

taper *v.i.* نریکول naray kawal

taper *n* کوچنشمع koochnay shama

tapestry *n.* غالولهپرده ghalay dawla parda

tar *n.* قیر،تارکول qeer; tarkol

tar *v.t.* پهقیرولل،تارکوللول pa qeero laral; tarkol lagawal

target *n.* موخه،هدف mokha; hadaf

tariff *n.* محصول mahsool

tarnish *v.t.* کدرکول،داغیکول kadar kawal; daghee kawal

task *n.* کار،چاره kar; chara

task *v.t.* پهکومکارمارل pa kom kar gumaral

taste *n.* ذایقه zayqa

taste *v.t.* ذایقهلرل zayqa laral

tasteful *a.* خوندور khwandawar

tasty *a.* خوندور khwandawar

tatter *n.* یرویرشی seeri weeri shay

tatter *v.t* یرویرکول seeri weeri kawal

tattoo *n.* خال khal

tattoo *v.i.* خالوهل khal wahal

taunt *v.t.* رل ratal

taunt *n* رنه ratana

tavern *n.* شرابخانه sharabkhana

tax *n.* مالیه maleeya

tax *v.t.* مالیهلول maleeya lagawal

taxable *a.* دمالیو da maleeyey war

taxation *n.* مالیهایودنه maleeya eekhodana

taxi *n.* کسی tiksee

taxi *v.i.* کسیکتلل tiksee ki tlal

tea *n* چای chay

teach *v.t.* ورزدهکول warzda kawal

teacher *n.* وونکی khowoonkay

teak *n.* یوولونه yaw dawl wana

team *n.* ډله dala

tear *v.t.* شلول،شکول shlawal; shkawal

tear *n.* اوکه ookhka

tear *n.* قهر،پ qahar; tap

tearful *a.* ژغونی zharghonay

tease *v.t.* اذارول azarawal

teat *n.* دتیوکه da tee sooka

technical *n.* تخنیکي takhneekee

technicality *n.* نه تخنیکي takhneekee garana

technician *n.* تخنیکيکارپوه takhneekee karpoh

technique *n.* فن؛طریقه fan; tareeqa

technological *a.* تخنیکپوراوند takhneek pori arwand

technologist *n.* تخنیکيکارپوه takhneekee karpoh

technology *n.* تخنيک پیژندنه takhneekee peyzhandana

tedious *a.* ستومانه کوونکی stomana kawoonkay

tedium *n.* ستوماني stomana

teem *v.i.* تشول tashawal

teenager *n.* نوی ځوان naway zwan

teens *n. pl.* نورلس کلن ځوان noorlas kalan zwan

teethe *v.i.* غاښونه کول ghakhoona kawal

teetotal *a.* دنشه یي موادو دپرولو په اروند da nashayee mawado da preykhwalo pa arwand

teetotaller *n.* دنشه یي موادو دپرولو ملا تی da nashayee mawado da preykhwalo mlataray

telecast *n.* درايويي يالمويزيوني پروګرام خپرونه da radyoyee ya talweezyonee parogram khparawana

telecast *v.t.* راديويي يالمويزيوني پروګرام خپرول radyoyee ya talweezyonee parogram khparawal

telecommunications *n.* لمفوني او د رابطی اریکی taylafoonee aw da rabitey areeki

telegram *n.* لر لیکنی lar leekanay

telegraph *n.* لمراف talgaraf

telegraph *v.t.* پملراف خبرول pa talgaraf khabrawal

telegraphic *a.* لمرافي talgarafee

telegraphist *n.* لمراف کارپوه talgaraf karpoh

telegraphy *n.* دلراف فن da talgaraf fan

telepathic *a.* فکري تاولرونکي fikree taraw laroonkay

telepathist *n.* په فکري تاو باوري pa fikree taraw bawaree

telepathy *n.* دانساني فکري تاو فن da insanee fikree taraw fan

telephone *n.* لمفون taylafoon

telephone *v.t.* پملفون غدل pa taylafoon ghageydal

telescope *n.* ستوراری لروین storsaray larween

telescopic *a.* ستوراری لروینی storsaray larweenee

televise *v.t.* پملويزيون خپرول pa talweezyon khparawal

television *n.* لمويزيون talweezyon

tell *v.t.* ویل wayal

teller *n.* ویاند،شمرونکی wayand; shmeyroonkay

temper *n.* مزاج mizaj

temper *v.t.* فلزته او به ورکول filiz ta oba warkawal

temperament *n.* خوی khooy

temperamental *a.* مزاجي mizajee

temperance *n.* طبیعت tabyat

temperate *a.* ملايم mulayim

temperature *n.* تودوخي tawdokhee

tempest *n.* توپان toopan

tempestuous *a.* توپاني toopanee

temple *n.* عبادت ځای ibadat zay

temple *n* رونرکی ranrookay

temporal *a.* مهالیز mahaleez

temporary *a.* لنمهالي land mahalee

tempt *v.t.* تحريکول tahreekawal

temptation *n.* لمسون lamsoon

tempter *n.* لمسوونکی lamsawoonkay

ten *n., a* لس؛لسمهشمره las; lasama shmeyra

tenable *a.* دساتنو da satani war

tenacious *a.* محکم muhkam

tenacity *n.* ینت teengakht

tenancy *n.* اجارهداري eejaradaree

tenant *n.* اجارهدار eejara

tend *v.i.* ميللرل mayl laral

tendency *n.* توجه tawajo

tender *n* دداوطلبمزايده da dawtalbay muzayda

tender *v.t.* دليلامياداوطلبپهمزايدهکونه اخستل da leelam ya dawtalbay pa muzayda ki wanda akheystal

tender *n* داجناسولدوونکة da ajnaso leygdawani kakhtay

tender *a* نرم؛لطيف naram; lateef

tenet *n.* عقيده aqeeda

tennis *n.* دنسلوبه da taynas loba

tense *n.* شدت؛دفعلزمانه shiddat; da fayl zamana

tense *a.* شديد shadeed

tension *n.* فشار fishar

tent *n.* خيمه khayma

tentative *a.* تجربوي tajrubawee

tenure *n.* دتصرفوخت da tasarruf wakht

term *n.* موده mooda

term *v.t.* نومپرايودل noom pri eekhodal

terminable *a.* پایتهرسدونی pay ta rasawal

terminal *a.* پهبیخکپروت pa beykh ki prot

terminal *n* آخر akhir

terminate *v.t.* ختمول khatmawal

termination *n.* پای؛ختمدا pay; khatmeyda

terminological *a.* نومپوهنیز noompohaneez

terminology *n.* نومپوهنه noompohana

terminus *n.* وروستنیتمای wrustanay tamzay

terrace *n.* چوتره؛برنه chawtra; baranda

terrible *a.* وحشتناک wahshatnak

terrier *n.* یوولکلیکوچنیکاريسپی yaw dawl khkulay koochnay khkaree spay

terrific *a.* فوقالعاده fawqul ada

terrify *v.t.* ترهول tarhawal

territorial *a.* سيمهییز seemayeez

territory *n.* سيمه seema

terror *n.* دار dar

terrorism *n.* ترهري tarhagaree

terrorist *n.* ترهر tarhagar

terrorize *v.t.* ترهول tarhawal

terse *a.* دک؛روزلشوی dak; rozal shaway

test *v.t.* آزمویل azmoyal

test *n* امتحان؛آزموینه imtihan; azmoyana

testament *n.* انجیل injeel

testicle *n.* خوه؛خصیه khota; khuseeya

testify *v.i.* تصدیقول tasdeeqawal

testimonial *n.* شهادتنامه shahadat nama

testimony *n.* تصدیق tasdeeq

tete-a-tete *n.* دوهپهدوه dwa pa dwa

tether *n.* پی paray

tether *v.t.* پزواني کول peyzwanee kawal

text *n.* عبارت؛متن ibarat; matan

textile *a.* اوبدل شوی obdal shaway

textile *n* منسوجات؛توکر mansoojat; tokar

textual *n.* لفظی lafzee

texture *n.* اوبدنه؛تنسته obdana; tanasta

thank *v.t.* منه ورته ویل manana warta wayal

thanks *n.* مننه manana

thankful *a.* منندوی manandoy

thankless *a.* ناشکره nashukra

that *a.* بل bal

that dem. *pron.* هغه hagha

that rel. *pron.* یو هغه hagha yaw

that *adv.* داول چ da dawl chi

that *conj.* چ دا da chi

thatch *n.* کابل؛لوخه kagal; lookha

thatch *v.t.* اخول akheyrawal

thaw *v.i* ویلکدل weeli keydal

thaw *n* رمموسم garam mosam

theatre *n.* تیاتر tyatar

theatrical *a.* تیاترپوراوند tyatar pori arwand

theft *n.* غلا ghla

their *a.* دهغوی da haghwee

theirs *pron.* د هغوی da haghwee

theism *n.* په خدای باور pa khuday bawar

theist *n.* په خدای باورلرونکی pa khuday bawar laroonkay

them *pron.* ته هغوی haghwee ta

thematic *a.* موضوعي mawzooee

theme *n.* موضوع؛مقاله mawzoo

then *adv.* کله چي kala chi

then *a* بیا bya

thence *adv.* له هغه لوري چ la hagha lori chi

theocracy *n.* دروحانیونوواکمني da roohaneeyoonu wakmanee

theologian *n.* ددیني علومو کارپوه da deenee uloomu karpoh

theological *a.* په الهي چاروپوراوند pa ilahee charo pori arwand

theology *n.* دین پوهنه deen pohana

theorem *n.* مسئله؛قاعده masala; qayda

theoretical *a.* نظري nazaree

theorist *n.* په نظري علم پوه pa nazaree ilam poh

theorize *v.i.* نظري کول nazaree seyrani kawal

theory *n.* نظري علم nazaree ilam

therapy *n.* معالجه mualija

there *adv.* هلته halta

thereabouts *adv.* په هغه شاوخوا ک pa hagha shawkhwa ki

thereafter *adv.* وروسته له wrusta la

thereby *adv.* له دی کبله la dey kabala

therefore *adv.* له دی لمله la dey lamala

thermal *a.* حرارتي hararatee

thermometer *n.* تودوخمچ tawdokhmeych

thermos flask *n.* دتودوخدرجه په خپل ځای خوندي ساتونکی لوی da tawdokhay daraja pa khpal zay khwandee satoonkay lokhay

thesis *n.* پوهنلیک pohanleek

thick *a.* راغوز raghond

thick *n.* غليظ ghaleez

thick *adv.* پهغليظول pa ghaleez dawl

thicken *v.i.* ضخيم كول zakheem kawal

thicket *n.* بوي ganr bootee

thief *n.* غل ghal

thigh *n.* ورون؛بنه wroon; panday

thimble *n.* وتمو gotmo

thin *a.* نرى naray

thin *v.t.* نرول dangarawal

thing *n.* شى؛يز shay; seez

think *v.t.* فكركول fikar kawal

thinker *n.* انگيريال angeyryal

third *a.* دريم dreyam

third *n.* دريمهبرخه dreyama barkha

thirdly *adv.* دريمداچ dreyam da chi

thirst *n.* تنده tanda

thirst *v.i.* تى كدل tagay keydal

thirsty *a.* تى tagay

thirteen *n.* ديارلس dyarlas

thirteen *a.* ديارلس dyarlas

thirteenth *a.* ديارلسم dyarlasam

thirtieth *a.* درشم deyrsham

thirtieth *n* درشمهبرخه deyrshama barkha

thirty *n.* درش deyrsh

thirty *a* درش deyrsh

thistle *n.* اغزى aghzay

thither *adv.* ته هخوا hakhwa ta

thorn *n.* اغزى aghzay

thorny *a.* اغزن aghzan

thorough *a* پوره؛مطلق poora; mutlaq

thoroughfare *n.* لويهلاره loya lara

though *conj.* ارچه agar chay

though *adv.* كههم ka sa ham

thought *n* اند؛فكر and; fikar

thoughtful *a.* اندپال andpal

thousand *n.* زر zar

thousand *a* دزروشمر da zaro shmeyr

thrall *n.* مريى mrayay

thralldom *n.* اسارت؛مرييتوب asarat; mrayeetob

thrash *v.t.* بولاودرزول dabawal aw drazawal

thread *n.* تار tar

thread *v.t* تارپكاچول tar paki achawal

threadbare *a.* شلشل shalag shalag

threat *n.* خطر khatar

threaten *v.t.* وال gwakhal

three *n.* در drey

three *a* ددروشمر da dreyo shmeyr

thresh *v.t.* كول؛كوترهكول takawal; kotra kawal

thresher *n.* دغلكولوماشين da galey masheen

threshold *n.* درشل darshal

thrice *adv.* درله در drey zala

thrift *n.* پاسرهشوشتمني pasra shawi shtamanee

thrifty *a.* پاسرهكوونكى pasra kawoonkay

thrill *n.* چ؛لز rach; larz

thrill *v.t.* چول rachawal

thrive *v.i.* هودهكول kha wada kawal

throat *n.* ستوني؛مر stoonay

throaty *a.* دلوىمرخاوند؛غلودلى da loy maray khawand; ghag lweydalay

throb *v.i.* درزدل drazeydal

throb *n.* درز؛ضرب draz; zarb

throe *n.* ددردیکه da dard sreeka

throne *n.* د،دپاچاتخت gaday; da pacha takht

throne *v.t.* پاچاکول pacha kawal

throng *n.* زیاتخلک zyat khalk

throng *v.t.* هوهجوول ganra goonra jorawal

throttle *n.* ستونى؛غاه stoonay; ghara

throttle *v.t.* ستونىورتختهکول stoonay wartakhta kawal

through *prep.* لهلور،پهواسطه la lori; pa wasta

through *adv.* سرترسره،لهپیلهترپایه sar tar sara; la payla tar paya

through *a* مستقیم mustaqeem

throughout *adv.* پهولنیزول pa tolaneez dawl

throughout *prep.* سرترسره sar tar sara

throw *v.t.* غورول ghorzawal

throw *n.* غوروونه ghorzawana

thrust *v.t.* پهزورسرهمنل pa zor sara mandal

thrust *n* مننه؛دننهکوونه mandana; danana kawana

thud *n.* درب drab drab

thud *v.i.* دربدربکول drab drab kawal

thug *n.* خونى؛انسانوژونکى khoonee; insan wazhoonkay

thumb *n.* بهوته bata gota

thumb *v.t.* پهبهوتهسولول pa bata gota soolawal

thump *n.* درب؛خرپ drab; khrap

thump *v.t.* درزول drazawal

thunder *n.* تندر tandar

thunder *v.i.* دتندرپهشانغکول da tandar pa shan ghag kawal

thunderous *a.* تندرتهورته tandar ta warta

Thursday *n.* پنجشنبه؛دزیارتور panjshamba; da zyarat wraz

thus *adv.* پهدول pa dey dawl

thwart *v.t.* لارهیبندول lara yi bandawal

tiara *n.* شاهيتاج shahee taj

tick *n.* دسموننه da samoon nakha

tick *v.i.* دسموننهلول da samoon nakha lagawal

ticket *n.* تکت teekat

tickle *v.t.* تخول takhnrawal

ticklish *a.* خانوزمه khangar wazma

tidal *a.* پهجذراومدپوراوند pa jazar aw mad pori arwand

tide *n.* دسمندرپه da samandar sapa

tidings *n. pl.* خبرونه khabroona

tidiness *n.* منظموالى munazzamwalay

tidy *a.* منظم munazzam

tidy *v.t.* منظمکول munazzam kawal

tie *v.t.* غوهکول ghota kawal

tie *n* غوه؛بند ghota; band

tier *n.* صف؛کتار saf; katar

tiger *n.* پانگ prang

tight *a.* کلک klak

tighten *v.t.* کلککول klakawal

tigress *n.* پازینه khazeena prang

tile *n.* كاشي كودوى kashee kawdoray

tile *v.t.* كاشي كودوىلول kashee kawdoray lagawal

till *prep.* ترهغهمهاله tar hagha mahala

till *n.* conj. چ د تر tar dey chi

till *v.t.* مكهدكتلپارهتيارول zmaka da kakht lapara tayarawal

tilt *v.i.* كدل kageydal

tilt *n.* كووالى kogwalay

timber *n.* لرى largay

time *n.* مهال mahal

time *v.t.* وختبرابرول،وختاكل wakht barabarawal

timely *a.* پرخپلوخت par khpal wakht

timid *a.* بزه bey zra

timidity *n.* بزهتوب bey zratob

timorous *a.* شرميندوكى sharmeendookay

tin *n.* قلعي qalee

tin *v.t.* پهقلعيسرهپول pa qalee sara pokhal

tincture *n.* يوولدرمل yaw dawl darmal

tincture *v.t.* رنول rangawal

tinge *n.* جزيىرنگ juzyee rang

tinge *v.t.* جزيىرنگوركول juzyee rang warkawal

tinker *n.* رات tatar

tinsel *n.* دفلسلاندهپ da filas zalanda patay

tint *n.* پيكهرنگ peeka rang

tint *v.t.* پيكهرنگوركول peeka rang warkawal

tiny *a.* كوچنى koochnay

tip *n.* سوكه sooka

tip *v.t.* بتولاكدولاملهراغورزيدل bey toley keydo lamala raghorzeydal

tip *n.* انعام eenam

tip *v.t.* انعاموركول eenam warkawal

tip *n.* مشوره mashwara

tip *v.t.* مشورهوركول mashwara warkawal

tipsy *a.* مست،نشه mast; nasha

tirade *n.* اودهاولهقهركهونا oogda aw la qahra daka wayna

tire *v.t.* ستىكدل،ستىكول staray keydal; staray kawal

tiresome *a.* ستومانهكوونكى stomana kawoonkay

tissue *n.* نسج nasj

titanic *a.* غر deyr ghat

tithe *n.* لسمهبرخه lasama barkha

title *n.* لقب laqab

titular *a.* افتخاري،رسمي iftikharee; rasmee

toad *n.* مكمشتىحشرهخور zmakmeyshtay hashra khor

toast *n.* يوولپستهو yaw dawl pasta doday

toast *v.t.* پههوروريتول pa hor wreetawal

tobacco *n.* تنباكو tambakoo

today *adv.* پهدوختونوك pa dey wakhtoono ki

today *n.* ور نن nan wraz

toe *n.* منول mangol

toe *v.t.* منوللول mangol lagawal

toffee *n.* كوچنكلكهشيريني koochnay klaka sheereenee

toga *n.* اودادر oogad sadar

together *adv.* پهەسره pa gada sara

toil *n.* کاو،لهزحمتهک کار karaw; la zehmata dak kar

toil *v.i.* د کختهک کار کول da karakhta dak kar kawal

toilet *n.* tatay

token *n.* نانه،کteekat nakhana;

tolerable *a.* دتحملو da tahammul war

tolerance *n.* زغم zgham

tolerant *a.* زغمونکی zghamoonkay

tolerate *v.t.* زغمل zghamal

toleration *n.* حوصله،صبر hawsala; sabar

toll *n.* دسکباج da sarak baj

toll *n* دبدپله کبلهزیاناوتلفات da badi peykhi la kabala zyan aw talfat

toll *v.t.* دزنپهکنولوسرهاعلانول da zang pa krangawalo sara aylanawal

tomato *n.* سوربانجان soor banjan

tomb *n.* قبر qabar

tomboy *n.* بدلمنیهلک badlamanay halak

tomcat *n.* نرپشی nar pashay

tome *n.* دکتابدوتن da keetab dotanay

tomorrow *n.* سبا saba

tomorrow *adv.* ته سبا saba ta

ton *n.* دوزنیوهپمانه da wazan yawa paymana

tone *n.* غ،آهنـ ghag; ahang

tone *v.t.* دبدنپهمضبوطول،رنورکول da badan pati mazbootawal; rang warkawal

tongs *n. pl.* انبور amboor

tongue *n.* ژبه zhaba

tonic *a.* مقوي،غن muqawee; ghagan

tonic *n.* مقويدرمل muqawee darmal

to-night *n.* نن شپه nan shpa

tonight *adv.* نندشپی nan da shpey

tonne *n.*

tonsil *n.* بغو baghot

tonsure *n.* سرخرینه sar khreyana

too *adv.* هم ham

tool *n.* آله ala

tooth *n.* غا ghakh

toothache *n.* دغاخو da ghakh khoog

top *n.* و که،اوج sooka; oj

top *v.t.* ترولولوایموندل tar tolo lwar zay moondal

top *n.* چت،بام chat; bam

topaz *n.* زیاقوت zeyr yaqoot

topic *n.* موضوع،مبحث mawzoo; mubhas

topical *a.* موضوعاتي mawzooatee

topographer *n.* نخچهک nakhcha kakh

topographical *a.* نخچهاخیستنوپور nakhcha akheestano pori arwand اوند

topography *n.* نخچهاخیستنه nakhcha akheestana

topple *v.i.* ندل nareydal

topsy turvy *a.* سرچپه sar chapa

topsy turvy *adv* پهسرچپهول pa sar chapa dawl

torch *n.* راغ sragh

torment *n.* کاو karaw

torment *v.t.* کول karawal

tornado *n.* هوايي‌توپان hawayee toopan

torpedo *n.* سمندريوني‌توغوندى samandaryoonay toghonday

torpedo *v.t.* په‌سمندريوني‌توغوندي ويشتل pa samandaryoonee toghondee weeshtal

torrent *n.* سلاب saylab

torrential *a.* سلابي saylabee

torrid *a.* تودده،ررم tawda; deyr garam

tortoise *n.* مكمشتةشمشتة zmakmeyshtay shamshatay

tortuous *a.* كلچلرونكى kagleych laroonkay

torture *n.* شكنجه،ربوونه shkanja; rabrawana

torture *v.t.* شكنجه‌كول shkanja kawal

toss *v.t.* شرخط‌كول sheyr khat

toss *n* شرخط sheyr khat

total *a.* ول tol

total *n.* حاصل،جمع hasil; jama

total *v.t.* جمع‌كول jama kawal

totality *n.* بشپارتوب bashpartob

touch *v.t.* لمس‌كول lams kawal

touch *n* لمس lams

touchy *a.* حساس،نازك hasas; nazak

tough *a.* توانمند twanmand

toughen *v.t.* كلكول،توانول klakawal; twanawal

tour *n.* يون،سفر yoon; safar

tour *v.i.* سفركول safar kawal

tourism *n.* رندويي garzandoyee

tourist *n.* سيلاني seelanee

tournament *n.* ورزشي‌سيالي warzishee syalee

towards *prep.* لورته lor ta

towel *n.* زان‌پاک zan pak

towel *v.t.* په‌زان‌پاک‌وچول pa zan pak wachawal

tower *n.* برج braj

tower *v.i.* هسكول haskawal

town *n.* خاروى khargotay

township *a.* خاروى khargotay

toy *n.* لوبتكه lobtaka

toy *v.i.* لوبدل lobeydal

trace *n.* خاپ،اثر khap; asar

trace *v.t.* تعقيبول taqeebawal

traceable *a.* دموندنى‌ور da moondani war

track *n.* مند،دپاى mand; da pkhey zay

track *v.t.* تعقيبول taqeebawal

tract *n.* دزمكي‌پراختيا da zmaki parakhtya

tract *n* مقاله maqala

traction *n.* كشش kashish

tractor *n.* دييوماشين da yeywi masheen

trade *n.* تجارت tijarat

trade *v.i* تجارت‌كول tijarat kawal

trader *n.* سودار sawdagar

tradesman *n.* سودار sawdagar

tradition *n.* دود،روايت dood; riwayat

traditional *a.* روايتي riwayatee

traffic *n.* ونه‌راونه،تراتگ wrana rawrana; tag ratag

traffic *v.i.* تراتگ‌كول tag ratag kawal

tragedian *n.* غم‌لپليكونكى gham larali peykhi leekoonkay

tragedy *n.* ويرللپه weer larali peykha

tragic *a.* ويرللى weer laralay

trail *n.* دپخاپونه؛جوهشولاره da pkhey khapoona; jora shawi lara

trail *v.t.* ازنپسکال zan pasi kagal

trailer *n.* بحركتهواون bey harakata wagon

train *n.* اورای orgaday

train *v.t.* تربيهوركول tarbeeya warkawal

trainee *n.* زدهكوونكى zda kawoonkay

training *n.* زدهكه؛تربيت zdakra; tarbeeyat

trait *n.* خصوصيت khasooseeyat

traitor *n.* خاين khayin

tram *n.* داردننهچلدونكىبرنايىواون da khar danana chaleydoonkay breykhnayee wagon

trample *v.t.* پايمالول paymalawal

trance *n.* جذبه؛بهوي jazba; bey hokhee

tranquil *a.* آسوده asooda

tranquility *n.* سكون sakoon

tranquillize *v.t.* دسكوندرملوركول da sakoon darmal warkawal

transact *v.t.* دپسوراكهوركهكول da peyso rakra warkra kawal

transaction *n.* دپسوراكهوركه da peyso rakra warkra

transcend *v.t.* پرمخككدل pri makhki keydal

transcendent *a.* برلاسى bar lasay

transcribe *v.t.* پهليكلىشكلكراوستل pa leekalee shakal ki rawastal

transcription *n.* نقلجوونه naqal jorawana

transfer *n.* وراستول؛منتقلي warastawal; muntaqilee

transfer *v.t.* منتقلكول muntaqil kawal

transferable *a.* انتقالكدونكى intiqal keydoonkay

transfiguration *n.* دشكلاوربدلون da shakal aw seyrey badloon

transfigure *v.t.* نورانيكول nooranee kawal

transform *v.* نوبهوركول nawi banra warkawal

transformation *n.* دببدلون da banri badloon

transgress *v.t.* ترترىكول tri teyray kawal

transgression *n.* سرغاوى sar gharaway

transit *n.* تريدنه teyreydana

transition *n.* انتقال؛بدلون intiqal; badloon

transitive *n.* ژرترىدونكى؛متعديفعل zhar teyreydoonkay; mutadee fayl

transitory *n.* ناپايدار napaydar

translate *v.t.* ژبال zhbaral

translation *n.* ژباه zhbara

transmigration *n.* دارواماانويوبلته نوتل da arwagano yaw bal ta nanawatal

transmission *n.* دمخابراتىپولدرالد da mukhabiratee sapo leygd raleygd

transmit *v.t.* داوسپنيزلارپهمرسته استول da ospaneezi lari pa mrasta astawal

transmitter *n.* مخابراتي‌پلادوونکی‌او استوونکی‌ماشين mukhabiratee sapey leygdawoonkay aw astawoonkay masheen

transparent *a.* رو roonr

transplant *v.t.* پیوندول peywandawal

transport *v.t.* لدول leygdawal

transport *n.* دلادولووسیله da leygdawalo waseela

transportation *n.* لدرالد leygd raleygd

trap *n.* دام dam

trap *v.t.* دام‌کرول dam ki geyrawal

trash *n.* ناکاره‌شی nakara shay

travel *v.i.* سفر‌کول safar kawal

travel *n* سفر safar

traveller *n.* مسافر musafar

tray *n.* پتنوس patnoos

treacherous *a.* خاینانه khaynana

treachery *n.* خیانت khyanat

tread *v.t.* پپرایودل pkhey pri eekhodal

tread *n* د گام‌اخیستن‌آواز da gam akheestani awaz

treason *n.* ژمنه‌ماتوونه zhmana matawana

treasure *n.* خزانه khazana

treasure *v.t.* ارزت‌ورکول kha arzakht warkawal

treasurer *n.* خزانه‌دار khazanadar

treasury *n.* خزانه‌داري khazana daree

treat *v.t.* چلند‌کول chaland kawal

treat *n* چلند؛رویه chaland; riwayya

treatise *n.* لیکلژمنه leekali zhmana

treatment *n.* چلند؛ملمستیا chaland; meylmastya

treaty *n.* میثاق meesaq

tree *n.* ونه wana

trek *v.i.* ستومانه‌سفر stomana safar

trek *n.* ستومانه‌کوونکی‌سفر‌کول stomana kawoonkay safar kawal

tremble *v.i.* رددل reygdeydal

tremendous *a.* شاندار shandar

tremor *n.* رددنه reygdeydana

trench *n.* مورچل morchal

trench *v.t.* مورچل‌جوول morchal jorawal

trend *n.* میلان meelan

trespass *v.i.* یوه‌لورته‌میلان‌لرل yawa lor ta meelan laral

trespass *n.* تری‌کول teyray kawal

trial *n.* محاکمه muhakama

triangle *n.* دروی drey gotay

triangular *a.* درویز drey goteez

tribal *a.* قبیلوي qabeelawee

tribe *n.* قبیله qabeela

tribulation *n.* سخته‌آزموینه sakhta azmoyana

tribunal *n.* محکمه mahkama

tributary *n.* دعزت‌پرزوینه da eezat peyrzoyana

tributary *a.* فرعي؛مرستیال faree; mrastyal

trick *n* چل؛دوکه chal; doka

trick *v.t.* چل‌کول chal kawal

trickery *n.* چلبازي chalbazee

trickle *v.i.* للراتل‌لل؛دل lag lag ratlal; saseydal

trickster *n.* دوکه‌مار dokamar

tricky *a.* چلباز chalbaz

tricolour *a.* دررنج drey rangee

tricolour *n.* دررنی drey rangay

tricycle *n.* ددریودورونوخاوند da dreyo dawro khawand

trifle *n.* کمارزتهیز kam arzakhta seez

trifle *v.i* نایزل na seez ganral

trigger *n.* دوسلماشه da wasley masha

trim *a.* متعادل،زهراکونکی mutaadil; zra rakhkoonkay

trim *n* سینار،سموونه seengar; samawana

trim *v.t.* تراشل،ترتیبول trashal; tarteebawal

trinity *n.* درونیتوب،تثلیث drey goonaytob; taslees

trio *n.* درکسیزهله drey kaseeza dala

trip *v.t.* ویدل،بکرخول khwayeydal; takar khwaral

trip *n.* سفر safar

tripartite *a.* دراخیز drey arkheez

triple *a.* درونی drey goonay

triple *v.t.,* درچندهکول drey chanda kawal

triplicate *a.* درچنده drey chanda

triplicate *n* دراخیزهتون drey arkheeza taroon

triplicate *v.t.* درچندهکول drey chanda kawal

triplication *n.* درچندهکوونه drey chanda kawana

tripod *n.* درپایه drey paya

triumph *n.* بریا،فتح barya; fata

triumph *v.i.* بریاکدل barya keydal

triumphal *a.* بریالی،فاتح baryalay; fatay

triumphant *a.* بریالی،فاتح baryalay; fatay

trivial *a.* بارزته bey arzakhta

troop *n.* دپویانوله da pawzyano dala

troop *v.i* پهلهکحرکتکول pa dala ki harakat kawal

trooper *n.* سرتری sar teyray

trophy *n.* دبریالیتوبیادار da baryaleetob yadgar

tropic *n.* دناستوایسیم da naray ustawayee seema

tropical *a.* استوایِ ustawayee

trot *v.i.* چکتلل chatak tlal

trot *n* چکت،داسغوندهتلل chatak tag; da as ghonda tlal

trouble *n.* ربروونه rabrawana

trouble *v.t.* ربرول rabrawal

troublesome *a.* ربروونکی rabrawoonkay

troupe *n.* دسندرغاوله da sandar gharo dala

trousers *n. pl* پتلون patloon

trowel *n.* دباغوانبلچه da baghwanay beylcha

truce *n.* لنمهالیاوربند lang mahalee orband

truck *n.* لار laray

true *a.* رتونی rakhtoonay

trump *n.* دلوبویوولپاه،بهاواهمسی da lobo yaw dawl panra; kha aw aham saray

trump *v.t.* بهتانلول buhtan lagawal

trumpet *n.* تروم،شپل trom; shpeylay

trumpet *v.i.* پهلوغاعلانول pa lwar ghag aylanawal

trunk *n.* تنه،دوزکنده tana; da wani kanda

trust *n.* اعتماد aytimad

trust *v.t* اعتمادکول aytimad kawal

trustee *n.* امین ameen

trustful *a.* امین ameen

trustworthy *a.* دباورو da bawar war

trusty *n.* دباوروسی da bawar war saray

truth *n.* رتیا rakhtya

truthful *a.* رتونی rakhtoonay

try *v.i.* هه کول hasa kawal

try *n* هه hasa

trying *a.* زیارک zyar kakh

tryst *n.* دخفیه خبرواتروای اووخت da khoofeeya khabaro ataro zay aw wakht

tub *n.* دلمبدویاجامووینلوتغاره da lambeydo ya jamo weenzalo taghara

tube *n.* نل nal

tuberculosis *n.* رنزنری naray ranz

tubular *a.* لهنل خهجوشوی la nal sakha jor shaway

tug *v.t.* پهزورهکشول pa zora kashawal

tuition *n.* تعلیم،بوونه taleem; khowana

tumble *v.i.* لوېدل lweydal

tumble *n.* رغدنه raghreydana

tumbler *n.* پیاله،ېلاس pyala; geelas

tumour *n.* سرطانی غوه sartanee ghota

tumult *n.* غوغا ghawgha

tumultuous *a.* بنظمه bey nazma

tune *n.* لحن،آهن lehen; ahang

tune *v.t.* موافق کدل،بهموزونآهنویل muwafiq keydal; pa mawzoon ahang wayal

tunnel *n.* تونل،داستنبهن toonal; da eystani bahanz

tunnel *v.i.* تونل کیندل toonal keendal

turban *n.* پکی patkay

turbine *n.* رخدونکیماشین sarkheydoonkay masheen

turbulence *n.* بلوا balwa

turbulent *a.* بلوایی balwayee

turf *n.* دخاوروپورتنبرخهچدووراو وراستهموادلري da khawro portanay barkha chi da wakho reykhi aw wrasta mawad laree

turkey *n.* ختمیچر khartamee charg

turmeric *n.* کورکمن koorkaman

turmoil *n.* دپرشانحالت da parayshanay halat

turn *v.i.* تاودل،رخدل taweydal; sarkheydal

turn *n* چورلدنه،بدلون،تاو choorleydana; badloon; taw

turner *n.* خراد،تراشوونکی kharad; tarashawoonkay

turnip *n.* پر teypar

turpentine *n.* رانه،ننده ranzara; nanzara

turtle *n.* شمشته shamshatay

tusk *n.* اوداوترهغا oogad aw teyra ghakh

tussle *n.* شخه،لانجه shkhara; lanja

tussle *v.i.* لانجهکول lanja kawal

tutor *n.* ووون khowan

tutorial *a.* درسي؛تعليمي darsee; taleemee

tutorial *n.* درسي كتاب darsee keetab

twelfth *a.* دولسم dolasam

twelfth *n.* دولسمهبرخه dolasama barkha

twelve *n.* دولس dolas

twelve *n* درجن darjan

twentieth *a.* شلم shalam

twentieth *n* شلمهبرخه shalama barkha

twenty *a.* شلم shalam

twenty *n* شل shal

twice *adv.* دومله dwa zala

twig *n.* كوچنىاخ؛طريقه koochnay khakh; tareeqa

twilight *n* سهاركـ sahar sark

twin *n.* جوه؛غبرولى jora; ghbargolay

twin *a* مركب murakab

twinkle *v.i.* پكدل parkeydal

twinkle *n.* پكـ park

twist *v.t.* نتل nakhteyzal

twist *n.* غنه gharana

twitter *n.* چوهار choonrar

twitter *v.i.* چوندل choonreydal

two *n.* دوه dwa

two *a.* دواه dwara

twofold *a.* دوهچنده dwa chanda

type *n.* قسم؛ول qisam; dawl

type *v.t.* چاپول؛لبندي كول chapawal; dalbandee kawal

typhoid *n.* دتايفوئيدتبه da tayfoyeed taba

typhoon *n.* سمندريتوپان samandaree toopan

typhus *n.* دتيفوسرنز da teefoos ranz

typical *a.* نوبتي؛بلهييز nobatee; beylgayeez

typify *v.t.* نمونهودل؛دمعياربهوركول namoona khodal; da mayar banra warkawal

typist *n.* چاپوونكى chapawoonkay

tyranny *n.* زورزياتى zor zyatay

tyrant *n.* ظالمجابر zalim jabir

tyre *n.* دايپايه da gadee paya

U

udder *n.* غولانه gholanza

uglify *v.t.* ناوهبهوركول nawara banra warkawal

ugliness *n.* بدشكلي bad shaklee

ugly *a.* بدشكله bad shakla

ulcer *n.* دمعدپ da maydey tap

ulcerous *a.* دمعدپپوراوند da maydey tap pori arwand

ulterior *a.* بعدي؛لر badee; leyri

ultimate *a.* آخري akhiree

ultimately *adv.* پهآخره كـ pa akhira ki

ultimatum *n.* مهلت muhlat

umbrella *n.* چتر chatray

umpire *n.* سرلوبارى sar lobsaray

umpire *v.t.,* سرلوباريكول sar lobsaree kawal

unable *a.* ناتوان natwan

unanimity *n.* همااندتوب ham andtob

unanimous *a.* پهيوهخوله pa yawa khula

unaware *a.* ناخبر،بپامه bey pama; na khabar

unawares *adv.* په‌بخبرسره pa bey khabray sara

unburden *v.t.* بار‌کوزول bar koozawal

uncanny *a.* خطرناک khatarnak

uncertain *a.* شکمن shakman

uncle *n.* تره،کاکا tra; kaka

uncouth *a.* بدرنه،ویجا bad rang; weejar

under *prep.* لاند landi

under *adv* په‌پول pa pat dawl

under *a* لاندینی landeenay

undercurrent *n.* پکار pat kar

underdog *n* هغه‌چاو‌مولنیزوضعیت ولري hagha chi nawara tolaneez wuzeeyat walaree

undergo *v.t.* زغمل zghamal

undergraduate *n.* نوی‌پوهنتونی زدکریال naway pohantoonee zdakryal

underhand *a.* مخفي makhfee

underline *v.t.* دکوميزلاندکره‌راکل da kom seez landi karkha rakkhal

undermine *v.t.* وروورو‌کمزوری‌کول wro wro kamzoray kawal

underneath *adv.* له‌لاندخه la landi sakha

underneath *prep.* لاندینی landeenay

understand *v.t.* پوهدل poheydal

undertake *v.t.* ژبه‌کول؛ژمنه‌کول zhaba kawal; zhmana kawal

undertone *n.* کمزوری‌او‌یه‌آواز kamzoray aw teet awaz

underwear *n.* لاندینه‌جام landeenay jamey

underworld *n.* دجنایتکارانوز da janayatkarano naray

undo *v.t.* باطلول batilawal

undue *a.* بایه،بوخته bey zaya; bey wakhta

undulate *v.i.* په‌ییزکول sapayeez kawal

undulation *n.* پاندوالی sapandwalay

unearth *v.t.* له‌خاوروخه‌راایستل la khawro sakha raeestal

uneasy *a.* پریشان parayshan

unfair *a* بانصافه bey insafa

unfold *v.t.* کاره‌کول khkara kawal

unfortunate *a.* بدمرغه bad margha

ungainly *a.* بمهارته bey maharata

unhappy *a.* خفه،ناکام khafa; nakam

unification *n.* یوکونز yaw kawang

union *n.* اتحادیه itihadeeya

unionist *n.* داتحادیغی da itihadeeyey gharay

unique *a.* بمثله bey misla

unison *n.* هم‌غیزتوب ham ghareetob

unit *n.* یوون yawoon

unite *v.t.* یوکول yaw kawal

unity *n.* یووالی yaw walay

universal *a.* نیوال nareewal

universality *n.* جامعیت jamieeyat

universe *n.* کائنات kaynat

university *n.* پوهنتون pohantoon

unjust *a.* غرمنصفانه ghayr munsifana

unless *conj.* مگرداچ magar da chi

unlike *a* مختلف mukhtalif
unlike *prep* برعكس bar aks
unlikely *a.* ناكدونى nakeydoonay
unmanned *a.* نامرد،بلهانساندوسيل na mard; bey la insana da waseelay
unmannerly *a* بادبي bey adabee
unprincipled *a.* بلار bey lari
unreliable *a.* باعتباره bey aytibara
unrest *n* اضطراب iztirab
unruly *a.* سرغاند sar gharand
unsettle *v.t.* نظمورخرابول nazam warkharabawal
unsheathe *v.t.* رندول sargandawal
until *prep.* چو so chi
until *conj* تردچ tar dey chi
untoward *a.* ورانكارى wrankaray
unwell *a.* ناپاك na pak
unwittingly *adv.* بخبرسره bey khabaray sara
up *adv.* پهواند،پورتهله pa wrandi; porta la
up *prep.* پورته porta
upbraid *v.t* رل،ناخوىكول ratal; nakhwakhee kawal
upheaval *n.* ناپىبدلون nasapee badloon
uphold *v.t* ملاتركول mla tar kawal
upkeep *n* دخونديساتندكارلت da khwandee satani da kar lagakht
uplift *v.t.* پورتهول porta wral
uplift *n* رفعت،سرلوي rifat; sar lwaree
upon *prep* پر،دپاسه par; da pasa
upper *a.* پورتنى portanay
upright *a.* نغ،ولا neygh; walar

uprising *n.* پاون pasoon
uproar *n.* غوغا ghawgha
uproarious *a.* لهشورهك la shora dak
uproot *v.t.* لهبخهراكل la beykha rakkhal
upset *v.t.* پرشانهكول parayshana kawal
upshot *n.* حاصل hasil
upstart *n.* نوىباىشوى naway baday shaway
up-to-date *a.* تازه taza
upward *a.* پورته porta
upwards *adv.* دپرمختياپههالك da parmakhtya pa hal ki
urban *a.* اري kharee
urbane *a.* مهذب muhazzab
urbanity *n.* اريتوب،بارمشتوالى khareetob; khar meyshtwalay
urchin *n.* دشطانبچى da shaytan bachay
urge *v.t* ينارسرهغوتل teengar sara ghokhtal
urge *n* ينار teengar
urgency *n.* اينتوب areentob
urgent *a.* اين areen
urinal *n.* متياز mityazanray
urinary *a.* پهمتيازوپوراوند pa mityazo pori arwand
urinate *v.i.* متيازكول mityazi kawal
urination *n.* دمتيازوكولوعمل da mityazo kawalo amal
urine *n.* متياز mityazi
urn *n* دمودايرولوى da maro da eero lokhay
usage *n.* كاراخيستنه kar akheestana
use *n.* استعمال istimal

use *v.t.* په‌کاراچول pa kar achawal
useful *a.* مفيد mufeed
usher *n.* لارود larkhod
usher *v.t.* رهنمايکول rehnumayee kawal
usual *a.* عادي adee
usually *adv.* معمولا mamoolan
usurer *n.* سودخور sood khor
usurp *v.t.* غصب‌کول ghasab kawal
usurpation *n.* په‌زوراخيستنه pa zor akheestana
usury *n.* سودخونه sood khwarana
utensil *n.* لوي‌اولري lokhee aw largee
uterus *n.* تخمدان tukhamdan
utilitarian *a.* دکوميزدورتوب‌له‌مخد هغه‌مطلوبيت da kom seez da gatawartob la makhi da hagha matloobeeyat
utility *n.* مفيديت mufeedeeyat
utilization *n.* کاروونه karawana
utilize *v.t.* کارول karawal
utmost *a.* ترولور tar tolo deyr
utmost *n* اعظمي azamee
utopia *n* يوخيالي‌هواد. yaw khyalee haywad
utopian *a.* خيالي khyalee
utter *v.t.* مکمل‌کول،اداکول mukamal kawal; ada kawal
utter *a* کامل kamil
utterance *n.* خپراوی،ونا khparaway; wayna
utterly *adv.* کاملا kamilan

vacancy *n.* تش‌ای tash zay
vacant *a.* خالي تش،؛ tash; khalee
vacate *v.t.* کول‌کاره‌بتشول،؛ tashawal; bey kara kawal
vacation *n.* رخصتي‌وزارتوب،؛ wuzgartob; rukhsatee
vaccinate *v.t.* ورکول‌واکسين wakseen warkawal
vaccination *n.* ورکوونه‌واکسين wakseen warkawana
vaccinator *n.* په‌واکسين‌ورکولومامور pa wakseen warkawalo mamoor
vaccine *n.* واکسين wakseen
vacillate *v.i.* زه‌نازه‌کدل zra nazra keydal
vacuum *n.* تشيال،خلا tashyal; khala
vagabond *n.* کوچی،کوال kochay; kadwal
vagabond *a* درپه‌در،کوه‌بی dar pa dar; koosa dabay
vagary *n.* خيال‌پرستي khyal parastee
vagina *n.* مهبل،تکی mahbal; teykay
vague *a.* مبهم،ون‌ز mubhim; goong
vagueness *n.* ونتوب goongtob
vain *a.* بايه bey zaya
vainglorious *a.* انکاری،بلو zankhkaray; batoo

vainglory *n.* لافاوبا lafi aw bati

vainly *adv.* بنتیج bey nateejey

vale *n.* دره dara

valiant *a.* مني meyranay

valid *a.* معتبر motabar

validate *v.t.* اعتبارورکول،نافذکول aytibar warkawal; nafiz kawal

validity *n.* اعتبار،تنفیذ aytibar; tanfeez

valley *n.* دره،وادي dara; wadee

valour *n.* مانه meyrana

valuable *a.* قیمتي qeematee

valuation *n.* ارزوونه arzawana

value *n.* بیه baya

value *v.t.* ارزت‌ورکول،نرخ‌اکل arzakht warkawal; narkh takal

valve *n.* ورخ warkh

van *n.* سرغندوی،سرلاری sar ghandaway; sar laray

vanish *v.i.* ورکدل wrakeydal

vanity *n.* فنا fana

vanquish *v.t.* بریالی‌کدل baryalay keydal

vaporize *v.t.* په‌بخاراول pa bukhar arawal

vaporous *a.* لوی‌لرونکی loogay laroonkay

vapour *n.* باس،لوی baras; loogay

variable *a.* بدلدونکی badleydoonkay

variance *n.* اختلاف،توپیر ikhtilaf; tawpeer

variation *n.* تغییر taghayyur

varied *a.* رنارن ranga rang

variety *n.* قسم،خل qisam; kheyl

various *a.* رنرنا ranga rang

varnish *n.* یوول‌لاورکوونکماده yaw dawl zala warkawoonki mada

varnish *v.t.* لاورکول zala warkawal

vary *v.t.* توپیرلرل tawpeer laral

vaseline *n.* واسلین wasleen

vast *a.* پراخ prakh

vault *n.* ومبته،مغاره gombata; maghara

vault *n.* وپ top

vault *v.i.* وپ‌وهل top wahal

vegetable *n.* سبزي sabzee

vegetable *a.* نباتي،سبزپوراوند nabatee; sabzay pori arwand

vegetarian *n.* سبزي‌خور sabzee khor

vegetarian *a* سبزي‌خور sabzee khor

vegetation *n.* نباتي‌ژوند nabatee zhwand

vehemence *n.* شدت،پیاوتیا shiddat; pyawartya

vehement *a.* شدید،توند shadeed; tond

vehicle *n.* ای gaday

vehicular *a.* داوپه‌اوند da gado pa arwand

veil *n.* پرده،برقع parda; burqa

veil *v.t.* پرده‌کول parda kawal

vein *n.* ر،ورید rag; wareed

velocity *n.* تزوالی teyzwalay

velvet *n.* بخمل bakhmal

velvety *a.* بخملي bakhmalee

venal *a.* فاسد،پسه‌خور fasid; paysa khor

venality *n.* بخونه badi khwarana

vendor *n.* لاسپلوری lasploray

venerable *a.* محترم؛معزز
muhtaram; moazzaz

venerate *v.t.* احترامۍکول ehtiram yi
kawal

veneration *n.* احترام ehtiram

vengeance *n.* کینه keena

venial *a.* دبنو da bakhani war

venom *n.* زهر zahar

venomous *a.* زهرجن zaharjan

vent *n.* هواکش؛سومه hawakash

ventilate *v.t.* هواورکول hawa
warkawal

ventilation *n.* هوارسوونه hawa
rasawana

ventilator *n.* هوارساند hawa rasand

venture *n.* لهخطرهکهچاره la khatara
daka chara

venture *v.t.* خطرناککارتهلاساچول
khatarnak kar ta las achawal

venturesome *a.* خطرناک
khatarnak

venturous *a.* خطرناک khatarnak

venue *n.* دلیدذکتناکلیۍای da leedani
katani takalay zay

veracity *n.* رتیاوینه rakhtya wayana

verendah *n.* برنه baranda

verb *n.* فعل؛کویی fayl; kroyay

verbal *a.* فعلوزمه؛کوزمه
faylwazma; karwazma

verbally *adv.* پهژبنيتوه pa
zhabanee toga

verbatim *a.* کیپهکی takay pa
takay

verbatim *adv.* وییپهویی wayay pa
wayay

verbose *a.* اوگد oogad

verbosity *n.* خبرهاودونه khabara
oogdawana

verdant *a.* تکشین tak sheen

verdict *n.* دقاضيحکم da qazee
hukam

verge *n.* ذه sanda

verification *n.* تصدیق tasdeeq

verify *v.t.* تصدیقول tasdeeqawal

verisimilitude *n.* دسموالیشونتیا da
samwalee shoontya

veritable *a.* رتینی rakhteenay

vermillion *n.* سوررنهحشرات soor
ranga hashrat

vermillion *a.* تکسور tak soor

vernacular *n.* سیمهییزهلهجهاووینه
seemayeeza lahja aw wayang

vernacular *a.* سیمهییز؛محلي
seemayeez; mahalee

vernal *a.* پسرلنی؛تازهاوتاند
pasarlanay; taza aw tand

versatile *a.* واخیز so arkheez

versatility *n.* رنارنتوب ranga
rangtob

verse *n.* نظم nazam

versed *a.* ماهر mahir

versification *n.* نظملیکنه nazam
leekana

versify *v.t.* نظملیکل nazam leekal

version n. روایت نسخه؛ nuskha;
riwayat

versus *prep.* پهواند pa wrandi

vertical *a.* عمودي؛نغ amoodee;
neygh

verve *n.* جوشاوشوق josh aw
kharosh

very *a.* و؛زیات deyr; zyat

vessel *n.* لوی lokhay

vest *n.* واسکه waskat

vest *v.t.* سپارل sparal

vestige *n.* آثار؛نه asar; nakha

vestment *n.* رسمي يا روحاني کالي rasmee ya roohanee kalee

veteran *n.* عسکري دوره پای ته رسولي پوي askaree dawra pay ta rasawalay pawzee

veteran *a.* تجربه کار tajruba kar

veterinary *a.* دارويو طبابت پور اوند da sarwayo tababat pori arwand

veto *n.* مخالفه رايه mukhalifa raya

veto *v.t.* مخالفه رايه ورکول mukhalifa raya warkawal

vex *v.t.* پرشانه کول parayshana kawal

vexation *n* پرشاني parayshanee

via *prep.* له لار la lari

viable *a.* وده کونکي؛عملي wada kawoonkay; amalee

vial *n.* کوچنی بوتل koochnay botal

vibrate *v.i.* رډدل reygdeydal

vibration *n.* رډدنه reygdeydana

vicar *n.* نايب؛پاينستي nayib; zaynastay

vicarious *a.* نيابتي nyabatee

vice *n.* اخلاقي فساد؛ګناه akhlaqee fasad; goona

viceroy *n.* دسلطنت نايب da saltanat nayib

vice-versa *adv.* برعکس baraks

vicinity *n.* نژدوالی nazhdeywalay

vicious *a.* شرير؛خبيث shareer; khabees

vicissitude *n.* بدلون؛لوو badloon; lwar zawar

victim *n.* ښکار khkar

victimize *v.t.* ښکار کول khkar kawal

victor *n.* بريالی baryalay

victorious *a.* بريالی baryalay

victory *n.* سوبه؛کاميابي soba; kamyabee

victuals *n. pl* رنګ رنګ خواه؛ماکولات ranga rang khwara; makoolat

vie *v.i.* سيالي؛رقابت syalee; raqabat

view *n.* منظر؛نظر manzar; nazar

view *v.t.* ليدل leedal

vigil *n.* سارنی لپاره ويښ پاتي کېدنه sarani lapara weekh pati keydana

vigilance *n.* ويښتوب؛سارنی ته ويښ پاتي کېدنه weekhtob; sarani ta weekh pati keydana

vigilant *a.* بيدار baydar

vigorous *a.* غتلی؛زواکمن ghakhtalay; zwakman

vile *a.* ناهار goonagar

vilify *v.t.* تورنول toranawal

villa *n.* کليوالي کور kaleewalee kor

village *n.* کلی kalay

villager *n.* کليوال kaleewal

villain *n.* فاسدسی fasid saray

vindicate *v.t.* تور يا بدګوماني لری کول tor ya badgoomanee leyri kawal

vindication *n.* دفاع؛رتينولي difa; rakhteenwalee

vine *n.* نرم ساقه؛تاک naram saqa; tak

vinegar *n.* سرکه sarka

vintage *n.* دشراب جوړونه موسم da sharab jorawani mawsam

violate *v.t.* تری کول؛توهين کول teyray kawal; tawheen kawal

violation *n.* سرغاوى،ترى sar gharaway; teyray

violence *n.* زورزياتى zor zyatay

violent *a.* غصهناک ghusanak

violet *n.* بنفش رنگ banafsh rang

violin *n.* د موسيقهآلهويلون da mawseeqay ala wayloon

violinist *n.* ويلونغوونکى wayloon ghagoonkay

virgin *n.* پغله،پاکلمنه peyghla; pak lamana

virgin *n* سوچه soocha

virginity *n.* بکارت،پغلتوب bakarat; peyghaltob

virile *a.* مردانه،لهجنسىپلوهفعال mardana; la jinsee palwa faal

virility *n.* نارينهجنسىواک،نارينتوب nareena jinsee zwak; nareentob

virtual *a* مجازى،واقعي majazee; waqiee

virtue *n.* کلا،فضيلت khkula; fazeelat

virtuous *a.* فضيلتلرونکى،متقي fazeelat laroonkay; muttaqee

virulence *n.* زهرجنتوب،ويروسيتوب zaharjantob; wayrooseetob

virulent *a.* زهرجن zaharjan

virus *n.* ويروس،دفسادتومنه wayroos; da fasad tomna

visage *n.* سره،ظاهريبه seyra; zahiree banra

visibility *n.* دليدوتيا da leed wartya

visible *a.* دليدو da leed war

vision *n.* بصيرت baseerat

visionary *a.* تصوري،خيالي tasawwuree; khyalee

visionary *n.* خياليانسان khyalee insan

visit *n.* راشهدرشه rasha darsha

visit *v.t.* راشهدرشهکول rasha darsha kawal

visitor *n.* ملمه،ليدونکىاوکتونکى melma; leedoonkay aw katoonkay

vista *n.* منظره،لرليد manzara; larleed

visual *a.* بصري basree

visualize *v.t.* مجسمکول mujassam kawal

vital *a.* اصلياومهم aslee aw muhim

vitality *n.* دپايتاوبقاواک da payakht aw baqa zwak

vitalize *v.t.* ژوندىکول zhwanday kawal

vitamin *n.* ويامين weetameen

vitiate *v.t.* خرابول kharabawal

vivacious *a.* خوشاله khoshala

vivacity *n.* تازهتوب،مستي tazatob; mastee

viva-voce *adv.* پهژبسره pa zhabi sara

viva-voce *a* ژبنى zhabanay

viva-voce *n* شفاهيآزموينه shafahee azmoyana

vivid *a.* فعال،هاند faal; hasand

vixen *n.* يده geedara

vocabulary *n.* ويبپانه،قاموس wayee panga; qamoos

vocal *a.* غيز ghageez

vocalist *n.* سندربول،سندرغاى sandarbol; sandar gharay

vocation *n.* رسالت،خدمتتهلوالتيا risalat; khidmat ta leywaltya

vogue *n.* دوديز؛رواجي doodeez; riwajee

voice *n.* انساني‌غ insanee ghag

voice *v.t.* بيانول؛غيزه‌به‌ورکول bayanawal; ghageeza banra warkawal

void *a.* بې‌گټ؛پوچ bey gati; pooch

void *v.t.* باطلول batilawal

void *n.* بې‌قانوني bey qanoonee

volcanic *a.* اورشيندى orsheenday

volcano *n.* اورشيندى‌غر orsheenday ghar

volition *n.* غوت؛اراده ghokht; irada

volley *n.* باران؛پرله‌پسز baran; parla pasi dazi

volley *v.t* پرله‌پسزکول parla pasi dazi kawal

volt *n.* دبرنايوپيمانه da breykhna yaw paymana

voltage *n.* قوه برنايي breykhnayee qawa

volume *n.* حجم؛مقدار،وله؛جلد hujam; miqdar; tolga; jild

voluminous *a.* لوى؛حجيم loy; hajeem

voluntarily *adv.* په‌داوطلبانه‌ول pa daw talbana dawl

voluntary *a.* داوطلبانه؛خپل‌په‌خوه daw talbana; khpal pa khwakha

volunteer *n.* داوطلب؛خپل‌په‌خوى daw talab; khpal pa khwakhi

volunteer *v.t.* داوطلب‌کدل daw talab keydal

voluptuary *n.* شهوتران shahwatran

voluptuous *a.* شهواني shahwanee

vomit *v.t.* کازکول kangi kawal

vomit *n.* کاز kangi

voracious *a.* حريص harees

votary *n.* راهب،راهبه rahib; rahiba

vote *n.* رايه raya

vote *v.i.* رايه‌ورکول raya warkawal

voter *n.* رايه‌ورکوونکى raya warkawoonkay

vouch *v.i.* ضمانت‌ورکول zamanat warkawal

voucher *n.* ضمانت‌ليک zamanat leek

vouchsafe *v.t.* اعطاکول ata kawal

vow *n.* کلک‌هو klak hod

vow *v.t.* په‌پينارسره‌ژمنه‌کول pa teengar sara zhmana kawal

vowel *n.* غن‌تورى ghagan toray

voyage *n.* هوايي‌ياسمندري‌يون hawayee ya samandaree yoon

voyage *v.i.* هوايي‌ياسمندري‌يون‌کول hawayee ya samandaree yoon kawal

voyager *n.* مسافر musafar

vulgar *a.* پوچ؛بادبه pooch; bey adaba

vulgarity *n.* بادبي؛پوچ‌خولتوب bey adabee; pooch khuleytob

vulnerable *a.* خرابدونکى kharabeydoonkay

vulture *n.* کجير kajeer

wade *v.i.* خوچيکوکردل khato cheekaro ki garzeydal

waddle *v.i.* دبتيه‌شان‌تلل da bati pa shan tlal

waft *v.t.* دبادپه‌شان‌ترېدل da bad pa shan teyreydal

waft *n.* نرم‌باد naram bad

wag *v.i.* مخ‌اوشاته‌حرکت‌کول makh aw sha ta harakat kawal

wag *n.* وکمار tokmar

wage *v.t.* جه‌کول jagara kawal

wage *n.* اجوره ajoora

wager *n.* شرطتنه shart tarana

wager *v.i.* شرطتل shart taral

wagon *n.* واون؛بارلادوونکوسیله wagon; bar leygdawoonki waseela

wail *v.i.* ویرکول weer kawal

wail *n.* ویر weer

wain *n.* ۱ gaday

waist *n.* ملا mla

waistband *n.* ملاوستن؛کمربند mla wastanay; kamar band

waistcoat *n.* بلستووکو bey lastonro kot

wait *v.i.* انتظارایستل intizar eestal

wait *n.* انتظار intizar

waiter *n.* دملمستون‌یاخونای‌خدمتار da meylmastoon ya khwaranzay khidmatgar

waitress *n.* دملمستون‌یاخونای‌خدمتاره da meylmastoon ya khwaranzay khidmatgara

waive *v.t.* مستثنی‌کول؛صرف‌نظرکول mustasna kawal; sarf nazar kawal

wake *v.t.* ویل؛ویدل weekhawal; weekheydal

wake *n.* ویوالی weekhwalay

wake *n.* من؛اثر mand; asar

wakeful *a.* بدار baydar

walk *v.i.* رمدل garzeydal

walk *n.* چکر؛پلی‌ت chakar; pali tag

wall *n.* دوال deywal

wall *v.t.* دوال‌جوول deywal jorawal

wallet *n.* دپیسوکوه da peyso kasora

wallop *v.t.* تزخودل teyz khwazeydal

wallow *v.i.* په‌خوکرغدل pa khato ki raghreydal

walnut *n.* چارمغز char maghaz

walrus *n.* سمندري‌فیل samandaree feel

wan *a.* رنالوتی؛نر rang alwatay; dangar

wand *n.* لته lakhta

wander *v.i.* سرودان‌رمدل sargardan garzeydal

wane *v.i.* کمزوری‌کدل kamzoray keydal

wane *n.* انحطاط؛کمزورتیا inhitat; kamzortya

want *v.t.* غوتل ghokhtal

want *n.* غوتنه ghokhtana

wanton *a.* جنایتکار؛بنظمه janayatkar; bey nazma

war *n.* جنگ jang

war *v.i.* جندل jangeydal

warble *v.i.* یوخاص‌طرزکسندره‌ویل yaw khas tarz ki sandara wayal

warble *n.* سرود؛چوهار sarood; choonrar

warbler *n.* یوول‌سندربوله‌مرغ yaw dawl sandar bola marghay

ward *n.* حصار؛خونه hisar; khoona

ward *v.t.* حفاظت کساتل hifazat ki satal

warden *n.* سرپرست sar parast

warder *n.* ساتندوی satandoy

wardrobe *n.* دجاموالمار da jamo almaray

wardship *n.* سرپرستي sar parastee

ware *n.* آلات؛يزونه alat; seezoona

warehouse *v.t* پهودام کساتل pa godam ki satal

warfare *n.* جه jagara

warlike *a.* جهپال jagara pal

warm1 *a.* تود؛رم tod; garam

warm *v.t.* تودول؛رمول todawal; garmawal

warmth *n.* تودوخه tawdokha

warn *v.t.* خبرداریورکول khabardaree warkawal

warning *n.* خبرداری khabardaree

warrant *n.* حواله؛رسميحکم hawala; rasmee hukam

warrant *v.t.* رسمياجازتلرل؛ تضمينول rasmee eejazat laral; tazmeenawal

warrantee *n.* ضمانت zamanat

warrantor *n.* ضامن zamin

warranty *n.* ضمانت zamanat

warren *n.* دسویودروزلوای da soyo da rozalo zay

warrior *n.* جنیالی jangyalay

wart *n.* زخه zakha

wary *a.* متوجه mutawajo

wash *v.t.* وینل weenzal

wash *n* ویننه weenzana

washable *a.* دوینلو da weenzalo war

washer *n.* دوبی dobee

wasp *n.* غومبسه ghombasa

waspish *a.* غومبستهورته ghombasi ta warta

wassail *n.* دشرابخورجشن da sharabkhoray jashan

wastage *n.* تلف کونه talf kawana

waste *a.* ضایع؛شا zaya; shar

waste *n.* ضایع کونه zaya kawana

waste *v.t.* تلف کول talf kawal

wasteful *a.* بایه bey zaya

watch *v.t.* لیدل؛کتل leedal; katal

watch *n.* لیدنه؛ساعت leedana; saat

watchful *a.* بدار؛بارو baydar; saro

watchword *n.* شعار shaar

water *n.* اوبه oba

water *v.t.* اوبهورکول oba warkawal

waterfall *n.* وبی zarobay

water-melon *n.* هندواله hindwanra

waterproof *a.* اوبضد؛نهلوندندونکی obzad; na loondeydoonkay

waterproof *n* بارانيوکر baranee tokar

waterproof *v.t.* اوبضدرول obzad garzawal

watertight *a.* اوبهنهاخیستونکی oba na akheestoonkay

watery *a.* اوبلن oblan

watt *n.* دبرناناپولویوپمانه da breykhna napawalo yaw paymana

wave *n.* په sapa

wave *v.t.* څاندکدل؛یکانخول sapand keydal; takan khwaral

waver *v.i.* زهنازهکدل zra nazra keydal

wax *n.* موم mom

wax *v.t.* مومورکول mom warkawal

way *n.* لاره lara

wayfarer *n.* لاروی laraway

waylay *v.t.* چاته‌لاره‌نيول cha ta lara neewal

wayward *a.* نافرمان nafarman

weak *a.* کمزوری kamzoray

weaken *v.t. & i* ناتوانه‌کول،ناتوانه‌ کدل natwana kawal; natwana keydal

weakling *n.* کمزوری kamzoray

weakness *n.* کمزوري kamzoree

weal *n.* پسوب،سوکالي parsob; sokalee

wealth *n.* مال،شتمني mal; shtamanee

wealthy *a.* بای baday

wean *v.t.* ماشوم‌له‌شدوورکولوبلول mashoom la sheydo warkawalo beylawal

weapon *n.* وسله wasla

wear *v.t.* اغوستل aghostal

weary *a.* ستی،بزاره staray; beyzara

weary *v.t. & i* ستومانه‌کول،بزاره‌کدل stomana kawal; beyzara keydal

weary *a.* زتوری‌کوونکی zartoray kawoonkay

weary *v.t.* کرکه‌کول kraka kawal

weather *n* موسم mosam

weather *v.t.* دموسم‌په‌واندبدلدل، زغمل da mosam pa wrandi badleydal; zghamal

weave *v.t.* تارونه‌سره‌نل taroona sara gandal

weaver *n.* جولا،اوبدونکی jola; obdoonkay

web *n.* جال،تنسته jal; tanasta

webby *a.* جال‌ته‌ورته jal ta warta

wed *v.t.* واده‌کول wada kawal

wedding *n.* واده wada

wedge *n.* دلری‌یااوسپنپه‌هیاوه da largee ya ospani panra ya tota

wedge *v.t.* په‌پانه‌ماتول pa pana matawal

wedlock *n.* نکاح nika

Wednesday *n.* چارشنبه charshamba

weed *n.* یوول‌سارانی‌بوی yaw dawl saranay bootay

weed *v.t.* ندهشی‌لمایه‌ایستل ganda shay la zaya eestal

week *n.* اونز oonay

weekly *a.* اونیز ooneez

weekly *adv.* په‌اووه‌ورو‌ک pa owa wrazo ki

weekly *n.* هره‌اونز hara oonay

weep *v.i.* ژل zharal

weevil *n.* یوول‌کوچنونه yaw dawl koochnay goongata

weigh *v.t.* وزن‌کول wazan kawal

weight *n.* وزن wazan

weightage *n.* وزن‌لرنه wazan larana

weighty *a.* دروند droond

weir *n.* داوبوکوچنی‌بند da obo koochnay band

weird *a.* عجیب ajeeb

welcome *a.* مهربانی،هرکلی mehrabanee; har kalay

welcome *n* هرکلی har kalay

welcome *v.t* استقبال‌کول istiqbal kawal

weld *v.t.* سره‌پوندول sara peywandawal

weld *n* یوکوونه yaw kawana

welfare *n.* ه kheygara

well *a.* نک،غوره،ه kha; ghwara; nayk

well *adv.* ه kha

well *n.* کوهی koohay

well *v.i.* داوبوسرتهراخولدل da obo sar ta rakhoteydal

wellington *n.* دنيوزيلنپلازمنه؛يوول آزادخولموزه da nyoozeelaynd plazmayna; yaw dawl azad khuley mooza

well-known *a.* مشهور mashahoor

well-read *a.* باخبر،کتابلوستی ba khabar; keetab lostay

well-timed *a.* پرای؛پهمناسبوخت par zay; pa munasib wakht

well-to-do *a.* کامياب kamyab

welt *n.* دبوتلواوجاموتلوکییوولتغمه da boot gandalo aw jamo gandalo ki yaw dawl taghma

welter *n.* وسامانيااسباب gadwad saman ya asbab

wen *n.* دانززيژبد w توری da angreyzay zhabi da w toray

wench *n.* ماشوم؛خدمتار mashoom; khidmatgar

west *n.* لويدیز lweydeez

west *a.* لويديوال lweydeez wal

west *adv.* دلويديپهلور da lweydeez pa lor

westerly *a.* لويديپوراوند lweydeez pori arwand

westerly *adv.* دلويديپهلور da lweydeez pa lor

western *a.* لويديه lweydeeza

wet *a.* لوند loond

wet *v.t.* لوندول loondawal

wetness *n.* لوندوالی loondwalay

whack *v.t.* پهپهوهل pa sapeyra wahal

whale *n.* يورستربدنیکب yaw deyr star badanay kab

wharfage *n.* پهلنرایکدکتدرولولت pa langar zay ki da kakhtay darawalo lagakht

what *a.* کوم؛کوميز kom; kom seez

what *pron.* هشی،به sa shay; sa

what *interj.* ه sa

whatever *pron.* کومهچ؛هرهچ kom sa chi; har sa chi

wheat *n.* غنم ghanam

wheedle *v.t.* غولول gholawal

wheel *a.* رخ؛پايه sarkh; paya

wheel *v.t.* رخول sarkhawal

whelm *v.t.* چهکول chapa kawal

whelp *n.* دسپيبچی da spee bachay

when *adv.* هوخت،کله sa wakht; kala

when *conj.* کلهچ kala chi

whence *adv.* لهکومايه la koma zaya

whenever *adv. conj* هروخت،هرکله؛ کله har wakht; har kala; kala

where *adv.* چر cheyri

where *conj.* چرته؛هلته charta; halta

whereabout *adv.* چرته cheyrta

whereas *conj.* کهمهم ka sa ham

whereat *conj.* کلهچ kala chi

wherein *adv.* به sanga

whereupon *conj.* لهمخي la makhi yi

wherever *adv.* هرچرته har cheyrta

whet *v.t.* ترهکول؛پارول teyra kawal; parawal

whether *conj.* آيا،پههرصورت aya; pa har soorat

which *pron.* کوم kom

which *a* کوميو چ kom yaw chi

whichever *pron* هريو har yaw

whiff *n.* ومه wagma

while *n.* موده،بوخت mooda; sa wakht

while *conj.* کله چ kala chi

while *v.t.* وخت‌ترول wakht teyrawal

whim *n.* هوس hawas

whimper *v.i.* غوريدل ghoreydal

whimsical *a.* هوس‌باز hawasbaz

whine *v.i.* کونجدل koranjeydal

whine *n* کونجدنه koranjeydana

whip *v.t.* په‌قمچينه‌وهل pa qamcheena wahal

whip *n.* قمچينه،شلاخه qamcheena; shalakha

whipcord *n.* غل‌شوی‌پندمزی gharal shaway pand mazay

whir *n.* چک‌پرواز chatak parwaz

whirl *n.i.* په‌دايروي‌لوربادحرکت‌کول pa dayrawee lori bandi harakat kawal

whirl *n* دايروي‌حرکت dayrawee harakat

whirligig *n.* رخنی sarkhanay

whirlpool *n.* اوبرنی obgarzanay

whirlwind *n.* ببوک barbokay

whisk *v.t.* په‌چک‌حرکت‌لرکول pa chatak harakat leyri kawal

whisk *n* کوچنی‌رب،بورس koochnay reybaz; bors

whisker *n.* دزمري‌ياپيشوبرت da zmaree ya peesho breyt

whisky *n.* يوول‌شراب yaw dawl sharab

whisper *v.t.* پس‌پس‌کول pas pas kawal

whisper *n* پس‌پسی،پخبر pas pasay; pati khabari

whistle *v.i.* شپلک‌وهل shpeylak wahal

whistle *n* شپلک shpeylak

white *a.* سپين speen

white *n* سپين‌رنز speen rang

whiten *v.t.* سپين‌رنور‌کول speen rang warkawal

whitewash *n.* دچوناوبه da chooney oba

whitewash *v.t.* دچونپه‌اوبورنول da chooney pa obo rangawal

whither *adv.* کوهای kom zay

whitish *a.* سپين‌وزمه speen wazma

whittle *v.t.* تراشل trashal

whiz *v.i.* بزيدل bazeydal

who *pron.* وک،کوميو sok; kom yaw

whoever *pron.* هروک‌چ،هرچاچ har sok chi; har cha chi

whole *a.* سالم،روغرمه salam; rogh ramat

whole *n* ول tol

whole-hearted *a.* صميمانه sameemana

wholesale *n.* غونپلورنه ghond plorana

wholesale *a* غونپلورونکی ghond ploroonkay

wholesale *adv.* په‌پراخه‌کچه pa parakha kacha

wholesaler *n.* غونپلوری ghond ploray

wholesome *a.* روغرمه rogh ramat

wholly *adv.* كاملا kamilan

whom *pron.* چاته،چالپاره cha ta; cha lapara

whore *n.* فاحشه fahisha

whose *pron.* چا da cha

why *adv.* ولې،دەلپاره wali; da sa lapara

wick *n.* با،فتيله،اورلوونی batay; fateela; orlagawoonay

wicked *a.* خبيث khabees

wicker *n.* چوکه chooka

wicket *n.* کوچندروازه،دکرکدلوبدر چوک koochnay darwaza; da krikat da lobi drey chooki

wide *a.* ارت،پلن art; plan

wide *adv.* پەپلنوالیسره pa planwalee sara

widen *v.t.* پلنول planawal

widespread *a.* پرانستی pranistay

widow *n.* کونه konda

widow *v.t.* کونول kondawal

widower *n.* کونډ kond

width *n.* پلنوالی planwalay

wield *v.t.* پەمهارتسرەکارول pa maharat sara karawal

wife *n.* ماينه mayna

wig *n.* مصنوعیوتان masnooee weykhtan

wight *n.* ژوندیموجود zhwanday mawjood

wigwam *n.* خمهولهکور khayma dawla kor

wild *a.* سارانی،وحشي saranay; wahshee

wilderness *n.* وحشيتوب،بيابان wahsheetob; bayaban

wile *n.* دوکه doka

will *n.* ارمان arman

will *v.t.* وصيتکول waseeyat kawal

willing *a.* راضي razee

willingness *n.* رضا raza

willow *n.* دوولونه da wali wana

wily *a.* مار دوکه dokamar

wimble *n.* برمه barma

wimple *n.* سرپونی sar patoonay

win *v.t.* کاميابدل kamyabeydal

win *n* کاميابي kamyabee

wince *v.i.* ځانلزول zan larzawal

winch *n.* لاستی،موی lastay; mootay

wind *n.* باد bad

wind *v.t.* کووتلل kogwog tlal

wind *v.t.* بادتەايوخدل bad ta eekhodal

windbag *n.* چاوو gapawoo

winder *n.* پچوونکی peychowoonkay

windlass *v.t.* دکوهيرخ da koohee sarkh

windmill *n.* باديژرنده badee zhranda

window *n.* کړکۍ karkay

windy *a.* توپانی toopanee

wine *n.* سرهشراب sra sharab

wing *n.* وزر wazar

wink *v.i.* سترکوهل stargak wahal

wink *n* سترک stargak

winner *n.* ونکی gatoonkay

winnow *v.t.* غلهبادول gala badawal

winsome *a.* زهراکونی zra rakhkoonay

winter *n.* ژمی zhamay

winter *v.i* ژمیترول zhamay teyrawal

wintry *a.* ژمنی zhamanay

wipe *v.t.* لهمنهول la manza wral
wipe *n.* پاکوونه pakawana
wire *n.* سیم seem
wire *v.t.* سیماومزيغول seem aw mazee ghazawal
wireless *a.* بسیم bey seem
wireless *n* بسیممخابره bey seem mukhabira
wiring *n.* سیمغوونه seem ghazawana
wisdom *n.* عقل،حکمت aqal; hikmat
wisdom-tooth *n.* دعقلغا da aqal ghakh
wise *a.* عقلمن aqalman
wish *n.* غوتنه ghokhtana
wish *v.t.* غوتل ghokhtal
wishful *a.* غوتونکی ghokhtoonkay
wisp *n.* غنچه ghuncha
wistful *a.* ويرللی weer laralay
wit *n.* شعور shaoor
witch *n.* کوره kodgara
witchcraft *n.* جادو jadoo
witchery *n.* جادو jadoo
with *prep.* سره،ورسره sara; warsara
withal *adv.* برسرهپرد bar seyra par dey
withdraw *v.t.* برتهاخيستل beyrta akheestal
withdrawal *n.* پرشات par sha tag
withe *n.* نرلته naray lakhta
wither *v.i.* ماوىکدل mraway keydal
withhold *v.t.* زانسرهساتل zan sara satal

within *prep.* پهشاوخواک pa shaw khwa ki
within *adv.* پهلرک pa lar ki
within *n.* دننه danana
without *prep.* دباند da bandi
without *adv.* پرتهلهدچ parta la dey chi
without *n* لهکورهوتلی la kora watalay
withstand *v.t.* دوامکول dawam kawal
witless *a.* ناپوه na poh
witness *n.* واه gawa
witness *v.i.* شاهدکدل،شاهديورکول shahid keydal; shahidee warkawal
witticism *n.* وکه toka
witty *a.* وکمار tokmar
wizard *n.* کوڈر kodgar
wobble *v.i* لزدل larzeydal
woe *n.* شديدغماووير shadeed gham aw weer
woebegone *a.* ويرجن weerjan
woeful *n.* غمپلی ghamzapalay
wolf *n.* لوه leywa
woman *n.* ﻪ khaza
womanhood *n.* منتوب khazmantob
womanish *n.* ینه khazeena
womanise *v.t.* دپهرکول da khazi pa seyr kawal
womb *n.* زنای zeyganzay
wonder *n* تعجب taajjub
wonder *v.i.* حراندل hayraneydal
wonderful *a.* حرانوونکی hayranawoonkay

wondrous *a.* حرانوونکی hayranawoonkay

wont *a.* رودی rogday

wont *n* عادت adat

wonted *a.* رودیز rogdeez

woo *v.t.* نجلاغوئل najlay ghokhtal

wood *n.* لری largay

woods *n.* نل zangal

wooden *a.* لرین largeen

woodland *n.* نلي‌سیمه zangalee seema

woof *n.* دسپي‌غپهار da spee ghapar

wool *n.* و waray

woollen *a.* وین wareen

woollen *n* وین‌وکر wareen tokar

word *n.* ویی،لغت wayay; lughat

word *v.t* غیدل ghageydal

wordy *a.* ژبنی zhabanay

work *n.* کار kar

work *v.t.* کارکول kar kawal

workable *a.* کدونی keydoonay

workaday *a.* ورنی wrazanay

worker *n.* کارر kargar

workman *n.* کارمند karmand

workmanship *n.* دکارکولوهنر da kar kawalo hunar

workshop *n.* کارای karzay

world *n.* نړ naray

worldling *n.* نړپال naraypal

worldly *a.* ددنړ da dey naray

worm *n.* چینجی cheenjay

wormwood *n.* یوول‌تریخ‌بوی yaw dawl treekh bootay

worn *a.* خراب‌شوی kharab shaway

worry *n.* پریشانی parayshanee

worry *v.i.* پریشانه‌کدل parayshana keydal

worsen *v.t.* بدتراکول،لاخرابول bad tara kawal; la kharabawal

worship *n.* عبادت ibadat

worship *v.t.* عبادت‌کول ibadat kawal

worshipper *n.* عبادت‌کوونکی ibadat kawoonkay

worst *n.* بدترین‌شی bad tareen shay

worst *a* ترولوناوه tar tolo nawara

worst *v.t.* ترولوبدوضعیت‌ته‌بول tar tolo bad wuzeeyat ta beywal

worsted *n.* وینه‌غل‌شوسن wareena gharal shawi sanay

worth *n.* قیمت،ارزت qeemat; arzakht

worth *a* ارزتمن arzakhtman

worthless *a.* بارزته bey arzakhta

worthy *a.* ارزتمن arzakhtman

would-be *a.* په‌خپل‌وومان pa khpal gooman

wound *n.* ټپ tap

wound *v.t.* ټپي‌کول tapee kawal

wrack *n.* ورانی؛خرابی wranay; kharabay

wraith *n.* روح؛اروا rooh; arwa

wrangle *v.i.* شخه‌کول shkhara kawal

wrangle *n.* شخه shkhara

wrap *v.t.* رانغال rangharal

wrap *n* ش sharay

wrapper *n.* پوونکی،لڼ pokhowoonkay; lang

wrath *n.* غضب ghazab

wreath *n.* دلوونوتاج da guloono taj

wreathe *v.t.* دا گولونو تاج جوړول da guloono taj jorawal

wreck *n.* دماتشو کتپارچ da mati shawi kakhtay parchey

wreck *v.t.* تباه کول taba kawal

wreckage *n.* تباهي tabahee

wrecker *n.* ورانوونکی wranawoonkay

wren *n.* یوه سندرغاوه مرغ yawa sandarghari wara marghay

wrench *n.* د نونو پرانستلو آله da natoono pranistalo ala

wrench *v.t.* په آله نونه پرانستل، راشکول pa ala natoona pranistal; rashkawal

wrest *v.t.* له بخه راکل la beykha rakkhal

wrestle *v.i.* زور آزمویل zor azmoyal

wrestler *n.* پروونکی parzawoonkay

wretch *n.* د کرکو شخص da kraki war shakhs

wretched *a.* بدبخت bad bakht

wrick *n* راوتل rag awukhtal

wriggle *v.i.* رغدل raghreydal

wriggle *n* رغدنه raghreydana

wring *v.t* غونول، تخته کول ghonzawal; takhta kawal

wrinkle *n.* ونز gonzi

wrinkle *v.t.* ونزکول gonzi kawal

wrist *n.* د لاس موند da las marwand

writ *n.* حکم، سند hukam; sanad

write *v.t.* لیکل leekal

writer *n.* لیکوال leekwal

writhe *v.i.* له درده غونجدل la darda ghonjeydal

wrong *a.* ناروا، غلط narawa; ghalat

wrong *adv.* په غلطا سره pa ghaltay sara

wrong *v.t.* ناروا کار کول narawa kar kawal

wrongful *a.* ناقانونه naqanoona

wry *a.* تاوخولی taw khwaralay

X

xerox *n.* د کاغذي نسخو نقل جوولو ماشین da kaghazee nuskho naqal jorawalo masheen

xerox *v.t.* د کاغذي نسخو ماشین باندنقل جوول da kaghazee nuskho masheen bandi naqal jorawal

Xmas *n.* د عیسائیانو اختر da eesayano akhtar

x-ray *n.* د وانماشین da warangi masheen

x-ray *a.* د وانماشین پواوند da warangi masheen pori arwand

x-ray *v.t.* د وانماشین سره طبي معاینه کول da warangi masheen sara tibee muayna kawal

xylophagous *a.* لرى خورى largay khoray

xylophilous *a.* په لرې کژوند کوونکی pa largee ki zhwand kawoonkay

xylophone *n.* د موسیقي پیانو ته ورته آله da mawseeqay pyano ta warta ala

Y

yacht *n.* تفریحي کښتۍ tafreehee kakhtay

yacht *v.i* تفریحي کښتۍ سمندريون کول tafreehee kakhtay ki samandaryoon kawal

yak *n.* دتبت يو دل غوايي da tibat yaw dawl ghwayay

yap *v.i.* غپېدل ghapeydal

yap *n* ناوه خبري nawara khabari

yard *n.* داوو والي مچولو يو پيمانه da oogadwalee meychawalo yaw paymana

yarn *n.* مزی، سپسين mazay; spanrseen

yawn *v.i.* ارمی استل argamay eystal

yawn *n.* ارمی argamay

year *n.* کال kal

yearly *a.* کلنی kalanay

yearly *adv.* لۍ هرکال يو زل har kal yaw zal

yearn *v.i.* زه کدل zra keydal

yearning *n.* آرزو arzoo

yeast *n.* تومنه tomna

yell *v.i.* نارې سورې کول narey soorey kawal

yell *n* نارې سور narey soorey

yellow *a.* زیر zeyr

yellow *n* زیر رنگ zeyr rang

yellow *v.t.* زیرول zeyrawal

yellowish *a.* زیربخن zeyrbakhan

Yen *n.* دچين رسمي سکه da cheen rasmee sika

yeoman *n.* خادم؛ کروندګر khadim; karwandagar

yes *adv.* هو، او ho; aw

yesterday *n.* پرون paroon

yesterday *adv.* ور تره teyra wraz

yet *adv.* لهدسره سره la dey sara sara

yet *conj.* تراوسه tar osa

yield *v.t.* محصول ورکول، اعطاکول mahsool warkawal; ata kawal

yield *n* پداوار؛بار paydawar; bar

yoke *n.* جغ jagh

yoke *v.t.* ترجغ لاندراوستل tar jagh landi rawastal

yolk *n.* دهزۍ da hagay zeyr

younder *a.* لر leyri

younder *adv.* هغه خواته hagha khwa ta

young *a.* ځوان zwan

young *n* کم عمره kam oomra

youngster *n.* زلموی zalmotay

youth *n.* ژکی zhanrkay

youthful *a.* شاداب shadab

Z

zany *a.* بعقل bey aqal

zeal *n.* شوق shawq

zealot *n.* شوقين shawqeen

zealous *a.* هيلهمن heelaman

zebra *n.* ورخر gorkhar

zenith *n.* ترولوهسک مقام tar tolo hask maqam

zephyr *n.* لوديزباد lweydeez bad

zero *n.* نشت؛صفر nasht; sifar

zest *n.* دماليمو اونارنج دپوستکي خوند da maltey leemoo aw naranj da postakee khwand

Pushto to English

A

aba *n* ابا dad, daddy

abadawal; meysht kawal *v.t.*
آبادول؛مشت‌کول people

abadawal; tasfeeya kawal *v.i.*
آبادول؛تصفیه‌کول settle

abadee *adj* ابدي eternal

abadeeyat *n* ابدیت eternity

abee rang *a* آبي‌رنگ blue

abeysey *n*. اب alphabet

abeysey *n*. اب spell

abeysey kawal; imla kawal *v.t.* اب
کول،املاکول spell

abroo *n*. آبرو repute

abroo *n*. آبرو prestige

abwalay karkeychanwalay *a.*
ابوالی ککیچنوالی
monochromatic

achar *n*. اچار pickle

achawal; tarha kawal *v. t.* اچول؛
طرحه‌کول cast

achawana; wozeeyat *n*. اچونه؛
وضعیت cast

ad kawoonkay adad *n*. عادکوونکی
عدد aliquot

ada kawal *v.t.* اداکول pay

adaa *n* ادعا claim

adaa kawal *v. t* ادعاکول claim

adab *n*. ادب mannerism

adabee *a.* ادبي literary

adabee aw farhangee nawakht
n. ادبي‌اوفرهني‌نوت renaissance

adabee ghorchanr *n*. ادبي‌غورچه
anthology

adad *n* عدد digit

adadee *a*. عددي numeral

adadee *a*. عددي numerical

adalat; mahkama *n*. عدالت؛
محکمه court

adat *n*. عادت addict

adat *n*. عادت habit

adat *n* عادت wont

adawat *n*. عداوت odium

adayana; jibran *n* ادینه؛جبران pay

adee *a*. عادي normal

adee *a*. عادي commonplace

adee *a*. عادي usual

adee halat *n*. عادي‌حالت normalcy

adee wagaray *n*. عادي‌وی
commoner

adeeb *n*. ادیب litterateur

adeeb; muhaqqiq *n*. ادیب؛محقق
scholar

adeebana *a*. ادیبانه oratorical

adsa *n*. عدسه lens

afat *n*. آفت calamity

afoonat zid *n*. عفونت‌ضد antiseptic

afrat *n* افراط excess

afratee shakhs *n* افراطي‌شخص
extremist

afraz; chrap chrap *n* افراز؛چپ
چپ splash

afrazawal; chrap chrap kawal
v.i. افرازول؛چپ‌چپ‌کول splash

afreen wayal *v.t.* آفرین‌ویل applaud

afsana *n*. افسانه fable

afsana *n* افسانه fiction

afsana *n*. افسانه legend

afsana dawla *a*. افسانه‌وله romantic

afsana peyzhandana *n.* افسانه پژندنه mythology

afsanawee *a* افسانوي fabulous

afsanawee *a.* افسانوي legendary

afsanawee *a.* افسانوي mythical

afsanawee *a.* افسانوي mythological

afsha kawal *v. t* افشاكول discover

afsha kawal *v. t* افشاكول divulge

afsos *n.* افسوس compunction

afsos *n.* افسوس remorse

afsos kawal *v.t.* افسوس كول rue

afsos kawal; ah kkhal *v.i.* افسوس كول؛آه كل sigh

afyoon *n.* افيون opium

agar chay *prep.* چ ار notwithstanding

agar chay *conj.* ارچه though

aghaz *n.* آغاز inception

aghaz *n.* آغاز initiative

aghaz; shoro *n.* آغاز؛شروع initial

agheyz *n* اغز effect

agheyz *n.* اغز influence

agheyz kawal; ijra kawal *v. t* اغز كول،اجراءكول effect

agheyz khandal *v.t.* اغيزندل affect

agheyz laral *v.t.* اغزلرل influence

agheyz man *a* اغزمن effective

agheyza achawal *v.i.* اغيزهاچول act

agheyznak *a.* اغزناك influential

agheyznaktob *n* اغزناكتوب efficacy

aghostal *v.t.* اغوستل wear

aghzan *a.* اغزنَ thorny

aghzay *n.* اغزى thistle

aghzay *n.* اغزى thorn

ah kkhana *n.* آهكنه sigh

ahak *n.* آهك lime

ahak kawal *v.t* آهككول lime

aham *a.* اهم important

aham juz *adj.* اهمجز component

aham; aslee *a* اهم،اصلي staple

ahan ruba *n.* آهنرُبا loadstone

ahdaa kawoonkay *n* اهداكوونكى donor

ahlee kawal *v.t.* اهليكول tame

ahmaq *a* احمق foolish

ahmaq *n.* احمق simpleton

ahmaq aw lawda *adj.* احمقاولوده crass

ahmaq saray *n* احمقسى blockhead

ahmaq saray *n.* سى احمق loggerhead

ahmaqana ehsasat *n.* احمقانه احساسات slush

ahmeeyat *n.* اهميت importance

ahmeeyat *n.* اهميت notability

ahmeeyat laral *v.i.* اهميتلرل matter

ahya; parawana *n* احيا؛پارونه animation

ajant *n* اجنٗ agent

ajar *n.* اجر gratuity

ajar warkawal *v.t.* اجروركول reward

ajar; jaza *n.* اجر،جزا reward

ajbari *a* اجبارى forcible

ajeeb *adj* عجيب bizarre

ajeeb *a.* عجيب queer

ajeeb *a.* عجيب weird

ajeeb aw ghareeb *a.* عجيباوغريب grotesque

ajeeb aw ghareeb shay *n.* عجيب او
غريب شى oddity
ajmal; landoon *n.* اجمال؛لنون
synopsis
ajoora *n.* اجوره wage
akademee *n* اکادیمی academy
akasee *n.* عکاسی photography
akhaz kawal *v. t.* اخذکول derive
akhbaree; rasa *a.* اخبارى؛رسا
expressive
akheyrawal *v.t.* اخول thatch
akheyree *a.* آخرى latter
akheystal; neewal *v.t* اخستل؛نيول
take
akheystoonkay *n.* اخستونکی
recipient
akhir *n* آخر terminal
akhiree *a.* آخرى ultimate
akhiree had *a.* اخرى حد maximum
akhiree had pori rasawal *v.t.*
اخرى حد پور رسول maximize
akhlaq khowoonkay *n.* اخلاق
ونکی moralist
akhlaq pohana *n.* اخلاق پوهنه
ethics
akhlaqee *a* اخلاقی ethical
akhlaqee *a.* اخلاقی moral
akhlaqee aseelwalay
ghokhtoonkay shakhs *n.*
اخلاقی اصیلولی غوتونکی شخص
puritan
akhlaqee chaland *n.* اخلاقی چلند
morality
akhlaqee fasad *n.* اخلاقی فساد
slough
akhlaqee fasad; goona *n.* اخلاقی
فساد؛ګناه vice

akhlaqee fikar warkawal *v.t.*
اخلاقی فکرورکول moralize
akhlaqee mayar *n.* اخلاقی معیار
norm
akhlaqeeyat *n.* اخلاقیات morale
akhoowat *n.* اخوت fraternity
akhor *n.* آخور crib
akhor *n.* آخور manger
akhta aw mubtila; tawrataw *n.*
اختەاو مبتلا؛تاوراتاو tangle
akhtar warkawal *v.t.* اخطارورکول
admonish
akhtar; tahdeed *n.* اخطار؛تهدید
denunciation
aks *n* عکس photograph
aks akheystal *v.t.* عکس اخستل
photograph
aks jorawoonkay *n.* عکس
جوورونکی photographer
aksee *a.* عکسی photographic
ala *a.* اعلی excellent
ala *n.* آله tool
ala; wasayal *n.* آله؛وسایل appliance
ala; waseela *n* آله؛وسیله device
ala; waseela *n.* آله؛وسیله
instrument
alama *n.* علامه symbol
alama *n.* علامه symptom
alama; larkhod *n.* علامه؛لارود
signal
alama; nakha *n.* علامه؛نه badge
alama; nakha *n.* علامه؛نه sign
alama; nakhan *n* علامه؛نان
emblem
alat; seezoona *n.* آلات؛ بیزونه ware
alatee *a.* آلاتی instrumental

albom *n.* البوم album

alee *a.* عالي stately

alee; lwar *a.* عالي؛لو high

aleehazrat *n.* اعليحضرت majesty

alim *a.* عالم learned

alimana *a.* عالمانه scholarly

aljabar *n.* الجبر algebra

almaray *n.* المار closet

almaray *n* المار cupboard

almas *n* الماس diamond

aloo *n.* الو potato

aloocha *n.* آلوچه plum

alwataka *n.* الوتكه aircraft

alwataka *n.* الوتكه aeroplane

alwataka *n.* الوتكه plane

alwatal *v.i* الوتل fly

alwatal; randa kawal *v.t.* الوتل، رنده كول plane

alwatana *n* الوتنه flight

alwatoonkay *n* الوتونكى bird

am *n* ام mango

am *a.* عام common

am khalk pri khabrawal *v.t.* عام خلك پرخبرول publicize

am wagaray *n.* عاموى populace

am wagaray *n.* snobbery

am wazhna *n.* عاموژنه holocaust

ama zhaba *n.* عامه‌ژبه slang

amada kawal *v. t* آماده‌كول equip

amadagee; meelan *n.* آمادي،ميلان inclination

amal *n.* عمل acting

amal kawal *n.* عمل‌كول act

amalee *a.* عملي practical

amalee *a.* عملي operative

amalee falsafa *n.* عملي‌فلسفه pragmatism

amalee kawal; areeza kawal *v.t.* عملي‌كول؛عريضه‌كول apply

amaleetob *n.* عمليتوب practicability

amaleeyat *n.* عمليات operation

amanat plorana *n.* امانت‌پلورنه consignment

amanat sparal *v.t.* امانت‌سپارل consign

amanat warsparal *v. t* امانت ورسپارل entrust

amar *n.* امر affair

amar kawal *v. t* امركول direct

amar; lar khodana *n* امر،لارودنه direction

amaree; lazimee *a.* امري،لازمي imperative

ambolans *n.* امبولانس ambulance

amboor *n. pl.* انبور tongs

ameen *a.* امين honest

ameen *n.* امين trustee

ameen *a.* امين trustful

ameen; khuday di wakree *interj.* آمين،خداى‌دوكي amen

ameerul bahar *n.* اميرالبحر admiral

ameyl *n.* امل garland

ameyl *n.* امل locket

ameyl *n.* امل necklace

ameyl *v.t.* اميل garland

amil *n* عامل factor

amirana *a.* آمرانه magisterial

amneeyat *n.* امنيت safety

amneeyat *n.* امنيت security

amneeyatee mamoor *n.* امنيتي مامور policeman

amneeyatee zwak; polees *n.* امنيتي واک؛پوليس police

amoodee; neygh *a.* عمودي؛نغ vertical

amoomee *a.* عمومي general

amoomee bakhana *n.* عمومي‌بخنه amnesty

amoomee har kalay *n.* عمومي‌هر کلی ovation

amoomee kaleesa *n.* عمومي کليسا cathedral

amoomee khwakha *n.* عمومي‌خوه consensus

amoomee; noomawaray *a.* عمومي؛نوموی popular

ampratooree *n.* امپراطوري imperialism

amree *a.* امر mandatory

amreeya *n.* امريه mandate

amrood *n.* امرود guava

ananas *n.* اناناس pineapple

anangay *n* انني cheek

and; fikar *n* اند؛فکر thought

andaza *n.* اندازه estimate

andaza geyree kawal *v.t.* اندازه يري‌کول survey

andaza geyree; daraja bandee *n.* اندازه‌ميري؛درجه‌بندي survey

andaza kawal *v.t* اندازه‌کول mete

andaza kawal *v.t.* اندازه‌کول size

andaza; daraja *n.* اندازه؛درجه gauge

andaza; hujam *n* اندازه؛حجم dimension

andaza; kach *n.* اندازه؛کچ size

andeykhman *adv* اندښمن agaze

andeykhna kawal *v.i.* اندښنه‌کول speculate

andi kawal *v.t.* انډی‌کول bale

andpal *a.* اندپال thoughtful

andwal; muadil *a.* انول؛معادل tantamount

angar *n* اﻧ compound

angar *n.* اﻧ outhouse

angaza kawoonkay *a.* انازه‌کوونکی resonant

angeyral *v.t.* انيرل account

angeyryal *n.* انريال thinker

angeyryal; tasawwuree *a.* انريال؛تصوري idealistic

angeyza *n.* انزه impulse

angeyzwee *a.* انزوي impulsive

angoor *n.* انور grape

angreyzee *n* انرزي English

anjuman *n* انجمن club

antan *n.* آنن antennae

antanee aw afoonee jisam *a.* انتاني‌او‌عفوني‌جسم septic

antanzid durmal *a.* انتان‌ضددرمل antiseptic

anzor *n* انور drawing

anzor *n.* انور picture

anzor akheystal *v.t.* انوراخستل picture

anzorawal *v.t* انورول draw

anzoreez *a.* انوريز pictorical

apalti wayal *v.i.* اپلتويل babble

apalti wayana *n.* اپلتوينه babble

apartman *n.* اپارتمان apartment

apartman *n.* اپارتمان compartment

apartman *n* اپارتمان flat

apartman aw da haghey lawazim *n.* اپارتمان او دهغلوازم suite

aqal; hikmat *n.* عقل؛حکمت wisdom

aqalman *a.* عقلمن wise

aqd *n* عقد contract

aqeeda *n* عقیده belief

aqeeda *n* عقیده concept

aqeeda *n.* عقیده tenet

aqeeda laral *v. t* عقیدهلرل believe

aqil *a.* عاقل sober

ar aw bansat *n.* آراوبنس rationale

ar kawal *v.t.* اکول necessitate

ara *n.* اره saw

ara laral *v. i* اهلرل belong

ara laral *v.i.* اهلرل pertain

aram *n.* ام lever

aram *n.* آرام comfort1

aram *n.* آرام relief

aram *n* آرام rest

aram bakhoonkay *a.* آرامبونکی sedative

aram samandar *a.* آرامسمندر pacific

aram warbakhal *v.t.* آراموربل relieve

aram warkawal *v. t* آراموركول comfort

aram warkawoonkay *a* آرام ورکوونکی comfortable

aram; kam walay *n.* آرام؛کموالی alleviation

arama *adj.* آرامه bland

arama *a.* آرامه leisurely

aramakht *n.* آرامت composure

aramakht *n.* آرامت leisure

aramakht *n.* آرامت lull

aramakht *n.* آرامت serenity

aramakht *n.* آرامت calm

aramawal *v.t.* آرامول allay

aramawal *v.t.* آرامول quell

aramawal *v.t.* آرامول quiet

aramawal *v.t.* آرامول soothe

aramawal *v.t.* آرامول still

aramawal; kamawal *v.t.* آرامول؛ کمول alleviate

aramawal; marawal *v.t.* آرامول؛ مول quench

aramowoonkay *adj* آراموونکی calmative

arawana *n* اونه convert

arayish *v.t.* آرایش furnish

arbab *n.* ارباب lord

arbabtob *n.* اربابتوب lordship

areeki ghosawal *v. t* ایکغوول disconnect

areeki warsara shookawal *v. t.* ایکورسرهشوکول excommunicate

areen *a.* این instant

areen *a.* این urgent

areen kach *n.* این کچ optimum

areen shart *n* اینشرط prerequisite

areen shart *a.* اینشرط requisite

areen; sharteeya *a.* این؛شرطیه prerequisite

areentob *n.* اینتوب urgency

argamay *n.* ارمی yawn

argamay eystal *v.i.* ارمیاستل yawn

arghawanee; arghawanee rang *adj./n.* ارغواني؛ارغواني رن purple arman *n.* ارمان will

armoonay *n.* ارمونی bastard

armoonay; gheyr qanoonee *a.* ارموني؛غرقانوني illicit

arooj *n.* عروج ascent

arq eystal *v. t* عرق‌استل distil

arsha jorawal *v. t* عرشه‌جوول deck

art; plan *a.* ارت؛پلن wide

artawol *v.t* ارتاوول fling

artya *n.* اتیا need

artya laral *v.t.* اتیالرل need

artya warta laral *v.t.* اتیاورته‌لرل require

arwa *n.* اروا ghost

arwa poh *n.* اروا‌پوه psychologist

arwa pohana *n.* اروا‌پوهنه psychology

arwa pohaneez *a.* اروا‌پوهنیز psychological

arwa; jazba *n.* اروا؛جذبه spirit

arwa; peyray *n.* اروا؛پری spectre

arwayeez narogh *n.* ارواییز‌نارو‌غ psychopath

arwayeez tababat *n.* ارواییز‌طبابت psychiatry

arwayeeza naroghee *n.* ارواییزه ناروغي neurosis

arz kawoonkay *n.* عرض کوونکی petitioner

arzakht warkawal; narkh takal *v.t.* ارزت‌ورکول؛نرخ‌اکل value

arzakht; bawar *n* ارزت؛باور credit

arzakhtman *a* ارزتمن worth

arzakhtman *a.* ارزتمن worthy

arzan *a* ارزان cheap

arzanawal *v. t.* ارزانول cheapen

arzawal *v. t* ارزول evaluate

arzawal *v.t.* ارزول praise

arzawana *n.* ارزوونه valuation

arzee mudat *n.* عارضي‌مدت interim

arzoo *n.* آرزو yearning

arzoo kawal *v.t.* آرزو‌کول covet

arzoo laral *v.t* آرزول‌رل desire

arzul balad *n.* عرض‌البلد latitude

as *n.* آس horse

as *n.* اس steed

asal oseydoonkay *n* اصل اوسیدونکی original

asal; ar *n.* اصل؛آر origin

asalat *n.* اصالت originality

asan *a* آسان easy

asana *a* آسانه facile

asana *a.* آسانه handy

asanawal *v. t* آسانول ease

asanawal *v.t* آسانول facilitate

asanee *n* آساني ease

asar *n.* اثر inspiration

asar; fishar *n.* اثر؛فشار impact

asar; ishara *n* اثر؛اشاره clue

asar; khyal *n.* اثر؛خیال impression

asar; nakha *n.* vestige

asarat; mrayeetob *n.* اسارت؛ مریيتوب thralldom

asasee qanoon *n* اساسي‌قانون constitution

asb *n.* عصب Nerve

asb peyzhandana *n.* عصب‌پژاند neurologist

asb peyzhandana *n.* عصب‌پژندنه neurology

asbab; kalee *n.* اسباب؛کالي apparel

asbab; lawazim *n.* اسباب،لوازم apparatus

asbab; lawazim *n.* اسباب،لوازم outfit

asbanee *a.* عصباني irritable

asbee *a.* عصبي nervous

aseeya *n* آسيا oriental

ashba *n.* اشباع saturation

ashiqana *a.* عاشقانه amorous

ashiqana *a.* عاشقانه melodramatic

ashna kawal *v.t.* اشناكول acquaint

ashna; nazhdey *a.* اشنا،نژد intimate

ashraf wakee *n.* اشراف واكي aristocracy

askaree dawra pay ta rasawalay pawzee *n.* عسكري دورهپايته رسولي پوي veteran

aslee *a.* اصلي genuine

aslee *a.* اصلي native

aslee *a.* اصلي original

aslee astogan *n* اصلي استون citizen

aslee aw muhim *a.* اصلي او مهم vital

aslee aw zarooree *a* اصلي او ضروري main

aslee banra *n.* اصلي به motif

aslee barkha; da bar yaw paymayish *n.* اصلي برخه؛دباريو پمائش gross

aslee namoona *n.* اصلي نمونه prototype

aslee tabieeyat *n.* اصلي تابعيت mainstay

aslee tatobay *n.* اصلي تابوبى metropolitan

aslee; soocha *a.* اصلي،سوچه indigenous

asman *n.* اسمان sky

asmanee *adj* آسماني celestial

asmanee *a.* آسماني heavenly

asmanee keetab *n.* اسماني كتاب scripture

asooda *a.* آسوده tranquil

aspanawee *n.* اسپانوي Spaniard

aspanawee *a.* اسپانوي Spanish

aspanawee wagaray ya zhaba *n.* اسپانوي وي ياژبه Spanish

astawana *n.* استوانه shaft

astawana; da astazo pandghalay *n.* استوونه نه؛داستازوپنغالي mission

astazay; rasool *n.* استازى،رسول apostle

astazeetob *n* استازيتوب deputation

astazeetob warkawal *v. t* استازيتوب ورکول depute

astogan *n.* استون inhabitant

astogan *n.* استون inmate

astoganzay *n.* استونای habitation

astoganzay *n.* استوۀ accommodation

astogna *n* استونه domicile

astogna kawal *v.t.* استونه کول inhabit

astogna laral *v.i.* استونه لرل reside

astogni pori arwand *a.* استونپور اوند resident

ata *n* اته eight

ata guteez *a.* اته ویز octangular

ata kawal *v. i* اعطاکول confer

ata kawal *v.t.* اعطاکول vouchsafe

ata makheez *n.* اته مخیز octagon

ata satree shayr *n.* اته سطري شعر octave

atal *n.* اتل champion

atal; qaharman *n.* اتل؛قهرمان hero

atalas *a* اتلس eighteen

atam; tar tolo koochnay basarkay *n.* اتم؛ترولوکوچنی برکی atom

atar *n.* عطر perfume

atar *n.* عطر scent

atardan *n* عطردان censer

atkal *n* اکل conjecture

atkal *n.* اکل guess

atkal *n.* اکل surmise

atkal *n.* اکل prediction

atkal kawal *v.i* اکل کول guess

atkal kawal *v.t.* اکل کول predict

atkal kawal *v.t.* اکل کول surmise

atkalawal *v. t* اکلول estimate

atkaray *n.* اتک handcuff

atkaray achawal *v.t* اتکاچول handcuff

atkaray achawal *v.t.* اتکاچول shackle

atkaray; zolanay *n.* اتک؛زولا shackle

atlawali kawal *v. t.* اتلولی کول champion

atlawee; qaharmanee *n.* اتلوي؛قهرماني heroism

atoboos *n* اتوبوس bus

atoboos; ustad *n* اتوبوس؛أستاد coach

atomee *a.* اومي atomic

atro aw khushbooyo sara ibadat kawal *v. t* عطرواوخوشبويوسره عبادات کول cense

atya *n* اتیا eighty

atya kalan *a.* اتیاکلن octogenarian

atya kalan insan *a* اتیاکلن انسان octogenarian

aw *conj.* او and

aw ka na *conj.* اوکه نه otherwise

aw nor; waghayra *n* اونور؛وغره etcetera

awakhtoon *n.* اوتون mutation

awakhtoon aw wanjoon *n.* اوتون اوونجون permutation

awar *a* اوار level

awarawal *v.t.* اوارول level

awaz pohana *a* اوازپوهنه acoustic

awaza *n.* اوازه rumour

awaza; gangosay *n.* آوازه؛بنوسی hearsay

awaza; shohrat *n* آوازه؛شهرت fame

awazey khparawal *v.t.* اوازخپرول rumour

awazey khparawoonkay *n.* آواز خپروونکی propagandist

awdas *n* اودس ablution

awlad *n* اولاد descendant

awlad; zay nastay *n.* اولاد؛ بای ناستی progeny

awrawal *v.t.* اورول hear

awreydal *v.i.* اوردل listen

awreydal; arawal *v.t. & i.* اودل؛ اول deflect

awreydoonkay *n.* اوردونکی listener

awreydoonkee *n.* اوردونکي audience

awreydyeez *a.* اوردییز sonic

awsar *a.* اوار observant

awsat takal *v.t.* اوسطاکل average

awya *n., a* اویا seventy

awyayam *a.* اویایم seventieth

awzar pa karawal; pa takali lar safar kawal *v.t.* اوزاربه کارول؛ پماکلالرسفرکول ply

ay hay *interj.* ای هی alas

aya; pa har soorat *conj.* آیا،په هر صورت whether

ayalat *n* ایالت federation

ayalat *n.* ایالت shire

ayash *n.* عیاش libertine

ayash *n.* عیاش reveller

ayash; masrafee *a.* عیاش،مسرفي sumptuous

ayashee *n.* عیاشی revel

ayashee kawal *v.i.* عیاشی کول revel

ayb *n* عب fallacy

ayb palatoonkay *adj* عب پلونکی censorious

aybjan *a* عبجن faulty

ayboona palatal *v. t* عبونه پلل cavil

ayidatee mahsool *n.* عایداتي محصول proceeds

aylameeya *n* اعلامیه declaration

aylameeya *n.* اعلامیه manifesto

aylan *n.* اعلان poster

aylan *n* اعلان advertisement

aylanawal *v.t.* اعلانول advertise

aylanawal *v.t.* اعلانول announce

aylanawal *v. t.* اعلانول declare

aylanawal *v.t.* اعلانول notify

aylanawal *v.t.* اعلانول proclaim

aynak jorawoonkay *n.* عینک جوروونکی optician

aysh *n.* عش jollity

aysh *n.* عیش mirth

aysh aw ishrat *n.* عش او عشرت joviality

aysh aw ishrat kawal *a.* عش او عشرت کول jovial

aysharee *a* اعشاري decimal

aytibar leek *n* اعتبارلیك affidavit

aytibar warkawal; nafiz kawal *v.t.* اعتباروركول؛نافذکول validate

aytibar; tanfeez *n.* اعتبار،تنفیذ validity

aytidal *n.* اعتدال mediocrity

aytidal *n.* اعتدال moderation

aytilafee *a* ایتلافي federal

aytimad *n.* اعتماد trust

aytimad kawal *v.t.* اعتمادکول accredit

aytimad kawal *v.t* اعتمادکول trust

aytiqad *n* اعتقاد creed

aytiraf *n.* اعتراف acknowledgement

aytiraz kawal *v. t* اعتراض کول demur

aytiraz kawal *v.t.* اعتراض کول object

aytiraz; shak *n* اعتراض،شک demur

ayzazee *a.* اعزازي honorary

azad *a.* آزاد free

azad palana *n.* آزادپالنه liberality

azada leekana *n.* آزاده لیکنه paraphrase

azadawal *v.t.* ازادول acquit

azadawal *v.t* آزادول free

azadawal *v.t.* آزادول liberate
azadawal *v.t.* آزادول rid
azadee *n.* آزادي liberation
azadee *n.* آزادي manumission
azadee *n.* آزادي freedom
azadee bakhkhoonkay *n.* آزادي
بخوونکی liberator
azam sargandawana; qarardad
n. عزمهرمندوونه،قرارداد resolution
azamee *n* اعظمي utmost
azarawal *v.t.* اذارول nettle
azarawal *v.t.* اذارول tease
azdawajee *a.* ازدواجي marital
azdawajee *a.* ازدواجي matrimonial
azeem *a* عظيم great
azeem *a.* عظيم luxuriant
azeem *a.* عظيم magnanimous
azeem *a.* عظيم magnificent
azeem; star *n* عظيم؛ستر august
azeeyat *n.* اذيت harassment
azeeyatawal *v.t.* اذيتول harass
azghan toot *n.* ازغنتوت
gooseberry
azhans *n.* اژانس agency
azmat *n.* عظمت glory
azmat *n.* عظمت luxuriance
azmat *n.* عظمت splendour
azmat warbakhal *v.t.* عظمتوربل
magnify
azmayakht *n.* آزمايت probation
azmoyal *v.t.* آزمويل probe
azmoyal *v.t.* آزمويل test
azmoyana *n* آزمينه experiment
azmoyana kawal *v.t.* آزمينهکول
quiz

azmoyantoon *n.* آزموينتون
laboratory
aztirab *a* اضطراب anxiety

B

ba aram *a* باآرام convenient
ba azmat *a.* باعظمت splendid
ba ba *n* بع بع bleat
ba ba kawal; amba amba kawal
v. i بعبعکول؛امباامباکول bleat
ba dawama *a* بادوامه evergreen
ba eeman; wafadar *a* باايمان؛وفادار
faithful
ba khabar *a.* باخبر aware
ba khabar *adj.* باخبر conversant
ba khabar *a.* باخبر informative
ba khabar; keetab lostay *a.* با
خبر،کتابلوستی well-read
ba shaoora *a* باشعوره conscious
ba sharfa *a.* باشرفه gentle
ba zawqa *adj* باذوقه elegant
bab; dars; saparkay *n.* باب؛درس؛
پرکی chapter
babara geera *n.* ببرهيره stubble
babozay *n* ببوزی fan
bachabaz; koonee *n.* بچهباز؛کوني
sodomite
bachabazee; kooneetob *n.* بچه
بازي؛کونيتوب sodomy
bachgay *n.* بچی offshoot
bachgay *n.* بچی offspring
bad *n.* باد wind
bad akhlaq *a.* بداخلاق immoral

bad akhlaqa kawal *v. t.* بداخلاقه کول demoralize

bad akhlaqee *n.* بداخلاقي immorality

bad akhlaqee kawal *n.* بداخلاقي کول misconduct

bad aw nawara leekana n. بداو ناوهلیکنه scribble

bad bakht *a.* بدبخت wretched

bad bakhta *a.* بدبخته miserable

bad bakhtee *n.* بدبختي mischance

bad been *a.* بدبین pessimistic

bad been kas *n.* بدبین کس pessimist

bad beenee *n.* بدبیني pessimism

bad booy laral *v.i.* بدبویلرل stink

bad booya *a.* بدبویه nosy

bad booyee *n.* بدبويي stench

bad booyee *n* بدبويي stink

bad chaland *n.* بدچلند mal-treatment

bad chaland *n.* بدچلند misdeed

bad chaleydal *v.i.* بادچلدل blow

bad chaleydana *n* بادچلدنه blow

bad ghokhtal *v.t.* بدغوتل malign

bad goomanee *n.* بدگوماني misgiving

bad kar *n.* بدکار malefactor

bad kharsa saray *n.* بدخرهسی prodigality

bad khooya *a.* بدخویه morose

bad lamana khaza *n.* بدلمنه slut

bad lamanee *n.* بدلمني prostitution

bad margha *a.* بدمرغه unfortunate

bad margha *a.* بدمرغه ominous

bad marghay *n.* بدمرغی affliction

bad marghee *n* بدمرغي disaster

bad marghee *n.* بدمرغي misfortune

bad meych *n* بادمچ anemometer

bad qismata *a.* بدقسمته luckless

bad rang; weejar *a.* بدرن؛ویجا uncouth

bad rooh; shaytan *n* بدروح؛شطان evil

bad salook kawal *v.t.* بدسلوک کول mistreat

bad shakla *a* بدشکله crook

bad shakla *a.* بدشکله ugly

bad shakla kawal *v. t* بدشکله کول distort

bad shaklee *n.* بدشکلي ugliness

bad ta eekhodal *v.t.* بادتهایودل wind

bad tara kawal; la kharabawal *v.t.* بدتراکول؛لاخرابول worsen

bad tareen shay *n.* بدترینشی worst

bad wahana *n* بادوهنه blight

bad wayana *n.* بدوینه malediction

bad weystana *n.* بادوستنه deflation

bada chara *n* بدهچاره ill

bada peykha *n.* بدهپه mishap

bada zhaba *n.* بدهژبه invective

badam *n.* بادام almond

badan *n* بدن body

badanee *a* بدني bodily

badanee *a* بدني corporal

badanee *a.* بدني physical

baday *a.* بای rich

baday *a.* بای wealthy

badaytob *n.* بایتوب opulence

badbakht *a* بدبخت adverse

barbandawal *v.t.* بربنول strip
barbandee *n.* باربندي packing
barbokay *n.* ببوک whirlwind
barghaz *n.* برغز dart
barkha *n* برخه canton
barkha *n.* برخه quota
barkha *n.* برخه section
barkha *n.* برخه segment
barkha *n.* برخه part
barkha akheystal *v.t.* برخهاخستل part
barkheez; juzayee *a.* برخيز؛جزيي partial
barkhleek *n* برخليک fate
barlasay *n* برلاسی domination
barlasay keydal *v.t.* برلاسی کدل attain
barlasay keydal *v.t.* برلاسی کدل overcome
barlasay keydal *v.i.* برلاسی کدل predominate
barma *n.* برمه auger
barma *n* برمه drill
barma *n.* برمه wimble
barma sara sooray kawal *v. t.* برمهسرهسوری کول drill
barmata kawal *v.t.* برمته کول snatch
barseyra par dey *adv.* برسرهپردې moreover
barseyran makh; sata *n.* برسرن مخ؛سطح surface
barseyran; sathee *a.* برسرن؛سطحي superficial
barseyrantob *n.* برسرنتوب superficiality

bartar *a.* برتر predominant
bartaree *n.* برتري excellence
bartaree *n.* برتري predominance
bartarfee *n* برطرفي dismissal
barwa *n.* بوا bawd
barya *n.* بريا success
barya keydal *v.i.* برياکدل triumph
barya; fata *n.* بريا؛فتح triumph
baryalay *a* بريالی successful
baryalay *a.* بريالی victorious
baryalay *n.* بريالی victor
baryalay keydal *v.i.* بريالی کدل succeed
baryalay keydal *v.t.* بريالی کدل vanquish
baryalay meena *n.* بريالمينه melodrama
baryalay; fatay *a.* بريالی؛فاتح triumphal
baryalay; fatay *a.* بريالی؛فاتح triumphant
baryaleetob *n.* بريالیتوب achievement
baryaleetob *n.* بريالیتوب attainment
baryazam *n* براعظم continent
baryazam pori arwand *a* براعظم پوراوند continental
barzakhee naray *n.* برزخي purgatory
basarkay *n.* برکی jot
basarkay *n.* برکی spark
baseerat *n.* بصيرت insight
baseerat *n.* بصيرت vision
baseerat laroonkay *a.* بصيرت لرونکی intuitive

bashar dosta *n.* بشردوسته philanthropy

bashar pal *a* بشرپال humanitarian

bashareeyat *n.* بشريت humanity

bashpar *a* بشپ accomplished

bashpar *a* بشپ complete

bashpar ghopa kawal *v.t.* بشپغوپه کول overwhelm

bashpar kawal *v.t.* بشپکول accomplish

bashpar wakman *n* بشپواکمن autocrat

bashpar wakman *a.* بشپواکمن omnipotent

bashpar wakmanee *n.* بشپواکمني omnipotence

bashpara mati warkawal *v.t.* بشپهماتورکول rout

bashparawal *v. t* بشپول complete

bashparawoonkay *a* بشپوونکی complementary

bashpartob *n.* بشپتوب totality

bashpartya *n.* بشپتيا accomplishment

baspana *n.* بسپنه donation

baspana warkawal *v. t* بسپنه ورکول bestow

basree *a.* بصري ocular

basree *a.* بصري visual

bata *n.* بته goose

bata gota *n.* بهوته thumb

batai *n.* بـ kiln

batay; fateela; orlagawoonay *n.* با؛فتيله؛اورلوونی wick

batil *a.* باطل null

batilawal *v.t.* باطلول counteract

batilawal *v. t* باطلول disprove

batilawal *v. t* باطلول elude

batilawal *v.t.* باطلول invalidate

batilawal *v.t.* باطلول undo

batilawal *v.t.* باطلول void

batilawal *v.t.* باطلول nullify

batilawal; hazafawal *v. t.* باطلول؛حذفول cancel

batilawona *n.* باطلوونه nullification

batoo *n* باو bouncer

batray *n* بر battery

bawafa *a.* باوفا loyal

bawar leek *n.* باورليک creed

bawaree *a* باوري credible

bawaree *a.* باوري reliable

bawaree *n.* باوري optimist

bawaree laraway *n.* باوريلاروی henchman

bawaseer *n.* بواسير piles

baya *n.* بيه price

baya *n.* بيه value

baya eekhodal *v.t.* بيهايودل rate

baya laral *v.t.* بيهلرل cost

baya moondal *v.t.* بيهموندل price

bayad *v.* بايد must

bayan *n* بيان express

bayan *n.* بيان statement

bayan; tawzee *n* بيان؛توضيح description

bayanawal *v. t* بيانول describe

bayanawal *v. t.* بيانول express

bayanawal *v.t* بيانول state

bayanawal *v.t.* بيانول represent

bayanawal; ghageeza banra warkawal *v.t.* بيانول؛غيزهبه وركول voice

bayanawoonkay *n.* بيانوونكى narrator

bayaneeya *a* بيانيه descriptive

bayaneeya *n.* بيانيه proclamation

baydar *a.* بدار cautious

baydar *a.* بدار vigilant

baydar *a.* بدار wakeful

baydar; saro *a.* بدار،بارو watchful

bayhooda *a.* بهوده frivolous

bayhooda wakht teyrawal *v.i.* بهودهوختترول dawdle

baysakal *n.* بايسكل bicycle

baysakal sawar *n* بايسكلسوار cyclist

baysakal; chakar *n* بايسكل؛چكر cycle

baytul khala *n.* بيتالخلا latrine

bayzwee jisam *n* بضويجسم oval

baz *n* باز falcon

bazar *n* بازار market

bazeydal *v.i.* بزدل whiz

bazhar *n.* بزهار murmur

be adabi *n* بىادبى disrespect

be asasa khabary *n.* بىاساسهخبرى gossip

be azami *n.* بىعزمى indecision

be da muhakimy la hukma da cha wajal *v.t.* بىدمحاكمىله حكمهدچاوژل lynch

be lari zai *n.* بلارىاى impasse

be mela *a.* بميله listless

be samara *adv* بثمره abortive

be tawaja *a* بىتوجه forgetful

beelyoon; da peyso yaw shmeyra *n* بيليون؛دپسويوشمره billion

beema *n.* بيمه insurance

beema kawal *v.t.* بيمهكول insure

beemar *n* بيمار invalid

beemaree *n.* بيماري illness

beer; afeen; ghorzay parzay *n* بير،افين؛غورىپرى hop

beer; yaw nalkawalay skhak *n* بير؛يونالكولىاک beer

beera *n.* بيه haste

beera kawal *v.i.* بيهكول hasten

beeranak *a.* ناک بيه hasty

beeranay halat *n* بينىحالت emergency

beezo *n.* بيزو monkey

beezo *n.* بيزو baboon

behes *n.* بحث debate

behes kawal *v. t.* بحثكول debate

behes kawal *v.t.* بحثكول argue

behree zwak *n.* بحريواک armada

behtaree *n* بهترى betterment

benzeen; naft *n.* بنزين؛نفت petrol

bera naak *adv.* بهناك headlong

bey adaba *a* بادبه discourteous

bey adaba *a.* بادبه impertinent

bey adaba *a.* بادبه impolite

bey adabee *n.* بادبي impertinence

bey adabee *a* بادبي unmannerly

bey adabee; pooch khuleytob *n.* بادبي؛پوچخولتوب vulgarity

bey andwala *n* بانوله antic

bey aqal *a.* بعقل silly

bey aqal *a.* بعقل zany

bey aqla *a.* بعقله idiotic

bey arzakhta *a.* بارزته invaluable
bey arzakhta *a.* بارزته trivial
bey arzakhta *a.* بارزته worthless
bey arzakhta kawal *v.t.* بارزته کول demonetize
bey arzakhta shay *n.* بارزته شی nothing
bey arzakhtob; deywaleeya *n.* بی ارزتوب؛دوالیه bankrupt
bey asba *a.* بعصبه nerveless
bey aytibara *a.* باعتباره unreliable
bey aytina *a.* باعتنا irrespective
bey aytinayee *n* باعتنائی disregard
bey aytinayee kawal *v. t* باعتنائی کول disregard
bey bahaney *adv* ببهانه bonafide
bey baka *a* بباکه dauntless
bey bakee *n.* بباکی hardihood
bey barkhi kawal *v. t* ببرخ کول dethrone
bey barkhiwalay *n.* ببرخوالی privation
bey bawaree *n.* بباوری mistrust
bey boonyada *a.* ببنیاده baseless
bey boonyada *a.* ببنیاده invalid
bey dagha *a.* بداغه spotless
bey daney mameez *n.* بدانممیز currant
bey dawama *a* بدوامه flimsy
bey eezata; kufreeya *a.* بعزته، کفریه profane
bey eezatee *n* بعزتی dishonour
bey eezatee kawal *v. t* بعزتی کول dishonour
bey ehteeyata *a.* باحتیاطه inconsiderate

bey faydey *a.* بفاید futile
bey faydeytob *n.* بفایدتوب futility
bey fikra *a.* بفکره careless
bey gati; pooch *a.* بگتی؛پوچ void
bey gatitob *n* بگتوب drawback
bey ghaga *a.* بغه silent
bey ghaga toray *n.* بغهتوری mute
bey gharaza *a.* بغرضه neuter
bey gharaza *a.* بغرضه selfless
bey goona *a.* بناه innocent
bey goonahtob *n.* بناهتوب innocence
bey hada *a* بحده extreme
bey harakat *a.* بحرکت immovable
bey harakata *a.* بحرکته motionless
bey harakata wagon *n.* بحرکته واون trailer
bey harakata; walar *a.* بحرکته؛ولا stagnant
bey hasila kawal *v.t.* بحاصله کول sterilize
bey haya *a.* بحیا immodest
bey hayayee *n.* بحیایی immodesty
bey his *a.* بحس insensible
bey hisa *a.* بحسه numb
bey hisa *a.* بحسه senseless
bey hisee *n.* بحسی apathy
bey hisee *n.* بحسی insensibility
bey hokha *n.* بهوه anaesthetic
bey hokha *n.* بهوی coma
bey hokha keydal *v.i* بهوه کدل swoon
bey hokhee *n* بهوی anaesthesia
bey honara *a.* بهنره artless
bey honara *a* بهنره clumsy

bey wano aw parakha dag wazma jalga *n.* اخاپراواونوب وزمهجله steppe

bey wasley kawal *v. t* بوسلكول disarm

bey wasley kawona *n.* بوسلكوونه disarmament

bey weyri *a.* بور intrepid

bey yara *a.* بياره lonesome

bey yara; bey madadgara *a.* ب يارهبمدكاره helpless

bey zaya *a.* بايه nonsensical

bey zaya *a.* بايه wasteful

bey zaya *a.* بايه vain

bey zaya garzeydal *v.t* بايهركدل maroon

bey zaya khabari *n.* بايهخبر prattle

bey zaya palatana kawal *v.t.* بايه پلنهكول poke

bey zaya wada kawal; bey tarteeba wada kawal *v.i.* بايه ودهكولبترتيبهودهكول straggle

bey zaya; bey wakhta *a.* بايهبوخته undue

bey zhwanda *a.* بژونده lifeless

bey zra *n.* بزه coward

bey zra *a.* بزه timid

bey zratob *n.* بزهتوب timidity

beydya; bey wafayee *n* بديابوفايي desert

beyjak *n.* بجک invoice

beykhee *adv* بيخي absolutely

beylawal *v.t.* بلول sunder

beylcha *n.* بلچه shovel

beylcha *n.* بلچه spade

beylchey sara leyri kawal *v.t.* بلچ سرهلركول shovel

beyleydana *n.* بلدنه abstraction

beylga *n.* بله specimen

beylga azmoyal *v.t.* بلهآزمويل sample

beylowanay *n.* بلووني midriff

beyltoon *n* بلتون detachment

beyltoon *n.* بلتون insulation

beyltoonpal *n.* بلتونپال secessionist

beynooma; na sarganda *a.* بنومه؛ نارنده anonymous

beyragh *n.* برغ banner

beyragh *n* برغ flag

beyranga *adj* بيرنه achromatic

beyray ki spareydal *v. t.* بكسپردل board

beyrta *adv.* برته aback

beyrta ada shaway heesab *n.* برته اداشوىحساب refund

beyrta akheestal *v.t.* برتهاخيستل withdraw

beyrta akheystal *v.t.* برتهاخستل retrieve

beyrta raghokhtal *v.t.* برتهراغوتل recall

beyrta rastaneydal *v.i.* برته راستندل rebound

beyrta staneydana *n.* برتهستندنه relapse

beyrta tar lasa kawal *v.t.* برتهتر لاسهكول recover

beyrta warkawal *v.t.* برتهوركول reimburse

beysareetob *a.* بساريتوب inimitable

beyt chi yawa qafeeya walaree *n.* بتچيوهقافيهولري couplet

beyzar *a.* بزار averse

beyzara kawal; marawal *n.* بزاره كول;مول surfeit

beyzaree *n.* بزاري aversion

bilkul *adv* بالكل due

birinj; zhar *n.* برنج;ژ brass

biskot *n* بسكو biscuit

blarbakht *n.* بلاربت pregnancy

blok; yawa dala hamkar ashkhas *n.* بلوک;يوهلههمكار اشخاص platoon

bodija; lagakht andwaltya *n* بودجه;لختانولتيا budget

boghay *n.* بوغ balloon

bojay *n.* بوج sack

bokam; rawataltya *n.* بوكام; راوتلتيا hunch

bokhar; loogay *n* بخار;لوى fog

bokht *a* بوخت busy

bokhtya *n.* بوختيا pastime

boonyad *n.* بنياد foundation

boonyadee *a.* بنيادي fundamental

boonyadee *n.* ادي gaiety

boonyadee; ibtidayee *a.* بنيادي; ابتدايي initial

boora warkawal *v.t.* بورهورکول sugar

boora; qand *n.* بوره;قند sugar

boot *n.* بت idol

boot *n.* بو shoe

boot parast *n.* بتپرست idolater

boot ta talay achawal *v.t* بوتهتلى اچول sole

boot; fayda *n* بو;فايده boot

bootan pa pkho kawal *v.t.* بوانپه پوکول shoe

bootay *n* بوى bush

bootay *n.* بوى plant

bootpohana *n* بوپوهنه botany

booy *n.* بوى fragrance

booy *n.* بوى smell

booyawal *v.i.* بويول inhale

booyawal *v.i.* بويول sniff

booyawal; booy warkawal *v.t.* بويول;بوىورکول smell

bordbaree *n* بردباري bearing

boseeda *adj* بوسيده carious

boshka; tyoob *n.* بشكه;تيوب barrel

botal *n* بوتل bottle

braj *n.* برج tower

brash *n* برش brush

brastan *n.* بستن coverlet

brayk lagawal *v. t* برکلول brake

breed *n.* بريد assault

breed *n* بريد dash

breed kawal *v.* بريدکول assail

breed kawal *v.t.* بريدکول assault

breed kawal *v.t.* بريدکول invade

breed kawal *v.i* بريدکول lunge

breed kawal *v.t.* بريدکول spearhead

breed; poola *n.* بريد;پوله frontier

breed; yarghal *n.* بريد;يرغل attack

breedoona aw hadood *n.* بريدونهاو حدود purview

breetanawee *adj* بريتانوي british

breykh *n* بر glow

breykhandoy *a* برندوى light

breykheydal *v.i.* بردل glow

breykheydana *n* بردنه dazzle

breykheydana *n.* بردنه scintillation

breykheydana *n.* برخدنه refulgence

breykhna *n* برنا electricity

breykhna warkawal *v. t* برنا ورکول electrify

breykhnayee *a* برنايي electric

breykhnayee qawa *n.* برنايي‌قوه voltage

breykhnayee sragh *n.* برنايي‌راغ bulb

breyt *n.* برت moustache

breytoona *n.* برتونه mustache

bronz; bronzee rang *n. & adj* برونز؛برونزي‌رن bronze

brudbaree *n.* بردباري endurance

buhran *n* بحران crisis

buhtan lagawal *v.t.* بهتان‌لول trump

bukhal *n* بخل grudge

bukhar kawal *v.i.* بخارکول steam

bukhar kawoonkay *n.* بخار کوونکی steamer

bukhar; lara *n* بخار؛له steam

bukharay *n.* بخار stove

bulbul *n.* بلبل nightingale

burdbar *a* بردبار endurable

burj; munara *n.* برج؛مناره steeple

bya *adv.* بيا again

bya *a* بيا then

bya chapawal *v.t.* بياچاپول reprint

bya katal *v.t.* بياکتل review

bya katana *n* بياکتنه review

bya neewana *n* بيانيوونه remand

bya paylawal *v.t.* بياپيلول resume

bya paylawana *n.* بياپيلوونه resumption

bya raghawana *n.* بيارغاوونه restoration

bya rastaneydal *v.t.* بياراستندل reclaim

bya rastaneydana; zmaksamoon *n* بياراستندنه؛مکسمون reclamation

bya razhwanday keydal *v.i.* بيا راژوندی‌کدل revive

bya razhwanday keydana *n.* بيا راژوندی‌کدنه resurgence

bya razhwanday keydana *n.* بيا راژوندی‌کدنه revival

bya razhwanday shaway *a.* بيا راژوندی‌شوی resurgent

bya tasal warkawal *v.t.* بياتسل ورکول reassure

bya tawleedawal *v.t.* بياتوليدول reproduce

bya tawleedawal; bya zeygeydal *v.t.* بياتوليدول؛بيازدل regenerate

bya tawleedawana *n* بياتوليدوونه reproduction

bya wadanawal *v.t.* بياودانول rehabilitate

bya wadantya *n.* بياودانتيا rehabilitation

bya zeygoon *n.* بيازون rebirth

byaleyda *n.* بيلدا secession

byatee kawal; skwalal *v.t.* بياتي کول؛سکولل shear

C

cha ta lara neewal *v.t.* چاته‌لاره‌نيول waylay

cha ta law warachawal v.t. چاته لاسوراچول tantalize

cha ta pateydal v.i. چاته پدل lurk

cha ta; cha lapara pron. چاته؛چا لپاره whom

chabak adj چابک alacrious

chabak a. چابک speedy

chadan n چدن cast-iron

chagh a چاغ fat

chaghakht n. چاغت obesity

chaghan ghag; faryad n چغن غ؛ فرياد squeak

chak; cheech n چک؛چيچ bite

chak; darz n چاک؛درز cut

chakar bandi da tlo patloon n. چکربانددتلوپتلون slacks

chakar wahal v.i. چکروهل meander

chakar wahal v.t. چکروهلsaunter

chakar wahana n چکروهنه stroll

chakar; pali tag n چکر؛پلی ټ walk

chakara; luab n. چکه،لعاب slime

chakaree a چکري،دوروي cyclic

chakchaki n چکچک acclaim

chakckahi kawal v.t چکچک کول acclaim

chaklayt n چاکلا chocolate

chal n چل deception

chal n. چل lurch

chal kawal v.t. چل کول trick

chal; chalbaz n. چل؛چلباز ruse

chal; doka n چل؛دوکه trick

chalak a چالاک cunning

chalakee n چالاکي cunning

chaland kawal v. t چلندکول conduct

chaland kawal v. i. چلندکول behave

chaland kawal v.t. چلندکول treat

chaland; akhlaq n چلند،اخلاق behaviour

chaland; amal n چلند؛عمل deed

chaland; meylmastya n. چلند؛ ملمستيا treatment

chaland; riwayya n چلند،رويهtreat

chalawal v.t. چلول steer

chalbaz a. چلباز artful

chalbaz n. چلباز impostor

chalbaz a. چلباز roguish

chalbaz a. چلباز shifty

chalbaz a. چلباز tricky

chalbazee n. چلبازي imposture

chalbazee n. چلبازي quackery

chalbazee n. چلبازي trickery

chalowoonkay n چلوونکی conductor

chalowoonkay; spor n. چلوونکی؛ سپور rider

cham aw chal n چماوچل disguise

chaman n. چمن lawn

chaman n. چمن sod

chamanzar n. چمنزار lea

chamtoo a. چمتو ready

chamtoo kawal v.t. چمتوکول assemble

chamtoowalay n. چمتووالی alacrity

chamtoowalay n. چمتووالی readiness

chang n. چ harp

changak n. چنک hook

changakh n چنا crab

changakha *n.* چنه frog
chanr *n* چا filter
chanrasay *n.* چاس mildew
chanrawal *v.t* چاول filter
chanrawana *n* چاونه sublime
chanrchanra *n.* چچه swallow
chanrowana; speenawana *n.* چاوونه،سپینوونه purgation
chanrzay *n.* چلای refinery
chap *n* چاپ edition
chap shaway shay *n.* چاپشویشی imprint
chap ta chamtoo kawal *v. t* چاپ تهچمتوکول edit
chap; khparawana *n* چاپ،خپرونه print
chapa kawal *v.t.* چپهکول whelm
chapaw kawal *v.i.* چپاوکول loot
chapawal *v.t.* چاپول print
chapawal *n.* چپاول havoc
chapawal *n.* چپاول loot
chapawal; dalbandee kawal *v.t.* چاپول،لبنديکول type
chapawoonkay *n.* چاپوونکی printer
chapawoonkay *n.* چاپوونکی typist
chapeyr garzeydal *v. i.* چاپرورلدل circulate
chapeyryal *n.* چاپریال environment
chapeyryal *n.* چاپریال periphery
chapeyryal *n.* چاپریال surroundings
chaplosa saray *n.* چاپلوسهسی sycophant
chaplosee *n* چاپلوسي flattery

chaplosee *v.t* چاپلوسيکول flatter
chaplosee *n* چاپلوسی adulation
chaplosee *n.* چاپلوسي sycophancy
chaplosee *n.* چاپلوسي insinuation
chaplosee kawal *v. t* چاپلوسيکول butter
chaplosee kawal *v.t.* چاپلوسيکول insinuate
chaqoo *n.* چاقو knife
char maghaz *n* چارمغز nut
char maghaz *n.* چارمغز walnut
chara saz *a.* چارهساز resourceful
charchari *n* چرچر chirp
charchari kawal *v.i.* چرچرکول chirp
charg *n* چر cock
charga *n.* چره fowl
charga *n.* چره hen
chargan satana *n.* چرگانساتنه poultry
charge warkawal *v.t.* چارجورکول lade
chargooray *n.* چروی chicken
chargooree eystal *v.i.* چرويایستل incubate
charj *n.* الیاژ چارج؛ alloy
chark *n* چرک dirt
chark; zoh *n.* چرک؛زوه pus
charmee waskat *n.* چرميواسک jerkin
charshamba *n.* چارشنبه Wednesday
charta; halta *conj.* چرته،هلته where
chartapee not *n.* چارتاپينو crotchet
chat *n.* چَت ceiling
chat *n.* چت roof

chat jorawal *v.t.* چت جوول roof

chat; bam *n.* چت،بام top

chatak *adj* چک brisk

chatak *a* چک express

chatak *a.* چک nimble

chatak *a.* چک quick

chatak *a.* چک swift

chatak aw chabak *a.* چکـاو چابک lively

chatak goozar *n* چکـوزار slash

chatak leekana *n.* چک ليکنه stenography

chatak leekoonkay *n.* چک ليکونکی stenographer

chatak parwaz *n.* چک پرواز whir

chatak tag; da as ghonda tlal *n* چک ت؛داس غوندهتلل trot

chatak tlal *v.i.* چکـتلل trot

chatak zghal *n.* چکـغل gallop

chatak zghalawal *v.t.* چکـغلول gallop

chatak zghaleydal *v.i.* چکـغلدل sprint

chataka teykhta *n* چکهتته scamper

chatakee zghastee syalee *n* چکی غاستيسيالي sprint

chataktya *n.* چکتيا rapidity

chatal *a* چل dirty

chatala ya jongara *n.* چلهياجونه slum

chatarbaz *n.* چترباز parachutist

chatee *n.* چی nonsense

chatray *n.* چتر umbrella

chawd; ayb *n* چاود؛عيب flaw

chawd; ghoswalay *n.* چاود؛غووالی slit

chawdal *v. t.* چاودول explode

chawdana *n* چاودنه blast

chawdana *n* چاودنه burst

chawdana *n.* چاودنه explosion

chawdeydal *v. i.* چاودول burst

chawkat; salor konja dara *n.* چوکا،څلور کونجهدده panel

chawkay *n.* چوکۍ seat

chawkay warkawal *v.t.* چوکۍ ورکول seat

chawtra; baranda *n.* چوتره؛برنه terrace

chay *n* چای tea

chay josha *n.* چایجوشه kettle

cheech *n.* چيچ sting

cheechal *v. t.* چيچل bite

cheechal *v.t.* چيچل pinch

cheechal *v.t.* چيچل sting

cheekar *n.* چيک mire

cheena; pasarlay *n* چينه،پسرلی spring

cheenee lokhee *n.* چينيلوی porcelain

cheenee lokhee *n.* چينيلوی china

cheenjay *n.* چينجی worm

cheetawal *v.t.* چيتول squeeze

cheetawal; bandawal *v.t.* چيتول؛بندول jam

cheygha *n* چغه cry

cheygha *n* چغه exclamation

cheygha soora *n* چغهسوره scream

cheygha wahal *v.i* چغهوهل exclaim

cheyghey aw kreeki *n.* چغاو کريک shriek

da aroozo ilam *n.* دعروضوعلم prosody

da arwagano pa naray bawar *n.* داروالانوپهنباور spiritualism

da arwagano yaw bal ta nanawatal *n.* داروالانویوبلته نوتل transmigration

da arwayeezo naroghyo daktar *n.* داروااییزوناروغیواکر psychiatrist

da as sheeshney *n.* داسشیشنۍneigh

da as sheeshneydal *v.i.* داسشیشنل neigh

da ashraf wakay palaway *n.* د اشرافواکپلوی aristocrat

da asnado aw kaghazo bakas; da wazarat danda aw maqam *n.* داسنادواوکاغذو بکس؛دوزارتدندهاومقام portfolio

da astogni aw da kar zay tr manz safar kawal *v. t* داستونۍ commuteاودکارایترمنسفرکول

da astogni war *a.* داستونو habitable

da astogni war *a.* داستونو inhabitable

da atom yawa manzanay zara *n.* داومیوهمننذره neutron

da atro booy warkawal *v.t.* د عطروبویورکول perfume

da awaz inikas *n* آوازانعکاسecho

da awreydo war *a* داوردورaudible

da aytimad namey khawand *adj* داعتمادنامخاوند accredited

da aytiraz war *a.* داعتراضو objectionable

da bad pa shan teyreydal *v.t.* دباد پهشانترلدل waft

da badan gharay *n.* دبدنغی limb

da badan jorakht *n.* دبدنجوت physique

da badan pata *n.* دبدنپه muscle

da badan pati mazbootawal; rang warkawal *v.t.* دبدنپ مضبوطول؛رنورکول tone

da badee ilam *n.* دبدیععلمrhetoric

da badi peykhi la kabala zyan aw talfat *n* دبدپلهکبلهزیاناو تلفات toll

da badnamay pa dar la cha sakha peysey akheystal *v.t* د بدنامپهارلهچاخهپساخستل blackmail

da badraft sah *n.* دبدرفتاهpuddle

da badwayani da falsafey pleewanay *n.* دبدويدفلسفه پليوني sceptic

da baghwanay beylcha *n.* دباغواز بلچه trowel

da bahar *n* دبهر outside

da bahar haywad mazdoor *a.* د بهرهوادمزدور mercenary

da bakhani war *a.* دبنو venial

da bal par zay eekhodal *v.t.* دبل پرایایودل substitute

da bal seez zay neewal *v.t.* دبلیز اینیول supersede

da balakhani balkun *n.* دبالاخاز بالکن balcony

da balot da koranay d yawi wani postakay *n.* دبلوطدکورنز پوستکی دیوز cork

da band deywal *n* دبنددوال bulwark

da bandeekhaney masool *n.* د بنديخانهمسؤل jailer

da bandeyz preykra *n* دبندزپرکه ban

da bandi *adv.* دباند out

da bandi *a.* دباند outdoor

da bandi *prep* دباند outside

da bandi *prep.* دباند without

da bandoono da dard ranz *n.* د بندونو ددردرنز rheumatism

da bandoono pa dard akhta kas *a.* دبندونوپهدرداختهکس rheumatic

da banri badloon *n.* دببدلون transformation

da banri yaw rangwalay *n.* دبیو رنوالی similitude

da barbat da rabab pakhwanay ala *n.* دبربطدرباب پخوازآله lyre

da barwrani karaya *n.* دباروزکرایه freight

da baryaleetob yadgar *n.* د بریالیتوبیادار trophy

da bati pa shan tlal *v.i.* دبتیپهشان تلل waddle

da bawar war *a.* دباورو trustworthy

da bawar war saray *n.* دباوروسی trusty

da baydminton da lobey parey laroonki ghondaska *n.* دبمنون دلوبهپرلرونکغونسکه shuttlecock

da baysakal rakab pa pkho wahal *v.t.* دبایسکلرکاب پهپو وهل pedal

da beemey peysey *n.* دبیمپس premium

da behes ghonda *n.* دبحثغونه seminar

da bey hokhay keymyayee mada *n* دبهو کمیایيماده chloroform

da bey istimala aw kharabo seezoono deyray *n* دباستعماله اوخرابویزونوری debris

da bey rahmay jinsee meena *n.* د برحمجنسيمينه sadism

da beyray khada *n.* دبخاده mast

da beyray takhta *n* دبتخته board

da boodayano butkhana *n.* د بودایانوبتخانه pagoda

da boot band *n.* دبوبند lace

da boot band taral *v.t.* دبوبندتل lace

da boot gandalo aw jamo gandalo ki yaw dawl taghma *n.* دبوځلواوجاموځلوکییو ولتغمه welt

da bootee koochnay sanga *n.* د بوي کوچنانه sprig

da breetaneeyey da sikey shalama barkha *n.* دبریتانید سکشلمهبرخه shilling

da breetaneeyey rasmee sika *n.* د سکه رسمي بريتانئ sterling

da breykhna jaryan ya shidat nap kawoonki peymana *n* د برناجريانياشدتناپ کوونکپمانه ampere

dabreykhnanapawaloyawpaymana *n.* دپوځانانولویوپمانه watt

da breykhna yaw paymana *n.* د برنایوپمانه volt

da bukharay da nal loogay *v.t.* د بخاردنللوی soot

da cha *pron.* د چا whose

da cha ghara takhta kawal *v.t.* د چاغاه تخته کول strangle

da chaland dawl *n.* دچلندول attitude

da chalowani qabil *a.* دچلوزقابل manageable

da chanrchanri awazoona *n.* د چچاواز ونه swallow

da chanrchanri pa shan awazoona kawal *v.t.* دچچ په شان اواز ونه کول swallow

da chawdo nakha *n.* دچاودونه nick

da chawkat amoodee barkha *n.* دچو کاعمودي برخه mullion

da cheechak naroghee *n.* د چیچک ناروغي smallpox

da cheen rasmee sika *n.* دچین رسمي سکه Yen

da cheeney pa shakal wareydal *v.i.* دچینه په شکل ورلدل spout

da chi *conj.* داچ since

da chi *conj.* داچ that

da chi *conj.* داچ now

da chooney oba *n.* دچوناوبه whitewash

da chooney pa obo rangawal *v.t.* دچونه په اوبو رنول whitewash

da dabaro skara *n* دبروسکاره coal

da daftar charwakay *n.* ددفتر چارواکی officer

da daftar qasid *n.* ددفترقاصد peon

da daftaree karmandano plaway ya idaree zay *n.* د دفتري کارمندانو پلاوی یا اداري یای secretariat e

da daktaray daraja *n* داکردرجه doctorate

da darak war *adj* ددرکو perceptible

da dard sreeka *n.* ددردیکه throe

da darmal pa arwand *a.* ددرمل په اوند medicinal

da darmalo yaw khorak *n* ددرملو یوخوراک dose

da darwazey da sar teer *n.* ددرواز دسرتیر lintel

da daryab sanda *n* ددریاب ئنه beach

da dawl chi *adv.* داول چ that

da dawl khalk; da dawl shayan *pron.* داول خلک؛داول شیان such

da dawtalbay muzayda *n* دداوطلبه مزایده tender

da dayrey muheet *n.* ددایرمحیط circumference

da dayri qutar *n* ددایرقطر diameter

da deenee uloomu karpoh *n.* د دیني علومو کارپوه theologian

da dey naray *a.* ددنی worldly

da doday pakhawani aw khwago jorawalo nanwayee *n* دوپخوناوخوو جوولونانوایی bakery

da doday parcha *n* دودی پارچه crumb

da dreyo dawro khawand *n.* د دریو دوورونوخاوند tricycle

da dreyo shmeyr *a* ددریوشمر three

da dwa payo motarsaykal *n.* ددوه پایومورسایکل scooter

da dwa shayano manz ki eekhodal *v.t.* ددوهشیانومنزک ایودل sandwich

da eejazey war *a.* داجازو permissible

da eemteeyaz khawand *n.* دامتیاز خاوند monopolist

da eesayano akhtar *n.* دعیسائیانو اختر Xmas

da eezat pa arwand *a.* دعزت په اوند prestigious

da eezat peyrzoyana *n.* دعزت پرزوینه tributary

da ehtiram war *a.* داحترامو reverend

da faaleeyat markaz *n.* دفعالیت مرکز hub

da fasfureek aseed malga *n.* د فسفریک اسیدماله phosphate

da faskh kawoni war *a.* دفسخ کوونو revocable

da fasloono law *n.* دفصلونو لو harvest

da feel ghakh *n.* دفیلغا ivory

da filam khodalo projektor *n* د فلمودلوپروجکور bioscope

da filas zalanda patay *n.* دفلس لاندهپ tinsel

da filizato da eystani aw weeli kawoni poha *n.* دفلزاتوداستناو ویلکوونپوهه metallurgy

da flaleen tokar *n* دفلالینوکر flannel

da foz astoganzay *n.* دفواستونای barrack

da gad zhwand wartya *n.* دژوند وتیا sociability

da gadee paya *n.* دایپایه tyre

da gadee sahoolat *n* دایسهولت conveyance

da gado pa arwand *a.* داوپهاوند vehicular

da galey masheen *n.* دغلکولوماشین thresher

da gam akheestani awaz *n* دام اخیستنآواز tread

da garmay mosam *n.* درموسم summer

da gawand pa arwand *a.* داونپه اوند neighbourly

da gaylan paymayish *n.* دلنپمایش gallon

da geetar da mawseeqay ala *n.* د اردموسیقهآله guitar

da geydi dananay barkha *n.* ددنه برخه bowel

da ghag angaza *n.* دغانازه resonance

da ghag lwarawalo ala *n.* دغلوولو آله microphone

da ghagoono da tarkeeb aw harfoono da wayang ilam *n.* دغونودترکیباوحرفونودوینعلم phonetics

da ghakh beykh *n.* دغابخ snag

da ghakh chark *n.* دغاچرک pyorrhoea

da ghakh khoog *n.* دغاخو toothache

da ghakhoono daktar *n* دغاونواکر dentist

da ghaley godam *n.* دغَلودام granary

da ghaley zeyrmatoon *n.* دغل زرمتون barn

da ghalo dano zeyrma *n.* دغلودانو زرمه lathe

da ghanamo ya joowaro wagay *n.* دغنمویاجوارووی spike

da ghanrey zala *n* دغاله cobweb

da hashrato larwa *n.* داروالوتارشحد
otter

da hawa *n.* دهوا aerial

da hawa chapeyryal *n.* دهوا
چاپريال space

da hawa pa shan *adj.* دهواپهشان
aeriform

da haydrojan gaz *n.* دهايروجنباز
hydrogen

da haywad dananay barkha *n.* د
هواددننبرخه midland

da haywad khwa ta *adv.* دهوادخوا
ته inland

da haywanato makhki pkhey *n* د
حواناتومخکپ foreleg

da hayz bandeyda *n.* دحضبندیدا
menopause

da hayz jaryan *n.* دحضجریان
menstruation

da hayz pa arwand *a.* دحضپهاوند
menstrual

da hayzey waba *n.* دهضوباcholera

da heelay ghag *n* دهیلغ quack

da heelay ghageydal *v.i.* دهیلغدل
quack

da heesaboono sabt keetab *n.* د
حسابونوثبتکتاب ledger

da heesaboono tasfeeya *n.* د
حسابونوتصفیه liquidation

da heywad rasmee sika *n* دهواد
رسمیسکه currency

**da heywadoono da nakhcho
keetab** *n.* دهوادونودنخچوکتاب
atlas

da hind aw pakistan sika *n.* دهند
اوپاکستانسکه rupee

**da hindso aw nakhcho pa
arwand** *a.* دهندسواونخچوپه
اوند graphic

da hisabdaray saroonkay *n.* د
حسابدارارونکی auditor

da ibadat koochnay zay *n.* د
عبادتکوچنیای chapel

da ibadat marasim *n.* دعبادت
مراسم ritual

**da ibadat marasimo pori
arwand** *a.* دعبادتمراسموپور
اوند ritual

da ibtidayee bashareeyat dawr
a. دابتداییبشریتدور primeval

da ida leek la makhi toranawal
v.t. دادعالیکلهمختورنولindict

**da ilat aw malool tar manz
areeka** *n* دعلتاومعلولترمنایکه
causality

da imaley darmal *n.* دامالدرمل
purgative

da inkar toray na *adv.* دانکارتوری
نه nay

da insan dawla beezo *adj.* دانسان
ولهبیزو anthropoid

da insan pa waseela pa karowal
v.t. دانسانپهوسیلهپهکاروولman

**da insanano da zhwand da nawi
dabareeney dawra** *a.* د
انسانانودژونددنوبریدنودوره
neolithic

da insanee fikree taraw fan *n.* د
انسانیفکريتاوفن telepathy

da intiqad hunar *n* دانتقادهنرcritic

da iqrar *a.* داقرار promissory

da ishq naz nakhrey kawal *v.i* د
عشقنازنخرهکول flirt

da ghari dasmal *n.* دغادسمال muffler

da gharmey doday *n.* دغرمو lunch

da gharmey doday khwaral *v.i.* د غرموخول lunch

da ghashee shatanay sanda *n.* د غشی‌شاتننه barb

da ghaybo ilam *n.* دغبوعلم prescience

da ghaza pa arwand *a.* دغذاپه‌اوند nutritive

da ghlo da saza chawbandee *n.* د غلودسزاچوبندي scaffold

da ghondaski pa shan eyrghareydal *v.i* دغونسکپه‌شان ارغدل bowl

da ghondaski wahalo danda *n* د غونسکوهلو نه bat

da ghondi da behes mawad *n.* دغوندبحث‌مواد agenda

da ghondyo ya ghroono laray *n.* دغونيوياغرونو اړ ridge

da ghwag kheeray *n.* دغوخيری mucus

da ghwag zawa *n* دغوزوه cerumen

da ghwameykho gala *n.* دغوامله cattle

da ghwayee ghwakha *n* دغوايي‌غوه beef

da ghwayee pa shan shkhwand wahal *v.t.* دغوايي‌په‌شان‌شخوند وهل munch

da gramofon da mawseeqay ala *n.* درامو فون‌دموسيقاآله gramophone

da gul panra *n.* دل‌پاه petal

da gulf loba *n.* دلف‌لوبه golf

da guloono taj *n.* دلونوتاج wreath

da guloono taj jorawal *v.t.* دلونو تاج‌جوول wreathe

da hadookee da postwalee ranz *n.* دهوکي‌دپوستوالي‌رنز rickets

da hagay speen *n* دهسپين albumen

da hagay yawa loba *n.* دهاکيوه‌لوبه polo

da hagay zeyr *n.* دهزير yolk

da hagha *pron.* دهغه his

da haghey *a* دهغ her

da haghey; haghey ta *pron.* دهغ؛ هغته her

da haghwee *a.* دهغوي their

da haghwee *pron.* دهغوي theirs

da hakay loba *n.* دهاکلوبه hockey

da hamley hasa *n.* دحمله stab

da haq ghla *n.* دحق‌غلا piracy

da har dard dwa aw moalij darmal *n.* دهردردوااومعالج درمل nostrum

da har maraz dawa *n.* دهرمرض دوا panacea

da har sa neem makh *n.* دهره‌نيم مخ silhouette

da har shee keenra khwa *n.* دهر شي‌کيه‌خوا left

da harkalee kota *n* دهرکلي‌خونه drawing-room

da harmoneeyom da mawseeqay ala *n.* دهارمونيوم‌دموسيقاآله harmonium

da hasharato zaharjan darmal *n* دحشراتوزهرجن‌درمل spray

da hashrato ilam *n.* دحشراتوعلم entomology

da ahangaray kora *n* دآهنرکوړه forge

da ajnaso leygdawani kakhtay *n* داجناسولدوونکت tender

da ajoorey peysey *n* داجورپسه emolument

da akasay kamra *n.* دعکاسکامره camera

da akseejan gaz *n.* دآکسیجنباز oxygen

da aksoono lapara yaw koochnay filam *n.* دعکسونو لپارهیوکوچنیفیلم microfilm

da alomeeneeyom filiz *n.* د الومینیومفلز aluminium

da alwatoonko zala *n.* دالوتونکوله aviary

da am karawani zhaba *n.* دعام کارونژبه lingua franca

da am wagaro raya *n.* دعامووراپه plebiscite

da amalee falsafey pa arwand *a.* دعملیفلسفهپهاوند pragmatic

da amoomee tafree zay *n.* دعمومي تفریحهای park

da amreeka rasmee sika *n* دامریکا رسمیسکه dollar

da anee harakat pa qawey pori arwand *a.* دآنيحرکتپهقوپپور اوند momentous

da anee harakat qawa *n.* دآني حرکتقوه momentum

da angooro sheera *n.* دانوروشیره must

da angreyzay zhabi da w toray *n.* توریwدانزيژبد wen

da angreyzay zhabi yaw makhtaray toray *pref.* دانرز ژبیومختایتوری be

da angreyzay zhabi yaw makhtaray toray *pref* دانرزژب یومختایتوری bi

da angreyzee kal atama myasht *n.* دانرزيکالاتمهمیاشت August

da angreyzee kal dolasama myasht *n* دانرزيکالدولسمه میاشت december

da angreyzee kal dreyma myasht *n.* دانرزيکالدریمه میاشت May

da angreyzee kal dwayama myasht *n* دانرزيکالدویمه میاشت February

da angreyzee kal lasama myasht *n.* دانرزيکاللسمهمیاشت October

da angreyzee kal nahama myasht *n.* دانرزيکالنهمه میاشت September

da angreyzee kal yawolasama myasht *n.* دانرزيکالیوولسمه میاشت november

da anzor akheystanai war *a.* د انوراخستنو picturesque

da anzwa zay *n.* دانزوامای hermitage

da apandeeks parsob *n.* داپانیکس پسوب appendicitis

da aqal ghakh *n.* دعقلغا wisdom-tooth

da aram kar *n.* دامکار leverage

da aram wraz *n.* دآرامور holiday

da areeko bandeyz *n* دایکوبندز boycott

cheyghey aw kreeki wahal *v.i.* چغ
او کریکوهل shriek

cheyghey wahal *v.i.* چغوهلscream

cheyghi soorey wahal *v.i.* چغسور
وهل squeak

cheyghi wahal *v. i* چغوهل crow

cheyghi wahal *v. i* چغوهل cry

cheyk *n.* چک cheque

cheyri *adv.* چر where

cheyrta *adv.* چرته whereabout

chobkhat; shmeyra *n.* چوبخط،
شمره tally

chogha *n* چوغه mantle

chogha aghostal *v.t* چوغهاغوستل
mantle

chokhawana *n.* چوخوونه poke

chola *n.* چوله notch

chola kawal *n.* چولهکول note

chooka *n.* چوکه wicker

choonrar *n.* چوهار twitter

choonreydal *v. i* چوندل cheep

choonreydal *v.i.* چودل twitter

choora; fataq *n.* چوره،فتق hernia

choorleez *n.* چورلي axis

choorleez *n.* چورلي pivot

choorleydal *v.i.* چورلدل revolve

choorleydal *v.i.* چورلدل roll

choorleydal *v.i.* چورلدل rotate

choorleydana *n.* چورلدنه rotation

choorleydana; badloon; taw *n*
چورلدنه،بدلون،تاو turn

choorleydoonkay *a.* چورلدونکی
rotary

chopar ta chamtoo *a.* چوپتهچمتو
serviceable

chopar warta kawal *v.t* چوپورته
کول service

choptya *n* چوپتیا hush

choptya *n.* چوپتیا quiet

choptya *n.* چوپتیا still

choptya *n.* چوپتیا silence

chowal; chawdal *v.i* چوول،چاودل
blast

chughandar *n* چغندر beet

churut wahana *n.* چرتوهنه doze

chust *a.* چست athletic

D

da payakht aw baqa zwak *n.* د
پایتاوبقاواک vitality

da ... pa oogdo ki; da ... pa
imtidad ki *prep.* د...پهاودو ک،د
...پهامتداد ک along

da ... pa waseela *prep* د...پهوسیله
by

da abeysey pa arwand *a.* دابهاوند
alphabetical

da abisi keetab *n.* دابکتاب primer

da abnoos bootay *n* دآبنوسبوی
ebony

da adabeeyato ilam *n.* دادبیاتوعلم
literature

da adaney stan *n.* داانستن stalk

da adayani war *n* داداینو due

da adayani war *a.* دادایینوpayable

da aflatoon da lari laraway *a.* د
افلاطوندلارلاروی platonic

bey parwa *a.* بپروا nonchalant

bey parwa *a.* بپروا negligent

bey parwayee *n.* بپروايي
negligence

bey parwayee *n.* بپروايي
nonchalance

bey patee kawal *v. t. & i* بپتيكول
blab

bey paymani *a.* بيماز measureless

bey qadra keydal / kawal *v.t.i.* بـ
قدرهكدل/كول depreciate

bey qanoona *a.* بقانونه lawless

bey qanoonee *n.* بقانوني void

bey qarar *adj.* بقرار agog

bey qaydagee *n.* بقاعلي
irregularity

bey qaydey *a.* بقاعد irregular

bey rahma *a.* برحمه ruthless

bey rehem *a.* برحم inexorable

bey rehma *a.* برحمه atrocious

bey rehma *a* برحمه brutal

bey rehma *adj.* برحمه merciless

bey rehma *a.* برحمه pitiless

bey rehmee *n* برحمي atrocity

bey rooha; jamid *a.* بروحه،جامد
inanimate

bey sabra *a.* بصبره impatient

bey sabree *n.* بصبري impatience

bey saray *a.* بساری matchless

bey seem *a.* بسيم wireless

bey seem mukhabira *n* بسيممخابره
wireless

bey sharafa *n.* بشرفه ruffian

bey sharam *a.* بشرم shabby

bey shari da wada zhwand
teyrawal *n* بشرعدوادهژوندترول
concubine

bey sharma *a.* بشرمه shameless

bey shmara *a.* بشماره incalculable

bey shmeyra *a.* بشمره countless

bey shmeyra *a.* بشمره innumerable

bey shmeyra *a.* بشمره numberless

bey shmeyra *a.* بشمره numerous

bey tafawat *a.* بتفاوت indifferent

bey tafawatee *n.* بتفاوتي
indifference

bey tajrubey *adj* بتجرب callow

bey taleema *a.* بتعليمه illiterate

bey tarafa *a.* بطرفه impartial

bey tarafa *a.* بطرفه neutral

bey tarafa kawal *v.t.* بطرفهكول
neutralize

bey tarafee *n.* بطرفي impartiality

bey tarbeeyey *a.* بتربيه rude

bey tarteeba *n* بترتيبه anomaly

bey tarteeba *a.* بترتيبه random

bey toley keydo lamala
raghorzeydal *v.t.* بتواكدولامله
راغوردل tip

bey wafayee *n.* بوفايي perfidy

bey wafayee kawal *v. t.* بوفاييكول
desert

bey wajdana *a.* بوجدانه miscreant

bey waka khandeydal *v.i.* بواكه
خندندل giggle

bey wakhta zeygeydana *n* بوخته
زدنه abortion

bey wakhta; bey moqa *a.* بوخته،بـ
موقع inopportune

bey insafa *a.* بانصافه injudicious

bey insafa *a* بانصافه unfair

bey insafee *n.* بانصافي injustice

bey itifaqee *n.* باتفاقي schism

bey itmaynanee *n.* باطميناني insecurity

bey itminanee *n* باطميناني dissatisfaction

bey jinsa noom *n* بجنسه نوم neuter

bey jorey *a.* بجو incomparable

bey jorey *a.* بجو peerless

bey jurata kawal *v. t.* بجرأته کول discourage

bey kara *a.* بکاره idle

bey kara *n.* بکاره idler

bey kara *a.* بکاره inactive

bey kara *a.* بکاره redundant

bey karee *n.* بکاري idleness

bey karee *n.* بکاري inaction

bey khabara *a.* بخبره oblivious

bey khabaray sara *adv.* بخبرسره unwittingly

bey khazi *n.* بـ bachelor

bey khwanda *a.* بخونده banal

bey khwanda *a.* بخونده humdrum

bey khwanda *a.* بخونده insipid

bey khwanda *a.* بخونده awkward

bey khwanda *a.* بخونده prosaic

bey khwandee *n.* بخوندي insipidity

bey kora *a* بکوره outcast

bey lari *a.* بلار unprincipled

bey lari kawal *v. t.* بلارکول derail

bey lari kawal *v.t.* بلارکول misguide

bey laritob *n.* بلارتوب aberrance

bey lastonro kot *n.* بلستوو کو waistcoat

bey maharata *a.* بمهارته ungainly

bey maharata kas *n.* بمهارته کس layman

bey mana *a* بمعنى absurd

bey mana *a.* بمانا insignificant

bey manatob *n.* بماناتوب insignificance

bey maney *a.* بماز meaningless

bey masheena koochnay alwataka chi da hawa pa waseela aloozee *n.* بماشينه کوچنالوتکه چددهوا په وسيله الوزي glider

bey misla *a.* بمثله unique

bey nateejey *adv.* بنتيج vainly

bey nazakata *a.* بنزاکته indecent

bey nazakatee *n.* بنزاکتي indecency

bey nazma *a.* بنظمه tumultuous

bey nazmee *n* بنظمي disorder

bey nazmee *n.* بنظمي indiscipline

bey nazmee *n.* بنظمي misrule

bey noomtya *n.* بنومتيا anonymity

bey pama *a.* بپامه imprudent

bey pama *a.* بپامه inattentive

bey pama *a.* بپامه rash

bey pama ghageydal *v. t* بپامه غدل blurt

bey pama; na khabar *a.* بپامه؛نا خبر unaware

bey pamee *n.* بپامي imprudence

bey parwa *a.* بپروا irresponsible

bey parwa *a.* بپروا mindless

bey parwa *a.* بپروا reckless

bangree *n.* بنی bangle
banjan *n* بانجان brinjal
bank ki hisab eekhodal *v. t* بانک کحساب‌ایودل deposit
bank ki peysey eekhodal *v.t.* بانک کپسای‌ودل bank
bank; kas *n.* ک،بانک bank
bankee hisab *n.* بانکی‌حساب deposit
bankwal *n.* بانکوال banker
banra *n* باه lash
banra badlawal *v. t* به‌بدلول disguise
banra laral; keedal keydal *v.t* به لرل،لیدل‌کدل figure
banras *n.* باس bamboo
bansat *n.* بنس base
bansat eekhodal *v.t.* بنسایودل base
bansat eekhodal *v.t.* بنسایودل found
bansat eekhodoonkay *n.* بنس ایودونکی founder
bansateez *a.* بنسیز basic
bansateez *a.* بنسیز cardinal
bansateez *a.* بنسیز rudimentary
bansateez samoonpal *a.* بنسیز سمونپال radical
baqa *n.* بقا survival
baqa warbakhal *v.t.* بقاوربل perpetuate
bar *n* بار burden
bar *n.* بار load
bar aks *prep* برعکس unlike
bar koozawal *v.t.* بارکوزول unburden
bar lasay *a.* برلاسی transcendent

bar seyra *adv.* برسره apart
bar seyra *prep* برسره besides
bar seyra par dey *adv.* برسره‌پر د further
bar seyra par dey *adv.* برسره‌پر د withal
barabar *a* برابر equal
barabar *n* برابر fit
barabar *a.* برابر parallel
barabarawal *v.t.* برابرول balance
barabarawal *v. t* برابرول equal
barabarawal *v.t.* برابرول parallel
barabarawoonkay *n.* برابروونکی regulator
barabaree *n* برابری equality
barabaree; nyalgee *n* برابري،نیالی offset
barabarwalay *n.* برابروال adequacy
barakat warkawal *v. t* برکت ورکول bless
baraks *adv.* برعکس vice-versa
baramnak *a.* برمناک gorgeous
baran wareydal *v.t.* باران‌ورېدل shower
baran; parla pasi dazi *n.* باران؛ پرله‌پسز volley
baranda *n.* برنه portico
baranda *n.* برنه verendah
baranee *a.* باراني rainy
baranee tokar *n* باراني‌وکر waterproof
baras; loogay *n.* باس؛لوی vapour
barawal *v. t* بارول burden
barawal *v.t.* بارول load
barband *a.* بربڼ naked
barbandawal *v.t.* بربنول bare

balakht *n* بالت pillow

balana *n.* بلنه call

balana *v.* بلنه invitation

balana warkawal *v.t.* بلنهورکول invite

balana; cheygha *n.* بلنه،چغه calling

balapokh *n.* بالاپو quilt

balaposh *n.* بالاپوش overcoat

balayee *a.* بلايي monstrous

baleydal *v.i.* بلدل lighten

baligh *a.* بالغ adolescent

baligh *a* بالغ adult

baligh kas *n.* بالغ کس adult

balogh *n.* بلوغ adolescence

balogh *n.* بلوغ maturity

baloghat *n.* بلوغت puberty

balor *n* بلور crystal

balot *n.* بلوط chestnut

balwa *n.* بلوا riot

balwa *n.* بلوا turbulence

balwa *n.* بلوا sedition

balwa kawal *v.t.* بلواکول riot

balwagar *n* بلوار anarchist

balwagarana *a.* بلوارانه seditious

balwagaree *n.* بلواري insurrection

balwayee *a.* بلوايي turbulent

bam *n* بم bomb

bam achowoonki alwataka *n* بم اچوونکالوتکه bomber

bam; da chawdani mawad *n.* بم، دچاودنمواد explosive

bambaree *n* بمباري bombardment

bambaree kawal *v. t* بمباري کول bomb

bambaree kawal *v. t* بمباري کول bombard

banafsh rang *n.* رنگ بنفش violet

band *a.* بند close

band; khand *n* بند،خ block

band; laswand *n* بند،لاسوند bond

bandakht *n* بندست deadlock

bandakht *n.* بندست restriction

bandakht *n.* بندست obstruction

bandal *n.* بنل pack

bandal kawal *v.t.* بنل کول pack

bandar *n.* بندر port

bandawal *v. t* بندول enclose

bandawal; rakkhata kawal *v.t.* بندول،راکته کول shut

bandee *n.* بندي captive

bandee *n.* بندي prisoner

bandeekhana *n.* بنديخانه jail

bandeekhana *n.* بنديخانه prison

bandeenay *a.* باندينی outer

bandeyz *n* بندنز ban

bandeyz *n* بندنز blockade

bandeyz *n.* بندنز sanction

bandeyz *n.* بندنز prohibition

bandeyz lagawal *n.* بندنزلول barrier

bandeyz lagawal *v.t.* بندنزلول prohibit

bandeyz lagawal *v.t.* بندنزلول sanction

bandinay makh warkawal *v.i* باننی مخورکول surface

bandol *n.* بنول pendulum

bang *n.* بن hemp

bangar *n.* بنار buzz

bangeydal *v. i* بندل buzz

bangeydal *v. i* بندل hum

bangeydana *n* بندنه hum

baghyana *a.* باغيانه mutinous

baghyana *a.* باغيانه rebellious

bahadaree *n.* بهادري gallantry

bahalee; beyrta gumarana *n.* بحالي؛برته‌مارنه reinstatement

bahana *n* بهانه pretext

bahand *n* بهاند fluid

bahanz; waseela *n* بهن؛وسيله channel

bahar *adv* بهر abroad

bahar kawal *v. t* بهركول displace

bahar kawal *v.t.* بهركول oust

bahar lor ta *adv* بهرلورته outward

bahar lor ta *adv.* بهرلورته outwardly

bahar ta *adv* بهرته outside

bahar ta *adv* بهرته outwards

bahar ta ghorzawal *v. t.* بهرته غورول eject

baharanay *a* بهرنى external

baharanay *a.* بهرنى outside

baharanay *a.* بهرنى outward

bahawal; pashal *v.t.* بهول؛پاشل shed

baheer *n.* بهير continuation

baheer; jaryan *n.* بهير؛جريان influx

baheydal *v.i* بهدل flow

baheydal; jaree keydal *v.i.* بهدل؛ جاري‌كدل stream

baheydana; sapara *n* بهدنه؛پره shed

baheydang *n* بهدنگ flow

bahimata *a* باهمته daring

bahree spay *n* بحري‌سپى beaver

bajlaka; khangaray *n.* بجلكه؛بنرى ankle

bak bak kawal *v.i.* بك‌بك‌كول gabble

bakarat; peyghaltob *n.* بكارت؛ پغلتوب virginity

bakhabar; hasas *a.* باخبر؛حساس sensible

bakhal *v.t* بخل absolve

bakhal *v.t* بخل forgive

bakhana kawal *v.t.* بخنه‌كول pardon

bakheel *n.* بخيل niggard

bakheelee kawal *v.t.* بخيلي‌كول grudge

bakhkhana *n.* بخنه apology

bakhkhana *n* بخنه concession

bakhkhana ghokhtal *v.i.* بخنه غوتل apologize

bakhmal *n.* بخمل velvet

bakhmalee *a.* بخملي velvety

bakhoonkay *a.* بونكى munificent

bakhshish *n.* بخشش octroi

bakht *n.* بخت luck

baks *n.* بكس case

bal *a* بل else

bal *a.* بل that

bal haywad ta leygdawal *v. t.* بل هوادته‌لدول export

bal wakht ta zandawal *v.t.* بل وختته‌منول adjourn

bal; juda *a.* بل؛جدا other

bal; nor *pron.* بل؛نور other

bala *n.* بلا bale

bala *n.* بلا monster

bala wraz *n.* بلهور morrow

balad *a* بلد familiar

balahisar *n.* بالاحصار citadel

balakht *n* بالت cushion

badbakhtee *n.* بدبختي misery

badee zhranda *n.* بادي‌ژرنده windmill

badee; leyri *a.* بعدي،لر ulterior

badgoomana insan *n* بدگومانه‌انسان cynic

badgoomana keydal *v.t.* بدگومانه کدل suspect

badi *n* بد bribe

badi *n.* بد corruption

badi khwaral *v.t.* بدخول misappropriate

badi khwarana *n.* بدخونه venality

badi radi wayal *v.t.* بدردويل insult

badi wahal / warkawal *v. t.* بوهل /ورکول bribe

badi; rishwat *n.* بدرشوت misappropriation

badkar *n.* بدکار seduce

badkara *a.* بدکاره nefarious

badkarana *a* بدکارانه seductive

badkaree *n.* بدکاري seduction

badla warkawal *v.t.* بدله‌ورکول requite

badlamanay halak *n.* بدلمنی‌هلک tomboy

badlawal *v. t.* بدلول change

badlawal *v.t.* بدلول alter

badlawal; da breykhna tanray kkhata porta kawal *v.t.* بدلول،دبریناکته‌پورته‌کول switch

badleydoonkay *a.* بدلدونکی variable

badloon *n.* بدلون change

badloon *n* بدلون alteration

badloon rawastal *v.t.* بدلون‌راوستل innovate

badloon rawastoonkay *n.* بدلون راوستونکی innovator

badloon; irtiqa *n* بدلون،ارتقا evolution

badloon; lwar zawar *n.* بدلون،لوو vicissitude

badloon; naway shay *n.* بدلون؛ نوی‌شی innovation

badmargha *a.* بدمرغه inauspicious

badmarghay *n.* بدمرغی adversity

badmash *n.* بدماش gangster

badmash *n.* بدماش knave

badmashee *n.* بدماشي knavery

badnam *a.* نام بد infamous

badnam *a* بدنام flagrant

badnam *a.* بدنام notorious

badnama *n.* بدنامه arrant

badnamawal *v.* بدنامول asperse

badnamawal *v.t.* بدنامول slander

badnamee *n.* بدنامي infamy

badnamee *n.* بدنامي slander

badnamtob *n.* بدنامتوب notoriety

badobaranee toopan *n.* بادوباراني توپان cyclone

badraga; da safar malgaray *n* بدره؛دسفرملری escort

badrang *n* بادرنگ cucumber

bagh *n.* باغ garden

baghawat *n.* بغاوت mutiny

baghawat *n.* بغاوت rebellion

baghawat kawal *v. i* بغاوت‌کول mutiny

baghee *n.* باغ insurgent

baghot *n.* بغو tonsil

baghwan *n.* باغوان gardener

baghyana *a.* باغیانه insurgent

zigzag *n.* خط منکسراومات و ایه so
zaya mat aw munkasir khat

zigzag *a.* پهزیزاول pa zeegzag dawl

zigzag *v.i.* پهزیزاولحرکت کول pa
zeegzag dawl harakat kawal

zinc *n.* دجستعنصر da jast unsar

zip *n.* زیپ،کشک zeep; kashak

zip *v.t.* پهکشکتل pa kashak taral

zip *n* فشار fishar

zonal *a.* مناومنطقهپوراوند mayni aw
mantaqey pori arwand

zone *n.* منطقه mantaqa

zoo *n.* ژوب zhobanr

zoological *a.* ژوپوهنپوراوند
zhopohani pori arwand

zoologist *n.* ژوپوه zhopoh

zoology *n.* ژوپوهنه zhopohana

zoom *n.* لویدنه،تزحرکت loyeydana;
teyz harakat

zoom *v.i.* لویول،لویدل loyawal;
loyeydal

da istiwa karkha *n* داستواکره
equator

da itihadeeyey gharay *n.* داتحادي
غى unionist

da izafat toray *n.* داضافتتورى
preposition

da iztirab halat *n.* داضطراب حالت
spasm

da jadee myasht *n* دجدي مياشت
Capricorn

da jama nakha; musbat *n* دجمع
نه،مثبت plus

da jamnastic da lobo mahir *n.* د
جمناسک دلوبوماهر gymnast

da jamnastic lobi *n.* دجمناسک لوبي
gymnastics

da jamnastic pa arwand; chust
a. دجمناسک په اوند،چست
gymnastic

da jamo almaray *n.* دجاموالمار
wardrobe

da jamo da gul booto patay *n.* د
جامو دل بووپ streamer

da jamo darz *n.* دجامودرز seam

da jamo gonji keydo wala darz *n*
دجامو ونج کدووالادرز crease

da janayatkarano naray *n.* د
جنايتکارانوز underworld

da janazey lmoonz *n.* دجنازلموز
requiem

da janazey marasim *n.* دجناز
مراسم funeral

**da jandaro pa yaw zay
zeygeydalee mashooman** *n* د
جانداروپه يوای زيدلي ماشومان
brood

da jangee tadbeeroono fan *n.* د
جنگي تدبيرونو فن strategy

da jangee tadbeeroono mahir *n.*
دجنگي تدبيرونوماهر strategist

da jarahay daktar *n.* دجراحاکر
surgeon

da jarahay meela *n* دجراحميله
probe

da jargey gharay *n* دجرغى
convener

da jashan war *a* دجشنو festive

da jast unsar *n.* دجست عنصر zinc

**da jazibey da qawey pa waseela
harakat kawal** *v.i.* دجاذبدقوپه
وسيله حرکت کول gravitate

da jismoonu da harkat mubhis
n. دجسمونو دحرکت مبحث
dynamics

**da jorabo aw banaynoono
jorawona ya ploranzay** *n.* د
جورابو او بنينونوجوونه يا پلورنى
hosiery

da jorabo band *n.* دجورابوبند
garter

**da jormaney da mawado
sarkaree nazir** *n.* دجرماند
موادوسرکاري ناظر bailiff

**da juram peykheydo pa mahal
bahana kawal** *n.* دجرمپدوپه
مهال بهانه کول alibi

da kab hagay *n.* دکبه spawn

da kab hagay achawal *v.i.* دکبه
اچول spawn

da kaghaz yawa raseed *n.* دکاغذ
يوه رسيد coupon

**da kaghazee nuskho masheen
bandi naqal jorawal** *v.t.* د
کاغذي نسخو ماشين باندنقل جوول
xerox

da kaghazee nuskho naqal jorawalo masheen *n.* د کاغذي نسخونقل جوولوماشين xerox

da kakhtay arsha *n* د کښتی عرشه deck

da kakhtay aw mal aw zan zhghoral *v.t.* د کښتاومال اوان ژغورل salvage

da kakhtay bar; mahmoola *n.* د کښتی بار؛محموله shipment

da kakhtay chalowani war *a.* د کښتی چلوونو navigable

da kakhtay karmandan *n.* د کښتی کارمندان crew

da kakhtay langar *n.* د کښتی لنگر anchor

da kakhtay langarzay *n* د کښتی لنگرځای anchorage

da kakhtay rashpeyl *n.* د کښتی راشپیل oar

da kakhtay rashpeyl *n.* د کښتی راشپیل row

da kakhtay rashpeyl wahal *v.t.* د کښتی راشپیل وهل row

da kakhtay stayring *n.* د کښتی سټیرنګ helm

da kakhtay ya da mal ya da zan zhghorana *n.* د کښتی یا د مال یا د ان ژغورنه salvage

da kalam nachor *n.* د کلم نچور gist

da kaleesa aw da haghi baharanee deywaloono manz ki chapeyra zmaka *n.* د کلیسا او د هغی بهرني دیوالونو من ک چاپیره ځمکه churchyard

da kaleesa da pap maqam *n.* د کلیسا د پاپ مقام papacy

da kaleesa da pap pori arwand *a.* د کلیسا د پاپ پور اروند papal

da kaleesa markaz *n.* د کلیسا مرکز nave

da kaleesa nazim *n.* د کلیسا ناظم beadle

da kam shee ghla kawal *v.t.* د کم شي غلا کول pilfer

da kaman pa banra arawal *v.t.* د کمان په بڼه اول arch

da kanfarans talar *n.* د کانفرانس تالار auditorium

da kankreeto jorawal *v. t* د کانکریو جوول concrete

da kankreeto mada *n* د کانکریو ماده concrete

da kanro dabaro yaw ghond *n.* د کانو بر و یو غون rubble

da kar eejaza leek *n.* د کار اجازه لیک licence

da kar haq *n* د کار حق patent

da kar kawalo hunar *n.* د کار کولو هنر workmanship

da kar takrar *n.* د کار تکرار reiteration

da kar zmaka *n* د کر ځمکه farm

da karakhta dak kar kawal *v.i.* د کاخته ک کار کول toil

da karani mahir *n.* د کرنماهر agriculturist

da karayi motar *n.* د کرایموټر cab

da karban filiz ya geys *n.* د کاربن فلزیاس carbon

da katan tukham *n.* د کتان تخم linseed

da katoleekee eesayano rehbar *n.* د کاتولیکي عیسائیانو رهبر pope

da kawdoree lokhee *n* د کو دوي لوي ceramics

da kaynato pa arwand *adj.* د
كائناتوپهاوند cosmic

da keena kakhay war *a* دكينهكو
enviable

da keetab dotanay *n.* دكتابدوتنه
tome

da keetab paysoor *n.* دكتابپايو
postscript

da keetab sareeza *n.* دكتابسريزه
preamble

da keetabtoon charwakay *n.* د
كتابتونچارواكى librarian

da khabaro ataro war *a.* دخبرو
اترو negotiable

da khabaro saray *a* دخبروسى
conversant

**da khakhto da darzoono da
neewani lapara zangari
khata** *n.* دختوددرزونودنيونلپارهزانز
خه lute

**da khandawoonko nandaro
honar mand** *n.* دخندونكو
نندارموهنرمند comedian

da khandeydo ghag *n.* دخنددوغ
laughter

**da khandoono pa mrasta
bandeyz** *n.* دخنونوپهمرستهبنلز
barricade

da khar bandanay barkhi *n.pl.* د
باربانندنبرخ outskirts

da khar da shawkhwa seema *n.*
دارդشاوخواسيمه suburb

**da khar da shawkhwa seemi
astogan** *a.* داردشاوخواسيم
استون suburban

**da khar danana chaleydoonkay
breykhnayee wagon** *n.* دار
دننهچلدونكىبرئايىواون tram

da khar nazim *n.* دارناظم mayor

**da kharabeydo
makhneewoonkay** *a.* دخرابدو
مخنيوونكى preservative

da kharakht ranz *n.* دخارترز
scabies

da kharatay masheen *n.* دخراط
مشين lathe

da kharwee daney *n.* دخرويدان
acorn

da khas moqey pa ara jashan *n*
دخاصموقعپهاهجشن festivity

da khash khash ghag *n.* دخشخش
غ rick

da khatar zang *n* دخطرزنز alarm

da khateez pa lor *adv* دختيزپهلور
east

**da khawro aw shago hifazatee
deywal** *n.* دخاورواوشوحفاظتي
دوال rampart

**da khawro portanay barkha chi
da wakho reykhi aw wrasta
mawad laree** *n.* دخاوروپورتنه
برخهچهدووراووراستهموادلري turf

da khawro teyl *n.* دخاوروتل
kerosene

da khazi pa seyr kawal *v.t.* دهمر
كول womanise

da khazo oogdey jamey *n.* دواود
جام gown

**da kheekhey baksa chi daryayee
makhlooq paki nandarey
lapara satalay shee** *n.* دبكسه
چدریائيمخلوقپكنندارلپارهساتلى
شي aquarium

da kheekhey pyala; kheekha *n.* د
پپياله،بيه glass

da khkuli banri khawand *a.* دكلب خاوند shapely

da khob kalee *n.* دخوب كالي nightie

da khob wakht *n.* دخوبوخت bed-time

da khoofeeya khabaro ataro zay aw wakht *n.* دخفيهخبرواتروای اووخت tryst

da khoog astoganzay *n.* دخو استونای sty

da khoog astoganzay *n.* دخو استونای stye

da khoog da ghwakhi landay *n.* دخودغولاندی bacon

da khoog ghwakha *n.* دخوغوه pork

da khoog wazda *n.* دخووازده lard

da khor pa shan *a.* دخورپهشان sisterly

da khorakee mawado sandooq *n.* دخوراكيموادوصندوق crate

da khowanzee da keetabono kasora *n.* دوونيدكتابونوكوه satchel

da khowanzee pori zdakri *n.* دوونيپورزدهک matriculation

da khowanzee rayees *n.* دووني رئيس principal

da khpali pohi bey zaya khodana *n.* دخپلپوهبايمودنه pedantry

da khra khazeena *n.* دخرهينه mare

da khra rambari *n* دخرهرمبا bray

da khuday da tolo peykho aw zwakoono majmoo ganral *n.* دخدای دولوپواووا كونومجموعهبلل pantheism

da khuday pa qudrat bawaree *n.* دخدایپهقدرتباوري pantheist

da khuday pa wajood bawar *n.* د خدایپهوجودباور deist

da khuday paman *interj.* دخدای پامان good-bye

da khuday qudrat *n.* دخدایقدرت providence

da khwago ploranzay *n* دخواو پلورنی confectionery

da khwakhay cheygha *n.* دخوچغه cheer

da khwakhay war *a.* دخوونو admirable

da khwandee satani da kar lagakht *n* دخونديساتندكارلت upkeep

da khwaralo war *a* دخولوو edible

da khwaro jazab aw tarkeeb *n* د خووجذباوتركيب assimilation

da khwaro naywleek *n.* دخواو نيوليک menu

da khwaro seezoona *n.* دخوويزونه eatable

da khwaro takali wanda *n.* دخواو اكلونه ration

da khwaro war *a* دخووو eatable

da kifayat tar kachi *adv* دكفايتتر كچ enough

da kilseeyum filiz *n* دكلسيمفلز calcium

da kipsool pa shakal *adj* دكپسول پهشكل capsular

da kirdar katana; neemrukh anzor *n.* دكرداركتنه؛نيمرخانور profile

da kobalt keymyayee onsar *n* د کوبالکميايي عنصر cobalt

da koch salatoaw khorakee mawado sakha jora doday *n.* د کوچ سلاتو او خوراکي موادو خه جوه و sandwich

da kolp zabancha *n* د کولپ زبانچه bolt

da kom seez da gatawartob la makhi da hagha matloobeeyat *a.* د کوميز د ورتوب له مخد هغه مطلوبيت utilitarian

da kom seez landi karkha rakkhal *v.t.* د کوميز لاند کره راکل underline

da koneen bootay *n.* د کونين بوی quinine

da koni da maqad pa arwand *adj.* د کوند مقعد په اوند anal

da koochnee dimagh pa arwand *adj* د کوچني دما غ په اوند cerebral

da koochno pa arwand *a.* د کوچنو په اوند infantile

da koochno wazhana *n.* د کوچنو وژنه infanticide

da koochnyo shayano da andazey ala *n.* د کوچنيو شيانو د انداز آله micrometer

da koochnyo shayano doorbeen *n.* د کوچنيو شيانو دوربين microscope

da koochnyo shayano ilam *n.* د کوچنيو شيانو علم micrology

da koohee sarkh *v.t.* د کوهي رخ windlass

da kookoo marghay *n* د کوکو مرغ cuckoo

da koolmey akhiree barkha *n.* د کولمي اخري برخه rectum

da koolmo pa arwand *a.* د کولمو په اوند intestinal

da kor asbab *n.* د کور اسباب furniture

da kor da istimal spaki saplay *n.* د کور د استعمال سپکپل slipper

da kor maloona aw lawazim *n.* د کور مالونه او لوازم movables

da korwadani ronra aw khwayndi *n.* د کورو دانر ونه او خوند in-laws

da kraki war shakhs *n.* د کرکو شخص wretch

da kulalay khata *n* د کلالاخه clay

da lafzoono lobey *n.* د لفظونو لوب pun

da lafzoono lobey kawal *v.i.* د لفظونو لوب کول pun

da lagyo geyday *n* د لريوی faggot

da lambeydo ya jamo weenzalo taghara *n.* د لمبدو ياجامو وينلو تغاره tub

da lams his pori arwand *a.* د لمس حس پور اوند tactile

da lams seez; mahsoos *a.* د لمس يز؛ محسوس tangible

da lams war *a.* د لمس و palpable

da largee dara *n.* د لري ده splinter

da largee hawara takhta *n.* د لري هواره تخته plank

da largee naray patay *n.* د لري نر پ lath

da largee teer *n.* د لري تير perch

da largee ya ospani panra ya tota *n.* دلري‌يااوسپنپاه‌ياوه wedge

da largee yaw pata *n* دلري‌يوپه ply

da larghono shayano nandarzay *n*دلرغونوشيانونندارای .museum

da laril da wani pa panro psolal shaway a. دلارل‌دونپه‌پاوپسولل شوی laureate

da las marwand *n.* دلاس‌موند wrist

da las pa sat goozar *n.* دلاس‌په‌سوزار backhand

da las takya *n.* دلاس‌تکیه maulstick

da las warghaway *n.* دلاس‌ورغوی palm

da laso kasano la manz sakha da yawa hagha wazhal *v.t.* دلسو کسانوله‌منخه‌دیوه‌هغه‌وژل decimate

da lasoono parkar *n* دلاسونوپکار clap

da laswandoono aw panro zabat *n.pl.* دلاسوندونواوپاوضبط archives

da laswandoono da sabt idara *n.* دلاسوندونودثبت‌اداره registry

da lateef zoq sakhtan *n.* دلطیف ذوق‌تن dainty

da law masheen; law garay *n.* د لوماشین؛لوری haverster

da leed war *a.* دلیدو visible

da leed war manzara *a.* دلیدو منظره spectacular

da leed wartya *n.* دلیدوتیا visibility

da leedani katani takalay zay *n.* دلیدذکتنا‌کلی‌ای venue

da leekaneezo wasayalo plooroonkay *n.* دلیکنیزووسایلو پلورونکی stationery

da leekani meyz *n* دلیکنمز desk

da leekani yawa barkha *n.* دلیک یوه‌برخه paragraph

da leekee cheenjay *n* دلیکی‌چینجی book-worm

da leekee nakhan *n.* دلیکی‌نان book-mark

da leekwal khpala leekalay lasleek *n.* دلیکوال‌خپله‌لیکلی لاسلیک autograph

da leelam war *a.* دلیلام‌و salable

da leelam ya dawtalbay pa muzayda ki wanda akheystal *v.t.* دلیلام‌یاداوطلبپه مزایده‌کونه‌اخستل tender

da leemoo sharbat *n.* دلیموشربت lemonade

da leygdawalo waseela *n.* دلدولو وسیله transport

da leygdawani war *a.* دلدونو portable

da leyri keydani war *a.* دلرکدنو removable

da leywanee spee naroghee *n.* د لونی‌سپی‌ناروغي rabies

da lmar rakhatana *v. i.* دلمراختل dawn

da lmar ranra ki badan khareydal *v.i.* دلمراکبدن‌خدل tan

da lobo dagar *n* دلوبور arena

da lobo yaw dawl panra; kha aw aham saray *n.* دلوبویول‌پاه؛به اواهم‌سی trump

da lokho khoona *n.* دلووخونه
pantry

da loogee la kabala sa bandeydal *v.t.* دلویله کبلهساه بندل smother

da loomranee aw dwayam por tar manz neem por *n.* دلومني او دویم پور ترمنیم پو mezzanine

da loy maray khawand; ghag lweydalay *a.* دلوی مرخاوند،غ لوندلی throaty

da loy munshee ya loomree wazeer danda ya maqam *n* د لوی منشي یالومي وزیر دندهیامقام chancery

da loyi darajey ghonda *n.* دلویدرجی غونه summit

da loyo koolmo landeenay barkha *n* دلویو کولمو لاندینی برخه colon

da lughato noomleek *n.* دلغاتو نوملیک glossary

da lwar himat khawand *a.* دلو همت خاوند ambitious

da lweydeez pa lor *adv.* دلودیپهلور west

da lweydeez pa lor *adv.* دلودیپهلور westerly

da madey aw naray da shtoon na manana *n.* دماداو ندشتوننه مننه nihilism

da maghfirat war *a.* دمغفرتو pardonable

da maghzo iltihab *n.* دمغزوالتهاب meningitis

da maide *a.* دمعدی gastric

da makh aks *n.* دمخعکس portrait

da makh anzor eystal *v.t.* دمخانور استل portray

da makh da barkhi naqashee *n.* دمخ دبرخنقاشي portraiture

da makh khwa ta *adv* دمخخواته forward

da makh las weenzalo khoona *n.* دمخلاس وینلوخونه lavatory

da makh palwa ta *adv.* دمخپلوهته onwards

da makh seengar kawal *a* دمخ سینارکول facial

da makh soorwalay *n* دمخسوروالی blush

da makha *prep.* دمخه past

da makha akheystal *v.t* دمخه اخستل forestall

da makha barkhleek takal *v.t.* د مخهبرخلیک اکل predetermine

da makha da krismas wraz *n.* د مخهدکرسمسور advent

da makha sanjawal *v.t.* دمخه سنجول premeditate

da makha soch *n.* دمخهسوچ premeditation

da makhi; makhamakh *a* دمخ، مخامخ front

da makhneewee waseela *a.* د مخنیوي وسیله scotch

da makoo safar kawal *v.t.* دماکو سفرکول shuttle

da mal da adloon badloon tijarat kawal *v.t.* barter1

da mal leygdawalo kakhtay *n.* د مالدولوکت barge

da maleeyey war *a.* دمالیو taxable

da malt aw khumree skhak *n.* د مالتاوخمريكاک mead

da maltey leemoo aw naranj da postakee khwand *n.* دماليمو اونارنجدپوستكيخوند zest

da manalo war *a* دمنلوو acceptable

da mandi musabiqa kawal *v.i* دمن مسابقهكول race

da manzanay darajey *a* دمننددرجه medium

da manzanyo peyryo tareekh pori arwand *a.* دمننيوپيوتاريخ پوراوند medieval

da mar ghonda tawrataw *n.* دمار غوندهتاوراتاو serpentine

da maree sozawani lapara da largyo zangari kota *n.* دمي سووزنلپارهدلريوانکوه pyre

da mareekh seeyara *n* دمريخسياره Mars

da marghano zala *n.* دمرغانوله cote

da marghano zala *n.* دمرغانوله roost

da marghay bachay *n.* دمرغبچی nestling

da markaz keenr las ta *n.* دمرکز کیلاسته mid-on

da markaz khee las ta *n.* دمرکزي لاسته mid-off

da marmar kanray *n.* دمرمرکانی marble

da maro arwagani *n.* دمواروانا manes

da maro da eero lokhay *n* دمود ايرولوی urn

da maro dua *n.* دمودعا memento

da maro pa mrasta ghayb wayana *n.* دموپهمرستهغبوینه necromancer

da maseehano akhtar *n* دمسیحانو اختر easter

da masharano jargey pori arwand *a* دمشرانوجرپورراوند senatorial

da masheeno ilam *n.* دماشینوعلم mechanics

da mashoom da zeygoon omeed shandawal *v.i.* دماشومدزونامید شنول miscarry

da mashoomano tanga *n.* د ماشومانوانه perambulator

da masko khar oseydoonkee *n.* د ماسکوارِاوسدونکی muscovite

da masoor dal *n.* دمسوردال lentil

da matal pa arwand *a.* دمتلپهاوند proverbial

da matbooato aw chalandoono sarana kawal *v. t.* دمطبوعاتواو چلندونوارنهکول censor

da matbooato aw chalandoono saroonkay *n.* دمطبوعاتواو چلندونوارونکی censor

da mati shawi kakhtay parchey *n.* دماتشوکتپارچ wreck

da mawarayee tabeeyat ilam *n.* د ماورايیطبیعتعلم metaphysics

da mawseeqay ala wayloon *n.* د موسیةآلهویلون violin

da mawseeqay da alato mahir *n.* دموسیةدآلاتوماهر instrumentalist

da mawseeqay dala *n.* دموسیةله orchestra

da mawseeqay pa arwand *a.* د موسيقپهاوند musical

da mawseeqay pyano ta warta ala *n.* دموسيقپيانوتهورتهآله xylophone

da maya shee da paymayish yawa paymana *n.* دمايعشي پمائشيوهپمانه litre

da mayar dalbandee *n.* دمعيار لبندي standardization

da mayato lapara payp *n* دمايعاتو لپارهپايپ cask

da maydey tap *n.* دمعدپ ulcer

da maydey tap pori arwand *a.* د معدپپوراوند ulcerous

da mazd pa badal ki sarawal *v.t.* دمزدپهبدلکرول agist

da mazooro lakray *n* دمعذورولک crutch

da meel la makhi sanjawana *n.* د ميللهمخسنجوونه mileage

da meylmastoon ya khwaranzay khidmatgar *n.* دملمستونيا خونایخدمتار waiter

da meylmastoon ya khwaranzay khidmatgara *n.* دملمستونيا خونایخدمتاره waitress

da meyrani khawand *a.* دمانخاوند manful

da meywa bagh *n.* دموهباغ orchard

da meywey ghwakhana barkha *n.* دموغونهبرخه pulp

da meywey oba *n* دمواوبه juice

da meywey oba laroonkay *a.* دمو اوبهلرونکی juicy

da meyzaree koochnay tokray *n.* دمزريکوچنوکر canister

da midal khawand *n.* دمالخاوند medallist

da milee shoora gharay *n.* دملي شوراغی parliamentarian

da mityazo kawalo amal *n.* د متيازوکولوعمل urination

da mla teer *n.* دملاتير backbone

da mla teer *n.* دملاتير spine

da mla teer pori arwand *a.* دملا تيرپورپراوند spinal

da moashirat da adabo ilam *n* د معاشرتدآدابوعلم etiquette

da moashirat da adabo keetab *n* دمعاشرتدآدابوکتاب facet

da moondani war *a.* دموندنو traceable

da moosalmanano deenee alim *n.* دمسلمانانودينيعالم mullah

da mor pa shan *a.* دمورپهشان motherlike

da mor plar pa arwand *a.* دمور پلارپهاوند parental

da mor plar wazhana *n.* دمورپلار وژنه parricide

da mosam pa wrandi badleydal; zghamal *v.t.* دموسمپهواند بدلدل؛زغمل weather

da mosam sara sam *a.* دموسمسره سم seasonable

da moseeqay nasta *n.* دموسيقناسته concert

da moseeqay yaw dawl badee ala *n.* دموسيقيولبادیآله bagpipe

da moseeqay yaw geetar chi dayrawee geyda laree *n.* د موسيقيويارچدايرويیدهلري banjo

da motar brayk *n* دموربرک brake

da motar jak *n.* دمورجک jack

da motar klach *n* دمورکلچ clutch

da motar raghawani ya darawani zay *n.* دمورغونيا درونای garage

da mozayeek anzor *n.* دموزائیک انور mosaic

da mreeni aylan *a.* دميناعلان obituary

da muchyo kor *n.* دمچیوکور hive

da mujaley khparowoonkay *n* د مجلخپروونکی editor

da mujaley sar maqala *n* دمجلسر مقاله editorial

da mukhabiratee sapo leygd raleygd *n.* دمخابراتيپولادرالد transmission

da mukhadira mawado yaw qisam *n* دمخدرومواديویوقسم cocaine

da munsifa plawee gharay *n.* د منصفهپلاويغی juror

da munsifa plawee gharay *n.* د منصفهپلاويغی juryman

da muqadaso seezoonu ghla *n.* د مقدسویزونوغلا sacrilege

da muqadaso seezoonu ghla kawoonkay *a.* دمقدسویزونوغلا کوونکی sacrilegious

da musafiro kakhtay *n* دمسافروکته ferry

da mustateelee shakal konj *n.* د مستطیليشکلکونج nook

da na manani war *a.* دنهمننو incredible

da na manfee kalma *adv.* دنهمنفي کلمه not

da naheeyey da mahkamey reeyasat *n.* دناحیدمحکمریاست magistracy

da naleegay da jorawani chara *n.* دنالیدجوونچاره padding

da nandarey fankara najlay *n.* د نندارفنکارهنجل mannequin

da nandarey sahna *n.* دنندارصحنه stage

da nandartoon beyzwee salon *n* دنندارتونبضويسالون amphitheatre

da naqashay da rangoono sakha kar akheystana *n.* دنقاشدرنونو خهکاراخستنه palette

da naqshey jorawalo kaghaz *n.* د نقشجوولوکاغذ chart

da naranj murabba *n.* دنارنجمربا marmalade

da naray ustawayee seema *n.* دذ استوایسیم tropic

da naree ranz da darmalani zay *n.* دنريرنزددرملنای sanatorium

da nareena jinsee ala *n.* دنارینه جنسيآله penis

da nargas gul *n* دنرسل narcissus

da naroghano da wralo dapara yaw dol kat *n.* دناروغانودولو دپارهیوولک litter

da naroghay nakha aw arz *a.* د ناروغنهاوعرض symptomatic

da nashayee mawado da preykhwalo mlataray *n.* د نشهیيموادوپرولوملاتی teetotaller da nashayee mawado da preykhwalo pa arwand *a.* د نشه‌یی موادو دپرولوپه‌اوند teetotal

da nasti zangaray meyz *n.* دناستة زنگ‌ری مز dais

da naswaro kadoo *n.* دنسواروکدو gourd

da natoono pranistalo ala *n.* د نونو پرانستلوآله wrench

da nawab meyrman *n.* دنواب مرمن countess

da nawalo obo bahanzoona *n* د ناولواوبوبهنونه sewer

da nawalo obo da zmaki landi bahanzoona *n.* دناولواوبودمک لاندبهنونه sewerage

da nawalo obo dand *n.* ز دناولواوبو swamp

da nawara gato da para jorjaray kawal *n* دناومودپاره جوجای‌کول collusion

da naykmarghay oj *n.* دنکمرغاوج heyday

da naytrojan gaz *n.* دنایتروجن‌گاز nitrogen

da naz nakhro tag *n* دنازنخروت strut

da neewani haq *n.* دنیونحق lien

da neewani hokam *n.* دنیونحکم injunction

da neewani preykra *n.* دنیونپرکه caption

da neyzey sooka *n.* دنزوکه spearhead

da nikal unsar *n.* دنکل‌عنصر nickel

da nikasee obo sooray *n.* دنکاسی اوبوسوری manhole

da niptoon seeyara *n.* دنپتون‌سیاره Neptune

da nisfun nihar karkha; gharma *a.* دنصف‌النهارکره،غرمه meridian

da nizamee dalgay tamzay *n.* د نظامي‌ډلتمهای cantonment

da nizamee masharano yawa dalgay *n.* دنظامي‌مشرانویوهٔ squadron

da noro da subak taqleed *n.* د نورودسبک‌تقلید parody

da nyoozeelaynd plazmayna; yaw dawl azad khuley mooza *n.* دنیوزیلنډپلازمینه،یوۍ آزادخولموزه wellington

da obdani masheen *n* داوبدنماشین loom

da obo bahanz *n* داوبوبهنز aqueduct

da obo band *n.* داوبوبند barrage

da obo band *n* داوبوبند dam

da obo koochnay band *n.* داوبو کوچنی‌بند weir

da obo pa sar lambo wahal *v.i* د اوبوپه‌سرلامبووهل float

da obo raeystani masheen *n.* د اوبورائستنماشین pump

da obo sar ta rakhoteydal *v.i.* د اوبوسرته‌راخوته‌دل well

da obo seyl ratlal *v.t* داوبوسل‌راتلل flood

da obo sheendani zangaray plasteekee nal *n.* داوبوشیندنذ ناني‌پلاستیکي‌نل hose

da obo zeyramtoon; tank *n.* داوبو زرمتون،ٻانک tank

da obo zeyrma *n.* داوبوزرمه rservoir

da ogad wali yawa mecha *n.* د
اودوالي‌يوه‌ميچه furlong

da oogad meel topak *n.* داودميل
وپک musket

**da oogadwalee meychawalo yaw
paymana** *n.* داودوالي‌مچولويو
پمانه yard

da oogadwalee yaw paymayish
n. داودوالي‌يوپمائش mile

da oogo porta harakat *n* داوڅپورته
حرکت shrug

**da or sheendee ghra weelee
mawad** *n.* داورشيندي‌غروويلي
مواد lava

**da orgadee aw kakhtay khob
khana** *n* داورايي‌اوکتخوب‌خانه
berth

da orgadee karkha *n.* داورايي‌کره
railway

**da ospaneezi lari pa mrasta
astawal** *v.t.* داوسپنيزلاري‌په‌مرسته
استول transmit

da ospani patlay ghazawal *v.t.* د
اوسپني‌پلغول rail

da pachayano koranay *n* داپاچايانو
کورن dynasty

da paf awaz khuley na watal *v.i.*
دپف‌اواز‌خولنه‌وتل puff

da pakh banay; sagay *n.* دپخ؛سى
bellows

**da pakhlanzee da lokho
weenzalo zay** *n.* دپخلني‌دلوو
وينلواى cesspool

da pakhlee lar khod *n.* دپخلي‌لار
ود cuisine

da pam na war *a* دپامنه‌و
aconsiderable

da pam war lamal *n.* دپامولامل
limelight

da pam war miqdar *n.* دپامومقدار
slump

da pamp pa waseela raeystal *v.t.*
دپمپ‌په‌وسيله‌رااستل pump

da parayshanay halat *n.* دپرشان
حالت turmoil

da parchoon sawdagar *n.* دپرچون
سودار retailer

da pareydani waseela *n.* دپاردن
وسيله stimulus

da parmakhtya pa hal ki *adv.* د
پرمختيا‌په‌حال‌ک upwards

da partalani war *a.* دپرتلنو
analogous

da pato yaw dawl loba *n.* دپتويو
ول‌لوبه rummy

**da pawzee lakhkar da yaw
tabqey tashkeel** *n.* دپوي‌لکرد
يوطبقه‌تشکيل legionary

da pawzee lakhkar yawa tabqa
n. دپوي‌لکريوه‌طبقه legion

da pawzyano dala *n.* دپويانوله
troop

da payey teer *n* دپايتير skid

**da peenzo sawo kaghazoonu
bandal** *n.* د٥٠٠کاغذونوبنل
ream

da peesho bachay *n.* دپيشوبچى
kitten

da peesho ghag *n.* دپيشوغ mew

da peesho ghag kawal *v.i.* دپيشوغ
کول mew

da peesho ghur ghur *n.* دپيشو
غُرغُر purr

da peesho ghureydal *v.i.* دپيشو
غُردل purr

da peykhi da tareekh pa zand leekal *v.t.* دپدتاريخپهزندليكل
post-date

da peyso adayana *n.* دپسواداينه
payment

da peyso kasora *n.* دپسوكوه purse

da peyso kasora *n.* دپسوكوه
wallet

da peyso rakra warkra *n.* دپسو راكهوركه transaction

da peyso rakra warkra kawal *v.t.* دپسوراكهوركهكول transact

da peywand zay *n.* دپوندای
commissure

da peywastoon zay *n.* دپوستونای
junction

da pkhey khapoona; jora shawi lara *n.* دپخاپونه،جوهشولاره trail

da pkhey palawan *n* دپپهلوان
bully

da pkhey ya boot talay *n.* دپيابو تلی sole

da pkho pa panjo kkheynastal *v.i.* دپوپهپنجوكناستل squat

da plar mreeni wrusta zeygeydalay *a.* دپلارمينوروسته زدلی posthumous

da plar wazhana *n.* دپلاروژنه
patricide

da pohantoon ya khowonzee laylya *n.* دپوهنتونياووني‌ليليه
hostel

da pohanzee rayees *n.* دپوهني رئيس dean

da pokhtani nakha *n* دپوتنه
interrogative

da pokhtani war *a.* دپوتنو
questionable

da poolas sarandoy *n* دپولس سارندوی constable

da poolo eekhodana *n.* دپولوايودنه
demarcation

da poolo takana *n.* دپولوباكنه
confinement

da poplayn tokar *n.* دپوپلين‌وكر
poplin

da poray dastakee *n.* دپودستكي
rung

da postakee yawa chanrasee saree naroghee *n.* دپوستكي‌يوه چاسي‌ساري‌ناروغي ringworm

da pozi danana *n* دپوزدننه nasal

da pozi sooray *n.* دپوزسوری
nostril

da pradeetob ehsas *n.* دپرديتوب احساس nostalgia

da pranasti lamani zanana kot *n.* دپرانستلمنزنانه‌كو skirt

da psa ghwakha *n.* دپسه‌غوه
mutton

da pust idara *n.* دپست‌اداره
post-office

da pust rayees *n.* دپست‌رئيس
postmaster

da putas filiz *n.* دپاس‌فلز potash

da putasyum unsar *n.* دپسيم‌عنصر
potassium

da pyano da mawseeqay ala *n.* د پيانودموسيقةآله piano

da pyano da mawseeqay ala ghagoonkay *n.* دپيانودموسيقةآله غوونكی pianist

da pyaz tamatar aw masalo roob *n.* دپيازمارواومسالوروب
ketchup

da qabar dabarleek *n* دقبربرليک epitaph

da qachaq danda *n.* دقاچاقدنده jobbery

da qadardanay war *a.* دقدردانو appreciable

da qanoonee mayar khawand *a.* دقانونيمعيارخاوند sterling

da qanoonee rabalani cheetay *n.* دقانونيرابلنچي summons

da qayd pa arwand *a.* دقدپهاوند adverbial

da qazee hukam *n.* دقاضيحکم verdict

da qazyano plaway *n.* دقاضيانو پلاوی judicature

da qutar neemayee *n.* دقطرنيمايي radius

da radyoyee ya talweezyonee parogram khparawana *n.* د رايويييالملويزيونيپرورامخپرونه telecast

da rag dard *n.* دردرد sprain

da ragheydo pa arwand *a* درغدو پهاوند curative

da rahat khoona *n.* دراحتخونه lounge

da rahibanu namazdak *n.* د راهبانونمزدک minster

da ramzee leekani ilam *n.* درمزي ليکنعلم cryptography

da rando lapara zangaray leek *n* دندولپارمانیليک braille

da rangarang shayano gadola *n.* درنارنشيانووله miscellany

da ranra aw tyarey tar manz wakht *n* درنااوتيارترمنوخت dusk

da ranz pr zid wakseen warkawal *v.t.* درنپرضدواکسين ورکول immunize

da ranzoor da wralo lasee waseela *n.* درنوردولودلاسي وسيله stretcher

da ratlonke gham khwarana *n* د راتلونکيغمخونه forethought

da rayi panra *n* درايپله ballot

da reeyazii pa arwand *a.* درياضي پهاوند mathematical

da rehem war *a.* درحمو pitiable

da roghtoon sarpayee narogh *n.* دروغتونسرپايينارو غ outpatient

da rokhantya nashtwalay *a.* د روانتيانشتوالی lacklustre

da roohaneeyoonu wakmanee *n.* دروحانيونوواکمني theocracy

da rooseeyi sika *n.* دروسيسکه rouble

da sa laroonko da noogi qismoona *n.* دساهلرونکودنو قسمونه species

da saboon zag *n.* دصابون lather

da sabt daftar *n.* دثبتدفتر register

da safar tokha *n.* دسفرتوه baggage

da sago iltihab *n* دسوالتهاب pneumonia

da sahib mansabano lakhta *n* د صاحبمنصبانولته baton

da sakht aw teyz ghag awaz *n* د سختاوتزغاواز slam

da sakino jismoono seyraneeza sanga *n.* دساکنوجسمونونيزمانه statics

da sakoon darmal warkawal *v.t.* دسکوندرملورکول tranquillize

da salami kaleezi jashan *n.* دسلم
کلیزجشن centenary

da salfar gaz *n.* دسلفرباز sulphur

da salo la makhi *n.* دسلولهمخ
percentage

da saltanat nayib *n.* دسلطنتنایب
viceroy

da samandar narmi sapey *n.* د
سمندرنرمپ lop

da samandar sapa *n.* دسمندرپه
tide

da samandar teeta sapa *a.* د
سمندریهپه neap

da samoon nakha *n.* دسموننه tick

da samoon nakha lagawal *v.i.* د
سمونهلول tick

da samwalee shoontya *n.* دسموالي
شونتیا verisimilitude

**da sandar bolo marghano yawa
dala** *n.* دسندربولومارغانویوهله
lark

da sandar gharo dala *n.* دسندرغاو
له troupe

da sandar gharo dalgay *n.* د
سندرغاوله chorus

da sanjawani war *a.* دسنجونو
measurable

da sanobar wana *n.* دصنوبرونه
pine

da sansor jargagay *n.* دسانسورجرهه
censorship

da sar khoogeydana *n.* دسرخولدنه
headache

da sar pakha *n* دسرپخه dandruff

da sar sangi ghosawal *v.t.* دسراز
غوول lop

da sar shmeyrani karpoh *n.* د
سرشمرنکارپوه statistician

da sarak baj *n.* دسربباج toll

da sarak da ghari meylmastoon
n. دسربدغاملمستون motel

da saree weykhtan *n.* دسيوتان
mane

da sari pa toga *adv.* دسارپهتوه
namely

da sarkh para ya meela *n.* درخ
پرهیامیله spoke

da sarmano ash kawana *n.* درمنو
آش کوونه tannery

**da sarwayo tababat pori
arwand** *a.* دارويوطبابتپوراوند
veterinary

da sat dad ghmbaray ranz *n.* د
غومبریرز mumps

da satani war *a.* دساتنو tenable

da sawdagaray war *a.* دسودارو
marketable

da sayins ilam *n.* دساینسعلم
science

da seemabo kan *n* دسیمابوکان
cinnabar

**da seemabo pa dagha alyazh
ghakhoona dakawal** *v.t.* د
سیمابوپهدغهالیاژغاونهکول
amalgamate

**da seemabo yaw alyazh chi da
ghakhoonu dakawalo
lapara pakareygee** *n* دسیمابو
یوالیاژچددغاونوکولولپارهپهکاري
amalgam

da seenama masheen *n.* دسینما
ماشین projector

da seenama ya talweezyon parda *n.* دسينماياتلويزيون‌پرده screen

da seend ghara *n* دسيندغاه strand

da seend pa lori *adv.* دسيندپه‌لور overboard

da seengar khoona *n.* دسينارخونه parlour

da seyri rang *n* درزرد complexion

da shabasee narey *n* دشاباسي‌نار acclamation

da shahadat gota *n* دشهادت‌گوته forefinger

da shahzada pa shan *a.* دشاهزاده په‌شان princely

da shakal aw banri badlawona *n.* دشكل‌اوببدلوونه metamorphosis

da shakal aw seyrey badloon *n.* دشكل‌اوربدلون transfiguration

da shakari naroghee *n* دشكر ناروغی diabetes

da shakhseeyat tajassum *n.* د شخصيت‌تجسم personification

da shambey wraz *n.* دشنبور sabbath

da shambey wraz *n.* دشنبور Saturday

da sharab jorawani mawsam *n.* دشراب‌جوونموسم vintage

da sharabkhoray jashan *n.* د شرابخورجشن wassail

da sharabo jam *n* دشرابوجام stalk

da sharam dagh *n.* دشرم‌داغ stigma

da sharamzay hadookay *n* د شرمای‌هوکی share

da shato da machyo rozana *n.* د شاتودمچيوروزنه apiculture

da shato da machyo zay *n.* دشاتود مچيوای apiary

da shato gabeen *n.* دشاتوبين honeycomb

da shato lokhay *n* دشاتولوی alveary

da shatranj pa loba ki kasht aw mat *n* دشطرنج‌په‌لوبه‌ککشت‌او مات checkmate

da shayr da bahar aw wazan ilam *a.* دشعردبحراووزن‌علم metric

da shayr warostay barkha *n* د شعروروستبرخه epilogue

da shaytan bachay *n.* دشطان‌بچی urchin

da shaytan manray *n.* دشطان‌ما pandemonium

da sheydo arwand shayan *n* د شدواوندشيان dairy

da sheydo qand *n.* دشدوقند lactose

da shmeyrani ilam *n.* دشمرنعلم statistics

da shomal pa lor *adv.* دشمال‌په‌لور northerly

da shomalee amreeka yaw dawl kab *a.* دشمالي‌امريکايوول‌کب hesitant

da shomalee amreeka yaw margha chi pa sar soor takay laree *n* دشمالي‌امريکايو مارغه‌چپه‌سرسورکي‌لري flicker

da shoora gharay *n.* دشوراغی councillor

da shpey *a.* دشپ nocturnal

da shpey *a* دشپ overnight

da shpey *adv.* دشپ nightly

da shpey la makhi *adv.* دشپلهمخ
overnight

da shpey pa asman ki tat gard *n.*
د دشپپهاسمانکتترد nebula

da shtamano wakmanee *n.* د
شتمنووا‌کمني oligarchy

da sinayma filam *n* دسینمافیلم
film

da skoondalo ya gareydalo
nakha *n.* دسکونلویارېدلونه prick

da sokht teyl *n.* دسوختتل fuel

da soli war *a.* دسولو peaceable

da sook goozar *n.* دسوکوزار
punch

da sook wahani loba *n* دسوکوهن
لوبه boxing

da soyo da rozalo zay *n.* دسویود
روزلوای warren

da sozawalo mawad *n.* دسوزولو
مواد stoker

da spee bachay *n.* دسپیبچی whelp

da spee bachay *n.* دسپیبچی
puppy

da spee ghapar *n.* دسپیغپهار woof

da spee khoona *n.* دسپیخونه
kennel

da spee kuranjeydana *n.* دسپی
کونجدنه bark

da speen sosan gul *n.* دسپینسوسن
لل lily

da speenawani war *a.* دسپینونو
justifiable

da speengeero da jargey gharay
n. دسپینیرودجرغی senator

da speengeero jarga *n.* دسپپینیرو
جرهه senate

da spogmay tandar neewana *n* د
سپومتندرنیونه eclipse

da sro zaro oba warkawal *v.t.* د
سروزروابهورکول gild

da sro zaro oba warkray
shaway *a.* دسروزرواوبهورکه
شوی gilt

da stargey shabkeeya *n.* دستر
شبکیه retina

da stargi gatay *n* دسترﻯ eyeball

da stargi gol *n.* دستریل cataract

da stargo banra *n* دستروباه
eyelash

da stargo dakdar *n.* دستروا‌کر
oculist

da stargo weenzalo doormal *n* د
سترووینلودرمل eyewash

da stargo zhghorandoya aynaki
n. دستروژغورندویهعنک goggles

da stayani sandara *n* دستاینسندره
laud

da stayani sandara wayal *v.t.* د
ستاینسندرهویل laud

da stayani war *a.* دستاینو laudable

da stayani war *a.* دستاینو
praiseworthy

da storo majma\ *n.* دستورومجمع
constellation

da storo pa arwand *a.* دستوروپه
اوند meteoric

da suroonw jorakht *n.* دسرونو
جوت chord

da swayl lor ta *adv* دسولﻟورته
south

da tabar mashra *n.* دبرمشره
matriarch

da tabieeyat haq warqawal *v.t.* د
تابعيت‌حق‌ورکول enfranchise

da taboot da eekheydo zay *n* د
تابوت‌دايوډوۍ bier

da tafree zay *n* دتفريح‌ۍ resort

da tahammul war *a.* دتحمل‌و
tolerable

da tal lapara *adv* دتل‌لپاره forever

da talgaraf fan *n.* دلراف‌فن
telegraphy

**da tameed da ghusal na
warkawana** *n* دتعميدغسل‌نه
ورکونه anabaptism

da tameed ghosal warkawal
+v.t. دتعميدغسل‌ورکول baptize

da tameereydo war *a.* دتعميرېدو
raparable

da tandar pa shan ghag kawal
v.i. دتندرپه‌شان‌غ‌کول thunder

da taoon naroghee *n.* دطاعون
ناروغي pestilence

da tap tarani patay ~*n.* دپ‌تڼ
bandage

da tap zay ya dagh *n* دپ‌ای‌ادا غ
scar

da tapoogano lar *n.* داپوګانوﻟ atoll

da taqaid tankha *n.* دتقاعدتنخوا
pension

da taqaid tankha akheystal *v.t.* د
تقاعدتنخوااخستل pension

**da tareekh aw neytey la makhi
da peykho lar leek** *n.* دتاريخ‌او
زله‌مخدپو‌اليک chronicle

da tarkanray randa *n* دتر‌کارنده
plane

da taroon mada *n.* دتون‌ماده
stipulation

da tasarruf wakht *n.* دتصرف‌وخت
tenure

da tasbeeh dana *n* دتسبيح‌دانه
bead

da tashannuj ranz *n.* دتشننج‌رز
hysteria

**da tashreefatee meylmastya
bandobast kawal** *v.t.* د
تشريفاتي‌ملمستيابندوبست‌کول
banquet

da tashreefato paband *a.* د
تشريفاتوپابند ceremonious

da taskeen darmal warkawal *v.t.*
دتسکين‌درمل‌ورکول sedate

da tawajo war *a.* دتوجهو
noteworthy

da tawan peysey *n.* دتاوان‌پس
ransom

da tawazo la makhi *a.* دتواضع‌له‌مخ
lowly

**da tawdokhay daraja pa khpal
zay khwandee satoonkay
lokhay** *n.* دتو‌دو‌خدرجه‌په‌خپل‌ای
خوندي‌ساتونکي‌لوی thermos
flask

da tawdokhay yaw paymayish *a.*
دتو‌دو‌خيو‌پمائش centigrade

**da tawdokhey da maloomawani
daraja** *n.* دتو‌دو‌خدمعلو‌موندرجه
calorie

da tayfoyeed taba *n.* دتايفوئيدتبه
typhoid

**da tayna loba chi pa yaw salon
ki ta sara keygee** *n.* دنس‌لوبه‌چ
په‌يو‌سالون‌کترسره‌کي badminton

da taynas loba *n.* دنس‌لوبه tennis

da taynas loba ki da ghondaski wahana *n.* دنس لوبه كدغونسك وهنه serve

da tee sooka *n.* دتي وكه teat

da tee sooka *n.* دتي وكه nipple

da teefoos ranz *n.* دتيفوس رنز typhus

da tehqeer cheygha *n.* دتحقير چغه hoot

da tehqeer cheygha wahal *v.i* د تحقير چغه وهل hoot

da teylo leygdawoonki laray *n.* د تلو لدونكلار tanker

da teyro panro aw drey konja zaree laroonki yawa wana *n.* دترو پلو او در كونجهزي لرونكيو ونه beech

da tibat aw mangoleeya haywanoono boodayee mula *n.* دتبت او منو ليا هو او دونو بودايي ملا lama

da tibat yaw dawl ghwayay *n.* د تبت يو ول غوايي yak

da tila aw speeno zaro bandi jor nakhan *n.* دطلا او سپينو زرو باند جونان hallmark

da tlo raftar *n* دتلو رفتار pace

da toori pokh *n.* دتوريو scabbard

da toro aw shakloono da manqooshay panra *n.* دتورو اوشكلونو دمنقوشپاله stencil

da toro aw shakloono da manqooshay panri pa mrasta naqsh jorawal *v.i.* د تورو اوشكلونو دمنقوشپاپه مرسته نقش جوول stencil

da tra, mama, ya tror zoy ya loor *n.* دتره,ماما,ياترورزوىيالور cousin

da trak trak awaz *n* دتك تك اواز snap

da traq traq ghag *n* دتق تق غ rattle

da ulampeek da nareewalo syalo lobgharay *n.* دالمپيك دنيوالو سيالولوبغاى olympiad

da usoolo pa shakal sargandawal *v.t* داصولو په شكل رندول formulate

da uzley aw maheechey dard *n.* دعضلاو ماهيچ درد myalgia

da wada loomranay myasht *n.* د وادهلومنمياشت honeymoon

da wada pa ara *a* دواده پهاه conjugal

da wada rasam *n.* دواده رسم nuptials

da wada war *a.* دواده و marriageable

da wada war *a.* دواده و nubile

da wadanay makh *n* دودانه مخ facade

da wahshee zanawar bachay *n* د وحشي ناوربچى cub

da wahshee zanawar zala *n.* د وحشي ناوراله lair

da wajood peenzam unsar *n.* د وجودپنم عنصر quintessence

da wakht sanjawani ala *n* دوخت سنجوآله chronograph

da wakht teyr watal *v.i.* دوخت تروتل lapse

da wali wana *n.* دولونه willow

da wananay da teer rawatali barkha *n.* دودادتیرراوتلبرخه corbel

da wani koonda *n.* دوڼکونده stump

da wanjoon tijarat *n.* دونجون تجارت barter2

da wano panri *n* دونوپا foliage

da warandi *adv.* دواند before

da warangi masheen *n.* دوانماشین x-ray

da warangi masheen pori arwand *a.* دوانماشینپوراوند x-ray

da warangi masheen sara tibee muayna kawal *v.t.* دوانماشین سره طبي معاینه کول x-ray

da wartya khawand *a.* دوتیاخاوند competent

da warzish karay ilam *n.* دورزش کارعلم athletics

da warzpanri gadoonbaya; nuskha leekana *n.* دورپاونبیه، نسخه لیکنه subscription

da wasley masha *n.* دوسلماشه trigger

da wat yaw paymayish *n.* دوایو پمائش metre

da watan yaw paymayish *n.* دوان یوپمائش inch

da watani lar; ikhraj *n.* دوتدلاره، اخراج exit

da wato lara *n.* دوتولاره passage

da wawri toopan *n* دواورتوپان blizzard

da wawri warookay ghar *n.* د واوریووکیغر iceberg

da wayna fan *n.* دونافن oratory

da wayyo ghwara kawana *n* د وییوغورهکونه diction

da wazan aw kach pa arwand *a.* دوزناوکچپهاوند metrical

da wazan yaw miqyas *n* دوزنیو مقیاس dram

da wazan yaw paymana *n.* دوزن یوپمانه ounce

da wazan yawa paymana *n.* دوزن یوهپمانه ton

da wazeerano da dalgay khoona *n.* دوزیرانودلخونه cabinet

da weeda keydani wagon *n.* دویده کدنواون sleeper

da weeda keydo kalee *n.* دویده کدوکالي bedding

da weeli keydano war *a.* دویلکدنو و soluble

da weeli keydano wartya *n.* دویل کدنوتیا solubility

da weeni pran shawi tota *n.* دوینه پرشووه clot

da weenzalo war *a.* دوینلوو washable

da weykhtano patawalo dasmal *n.* دوتانوپولودسمال scarf

da weykhtano taw aw klokhta *n* دوتانوتاواوکلوته crimp

da weykhto weenzalo maya murakkab *n.* دوتووینلومایع مرکب shampoo

da wrazi khob *n.* دورخوب reverie

da wreykhmo cheenjay *n* دورمو چینجی caterpillar

da wrorwalay tolana *n.* دوورول ولنه confraternity

da yadakhtoono kitabgotay *n* د یادتونوکتابوی diary

da yadawani ghonda jorawal *v. t.* ديادونغونه‌جوول
commemorate

da yadawani war *a.* ديادونو
notable

da yasmeen gul *n.* دياسمين‌ل
jasmine, jessamine

da yaw kab noom *n.* ديوكب‌نوم
bass

da yaw kashoghi pa andaza *n.* د يوكاشوغپه‌انداز ه spoonful

da yaw khuday ibadat *n.* ديو خداى‌عبادت monolatry

da yaw lori pa gata *adv* ديولوريه
ex-parte

da yaw seemi da nabatato qismoona *n.* ديوسيمدنباتاتو قسمونه flora

da yaw seemi da zanawaro aw booto qismoona *n.* ديوسيمد ناورواوبوؤ‌قسمونه fauna

da yawa payp dakhilee sooray *n.* ديوه‌پايپ‌داخلي‌سورى bore

da yawey khazi larana *n.* ديولرنه
monogamy

da yeywi masheen *n.* دييوماشين
tractor

da yoonanee abeysey akhiree toray *n.* ديوناني‌ابآخري‌توري
omega

da yoonanee abeysey loomray toray *n* ديوناني‌ابلومى‌توري
alpha

da zafran pa shan *a* دزعفران‌په‌شان
saffron

da zan mukhalif jorawal *v.t.* دان مخالف‌جوول alienate

da zanawaro aw marghano da oseydo zay *n.* د دناورواومارغانود اوسدواى habitat

da zanawaro post weykhtan *n.* د ناورو پوست‌وتان fur

da zang pa krangawalo sara aylanawal *v.t.* دزنپه‌كنولوسره اعلانول toll

da zarab nakha; shkhara *n* د ضرب‌نه،؛شخه cross

da zaro shmeyr *a* دزروشمر
thousand

da zay badloon *n* دای‌بدلون shift

da zdakri da dawrey mazameen *n.* دزدكددور‌مضامين syllabus

da zdakri dawra *n.* دزده‌كدوره
semester

da zdakro dawra *n.* دزده‌كودوره
course

da zhabi lahja *n* دژبلهجه dialect

da zhabi pa sooka khabari kawal *v.t.* دژبهو‌كه‌خبركول
lisp

da zhabi pa sooka khabari kawona *n* دژبهو‌كه‌خبركونه
lisp

da zhamee mosam pa khob teyrowana *n.* دژمي‌موسم‌په خوب‌تروونه hibernation

da zhghorani chatray *n.* دژغورن چتر parachute

da zhrandi masheen *n.* دژرند ماشين grinder

da zhwand kranlar *n.* دژوندكنلاره
career

da zhwand malgaray *n.* دژوند ملرى helpmate

da zhwand malgaray n. دژوند ملری spouse

da zhwand muhima dawra n. د ژوندمهمهدوره milestone

da zmaki breedoono ki danana a. دمکبریدونوکدننه inland

da zmaki makh; por n دمکمخ;پو floor

da zmaki naray taranga n. دمکنر تانه strait

da zmaki parakhtya n. دمکپراختیا tract

da zmakpeyzhandani pa arwand a. دمکپژندنپهاوند geological

da zmakpohani pa arwand a. د مکپوهنپهاوند geographical

da zmaree burj n. دزمريبرج Leo

da zmaree ya peesho breyt n. د زمريیاپیشوبرت whisker

da zor tokar tota n. دزووکروه rag

da zor zyatee zana n. دزورزیاتيزنا rape

da zra da sharyanoonu dard n د زهدشریانونودرد angina

da zra draza n. دزهدرزا palpitation

da zra khwala kawal v. t دزهخواله کول commune

da zulfano chatar n. دزلفانوچتر frill

da zwak aw zor sakhtan adj. د واکاوزورتن cogent

da zwanay war a. دوانو juvenile

da zyar nargas gul n. دزینرسگل daffodil

da zyaree ranz n. دزیيرنز jaundice

da; hagha pron. دا;هغه it

dabagh n. دباغ tanner

dabar zaray a. برزی obdurate

dabara; kanray n. بره;کانی stone

dabareen a. برین stony

dabareena takhta n. برینهتخته slab

dabawal aw drazawal v.t. بولاو درزول thrash

dabdaba n. دبدبه pomp

dad n. ١ assurance

dad laral v.i. الرل rely

dad warkawal v.t. اورکول assure

dad warkawal v. t اورکول console

dada kawal v.i. هکول abstain

dada kawal v.t. هکول avoid

dada kawona n هکونه evasion

dada; ijtinab n. ه;اجتناب avoidance

dadeena n اینه consolation

dadeena warkawal v. t اینهورکول ensure

dadman a. امن placid

dadman; yaqeenee a. امن;یقیني sure

dafa kawal v.t. دفعکول repulse

dafa kawal; beyrta garzawal v.t. دفعکول;برتهرول avert

daftar n. دفتر bureau

daftaree a. دفتري official

daftaree monshee n دفتريمنشي clerk

dag n. ١ moor

dag a. ١ plain

dagar n. ر ground

dagar; zay n. ر;ای place

dagar; zmaka n ر;مکه field

dagh n داغ blemish

dagh *n.* داغ blot

dagh *n.* داغ stain

dagh lagawal *v. t* داغلول blot

dagh lagawal *v.t.* داغلول scar

dagh; kakartya *n.* داغ،ككتيا smear

dagh; kakartya *n.* داغ،ككتيا taint

dagha zay ta *adv.* دغمایته hither

daghee kawal *v.t.* داغيكول smear

dainamik *a* داينامک dynamic

dak; rozal shaway *a.* ک،روزل شوی terse

dak; shtaman *a.* ک،شتمن fraught

dakawal *v.t* كول fill

dakhalat *n.* دخالت interference

dakhalat kawal *v.i.* دخالتكول interfere

dakhila *n.* داخله admission

dakhilawal; darak kawal *v.t.* داخلول،درككول induct

dakhilee *a.* داخلي inner

dakhilee *a.* داخلي interior

dakhilee *a.* داخلي internal

dakhileyda *n.* داخلدا induction

dakowoonkay watan *n.* دکوونکی وان interlude

daktar *n.* اکر physician

dal *n.* ال shield

dala *n* له deligate1

dala *n.* له gang

dala *n* له shoal

dala *n.* له team

dala *n.* له group

dala yeez *a* لهييز factious

dala yeeza honaree warzishee nasa *sn.* لهييزههنريورزشينا ballet

dala yeeza mawseeqee *a.* لهييزه موسيقي orchestral

dala; tabqa *n.* له،طبقه category

dalaeez *a* لهييز communal

dalal *n.* دلال middleman

dalal *n.* دلال monger

dalalat; ishara *n.* دلالت،اشاره indication

dalan *n.* دالان lobby

dalan *n.* دالان porch

dalan; talar *n.* دالان،تالار hall

dalay *n.* ال gift

dalay *n.* ال largesse

dalay *n.* ال present

dalay kawal *v. t.* الكول dedicate

dalayeez chakar *n.* لهييزچکر picnic

dalayeez chakar ta tlal *v.i.* لهييز چکرتهتلل picnic

dalayeez harakat kawal *v.i* لهييز حرکتکول stampede

dalayeez khozakht *n.* لهييزخوت procession

dalayeez saz *n.* لهييزساز symphony

dalayeeza ghonda *n* لهييزهغونه rally

dalayeeza ghonda ratolawal *v.t.* لهييزهغونهراولول rally

dalbandee *n* لبندي classification

dalbandee kawal *v.t.* لبنديكول assort

dalbandee kawal *v. t* لبنديكول classify

dalbaz *n.* الباز acrobat

daleel *n.* دليل proof

daleel wrandi kawal *v.i.* دليل‌واند كول reason

dalgay n ل batch

dalwakee *a* لواكي feudal

dam *n.* دام pitfall

dam *n.* دام trap

dam *n.* دام snarl

dam ki geyrawal *v.t.* دام‌كرول trap

dam; doa *n.* دم،دعا invocation

dam; nayee *n.* م،نايي barber

dama kawal *v.t.* دمه‌كول relax

dama kawoonkay *n.* دمه‌كونكى relay

dama; aram *n.* دمه،ارام relaxation

damaval *v.t.* دمول infuse

dana *n* دانه abscess

dana *n.* دانه pill

danana *n.* دننه interior

danana *a.* دننه inward

danana *n.* دننه within

danana *prep.* دننه inside

danana khwa ta *adv.* دننه‌خواته inwards

danana; pa ... ki *prep.* دننه،په‌ـــ‌ك into

danananay; dakhilee *a.* دنني، داخلي indoor

danananay; dakhilee *a* دنني، داخلي inside

dand *n.* ډ lagoon

dand *n.* ډ pond

danda *n.* دنده job

danda *n.* دنده occupation

danda sparal; tohmat lagawal *v.t.* دنده‌سپارل،تهمت‌لول charge

dandana *n* دندانه cog

dangar *a.* نر haggard

dangar *n.* نر slender

dangar keydal *v.i.* نركدل slim

dangarawal *v.t.* نرول thin

dangawal *v. t* دنول exalt

danrya *n.* ديا coriander

dar *n.* ار awe

dar *n.* ار terror

dar pa dar garzeydal *v.i.* درپه‌در ګرځدل stray

dar pa dar; koosa dabay *a* درپه در؛ كوهبى vagabond

dar sakha zra chawdal *v.i.* ارخه‌زه چاودل cower

dara *n.* داه dacoity

dara *n.* دره vale

dara achowoonkay *n.* داهاچوونكى dacoit

dara mar *n.* داهمار bandit

dara; wadee *n.* دره،وادي valley

daraja; tolgay *n* درجه‌بولى class

darak kawal *v.t.* درک‌كول realize

darak kawal; moondal *v.t.* درک كول؛موندل perceive

darak; ehsas *n.* درک،احساس perception

darantoob *n.* ارنتوب cowardice

darawal *v.t.* درول stop

darawal; beyrawal *v. t.* درول؛برول cow

daraz *n* دراز drawer

darbaree *n.* درباري courtier

darbaree fahisha *n.* درباري‌فاحشه courtesan

darcheenee *n* دارچيني cinnamon

dard *n.* درد ache

dard *n.* درد agony

dard *n.* درد pain

dardawal *v.t.* دردول pain

dardnak *a.* دردناک painful

dardnak; tapee *a.* دردناک؛پی sore

dareez warta eekhodal *v.t.* درېز ورته ايودل stage

dareez; mimbar *a.* درېز؛منبر pulpit

dareyda *n* درېدا erection

dareydal *v. t.* درېدل halt

dareydal *v.i.* درېدل stand

dareydana *n* درېدنه halt

dareydana *n* درېدنه stop

dareydana; da dareydo zay *n.* درېدنه؛ددرېدوای stand

dareydana; qayam *n* درېدنه؛قيام stay

darga *n.* دره junk

dari wari kawal *v.t.* دوکول smash

darj kawal *v. t.* درجکول book

darja bandee *n.* درجهبندي gradation

darja bandee kawal *v.t* درجهبندي کول grade

darjan *n* درجن dozen

darjan *n* درجن twelve

darlodal *v.t.* درلودل have

darmal *n* درمل drug

darmal *n.* درمل medicine

darmal ploroonkay *n* درمل پلورونکی druggist

darmalana *n* درملنه cure

darmalana *n.* درملنه medicament

darmalana kawoonkay *a.* درملنه کوونکی remedial

darmalana yi kawal *v. t.* درملنهيی کول cure

darmaleez mahlool *n.* درملیز محلول syrup

darmaltoon *n.* درملتون pharmacy

darmaltoon *n* درملتون dispensary

darogh *n* دروغ lie

darogh wayal *v.i.* دروغويل lie

darogh; palma *n* دروغ؛پلمه sham

daroghjan *n.* دروغجن liar

daroghjan khabar *n* دروغجنخبر canard

darowoonakay *a.* اروونکی awful

darowoonkay *a* اروونکی formidable

darowoonkay khob *n.* اروونکی خوب nightmare

dars *n.* درس lecture

dars warkawal *v* درسورکول lecture

dars warkowoonkay *n.* درس ورکوونکی instructor

dars; hidayat *n.* درس؛هدايت instruction

darsee keetab *n.* درسيکتاب tutorial

darsee nisab *n* درسينصاب curriculum

darsee; taleemee *a.* درسي؛تعليمي tutorial

darshal *n.* درشل threshold

darwagh *a* درواغ bogus

darz *n* درز cleft

darz *n* درز crack

darz *n* درز fissure

darz moondal; mateydal *v. i* درز موندل؛ماتدل crack

darz; chawd *n.* درز؛چاود scotch

darz; nifaq *n* درز؛نفاق split

darzoona bandawal *v.t.* درزونه بندول seam

daseesa *n.* دسیسه conspiracy

dasi na chi *conj.* داسنه‌چ lest

dasmal *n.* دسمال kerchief

dasmal *n.* دسمال napkin

dasta; bandal *n.* دسته،بنل sheaf

dastak; magaway *n.* دستک؛موی picket

dastan *n.* داستان narrative

dastanee *a.* داستانی narrative

dastawayz *n* دستاوز document

dastmal *n.* دستمال handkerchief

daw talab keydal *v.t.* داوطلب‌کدل volunteer

daw talab; khpal pa khwakhi *n.* داوطلب؛خپل‌په‌خوی volunteer

daw talbana; khpal pa khwakha *a.* داوطلبانه؛خپل‌په‌خوه voluntary

dawa kawoonkay *n.* دعواکوونکی plaintiff

dawam *n.* دوام consistence,-cy

dawam *n.* دوام permanence

dawam kawal *v.t.* دوام‌کول withstand

dawam laral *v. i.* دواملرلcontinue

dawamdar *a.* دوامدار lasting

dawamdar shay *n.* دوامدارشی perennial

dawlatee aylan *n.* دولتی‌اعلان communiqué

dawoodee gul *n* داودیل daisy

dawra; chapeyryal *n.* دوره؛چاپریال circuit

dawra; da nawee mosam payl *n* دوره؛دنوي‌موسم‌پیل epoch

dawra; dawran *n* دوره؛دوران spell

dawran *n* دوران era

dawrayee; musalsal *a.* دورهیی؛ مسلسل serial

dayee *n.* دایی midwife

daymee *a.* دایمي permanent

daymee *a.* دایمي perpetual

daymee pam kawal *v. t* دایمي‌پام کول contemplate

dayra *n.* دایره circle

dayra *n.* دایره sphere

dayrawee *a* دایروي circular

dayrawee *a.* دایروي spherical

dayrawee harakat *n* دایروي‌حرکت whirl

daz bandee *n.* زبندي armistice

deen *n.* دین religion

deen pohana *n.* دین‌پوهنه theology

deendar *a.* دیندار saintly

deenee *a.* دیني religious

deenee aqeeda *n* دیني‌عقیده dogma

deenee aw mazhabee dood *n.* دیني‌اومذهبي‌دود sacrament

deewa *n.* دیوه lantern

deeyanat *n.* دیانت honesty

dehleez *n.* دهلیز corridor

dendar *a.* دیندار godly

dew *n.* دیو demon

dey dawran ki *prep* ددوران‌ک during

deykhwa; dalta *adv.* دخوا،دلته here

deyo *n* دیو fiend

deyr arkheez fanee aw takhneekee pohantoon *n.* ر اخيزفني‌اوتخنيكي‌پوهنتون polytechnic

deyr arkheez fanoono pori arwand *a.* ر اخيزفنونوپوراوند polytechnic

deyr bad shakla *a.* ربدشكله hideous

deyr ghat *a.* رغ titanic

deyr kam *adv.* ركم seldom

deyr khandowoonkay *a.* ر خندوونكى hilarious

deyr koochnay *a.* ركوچنى minute

deyr koochnay cheenjay *n.* ر كوچنى‌چينجى mite

deyr loy *a* رلوى enormous

deyr loy *a* رلوى mammoth

deyr muhim *a.* رمهم salient

deyr oomar laral *v.i.* رعمرلرل outlive

deyr pakhwanay *a.* رپخوانى immemorial

deyr porta kawal *v.t.* رپورته‌كول sky

deyr sakht *adj.* رسخت crucial

deyr sor *a.* رسو frigid

deyr warta *prep.* رورته near

deyr zala *adv.* رله oft

deyr zala *adv.* رله often

deyr zarooree *a* رضروري dire

deyr zhar *adv.* رژر anon

deyr zhar *adv.* رژر soon

deyr; zyat *a.* ر؛زيات very

deyra kkhata barkha *n.* ره‌كته برخه nadir

deyrakht *n.* رت immensity

deyrakht *n.* رت increment

deyrakht *n.* رت superabundance

deyrkay *n.* ركى majority

deyrsh *n.* درش thirty

deyrsh *a* درش thirty

deyrsham *a.* درشم thirtieth

deyrshama barkha *n* درشمه‌برخه thirtieth

deyw *n.* دو giant

deywal *n.* دوال wall

deywal *n.* دوال mural

deywal jorawal *v.t.* دوال‌جورول wall

deywalee *a.* دوالى mural

deywaleeya keydang *n.* دواليه‌كدن ___ bankruptcy

difa *n* دفاع defence

difa kawal *v. t* دفاع‌كول defend

difa kawal *v.t* دفاع‌كول fend

difa kawal *v.i.* دفاع‌كول plead

difa kawoonkay *n* دفاع‌كوونكى defendant

difa; rakhteenwalee *n.* دفاع؛ رتينولي vindication

difaee khozakht *n.* دفاعي‌خوت parry

difaee zawab *n.* دفاعي‌واب rejoinder

dimagh *n* دماغ brain

dobara chap *n.* دوباره‌چاپ reprint

dobara raghondawal *v.t.* دوباره راغونول recollect

dobara yaw keydal *v.t.* دوباره‌يو كدل rejoin

dobara zandan ta astawal *v.t.* دوباره‌زندان‌ته‌استول remand

dobara zwanawal *v.t.* دوبارهوانول rejuvenate

dobee *n.* دوبي washer

dobee khana *n.* دوبيخانه laundry

doday *n* و bread

doday khwaral *v. t.* وخول dine

dok *n.* دوک spindle

doka *n.* دوکه cheat

doka *n* دوکه deceit

doka *n* دوکه dodge

doka *n.* دوکه fraud

doka *n.* دوکه wile

doka kawal *v. t* دوکهکول deceive

doka kawal *v.t.* دوکهکول hoodwink

doka kawal *v.t.* دوکهکول lure

doka kawal *v.t.* دوکهکول rook

doka; doka warkawal *n.t.* دوکه، دوکهورکول delude

dokamar *n.* دوکهمار trickster

dokamar *a.* دوکهمار wily

dokamar aw bey haya *n.* دوکهمار اوبحيا rascal

dokey baz *a.* دوکباز fraudulent

dol *n* ول drum

dol wahal *v.i.* ولوهل drum

dol; seengar *n* ول،سينار fashion

dol; zan sambalawana *n.* ول،بان سمبالونه mode

dolas *n.* دولس twelve

dolasam *a.* دولسم twelfth

dolasama barkha *n.* دولسمهبرخه twelfth

dolay *n.* ول palanquin

dolcha *n* ولچه bucket

dolcha *n.* ولچه pail

doobeydal *v.t.* وبدل swamp

doobeydana *n* وبدنه sink

dood *n.* دود custom

dood shaway *a.* دودشوی prevalent

dood; riwayat *n.* دود،روايت tradition

doodeez; riwajee *n.* دوديز،رواجي vogue

doodeydal *v.i.* دودﺪل prevail

dookhmanee *n.* دنمي feud

doongeydal *v.i.* وندل grumble

doonyawee *a* دنياوي earthly

doonyawee *a.* دنيوي mundane

doonyayee mal *n.* دنياييمال pelf

doora *n.* دوه powder

doora achawal; sheendal *v.t.* دوه اچول،شيندل powder

doorbeenee *a.* دوربيني microscopic

doori *n* دو dust

doori pakawal *v.t.* دوپاکول dust

doori pakawoonkay *n* دوپاکوونکی duster

doshamba *n.* دوشنبه Monday

dostana *adj.* دوستانه amicable

dostana *a.* دوستانه fraternal

dostana majlis *n.* دوستانهمجلس symposium

dotanay; doseeya *n* دوتن،دوسيه file

dozakh *a.* دوزخ hell

dozakhee *a.* دوزخي infernal

drab drab *n.* دربدرب thud

drab drab kawal *v.i.* دربدرب کول thud

drab; khrap *n.* درب،خرپ thump

drabowal *v.t.* دربوول bang

drabowana *n.* دربوونه bang
drama; nandara *n* رامه;ننداره drama
drana toora *n.* درنهتوره sabre
dranaway *n* درناوی esteem
dranaway *a.* درناوی reverential
dranaway kawal *v.t.* درناوی‌کول respect
dranaway warkawal *v. i.* درناوی ورکول crouch
dranaway warkawal *v. t* درناوی ورکول esteem
dranaway warta kawal *v. t* درناوی‌ورته‌کول honour
draz; zarb *n.* درز;ضرب throb
drazawal *v.t.* درزول thump
drazeydal *v.i.* درزدل palpitate
drazeydal *v.i.* درزدل pulse
drazeydal *v.i.* درزدل throb
drey *n.* در three
drey arkheez *a.* دراخیز tripartite
drey arkheeza taroon *n* دراخیزه تون triplicate
drey chanda *a.* درچنده triplicate
drey chanda kawal *v.t.,* درچنده کول triple
drey chanda kawal *v.t.* درچنده کول triplicate
drey chanda kawana *n.* درچنده کوونه triplication
drey goonay *a.* درونی triple
drey goonaytob; taslees *n.* درونی توب;تثلیث trinity
drey gotay *n.* دروی triangle
drey goteez *a.* درویز triangular

drey kaseeza dala *n.* درکسیزه‌دله trio
drey paya *n.* درپایه tripod
drey rangay *n* دررنی tricolour
drey rangee *a.* دررني tricolour
drey zala *adv.* درله thrice
dreyam *a.* دریم third
dreyam da chi *adv.* دریم‌داچ thirdly
dreyama barkha *n.* دریمه‌برخه third
droond *a.* دروند hefty
droond *a.* دروند weighty
droond aw patman *a.* درونداوپتمن superb
droond goozar *n.* دروندوزار pound
droond; sabit *a.* دروند;ثابت staid
drost *a* درست correct
drostawal *v. t* درستول correct
drust *a.* درست accurate
drustwalay *n.* درستوال accuracy
dukhman *n* دښمن enemy
dukhmanee *n* دښمني animosity
dukhmanee *n* دښمني enmity
dwa *n.* دوه two
dwa arkheez *n* دوه‌اخیز double
dwa arkheez *a* دوه‌اخیز equivocal
dwa arkheez agheyz *n.* دوه‌اخیزاغیز interplay
dwa arkheeza *adj* دوه‌اخیز amphibious
dwa chanda *a.* دوه‌چنده twofold
dwa chanda kawal *v.t.* دوه‌چنده کول redouble
dwa kalan war *adj* دوه‌کلن‌وار biennial

dwa khazi larana *n* دوهلرنه
bigamy

dwa makhay; reeya *n.* دوهمخي؛ريا
insincerity

dwa makhee *n* دوهمخي duplicity

dwa myashtanay *adj.* دوهمياشتنه
bimonthly

dwa ooneeza *adj* دوهاونيزه
bi-weekly

dwa pa dwa *n.* دوهپهدوه tete-a-tete

dwa pkhey laroonkay jandar *n*
دوهپلرونکیجاندار biped

dwa raga *a.* دوهره mulish

dwa raga haywan *a* دوهرهحوان
mongrel

dwa raga; dwa jinsa *adj.* دوهره؛
دوهجنسه bisexual

dwa raga; mukhalif *a* دوهره؛
مخالف cross

dwa saray kalang *n.* دوهسریکلن
mattock

dwa sawa kalan *adj* دوهسوهکلن
bicentenary

dwa stargeez doorbeen *n.* دوه
ستریزدوربین binocular

dwa zala *adv.* دوهله twice

dwa zaray *n.* دوهزی shilly-shally

dwa zaweeyi laroonkay *adj.* دوه
زاویلرونکی biangular

dwa zhabeez *a* دوهژبیز bilingual

dwara *a* دواه both

dwara *a.* دواه two

dwara; ham ... ham *pron* دواه؛هم
هم___ both

dwayam *a.* دویم second

dwayam breedman *n.* دویمبریدمن
lieutenant

dwayma nuskha *n* دویمهنسخه
duplicate

dwey oonay *n.* دواوونز fort-night

dyarlas *n.* دیارلس thirteen

dyarlas *a* دیارلس thirteen

dyarlasam *a.* دیارلسم thirteenth

eejara *n.* اجاره lease

eejara *n.* دار اجاره tenant

eejara daree *n.* اجارهداري
monopoly

eejara kawal *v.t.* اجارهکول lease

eejaradaree *n.* اجارهداري tenancy

eejaza *n.* اجازه permission

eejaza *n.* اجازه permit

eejaza leek *n.* اجازهلیک conge

eejaza leek akheystoonkay *n.*
اجازهلیکاخستونکی licensee

eejaza leek warkawal *v.t.* اجازه
لیکورکول license

eejaza leek; qarardad *n* اجازه
لیک؛قرارداد charter

eejaza warkawal *v.t.* اجازهورکول
let

eejaza warkawal *v.t.* اجازهورکول
permit

eejaza warkawona *n.* اجازهورکونه
indulgence

eekhodal *v.t.* ایودل position

eekhodal *v.t.* ایودل put

eela *adv.* ایله barely

eela; bas ham domra *a.* ايله؛بس‌هم دومره mere

eeman *n* ايمان faith

eemandaree *n.* ايمانداري integrity

eemteeyaz *n.* امتياز privilege

eemtiyaz *n* امتياز distinction

eenam *n* انعام bonus

eenam *n* انعام bounty

eenam *n.* انعام prize

eenam *n.* انعام tip

eenam warkawal *v.t.* انعام‌ورکول prize

eenam warkawal *v.t.* انعام‌ورکول tip

eengleesee abjoo *n* انليسي‌آبجو ale

eerey *n.* اير ash

eerey kawona *n* ايرکونه cremation

eerlayndee *a.* ايرليني Irish

eerlayndee wagaray ya zhaba *n.* ايرليني‌وي‌يازبه Irish

eesaeeyat *n.* عيسائيت Christianity

eesarawal; zandawal *v. t* ايسارول؛زندول‌ detain

eesawee *a.* عيسوي Christian

eesayee *n* عيسائي Christian

eetalwee *a.* ايالوي Italian

eetalwee wagaray ya zhaba *n.* ايالوي‌وي‌يازبه Italian

eetar; sheen asman *n* ايتر؛شين آسمان ether

eezat *n* عزت dignity

eezat kamawal *v. t* عزت‌کمول degrade

eezat mab *n.* عزت‌مأب Highness

ehsan; zhmana *n.* احسان؛ژمنه obligation

ehsas *n.* احساس sentiment

ehsasatee aw ghinayee *a.* احساساتي‌اوغنايي lyrical

ehsasee; jazbatee *a.* احساسي؛ جذباتي sentimental

ehteeyaj *n* احتياج requiste

ehteeyat *n.* احتياط precaution

ehteeyat *n.* احتياط prudence

ehteeyatee *a.* احتياطي precautionary

ehtikar *n.* احتکار speculation

ehtimal *n.* احتمال contingency

ehtimal *n.* احتمال probability

ehtimal; sahee gooman *n.* احتمال؛ صحيح‌ومان presumption

ehtimalan *adv.* احتمالاً probably

ehtiram *n.* احترام compliment

ehtiram *n.* احترام courtesy

ehtiram *n.* احترام homage

ehtiram *n.* احترام honour

ehtiram *n.* احترام respect

ehtiram *n.* احترام obeisance

ehtiram *n.* احترام veneration

ehtiram aw dranaway kawal *v. t* احتراماودرناوى‌کول compliment

ehtiram kawal *v.t.* احترام‌کول revere

ehtiram satowoonkay *a.* احترام ساتوونکى considerate

ehtiram warkawal *v.t* احترام ورکول dignify

ehtiram yi kawal *v.t.* احترام‌ي‌کول venerate

etifaq ta raseydal *v.t.* اتفاق ته رسدل accede

etihadeeya shirkat *n* اتحادیه شرکت corporation

eyshawal *v.i.* اشول boil

eysheydal *v.i.* اشدل seethe

eystana *n* استنه eviction

eystana *n.* استنه expulsion

F

faal *a.* فعال strenuous

faal *a.* فعال active

faal; gatawar *a* فعال،ءور efficient

faal; hasand *a.* فعال،ءاند vivid

faalawal *v.t.* فعالول activate

faaleeyat *n.* فعالیت activity

faaleeyat; gatawartob *n* فعالیت، ورتوب efficiency

fahashtob *n.* فحشتوب obscenity

fahish *a.* فاحش obscene

fahish insan *n.* فاحش انسان prostitute

fahisha *n.* فاحشه cuckold

fahisha *n.* فاحشه whore

fahisha *n.* فاحشه strumpet

fahisha khana *n* فاحشه خانه brothel

faks masheen *n* فاکس ماشین fac-simile

fal *n.* فال auspice

falij *n.* فالج mutilation

faljawal *v.t.* فلجول mutilate

falsafa *n.* فلسفه philosophy

fan *n.* فن art

fan; tareeqa *n.* فن،طریقه technique

fana *n.* فنا vanity

fanee *a.* فانی mortal

fanee bashar *n* فانی بشر mortal

fankar *n.* کار فن actor

fankara *n.* کاره فن actress

faransawee *a.* فرانسوی french

faransawee wagaray ya zhaba *n* فراسوی وی یاژبه French

farayb *n.* فرب swindle

farayb; wehem *n.* فرب،وهم illusion

faree lar *n* فرعی لار bypass

faree mahsool *n* فرعی محصول by-product

faree mustajar ta da eejarey haq warkawal *v.t.* فرعی مستاجر ته د اجاره حق ورکول sublet

faree; mrastyal *a.* فرعی،مرستیال tributary

fareyb *n.* فریب delusion

farhangee *a* فرهنی cultural

farigh *a* فارغ leisure

farikhta *n* فرته angel

farman *n* فرمان decree

farman *n.* فرمان order

farman sadirawal *v. i* فرمان صادرول decree

farman warkawal *v.t* فرمان ورکول order

farman warkawal; masharee kawal *v. t* فرمان ورکول،مشری کول command

farman; masharee *n* فرمان،مشری command

farmanbardar *adj.* فرمانبردار compliant

farmanbardar *a* فرمانبردار docile

farmanbardaree *n.* فرمانبرداري compliance

faryadee *a.* فريادي rowdy

farz kawal *v.i.* فرض كول deem

farzee ya daroghee noom *n.* فرضي يادروغي نوم alias

fasadee *a* فسادي decadent

fasahat aw balaghat *n* فصاحت او بلاغت eloquence

fasahat aw balaghat *a.* فصاحت او بلاغت rhetorical

fasakh kawoonkay *a.* فسخ كوونكى irritant

fasee *a* فصيح eloquent

fasfuras laroonkay *n.* فاسفرس لرونكى phosphorus

fasid *a.* فاسد corrupt

fasid saray *n.* فاسدسى villain

fasid; paysa khor *a.* فاسد؛پسه خور venal

fasidawal *v. t.* فاسدول corrupt

fasiq *n* فاسق debauchee

faskh kawal *v.t.* فسخ كول revoke

faskh kawana *n.* فسخ كوونه revocation

fasq *n* فسق debauchery

fastayee *n.* فسطايي sophist

fata kawal *v.t.* فتح كول overpower

fawara *n.* فواره fountain

fawqul ada *a.* فوق العاده terrific

fawree *a* فوري immediate

fawree *a.* فوري prompt

fayda *n.* فايده advantage

fayda mand *a.* فايده مند advantageous

fayl ta arwand; qayd *n.* فعل ته اوند؛ قد adverb

fayl; kroyay *n.* فعل؛كويى verb

faylwazma; karwazma *a.* فعل وزمه؛كوزمه verbal

faysala kon *a* فصله كن decisive

faysala kun *a* فصله كن conclusive

faza *n.* فضا atmosphere

faza ki garzeydal; zay warkawal *v.t.* فضا كردل؛ځاى وركول space

fazeelat laroonkay; muttaqee *a.* فضيلت لرونكى؛متقي virtuous

feedeeya *n.* فديه scapegoat

feel *n* فيل elephant

feelasof *n.* فيلسوف philosopher

feelasofyana *a.* فيلسوفيانه philosophical

feelwan *n.* فيلوان mahout

fehem *n.* فهم intellect

fidakarana *a.* فداكارانه sacrificial

fikar kawal *v.i.* فكر كول muse

fikar kawal *v.t.* فكر كول think

fikar; and *n.* فكر؛آند notion

fikar; arwa *n.* فكر؛اروا psyche

fikar; ghor *n* فكر؛غور muse

fikarmand *a.* فكرمند mindful

fikree *a.* فكري intellectual

fikree *a.* فكري notional

fikree tamayal *n* فكري تمايل complex

fikree taraw laroonkay *a.* فكري تاولرونكى telepathic

fikree twan *n.* فكري توان mentality

fikree; jazbatee *a.* فكري؛جذباتي
spirited

filam chamtoo kawal *v.t* فيلم چمتو
كول film

filiz *n.* فلز metal

filiz ta oba warkawal *v.t.* فلزتهاوبه
وركول galvanize

filiz ta oba warkawal *v.t.* فلزتهاوبه
وركول temper

filizee *a.* فلزي metallic

filizee khwalay *n.* فلزي خول helmet

filizee pokh warkawal *v.t.* فلزي پو
وركول plate

finar; bampar *n.* فنر؛بمپر bumper

firasat *n.* فراست intuition

firasat *n.* فراست keenness

firasat *n.* فراست sagacity

fishar *n* فشار depression

fishar *n.* فشار tension

fishar *n.* فشار pressure

fishar *n* فشار zip

fishar achawal *v.t.* فشاراچول
pressurize

fishar landi rawastal *v. t* فشارلاند
راوستل depress

fishar landi rawastal *v.t.* فشارلاند
راوستل strain

fishar; zor *n* فشار؛زور strain

fitna *n.* فتنه incense

fitna achawal *v.t.* فتنهاچول incense

fitrat *n.* فطرت mettle

fitree *a.* فطري inborn

fitree *a.* فطري natural

fitwa warkawal *v.t.* فتواوركول
award

fitwa; bakhana *n.* فتوا؛بنه award

fizeek *n.* فزیک physics

foq bashar *a.* فوق بشر superhuman

**foq bashar khusooseeyat
laroonkay insan** *n.* فوق بشر
خصوصیات لرونکی انسان
superman

foqul ada *a.* فوق العاده supernatural

fosil *n.* فوسیل fossil

frak *n.* فراک frock

frekvency *n.* فریکوینسی frequency

funji *n.* فنجی fungus

fyooz *n* فیوز fuse

G

gabeen *n.* بین beehive

gad jaryan *n* جریان confluence

gad zhwand sara kawal *v. i* ژوند
سره کول co-exist

gad zhwandoon *n* ژوندون
co-existence

gada; darweyzgar *n* دا؛درورز
beggar

gada; nasa *n* نا؛ dance

gadaval *v.t.* ول intermingle

gadawana; yaw zay kawana *n* ؛رنه
کونه ای یو amalgamation

gaday *n.* ا wain

gaday *n.* ای vehicle

gaday chalawal *v. t* ای چلول drive

gaday; da pacha takht *n.* د؛دپاچا
تخت throne

gadayee kawal *v. t.* دایی کول beg

gadayee kawal *v. i* دایی کول cadge

gadayee kawal *v.t.* ګدايي کول
maunder

gadey hasi *n* ه collaboration

gadeydal *v. t.* ګد dance

gadwad ash n. آش ګډ hotchpotch

gadwad kawal *v.t.* ګډول و jumble

gadwad saman ya asbab *n.* و
سامان يا اسباب welter

gadwadawal *v.t.* ګډول mate

gadwadawal *v.i* ګډول mix

gadwadee *n.* ګډوي chaos

gadwadee *n.* ګډوي muddle

gadwadee palana *n.* پالنه ګډوي
anarchism

gadwadee; baghawat *n* ګډوي؛بغاوت
anarchy

gadwalay *n* ګډوالی combination

gaheez *n.* هير morning

gala badawal *v.t.* غله بادول
winnow

galal; zeygeydal; zeygawal *v.t*
ګالل؛زېدل؛زول bear

galay *n.* ږلی hail

galay wareydal *v.i* ږلی ورېدل hail

gam pa gam *a.* ګام په ګام gradual

gam pa gam seyral *v.t.* ګام په ګام
scan

ganda *a.* ګنده insane

ganda shay la zaya eestal *v.t.* ګنده
شی له ضايع ايستل weed

gandal *v.t.* ګنل sew

gandana *n.* ګننه stitch

gandoonkay *n.* ګنونکی tailor

gangas kawal *v.t.* ګنس کول puzzle

gangas kawal *v. t* ګنس کول
bewilder

gangasawal *v. t* ګنسول confuse

gangastob *n.* ګنستوب puzzle

gangosawal *v.t* ګنوسول astound

ganr bootee *n.* ګنر بوټی thicket

ganr nafoosa *a.* ګنر نفوسه populous

ganr shmeyr khazi larana *n.* ګنر شمېر
خزي لرنه polygamy

ganr shmeyr khazi laroonkay *a.*
ګنر شمېر خزي لرونکی polygamous

ganr syoray *n.* ګنر سيوری gloom

ganra *n* ګنره density

ganra gonra *n* ګنره ګونره crowd

ganra goonra *n.* swarm

ganra goonra *n.* ګنره ګونره mob

ganra goonra jorawal *v.i.* ګنره ګونره
جوړول swarm

ganra goonra jorawal *v.t.* ګنره ګونره
جوړول throng

ganra goonra kawal *v.t.* ګنره ګونره کول
mob

ganri wani *n.* ګنري ونه coppice

gapawoo *n.* ګپاوو windbag

garam aw namjan *a.* ګرم او نمجن
sultry

garam aw tod *a.* ګرم او تود hot

garam mosam *n* ګرم موسم thaw

garana; ibarat *n.* ګرنه؛عبارت phrase

garanday kawal *v.t* ګندی کول
accelerate

garanday kawal *v. t.* ګندی کول
expedite

garanday; teyz *a* ګندی؛تېز fast

garandeetob *n* ګندیتوب
acceleration

garandeetob *n* ګندیتوب expedition

garang *n.* ګرنه cliff

gararay; abzar *n.* رار؛ابزار gear

garay *n.* clock

gard *n.* درمmist

gard chapeyra *prep.* ردچاپره around

gard; golay *a.* ردبول round

gardawal; raghondawal *v.t.* ردول؛راغونول round

garday *n.* ردی globe

gardjan *a.* ردجن hazy

gareydal; garawal *v.t.* ردل؛برول scratch

gareydana; nasht *n.* ردنه؛نشت scratch

garm aw naram; hosa *a.* گرماو نرم؛هوسا cosy

garmaka; dana *n.* رمكه؛دانه pimple

garweygna *n.* رونه inquest

garweygna *n.* رونه interrogation

garz bandee *n* ربندي curfew

garzand *n.* رند rover

garzand ploroonkay *n* رند پلورونكى hawker

garzand plorowoonkay *n.* رند پلوروونكى badger

garzand; mutaharik *a.* رند؛ متحرک mobile

garzanda; mutaharik *adj* رنده؛ متحرک ambulant

garzandoyee *n.* رندويى tourism

garzeydal *v.i.* ردل walk

garzeydana *n.* ردنه mobility

gasht *n* شت patrol

gasht kawal *v.i.* شت كول patrol

gasht kawal *v.i.* شت كول roam

gata *n.* گ profit

gata akheystal *v.t.* گاخيستل advantage

gata kawal *v.t.* گكول profit

gata rasawal *v. t.* گرسول benefit

gata; fayda *n* گ؛فايده benefit

gata; hasil *n.* گ؛حاصل income

gatandoya *a.* گندويه profitable

gatandoyay *n.* گندويى profiteer

gatavar *a.* گور fruitful

gatavar *a.* گور lucrative

gatawar *a* گور beneficial

gatoonkay *n.* گونكى winner

gawa *n.* گواه witness

gawahee warkawal; tasqeekawal *v.t.* گواهى وركول؛ تصديقول attest

gawand *n.* گاوند neighbourhood

gawandee *n.* گاوني neighbour

gawandyan *n.* گاونيان kith

gaz *n.* گاز gas

gazara *n.* گازره carrot

gdan; bajra *n.* گدن؛باجره millet

gebon *n.* گيبون gibbon

gedara *n.* گده fox

geedara *n.* گيده vixen

geela *n* گيله complaint

geela kawal *v. i* گيله كول complain

geela; shikayat *n.* گله؛شكايت grievance

geera *n* گيره beard

geera khrayna *n* گيره خرينه shave

geometry *n.* گيوميرى geometry

geyda *n* گيده belly

geyda yeez *a.* گييز abdominal

geyday *n* cluster

geyday *n.* ى package

geyday kawal *v. i.* کول cluster

geyr mustaqeem maleeyat *n* غر مستقیم‌مالیات excise

geyr ratlana *n* رراتلنه fix

ghabee *a* غبي dull

ghabee kawal *v. t.* غبي‌کول dull

ghaflat *n* غفلت neglect

ghaflat kawal *v.t.* غفلت‌کول neglect

ghag *n* غ sound

ghag khpareydal *v.i.* غخپریدل sound

ghag rasand *n.* غرساند megaphone

ghag ta inikas warkawal *v. t* غته انعکاس‌ورکول echo

ghag; ahang *n.* غ،آهن tone

ghagan toray *n.* غن‌توری vowel

ghagana macho tri akheystal *v.i.* غنه‌مچوتراخستل smack

ghagantob *n.* غنتوب sonority

ghageez *a.* غیز phonetic

ghageez *a.* غیز vocal

ghageeza noomawana *n.* غیزه نوموونه onrush

ghageydal *v.i.* غدل speak

ghageydal *v.t* غیدل word

ghageydal; khabari kawal *v.i.* غدل،خبرکول talk

ghageydoonkay *n.* غدونکی speaker

ghagowona *n.* غوونه lyric

ghakh *n.* غا tooth

ghakhoona kawal *v.i.* غاوونه‌کول teethe

ghakhtalay *adj.* غتلی deft

ghakhtalay *a* غتلی drastic

ghakhtalay kawal *v.t.* غتلی‌کول corroborate

ghakhtalay; hodman *a.* غتلی؛هو من stalwart

ghakhtalay; zwakman *a.* غتلی؛ واکمن vigorous

ghal *n* غل burglar

ghal *n.* غل pirate

ghal *n.* غل thief

ghala *n.* غَله cereal

ghala *n.* غله grain

ghala; fasal *n* غله؛فصل crop

ghalaba *n* غلبه conquest

ghalaba kawal *v. t* غلبه‌کول conquer

ghalaba laral *v. t* غلبه‌لرل dominate

ghalat *a* غلط false

ghalat *a.* غ incorrect

ghalat chap *n.* غلط‌چاپ misprint

ghalat chapawal *v.t.* غلط‌چاپول misprint

ghalat goomat *n.* غلطومان misconception

ghalat khabar warkawal *v.t.* غلط خبرورکول misgive

ghalat noom *n.* غلط‌نوم misnomer

ghalat qazawat kawal *v.t.* غلط قضاوت‌کول misjudge

ghalat tabeer *n.* غلط‌تعبیر misunderstanding

ghalata larkhowana kawal *v.t.* غلطه‌لاروونه‌کول misdirect

ghalatee *n* غلطي error

ghalatee *n* غلطي fault
ghalatee kawal *v. i* کول غلطي err
ghalay *n.* غال carpet
ghalay *n.* غال rug
ghalay dawla parda *n.* غالولهپرده tapestry
ghalay kawal *v.t.* کول غلى silence
ghalay kawoonkay *n.* غلى کوونکى silencer
ghalay; sakin *a.* غلى;ساکن quiet
ghalay; sakit *a.* غلى;ساکت still
ghalayeez *a* غَلَـييز cereal
ghalbeyl *n.* غلبل riddle
ghalbeyl *n.* غلبل sieve
ghalbeylawal *v.t.* غلبلول sieve
ghalbeylawal *v.i.* غلبلول riddle
ghaleez *n.* غليظ thick
ghaleeza aw tata lara *n.* غليظهاوتته له smog
ghalmaghalee *a.* غالمغالي noisy
ghalmaghalee *n.* غالمغالي rampage
gham *n.* غم grief
gham larali peykhi leekoonkay *n.* غملاپليکونکى tragedian
ghamay *n* غمى gem
ghamjan *a.* غمجن lamentable
ghamjan *a.* غمجن rueful
ghamjan *a.* غمجن grievous
ghamjanawal *v.t.* غمجنول aggrieve
ghamjanawal *v.t.* غمجنول grieve
ghamjanee *n.* غمجني anguish
ghamjaneydal *v.i.* غمجندل sorrow
ghamrazee; gad masooleeyat *n.* غمرازي;مسؤليت solidarity
ghamzapalay *n.* غمپلى woeful

ghanam *n.* غنم wheat
ghanayee *a.* غنايي lyric
ghandana *n.* غندنه damnation
ghandana *n.* غندنه reproof
ghandanleek *n.* غندنليک satire
ghanra *n.* غه spider
ghanra *n.* ڼه computation
ghanra kawal *v.t.* ه کول compute
ghapal; kuranjeydal *v.t.* غپل; کونجدل bark
ghapeydal *v.i.* غپدل yap
ghar *n* غار den
ghar *n.* غر mountain
ghar ghara kawal *v.i.* غغهکول gargle
ghar khatoonkay *n* غرختونکى alpinist
ghar khatoonkay *n.* غرختونکى mountaineer
ghara *n* غاه collar
ghara eekhodal *v.i.* غاهايودل acquiesce
ghara eekhodal *v. i* غاهايودل comply
ghara eekhodal *v.t.* غاهايودل obey
ghara eekhodana *n.* غاهايودنه acquiescence
ghara eekhodana *n.* غاهايودنه submission
ghara warkawal *v. t.* غاهورکول embrace
ghara; sat *n.* غاه; neck
gharakay *n* کغاﺀ anadem
gharal shaway pand mazay *n.* غلشوىپندمزى whipcord
gharana *n.* غڼه twist

gharay *n.* غى member

gharay; had *n.* غى،ه organ

gharayeez *a.* غرهييز mountainous

ghareetob *n.* غيتوب membership

ghari eekhodalo ta rabalal *v.t.* غا
ايودلوتهرابلل summon

gharma *n.* غرمه noon

gharmanay khob *n.* غرمنىخوب
siesta

gharoor laral *n* غرورلرل conceit

gharqeydal; tanazzul kawal *v.i.*
غرقدل؛تنزلكول sink

gharsa *n* غره deer

gharsa *n.* غره antelope

ghasab kawal *v.t.* غصبكول usurp

ghasha *n.* غشا membrane

ghashay *n* غشى arrow

ghata pyala *n.* غهپياله mug

ghawalaunkay *a* غولونكى elusive

ghawgha *n* غوغا din

ghawgha *n.* غوغا tumult

ghawgha *n.* غوغا uproar

ghayb pohana *n.* غبپوهنه
foreknowledge

ghaybat kawal *v.t.* غيبتكول
backbite

ghayr akhlaqee *a.* غراخلاقي
amoral

ghayr ashrafee shakhs *n.* غر
اشرافىشخص snob

ghayr faal *a.* غرفعال inoperative

ghayr faal *a.* غرفعال passive

ghayr hazir *a* غرحاضر absent

ghayr haziree *n* غرحاضري
absence

ghayr insanee *a.* غرانساني
inhuman

ghayr mamoolee *a.* غرمعمولي
outsize

ghayr masawee *a.* غرمساوي
nonpareil

ghayr mehfooz *a.* غرمحفوظ
insecure

ghayr moassar *a.* غرمؤثر
ineffective

ghayr munsifana *a.* غرمنصفانه
unjust

ghayr qanoonee *a.* غرقانوني
invalid

ghayr rasmee *a.* غررسمي informal

ghayr zaroree *a.* غرضروري
needless

ghaza *n* غذا diet

ghaza *n.* غذا nutrition

ghazab *n.* غضب ire

ghazab *n.* غضب outrage

ghazab *n.* غضب wrath

ghazabnak *a* غضبناک ferocious

ghazabnak *a* غضبناک fierce

ghazabnak *a.* غضبناک furious

ghazal *n.* غزل sonnet

ghazal leekoonkay *n.* غزلليكونكى
lyricist

ghazawal; parakhtya warkawal
v.t. غول؛پراختياوركول stretch

ghazawana *n* غوونه stretch

ghazayee *a.* غذايي nutritious

ghazayee ishtiha *n.* غذايياشتها
appetite

ghazeydal *v.i* غدل lie

ghazeydal *v.i.* غدل loll

ghbarg *a* غبر double

ghbarg; dwa kasee *a* غبر،دوه‌کسي dual

ghbargawal *v. t.* غبرول double

ghbargoon *n.* غبرون reaction

ghbargoon khowal *v.i.* غبرون‌وول react

gheyg *n.* غ lap

gheyga; ghara *n* غه،غاه embrace

gheyr madee *a.* غرمادي immaterial

gheyr mehdood *a.* غرمحدود indefinite

gheyr qanoonee *a.* غرقانوني illegal

gheyr shakhsee *a.* غرشخصي impersonal

ghla *n* غلا burglary

ghla *n.* غلا theft

ghla kawal *v.i.* غلاکول steal

ghla kawal *v.* غلاکول pinch

ghla kawal *v.t* غلاکول pirate

ghla shaway a. غلاشوى rapt

ghobar *n.* غبار haze

ghojal; pand ghalay *n* غوجل؛ پنغالى stable

ghojala *n* غوجله byre

ghokht; irada *n.* غوت،اراده volition

ghokhtal *v.t.* غوتل crave

ghokhtal *v.t.* غوتل want

ghokhtal *v.t.* غوتل wish

ghokhtana *n* غوتنه demand

ghokhtana *n* غوتنه desire

ghokhtana *n.* غوتنه wish

ghokhtana *n* غوتنه want

ghokhtana kawal *v. t* غوتنه‌کول demand

ghokhtana; zaray *n.* غوتنه،زار solicitation

ghokhtanleek *n.* غوتلیک application

ghokhtanleek *n.* غوتنیک petition

ghokhtoonkay *a.* غوتونکى wishful

ghokhtoonkay; ghokhtan leek warkawoonkay *n.* غوتونکى؛ غوتن‌لیک‌ورکوونکى applicant

gholam azadawal *v.t.* غلام‌آزادول manumit

gholanza *n.* غولانه udder

gholawal *v. t* غولول beguile

gholawal *v. t.* غولول bilk

gholawal *v. t.* غولول cheat

gholawal *v.t.* غولول swindle

gholawal *v.t.* غولول wheedle

gholawoonkay *a.* غولوونکى sophisticated

gholawoonkay *n.* غولوونکى swindler

gholay *n.* غولى courtyard

gholowona *n.* غولونه lure

ghombar *n* غومبر coo

ghombar kawal *v. i* غومبرکول coo

ghombasa *n.* غومبسه wasp

ghombasi ta warta *a.* غومبسه‌ورته waspish

ghoncha *n* غنچه bud

ghond *n.* غوند brigade

ghond plorana *n.* غوندپلورنه wholesale

ghond ploray *n.* غوندپلورى wholesaler

ghond ploroonkay *a* غوندپلورونکی wholesale

ghonda *n* غونه conference

ghonda *n* غونه delegation

ghondaska *n.* غونسکه ball

ghondawal *v.t.* غونول accumulate

ghondawal; jala kawal *v.t.* غونول، جلاکول pick

ghondawal; tawowal *v.t.* غونول، تاوول furl

ghonday *n.* غوز hill

ghonday *n.* غوز mount

ghondeydal *v. t* غوندل convene

ghondeydal *v.i* غوندل flock

ghondeydana *n* غونیدنه accumulation

ghondla jorawal; saza warkawal *v.t.* غونله‌جوول؛سزاورکول sentence

ghondla poha; da nahwi ilam *n.* غونله‌پوهه،دنحوعلم syntax

ghondla; saza *n.* غونله،سزا sentence

ghonzawal; takhta kawal *v.t* غونول؛تخته‌کول wring

ghopa *n* غوپه dive

ghopa kawal *v. t* غوپه‌کول dip

ghopa kawana *n.* غوپه‌کونه soak

ghopa kawona *n.* غوپه‌کوونه immersion

ghopa wahal *v. i* غوپه‌وهل dive

ghor ghor *n.* غورغور grunt

ghor ghor kawal *v.i.* غورغورکول grunt

ghor kawal *v.t.* غورکول mull

ghor kawal *v.t.* غورکول ponder

ghora malee kawal *v. t* غوه‌مالی کول coax

ghorap ghorap skhal *v.i.* غوپ غوپل sup

ghoravy *n.* غوروی hag

ghoraway *n.* غوراوی choice

ghoraway *n.* غوراوی option

ghoraway *n.* غوراوی pre-eminence

ghoraway *n.* غوراوی preference

ghorchanr shaway keetab *n.* غورچاشوی کتاب breviary

ghoreydal *v.i.* غوریدل snort

ghoreydal *v.i.* غوریدل whimper

ghoreydal *v.i.* غوریدل roar

ghoreydana *n.* غوریدنه roar

ghorzang *n* غورز commotion

ghorzang kawal *v.i.* غورزکول sally

ghorzawal *v.t.* غورول throw

ghorzawana *n* غورونه overthrow

ghorzawana *n.* غوروونه throw

ghorzeydana *n* انحطاط غوریدنه، fall

ghosa *n.* غصه fury

ghosa kawona *n.* کوونه غصه aggravation

ghosawal *v.t.* غوول rip

ghosawana *n* غوونه dissection

ghoswalay *n.* غووالی rift

ghota *n.* غوه knot

ghota kawal *v.t.* غوه‌کول knot

ghota kawal *v.t.* غوه‌کول plunge

ghota kawal *v.t.* غوه‌کول tie

ghota; band *n* غوه،بند tie

ghota; ghopa *n.* غوه؛غوپه dip

ghota; ghopa *n* غوه،غوپه plunge

ghotay *n* غو bloom

ghotay *n* غو blossom

ghotay kawal *v.i.* غوكول bloom

ghotay kawal *v.i* غوكول blossom

ghozh khwaroonkay *a.* غوژ
خوونکی supple

ghrambahar *n.* غمبهار rumble

ghrambar *n* غمبار growl

ghrambeydal *v.i.* غمبدل growl

ghrap *n.* غپ sip

ghreew rawastoonkay *a.* غرو
راوستونکی pathetic

ghreew; hya hoo *n.* غرو،هياهو
hubbub

ghroombeydal *v.i.* غومبدل rumble

ghulam jorawal *v.t.* غلامجوول
enslave

ghuncha *n.* غنچه wisp

ghusa *n.* غصه anger

ghusa *n.* غصه rage

ghusa keydal *v.t.* غصهکدل loathe

ghusa; pa qahar *a.* غصه،پهقهر
angry

ghusanak *a.* غصهناک loath

ghusanak *a.* غصهناک violent

ghusanak keydal *v.i.* غصهناککدل
rage

ghwa *n.* غوا cow

ghwag *n* غو ear

ghwag pakowoonkay *n.* غو
پاکوونکی aurilave

ghwakha *n* غوه flesh

ghwakha *n.* غوه meat

ghwakhan *a.* غون pulpy

ghwakhan keydal *v.t.* غونکدل
pulp

ghwalaval *v.t* غولول gull

ghwand; da hukoomat
wakmanee *n.* غند؛دحکومت
واکمنی regiment

ghwar *a.* غو oily

ghwara *a* غوره better

ghwara *a* غوره select

ghwara aw ala *a* غورهاواعلئ
classic

ghwara aw mumtaz *a.* غورهاوممتاز
superfine

ghwara kawal *v. t.* غورهکول
choose

ghwara kawal *v.t.* غورهکول select

ghwara keydal; ghwara kawal *v.
t* غورهکدل؛غورهکول better

ghwara mal *n.* غوهمال minion

ghwaramalee kawal *v. t.* غوهمالي
کول court

ghwarawal *v.t.* غوول lubricate

ghwarowana *n.* غوونه lubrication

ghwarowoonkay mawad *n.*
غووونکیمواد lubricant

ghwayay *n* غوایی bull

ghwayay *n.* غویی ox

ghwayee sara loba kawoonkay *n*
غویيسرهلوبهکوونکی. matador

glicrine *n.* لیسرین glycerine

gmanz *n* مه comb

godam *n.* ودام storage

godam ki satal *v.t.* ودامکساتل
store

gokha *v.t.* وه isolate

gokha kawal *v. t* وهکول depose

gokha keydal *n* وهکیدل abdication

gol *n* ل flower

gol gopee *n.* لوپی cauliflower

golalay; safa *a* صفا،للای fair
golay *n.* لوگ tablet
gomaral shaway *n.* ﻫﺎرلشوی assignee
gombata; maghara *n.* مغاره،ومبته vault
gomra kawal *v.t.* ﻫﺮاهکول mislead
gond *n* وند faction
gond *n.* وند party
gonda *n.* وﻧﻪ knee
gonda kedal *v.i.* وﻧﻪکیدل kneel
gongosay *n* وﻧﻮسی bruit
gonzi *n.* وﻧﺰ wrinkle
gonzi gonzi *a.* وﻧﻮز slovenly
gonzi kawal *v.t.* وﻧﺰکول wrinkle
gonzi kawana *n.* وﻧﺰکوﻧﻪ shrinkage
gonzi keydal *v.i* وﻧﺰکدل shrink
gonzi warkawal *v.t.* وﻧﻮرکول crimple
gooman aw atkal kawal *v.t.* وﻣﺎن اوﻛﻞکول imagine
gooman kawal *v. t* وﻣﺎنکول conjecture
gooman kawal *v.t.* وﻣﺎنکول assume
gooman; hod *n.* ﻫﻮ؛وﻣﺎن assumption
goombat *n* وﻣﺒﺖ dome
goona *n.* ﻧﺎه misdemeanour
goona *n.* ﻧﺎه sin
goona gar *n.* ﻧﺎﻫﺎر offender
goona kawal *v.t.* ﻧﺎهکول offend
goona kawal *v.i.* ﻧﺎهکول sin
goonagar *a.* ﻧﺎﻫﺎر sinful
goonagar *n.* نهار sinner

goonagar *a.* ﻧﺎﻫﺎر vile
goong *n.* وﻧﮓ owl
goong bayan *n* وﻧﺒﻴﺎن enigma
goonga stoonza *n* وﻧﻪستوﻧﺰه dilemma
goongay *a* وﻧﯽ dumb
goongtob *n.* وﻧﺘﻮب vagueness
goozan wahal *v.t.* وزنوﻫﻞ lame
goozan wahalay *a.* وزنوﻫﻠﯽ lame
goozanr *n.* وز palsy
goozanr *n.* وز paralysis
goozanr wahal *v.t.* وزوﻫﻞ paralyse
goozanr wahalay *a.* وزوﻫﻠﯽ paralytic
goozar kawal; las pri rakakhal *v.t.* وزارکول؛لاسﭘﺮراکل stroke
gopee *n.* وﭘﯽ cabbage
goreela beezo *n.* وریلابﻴﺰو gorilla
gorkhar *n.* ورﺧﺮ zebra
gosha nasheen zahid *n.* وﺷﻪﻧﺸﻴﻦ زاﻫﺪ hermit
gostakh *a.* ستاخ insolent
got nastay keydal *v.i.* وﻧﺎستیکدل retire
gota *n* وﺗﻪ finger
gota pa ghakh *adv.,* وﺗﻪﭘﻪﻏﺎ agape
gota warwral *v.t* وﺗﻪورول finger
gotmeyshtaytob *n.* وﻣﺸﺘﯽﺗﻮب agoraphobia
gotmo *n.* وﺗﻤﻮ thimble
gran *a* ﮔﺮان expensive
gran *a.* ﮔﺮان herculean
gran *a.* ﮔﺮان lovely

grana joreydal; bey payle preykhodal v. t. جوددل;بپايل رانه برودل baffle

grees n ريس grease

grees warkawal v.t ريسوركول grease

grees warkray shaway a. ريس وركى شوى greasy

groha sargandawana n. روهه رنډونه suggestion

gul meykhay n. ل مخ stud

gul ploroonkay n ل پلورونكى florist

gul sang n. ل سن moss

gul sanga n. ل انه nosegay

gulab n. لاب rose

gulabee a لابي pink

gulabee rang n. لابي رن pink

gulabee rang ta mayil a. لابي رنته مايل pinkish

gulalay n لالى dandy

gulalay a. لالى hale

gulalay a. لالى handsome

gulalay a لالى pretty

gulalay insan n لالى انسان smart

guldasta n لدسته bouquet

guldozee n لدوزي embroidery

gulucose n. لوكوز glucose

gulwareen a. لورين rosy

gulwareen; gulwazma a. لورين;بل وزمه roseate

gustakh a. ستاخ petulant

gustakh saray ya khaza n. ستاخ سرى ياه minx

gustakhee n ستاخي flippancy

gustakhee n. ستاخي petulance

---

gut n و corner

gwakhal v.t. واښل threaten

had a. حاد keen

had n. حد extent

had n. حد limit

hadaf n. هدف objective

hadee seem n. هادي سيم lead

hadeera n. هديره necropolis

hadeeya n. هديه offering

hadeeya warkawal v. t هديه وركول donate

hadisa n. حادثه incident

hadisatee a. حادثاتي incidental

hadokeez kawal v.t. هوكيز كول ossify

hadookay n. هوكى bone

hafiza n. حافظه memory

hafiza n. حافظه remembrance

hafizey ta rawastal v. t حافظته راوستل evoke

hagay n ه egg

hagay dawla a. هوله oval

hagha pron. هغه he

hagha dem. pron. هغه that

hagha ameyl chi da karay pa seyr zareygee n هغه امل چد کپهر ي festoon

hagha chi nawara tolaneez wuzeeyat walaree n هغه چناوه ولنيز وضعيت ولري underdog hagha kach; kala chi; saranga chi *adv.* هغه کچ؛کله چ؛رنه چ as

hagha kas chi khwaley kawee; garmowoonkay jakat *n.* هغه کس چ خواکوي؛رموونکي جاک sweater

hagha khaza *pron.* هغه she

hagha khwa deykhwa khozeydal *v.t.* هغه خوادخواخوبدل rock

hagha khwa leyri *prep.* هغه خوالر beyond

hagha khwa ta *adv.* هغه خواته younder

hagha loybadana beezo chi pa wano ki zhwand kawee *n.* هغه لوی بدنه بیزو چپهونو کژوند کوي chimpanzee

haghamasheenchipaharakat kawalotrinabreykhnapayda keygee n حرکت په چ ماشین هغه کي پدا برنا ترینه کولو dynamo

hagha ta *pron.* هغه ته him

hagha yaw rel. *pron.* هغه یو that

hagha zai che weele shavi falz pa qalabo ke achavi *n.* هغه ای چه ویلی شوی فلز په قالبو کي اچوی foundry

haghwee ta *pron.* هغوي ته them

hajoom *n.* هجوم irruption

hakakee kawal *v. t* حکاکي کول engrave

hakeem; darmal jorawoonkay *n.* حکیم؛درمل جووونکی physicist

hakhwa deykhwa harakat kawal *v.i.* هنخوادخواحرکت کول shuffle

hakhwa deykhwa zambeydal *v.i.* هنخوادخوامبدل sway

hakhwa ta *adv.* هنخواته thither

hakim *n* حاکم dictator

hal kaval *v.t* حل کول fathom

hal kawal *v.t* حل کول dissolve

hal kawal *v.t.* حل کول resolve

hal lara *n.* حل لاره solution

hal lara warta moondal *v.t.* حل لارهورته موندل solve

hal; soorat; sarangwalay *n؛* حال؛ صورت؛برنوالی circumstance

halak *n* هلک boy

halaktob *n* هلکتوب boyhood

halat *n.* حالت standing

halat *n.* حالت situation

halat; keyfeeyat *n.* حالت؛کفیت posture

halat; martaba *n.* حالت؛مرتبه status

halat; reeyasat; dawlat *n.* ؛حالت؛ ریاست؛دولت state

halat; shart *n* حالت؛شرط condition

halbee lokhay *n.* حلبي لوی can

haleem *a.* حلیم meek

haleydana *n.* حلدنه solvency

halta *adv.* هلته there

halweeyat *n.* حلویات sweetmeat

ham *adv.* هم too

ham agangee *n.* هم آهني consonance

ham andtob *n.* هم اندتوب unanimity

ham andtob *n.* هم اندتوب sympathy

ham ara *adj* هم آره cognate

ham ghareetob *n.* همغيزتوب
unison

ham khooya *a* همخويه congenial

ham mahala *a* همهاله
contemporary

ham mana *a.* همانا synonymous

ham maneez wayay *n.* هممانيزويى
synonym

ham nooma *n.* همنومه namesake

ham por *n* همپو equal

ham rotba *a.* همرتبه co-ordinate

ham taroonay; zhman *n.* همتونى،
ژمن ally

ham waznee *b.* هموزني rhythm

hamaysha bahar gul *n.* همشهبهار
گل marigold

hamaysha; tar dey chi *adv.*
همشه،تردچ still

hamda shan *adv.* همداشان
likewise

hamda shan; da ranga *a.* همدا
شان،دارنه such

hamda shan; hamda dawl *adv.*
همداشان،همداول also

hamdardee kawal *v. i.* همدردي
کول condole

hamghardi *a.* همغاى harmonious

hamjinsa *a.* همجنسه
homogeneous

hamkar *n* همکار colleague

hamkaree *n* همکاري co-operation

hamkaree *n* همکاري co-ordination

hamkaree kawal *v. i* همکاري کول
co-operate

hamla *n.* حمله invasion

hamla *n.* حمله onset

hamla; da zang ghag *n* حمله،دزنغ غ
stroke

hamsafar *n.* همسفر consort

hangeydal *v. i* هندل bray

haq peyzhandana *n.* حقپژندنه
gratitude

haqarat *n* حقارت contempt

haqdar *a* حقدار eligible

haqdar garzeydal *v. t.* حقدارګرېدل
deserve

haqeeqat *n* حقيقت fact

haqeeqat *n.* حقيقت reality

haqeeqee *a.* حقيقي real

haqeeqee *a.* حقيقي realistic

haqiki *a.* حقيقى intrinsic

haqooqee dawa *n.* حقوقيدعوا plea

haqooqee salakar *n.* حقوقيسلاکار
solicitor

haqul wakala *n.* حقالوکاله
honorarium

har arkheeza manzara *n.* هراخيزه
منظره panorama

har cheyrta *adv.* هرچرته wherever

**har dawl rakakhta keydoonkay
chaparkat ya bistara** *n* هرول
راکته کدونکى چپر کيابستره
bunk

har kal yaw zal *adv.* هرکاليول
yearly

har kalay *n* هرکلى welcome

har kas *pron.* هرکس each

har lori ta *adv.* هرلورته round

har shay; pa hees dawl *n.* هرشى،
پههيول aught

har sok chi; har cha chi *pron.* هر
وک چ؛هرچاچ whoever

har sok; har cha *pron* هروک؛هر
چا all

har wakht; har kala; kala *adv.*
conj هروخت؛هركله؛كله
whenever

har yaw *a* هريو each

har yaw *adv.* هريو either

har yaw *a* هريو every

har yaw *pron* هريو whichever

har zay mawjoodgee *n.* هرای
موجودي omnipresence

har zay ta hazir *a.* هرایته‌حاضر
omnipresent

hara myasht *adv* هره‌مياشت
monthly

hara oonay *n.* هره‌اوونۍ weekly

hara waraz *adv.* هره‌ورځ daily

harakat *n.* حركت motion

harakat *n.* حركت movement

harakat kawal *v.i.* حركت‌كول
motion

harakat warkawal *v.i.* حركت
وركول motor

harakat warkawal *v.i.* حركت
وركول stir

harakat; takan *n.* حركت؛بكان
move

haram *a* حرام taboo

haram ganral *v.t.* حرامل taboo

haran *n.* هارن siren

hararatee *a.* حرارتي thermal

hareef *n.* حريف adversary

hareef; dukhman *n* حريف؛دمن
foe

harees *a.* حريص voracious

harfi nida; dakhalat *n.* حرف‌ندا؛
دخالت interjection

hasa *n.* هه attempt

hasa *n.* هه conation

hasa *n* هه effort

hasa *n* هه try

hasa aw hand *n* هه‌اوهاند diligence

hasa kawal *v.t.* هه‌كول attempt

hasa kawal *v.i.* هه‌كول try

hasakaval *v.i.* هسكول heave

hasand *n* هاند quick

hasas *a* حساس critical

hasas; nazak *a.* حساس؛نازک
sensitive

hasas; nazak *a.* حساس؛نازک
touchy

hasaseeyat *n.* حساسيت sensibility

hasaseeyat larana *n.* حساسيت‌لرنه
allergy

hasawal *v.t.* هول persuade

hasawal; kropawal *v.i.* هول؛
كپول incline

hasawana; tahreek *n.* هوونه؛
تحريک persuasion

hashara khoray mogak *n.* حشره
خوری‌موک shrew

hasheeya *n.* حاشيه margin

hasheeya warkawal *v.t* حاشيه
وركول fringe

hasheeya; charma *n.* حاشيه؛چرمه
fringe

hasheeyawee *a.* حاشيوي marginal

hashra *n.* حشره insect

hashra *n.* حشره moth

hashra wazhoonkay *n.* حشره
وژونكی insecticide

hasil *n.* حاصل output

hasil *n.* حاصل product

hasil *n.* حاصل upshot

hasil warkawoonkay *a.* حاصل ورکوونکی prolific

hasil; jama *n.* حاصل؛جمع total

hask *n* هسک over

hask; jag *a.* هسک؛ج tall

hask; watalay *a.* هسک؛وتلی outstanding

haskawal *v.i.* هسکول tower

hasta *n.* هسته kernel

hastawee *a.* هستوي nuclear

hastee *n* هستی entity

hawa *n* هوا air

hawa meych *n* هوامچ barometer

hawa peyzhand *n.* هواپژاند meteorologist

hawa peyzhandana *n.* هواپژندنه meteorology

hawa rasand *n.* هوارساند ventilator

hawa rasawana *n.* هوارسوونه ventilation

hawa warkawal *v.t.* هواورکول ventilate

hawa zid wasla *a.* هواضدوسله anti-aircraft

hawabazee *n.pl.* هوابازي aeronautics

hawadar star zay *a.* هوادارسترای palatial

hawakash *n.* هواکش؛سومه vent

hawala; rasmee hukam *n.* هواله؛ رسمي حکم warrant

hawar *n.* هوار plain

hawara sata *a.* هواره سطح plane

hawarawal *v. t* هوارول even

hawas *n.* هوس longing

hawas *n.* هوس whim

hawas kawal *v.i.* هوس کول hanker

hawasbaz *a.* هوس باز whimsical

hawayee *a.* هوايي aerial

hawayee *a.* هوايي spatial

hawayee *a.* هوايي airy

hawayee toopan *n.* هوايي توپان tornado

hawayee ya samandaree yoon *n.* هوايي ياسمندري يون voyage

hawayee ya samandaree yoon kawal *v.i.* هوايي ياسمندري يون کول voyage

hawayoon *n.* هوايون aviation

hawayoonee *n.* هوايوني aviator

haweeyat; shakhseeyat *n.* هويت؛ شخصيت personality

hawsala; sabar *n.* حوصله؛صبر toleration

haya *n* حيا modesty

hayanak *a.* حياناک modest

hayatee awakhtoon *n.* حياتي اوتون metabolism

haybatnak *a.* هبتناک horrible

hayjan *n.* هجان sensation

hayjanee *a.* هجاني sensational

hayran *a.* حيران aghast

hayranawal *v.t.* حرانول mystify

hayranawal *v.t.* حرانول perplex

hayranawal *v.t.* حرانول stun

hayranawal *v.t.* حرانول surprise

hayranawal *v.t.* حرانول stupefy

hayranawoonkay *a.* حرانوونکی marvellous

hayranawoonkay *a.* حرانوونکی wonderful

hayranawoonkay *a.* حرانوونکی
wondrous

**hayranawoonkay warzashee
kartab kawal** *v.t.* حرانوونکی
ورزشي کرتب کول stunt

hayranawoonkay; ajeeb *a.*
حرانوونکی،عجیب stupendous

hayraneydal *v.i.* حراندل wonder

hayrantya *n.* حرانتیا surprise

haywad pal *a.* هوادپال patriotic

haywad palana *n.* هوادپالنه
partiotism

haywad wal *n.* هوادوال patriot

haywanee shaoor *n.* حوانيشعور
instinct

haywanee shaoor laroonkay *a.*
حواني‌شعورلرونکی instinctive

hayz *n.* حض menses

hazaf; faskh *n* حذف،فسخ
cancellation

hazafawal *v. t* حذفول delete

hazafawal *v.t.* حذفول omit

hazafawana *n.* حذفونه omission

hazam; mujalla *n.* هضم،مجله
digest

hazima *n* هاضمه digestion

hazir zawabee *n.* حاضروابي
repartee

hazirawal *v.t.* حاضرول manifest

haziree akheystana *n.* حاضري
اخستنه roll-call

haziree; sar *n.* حاضري،بار
attendance

hazireydal; pam kawal *v.t.*
حاضردل؛پام‌کول attend

hazmawal *v. t.* هضمول digest

hazrat eesa alayhissalam *n.*
حضرت‌عیسی‌علیه‌السلام Christ

hazyanee *a.* هذیاني frantic

heefazat kawal *v.t.* حفاظت‌کول
secure

heefazat; masuntya *n.* حفاظت،
مصئونتیا immunity

heela kawal *v. t* هیله‌کول expect

heela laral *v.i* هیله‌لرل long

heela man *a* هیله‌من desirous

heela man; arzoo man *adj.* هیله
من،آرزومن appetent

heela; arzoo *n.* هیله،آرزو ambition

heela; ishteeyaq *n.* هیله،اشتیاق
appetence

heela; tama *n.* هیله،طمع
expectation

heelaman *n.* هیله‌من aspirant

heelaman *adj.* هیله‌من avid

heelaman *a.* هیله‌من hopeful

heelaman *a.* هیله‌من zealous

heelaman; narama *a.* هیله‌من،نارامه
solicitious

heelay *n.* هیل duck

hees *adv.* هی any

hees cheyrta *adv.* هیچرته nowhere

hees yaw *pron.* هییو none

hees; har *a.* هی،هر any

hees; nafee *n* هی،نفي no

heesab *n.* حساب account

heesab beyrta warkawal *v.t.*
حساب‌برته‌ورکول refund

heesab speenawal *v.t.* حساب
سپینول recompense

heesabawal *v. t.* حسابول
enumerate

heeskala *adv.* هيكله nothing

heeskala *adv.* هيكله none

heeskala; hees wakht *adv.* هيكله، هيوخت never

heesok *pron.* هيوک nobody

heyl *n.* هل cardamom

heyranawal *v.t.* حرانول astonish

heyranawal *v. t* حرانول daze

heyranawal *v.t.* حرانول amaze

heyranawoonkay *n.* حرانوونکی marvel

heyranawoonkay *a.* حرانوونکی phenomenal

heyraneydal *v.i* حراندل marvel

heyrantya *n.* حرانتيا amazement

heyrantya *n.* حرانتيا astonishment

heyrantya *n* حرانتيا daze

heyrawal *v.t* هرول forget

heyrawana *n.* هروونه oblivion

heywad *n.* هواد country

heywan *n* حيوان beast

heywan dawla *a* حيوان‌وله beastly

hifazat ki satal *v.t.* حفاظت‌کساتل ward

hija; sapa *n.* هجا،په syllable

hijayee; da yawey sapey astazay *n.* هجايي،ديوهاستازی syllabic

hijoleekoonkay *n.* هجوليکونکی satirist

hilzonee sadaf *n.* حلزوني‌صدف conch

himaqat *n.* حماقت infatuation

himaqat kawal *v.t.* حماقت‌کول infatuate

himat kawal *v. i.* همت‌کول dare

hindee imlee *n.* هندي‌املي tamarind

hindee; hindoostanee *a.* هندي، هندوستاني Indian

hindsee mumayish *n.* هندسي‌نمايش graph

hindsee zay *n.* هندسي‌ای locus

hindsi *a.* هندسی geometrical

hindwana *n.* هندوانه melon

hindwanra *n.* هندواله water-melon

hiras *n.* حرص avarice

hiras *adv.* حرص avidity

hiras *n.* حرص greed

hirasee *a.* حرصي greedy

his *n.* حس sense

hisabawal; tareekh maloomawal *v. t* حسابول،تاريخ‌معلومول date

hisabdaree *n.* حسابداري accountancy

hisar *n.* حصار enclosure

hisar; khoona *n.* حصار، خونه ward

ho; aw *adv.* هو،او yes

hod *n.* هو intent

hod laral *v.t.* هولرل purpose

hojam *n* حجم bulk

hokam chalawal *v. t* حکم‌چلول dictate

hokam; hakimeeyat *n* حکم، حاکميت dictation

honar *n* هنر craft

honar *n.* هنر forte

honar mand *n* هنرمند craftsman

honaree *a.* هنري artistic

honaree lasleek *n.* هنري‌لاسليک monograph

honarmand *n.* هنرمند artist

hookhyar *a.* هوښيار clever

hookhyar *a.* هوښيار intelligent

hookhyar *a.* هوشيار sagacious
hookhyar *a.* هوشيار sage
hookoomat kawal *v.t.* حکومت کول rule
hoora *n.* حوره sylph
hujam; miqdar; tolga; jild *n.* حجم،مقدار،بوله،جلد volume
hujra *n.* هجره forum
hukam *n.* حکم ordinance
hukam *n.* حکم ruling
hukam *n.* حکم precept
hukam; sanad *n.* حکم،سند writ
hukamranee *n.* حکمراني governance
hukamranee kawal *v.t.* حکمراني کول govern
hukoomat *n.* حکومت government
hukoomat kawal *v.i.* حکومت کول reign
hukoomatee nizam *n.* حکومتي نظام regime
hunar *n.* هنر skill

I

ibadat *n* عبادت cult
ibadat *n.* عبادت worship
ibadat kawal *v.t.* عبادت کول worship
ibadat kawoonkay *n.* عبادت کوونکی worshipper
ibadat zay *n.* عبادتای temple
ibadatee *a.* عبادتي liturgical
ibadatzay *n.* عبادتای sanctuary

ibarat *n* عبارت clause
ibarat karawana; kalma bandee *n.* عبارت کاروونه،کلمهبندي phraseology
ibarat; matan *n.* عبارت،متن text
ibham *n.* ابهام obscurity
ibham wayal *v.i.* ابهام ويل quibble
ibham; goongtob *n.* ابهام،ونتوب ambiguity
ibtidayee *a.* ابتدايي preliminary
ibtidayee *a.* ابتدايي preparatory
ibtidayee *a.* ابتدايي primary
ibtidayee *a* ابتدائي elementary
ida kawal *v.t.* ادعا کول affirm
idama *n.* ادامه resume
idama darawal *v.* ادامهدرول discontinue
idama laral *v.i.* ادامهلرل last
idama warkawal *v.t.* ادامهورکول maintain
idama warkawal; khwandee satal *v.t.* ادامهورکول،خوندي ساتل sustain
idara *n.* اداره administration
idara *n.* اداره organization
idara kawal *v.t.* اداره کول administer
idara kawal; pa so ghwandoono weyshal *v.t.* اداره کول،پهوغنونو وشل regiment
idara kawoonkay *n.* اداره کوونکی operator
idaree *a.* اداري administrative
idaree charwakay *n* اداري چارواکی official
idaree charwakay *n.* اداري چارواکی rum

idaree mamoor *n* اداري،مأمور bureaucrat

idaree sanga *n* اداريخانه department

idaree taseesat *n.* اداري،تأسيسات Bureaucuracy

idaree; masoolee *a.* اداري،مسؤولي officious

idrak *n* ادراك conception

idrak *n.* ادراك sentience

idrak *n.* ادراك realization

idrakee *a.* ادراكي perceptive

idrakee *a.* ادراكي sentient

iftikhar ta raseydana *n* افتخارته رسدنه accession

iftikharee; rasmee *a.* افتخاري، رسمي titular

ihanat *n.* اهانت insolence

ihata kawal *v. t* احاطه،كول encompass

ihata kawal *v.t.* احاطه،كول surround

ihda *n* اهداء grant

ijara kaonke *n.* اجاره،كوونكی lessee

ijaza warkawal *v.t.* اجازه،وركول allow

ijra kawal *v. t.* اجراكول enforce

ijra kawal *v.t.* اجراكول perform

ijra kawoonkay *n.* اجراكوونكی performer

ijraywee charwakay *n.* اجرايوي چارواكی sergeant

ijtinab *n* اجتناب refrain

ijtinab kawal *v.i.* اجتناب،كول refrain

ikhlaqee keesa *n* اخلاقي كيسه apologue

ikhlas *n* اخلاص devotion

ikhrajawal *v. t.* اخراجول expel

ikhtilaf *n.* اختلاف conflict

ikhtilaf *n* اختلاف discord

ikhtilaf laral *v. i* اختلاف،لرل disagree

ikhtilaf peyda keydal *v. i* اختلاف پداكدل conflict

ikhtilaf; tawpeer *n.* اختلاف،توپیر variance

ikhtira *n.* اختراع concoction

ikhtira kawal *v. t* اختراع،كول concoct

ikhtira kawal *v. t* اختراع،كول devise

ikhtira kawal *v.t.* اختراع،كول invent

ikhtiraee *a.* اختراعي inventive

ikhtisas *n.* اختصاص specialization

ikhtisasee; malkeeyatee *a.* اختصاصي،ملكيتي proprietary

ikhtyar *n.* اختيار liberty

ikhtyaree *a.* اختياري optional

iktibas kawal *v. t* اقتباس،كول extract

iktishaf *n* اكتشاف exploration

iktishafee safar kawal *v.t* اكتشافي سفركول explore

ilaha *n.* الهه goddess

ilahee; khuday *n* الهي،خداى divinity

ilaj *n.* علاج remedy

ilaqa *n.* علاقه county

ilham *n.* الهام oracle

ilhamee *a.* الهامي oracular

iltihab; sozeydanə *n.* التهاب؛سوبلدنه inflammation

iltihabee *a.* التهابي inflammatory

iltihabee parsob *n* التهابي؛پسوب blain

iltimas kawal; murajia kawal *v.t.* التماس كول؛مراجعه كول appeal

iltimas; zaree *n.* التماس؛زاري appeal

ilzam lagawal; adaa kawal *v.t.* الزام لول،ادعا كول allege

ilzam; adaa *n.* الزام؛ادعا allegation

imala; tazreeq *n.* اماله؛تزريق injection

imteeyazee *a.* امتيازي preferential

imtihan akheystal *v. t* امتحان اخستل examine

imtihan akheystoonkay *n* امتحان اخستوونكی examiner

imtihan warkowoonkay *n* امتحان وركوونكی examinee

imtihan; azmoyana *n* امتحان، آزموينه test

imza kawal *v. t.* امضا كول countersign

infijaree *a* انفجاري explosive

infiradee *a.* انفرادي sporadic

inglastan ki tar shahzada landi laqab *n* انلستان كتر شاهزاده لاند لقب duke

inhidam *n.* انهدام subversion

inhiraf *n* انحراف lapse

inhisar laral *v. i.* انحصارلرل depend

inhisar laroonkay *n* انحصارلرونكی dependant

inhisaree eemteeyaz akheystal *v.t.* انحصاري امتيازاخستل monopolize

inhisaree haq warkawal *v.t.* انحصاري حق ور كول patent

inhitat; kamzortya *n* انحطاط، كمزورتيا wane

inikas *n.* انعكاس reflection

inikas *n.* انعكاس reflex

inikasee *a.* انعكاسي reflective

injeel *n* انجيل bible

injeel *n.* انجيل gospel

injeel *n.* انجيل testament

inkar *v.t.* انكار gainsay

inkar *n* انكار abnegation

inkar *n.* انكار repudiation

inkar kawal *v. t* انكار كول abnegate

inkar kawal *v. t.* انكار كول deny

inkar kawal *v.t.* انكار كول renounce

inkar kawal *v.t.* انكار كول repudiate

inqilabee *a.* انقلابي revolutionary

inqilabee wagaray *n* revolutionary

insan *n.* انسان man

insan pal *n.* انسان پال philanthropist

insan pala *a.* انسان پاله philanthropic

insanawal; saray kawal *v.t.* انسانول؛سی كول humanize

insanee *a.* انساني human

insanee *a.* انساني manlike

insanee ghag n. انساني غ voice

insanee nizhad n. انساني نژاد mankind

intikhab n. انتخاب selection

intikhabatee hoza n انتخاباتي حوزه constituency

intikhabawal v. t انتخابول constitute

intikhabee a. انتخابي selective

intikhabee plaway n انتخابي پلاوی electorate

intiqad n انتقاد criticism

intiqal keydoonkay a. انتقال کدونکی transferable

intiqal; badloon n. انتقال؛بدلون transition

intishar; tableegh n. انتشار؛تبليغ propagation

intizam kawal v.t. انتظام کول manage

intizar n. انتظار wait

intizar eestal v.i. انتظار ايستل wait

intizar eystal v.t. انتظار استل await

inzimam; zameema kawana n انضمام؛ضميمه کونه annexation

iqama; yawa zangaray wuzeeyat n. اقامه؛يو ماني وضعيت pose

iqrar n اقرار confession

iqrar kawal v. t. اقرار کول confess

iqrarawal v.t. اقرارول admit

iqtibas; bayan n. اقتباس؛بيان quotation

iqtisad n اقتصاد economy

iqtisad pohana n. اقتصاد پوهنه economics

iqtisadee a اقتصادي economic

iqtisadee parsob n. اقتصادي پسوب inflation

irada kawal v.t. اراده کول intend

irada; nyat n اراده؛نيت animus

iradee a ارادي deliberate

irtiash v.i. ارتعاش shiver

irtibat n. ارتباط correlation

irtibat laral v.t. ارتباطلرل associate

irtibat laral v.t. ارتباطلرل relate

irtibat warkawal v.t. ارتباطورکول correlate

irtibat; nisbat n. ارتباط؛نسبت relation

isam; noom n. اسم؛نوم noun

ishal n اسهال diarrhoea

ishara n. اشاره gesture

ishara n. اشاره hint

ishara kawal v.i اشاره کول hint

ishara kawoonkay a. اشاره کوونکی indicative

ishara kawoonkay n. اشاره کوونکی indicator

ishara warkawal v.t. اشاره ورکول beckon

ishara; khabartya n. اشاره؛خبرتيا intimation

ishara; peywand n. اشاره؛پوند slur

ishqeeya; jinsee a عشقيه؛جنسي erotic

ishtiba kawal v.i. اشتباه کول fumble

isla n. اصلاح reformation

isla n. اصلاح modification

isla kawal v.t. اصلاح کول modify

isla kawal v.t. اصلاح کول restore

isla kawal *v.t.* اصلاح کول revise
isla kawal *v.i.* اصلاح کول rectify
isla kawoonkay *n.* اصلاح کوونکی
reformatory
isla kawoonkay *a* اصلاح کوونکی
reformatory
isla; naway nazar *n.* اصلاح؛نوی
نظر revision
isla; samowoonkay *n.* اصلاح؛
سموونکی rectification
israf *n* اسراف extravagance
israf kawal *v.t.* اسراف کول lavish
israf kawoonkay *a* اسراف کوونکی
extravagant
israfee *a.* اسرافي lavish
israr *n.* اصرار insistence
israr *n.* اصرار persistence
israr kawal *v.i.* اصرار کول haggle
israr kawal *v.t.* اصرار کول insist
israr kawal *v.i.* اصرار کول persist
israr kawoonkay *a.* اصرار کوونکی
insistent
israr kawoonkay shakhs *n.* اصرار
کوونکی شخص stickler
isteyhsalee *adj.* استحصالي
corrosive
istiara *n.* استعاره metaphor
istifa *n.* استعفا resignation
istifada *n* استفاده gain
istikhbarat *n.* استخبارات
intelligence
istikhdamawal *v. t* استخدامول
engage
istikhdamowoonkay *n*
استخداموونکی employer
istimal *n.* استعمال use

istimbat *n.* استنباط inference
istiqamat laral *v.i.* استقامت لرل
persevere
istiqbal kawal *v.t* استقبال کول
welcome
istirahat *n.* استراحت repose
istirahat kawal *v.i.* استراحت کول
repose
istisna *n* استثناء exception
itaat *n.* اطاعت obedience
itaat *n.* اطاعت subordination
itaat *n.* اطاعت subjection
itaat *n.* اطاعت subjugation
itaat kawal *v.t.* اطاعت کول
subordinate
itaat kawoonkay *n* اطاعت کوونکی
subordinate
italat *n.* عطالت inertia
itehadeeya *n.* اتحادیه league
itifaqan *adv.* اتفاقا occasionally
itifaqee *a.* اتفاقي occasional
itihadeeya *n.* اتحادیه union
itisal *n.* اتصال juncture
itmaynan *n.* اطمینان surety
itminan *n* اطمینان confidence
izafee *a* اضافي extra
izafee *a* اضافي spare
izafee *a.* اضافي superfluous
izafee *a.* اضافي supplementary
izafee *a.* اضافي additional
izafee *adj* اضافي adscititious
izafee kar *n* اضافي کار overtime
izafee kar kawal *v.i.* اضافي کار کول
overwork
izafee maleeya *n.* اضافي مالیه
surcharge

izafee maleeya lagawal *v.t.* اضافي ماليهلول surcharge

izhar *n.* اظهار expression

iztirab *n* اضطراب distress

iztirab *n* اضطراب unrest

iztirab *n.* اضطراب panic

J

jaba *n* جبه bog

jaba *n* جعبه cist

jaba ki doobeydal *v.i* جبهكوبدل bog

jadoo *n.* جادو witchcraft

jadoo *n.* جادو witchery

jadoo kawal *v.t* جادوكول bewitch

jadooyee *a.* جادويي magical

jadwalee *a.* جدولي tabular

jag awaza zang *n.* جآوازهزن gong

jagara *n.* جه warfare

jagara kawal *v.t.* جهكول wage

jagara pal *a.* جهپال warlike

jageerdarana *a.* جايردارانه manorial

jagh *n.* جغ yoke

jagra *n* جه combat1

jagra kawoonkay *n* جهكوونكى belligerent

jagra mar *n* جهمار combatant1

jagra mar *a.* جهمار militant

jagra maree *a.* جهمارى combatant

jagra maree *n* جهمارى militant

jagramaree *n* جهماري belligerency

jagran *n* جن major

jagrawoo *a* جاوو bellicose

jagrayeez; jagrawoo *a* جهييز؛جاوو belligerent

jagtooran; mashar *n.* جتورن؛مشر captain

jahalat *n.* جهالت nescience

jahayz *n* جهز dowry

jahayz *n. pl* جهز paraphernalia

jai *n.* ز hemisphere

jajoora *n.* ججوره craw

jaka *n.* جكه jerk

jakat *n.* جاكت jacket

jakat dawla kamees *n* جاكوله كميس blouse

jal *n.* جال net

jal *n.* جال network

jal ghorawal *v.t.* جالغوول net

jal kari *n* جعلكارى forgery

jal saz *n.* جعلساز counterfeiter

jal ta warta *a.* جالتهورته webby

jal; looma *n.* جال؛لومه mesh

jal; tanasta *n.* جال؛تنسته web

jala kawal *v. t* جلاكول divide

jala kawal *v.t.* جلاكول insulate

jala kawal *v.t.* جلاكول seclude

jala kawal *v.t.* جلاكول separate

jala kawal *v.t.* جلاكول sequester

jala kawal *n.* جلاكوونه severance

jala kawana *n.* جلاكوونه pick

jala kawoonkay *n.* جلاكوونكى insulator

jala keydal *v. i.* جلاكدل depart

jala keydana *n* جلاكدنه departure

jala keydoonkay *a.* جلاكدونكى separable

jala shaway *a.* جلاشوى secluded
jala shaway *a.* جلاشوى separate
jalad; tameelawoonkay *n.* جلاد،
تعميلوونکى executioner
jalatob *n.* جلاتوب seclusion
jalatob *n.* جلاتوب segregation
jalatob *n.* جلاتوب separation
jalawatan kawal *v. t* جلاوطن کول
exile
jalawatnee *n.* جلاوطني exile
jalib *a.* جالب interested
jalibeeyat *n.* جالبيت interest
jalwa warkawal *v.t* جلوه ورکول
foil
jam *n.* جام goblet
jama *a.* جمع plural
jama kawal *v.t.* جمع کول total
jama kawal *v.t.* جمع کول sum
jamadar *n* جمعدار foreman
jamay *a* جامع overall
jamay *n.* جامع precise
jamhooree *a* جمهوري democratic
jamhooree *n.* جمهوري republic
jami *n.* جام clothes
jami *n* جام dress
jami aghostal *v. t* جاماغوستل
clothe
jami aghostal *v. t* جاماغوستل dress
jamid *a.* جامد solid
jamieeyat *n.* جامعيت universality
janab *n* جناب excellency
janat *n.* جنت heaven
janat *n.* جنت paradise
janayat *n* جنايت crime
janayat kar *n* جنايت کار criminal

janayatkar; bey nazma *a.*
جنايتکار، بنظمه wanton
janayee *a* جنايي criminal
janeen *n* جنين embryo
jang *n* جنگ battle
jang *n.* جنگ war
jangay; tar zangoonano land
patloon *n. pl.* جانى،ترزنونانو لنډ
پتلون shorts
jangee *a.* جنگي martial
jangee beyray *n* جنگي بيړ fleet
jangee chal *n.* جنگي چال strategem
jangee krachay *n* جنگي کراچ chariot
jangeydal *v. i.* جنډل battle
jangeydal *v. t.* جنډل combat
jangeydal *v.i.* جنډل militate
jangeydal *v.i.* جنډل war
jangyalay *n.* جنيالى warrior
janjal *n* جنجال affray
janjal *n* جنجال botheration
janjal joreydal; tasadum kawal
v.t. جنجال جوډل،تصادم کول rush
janjal kawal *v.i.* جنجال کول
quarrel
janjal; hasa aw hand *n.* جنجال،هه
او هاند strife
janjalee *a.* جنجالي quarrelsome
jar wahal *v. t* جاروهل blare
jarahee *n.* جراحي surgery
jaraseem *n.* جراثيم germ
jaraseem *n.* جراثيم leech
jaraseem *n.* جراثيم parasite
jaraseem wazhoonkay *n.* جراثيم
وژونکى germicide
jarchee; aylchee *n.* جارچي،المجي
herald

jaree *a* جاري continuous

jaree *n.* جاري instant

jaree *a.* جاري affluent

jareeda *n.* جريده journal

jareema *n* جريمه fine

jareema *n.* جريمه penalty

jareema kawal *v.t* جريمه‌كول fine

jareema kawal *v.t.* جريمه‌كول penalize

jareema warkawal *v.t* جريمه وركول forfeit

jarga *n.* جرهه assembly

jaroo *n* جارو broom

jaryan *n* جريان circulation

jaryan *n.* جريان progress

jaryan laral *v.i.* جريان‌لرل progress

jashan *n.* جشن ceremony

jashn *n* جشن carnival

jasoor *adj.* جسور hardy

jasoos *n* جاسوس emissary

jawahirat ploranzay *n.* جواهرات پلورنۍ jewellery

jaydad *n* جايداد estate

jaydad *n.* جايداد property

jazam *n.* جذام leprosy

jazamee *n.* جذامي leper

jazamee *a.* جذامي leprous

jazayee *a.* جزايي penal

jazba *n* جذبه emotion

jazba *n.* جذبه passion

jazba; bey hokhee *n.* جذبه؛بهوي trance

jazbatee *a* جذباتي emotional

jazbatee *a.* جذباتي passionate

jazbawal *v.t* جذبول absorb

jazbawal *v. t* جذبول devour

jazbawal; gharqawal *v.t.* جذبول؛ غرقول immerse

jeel *n.* جيل lake

jeereb *n.* جريب acre

jeerebana *n.* جريبانه acreage

jeyb *n.* جب pocket

jeyb ki eekhodal *v.t.* جب كايو دل pocket

jibran *n* جبران compensation

jibranawal *v.t* جبرانول compensate

jibranawal *v.t.* جبرانول recoup

jilogeeree *n.* جلويري repression

jins; qisam *n.* جنس؛قسم sort

jins; shahwat *n.* جنس؛شهوت sex

jinsee kamzortya *n.* جنسي كمزورتيا impotence

jisam warkawal *v. t.* جسم وركول embody

jisman; yaw zay *adv.* جسم؛يواى bodily

jismee twan *n.* جسمي‌توان fortitude

jogha *n* جوغه aigrette

jola; obdoonkay *n.* جولا؛اوبدونكى weaver

jongara *a.* جونه shanty

joodar; tor ghanam *n.* جودر؛تور غنم rye

jooma *n.* جمعه Friday

joomat *n.* جومات mosque

joowar *n.* جوار maize

joowaray *n* جوارى corn

jor *n* جوړ make

jor jaray *n.* جوړجاى accord

jor jaray *n.* جوړجاى harmony

jor jaray kawal *v.i.* جوجای‌کول tamper

jor jaray kawoonkay *n.* جوجای کوونکی negotiator

jor jaree *n.* جوجای assent

jor jaree kawal *v.i.* جوجای‌کول assent

jora *n* جوه couple

jora *n* جوه mate

jora *n.* جوه pair

jora *n.* جوه mediation

jora kawal *v. t* جوه‌کول couple

jora kawal *v.t.* جوه‌کول mate

jora kawal *v.i.* جوه‌کول mediate

jora keydal *v.t.* جوه‌کدل pair

jora; ghbargolay *n.* جوه‌،غبرولی twin

jora; naqlee *a* جوه‌،نقلي duplicate

jorabey *n.* جوراب sock

jorakht *n* جوت build

jorakht *n* جوت formation

jorakht *n.* جوت structure

jorakht aw tarkeeb *n.* جوت‌او ترکیب norm

jorakhtaneez *a.* جوتیز structural

jorat; himat *n.* جرأت‌،همت daring

jorawal *v. t.* جوول construct

jorawal *v.t.* جوول make

jorawal; wadanawal *v.t* جوول، ودانول set

jorawana; sakht *n* جوونه‌،ساخت fabrication

jorjaray; astogna *n.* جوجای‌،استونه settlement

jorowoonkay *n.* جووونکی maker

josh *n* جوش boil

josh aw kharosh *n* جوش‌او‌خروش enthusiasm

josh aw kharosh *n.* جوش‌او‌شوق verve

joshawoonkay *n* جوشوونکی boiler

judagana *n.* جداانه aside

juft; jora *a* جفت‌،جوه even

juram *n.* جرم guilt

juram *n.* جرم offence

juz *n* جز portion

juz; wasayil *n* جز‌،وسایل appurtenance

juzee *n.* جزیي nuance

juzyee jagara *n.* جزیي‌جه skirmish

juzyee rang *n.* جزیي‌رنگ tinge

juzyee rang warkawal *v.t.* جزیي‌رنگ ورکول tinge

K

ka kor khaza *n.* دکوره matron

ka sa ham *conj.* کهه‌هم albeit

ka sa ham *conj* کهه‌هم however

ka sa ham *conj.* کهه‌هم nevertheless

ka sa ham *conj.* کهه‌هم notwithstanding

ka sa ham *adv.* کهه‌هم though

ka sa ham *conj.* کهه‌هم although

ka sa ham *conj.* کهه‌هم whereas

ka; ay kash *conj.* که‌،ای کاش if

kab *n* کب fish

kab neewal *v.i* کب‌نیول fish

kab neewoonkay *n* کب نیوونکی fisherman

kabar *n.* کبر pride

kabar kawal *v.t.* کبر کول pride

kabarjan *a.* کبرجن arrogant

kabarjan *a.* کبرجن haughty

kabarjan; adee *v* کبرجن؛عادي snobbish

kach; miqdar *n* کچ؛مقدار amount

kach; miqdar *n.* کچ؛مقدار quantum

kach; miqyas *n* کچ؛مقیاس criterion

kachar *n.* کچر mule

kada kawal *v. i* که کول decamp

kada kawal *v.i.* که کول migrate

kadar kawal; daghee kawal *v.t.* کدرکول؛داغي کول tarnish

kadoo *n.* کدو pumpkin

kadwal *n.* کوال immigrant

kadwal *n.* کوال migrant

kadwalee *n.* کوالي migration

kadwaltob *n.* کوالتوب immigration

kafan waraghostal *v.t.* کفن وراغوستل shroud

kafan; pokh *n.* کفن؛پو shroud

kafara *n.* کفاره atonement

kafara warkawal *v.i.* کفاره ورکول atone

kafee *a* کافي enough

kafee keydal *v.i.* کافي کدل suffice

kafee; poora *a.* کافي؛پوره sufficient

kafoor *n.* کافور camphor

kaga karkha *n* که کره slant

kagal; lookha *n.* کال؛لوخه thatch

kagawana *n* کونه stoop

kageydal *v.i.* کدل stoop

kageydal *v.i.* کدل tilt

kageydal; kagawal *v. t* کدل؛کول bend

kagh kagh kawal *v. i.* کاغ کاغ کول caw

kaghaz *n.* کاغذ paper

kaghaz bad *n.* کاغذباد kite

kagleych *n.* کلچ labyrinth

kagleych laroonkay *a.* کلچلرونکی tortuous

kahil *a.* کاهل indolent

kahil *n.* کاهل slothful

kahilee *n.* کاهلي sloth

kahintob; mulatob *n.* کاهنتوب، ملاتوب priesthood

kahkashan *n.* کهکشان galaxy

kajawa *n.* کجاوه sedan

kajeer *n.* کجیر vulture

kajoora *n.* کجوره palm

kakar *a.* کک infectious

kakar *a.* کک nasty

kakarawal *v.t.* ککول infect

kakarawal *v.i* ککول mess

kakarawal *v.t.* ککول muddle

kakari wahal *v. i* ککوهل cackle

kakartya *n.* ککتیا infection

kakhtay *a* کتی downward

kakhtay *n* کت ark

kakhtay *n.* کت ship

kakhtay chalawal *v.i* کتچلول boat

kakhtay chalawal *v.i.* کتچلول navigate

kakhtay chalawoonkay *n.* كه
چلوونكى sailor
kakhtay ki tlal *v.i.* كتكتلل sail
kal *n.* كال year
kala *n.* كلا castle
kala *n.* كلا fort
kala chi *conj.* كله چ when
kala chi *conj.* كله چ whereat
kala chi *conj.* كله چ while
kala chi *adv.* كلهچي then
kala na kala *adv.* كلهناكله
sometime
kalanay *a.* كلنى annual
kalanay *a.* كلنى yearly
kalanay moash *n.* كلنىمعاش
annuity
kalang; zanra *n* كلنگ;زاله crane
kalay *n.* كلى village
kalbad peyzhandana *n.* كالبد
پژندنه anatomy
kalbad; jorakht *n.* كالبد;جوت
skeleton
kalee *n* كالي clothing
kalee *n.* كالي garb
kalee *n.* كلي key
kalee aw saman *n.* كالياوسامان
belongings
kalee weenzoonki khaza *n.* كالي
وينونكه laundress
kalee; marham *n* كالي;مرهم
dressing
kaleesa *n.* كليسا church
**kaleesha aw feelam
barabarawal** *v.t.* كليشهاوفيلم
برابرول stereotype

**kaleesha; da kaleeshey jorawani
fan** *n.* كليشه;دكليشهجوروفن
stereotype
kaleewal *n.* كليوال peasant
kaleewal *a.* كليوال rural
kaleewal *n.* كليوال villager
kaleewal saray *n* كليوالسى rustic
kaleewal zhwand kawal *v.t.*
كليوالژوندكول rusticate
kaleewala khooy *n.* كليوالهخوى
peasantry
kaleewalee banra warkawana *n.*
كليوالىبهوركوونه rustication
kaleewalee kor *n.* كليوالىكور villa
kaleeza *n.* كليزه almanac
kaleeza; har kal *n.* كليزه;هركال
anniversary
kalhindara *n.* كالهنداره calendar
kali pa aghostal *v.t* كالىپهاغوستل
garb
kalma bandee kawal *v.t.* كلمه
بنديكول phrase
kaltoor *n* كلتور culture
kam *a.* كم lesser
kam arzakhta *a* كمارزته
economical
kam arzakhta seez *n.* كمارزتهيز
trifle
kam asal *a.* كماصل ignoble
kam asla *a* كماصله bastard
kam kharsa *a.* كمخره inexpensive
kam khorakee *n.* كمخوراكي
malnutrition
kam na kam had *a* كمنهكمحد
minimum
kam oomra *n* كمعمره young

kam ratlana *n.* کمراتلنه shortcoming

kam; lag *a.* کم،لګ minor

kam; naseez *a.* کم،نایز slight

kamakht *n* کمت dearth

kamakht *n* کمت decrease

kamakht *n.* کمت lack

kamakht *n.* کمت shortage

kamakht *n.* کمت rabate

kamakht *n.* کمت mitigation

kamakht; sapma *n.* کمت،سپما retrenchment

kaman *n.* کمان arch

kaman *n* کمان bow

kamanee lara *n* کمانۍلاره arcade

kamar band *n* کمربند belt

kamarband taral *v.t* کمربندتل girdle

kamawal *v.t.* کمول assuage

kamawal *v. t* کمول decrease

kamawal *v. t* کمول dwindle

kamawal *v. i* کمول ebb

kamawal *v.t.* کمول lack

kamawal *v.t* کمول lessen

kamawal *v.t.* کمول reduce

kamawl *v.t.* کمول deduct

kamay *n.* کمۍ reduction

kamedonkay *a* کمیدونکی flexible

kameen warta neewal *n.* کمین ورتهنیول ambush

kameenatob *n.* کمینهتوب meanness

kamees *n.* کمیس shirt

kamees landi aghostal keydoonkay khazeena laman *n.* کمیسلاندۍاغوستل کدونکینهلمن petticoat

kameydana *n* کمدنه ebb

kamil *a.* کامل full

kamil *a* کامل utter

kamil; mukamal *a.* کامل،مکمل implicit

kamila khwakhee *n* کاملهخوي bliss

kamila mati *n* کاملهمات rout

kamilan *adv* کاملا downright

kamilan *adv.* کاملا utterly

kamilan *adv.* کاملا wholly

kamilan roond *n.* کاملاوند purblind

kamilan; hamda ranga *adv* کاملا؛ همدارنه even

kamooneezam *n* کمونیزم communism

kamtar *a.* کمتر inferior

kamtaree *n.* کمتري inferiority

kamyab *a.* کمیاب scarce

kamyab *a.* کامیاب well-to-do

kamyabay lapara sakht intizar kawal *v. t* کامیابلپارهسختانتظار کول bide

kamyabee *n* کامیابي win

kamyabeydal *v.i.* کامیابدل prosper

kamyabeydal *v.t.* کامیابدل win

kamzoray *a* کمزوری feeble

kamzoray *v.t.* کمزوریکول handicap

kamzoray *a.* کمزوری weak

kamzoray *n.* کمزوری weakling

kamzoray aw teet awaz *n.* كمزورىاويـآواز undertone

kamzoray insan *a.* كمزورىانسان sickly

kamzoray keydal *v.i* كمزورىكدل faint

kamzoray keydal *v.i.* كمزورىكدل wane

kamzoray; bey zra *a* كمزورى؛بزه faint

kamzoree *n.* كمزورﻯ weakness

kamzortia *n.* كمزورتيا incapacity

kamzortya *n* كمزورتيا debility

kamzortya *n.* كمزورتيا sickness

kamzortya *n.* كمزورتيا swoon

kan keendoonkay *n.* كانكيندونكى miner

kan peyzhandana *n.* كانپژندنه mineralogy

kan peyzhandoonkay *n.* كان پژندونكى mineralogist

kan; madan *n* كان،معدن mine

kanastal *v.t.* كنستل dig

kanaya; hikayat *n.* كنايه،حكايت allegory

kanda *n.* كنده cavity

kanda *n* كنده ditch

kanda *n.* كنده pit

kanda *n.* كنده moat

kanda keendal *v.t.* كندهكيندل moat

kandak *n* كنک battalion

kanee dabar *n.* كانيبر mineral

kanee dabara *n.* كانيبره ore

kanee kheekha *n.* كانيـيه mica

kanee; madanee *a* كاني،معدني mineral

kanfarans *n.* كانفرانس convention

kangal keydal *v.i.* كنلكدل freeze

kangi *n* كاﻧﮔ vomit

kangi kawal *v.t.* كاﻧﮔكول vomit

kanjkaw; daqeeq *a* كنجكاو،دقيق curious

kanjoos *n.* كنجوس miser

kanray *n.* كانى rock

kanree dabari raistal *v.i.* كانيبر راالستل quarry

kanzal kawal *v.t.* كنلكول scold

kar *n.* كار function

kar *n.* كار work

kar akheestana *n.* كاراخيستنه usage

kar bandeyz kawal; weeshtal *v.t.* كاربنلزكول؛ويشتل strike

kar kawal *v.i* كاركول function

kar kawal *v.t.* كاركول work

kar poh *n* كارپوه expert

kar ta hasawal *v. t* كارتههول employ

kar; chara *n.* كار،چاره task

kara *a* كره exact

kara katana *n.* كرهكتنه perusal

kara katana *n.* كرهكتنه scrutiny

kara katana kawal *v.t.* كرهكتنه كول scrutinize

karakht *a.* كرخت obtuse

karal *v. t* كرل cultivate

karal; nyalawal *v.t.* كرل؛نيالول plant

karana *n* كرنه agriculture

karaneez *a* كرنيز agricultural

karaneeza zmaka *adj* کرنیزهمکه arable

karanpohana *n.* کرنپوهنه agronomy

karaw *n.* کاو torment

karaw; la zehmata dak kar *n.* کاو،لهزحمتهکـکار toil

karaw; mazdooree *n.* کاو،مزدوري labour

karawal *v.t.* کارول utilize

karawal *v.i.* کول pine

karawal *v.t.* کول torment

karawal; amal ki rawastal *v.t.* کارول،عمل کراوستل implement

karawalay *n.* کرهوالی precision

karawana *n.* کاروونه utilization

karawona *n.* کارونه implement

karay *n.* ک curl

karay *n.* ک link

karay *n.* ک ring

karay; dawra *n.* کـ،دوره round

karaya *n* کرایه fare

karaya *n.* کرایه rent

karaya kawal *v.t* کرایهکول hire

karaya kawal *v.t.* کرایهکول rent

karaya; eejara *n.* کرایه،اجاره hire

karee baheer *n.* کاري بهیر proceeding

karee dawra *n.* کاري دوره process

karee khoona *n.* کاري خونه studio

karee plan *n.* کاري پلان programme

karee plan jorawal *v.t.* کاري پلان جوول programme

kareekatoor *n.* کاریکاور cartoon

kareeza nakha *n.* کیزهنه ringlet

kareydoonkay *a.* کاردونکی practicable

kargadan *n.* کرگدن rhinoceros

kargar *n.* کارر worker

kargheyran *a.* کرغن obnoxious

kargheyran *a.* کرغن offensive

karhanra; baghbanee *n.* کرهه، باغباني husbandry

karkay *n.* کک window

karkha *n.* کره line

karkhana *n* کارخانه factory

karmand *n* کارمند employee

karmand *n.* کارمند workman

karmandan *n.* کارمندان staff

karmandan *n.* کارمندان personnel

karpoh *n.* کارپوه detective

karpoh *a.* کارپوه skilful

karpoh *n.* کارپوه speciaiist

karpoh shakhs *n.* کارپوهشخص tactician

karray *n* کړی cricket

kart; panra *n.* کارت،پاه card

kartoon *n* کارون comic

kartoos; marmay *n.* کارتوس،مرم cartridge

karwanda *n.* کرونده plantation

karwandagar *n* کرونسر farmer

karwandagar *n.* کرونسر ploughman

karzay *n.* کارای workshop

karzay; daftar *n.* کارای،دفتر office

kasa *n* کاسه bowl

kasab; danda *n.* کسب،دنده profession

kasabee; mahir *a.* ماهر؛كسبي professional ،

kasad; rakood *n.* ركود؛كساد stagnation

kasafat *n.* كثافت garbage

kasafat aw chatalay *a.* چل او كثافات paltry

kasar; mateydana *n.* ماتدنه؛كسر fraction

kasat akheystal *v.t.* اخستل كسات avenge

kasat akheystal *v.t.* اخستل كسات revenge

kasat; ghach *n.* غچ؛كسات revenge

kashar *n.* كشر junior

kashee kawdoray *n.* كودوى كاشي tile

kashee kawdoray lagawal *v.t.* كاشي كودوىلول tile

kashish *n.* كشش gravitation

kashish *n.* كشش traction

kashmalay *n.* كشمالى basil

kashogha *n.* كاشوغه spoon

kasora *n.* كوه bag

kasora *n.* كوه pouch

kasora ki achawal *v. i.* اچول كوه bag

kasora laroonkay *n.* كوهلرونكى marsupial

kata pri eekhodal *v.t.* ايودل كتهپر panel

katal *v.i* كتل look

katal aw palatal *v.t.* اوپلل كتل peruse

katal; leedal *v.t.* ليدل؛كتل see

katana *a* كتنه look

katanee tokar *n.* توكر كتاني linen

katar pri ragarzawal *v.t* كارهپر رارول fence

katar; leeka *n.* ليكه؛كتار queue

katara *n* كاره fence

katara *n.* كاره railing

kateeba *n.* كتيبه inscription

katoleek eesayee *a.* عيسائ كاتوليك catholic

katoonkay *n.* كتونكى on-looker

katoray *n* كورى beaker

kawal *v. t* كول do

kawsay *n* كو lock

kawsheyr *n.* كوشر solder

kawsheyrawal *v.t.* كوشرول solder

kawtara *n.* كوتره culvert

kawtara *n* كوتره dove

kawtara *n.* كوتره pigeon

kayfeeyat *n.* كفيت modality

kayfeeyat *n.* كفيت phenomenon

kayk *n.* كك cake

kayla *n.* كله banana

kayla *n.* كله plantain

kaynat *n.* كائنات universe

kedonkay *a* كيدونكى feasible

keemyagaree *n.* كيماري alchemy

keena *n.* كينه spite

keena *n.* كينه rancour

keena *n.* كينه vengeance

keena kakh *a* كينه envious

keeha satal *v. t* كينهساتل envy

keendana *n* كيندنه dig

keendana *n.* كيندنه excavation

keendawal *v. t.* كيندول excavate

keendoonkay *n.* كيندونكى pitman

keenr *a.* كې left

keenr lasay *a.* کیلاسی sinister

keesa *n.* کیسه tale

keesa *n.* کیسه story

keesa kawal *v.t.* کیسه کول narrate

keesa leekoonkay *n.* کیسهلیکونکی novelist

keesa; bayan *n.* کیسه،بیان narration

keetab *n.* کتابی bookish

keetab lostay *a.* کتابلوستی studious

keetabgotay *n* کتابوی booklet

keetabploray *n.* کتابپلوری stationer

keetabtoon *n.* کتابتون library

keydal *v. i* کدل become

keydal (da shtoon rabita fayl) *v.t.* کدل(دشتونرابطهفعل) be

keyday *n* bundle

keyday shee; shayad *adv.* کدای شی،شاید perhaps

keydoon *n.* کدون possibility

keydoonay *a.* کدونی likely

keydoonay *a.* کدونی possible

keydoonay *a.* کدونی workable

keymya poh *n.* کمیاپوه chemist

keymya pohana *n.* کمیاپوهنه chemistry

keymyayee *a.* کیمیایی chemical

keymyayee mawad *n.* کیمیاییمواد chemical

kha *a.* ﺨ good

kha *adv.* ﺨ well

kha arzakht warkawal *v.t.* ﺨارزت ورکول treasure

kha noom laral *v.t.* ﺨنوملرل repute

kha noom; aytibar *n.* ﺨنوم،اعتبار reputation

kha nyat *n.* ﺨنیت goodwill

kha raghalay; har kalay *n.* ﺨ راغلی،هرکلی reception

kha shagoon *n.* ﺨشون mascot

kha wada kawal *v.i.* ﺨودهکول thrive

kha walay *n.* ﺨوالی goodness

kha; ghwara; nayk *a.* ﺨ،غوره،نک well

khabar panra *n* خبرپاه bulletin

khabar panra *n.* خبرپاه prospectus

khabara oogdawana *n.* خبرهاودونه verbosity

khabara ya lost takrarawal *v.t.* خبرهیالوستتکرارول repeat

khabardaray *n.* خبرداری caution

khabardaray warkawal *v. t.* خبرداریورکول caution

khabardaray warkawal *v.t* خبرداریورکول forewarn

khabardaree *n.* خبرداري premonition

khabardaree *n.* خبرداری warning

khabardaree warkawal *v.t.* خبرداریورکول warn

khabari *n* خبر talk

khabari atari *n.* خبراتر chat1

khabari atari kawal *v. i.* خبراتر کول chat2

khabari atari kawal *v. t* خبراتر کول communicate

khabari atari kawal *v.t.* خبراتر کول converse

khabartya *n* خبرتیا cognizance

khabartya *a.* خبرتیا notice

khabartya; aylan n. خبرتيا،اعلان
announcement

khabaryal n. خبريال
correspondent

khabaryal n. خبريال reporter

khabasat n. خباثت malignity

khabees a. خبيث malignant

khabees a. خبيث wicked

khabrawal v.t. خبرول apprise

khabrawal v.t. خبرول inform

khabrawal v.t. خبرول notice

khabrawana n. خبروونه
notification

khabrawona n. خبرونه news

khabrawoonkay n. خبروونکی
informer

khabroona n. pl. خبرونه tidings

khach pach kawal v.t. خچ پچ کول
squash

khach pach shaway n خچ پچ شوی
squash

khachantob n. خچنتوب insanity

khadim a. خادم ministrant

khadim n. خادم steward

khadim; karwandagar n. خادم؛
کروندر yeoman

khafa; nakam a. خفه،ناکام
unhappy

khageena n. خاینه omelette

khaghalay n. اغلی Messrs

khaghalay n. اغلی mister

khaghalay; hazrat n. اغلی؛حضرت
sir

khaj n خج accent

khaka n خاکه contour

khaka n خاکه diagram

khakhawal v. t. خول bury

khakhowana n خوونه burial

khakhta n. خته adobe

khakhta n خته brick

khakrayz n. خاکرز mound

khaksar a. خاکسار humble

khaksaree n. خاکساري humility

khal n. خال mole

khal n. خال tattoo

khal khal n. خال خال mottle

khal wahal v.t. خال وهل inoculate

khal wahal v.i. خال وهل tattoo

khal wahana n. خال وهنه
inoculation

khalee; pooda a. خالي؛پوده hollow

khaleefa n. خليفه prelate

khaleej n. خليج gulf

khaliq n خالق creator

khalis a خالص net

khalq n. خلک people

kham a خام crude

kham a. خام raw

kham aw nawara a. خام او ناوه
maladroit

khamar n امار dragon

khamdar adj خم دار anfractuous

khameera n. خميره paste

khamosh a. خاموش mum

khamosh a. خاموش serene

khamosh a. خاموش taciturn

khamosh a. خاموش mute

khamosh a. خاموش reticent

khamosh aw janjal sakha leyri
prot insan n. خاموش او جنجال
سخه لري پروت انسان
stoic

khamoshawal *v. t.* خاموشول calm
khamoshawal *v.i* خاموشول hush
khamoshawal *v.t.* خاموشول lull
khamoshawal *v.t.* خاموشول pacify
khamoshawal *v.t.* خاموشول slake
khamoshee *n.* خاموشي calm
khamoshee *n.* خاموشي stillness
khamoshee *n.* خاموشي reticence
khamosheydal *v.i.* خاموشدل subside
khand darawal; katara tri tawowal *v.t* خندرول،کاره‌تر تاوول hurdle2
khand keydal; bandawal *v.t* خند کدل،بندول block
khand keydana *n.* خندکدنه impediment
khand ya katara ratawowal *v.t* خنیاکاره‌راتاوول hedge
khand; katara *n.* خند،کاره hedge
khand; katara tawowan *n.* خند، کاره‌تاوونه hurdle1
khand; muzahimat *n.* خند،مزاحمت hindrance
khanda *n.* خندا laugh
khanda *n.* خندا smile
khandal *v.i* خندل laugh
khandan *a.* خندان cheerful
khandan *adj.* خندان convivial
khandawoonkay *a* خندوونکی comic
khandawoonkay *a* خندوونکی comical
khandawoonki hunaree nandara warandi kawal *v.t.* خندوونکهنري‌ندارهواندکول parody

khandawoonki nandara *n.* خندوونکنداره comedy
khandoonkay *a.* خندونکی jocular
khandoonkay *a.* خندونکی laughable
khandowoonkay *n.* خندوونکنداره mime
khandowoonkay *n.* خندوونکی funny
khandowoonki nandara *n* خندوونکنداره farce
khangar wazma *a.* خانوزمه ticklish
khanjar *n.* خنجر dagger
khanqa *n.* خانقا abbey
khanqa *n.* خانقا cloister
khanqa *n.* خانقا monastery
khap; asar *n.* خاپ،اثر trace
khapa *a.* خپه sad
khapa kawal *v. t* خپه‌کول displease
khapa kawal *v.t.* خپه‌کول sadden
khapa kawoonkay *a.* خپه‌کوونکی muggy
khapara *n.* خپه paw
khaparak *n* اپرک bat
khapeyray *n* اپر fairy
khapgan *n* خپان displeasure
khapgan *n.* خپان sorrow
khapgan kawal *v.i.* خپان‌کول regret
khapgan; pkheymanee *n* خپان، پماني regret
khapori *n* خاپو crawl
khapori kawal *v. t* خاپوکول crawl
khar *n.* خر ass
khar *n* خر donkey

khar *n* ‫کار‬ city
khar dawla *adj.* ‫خروله‬ asinine
khar khar *n* ‫خرخر‬ snore
khar mach *n.* ‫خرمچ‬ gadfly
kharab shaway *a.* ‫خرابشوی‬
worn
kharabawal *v. t* ‫خرابول‬ bungle
kharabawal *v.t.* ‫خرابول‬
contaminate
kharabawal *v. t.* ‫خرابول‬ debauch
kharabawal *v.t.* ‫خرابول‬ vitiate
kharabawana *n* ‫خرابونه‬ bungle
kharabawana *n* ‫خرابونه‬ debauch
kharabee *n* ‫خرابي‬ spoil
kharabeyda *n.* ‫خرابدا‬ rot
kharabeydal *v. i* ‫خرابدل‬ decay
kharabeydal *v.i.* ‫خرابدل‬ low
kharabeydal; wrusteydal *v.i.*
‫خرابدل;وُرستدل‬ rot
kharabeydoonkay *a.* ‫خرابدونکی‬
vulnerable
kharabtya *n* ‫خرابتیا‬ malady
kharad; tarashawoonkay *n.*
‫خراد;تراشوونکی‬ turner
kharakh *n.* ‫خار‬ itch
kharakh laral *v.i.* itch
kharashkay *n.* ‫خراشکی‬ sputum
khard *a.* ‫خ‬ grey
khardal *n.* ‫خردل‬ mustard
kharee *a.* ‫باري‬ municipal
kharee *a.* ‫باري‬ urban
khareedaree kawal *v. t.* ‫خریداري‬
‫کول‬ buy
khareetob; khar meyshtwalay *n.*
‫باریتوب;بارمشتوالی‬ urbanity
khargotay *n.* ‫باروی‬ town

khargotay *a.* ‫باروی‬ township
kharhar *n.* ‫خرهار‬ snort
kharhar kawal *v.i.* ‫خرهارکول‬
snore
kharij qismat *n.* ‫خارجقسمت‬
quotient
kharijawal *v. t* ‫خارجول‬ emit
kharijee *a* ‫خارجي‬ foreign
kharijee heywadwal *n* ‫خارجي‬
‫هوادوال‬ foreigner
kharob; seyl *n* ‫خوب;سل‬ flood
khars *n* ‫خر‬ expenditure
khars *n.* ‫خر‬ alimony
kharsawal *v.t.* ‫خرول‬ sell
khartamee charg *n.* ‫ختمي‌چر‬
turkey
kharwalee *n.* ‫باروالي‬ municipality
khas *a.* ‫خاص‬ peculiar
khas *a.* ‫خاص‬ special
khas *a.* ‫خاص‬ particular
khas saray *n.* ‫خاص‌سی‬ particular
khasee kawal *v.t.* ‫خصي‌کول‬ geld
khasees; badlaray *a.* ‫خسیس;‬
‫بدلاری‬ sordid
khasees; kanjoos *a.* ‫خسیس;‬
‫کنجوس‬ miserly
khaseeyat *n.* ‫خاصیت‬ peculiarity
khasha *n.* ‫خاشه‬ mote
khasoosee *a.* ‫خصوصي‬ respective
khasoosee malkeeyat *n.* ‫خصوصي‬
‫مالکیت‬ propriety
khasoosee; khpal zatee *a.*
‫خصوصي;خپل‌ذاتي‬ private
khasooseeyat *n.* ‫خصوصیت‬ trait
khasozey aw khoshaya *n.* ‫خوزاو‬
‫خوشایه‬ scrap

khat kashee *n* خط‌كشي lining
khata *n*. خه mud
khata sara makhamakhawal *v.t*
خطرسره‌مخامخول hazard
khata; laha *n*. خه،لهه silt
khatar *n*. خطر danger
khatar *n*. خطر hazard
khatar *n*. خطر peril
khatar *n*. خطر jeopardy
khatar *n*. خطر threat
khatar *n*. خطر risk
khatar sara makhamakhawal
v.t. خطرسره‌مخامخول
jeopardize
khatar sara makhamakhawal
v.t. خطرسره‌مخامخول risk
khatarnak *a* خطرناک dangerous
khatarnak *a.* خطرناک perilous
khatarnak *a.* خطرناک risky
khatarnak *a* خطرناک serious
khatarnak *a.* خطرناک uncanny
khatarnak *a.* خطرناک venturous
khatarnak *a.* خطرناک
venturesome
khatarnak kar ta las achawal
v.t. خطرناک‌کارته‌لاس‌اچول
venture
khatarnak; nazhdey *a.* خطرناک،
نژد imminent
khatee *n*. خطي manuscript
khateez *n* ختيز east
khateez *n*. ختيز orient
khateez ta tlal *v.t*. ختيزته‌تلل orient
khateezwal *a* ختيزوال east
khateezwal *a* ختيزوال eastern
khateezwal *a*. ختيزوال oriental

khatgar *n*. خر mason
khatgaree *n*. خري masonry
khatima *n* خاتمه expiry
khatir jamee *n* خاطرجمعي
affirmation
khatir; loray *n* خاطر،لورى behalf
khatira; yadgar *n*. خاطره،یادگار
reminiscence
khatirdaree kawal *v. t* خاطرداري
کول entertain
khatirdaree; har kalay *n*. خاطر
داري؛هرکلی entertainment
khatmawal *v.t*. ختمول terminate
khato cheekaro ki garzeydal *v.i.*
خوچیکرو کرپدل wade
khato ki lweydal *v.t*. خوکلوپدل
puddle
khawra *n*. خاوره soil
khawran lokhay *n*. خاورن‌لوی
crockery
khawreen *a* خاورین earthen
khay las; sam kar *n* ىلاس؛سم‌کار
right
khayanat kawal *v.t*. خیانت‌کول
betray
khayanat; ghadaree *n* خیانت،
غداري betrayal
khayatee kawal *v.t*. خیاطي‌کول
tailor
khayin *n*. خاین conspirator
khayin *a* خاین dishonest
khayin *n*. خاین traitor
khayma *n*. خیمه tent
khayma dawla kor *n*. خمه‌وله‌کور
wigwam
khaynana *a.* خاینانه treacherous
khayraza *a* رازه fertile

khayraza kawal *v.t* رازه‌كول
fertilize

khayrazee *n* رازي fertility

khayza satha *n.* خزه‌سطحه crust

khaza *n* ه female

khaza *n.* ه woman

khazana *n.* خزانه treasure

khazana dar *n.* خزانه‌دار cashier

khazana daree *n.* خزانه‌داري
treasury

khazanadar *n.* خزانه‌دار treasurer

khazanda *n.* خزنده bug

khazanda *n* خزنده creeper

khazdaka *n* خزدكه beetle

khazeena *a* ينه effeminate

khazeena *a* ينه female

khazeena *n.* ينه womanish

khazeena khoog *n.* خوينه sow

khazeena khwali jorawoonkay
n. ينه‌خواجووونكى milliner

khazeena khwali plorawana *n.*
ينه‌خوالپلورونه millinery

khazeena padree *n.* ينه‌پادري
priestess

khazeena prang *n.* ينه‌پان tigress

khazeena somia *n.* ينه‌صومعه
nunnery

khazeena tawas *n.* ينه‌طاوس
peahen

khazeena zangaray noom *a* ينه
مانى‌نوم maudlin

khazeena zayr parahanee *n.* ينه
زرپراهني smock

khazmantob *n.* منتوب
womanhood

kheekha *n* يه mirror

kheekha ghosowoonkay *n.* يه
غووونكى glazier

kheeran *a.* خيرن squalid

kheeray *n* خيرى filth

kheygara *n* ه favour1

kheygara *n.* ه benefaction

kheygara *n.* ه welfare

kheygara kawal *v.t* ه‌كول favour

kheymey darawal *v. i.* خمدرول
camp

kheyran *a* خرن filthy

kheyranawal *v. t.* خرنول daub

kheyranawal *v.t.* خيرنول stain

kheyraneydal *v.t.* خرندل soil

kheyrantya *n.* خرنتيا defile

kheyrat *n.* خرات charity

kheyrat *n.* خرات alms

kheyratee *a.* خراتي charitable

kheyta *n* خه abdomen

kheyta *n.* خه stomach

khidmat *n.* خدمت service

khidmat kawal *v.t* خدمت‌كول
nurse

khidmat kawal *v.t.* خدمت‌كول
serve

khidmatgar *n.* خدمتار attendant

khidmatgar *n.* خدمتار servant

khidmatgarana *a.* خدمتارانه
servile

khilwat *n.* خلوت solitude

khilwat *n.* خلوت privacy

khitab kawal *v.t.* خطاب‌كول
address

khkanza *n* كنا abuse

khkanzal *v.t.* كنل abuse

khkar *n.* كر horn

khkar *n.* کار victim

khkar *n.* کار prey

khkar *n* کار hunt

khkar kawal *v.t.* کارکول hunt

khkar kawal *v.t.* کارکول victimize

khkar kawal *v.i.* کارکول prey

khkar shaway zanawar ya insan *n.* کارشوی‌ناوریاانسان quarry

khkar ta dam ki da khwaro mawad eekhodal *v.t.* کارته‌دام کدخووموادایودل bait

khkara kawal *v. t* کاره‌کول disclose

khkara kawal *v.t.* کاره‌کول unfold

khkaree *n.* کاري hunter

khkaree saray *n.* کاری‌سی huntsman

khkaree spay *n.* کاري‌سپی hound

khkeylakee *a* کلاکي colonial

khkeylakee seema *n* کلاکي‌سیمه colony

khkula *n* کلا beauty

khkula *n.* کلا prettiness

khkula *a.* کلاپالونکی aesthetic

khkula peyzhandana *n.pl.* کلا پژندنه aesthetics

khkula warbakhal *v.t.* کلاوربل grace

khkula warbakhal *v.t* کلاوربل groom

khkula; fazeelat *n.* کلا؛فضیلت virtue

khkulawana aw machaka *n.* کلونه‌اومچکه smack

khkulay *a* کلی beautiful

khkulay kawal *v. t* کلی‌کول beautify

khkuli manzara laroonkay *a.* کلا منظره‌لرونکی scenic

khkuli najlay *n* کلنجلا belle

khlasoon *n.* خلاصون acquittal

khlasoon *n.* خلاصون salvation

kho bya ham *adv.* خوبیاهم however

kho; wali *conj.* خو،ولا but

khob *n* خوب dream

khob *n.* خوب sleep

khob leedal *v. i.* خوب‌لیدل dream

khobawalay *a.* خوبولی sleepy

khobawalay *n.* خوبولی somnolent

khobawalay halat *n.* خوبولی‌حالت somnolence

khodana *n.* ودنه pageant

khog *a.* خو sweet

khog kalam *n* خوکلام epigram

khog malgaray *n* خوملری chum

khogwalay *n.* خووالی sweetness

khola *n.* خوله mouth

kholpotay paki eekhodal *v.t.* خولپوی‌پکایودل plug

kholpotay; plag *n.* خولپوی؛پل plug

khoofeeya *a.* خفیه secret

khoofeeya *a.* خفیه secretive

khoogeydal *v.i* خودل smart

khoogeydal *v.i.* خویدل ache

khoona *n.* خونه chamber

khoona *n.* خونه room

khoonee peychash *n* خونی‌پچش dysentery

khoonee; insan wazhoonkay *n.* خوني،انسان‌وژونکی thug

khoosa kawal; soolawal v. t خوسا
كول؛سولول erode
khooshaya n خوشايه dung
khooshbooya a. خوشبويه fragrant
khooy n خوى conduct
khooy n. خوى temperament
khor n. خور sister
khora deyr adv. خورار full
khora deyr a. خورار immense
khora deyr a. خورار
superabundant
khorak n. خوراك meal
khorawal v.t. خورول jog
khorma; neyta n خرما؛نه date
khorwa n وروا broth
khorwa n. وروا soup
khorwa pakhowoonkay n. وروا
پخوونكى stew
khorwalee n. خورولي sisterhood
khosa a. خوسا morbid
khosh khalqa a. خوش خلقه affable
khoshal a. خوشال glad
khoshala a. خوشاله gay
khoshala a. خوشاله jubilant
khoshala a خوشاله merry
khoshala a. خوشاله vivacious
khoshala kawal v.t. خوشاله كول
gladden
khoshalawal v. t. خوشالول delight
khoshalee n خوشالي delight
khoshalee n. خوشالي frolic
khoshalee n. خوشالي hilarity
khoshalee n. خوشالي merriment
khoshalee kawal v.i. خوشاي كول
frolic
khoshaleydal v.i. خوشالدل rejoice

khoshay kawal v.t. خوشى كول
relinquish
khoshbakhtee adv. خوشبختهسره
luckily
khoshbooya n. خوشبو odour
khoshbooya a. خوشبويه odorous
khoshbooya kawal v. t خوشبويه
كول embalm
khoshhalee n. خوشحالي prosperity
khota; khuseeya n. خوه؛خصيه
testicle
khotawal v.t. خوول agitate
khowal v.t. وول show
khowan n. وون tutor
khowana n. وونه show
khowana aw rozana n. وونهاوروزنه
lore
khowana aw rozana n. وونهاوروزنه
pedagogy
khowana kawal v.t. وونه كول
instruct
khowana; tarbeeya n وونه؛تربيه
education
khowanzay n. ووني school
khowanzay tar sara kawal v.t.
ووني ترسره كول matriculate
khowoonkay n. وونكه governess
khowoonkay n. وونكى monitor
khowoonkay n. وونكى pedagogue
khowoonkay n. وونكى teacher
khozakht manoonkay a. خوت
منونكى movable
khozakht warkawal v.t. خوت
ورکول jostle
khozanda aw khwayanda shaga
n. خوندهاووينده شه quicksand

khozanda meela *n.* خوندهميله
piston

khozanda waseela *n.* خوندهوسيله
motor

khozawoonkay *n.* خووونکی mover

khpal haywad ta beyrta ragarzeydal *v.t.* خپل‌هوادته‌برته
رارمل repatriate

khpal haywad ta beyrta staneydana *n.* خپل‌هوادته‌برته
ستندنه repatriation

khpal haywad ta staneydoonkay *n*
خپل‌هوادته‌برته‌ستندونکی
repatriate

khpal karay *a.* خپل‌کاری
automatic

khpal lasay zhwand leek *n.* خپل
لاسی‌ژوندلیک autobiography

khpal palana *n.* خپل‌پالنه nepotism

khpal saray *a.* خپل‌سری
headstrong

khpal saray *a.* خپل‌سری perverse

khpal saray *a.* خپل‌سری stubborn

khpal saree *n.* خپل‌سري perversion

khpal saree; fasad *n.* خپل‌سري،
فساد perversity

khpal zat *n* خپل‌ذات ego

khpal; zanee *a.* خپل،ذاني own

khpala groha khkara kawal *v.t.*
خپله‌ورهمکاره‌کول suggest

khpalawal *v.t.* خپلول adopt

khpalawana *n* خپلونه adoption

khpalawana *n.* خپلونه occupancy

khpalwak hukoomat *a* خپلواک
حکومت autonomous

khpalwaka *a.* خپلواکه independent

khpalwaka hookoomat *n* خپلواکه
حکومت autocracy

khpalwaka preykhodal *v.t.*
خپلواکه‌پرودل indulge

khpalwaka preykhodalay shaway *a.* خپلواکه‌پرودلی‌شوی
indulgent

khpalwakee *n.* خپلواکي
independence

khpalwalee *n.* خپلولي kinship

khpalwan *n.* خپلوان kin

khpalwan *n.* خپلوان relative

khparandoy *n.* خپرندوی publisher

khparawal *v. t* خپرول broadcast

khparawana *n* خپرونه broadcast

khparaway *n.* خپراوی prevalance

khparaway; wayna *n.* خپراوی،ونا
utterance

khpor shaway; parakh *a.* خپور
شوی،پراخ rampant

khuday *n.* خدای deity

khuday *n.* خدای god

khuday *n.* خدايي godhead

khuday di mal sha *interj.* خدای‌د
مل‌شه bye-bye

khuday di mal sha *n.* خدای‌دی‌مل
شه adieu

khuday pa amanee *interj.* خدای‌په
اماني adieu

khuday warkaray shay *n.* خدای
ورکی‌شی godsend

khulasa *n* خلاصه abstract

khulasa shaway *a.* خلاصه‌شوی
compact

khulasa; iqtibas *n* خلاصه،اقتباس
extract

khuloos *n.* خلوص sincerity

khush tabee *n.* خوشطبعي humour
khuskay *n.* خوسکی calf
khusoosee *a* خصوصي especial
khwa badoonkay *a.* خوابدوونکی odious
khwa; arkh *n.* خوا،ارخ side
khwabadee *n.* خوابدي resentment
khwaga jorowoonkay *n* خواه جوورونکی confectioner
khwaga patasa *n.* خوهپتاسه lollipop
khwaga sandara *n.* خوهسندره melody
khwagawal *v.t.* خوول sweeten
khwakh *a.* خو happy
khwakh tabee *n.* خوطبعي pleasantry
khwakhawal *v.t.* خوول like
khwakhee *n.* خوی revelry
khwakhee *n.* خوي happiness
khwakhee *n.* خوي jubilation
khwakhoogee *n* خواخوي condolence
khwakhoogee khkara kawal *v.i.* خواخويکاره کول sympathize
khwalay *n.* خول cap
khwalay *n.* خول hat
khwaley *n.* خول sweat
khwaley keydal *v.i.* خوالکدل sweat
khwana *a.* خوانا legible
khwand *n* خوند smack
khwand akheystal *v. t* خونداخستل enjoy
khwand akheystal *v.t.* خونداخستل relish

khwand aw booy *n* خونداوبوی flavour
khwand warkawal *v.t.* خوندورکول please
khwandawar *a* خوندور delicious
khwandawar *n.* خوندور joyful, joyous
khwandawar *a.* خوندور tasteful
khwandawar *a.* خوندور tasty
khwandawar sharab *n.* خوندور شراب nectar
khwandee kawoonkay *n.* preservative
khwandee satal *v.t.* خونديساتل preserve
khwandeeyeena *n.* خونديينه preservation
khwandeyana; satana *n.* خوندينه، ساتنه sustenance
khwar *a.* خوار abject
khwar *a* خوار despicable
khwara *n* خواه food
khwara *n* خواه feed
khwara chamtoo kawal *v.* خواه چمتوکول cater
khwara warkawal *v.t* خواهورکول feed
khwara warkawal *v.t.* خواهورکول nourish
khwara; ghaza *n.* خواه،غذا aliment
khwaral *v. t* خول eat
khwaranzay *n.* خوانای restaurant
khwaree ke *a.* خواري کی laborious
khwasheenawoonkay *a* خواشينوونکی deplorable
khwasheenee *a* خواشينی cheerless
khwasheenee *a.* خواشيني sorry

khwasheenee kawal *v.t.* خواشینی كول incur

khwayand *a.* ویند slippery

khwayandoy *n.* ویندوی roller

khwayeyda *n.* ویدا jostle

khwayeydal *v.t.* ویدل glide

khwayeydal; khoshay kawal *v.i.* ویدل،خوشی كول slip

khwayeydal; takar khwaral *v.t.* ویدل،ٻكرخول trip

khwayeydana *n* ویدنه slide

khyal palana *n.* خیال پالنه idealism

khyal parasta *a.* خیال پرسته quixotic

khyal parastee *n.* خیال پرستي vagary

khyal; fikar *n.* خیال،فكر idea

khyalee *a.* خیالي imaginary

khyalee *a.* خیالي utopian

khyalee banra warkawal *v.t.* خیالي بهوركول idealize

khyalee insan *n.* خیالي انسان idealist

khyalee insan *n.* خیالي انسان visionary

khyalee keesa *n.* خیالي كیسه myth

khyalee; mafroozee *a.* خیالي، مفروضي hypothetical

khyalee; tasawwuree *a.* خیالي، تصوري ideal

khyanat *n.* خیانت dishonesty

khyanat *n.* خیانت treachery

khyanat kawal *v. i.* خیانت كول conspire

ki; da ... pa lori *prep.* ك؛د___په لور at

kifayat; kafee miqdar *n.* كفایت، كافي مقدار sufficiency

kimkhab *n* كمخاب brocade

kinaya *n.* كنایه quibble

kinayawee; ramzee *a.* كنایوي، رمزي allusive

kinayee *a.* كنایي sarcastic

kitab peyzhand *n* كتاب پژاند bibliographer

kitab peyzhandana +*n* كتاب پژندنه bibliography

kitabgotay *n* كتابوی brochure

kkhata *adv* كته down

kkhata *a.* كته low

kkhata aw porta top *n* كته او پورته توپ skip

kkhata kawal *v.t.* كته كول lower

kkhata kawal; raparzawal *v. t* كته كول؛راپرول down

kkhata keydal *v. i.* كته كدل descend

kkhata keydana; nasal *n.* كته كدنه؛نسل descent

kkhata walay *n.* كته والی lowliness

kkheynastal *v.i.* كناستل sit

klak *a.* كلك adamant

klak *a* كلك concrete

klak *a* كلك firm

klak *a.* كلك tight

klak aw rasikh *a.* كلك او راسخ impenetrable

klak hod *n.* كلك هو vow

klakawal *v.t.* كلكول tighten

klakawal *v.t.* كلكول stiffen

klakawal; twanawal *v.t.* كلكول؛ توانول toughen

kochay *n.* کوچی nomad

kochay; kadwal *n.* کوچی؛کوال vagabond

kochyana *a.* کوچیانه nomadic

kod warkawal *v.t.* کوورکول manure

kod; ramzee shmeyra *n* کو؛رمزي شمره code

kodgar *n.* کو ر magician

kodgar *n.* کو ر sorcerer

kodgar *n.* کو ر wizard

kodgara *n.* کو ره witch

kodgaree *n.* کوري sorcery

kodi *n.* کوي talisman

kodi kawal *v.i.* کوکول conjure

kodi; dam durha *n.* کو؛دمدرها amulet

kog *adj.* کو crump

kog rakog *n* کوراکو bight

kog stargay keydal *v.i.* کوستری کدل squint

kog stargtob *n* کوسترتوب squint

kog walay *n* کووالی curve

kog walay warkawal *v. t* کووالی ورکول curve

kog; da spee pa seyr yaw zanawar *n.* کو؛دسپيپهريوناور hyaena, hyena

kogwalay *n* کووالی bend

kogwalay *n* کووالی bent

kogwalay *n.* کووالی tilt

kogwog tlal *v.t.* کوتلل wind

kokhakh *n.* کو quest

kokhakh kawal *v.t.* کوکول quest

kokhakh; fishar *n.* کو؛فشار stress

kolp *n.* کولپ lock

kolp bandawal *v. t* کولپبندول bolt

kolp laroonki almaray *n.* کولپ لرونکالمار locker

kolpawal *v.t* کولپول lock

kom *pron.* کوم which

kom kas *pron.* کوم کس somebody

kom kas; yaw sok *pron.* ؛ کوم کس یووک someone

kom sa chi; har sa chi *pron.* کومه چ؛هرهچ whatever

kom yaw chi *a* کوميوچ which

kom zay *adv.* کوهای whither

kom; kom seez *a.* کوم؛کوميز what

komakee *a.* کومکي helpful

komakee *a.* کومکي subsidiary

konatay *n* کونای buttock

konatay *n* کونای hip

kond *n.* کو ز widower

konda *n* کونده bloc

konda *n.* کونده log

konda *n.* کونه widow

kondawal *v.t.* کونول widow

konj; gokha *n* کونج؛گوه angle

konr *a* کو ز deaf

koocheydal *v.i.* کوچیدل immigrate

koochnay *n.* کوچنی babe

koochnay *n.* کوچنی baby

koochnay *a.* کوچنی small

koochnay *a.* کوچنی tiny

koochnay *n.* کوچنی infant

koochnay *n* کوچنی minor

koochnay *a.* کوچنی least

koochnay as *n.* کوچنیاس pony

koochnay astoganzay *n.* کوچنی استونای lodge

koochnay baks *n* كوچنبکس casket

koochnay botal *n.* كوچنی بوتل vial

koochnay dabarleek *n.* كوچنی برليک miniature

koochnay dabay *n.* كوچنی بی packet

koochnay dara *n* كوچندره dale

koochnay darwaza; da krikat da lobi drey chooki *n.* كوچنی دروازه؛د کر کدلوبدرچوک wicket

koochnay drey payey laroonkay gaday *n.* كوچنی درپايلرونکی ای rickshaw

koochnay ghonday *n.* كوچنغو hillock

koochnay kakhtay *n* كوچنکت boat

koochnay kalay *n.* كوچنی کلی hamlet

koochnay kawal *v. t* كوچنی کول diminish

koochnay khakh; tareeqa *n.* كوچنی اخ؛طريقه twig

koochnay khaleej *n* كوچنی خليج bay

koochnay khaleej *n.* كوچنی خليج creek

koochnay khoona *n.* كوچنخونه cabin

koochnay khoona *n.* كوچنخونه snug

koochnay klaka sheereenee *n.* كوچنکلکه شيريني toffee

koochnay koranay charg *n.* كوچنی کورنی چر bantam

koochnay la sheydo beylawal *v. t* كوچنی له شدوبلول ablactate

koochnay largeena khoona *n.* كوچنلرينه خونه stall

koochnay meykh *n.* كوچنی مخ pin

koochnay miqnateesee sapa *n.* كوچنمقناطيسي په microwave

koochnay panra *n.* كوچنپاه leaflet

koochnay reybaz; bors *n* كوچنی رب؛بورس whisk

koochnay seegar *n.* كوچنی سيار cigarette

koochnay shama *n* كوچنشمع taper

koochnay sooray *n.* كوچنی سوری pore

koochnay taj *n.* كوچنی تاج coronet

koochnay wyala *n.* كوچنويا streamlet

koochnay; warookay *a.* كوچنی؛ووکی minuscule

koochneetob *n.* كوچنيتوب infancy

koodala *n.* کوله hut

koog *n.* خو pig

koohay *n.* کوهی well

kooki *n* کوک howl

kooki kawal; cheyghi wahal *v.t.* کوکول؛چغوهل howl

koolmey *n.* کولمه intestine

koolmey aw ahsha *n.* کولماواحشاء inside

koonda; reekha *n.* کونده؛ريه stub

koonr kawoonkay ghag *a.* کوکوونکی غ strident

koorkaman *n.* کورکمن turmeric

koosa *n.* کوه lane

koosa *n.* کوه street

koosa dabay saray *n.* کوهی سی loafer

koosa dabay; wrusto pati shaway *n.* كوهبى؛وروستوپات شوى straggler

koosa; lara *n.* كوه؛لاره alley

koota kawal *v.t.* كوهكول mow

kooza *n.* كوزه pitcher

kopra *n* كوپره coconut

kopray *n* كوپ scalp

kopray *n.* كوپ skull

kor *n.* كور home

kor; sray *n* كور؛سراى house

koranay *n* كورنۍ family

koranay khowoonkay *n.* كورنۍ وونكى pedant

koranay marghay *n.* كورنمرغ sparrow

koranay noom *n.* كورنۍنوم nickname

koranay noom *n.* كورنۍنوم surname

koranay noom eekhodal *v.t.* كورنۍنومايودل nickname

koranay seez *n* كورنۍيز domestic

koranay; ahlee *a.* كورنۍ؛اهلي tame

koranay; aslee *a* كورنۍ؛اصلي domestic

koranjeydal *v.i.* كونجدل whine

koranjeydana *n* كونجدنه whine

korba *n.* كوربه host

kornastay *a.* كورناستى sedentary

kot *n* كو coat

kotangay *n* كوټ cottage

krachay *n.* كراچ cart

kragh kragh *n.* كاغ كاغ caw

kragha; kargha *n* كاغه؛كارغه crow

kraka *n.* كركه hate

kraka *n.* كركه malice

kraka *n.* كركه abhorrence

kraka kawal *v.t.* كركهكول abhor

kraka kawal *v. t* كركهكول despise

kraka kawal *v. t* كركهكول dislike

kraka kawal *v.t.* كركهكول hate

kraka kawal *v.t.* كركهكول weary

kraka; na khwakhee *n* كركه؛نا خوي dislike

krakjan *a* كركجن abominable

krakjan *a.* كركجن revengeful

krakjan *a.* كركجن malicious

krana *n.* كنه action

kranjay *n* كنجى creak

kranjeydal *v. i* كنجدل creak

kranlara *n.* كنلاره policy

kranlara warta jorawal *v.t.* كنلارهورتهجوول systematize

kranlara; mimbar *n.* كنلاره؛منبر platform

krap *n.* كپ click

krasan *a.* كسن brittle

krati prati kawal *v. t.* كپتۍكول chatter

kreeka wahal *v.i.* كرۍكهوهل shout

kreeka; faryad *n.* كرۍكه؛فرياد shout

krega kawal *n.* كرۍهكول gobble

krismis (da eesayano akhtar) *n* كرسمس(دعيسائيانواختر) Christmas

kubra mar *n* كبرامار cobra

kuch *n* كوچ butter

kufar kawal *v.t.* کفرکول profane
kulal *n.* کلال potter
kulalee *n.* کلالی pottery
kura *n.* کره orb
kursay *n.* کرسۍ chair
kwata *n.* کوه pile
kwata kawal *v.t.* کوهکول pile

L

la ... leyri *adv.* له___لر far
la ... porta *adv.* له___پورته beyond
la ... sakha *prep.* له___خه from
la ... sakha sha ta *prep* له___خهشا ته behind
la ... sakha warandi *prep* له___خه واند before
la arakha *adv* لهاخه by
la aytibar sakha zyat tar lasa shaway *n.* لهاعتبارخهزیاتترلاسه شوی overdraft
la bad sakha khwandee zay *n.* له بادخهخوندیای lee
la beykha rakkhal *v.t.* لهبخهراکل wrest
la beykha rakkhal *v.t.* لهبخهراکل uproot
la blarbakht sakha makhneeway *n.* لهبلاربتخه مخنیوی contraception
la dandi rukhsatawal *v. t.* لهدند رخصتول dismiss
la dandi sakha kharijawal *v.t.* له دندخهخارجول sack

la darda ghonjeydal *v.i.* لهدرده غونجدل writhe
la dey amala *adv.* لهداملـه accordingly
la dey kabala *adv.* لهدکبله thereby
la dey kabala; par dey asas *adv.* له دکبله،پر داساس so
la dey khwa hagha khwa ta *prep.* لهدخواهغهخواته athwart
la dey lamala *adv.* لهدلاملـه hence
la dey lamala *adv.* لهدلاملـه therefore
la dey parta *adv.* لهدپرته otherwise
la dey sara sara *adv.* لهدسرهسره nonetheless
la dey sara sara *adv.* لهدسرهسره notwithstanding
la dey sara sara *adv.* لهدسرهسره yet
la dooda bahar *a* لهدودهبهر anomalous
la dwa hindso jor *adj* لهدوهندسو جو binary
la dwa sakha yaw *a.,* لهدوخهیو either
la garda dak *a.* لهردهک misty
la garway sakha khlasawal *v.t.* له روخهخلاصول redeem
la garway sakha khlasoon *n.* لهرو خهخلاصون redemption
la ghag porta *a.* لهغپورته supersonic
la gharmey makhki *n* لهغرمهمخک forenoon
la ghusey khoteydal *v.i.* لهغصه خودل simmer

la had sakha zyata stayana *n.* له ستاينه حدخهزياته apotheosis

la hada zyat *adv* له حدهزيات extra

la hagha lori chi *adv.* له هغه لوري چ thence

la hagha wakhta chi *adv.* له هغه وخته چ since

la haqooqo mahroomawal *v.t* له حقوقو محرومول outlaw

la harakata ghorzawal *v.t.* له حركته غورول stall

la ilaj *a.* لاعلاج incurable

la insanano aw basharee tolani sakha beyzara insan *n.* له انسانانو او بشري يو لنخه بزار انسان misanthrope

la josha dak *a* له جوشه ك enthusiastic

la kamakht aw zyadakht parta *adv.* له كمت او زيادت پرته sharp

la kara ghorzawana *n.* له كاره غورونه sterilization

la kara lweydalay *a.* له كارهلويدلى obsolete

la karawa dak *a.* له كاوه ك arduous

la karawa daka azmoyana *n.* له كاوه كه آزموينه ordeal

la khatar sakha khabrawal *v.t* له خطر خه خبرول alarm

la khatar sara makahmakhawal *v. t.* له خطر سره مخامخول endanger

la khatara daka chara *n.* له خطره كه چاره venture

la khato aw laho dak zay *n.* له خو او لهو ك ساى slough

la khawro sakha raeestal *v.t.* له خاورو خه راايستل unearth

la kholi sakha leyri *adj* له خولى خه ليرى aboral

la khudaya monkar *n* له خدايه منكر atheist

la khwaro da makha ishtiha rawastoonkay skhak *n* له خو دمخه اشتهار او ستونكى اك appetizer

la koma zaya *adv.* له كومه يه whence

la kor sakha leyri *adv.* له كور خه لر forth

la kora watalay *n* له كوره وتلى without

la kraghi da koranay yaw margha *n.* له كاغد كورنى يو مارغه jay

la landi sakha *adv.* له لاندخه underneath

la lari *prep.* له لار via

la lasa warkawal *v.t.* له لاسه ور كول miss

la lasa wrakawal *v.t.* له لاسه ور كول lose

la lori; pa wasta *prep.* له لور؛ په واسطه through

la lwagi mreydal *v.i.* له لو مدل starve

la makhi yi *conj.* له مخي whereupon

la maleeyey sakha maf *a.* له ماليخه معاف scot-free

la manza tlal *v. i* له منه تلل collapse

la manza tloonkay *a.* له منه تلو نكى perishable

la manza waral *v.t.* له منه ول annihilate

la manza wral *v.t* لهمنهول abolish

la manza wral *v. t* لهمنهول
eliminate

la manza wral *v. t* لهمنهول
eradicate

la manza wral *v.t.* لهمنهول slay

la manza wral *v.t.* لهمنهول wipe

la manza wrana *v* لهمنهونه
abolition

la manza wrana *n.* لهمنهونه
removal

la markaz sakha rakhkoonkay *adj.* لهمرکزخهراکونک
centrifugal

la mashoom sara lobi kawal *v.t.* لهماشومسرهلوبکول dandle

la maskharo dak *a.* لهمسخروک
ridiculous

la meeni dak *adj* لهمينک amatory

la mehdood *a.* لامحدود infinite

la mehdood *a.* لامحدود limitless

la mehdoodeeyat *n.* لامحدوديت
infinity

la nacharay sakha *adv.* لهناچارخه
needs

la nakamay sakha *adv.* لهناکامخه
perforce

la nal sakha jor shaway *a.* لهنلخه جوشوى tubular

la nasyal sara wada kawoonkay *a.* لهناسيالسرهوادهکوونکى
morganatic

la nawee sara raghawal *v.t.* لهنوي سرهرغول renovate

la nizam sara sam *a.* لهنظامسرهسم
systematic

la noro sara weyshal *v.t.* لهنورو سرهوشل share

la palatani parta qazawat kawal *n.* لهپلنپرتهقضاوتکول prejudice

la pkho achawal *v.t.* لهپواچول
overthrow

la pkho lweydal *v.i.* لهپولودل
succumb

la qanoon sara barabarawal *v.t.* لهقانونسرهبرابرول regulate

la qanoon sara sam *a.* لهقانونسره
سم statutory

la qanoonee lari zay sakha weystal *v. t* لهقانونىلارىخه وستل evict

la qazayee preykri aw hod parta *a.* لهقضايىپرکاوهوپرته
subjudice

la reekhtanee tareekh sakha makhki tareekh wayal *n* له ريتيتاريخخهمخکيتاريخويل
antedate

la sakht kaghaza jora shawi naray gata *n.* لهسختکاغذه جوهشونرته cardboard

la sami lari arawal *v.t.* لهسملاراول
pervert

la sara *adv.* لهسره afresh

la sara ada kawal *v.t.* لهسرهاداکول
repay

la sara adaygee *n.* لهسرهادايى
repayment

la sara bya sanjawana *n.* لهسرهبيا سنجونه overhaul

la sara shmeyral *v.t.* لهسرهشمرل
recount

la sara zeyrma kawal *v.t.* لهسره زرمهکول replenish

la sara; dobara *adv.* لهسره،دوباره
anew

la sarkey aw meywey jor skhak
n. لهسركاومو جوماك shrub

la saza sakha bakhana *n.* لهسزاخه
بنه impunity

**la shahay sara yaw zay
takhteydal** *v. i* لهشهسرهیوای
تتدل elope

la sharmeydo makh sooreydal
v.i لهشرمدومخسوریدل blush

la sheydo beyleyda *n* لهشدوبلدا
ablactation

la sheydo dak *a.* لهشدوک milky

la shmeyra awreydal *v.t.* لهشمره
اولدل outnumber

la shora dak *a.* لهشورهک
uproarious

**la shta pangi sakha deyr
akheystal** *v.t.* لهشتهپانخهر
اخستل overdraw

la storo dak *a.* لهستوروک starry

**la tareekh sakha da makha
dawri loy feel** *n.* لهتاریخهخهد
مخهدورلوی فیل mammoth

**la tashreefato sara tar sara
kawal** *v.t.* لهتشریفاتوسرهترسره
کول solemnize

la toko aw maskharo dak anzor
n. لهتوکواومسخروکانور
caricature

la trakahar sara matawal *v.t.* له
تکهارسرهماتول snap

la wada makhkeenay *a.* لهواده
مخکینی premarital

la wada warandi *adj.* لهوادهواند
antenuptial

la wakhta awookhtal *v. t* لهوخته
اوتل elapse

la wara *adv.* لهورا afar

la warandi; da makha *adv.* له
واند،دمخه beforehand

la watana sharal *v.t.* لهوطنهشل
banish

la watana sharal *v.t.* لهوطنهشل
deport

la watana sharana *n.* لهوطنهشنه
banishment

**la wrandi chamtoo shaway;
muayyan** *a* لهواندچمتوشوی،
معین set

la yada lostal *n.* لهیادهلوستل
recitation

la yada wayal *v.t.* لهیادهویل recite

la yawa sara; har dawal *adv* لهیوه
سره،هرول all

la zan sara ghageydana *n.* لمان
سرهغدنه soliloquy

la zan sara khandal *v. i* لمانسره
خندل chuckle

la zaya porta kawal *v.t.* لمایهپورته
کول remove

la zaya top wahal *v.t.* لمایوپوهل
startle

la zeygeydoon warandi *adj.* له
زلدونواند antenatal

la zor asar sara ara laroonkay *n*
لهزوعصرسرهاهلرونکی
anachronism

la zyan sakha khwandee *a* لهزیان
خهخونديي proof

laas *n* لاس hand

laas achawal *v.t.* لااساچول infringe

laas pa las khparowoonki khabartya *n.* لاس‌په‌لاس خپروونکخبرتیا handbill

laasee kaar *n.* لاسی‌کار handiwork

laasee sanat *n.* لاسی‌صنعت handicraft

laasi kitab *n.* لاسی‌کتاب handbook

lafi *n* لاف boast

lafi aw bati *n.* لافاوبا vainglory

lafi wahal *v.i* لافوهل boast

lafzee *a.* لفظي literal

lafzee *n.* لفظي textual

lafzee shkhara *n* لفظي‌شخه row

lag *a.* ل little

lag *a.* ل less

lag lag *n.* ل‌ل stork

lag lag ratlal; saseydal *v.i.* للراتلل، سدل trickle

lag miqdar *n.* لمقدار little

lag sa *adv.* له little

lag sa khwara *n.* له‌خواه snack

lag shan *n.* لشان handful

lag wakht makhki *adv.* لوخت‌مخک recently

lag zhawar *n.* لژور shoal

lag; kam *a.* ل،کم scant

lagakht *n* لت consumption

lagakht *n.* لت cost

lagakhtoona kamawal *v.t.* لتونه کمول retrench

lagawal *v.t.* لول abate

lagawal *v.i.* لول adhere

lagawal *v.t.* لول affix

lagawana *n.* لونه abatement

laghar *a.* لغ nude

laghara mujasima *n* لغه‌مجسمه nude`

laghartob *n.* لغتوب nudity

laghata *n* لَغَته clamp

laghata *n.* لغته kick

laghata wahal *v.t.* لغته‌وهل kick

lagkay *n.* لاکی minority

lagtob *n.* لتوب paucity

lagya kawal *v.t.* لیاکول occupy

lahoo *adv.* لاهو afloat

lajanzar *n.* لجنزار marsh

lajanzara *a.* لجنزاره marshy

lak *n* لاک lac, lakh

lak; neygh *a* لک،نغ erect

laka; ghondi *pron.* لکه،غوند as

lakara; amsa *n.* لکه،امسا stick

lakara; musafir khana *n.* لکه، مسافرخانه cane

lakay *n.* لک tail

lakay wal storay *n* لکوال‌ستوری comet

lakay wal storay *n.* لکوال‌ستوری meteor

lakhta *n.* لته wand

lakhtay *n* لت drain

lakhtay *n.* لتی gutter

lakhtleek jorawana *n.* لتلیک جوونه tabulation

lakhtleek jorawoonkay *n.* لتلیک جوونکی tabulator

lalo lalo *n.* للولو lullaby

lamal garzeydal *v.t* لامل‌ردل cause

laman warachawal *v.t.* لمن‌وراچول skirt

lamanleek *adj.* لمنلیک adscript

lamba *n* لمبا bath

lamba *n* لمبه flame

lamba keydal; zor akheystal *v.i* لمبه كدل؛زوراخستل blaze

lamba warta kawal *v.i* لمبهورته كول flame

lambeydal *v. t* لمبدل bathe

lambo wahal *v.i.* لامبووهل swim

lambo wahana *n* لامبووهنه swim

lambo wahoonkay *n.* لامبووهونكى swimmer

lambowahana *n* لامبووهنه buoyancy

lambozan tokay *n* لامبوزنتوكى buoy

lamda karee ora *n* لمده كىياوه dough

lamdawal *v. i.* لمدول dabble

lamdawal *v. t.* لمدول damp

lamdawal *v.t.* لمدول steep

lamdawal *v.t.* لمدول soak

lamdeydal *v.i.* لمدل sob

lamdwalay *n* لمدوالى damp

lamehdood *a.* لا محدود immeasurable

lams *n* لمس touch

lams kawal *v.t.* لمسكول touch

lams; ehsas *n* لمس،احساس feeling

lamsawal *v.t.* لمسول abet

lamsawal *v.t.* لمسول incite

lamsawal *v.t.* لمسول instigate

lamsawal; darak kawal *v.t* لمسول؛درككول feel

lamsawana *n.* لمسونه provocation

lamsawona *n* لمسونه agitation

lamsawoonkay *a.* لمسوونكى provocative

lamsawoonkay *n.* لمسوونكى tempter

lamsoon *n.* لمسون abetment

lamsoon *n.* لمسون instigation

lamsoon *n.* لمسون temptation

lanat *n* لعنت curse

lanat warkawal *v. t* لعنتوركول curse

lanat wayal *v. t.* لعنتويل damn

lanatee *a.* لعنتي accursed

land *a* لند curt

land *a.* لند short

land *a* لند summary

land fikray *a.* لندفكرى insular

land fikree *n.* لندفكري insularity

land mahala astogna kawal *v.t.* لند مهالهاستونهكول lodge

land mahalay zand *n.* لندمهالىز adjournment

land mahalay; nasapee *a* لندمهالى، ناپي snap

land mahalee *a.* لندمهالي temporary

land mahalee astogna *n* لندمهالي استونه sojourn

land mahalee bandobast *a.* لند مهاليبندوبست provisional

landa aw teyza sa akheystal *v.i.* لنداوتزهساهاخستل pant

landa azmoyana *n.* لندهآزموينه quiz

landa keesa *n.* لندهكيسه anecdote

landa keesa *n.* لندهكيسه novelette

landa weyna *n* لندهونا aphorism

landawal *v.t.* لنول abbreviate

landawal *v.t* لنول abridge

landawal *v.t.* لنول shorten

landay ya koochnay *a.* لنۍياکوچنی puny

landeenay *a.* لاندینی nether

landeenay *a* لاندینی under

landeenay *prep.* لاندینی underneath

landeenay jamey *n.* لاندینجام underwear

landeenay por *n.* لاندینیپو basement

landeez *n* لنیز abbreviation

landeez *n* لنیز abridgement

landi *prep* لاند below

landi *prep.* لاند under

landi kawal *v.t.* لاندکول overtake

landi khwa ta *adv* لاندخواته downwards

landi; teet *prep* لاند؛ټ beneath

landoon *n* لنون brevity

landoon *n.* لنون summary

landoon; ghorchanr *n.* لنون؛غورچا precis

lang mahalee orband *n.* لنمهالي اوربند truce

langar zay *n.* لنرای dock

langaree; hawan *v.t.* لنر؛هاون mortar

langarzay *n.* لنرای harbour

lanja kawal *v.i.* لانجهکول tussle

lanzaka *n* لانکه doll

lapara *prep* لپاره for

lapara; haq *n.* لپاره؛حق sake

lapaya pohana *n.* لاپايهپوهنه omniscience

lapreydal *v.i.* لپدل shudder

lapreydana *n* لپدنه shudder

laqab *n.* لقب title

lar khod *n.* لار ود guide

lar khod lar leek *n.* لارودالیک index

lar khowana *n.* لاروونه guidance

lar khowana *n.* لاروونه lead

lar khowana kawal *v.t.* لاروونه کول guide

lar khowoonki khabara *n* لار وونکیخبره cue

lar leed *n.* لرلید background

lar leek *n.* الیک catalogue

lar leekanay *n.* لرلیکنی telegram

lar moondal *v.t.* لارموندل orientate

lar wrakay *a* لارورکی erroneous

lara *n.* لاره way

lara yi bandawal *v.t.* لارهيبندول thwart

laral *v.t.* لرل own

laram *n.* لم scorpion

laramay *n.* لم nettle

larana; neewana *n.* لرنه؛نیونه possession

laraway *n.* لاروی passenger

laraway *n.* لاروی wayfarer

laray *n.* لار truck

laray *n.* لار lorry

laray *n.* ل series

laray; tarteeb *n.* ل ترتیب range

laray; tasalsul *n.* ل تسلسل sequence

largay *n.* لری timber

largay *n.* لری wood

largay khoray *a.* خوری لری xylophagous

largeen *a.* لرين wooden

largeen satak *n.* لرينسک maul

largeena lakara *n* لرينهلکه stake

larghon peyzhandoonkay *n* لرغونپژندونکی antiquarian

larghon peyzhandoonkay *n.* لرغونپژندونکی antiquary

larghonay *a.* لرغونی ancient

larghonay *a.* لرغونی antiquarian

larghonay *a.* لرغونی antique

larghonay; zor *a.* زو؛لرغونی archaic

larghonee *a* لرغوني classical

larghonee asar *n.* لرغونيآثار relic

larghonee oloom *n* لرغونيعلوم classic

larghonee tamaddun pori arwand *a.* لرغونيتمدنپوراوند primitive

larghoni zamana *n.* لرغونزمانه antiquity

lari *n.* لا saliva

larkhod *n* لارود forerunner

larkhod *n.* لارود precepter

larkhod *n.* لارود leader

larkhod *n.* لارود usher

larkhod keetabgotay *n* لارود کتابوی directory

larkhowana *n.* لارونه leadership

larleed *n.* لرليد landscape

larleed *n.* لرليد outlook

larleed; qyafa *n.* قيافه؛لرليد prospect

laroonkay; malik *n.* مالک؛لرونکی owner

laryoon *n* لاريون march

larza *n.* لزه quiver

larza *n* لزه shake

larzand *a.* لزاند seismic

larzanda taba *n* لزندهتبه ague

larzeydal *v. i* لرزدل erupt

larzeydal *v.i.* لزدل pulsate

larzeydal *v.i.* لزدل quake

larzeydal *v.i.* لزدل quiver

larzeydal *v.i.* لزدل shake

larzeydal *v.i* لزدل wobble

larzeydal *v.t* لزدل flicker

larzeydal *v.t* لزدل flutter

larzeydana *n* لرزدنه eruption

larzeydana *n* لزدنه flutter

larzeydana *n* لزدنه quake

larzeydoonkay *a.* لزدونکی shaky

las akheystal *v. i.* لاساخستل cease

las aw greywan keydal *v.i.* لاساو روانکدل grapple

las aw greywan keydana *n.* لاساو روانکدنه grapple

las kakhana *n* لاسکنه manual

las laka *n.* لسلکه million

las magho *n.* لاسماغو glove

las neeway *n.* لاسنيوی adhesion

las paki wahal *v.t.* لاسپکوهل retouch

las raseydana *n* لاسرسدنه access

las ta rawastal *v.t.* لاستهراوستل achieve

las ta rawastal *n* لاستهراوستل acquest

las ta rawastana *n.* لاستهراوستنه acquisition

las ta rawral *v.t.* لاستهراول get

las ta rawral *v.t.* لاستهراول obtain

las ta rawral *v.t.* لاستهراول seize
las tapawal *v.t.* لاسپول grope
las warkawal *v.t.* لاسورکول palm
las warsakha akheystal *v.t.* لاس ورخهاخستل quit
las zara *n.* لسزره myriad
las zareez *a* لسزریز myriad
las; lasama shmeyra *n., a* لس؛ لسمهشمره ten
lasama barkha *n.* لسمهبرخه tithe
lasee *a.* لاسي manual
lasee bam *n.* لاسيبم grenade
laseeza *n* لسیزه decade
lashkhor zanawar ya margha *n.* لاشخورناوریامارغه scavenger
lasleek *n.* لاسلیک signature
lasleekoonkay *n.* لاسلیکونکی signatory
lasoona aw nookan seengarawal *n.* لاسونهاونوکانسیناول manicure
lasoona parkawal *v. i.* لاسونهپکول clap
lasploray *n.* لاسپلوری vendor
lasposay; goodagay *n.* لاسپوی؛ای puppet
lastay *n.* لاستی handle
lastay; kalawa *n.* لاستی؛کلاوه skein
lastay; mootay *n.* لاستی؛موی winch
lastee loya pyala *n.* لاستيلويهپیاله jug
lastonr khula *n* لستوخوله cuff
lastonr khula warchawal *v. t* لستوخولهوراچول cuff
lastonray *n* لستوی sleeve

lat saray *n.* لسی sluggard
latarawal *v.t.* لتاول afflict
lateef *a.* لطیف dainty
lateef *a* لطیف delicate
lawang *n* لونگ clove
lawda *n.* لوده idiot
lawda *a* لوده stupid
lawda; bey aqla *a.* لوده؛بعقل indiscriminate
lawda; ganr *a* لوده؛ dense
lawdatob *n.* لودهتوب stupidity
lawgaree; da law masheen *n.* لوری؛دلوماشین reaper
lawreena *a* لورینه bountiful
laya *n.* لایه layer
lazat *n* لذت enjoyment
lazat *n.* لذت pleasure
lazat *n.* لذت joy
lazimee fayl *a. verb* لازميفعل intransitive
lazimee kawona *n.* لازميکوونه imposition
lazmee *a* لازمي compulsory
lazoom *n* لزوم must
leed; manzara *n.* لید؛منظره perspective
leedal *v.t.* لیدل sight
leedal *v.t.* لیدل view
leedal keydoonay; tar pam landi *a.* لیدلکدونی؛ترپاملاند sightly
leedal; katal *v.t.* لیدل؛کتل watch
leedana *n.* لیدنه sight
leedana katana *n.* لیدنهکتنه meeting
leedana; saat *n.* لیدنه؛ساعت watch
leedoonkay *n.* لیدونکی spectator

leedoonkay *n.* ليدونکی seer

leek *n* ليک letter

leek lost *n.* ليک‌لوست literacy

leek ya saman pa pust leygdawal *v.t.* ليک‌یاسامان‌په‌پُست‌لدول post

leeka *n* ليکه column

leeka *n.* ليکه row

leeka leeka kawal *v.t.* ليکه‌ليکه‌کول stripe

leeka pri kakhal *v.t.* ليکه‌پرکل line

leekal *v.t.* ليکل write

leekal; pa band ki achawal *v.t.* ليکل؛په‌بندکاچول pen

leekali zhmana *n.* ليکلژمنه treatise

leekanay banra *n* ليکه‌به calligraphy

leekay *n* ليکی book

leekay satoonkay *n* ليکی‌ساتونکی book-keeper

leekee plorowoonkay *n* ليکي پلورونکی book-seller

leekoonkay *n.* ليکونکی notary

leekwal *n.* ليکوال author

leekwal *n.* ليکوال writer

leelam *n* ليلام auction

leelamawal *v.t.* ليلامول auction

leemoo *n.* ليمو lemon

leendakay *n.* ليندک parenthesis

leenday wala; khakht karay *n* ليندوالا؛خت‌کاری archer

leengay *n.* لينی shin

leesansa sar ta rasawal *v.i.* ليسانسه‌سرته‌رسول graduate

leeyaqat *n.* لياقت merit

leeyaqat *n.* لياقت prowess

leeyaqat laral *v.t* لياقت‌لرل merit

leeyaqat; twan *n.* لياقت؛توان potency

lehen; ahang *n.* لحن؛آهنگ tune

lehja; garana *n.* لهجه؛نه idiom

lehjawee *a.* لهجوي idiomatic

levaltia *n* ليوالتيا fervour

leycha *n* لجه forearm

leygd raleygd *n.* لدرالد transportation

leygdawal *v.t.* لدول send

leygdawal *v.t.* لدول transport

leygdawana *n.* لدونه carriage

leygdawana *n.* لدونه portage

leygdawoonkay *n.* لدوونکی carrier

leyri *a* لر distant

leyri *a* لر far

leyri *a.* لر remote

leyri *a.* لر younder

leyri kawal; ghorzawal *v. t* لر کول؛غورول dispose

leyri kawona *n* لرکوونه disposal

leyri walay *n* لروالی far

leyri; pa gokha ki *adv.* لر؛په‌وه‌که aloof

leyri; yaw lori ta *adv.* لر؛يولورته away

leywa *n.* لوه wolf

leywal *a* لوال eager

leywal; munasib *a.* لوال؛مناسب apt

leywanay *a* لونی crazy

leywanay *n.* لونی maniac

leywanay *a.* لونی lunatic

leywanay kas *n.* لونی‌کس lunatic

leywanay kawal *v.t* لونی‌کول dement

leywantob *n.* لونتوب lunacy
leywantob *n* لونتوب mania
leywantob *n.* لونتوب psychosis
leywantob *v.i.* لونتوب كول rampage
libas *n.* لباس attire
libas *n.* لباس costume
lifafa *n* لفافه envelope
lmanzal *v. t. & i.* لمانل celebrate
lmanzana *n.* لماننه celebration
lmar *n.* لمر sun
lmar khwalay *n* لمرخول belvedere
lmar rakhatana *n* لمرراختنه dawn
lmar ta eekhodal *v.t.* لمرتهايودل sun
lmareen *a.* لمرين solar
lmareen *a.* لمرين sunny
lmareen *a.* لمرين shiny
lmoonz *n.* لمونز prayer
lmoonz kawal *v.i.* لمونزكول pray
loab *n.* لعاب mucilage
loba *n.* لوبه play
loba *n.* لوبه sport
loba kawal *v.i.* لوبه كول sport
loba panra *n* لوبه پاه foolscap
loba; musabiqa *n.* لوبه؛مسابقه game
lobeydal *v.i.* لوبدل toy
lobghalay *n.* لوبغالی gymnasium
lobghalay *n.* لوبغالی stadium
lobgharay *n.* لوبغای player
lobgharay *n.* لوبغای sportsman
lobi kawal *v.i.* لوبكول play
lobsaray *n.* لوباری referee
lobtaka *n.* لوبتکه toy
lobya *n.* لوبیا bean

lochak *n.* لوچك scoundrel
loga *n* لوه hunger
logareetam *n.* لوباریتم logarithim
lokhay *n* لوی dish
lokhay *n.* لوی plate
lokhay *n.* لوی vessel
lokhay *n.* لوی pot
lokhee aw largee *n.* لوی او لري utensil
loochak *a.* لوچک profligate
loochak aw koosa dabay zwan *n.* لوچک او کوه بی وان hooligan
loochkay *n.* لوچکی profligacy
loogay *n.* لوی smoke
loogay *n.* لوی soot
loogay keydal *v.i.* لوی کدل smoke
loogay laroonkay *a.* لوی لرونکی vaporous
loogay wahalay *a.* لوی وهلی smoky
looma *n.* لومه noose
looma *n.* لومه snare
loomranay *a.* لومنی premier
loomranay; muhim *a.* لومنی؛مهم prime
loomranee maqam ta stanawal *v.t.* لومنی مقام ته ستنول reinstate
loomray *a* لومی first
loomray *n* لومی preliminary
loomray gam porta kawal *v.t.* لومی ام پورته کول initiate
loomray wraz *n* لومور first
loond *a.* لوند wet
loondawal *v.t.* لوندول wet
loondwalay *n.* لوندوالی wetness
loor *n* لور daughter
loosawal *v.t.* لوول denude

loot talan *n.* تالان لو ravage
loota *n.* لوه clod
lootal *v.t.* لول depredate
lootal *v.i.* لول maraud
lootal *v.t.* لول plunder
lootal *v.t.* لول rob
lootal; tala kawal *v.t.* لول،تالاکول ravage
lootmar *n.* لوهمار marauder
lor *n.* لور sickle
lor *n.* لور scythe
lor ta *prep.* لورته towards
lora *n.* لوه oath
lorand *a.* لوراند merciful
lorand; mehraban *a.* لوراند،مهربان amiable
loreenee; mehrabanee *n.* لوريني، مهرباني amiability
los; barband *a.* لو،بربند bare
lost *n.* لوست lesson
lostal *v.t.* لوستل read
lostay *a.* لوستی literate
lostoonkay *n.* لوستونکی reader
loy *a* لوی big
loy askar *n.* لوىسم cavern
loy asqaf *n.* لوىاسقف archbishop
loy aw azeem *a.* لوىاوعظيم massive
loy badanay *a.* لوىبدذ gigantic
loy badanay *a.* لوىبدنی massy
loy chamanzar *n.* لوىچمنزار meadow
loy jageer *n.* لوىجاير manor
loy kar kawal *v. t* لوىکارکول exploit
loy khamar *n.* لوىامار python

loy khar pori arwand *a.* لوىارپور اوند metropolitan
loy loy gamoona akheystal *v.i.* لوىلوىهامونهاخستل stride
loy loy leekal *v.t* لوىلوىليکل engross
loy munshee; loomray wazeer *n.* لوىمنشي،لومىوزير chancellor
loy or *n* لوىاور bonfire
loy samandar *n.* لوىسمندر ocean
loy toray *a.* لوىتورى capital
loy wat *n.* لوىوا avenue
loy; hajeem *a.* لوى،حجيم voluminous
loya darwaza *n.* لويهدروازه gate
loya gol dabara *n* لويمولبره boulder
loya karnama *n* لويهکارنامه feat
loya keygday *n.* لويهکد pavilion
loya khoona *n.* لويهخونه saloon
loya lar *n.* لويهلار highway
loya lara *n.* لويهلاره thoroughfare
loya musafiree kakhtay *n* لويه مسافري کٹ cruiser
loya namray *n.* لويهنمه gulp
loya sapa *n* لويهپه billow
loya sawdagaree *n* لويهسوداري enterprise
loya teyrwatana *n* لويهتروتنه blunder
loya tota *n.* لويهلوه lump
loyawal; loyeydal *v.i.* لويول،لويدل zoom
loyee *n.* لويي grandeur
loyee *n.* لويي magnanimity

loyeydana; teyz harakat *n.* ،لویدنه،‏ تزحرکت zoom

loyidal *v.t.* لویدل lump

lozh *n.* لوژ gallery

lugho kawal *v. t.* لغوکول abrogate

lughwa kawal *v.t.* لغوه‌کول countermand

lughwa kawal *v.t.* لغوه‌کول annul

luqma *n.* لقمه mouthful

lwaga; qahtee *n.* لوه؛قحطي starvation

lwar awazay *a.* لواوازی loud

lwar ghag *n.* لوغر alp

lwar narkh warandi kawal *v.t.* لو نرخواندکول outbid

lwar poray *n* لوپوی eminance

lwar poray hakim *n.* لوپوی‌حاکم paramount

lwar poray rahib *n* لوپوی‌راهب prior

lwar pori rahiba *n.* لوپوراهبه prioress

lwar walay *n.* لووالی altitude

lwar walay maloomowoonkay *n* لووالی‌معلومونکی altimeter

lwar zhawar *a.* لوژور rough

lwara alwatana kawal *v.i.* لوه الوتنه‌کول soar

lwara baya warkawal *v.t.* لوه‌بیه ورکول overrate

lwara sapa *n.* لوهپه surge

lwara sata *n.* لوهسطح plateau

lwara sawkay *n.* لوهوک stool

lwarawal *v. t* لوول elevate

lwarawal *v.t.* لوول heighten

lwarawana *n* لووونه elevation

lwaraway *n.* لواوی reverence

lwaraway *n.* لواوی supremacy

lwarwalay *n.* لووالی height

lweydal *v.i.* لودل tumble

lweydeez *n.* لودیز west

lweydeez *n.* لودیز occident

lweydeez bad *n.* لودیزباد zephyr

lweydeez pori arwand *a.* لودیزپور اوند westerly

lweydeez wal *a.* لودیزوال west

lweydeeza *a.* لودیزه western

lweydeeza naray *a.* لودیزهـ occidental

lweyshtakay *n* لوشتکی dwarf

lweyshtakay saray *n.* لوشتکی‌سی midget

lweyshteenak insan *n.* لوشتینک انسان pygmy

M

ma khpala *pron.* ماخپله myself

ma la *pron.* ماله me

maaf; khwandee *adj* معاف؛خوندي exempt

maafawal *v.t* معافول excuse

maafawal; takhfeefawal *v.t.* معافول؛تخفیفول remit

maafeeyat *n.* معافیت remission

maafeeyat; bakhana *n* معافیت؛ بخنه excuse

maamila *n.* معامله issue

mach *n* مچ fly

machak *n.* مچک goad

machay *n.* مچ bee

machnoghza *n.* مچنوغزه sling

macho *n.* مچو kiss

macho kawal *v.t.* مچوکول kiss

mada *n.* ماده matter

mada *n* ماده material

mada parastee *n.* مادهپرستي materialism

mada; seez *n.* ماده،یز stuff

mada; zat *n.* ماده،ذات substance

madanee *a* مدني civic

madanee oloom *n* مدنيعلوم civics

madanee; oolasee *a* مدني،اولسي civil

madawam *adj.* مداوم continual

madee *a.* مادي material

madee banra warkawal *v.t.* مادي بهورکول substantiate

madha *n.* مدحه panegyric

mafad *n.* مفاد content

mafad aw gata *n.* مفاداوه scope

mafhoom; mana *n.* مفهوم،مانا purport

mafhoomee kawal *v.t.* مفهوميکول purport

mafrooza; yaw khyal *n.* مفروضه، یوخیال hypothesis

mafsal *n.* مفصل joint

mag; wray *n.* مږ،وری ram

magar da chi *prep* مرداچ but

magar da chi *conj.* مرداچ unless

magar da chi *prep* مرداچ save

magar; prata la *prep* مر،پرتهله except

magaway; sanjaq *n.* موی،سنجاق peg

maghfirat *n.* مغفرت pardon

maghroor *n* مغرور swagger

maghroorana *a.* مغرورانه lofty

mahal *n.* محل locality

mahal *n.* مهال time

mahaleez *n.* مهالیز periodical

mahaleez *a.* مهالیز temporal

mahalweysh *n.* مهالویش schedule

mahalweysh ki wakht warkawal *v.t.* مهالویشکوخترورکول schedule

maharat *n.* مهارت speciality

maharat *n.* مهارت tact

maharat *n.* مهارت manipulation

maharat *n.* مهارت mastery

maharat *n.* مهارت sleight

maharat *n.* مهارت proficiency

maharatoona aw tadbeeroona *n.* مهارتونهاوتدبیرونه tactics

mahbal; teykay *n.* مهبل،تکی vagina

mahboob *a* محبوب beloved

mahboob *n* محبوب sweet

mahdood *a* محدود finite

mahdood *a.* محدود limited

mahdoodawal *v. t* محدودول confine

mahdoodawal *v. t* محدودول curb

mahdoodawal *v.t.* محدودول limit

mahdoodawal *v.t.* محدودول restrict

mahdoodawoonkay *a.* محدودوونکی restrictive

mahdoodeeyat *n.* محدودیت limitation

mahfooz *a.* محفوظ safe

mahir *n.* ماهر adept

mahir *a.* ماهر proficient

mahir *a.* ماهر versed

mahir; chalbaz *a* ماهر،چلباز crafty

mahirana *a* ماهرانه elaborate

mahirana *a.* ماهرانه tactful

mahkama *n.* محكمه tribunal

mahkamey ta hazirawal *v.* محكمې ته حاضرول arraign

mahrak *n.* محرک locomotive

mahramana *a.* محرمانه confidential

mahroomawal *v. t.* محرومول bereave

mahroomeeyat *n* محروميت bereavement

mahsool *n.* محصول tariff

mahsool warkawal; ata kawal *v.t.* محصول وركول،اعطاكول yield

mahsoor zay *n.* محصورځای closure

mahwa kawal *v. t* محوه كول erase

mahwa kawal *v.t.* محوه كول obliterate

majazee; kanayawee *a.* مجازي؛ كنايوي allegorical

majazee; waqiee *a* مجازي؛واقعي virtual

majboor *a.* مجبور needful

majboorawal *v. t* مجبورول compel

majboorawal *v.t.* مجبورول induce

majlis *n* مجلس congress

majlis *n.* مجلس session

majmooa jorawal *v.t.* مجموعه جورول aggregate

makab *n* مكعب cube

makab dawla *adj.* مكعب وله cubiform

makabee *a* مكعبي cubical

makalima *n.* مكالمه parley

makan; tar wadanay landi zmaka *n.* مكان؛تر ودانځلاندمكه site

makar; heela *n.* مكر؛حيله guile

makar; mozee *a.* مكار؛موذي sly

makashifa *n.* مكاشفه revelation

makatiba *n.* مكاتبه correspondence

makatiba kawal *v. i* مكاتبه كول correspond

makh *n* مخ face

makh aw sha ta harakat kawal *v.i.* مخ او شاته حركت كول wag

makh khwa ta *a.* مخ خواته onward

makh pa kkhata *adv* مخ په كته downward

makh pa shomal *adv.* مخ په شمال north

makh pa zwar *prep* مخ پمو down

makh pa zwara *adv.* مخ پمو ه backward

makha *n.* مخه front

makha dap kawal *v.t.* مخه پ كول resist

makha dap kawal *v.t.* مخه پ كول restrain

makha kha *n* مخه farewell

makha neewal *v.t.* مخه نيول tackle

makha neewana; karee wasayal *n.* مخه نيونه؛ كاري وسايل tackle

makha yi ragarzawal *v.t.* مخه يې رارول rein

makham *n* ماخام evening

makham *n.* ماخام supper

makhamakh keydal *v.t* مخامخ كدل face

makhamanay doday *n* مخامنو دودي dinner

makhfee *adj.* مخفي clandestine

makhfee *a.* مخفي underhand

makhfee *a.* مخفي occult

makhfee kawal; patawal *v.t.* مخفي كول؛پول stow

makhkakh *n.* مخخ pioneer

makhkanay; warandi *n.* مخكني، واند antecedent

makhki *adv.* مخكي ahead

makhki *adv.* مخخ ago

makhki keydal *v.* مخخكدل precede

makhki keydal *v.t.* مخخكيدل advance

makhki la dey chi *conj* مخكله‌دچ before

makhki la dey; qablan *adv.* مخخ له‌د،قبلا already

makhki la makhki chamtoo kawal *v.t* مخكله‌مخخكچمتوكول forearm

makhki la; albata *adv.* مخكله،البته rather

makhlooq *n* مخلوق creature

makhloot shaway shorba *n.* مخلوط‌شوشوربا porridge

makhloot taleem *n.* مخلوط‌تعليم co-education

makhloot; gadola *n* مخلوط؛وله blend

makhlootawal *v. t* مخلوطول blend

makhneeway *n* مخنيوي control

makhneeway *n.* مخنيوي interception

makhneeway *n.* مخنيوي inhibition

makhneeway *n.* مخنيوي prevention

makhneeway aw waqaya *n.* مخنيوىاووقايه repercussion

makhneeway kawal *v. t* مخنيوى كول control

makhneeway kawal *v.t.* مخنيوى كول inhibit

makhneeway kawal *v.t.* مخنيوى كول prevent

makhneeway kawoonkay *a.* مخنيوىكوونكى obstructive

makhneewoonkay *a.* مخنيوونكى preventive

makhneewoonkay *a.* مخنيوونكى repellent

makhooka *n* موكه beak

makhroot *n.* مخروط cone

makhsoos *a.* مخصوص extraordinary

makhsoos *a.* مخصوص specific

makhtaray *n.* مختاى prefix

larghonaya. *a* مكنون latent

makoo *n.* ماكو shuttle

makoos; makoos fayl *a* معكوس؛ معكوس‌فعل reflexive

makoosawana *n.* معكوسوونه reversal

mal *n* مل fellow

mal *n.* مال lucre

mal keydal *v.t.* مل كيدل accompany

mal; shtamanee *n.* مال؛شتمني wealth

malak; khan *n.* ملک،خان squire

malakush shoara *n* ملک‌الشعرا
laureate

malamat ganral *v. t* ملامتل blame

malamatawal *v. t.* ملامتول
condemn

malamatawal *v. t.* ملامتول convict

malamatawal *v.t.* ملامتول impute

malamatawal *v.t.* ملامتول rebuke

malamatawal *v. t.* ملامتول chide

malamatee *n.* ملامتي reproach

malamatya *n* ملامتيا condemnation

malamatya *n.* ملامتيا rebuke

malamatya; ilzam *n* ملامتيا،الزام
blame

malande *n.* ملند lampoon

malande kawal *v.t.* ملندکول
lampoon

malandi *n* ملند gibe

malandi pri kawal *v.i.* ملندپرکول
mock

malandi wahal *v.i.* ملندوهل gibe

malandi; peyghor *adj* ملند،پغور
mock

maldara; shtaman *n.* مالداره،شتمن
millionaire

malee *a* مالي fiscal

malee mrasta *n.* مالي‌مرسته subsidy

malee mrasta kawal *v.t.* مالي‌مرسته
کول subsidize

maleeya *n.* ماليه revenue

maleeya *n.* ماليه tax

maleeya eekhodana *n.* ماليه‌ايودنه
taxation

maleeya lagawal *v.t.* ماليه‌لول tax

maleeyat *n* ماليات finance

maleeyat *n.* ماليات levy

maleeyat lagawal *v.t.* ماليات‌لول
levy

maleeyatee *a* مالياتي financial

maleeyatee jareema *n.* مالياتي
جريمه surtax

malga *n.* ماله salt

malga pri mokhal *v.t* ماله‌پرمول
salt

malga pri mokhal *v.t.* ماله‌پرمول
season

malgaray *n* ملری accomplice

malgaray *n.* ملری comrade

malgaray *n.* ملری friend

malgaray *n.* ملری mate

malgaray; mal; warsara *adv.*
ملری،مل،ورسره along

malgartya; ashnayee *n.* ملرتيا،
آشنايي amity

malgary *n.* ملری companion

malgeen *a.* مالين saline

malgeen *a.* مالين salty

malghalara *n.* ملغلره pearl

malham *n.* ملهم balm

malham *n.* ملهم ointment

malik *n.* مالک proprietor

malika *n* ملکه empress

malika *n.* ملکه queen

malkee wagaray *n* ملکي‌وی
civilian

malmal *n.* ململ mull

maloom *a.* مالوم conspicuous

maloom *a.* معلوم overt

maloomat *n.* معلومات information

maloomawal *v.t.* معلومول ascertain

maloomawal *v. t* معلومول detect

maloomawal v. t معلومول diagnose

maloomeydal v.i. معلومدل loom

maloona lootal v.t. مالونه‌لول ransack

malt laroonkay skhak jorawal n. مالت‌لرونکی‌ياک‌جوول malt

malta n. ماله lime

maltya n ملتا accompaniment

malyatee wazeeyat; atkal n. مالياتي‌وضعيت،اكل assessment

mamas n. مماس tangent

mamnooa a. ممنوعه prohibitive

mamnooa a. ممنوعه prohibitory

mamoli a. معمولی mean

mamoolan adv. معمولا usually

mamoolee a. معمولي ordinary

mamoor n. مأمور commissioner

mamoor; amil n. مأمور،عامل functionary

mamooreeyat n. مأموريت commission

man aw salwa n. من‌او‌سلوا manna

mana n. مانا meaning

mana akheystal v.t مانا‌اخستل mean

mana kawal v. t. منع‌كول debar

mana kawal v. t منع‌كول dissuade

mana kawal v.t منع‌كول forbid

mana kawal v.t. منع‌كول rebuff

mana warkawal v.t. ماناور‌كول signify

mana; loyakht n. مانا،لويت signification

mana; radawana n. منع،ردونه rebuff

manadee n. منادي precursor

manakhta kawal v.t. منته‌كول avow

manal & منل accept

manana n. مننه thanks

manana warta wayal v.t. مننه‌ورته‌ويل thank

manandoy a. مننډوی grateful

manandoy a. مننډوی thankful

manay n. مانع obstacle

manay kawal v.t. مانع‌كول mar

manay keydal v.t. مانع‌كدل impede

manay keydal v.t. مانع‌كدل obstruct

manay; khazan n. مني،خزان autumn

mand; asar n منډ،اثر wake

mand; da pkhey zay n. منډ،دپای track

manda n. منډه run

manda wahal v.i. منډه‌وهل run

mandana; danana kawana n مندنه،دننه‌كوونه thrust

mandaroo n. منداو churn

manfee a. منفي no

manfee a منفي minus

manfee a. منفي negative

manfee adad n. منفي‌عدد negative

mangol n. منګول toe

mangol lagawal v.t. منګول‌لول toe

mangoley n منګول claw

mangoli prey khakhawal v.t. منګول‌پرخول paw

manoonkay; darak kawoonkay a. منونکی،درک‌كوونکی receptive

manra *n.* مه apple

manray *n* ما bungalow

manray *n* ما edifice

manray *n.* ما palace

manroo *n.* مالو mariner

manroo *n.* مالو navigator

mansoobawal *v.t.* منسوبول ascribe

mansoojat; tokar *n* منسوجات،ټوکر textile

mansookh *a.* منسوخ outdated

mansookh shaway *a.* منسوخشوی antiquated

mantaj *a* منتج consequent

mantaq *n.* منطق logic

mantaq poh *n.* منطق پوه logician

mantaqa *n.* منطقه zone

mantaqee *a* منطقي coherent

mantaqee *a.* منطقي logical

mantaqee banra warkawal *v.t.* منطقي بهورکول rationalize

manz *a.* مٔ mid

manz *a.* مٔ middle

manzanay barkha *a.* مننربرخه innermost

manzanay had *n.* مننی حد average

manzani takay *n.* مننی کی mean

manzar *n.* منظر scenery

manzar; nazar *n.* منظر،نظر view

manzara *n.* منظره scene

manzara; larleed *n.* منظره،لرليد vista

manzara; tamasha *n.* منظره،تماشا spectacle

manzgaray *n.* مننی arbitrator

manzgaray *a.* مننی intermediate

manzgaray *n.* مننی mediator

manzgartob *n.* منتوب arbitration

manzil *n* منزل destination

manzoor *a.* منظور intent

maqad *n.* مقعد anus

maqala *n* مقاله article

maqala *n* مقاله tract

maqala leekal *v. t.* مقاله ليکل essay

maqala leekoonkay *n* مقاله ليکونکی essayist

maqala; namoona *n.* مقاله،نمونه essay

maqam laral *v.t.* مقام لرل rank

maqam; halat *n.* مقام،حالت position

maqam; poray *n.* مقام،پو rank

maqar *adj.* مقعر concave

maqawam; payand *a.* مقاوم،پايند resistant

maqawmat *n.* مقاومت resistance

maqbara *n.* مقبره mausoleum

maqbara *n.* مقبره sepulchre

maqbara *n.* مقبره sepulture

maqool *a.* معقول reasonable

maqooleeyat; hookhyaree *n.* معقوليت؛هوياري sobriety

maqsad *n.* مقصد goal

mar *a* مه dead

mar *n.* مار serpent

mar *n.* مار snake

mar keydal *v. i* مکدل decease

mar peych; bandol *n.* مارپچ؛بنول spiral

mar postakay ghorzawal *v.t.* مه پوستکی غورول slough

maraka *n* مرکه dialogue

maraka *n.* مرکه interview

maraka kaval *v.t.* مرکه‌کول interview

maraka kawal *v. t.* مرکه‌کول discuss

marawal *v.t.* مَول glut

maray *n.* مه morsel

maray *n* مى corpse

maraz; krak *n.* مز؛کرک quail

marboot *a.* مربوط pertinent

marboot *a.* مربوط relative

mardana; la jinsee palwa faal *a.* مردانه؛له‌جنسي‌پلوه‌فعال virile

mareez *n* مريض patient

marg ta sparal *v. t.* مرته‌سپارل doom

margee *a* مري fatal

margee hal *a.* مري‌حال moribund

margharay *n.* مرغى gland

marhala *n.* مرحله phase

marifat; fikree zhawarwalay *n.* معرفت؛فکري‌ژوروالى profundity

marifee kawal *v.t.* معرفي‌کول introduce

marifee kawana *n.* معرفي‌کوونه representation

marjan *n* مرجان coral

markaz *n* مرکز center

markaz *n* مرکز centre

markaz *n* مرکز middle

markaz; sazman *n.* مرکز؛سازمان institution

markazee *a.* مرکزي central

markazee barkha *n.* مرکزي‌برخه midst

markazee hasta *n.* مرکزي‌هسته nucleus

markazi *a* مرکزى focal

markheyray *n.* مرخى mushroom

marmay *n* مرم bullet

marmay; da nakhi weeshtana *n.* مرم؛دنوي‌شتنه shot

marseeya *n* مرثيه elegy

marseeya *n.* مرثيه monody

martaba *n.* مرتبه grade

masadira *n.* مصادره requisition

masadira kawal *v.t.* مصادره‌کول requisition

masahat *n* مساحت area

masala *n.* مساله spice

masala pri doorawal *v.t.* مساله‌پر دوول spice

masala; qayda *n.* مسئله؛قاعده theorem

masaleydar; khwandawar *a.* مسالدار؛خوندور spicy

masana *n* مثانه bladder

masawee *a* مساوي equivalent

masawee ganral *v. t* مساوي‌ل equate

masawee kawal *v. t.* مساوي‌کول equalize

masaweetob *n.* مساويتوب parity

masee alayhis salam *n.* مسيح‌عليه السلام messiah

maseehee naray *n.* مسيحي‌نز Christendom

mashahoor *a.* مشهور renowned

mashahoor *a.* مشهور well-known

mashar *a* مشر elder

mashar saray *n.* مشرسرى senior

mashar; rahbar *n* مشر؛رهبر premier

mashar; zor *a.* مشر،زو senior
masharee *n.* مشري captaincy
masharee *a* مشرى elderly
masharee kawal *v.i.* مشري‌كول preside
mashartob *n.* مشرتوب seniority
mashboo kawal *v.t.* مشبوع‌كول saturate
masheen *n* ماشين engine
masheen poh *n.* ماشين‌پوه mechanic
masheenee saray *n.* ماشيني‌سى robot
mashghola *n.* مشغولا hobby
mashghulawal *v.t.* مشغولول amuse
mashghultya; tafreeh *n* مشغولتيا، تفريح amusement
mashhoorawal *v.t.* مشهورول popularize
mashkook *a.* مشكوک suspect
mashoom *n.* ماشوم kid
mashoom *n* ماشوم child
mashoom la sheydo warkawalo beylawal *v.t.* ماشوم‌له‌شدو وركولوبلول wean
mashoom; khidmatgar *n.* ماشوم، خدمتار wench
mashoomana *a.* ماشومانه childish
mashoomana *a.* ماشومانه puerile
mashoomtob *n.* ماشومتوب childhood
mashooq *n* معشوق beloved
mashoor *a.* مسحور captive
mashoorawal *v. t.* مسحورول captivate
mashq kawal *v.t.* مشق‌كول practise

mashq; tajruba *n.* مشق،تجربه practice
mashra; rahbara *n.* مشره،رهبره premiere
mashroob *n.* مشروب liquor
mashwara *n* مشوره consultation
mashwara *n.* مشوره tip
mashwara kawal *v. t* مشوره‌كول consult
mashwara warkawal *v.t.* مشوره وركول tip
mask aghostay lobgharay *n.* ماسک‌اغوستى‌لوبغاى mummer
maskan *n* مسكن abode
maskhara *n.* مسخره bantling
maskhara *n* مسخره buffoon
maskhara *n* مسخره clown
maskhara *n.* مسخره joker
maskhara kawal *v.t.* مسخره‌كول satirize
maskhara; malanda *n* مسخره،ملنده sneer
maskharey *n.* مسخر raillery
maskharey *n.* مسخر ridicule
maskoona aghostee lobgharee *n.* ماسكونه‌اغوستى‌لوبغاى pantomime
maslak *n.* مسلک sect
maslakee *a.* مسلكي sectarian
maslihat *n* مصلحت advisability
maslihat *n.* مصلحت opportunism
maslihatee gatawar *a* مصلحتي‌ور expedient
masnad *n.* مسند predicate
masnad; mutee *a* مسند،مطيع subject

masnooee *a.* مصنوعي artificial

masnooee *a.* مصنوعي counterfeit

larghonaya *a* مصنوعي fictitious

masnooee *a.* مصنوعي synthetic

masnooee khobawana *n.* مصنوعي خوبونه mesmerism

masnooee seez *n* مصنوعي‌يز synthetic

masnooee weykhtan *n.* مصنوعي وتان wig

masool *a.* مسؤل liable

masool *a* مسؤل accountable

masoolana *a* مسؤلانه amenable

masooleeyat *n* مسؤليت post

masooleeyat *n.* مسؤليت liability

masooleeyat warkawal *v.t.* مسؤليت‌ورکول sponsor

masraf *n* مصرف consumption

masraf keydal *v. t* مصرف‌کدل consume

masraf; lagakht *n.* مصرف،‌لت expense

masrafawal *v. t* مصرفول expend

masrafawal *v.t.* مصرفول spend

mast *a.* مست jolly

mast; nasha *a.* مست،‌نشه tipsy

mastawal *v. t* مستول bemuse

mastawal *v. i* مستول booze

mastee *n.* مستي spree

mastey *n* مستة curd

mat *n.* م arm

mat band *a* مبند armlet

matal *n.* متل adage

matal *n* متل byword

matal; zareena wayna *n.* متل؛زرینه ونا proverb

matam *n.* ماتم lamentation

matam *n.* ماتم mourning

matam kawal *v.i.* ماتم‌کول mourn

matam kawal *v. t* ماتم‌کول bewail

matam kawoonkay *n.* ماتم‌کوونکی mourner

matawal *v. t* ماتول contradict

matawal *v.t* ماتول fracture

matawal; beylawal *v.i.* ماتول؛بلول split

matey warkawal *v. t* ماتورکول crush

mateydal; matawal *v. t* ماتدل؛ ماتول break

mateydana *n* ماتدنه breakage

mateydoonkay *n* ماتدونکی cracker

mati *n* ماتِ defeat

mati warkawal *v. t.* مانورکول defeat

matlab rasawal *v.t.* مطلب‌رسول intimate

matrah kawal *v.t.* مطرح‌کول propound

matrooka *n.* متروکه scourge

matwalay *n.* ماتوالی fracture

matwalay; zand *n* ماتوالی؛ز break

mawafiqi areeki *n.* موافقایک rapport

mawarayee tabeeyat pori arwand *a.* ماورایي‌طبیعت‌پوراوند metaphysical

maweez *n.* مویز raisin

mawhoom parast *a.* موهوم‌پرست superstitious

mawhoom parastee *n.* موهوم‌پرستي superstition

mawjood *a* موجود available

mawjood *a.* موجود present

mawjood; zeyrma shaway *a.*
موجود؛زرمهشوى stock

mawjooda *a* موجوده current

mawjoodgee *n.* موجودي presence

mawroosee *n.* موروثي hereditary

mawseeqee *n.* موسيقي music

mawseeqee jorawoonkay *n.*
موسيقيجوونكى musician

mawzoo *n.* موضوع؛مقاله theme

mawzoo; mubhas *n.* موضوع؛مبحث
topic

mawzoo; wayna *n* موضوع؛ونا
discourse

mawzooatee *a.* موضوعاتي topical

mawzooee *a.* موضوعي thematic

mawzooee; failee *a.* موضوعي؛فاعلي
subjective

mawzoon; ham wazan *a.* موزون؛
هموزن rhythmic

mawzoonawal *v. t* موزونول
co-ordinate

maya *n* مايع liquid

maya kawal *v.t.* مايعكول liquefy

maya kawal *v.t.* مايعكول liquidate

mayan *n.* مين lover

mayantob *n.* مينتوب affection

mayar *n.* معيار standard

mayaree *a* معياري standard

mayaree kawal *v.t.* معياريكول
standardize

mayda keydal *v.i.* مدهكدل grind

maydawal *v. t* مدول crumble

maydawal *v.t* مدول mash

maydawal *v.t.* مدول shatter

mayl laral *v.i.* ميللرل tend

mayla *n.* ملا fair

mayla *n* مله festival

maymar *n.* معمار architect

maymaree *n.* معماري architecture

mayna *n.* ماينه wife

**mayni aw mantaqey pori
arwand** *a.* مداومنطقهپوراوند
zonal

mayoosa kawal *v.t.* مأيوسهكول
frustrate

mayoosawal *v. t* مايوسول deject

mayoosawal *v. t.* مأيوسول
disappoint

mayoosee *n* مايوسي dejection

mayoosee *n.* مأيوسي frustration

maza akheystal *v.t.* مزهاخستل
savour

mazanak *a.* مزهناك palatable

mazay; spanrseen *n.* مزى؛سپسين
yarn

mazay; tar *n.* مزى؛تار string

mazd; fees *n* مزد؛فيس fee

mazd; zeyra *n.* مزد؛يره allowance

mazdeegaray meylmastya *n.*
مازديرملمستيا matinee

mazdoor *n.* مزدور hireling

mazdoor *n.* مزدور labourer

mazdooree kawal *v.i.* مزدوريكول
labour

mazhabee hukoomat *n.* مذهبي
حكومت hierarchy

mazhabee qanoon *n* مذهبيقانون
canon

mazhabee tarana *n.* مذهبيترانه
hymn

mazhabee tashreefat *n.* مذهبي
تشريفات rite

mazoor *n* معذور handicap
mazroob *n.* مضروب multiplicand
meela; lakara *n.* ميله،لكه rod
meelan *n.* ميلان trend
meena *n* مينه love
meena kawal *v.t.* مينه كول love
meena toree *a.* ميناتوري miniature
meena warkawal *v.t* مينه وركول endear
meena; ishq *n* مينه،عشق amour
meenakaree *n* ميناكاري enamel
meenanak *a.* مينه ناك adorable
meenanak *a.* مينه ناك affectionate
meenanak *a.* مينه ناك loving
meenanak *a.* مينه ناك sociable
meenawal; shoqeen *n.* مينه وال، شوقين amateur
meenzal *v.t.* مينل leach
meeras *n.* ميراث heredity
meeras *n.* ميراث heritage
meeras *n.* ميراث legacy
meeras *n.* ميراث inheritance
meeras ki preykhodal *v. t.* ميراث كپرودل bequeath
meerasee *a.* ميراثي inherent
meesaq *n.* ميثاق treaty
mehboob *n* محبوب darling
mehboob *a.* محبوب lovable
mehfooz *a.* محفوظ immune
mehfooz *a.* محفوظ secure
mehraban *adj* مهربان benign
mehraban *adj.* مهربان complaisant
mehraban *a.* مهربان courteous
mehraban *a.* مهربان humane
mehraban *a* مهربان kind

mehrabana *a.* مهربانه gracious
mehrabanee *n.* مهرباني complaisance
mehrabanee; har kalay *a.* مهرباني،هر كلى welcome
mehroomawal *v. t* محرومول deprive
mehsoosawal *v.t.* محسوسول sense
melma; leedoonkay aw katoonkay *n.* ملمه،ليدونكى او كتونكى visitor
meyda meyda kawal *v.t.* مده مده كول mince
meydawoonkay *a* مدوونكى molar
meydeydana *n* ميددنه bruise
meyga *n* مه ewe
meygay *n* مى ant
meykh toombal *v.t.* مخ و مبل pin
meykha *n.* مه buffalo
meykhanikee *a* ميخانيكي mechanic
meykhanikee *a.* ميخانيكي mechanical
meyl *n.* مل liking
meylma *n.* ملمه guest
meylma pal *a.* ملمه پال hospitable
meylmastoon *n.* ملمستون hotel
meylmastya *n.* ملمستيا hospitality
meylmastya; jashan *n* ملمستيا، جشن feast
meyra *n* مه husband
meyrana *n* مانه bravery
meyrana *n.* مانه valour
meyranay *a.* منى valiant
meyrgee *n* مرى epilepsy
meyrman *n.* مرمن dame

meyrman *n.* مرمن lady
meyrman *n.* مرمن mistress
meysht kawal *v.t* مشت‌کول house
meysht kawal *v.t.* مشت‌کول populate
meysht zay *n* مشتـای dwelling
meysht zay *n.* مشتـای lodging
meysht zay *n.* مشتـای residence
meywa *n.* موه fruit
meyz *n.* مز table
midal *n.* مال medal
milawawal *v.t.* ملاوول meet
milee kawal *v.t.* ملی‌کول nationalize
milee keydana *n.* ملی‌کدنه nationalization
milee sarood *n* ملی‌سرود anthem
milee shoora *n.* ملی‌شورا parliament
milee; amoomee *a.* ملی؛عمومي public
mileeyat *n.* ملیت nationality
milkeeyat *n.* ملکیت ownership
mimbar; dareez *n.* ممبر؛دریه rostrum
miqnatees *n.* مقناطیس magnet
miqnatees *a.* مقناطیسي magnetic
miqnateeseeyat *n.* مقناطیسیت magnetism
miqyas *n.* مقیاس meter
mis *n* مس copper
misgar *n.* مسر smith
miskeen *a.* مسکین poor
misree haram *n.* مصری‌هرم pyramid
mityazanray *n.* متیاز urinal

mityazi *n.* متیازی urine
mityazi kawal *v.i.* متیازکول urinate
mizaj *n.* مزاج mood
mizaj *n.* مزاج temper
mizajee *a.* مزاجي temperamental
mla *n.* ملا waist
mla tar kawal *v.t* ملاتر‌کول uphold
mla wastanay *n.* ملاوستنـ girdle
mla wastanay; kamar band *n.* ملاوستن؛کمربند waistband
mlatar kawal *v.t.* ملاتر‌کول prop
mlatar kawal *v.t.* ملاتر‌کول support
mlataray *n.* ملاتی support
moadab *a* مؤدب decent
moadab; satandoy *n* مؤدب، ساتندوی gallant
moallaq *prep.* معلق pending
moama *n.* معما conundrum
moamila *n* معامله deal
moamila *n.* معامله entreaty
moamila kawal *v. i* معامله‌کول deal
moamila kawoonkay *n* معامله کوونکی dealer
moamilagar *n.* معاملهر coper
moannas *a* مؤنث feminine
moash akheystoonkay *n* معاش اخیستونکی annuitant
moassar *a.* مؤثر impressive
moassisa *n.* مؤسسه institute
moattar kawal *v.t.* معطر‌کول scent
moayina; imtihan *n.* معاینه؛امتحان examination
moayna *n* معاینه check
moayna kawal *v. t.* معاینه‌کول check

mobariza ghokhtoonkay *n.* مبارزه غوتونکی appellant

mochee *n* موچی cobbler

modaee *n* مدعي claimant

moeen *a* معین definite

mogak *n.* موک mouse

mogak *n.* موک rat

moheet; parkar *n* محیط؛پرکار compass

mohrik *n.* محرک incentive

mohtaram *a* محترم dear

mohtaram *n.* محترم gentleman

mohtaram *a.* محترم honourable

mojee harakat *n* موجي‌حرکت sway

mojiza *n.* معجزه miracle

mojizatee *a.* معجزاتي miraculous

mokha *n.* موخه aim

mokha; hadaf *n.* موخه؛هدف purpose

mokha; hadaf *n.* موخه؛هدف target

mokhal *v.t.* مولل massage

mokhana *n.* مونه friction

mokhana *n.* مونه massage

mokhowoonkay *n.* مووونکی masseur

mom *n.* موم wax

mom warkawal *v.t.* موم‌ورکول wax

momin *n.* مؤمن monotheist

momyayee shaway maray *n.* مومیایي‌شوی‌می mummy

mooda *n* موده duration

mooda *n.* موده term

mooda; dama *n.* موده؛دمه interval

mooda; sa wakht *n.* موده؛هوخت while

moolakh *n.* ملخ locust

moolay *n.* مول radish

moondal *v.t* موندل find

moondal *v.t.* موندل procure

moondana *n.* موندنه discovery

moondana *n.* موندنه procurement

moosafar khana *n.* مسافرخانه inn

mootay wahal *v.i.* مووی‌وهل masturbate

mootay; sook *n* مووی؛سوک fist

moqa *n.* موقع occasion

moqa *n.* موقع opportunity

moqa rapeykheydal *v.t* موقع‌راپدل occasion

moqa; fursat *n.* موقع؛فرصت chance

moqarraba farikhta *n* مقربه‌فرته archangel

moqeeyat *n.* موقعیت location

mor *n* مور mother

mor *n* مور mum

mor *n* مور mummy

mor plar *n.* مورپلار parent

mor wazhana *n.* موروژنه matricide

mor wazhoonkay *a.* موروژونکی matricidal

moram *v.i.* مرام aim

moranay *a.* مورنه motherly

moranay *a.* مورني maternal

morchal *n.* مورچل trench

morchal jorawal *v.t.* مورچل‌جوول trench

morwalay *n.* موروالی motherhood

mosam *n.* موسم climate

mosam *n.* موسم season

mosam *n* موسم weather

mosam sara zan adatawal *v.t*
موسمسرهانعادتول acclimatise

mosamee *a.* موسمي seasonal

moseeqee wala meylmastoon *n.*
موسيقيواهملمستون cabaret

mosh khurma *n.* موشخرما marten

mosh khurma *n.* موشخرما
mongoose

mosh khurma *n.* موشخرما
squirrel

moshahida kawal *v. t* مشاهدهکول
behold

moska kawal *v.i* smile

mostaqeem *adv* مستقيم aright

mostaqeeman *adv.* مستقيما aright

motabar *a* معتبر creditable

motabar *a.* معتبر valid

motadil *a.* معتدل mediocre

motadil *a.* معتدل moderate

motadil kawal *v.t.* معتدلکول
moderate

motamadin garzawal *v. t* متمدن
رول civilize

**motanawab; tar dwa barkho
pori zangaray** *n.* متناوب;تردوه
برخوپورانی alternative

motar *n.* مور automobile

motar *n.* مور car

motar chalowoonkay *n.* مور
چلوونکی motorist

motarwan *n.* موروان chauffeur

motarwan *n* موروان coachman

motasib kas *n* متعصبکس bigot

motor wan *n* موروان driver

motor wanee *n* موروانی drive

mozeekala drama *n.* موزیکالهرامه
opera

mrasta *n* مرسته aid

mrasta *n.* مرسته assistance

mrasta *n* مرسته help

mrasta ghoshtal *v.t.* مرستهغوشتل
invoke

mrasta kawal *v.t* مرستهکول aid

mrasta kawal *v.t.* مرستهکول assist

mrasta kawal *v.t* مرستهکول hand

mrasta kawal *v.t.* مرستهکول help

mrasta warsara kawal *v.t.* مرسته
ورسرهکول staff

mrastandoy *n.* مرستندوی auxiliary

mrastandoya *a.* مرستندویه
auxiliary

mrastandoya *a* مرستندویه
co-operative

mrastyal *n.* مرستیال assistant

mraway *n.* ماوی low

mraway keydal *v.i* ماویکدل fade

mraway keydal *v.i.* ماویکدل
languish

mraway keydal *v.i.* ماویکدل
wither

mrayay n. مریی slave

mrayay *n.* مریی thrall

mrayay *n.* مریی serf

mrayay dawla *a.* مرییوله slavish

mrayeetob *n* مرییتوب bondage

mrayeetob *n.* مرییتوب slavery

mrayeetob ta wral *v.i.* مرییتوبته
ول slave

mreena *n* مینه death

mreena *n* مینه decease

mreena *n.* مينه mortality

mreestoon *n.* ميستون cemetery

mreestoon *n.* ميستون morgue

mreydal *v. i* مدل die

mrich *n.* مرچ chilli

mrich *n.* مرچ pepper

muahida *n.* معاهده pact

mualija *n.* معالجه therapy

muallaq *n.* معلق suspense

muallaq kawal; zandawal *v.t.* معلق کول،بنول suspend

muash *n.* معاش livelihood

muayna kawal *v.t.* معاينه کول observe

mubadil *n.* مبادل interchange

mubadila kawal *v. t* مبادله کول exchange

mubadila kawal *v.* مبادله کول interchange

mubadila; safaree *n* مبادله،صرافي exchange

mubahisa *n* مباحثه contention

mubahisa *n* مباحثه controversy

mubahisa; daleel *n.* مباحثه،دليل argument

mubaligha *n.* مبالغه exaggeration

mubaligha kawal *v. t.* مبالغه کول exaggerate

mubaligha wayna *n.* مبالغهونا hyperbole

mubarak *a.* مبارک auspicious

mubarakee *n* مبارکي congratulation

mubarakee wayal *v. t* مبارکي ويل congratulate

mubariza *n.* مبارزه campaign

mubariza *n.* مبارزه challenge

mubarizey ta tlal *v. t.* مبارزتهبلل challenge

mubhim *a.* مبهم obscure

mubhim; goong *a.* مبهم،بونۍ vague

mubhim; shakman *a.* مبهم،شکمن ambiguous

mudaee *n.* مدعي suitor

mudafay wakeel *n* مدافعوکيل advocate

mudafay wakeel *n.* مدافعوکيل pleader

mudakhila *n.* مداخله intervention

mudakhila kawal *v.i.* مداخله کول intervene

mudakhila kawoonkay *v.i.* مداخله کوونکی meddle

mudarris *n.* مدرس lecturer

mudat; takal shaway wakht *n.* مدت،باکل شوی وخت span

mudeer *n.* مدير administrator

mudeer *n.* مدير director

mudeer *n.* مدير manager

mudeeree *a* مديري editorial

mudeeree *a.* مديري managerial

mudeereeyat *n.* مديريت management

mudeereeyat *n.* مديريت superintendence

mufakkir *n.* مفکر intellectual

mufassir *n* مفسر commentator

mufeed *a.* مفيد subservient

mufeed *a.* مفيد useful

mufeedeeyat *n.* مفيديت utility

mufrad; yaw *a.* مفرد،يو singular

muhafiza kar *a* محافظه کار conservative

muhafiza karee khokhawoonkay *n* محافظه کاري خووونکی conservative

muhakama *n*. محاکمه trial

muhamat; aslaha *n*. مهمات،اسلحه ammunition

muhandis *n* مهندس engineer

muhar lagawal *v.i.* مهر لول stamp

muhar; tapa *n* مهر،ټاپه die

muhasib *n*. محاسب accountant

muhasira kawal *v. t* محاصره کول besiege

muhasira; kalabandee *n*. محاصره،کلابند siege

muhazzab *a*. مهذب politic

muhazzab *a*. مهذب urbane

muheet *n*. محیط milieu

muhim *n* مهم adventure

muhim *a*. مهم chief

muhim *a* مهم earnest

muhim *a* مهم principal

muhim *a*. مهم significant

muhim shakhseeyat *n*. مهم شخصیت personage

muhimatee *a*. مهماتي adventurous

muhkam *a* محکم consistent

muhkam *a*. محکم tenacious

muhlal *n* محلل solvent

muhlat *n*. مهلت ultimatum

muhrak *n*. محرک motive

muhtaj *a*. محتاج needy

muhtajee *n*. محتاجي necessity

muhtaram *a*. محترم respectful

muhtaram; moazzaz *a.* محترم؛ معزز venerable

muhtat *adj.* محتاط circumspect

muhtat *a*. محتاط painstaking

muhtat *a*. محتاط prudential

muhtat *a*. محتاط prudent

muhtat insan *n*. محتاط انسان prude

muhur; tapa *n*. مهر،ټاپه seal

mujala *n*. مجله circular

mujala *n*. مجله gazette

mujarrad *adj* مجرد abstract

mujassam *a*. مجسم incarnate

mujassam kawal *v.t.* مجسم کول incarnate

mujassam kawal *v.t.* مجسم کول materialize

mujassam kawal *v.t.* مجسم کول visualize

mujassam kawana *n*. مجسم کونه portrayal

mujassima *n*. مجسمه statue

mujassima *n*. مجسمه sculpture

mujassima dawla *a.* مجسمهوله sculptural

mujassima jorawoonkay *n*. مجسمه جوروونکی sculptor

mujrim *n* مجرم convict

mujrim *a*. مجرم guilty

mujrimeeyat *n* مجرمیت conviction

mukalima *n* مکالمه conversation

mukamal aw bashbar insan *n* مکمل او بشپان سان ideal

mukamal kawal; ada kawal *v.t.* مکمل کول،ادا کول utter

mukarrar *n*. مکرر frequent

mukhabiratee sapey leygdawoonkay aw astawoonkay masheen *n.* مخابراتي‌پلادوونكى‌او‌استوونكى ماشين transmitter

mukhalif *prep.* مخالف against

mukhalif *a* مخالف contrary

mukhalif *a.* مخالف hostile

mukhalif *n.* مخالف opponent

mukhalif *a.* مخالف opposite

mukhalif *a.* مخالف repugnant

mukhalif mafhoom warkawal *v.t.* مخالف‌مفهوم‌ور‌كول contrapose

mukhalif; dukhman *n.* مخالف، دمن antagonist

mukhalif; par zid *pref.* مخالف؛پر ضد anti

mukhalifa raya *n.* مخالفه‌رايه veto

mukhalifa raya warkawal *v.t.* مخالفه‌رايه‌ور‌كول veto

mukhalifana ihsas *n.* مخالفانه احساس antipathy

mukhalifat *n.* مخالفت hostility

mukhalifat kawal *v.t.* مخالفت‌كول antagonize

mukhalifat kawal *v.t.* مخالفت‌كول oppose

mukhalifat kawal; zawab warkawal *v. t* مخالفت‌كول، وابور‌كول counter

mukhalifat khkara kawal *v.i* مخالفت‌كاره‌كول frown

mukhalifat; dukhmanee *n* مخالفت،دمني antagonism

mukhatib *n.* مخاطب addressee

mukhlis *a.* مخلص sincere

mukhtalif *a* مختلف different

mukhtalif *a* مختلف unlike

mukhtasar *a* مختصر abstract

mukhtasar *a.* مختصر brief

mukhtasar *a* مختصر concise

mukhtasar leekal *v.t.* مختصرليكل jot

mulaqat *n.* ملاقات meet

mulaqat aw khabari atari *n.* ملاقات‌او‌خبراتر rendezvous

mulawwis kawal *v.t.* ملوث‌كول taint

mulayam *adj.* ملايم daft

mulayim *a.* ملايم temperate

mulazim; nawkar *n.* ملازم؛نوكر retinue

mulhidtob *n* ملحدتوب atheism

mumtaz *a* ممتاز distinct

munakis jisam *n.* منعكس‌جسم reflector

munakis kawal *v.t.* منعكس‌كول reflect

munakis shaway *a* منعكس‌شوى reflex

munakisawal *v.t.* منعكسول mirror

munakkis keydal *v.i.* منعكس‌كدل resound

munara *n.* مناره minaret

munasib *a.* مناسب adequate

munasib *adj* مناسب apposite

munasib *a.* مناسب appropriate

munasib *a* مناسب due

munasib *a* مناسب fit

munasib *a* مناسب optimum

munasib *a.* مناسب proper

munasib; da ijra war *a.* د،مناسب اجراو applicable

munasibat *n.* مناسبت relevance

munasibat; wartya *n.* مناسبت،وتيا appropriation

munasibawal; zangaray kawal *v.t.* مناسبول،بانىکول appropriate

munazira *n.* مناظره moot

munazza; mehfooz *a.* منزه،محفوظ inviolable

munazzam *a.* منظم regular

munazzam *a* منظم rum

munazzam *a.* منظم tidy

munazzam harakat *n.* منظمحرکت march

munazzam kawal *v.t.* منظمکول tidy

munazzamwalay *n.* منظموالى tidiness

munfajira mawad *n* منفجرهمواد dynamite

munharif *adv.,* منحرف astray

munharif kawal *v.t.* منحرفکول shunt

munharif keydal *v. i* منحرفکدل deviate

munqabiz kawal *v. t* منقبضکول condense

munqal; nagharay *n.* منقل،نغرى hearth

munqata kawal *v. t* منقطعکول disrupt

munsarif kawal *v. t* منصرفکول divert

munshee *n.* منشي secretary

muntaqil kawal *v.t.* منتقلکول transfer

muqabil takee *n.* مقابلکي antipodes

muqabila *n.* مقابله confrontation

muqabila kawal *v. t* مقابلهکول contest

muqadas *a.* مقدس holy

muqaddas *a.* مقدس sacred

muqaddas; na badleydoonkay *a.* مقدس،نابدلدونکى sacrosanct

muqadima *n.* مقدمه prelude

muqadima chamtoo kawal *v.t.* مقدمهچمتوکول prelude

muqannana plaway *n.* مقننهپلاوى legislature

muqaribat; moamila *n.* مقاربت،معامله intercourse

muqawee darmal *n.* مقويدرمل tonic

muqawee; ghagan *a.* مقوي،غن tonic

muqawmat *n.* مقاومت opposition

muqtazee *a.* مقتضي advisable

muraba *n.* مربا jam

muraba; zangari inhisaree seema *n.* مربا،زانحصاريسيمه preserve

murafia *n.* مرافعه litigation

murafia kawal *v.t.* مرافعهکول litigate

murafia kawoonkay *n.* مرافعه کوونکى litigant

murafia; yawa jor jamey *n.* مرافعه،يوهجوجام suit

murajia *n.* مراجعه recourse

murajia kawal; beyrta katana kawal *v.t.* مراجعه کول؛برته کتنه کول refer

murakab *a* مرکب compound

murakab *n* مرکب multiple

murakab *a* مرکب twin

murakab jisam *n* مرکب جسم compound

murakab; gadola *n.* مرکب؛وله mixture

muratab kawal *v. t* مرتب کول concert2

murda khana *n.* مرده خانه mortuary

murdaree *n.* مرداري squalor

mureed *n* مرید follower

mureed; shagard *n* مرید؛شارد disciple

murtahin *n.* مرتهن mortagagee

murtakib keydal *v. t.* مرتکب کدل commit

musabiqa *n.* مسابقه competition

musabiqa *n.* مسابقه contest

musabiqa *n* مسابقه match

musabiqa kawal *v.i* مسابقه کول game

musabiqana *a* مسابقانه competitive

musadira *n* مصادره confiscation

musadira kawal *v. t* مصادره کول confiscate

musafar *n.* مسافر voyager

musafar *n.* مسافر traveller

musakkan darmal *n* مسکن درمل sedative

musalihat kawoonkay *n.* مصالحت کوونکی intermediary

musallam *a.* مسلم indisputable

musallam ganral; sahee gooman kawal *v.t.* مُسَلم؛صحیح و مان کول presume

musallat *a.* مسلط imposing

musallatawal *v.t.* مسلطول impose

musalsal dard laral *v.t.* مسلسل درد لرل nag

musarat *n.* مسرت gratification

musawida *n* مسوده draft

musawida chamtoo kawoonkay *a* مسوده چمتو کوونکی draftsman

musawwida *n.* مسوده script

musbat *a* مثبت affirmative

musbat *a.* مثبت plus

musbat *a.* مثبت positive

musbat agheyz laroonkay *a.* مثبت اغیز لرونکی salutary

mushabay *a.* مشابه identical

mushal; pakówoonkay *a* مُسهل؛ پاکوونکی purgative

mushk *n.* مشک musk

mushkil *a* مشکل difficult

mushtarik amil *n.* مشترک عامل coefficient

mushtree *n.* مشتري jupiter

musraf *a.* مُسرف prodigal

mustaid *a.* مستعد gifted

mustaid *a.* مستعد prone

mustaqar kawal; tamzay ki preykhwal *v.t.* مستقر کول؛تمای کپرول station

mustaqbil *n* مستقبل future

mustaqeem *a* مستقیم through

mustaqeeman *adv.* مستقیماً outright

mustaqeeman *adv.* مستقیماً
straightway

mustaqil *a* مستقل constant

mustasna garzawal *v. t* مستثنی‌رول
exclude

mustasna kawal *v. t* مستثنی‌کول
except

mustasna kawal *v. t.* مستثنی‌کول
exempt

mustasna kawal; sarf nazar
kawal *v.t.* مستثنی‌کول؛صرف‌نظر
کول waive

mustateel *n.* مستطیل oblong

mustateel *n.* مستطیل rectangle

mustateel shakal laroonkay *a.*
مستطیل‌شکل‌لرونکی rectangular

mutaadad *a.* متعدد many

mutaadil; zra rakhkoonkay *a.*
متعادل؛زه‌راکونکی trim

mutaal; tar tolo lwar *a.* متعال؛تر
ولولو supreme

mutaasib shakhs *n* متعصب‌شخص
fanatic

mutaasib; mutashadad *a* متعصب؛
متشدد fanatic

mutabiat kawal *v.t* متابعت‌کول
follow

mutabiq; arwand *a.* مطابق؛اوند
relevant

mutakhassas keydal *v.i.* متخصص
کدل specialize

mutalia; lost *n.* مطالعه؛لوست study

mutanasib *a.* متناسب symmetrical

mutanasib *a.* متناسب proportional

mutanasib *a.* متناسب
proportionate

mutanasib kawal *v.t* متناسب‌کول
fit

mutanasib kawal *v.t.* متناسب‌کول
proportion

mutanaway *a.* متنوع
miscellaneous

mutaqabal amal kawal *v.t.* متقابل
عمل‌کول reciprocate

mutaqabal; mutanawab *a.* متقابل؛
متناوب reciprocal

mutaqabil warandeyz *n.* متقابل
واندز paradox

mutaqabil zawab *n.* متقابل‌واب
retort

mutaqabil zawab warkawal *v.t.*
متقابل‌واب‌ورکول retort

mutaqaid *n.* متقاعد pensioner

mutasavi ul azla *a* متساوی‌الاضلاع
equilateral

mutasil *a.* متصل adjacent

mutasil *adj.* متصل conjunct

mutasil kawal *v.t.* متصل‌کول
adjoin

mutasirawal *v.t.* متاثرول impress

mutasirawal *v.t.* متاثرول inspire

mutawajo *a.* متوجه attentive

mutawajo *a.* متوجه wary

mutawajo kawal *v.* متوجه‌کول
advert

mutawajo keydal *v.t.* متوجه‌کدل
overlook

mutawajo oseydal *v.i.* متوجه‌اوسدل
beware

mutawasit *a.* متوسط average

mutawatir *adj.* متواتر consecutive

mutawazeeul azla *n.* متوازی
الاضلاع parallelogram

mutazad *a.* متضاد paradoxical
mutee *a* مطيع dutiful
mutee *a.* مطيع submissive
mutee kawal *v.t.* مطيع کول subdue
mutmain *a.* مطمئن confident
muwafaq; khoshhala *a.* موفق، خوشحاله prosperous
muwafiq *a.* موافق agreeable
muwafiq *a.* موافق suitable
muwafiq keydal *v.t.* موافق کيدل accord
muwafiq keydal; pa mawzoon ahang wayal *v.t.* موافق کدل؛ په موزون آهنويل tune
muwafiqat *n.* موافقت suitability
muwafiqat kawal *v.i.* موافقت کول agree
muzahimat kawal *v.i.* مزاحمت کول scuffle
muzahimat; shormashor *n.* مزاحمت؛شورماشور scuffle
muzakira *n.* مذاکره nagotiation
muzakira kawal *v.t.* مذاکره کول negotiate
muzakira kawal *v.i* مذاکره کول parley
muztarib *a.* مضطرب anxious
muztarib kawal *v. t* مضطرب کول distress
myashay *n.* مياشى mosquito
myasht *n.* مياشت month
myashtanay *a.* مياشتنى monthly
myashtanay mujala *n* مياشتنمجله monthly

N

na *adv.* نه no
na amalee *a.* ناعملي impracticable
na amaleetob *n.* ناعملي توب impracticability
na andwaltob *n.* ناانولتوب odds
na arama *n* نارامه disquiet
na arwand *a.* نااروند incoherent
na awreydoonkay *a.* نه اورىدونکى inaudible
na badleydoonkay; na kageydoonkay *a.* نه بدلدونکى، نه کدونکى inflexible
na basya; pati raghalay *a.* نابسيا، پاتراغلى insolvent
na beyleydoonkay *a.* نه بلدونکى inseparable
na cheez *a.* ناچيز negligible
na darana *n.* نه ارنه intrepidity
na gholeydoonkay *a.* نه غولدونکى infallible
na hazmeydana *n.* نه هضمدنه indigestion
na hazmeydoonkay *a.* نه هضمدونکى indigestible
na heelay keydal *v. i* ناهيلى کدل despair
na heelee *n* نا هيلي despair
na ijra *a* نااجرا pending
na istimaleyda *n.* نه استعمالدا redundance
na jor *a.* ناجو inapplicable
na kharabeydoonkay *a.* نه خرابدونکى incorruptible
na khu *conj.* نه خو neither

na khu *conj* نه‌خو nor
na khwakhee khkara kawal *v.t.*
ناخوي‌كاره‌كول resent
na leeda *n* نه‌ليدا blindness
na leedoonkay *a.* نه‌ليدونكى
invincible
na lostal keydal *n.* نه‌لوستل‌كدل
illegibility
na lostal keydoonkay *a.* نه‌لوستل
كدونكى illegible
na manal; lughwa kawal *v.t.* نه
منل؛لغوه‌كول repeal
na manana *n* نه‌مننه denial
na manana *n.* نه‌مننه refusal
na manana *n.* نه‌مننه refutation
na manana *n* نه‌مننه repeal
na mard; bey la insana da
waseelay *a.* نامرد؛بله‌انسان‌دوسيله
unmanned
na mashroo gad zhwand *n.* نا
مشروع‌ژوند concubinage
na mateydoonkay *n.* نه‌ماتدونك
adamant
na mehraban *a.* نامهربان
inhospitable
na mehsoos *a.* نامحسوس
intangible
na munasib *a.* نامناسب improper
na mushakhkhas *a.* نامشخص
indistinct
na mustaqeem *a.* نامستقيم indirect
na omeeda *a.* نااميده hopeless
na oomeeda *a* نااميده desperate
na pak *a.* ناپاک unwell
na peywastoon *n.* نه‌پوستون
non-alignment
na poh *a.* ناپوه witless

na qararee *n.* ناقراري malaise
na radeydoonkay *a.* نه‌رددونكى
irrefutable
na ragheydoonkay *a.* نه‌رغدونكى
incorrigible
na raz *n* ناراض malcontent
na raza *a.* ناراضه malcontent
na razayat kawal *v. t.* نارضايت
كول dissatisfy
na razee keydoonkay *a.* نه‌راضه
كدونكى insatiable
na roghwalay *n* ناروغوالى
morbidity
na sam *a* ناسم abnormal
na seez ganral *v.i* نايزل trifle
na sharha keydoonkay *a.* نه‌شرحه
كدونكى indescribable
na shmeyri khabari kawal *v.t.* نا
شمرخبركول jabber
na shukree *n.* ناشكري ingratitude
na tajroba kar *n.* ناتجربه‌كار
inexperience
na tajruba kar *a.* ناتجربه‌كار junior
na wada shawi khaza *n.* ناوادهشو
ه maid
na wara kar kawona *n.* ناوه‌كار
كونه malpractice
na wara nyat *a.* ناوه‌نيت malafide
na wara; kharab *a* ناوه؛خراب evil
na wayla keydana *n.* نه‌ويلكدنه
insolvency
na waylay keydoonkay *n.* نه‌ويل
كدونكى insoluble
na yawazi *conj* نه‌يواز both
na zghamana *n.* نه‌زغمنه
intolerance

na zghamowoonkay a. نه زغموونکی intolerable

na zghamowoonkay a. نه زغموونکی intolerant

na zhghoroonkay a. نه‌ژغورونکی indefensible

na zhranda shawi wareeji n. نه ژرنده‌شووریج paddy

naarama n ناآرامه discontent

naaramee n ناآرامي discomfort

naashna a. ناآشنا strange

nabaligh a. نابالغ premature

nabaryalay balal v. t. نابريالی‌بلل disqualify

nabatee koch n. نباتي‌کوچ margarine

nabatee koochnee sporawan n. نباتي کوچني‌سپورونه pollen

nabatee sheera n. نباتي‌شيره sap

nabatee zhwand n. نباتي‌ژوند vegetation

nabatee; sabzay pori arwand a. نباتي؛سبزپوراوند vegetable

nabawara kawal v. t. ناباوره‌کول distrust

nabawaree n ناباوري distrust

nabawee a. نبوي prophetic

nabaz n. نبض pulse

nabee n. نبي prophet

naboowat n. نبوت prophecy

nachar a. ناچار inevitable

nachar kawal v.t. ناچارکول oblige

nacheez a. ناچيز petty

nadooda a. نادوده outmoded

nadrust a. نادرست inexact

nafar; shakhs n. نفر،شخص person

nafarman a. نافرمان insubordinate

nafarman a. نافرمان wayward

larghonayn. n نافرماني insubordination

nafee n. نفي negation

nafoos n. نفوس population

nafooz kawal v.t. نفوذکول pervade

nafooz; nanawatana n. نفوذ،ننوتنه penetration

nafrat n. نفرت repugnance

naftee mawad n. نفتي‌مواد petroleum

naghdey a. نغدي pecuniary

naghdi peysey n. نغدپسـه cash

nagheeree kawal v.t. ناغيي‌کول shirk

nagheeree kawoonkay n. ناغي‌کوونکی shirker

naghota kawoonkay a. نغوته کوونکی suggestive

nagokheydal v.i. نوکل plod

naha n. نهه nine

naham a. نهم ninth

nahang n نهه alligator

nahang n نهه crocodile

nahawar a. ناهوار rugged

nahawarawal v.t. ناهوارول ruffle

naheelay kawal v. t ناهيلی‌کول daunt

naheeya n. ناحيه region

naheeya n. ناحيه sector

naheeya; ilaqa n علاقه،ناحيه. parish

najabat n. نجابت nobility

najeeb zada n. نجيب‌زاده magnate

najlay n. نجل girl

najlay ghokhtal v.t. نجلغوتل woo

najlay ghonde *a.* نجلغوند girlish

nak *n.* ناک pear

nakafee *a.* ناكافي insufficient

nakafee *a.* ناكافي scanty

nakamee *n* ناكامي failure

nakamee *n* ناكامي fiasco

nakar; lat *a.* ناكار،لت sluggish

nakara shay *n.* ناكارهشى trash

nakarara *a* ناكراره fitful

nakeydoonay *a.* ناكدونى unlikely

nakha eekhodal *v. i* نهايودل denote

nakha eekhoodoonkay *n.* نه ايودونكى marker

nakha laroonkay *a.* نهلرونكى symbolic

nakha weeshtoonkay *n.* نه ويشتونكى marksman

nakhalis; barjasta *a* ناخالص، برجسته gross

nakhan *n.* نان mark

nakhan lagawal *v.t* نانلول mark

nakhana; teekat *n.* نانه،بک token

nakhcha *n* نخچه map

nakhcha akheestana *n.* نخچه اخيستنه topography

nakhcha akheestano pori arwand *a.* نخچهاخيستنوپوراوند topographical

nakhcha jorawal *v.t.* نخچهجوول map

nakhcha kakh *n.* نخچهك topographer

nakhlawal *v.t.* نلول attach

nakhleydal; pa lakari wahal *v.t.* نلدل،پهلكوهل stick

nakhleydal *n* نخر،مكز flirt

nakhtar *n* نتر fir

nakhteyzal *v.t* نتل nip

nakhteyzal *v.t.* نتل twist

nakhwakh *a.* خو نا disagreeable

nakhwakhee *n.* ناخوي disagreement

nakhwakhee *n* ناخوي disapproval

nakhwakhee *n.* ناخوي reluctance

nakreezi *n.* نكرِه myrtle

nal *n.* نل tube

nal; nawa; fawara *n.* نل،ناوه،فواره spout

nal; necha *n* نل،نيچه fistula

nal; soornray *n.* نل،سورى pipe

nalay *n.* نا nozzle

nalayiq *a.* نالائق incompetent

nalbakay *n.* نالبكى saucer

naldawan; sarp kar *n.* نلدوان، سرپكار plumber

naleedalay *a.* ناليدلى invisible

naloono ki oba rasawal *v.i* نلونوكى اوبهرسول pipe

nam *a* نم damp

nam *n.* نم moisture

nam payda kawal *v.t.* نمپداكول moisten

namafhooma shor aw zwag *n* نامفهومهشوراوزو babel

namahirana peywandawal *v. t* ناماهرانهپوندول botch

namak haram *a* نمکحرام disloyal

namaqool *a.* نامعقول illogical

namaqoola *a.* نامعقوله irrational

namasaid halat n. نامساعدحالت predicament

namjan a. نمجن moist

namjan; loond a. نمجن،لوند humid

namnak adj. نمناک dank

namoona n نمونه mould

namoona n. نمونه sample

namoona n. نمونه parable

namoona khodal; da mayar banra warkawal v.t. نمونه ودل؛دمعياربهوركول typify

namoona; beylga n. نمونه،بله instance

namoona; mayar n. نمونه،معيار paragon

namtoo a نامتو brilliant

namtoo; alee janaba a نامتو،عال جنابه eminent

namunasib a. نامناسب irrelevant

namzadgee n. نامزدي betrothal

nan da shpey adv. نن دشپ tonight

nan shpa n. نن شپه to-night

nan wraz n. ور نن today

nana estana v.t. ننه ايستنه jab

nanawatal; dakhileydal v. t ننوتل؛ داخلدل enter

nanawatana n. ننوتنه admittance

nanawatana n ننوتنه entrance

nanawatana n ننوتنه entry

nanaweystal; zayawal v.t. ننوستل؛ زايول insert

nanaweystana n. ننوستنه insertion

nandara n. ننداره exhibit

nandara jorawoonkay n ننداره جوروونکی dramatist

nandaray wahal; nandaray v. i. ناندروهل،ناندر n & brawl

nandarey ta zahirawal v. t نندارته ظاهرول display

nandarey; nandarey wahal n&. ناندر،ناندروهل v.i clack

nandari ta wrandi kawal v. t ننداره تهواندکول exhibit

nandartoon n. نندارتون exhibition

naneydal v.i. نندل ooze

naneydal; teetawal v. t. نندل؛تيتول sprinkle

naneydana; sheendana n. نندنه؛ شيندنه spray

napakee n. ناپاکي impurity

napawal; wazan kawal v.t. ناپول؛ وزنکول scale

napaydar a ناپايدار fickle

napaydar n. پايدار نا transitory

napoh a. پوه نا apish

napoh n ناپوه fool

napoh a. ناپوه ignorant

napohee n ناپوهي folly

napohee n. ناپوهي ignorance

napohee; kam taleemee n. ناپوهي، کمتعليمي illiteracy

napukhta a. ناپخته immature

napukhtagee n. ناپختي immaturity

naqab n. نقاب mask

naqab achowal v.t. نقاب اچول mask

naqal n نقل copy

naqal jorawal v. t نقلجورول copy

naqal jorawal v. t نقلجورول duplicate

naqal jorawana *n.* نقل‌جورونه transcription

naqanoona *a.* ناقانونه wrongful

naqashee; anzorgaree *n.* نقاشي؛ انورږري painting

naqis *a.* ناقص imperfect

naqras *n.* نقرس gout

naqrayee *a* نقرهيي silver

naqsh kawal *v.t.* نقش‌کول inscribe

naqsh; banra *n* نقش؛به figure

naqsh; muhar *n.* نقش،مهر stamp

nar khazay *n* نرى eunuch

nar pashay *n.* نرپشى tomcat

nara; shuar *n.* ناره،شعار slogan

naram *a.* نرم lenient

naram *a.* نرم mellow

naram *a.* نرم mild

naram *a.* نرم polite

naram aw teeng *a.* نرماوینه sedate

naram bad *n* نرم‌باد waft

naram saqa; tak *n.* نرم‌ساقه،تاک vine

naram; lateef *n.* نرم،لطیف soft

naram; lateef *a* نرم،لطیف tender

naram; sayqalee *a.* نرم؛صیقلي sleek

narama *a.* نارامه inconvenient

narama *a.* نارامه restive

narama kawal *v.t.* نارامه‌کول hinder

narama kawal *v.t.* نارامه‌کول obsess

narama kawal *v.t.* نارامه‌کول perturb

naranj *n.* نارنج orange

naranjee *a* نارنجي orange

narasmee jangyalay *n.* نارسمي جنیالى guerilla

narawa *a.* ناروا inadmissible

narawa kar kawal *v.t.* ناروا‌کارکول wrong

narawa; armoonay *a.* ناروا؛ارموني illegitimate

narawa; ghalat *a.* ناروا؛غلط wrong

narawal *v.t.* نول subvert

naray *a.* نرى thin

naray *n.* ن world

naray kawal *v.i.* نرى‌کول taper

naray lakhta *n.* نرلته withe

naray ranz *n.* نرى‌رنز tuberculosis

naray warakht *n* نرى‌ورت drizzle

naray warakht wareydal *v. i* نرى ورت‌ورېدل drizzle

naraypal *n.* نپال worldling

nareekhtoonay *a* ناریتوني sham

nareekhtoonay; armoonay *a.* ناریتوني؛ارموني spurious

nareena *a.* نارینه male

nareena *a.* نرینه masculine

nareena as *n.* نارینه‌اس stallion

nareena jinsee zwak; nareentob *n.* نارینه‌جنسي‌واک؛نارینتوب virility

nareena sra gowaza *n.* نارینه‌سره وزه stag

nareentob *n.* نارینتوب manhood

nareentob *n* نارینتوب manliness

nareewal *a.* نیوال global

nareewal *a.* نیوال international

nareewal *a.* نیوال universal

narey soorey *a.* نارسور outcry

narey soorey *n* نار سور yell
narey soorey kawal *v.i.* نارسور کول yell
nareydal *v.i.* ندل topple
nareydalay *a.* ندلی subversive
narkh; sharah *n.* نرخ؛شرح rate
narma khata *n.* نرمهخه ooze
narma oogda sawkay *n.* نرمهاوده وک sofa
narmakht *n.* نرمت lenience, leniency
narmakht *a.* نرمت rickety
narmawal *v.t.* نرمول masticate
narmawal *v.t.* نرمول smooth
narmawal; mulayim keydal *v.t.* نرمول؛ملايمکدل soften
narmee *n.* نرمي laxity
narmee *n.* نرمي politeness
narmeydal *v.i.* نرمدل relent
narogha *a.* ناروغه sick
naroghee *n.* ناروغي ailment
narogheydal *v.t.* ناروغدل ail
nasab *n.* نسب parentage
nasab kawal; toghawal *v.t.* نصب کول؛توغول pitch
nasab shaway zay *n.* نصبشوىاى pitch
nasabnama *n.* نسبنامه pedigree
nasal *n.* نسل generation
nasal *n.* نسل posterity
nasam *a.* ناسم inaccurate
nasam chaland kawal *v.i.* ناسم چلندکول misbehave
nasam darak kawal *v.t.* ناسمدرک کول misapprehend

nasam karawal *v.t.* ناسمکارول misuse
nasam karowana *n.* ناسمکارونه misuse
nasam khodal *v.t.* ناسمودل misrepresent
nasam poheydal *v.t.* ناسمپوهدل misconceive
nasam poheydal *v.t.* ناسمپوهدل misunderstand
nasam shay *n.* ناسمشى misfit
nasam shmeyral *v.t.* ناسمشمرل miscalculate
nasam tabeerawal *v.t.* ناسمتعبيرول misconstrue
nasam; najor *adv.* ناسم؛ناجو ill
nasama larkhowana *n.* ناسمه لاروونه misdirection
nasama shmeyra *n.* ناسمهشمره miscalculation
nasamee *n.* ناسمي mal adjustment
nasapa *a* ناپه abrupt
nasapa *adv.* ناپه forthwith
nasapa breed *n* ناپهبريد pounce
nasapa breed landi neewal *v.i.* ناپهبريدلاندنيول swoop
nasapa kharabtya *n* breakdown
nasapa lambey lageydal *v.i* ناپه لمب لدل flare
nasapa surat zyatawal *v.i.* ناپه سرعتزياتول spurt
nasapa takan *n.* ناپهکان jolt
nasapa takar *n* ناپهکر crash
nasapaee breed kawal *v.i.* ناپهبريد کول storm
nasapee *n* ناپي abruption
nasapee *a* ناپي dramatic

nasapee aw chatak faaleeyat n. نساپۍاوچکفعاليت sally

nasapee aw gadwad harakat n. نساپۍاووحرکت rush

nasapee badloon n. نساپۍبدلون upheaval

nasapee breed n نساپۍبريد swoop

nasapee dalayeez harakat n. نساپۍ لهييزحرکت stampede

nasapee dar n. نساپۍار fright

nasapee darawal v.t. نساپۍارول frighten

nasapee hasa n نساپۍهه spurt

nasapee park ya baheer n نساپۍ پکـيابهير flush

nasapee parkeydal ya baheydal v.i نساپۍپکدليابهدل flush

nasapee peykha n. نساپۍپه sudden

nasapee toghawona n. نساپۍتوغونه lunge

nasapeetob n. نساپۍتوب spontaneity

nasapi a. نساپۍ haphazard

nasar n. نثر prose

nasaz a. ناساز indisposed

nasbawal v. t نصبول erect

nasbawal v.t نصبول fix

nasbawoonkay n نصبوونکی fitter

naseehat n نصيحت advice

naseehat n. نصيحت maxim

naseehat kawal v.t. نصيحتکول advise

nasha kawal v.t. نشهکول intoxicate

nasha kawona n. نشهکونه intoxication

nasha saray n نشهسی drunkard

nashar; khparaway n. نشر، خپراوی publication

nashayee mawad n. نشهيۍمواد narcosis

nashayee mawad n. نشهيۍمواد narcotic

nashayee skhak n. نشهياک intoxicant

nashoonay a. ناشونی impassable

nashoonay a. ناشونی impossible

nashoontya n. ناشونتيا impossibility

nashrawal v.t. نشرول publish

nasht n. نشت nil

nasht; sifar n. نشت،صفر nought

nasht; sifar n. نشت،صفر zero

nashtoon; da manfee alama n نشتون،دمنفيعلامه minus

nashukra a. ناشکره thankless

nasj n. نسج tissue

nasoor; changakh n. ناسور،چنا cancer

naswar n. نسوار snuff

naswaree a نصواري brown

naswaree rang n نصواريرنـ brown

nasyan; heyrawana n نسيان،هرونه amnesia

natajruba karee n. ناتجربهکاري naivety

natakmeel a . ناتکميل incomplete

natanzeemee n. ناتنظيمي mal administration

nateeja n. نتيجه conclusion

nateeja n. نتيجه result

nateeja warkawal v.i. نتيجهورکول result

nateekawtob *n.* نايكاوتوب instability

natwan *a* ناتوان disabled

natwan *a.* ناتوان incapable

natwan *a.* ناتوان unable

natwan kawal *v.t.* ناتوان کول impoverish

natwana kawal *v. t* ناتوانه کول disable

natwana kawal *v. t.* ناتوانه کول enfeeble

natwana kawal; natwana keydal *v.t&.i* ناتوانه کول؛ناتوانه کدل weaken

natwanee *n* ناتواني disability

natwanee *n.* ناتواني inability

nawa; kanal *n.* ناوه؛کانال groove

nawab *n.* نواب nabob

nawada kari najlay *n.* ناواده کنجل spinster

nawakht *n.* نوت invention

nawakht *n.* نوت novelty

nawakhtgar *n.* نوتر inventor

nawalay *a.* ناولی impure

nawalay *n.* ناولی rubbish

nawalay kawal *v.t.* ناولی کول pollute

nawalay shay *n.* ناولشی mess

nawalay; kheyran *a.* ناول؛خرن foul

nawaleetob *n.* ناولیتوب pollution

nawali aw chatali oba *n.* ناولاو چل او به sewage

nawara *a* ناوه abusive

nawara *a.* ناوه bad

nawara *a.* ناوه heinous

nawara aw past saray *n.* ناوهاو پست سی skate

nawara banra warkawal *v.t.* ناوه بهور کول uglify

nawara bawar *n.* ناوهباور misbelief

nawara chaland *n.* ناوهچلند misbehaviour

nawara chaland *n.* ناوهچلند miscarriage

nawara chalowana *n.* ناوهچلوونه mismanagement

nawara gata porta kawal *v. i* ناوه هپورته کول encroach

nawara ghageydal *v. i* ناوهغدل blether

nawara istimal *n.* ناوهاستعمال misapplication

nawara khabari *n* ناوهخبر yap

nawara leekana *n* scrawl

nawara peykha *n.* ناوهپه misadventure

nawara saray *a* ناوهسی forlorn

nawara teyrwatana kawal *v.i* ناوه تروتنه کول blunder

nawara yawwalay *n.* ناوهیووالی misalliance

nawara; nasam *adv.* ناوه؛ناسم amiss

nawara; wazhoonkay *a* ناوه؛وژونک deadly

nawarta *a* ناورته dissimilar

nawarta walay *n* ناورته والی disparity

nawartob *n.* ناوتوب impropriety

nawartob *n* ناوتوب disqualification

nawartya *n* ناوتیا demerit

naway *a.* نوی new

naway *a.* نوی novel

naway askar *n.* نوی‌عسکر recruit

naway baday shaway *n.* نوی‌بای شوی upstart

naway kadwal *n.* نوی‌کوال settler

naway kar *n.* نوی‌کار novice

naway pohantoonee zdakryal *n.* نوی‌پوهنتونی‌زدکیال undergraduate

naway tawleed *n.* نوی‌تولید regeneration

naway zwan *n.* نوی‌وان teenager

nawbatee *a.* نوبتی periodical

nawee *n.* نوی ninety

nawi *n* ناو bride

nawi banra warkawal *v.t.* نوبه ورکول modernize

nawi banra warkawal *v.* نوبه ورکول transform

nawi zwanee *n.* نووانی rejuvenation

nawkar *n.* نوکر lackey

nawkar *n* نوکر menial

nawkar sifatee *n.* نوکرصفتی servility

nawyam *a.* نویم ninetieth

nayab *a* نایاب extinct

nayab *a.* نایاب rare

nayib; zaynastay *n.* نایب،بایناستی vicar

naylon *n.* نایلون nylon

naymat *n* نعمت boon

naz nakhra *n* نازنخره ogle

naz; bati *n* ناز؛با brag

nazak *a.* نازک frail

nazak; wreykhmeen *a.* نازک؛ ورمین sheer

nazakat *n* نزاکت decency

nazam *n.* نظم verse

nazam leekal *v.t.* نظم‌لیکل versify

nazam leekana *n.* نظم‌لیکنه versification

nazam warkharabawal *v.t.* نظم ورخرابول unsettle

nazar *n.* نذر oblation

nazarat *n.* نظارت surveillance

nazarat *n.* نظارت supervision

nazarat kawal *v.t.* نظارت‌کول supervise

nazaree *a.* نظری theoretical

nazaree ilam *n.* نظري‌علم theory

nazaree seyrani kawal *v.i.* نظري‌ کول theorize

nazaree teyrwatana *n.* نظري‌تروتنه oversight

nazawal *v. t.* نازول caress

nazawal *v. t.* نازول cherish

nazawal *v.t* نازول fondle

nazawal *v.t.* نازول pat

nazawal *v.t.* نازول pet

nazawalay; gran *n.* نازولی؛ران pet

nazawana *n* نازوونه pat

nazeydal *v. i* نازدل brag

nazhad *n* نژاد caste

nazhdey *adv.* نژد anigh

nazhdey *a.* نژد approximate

nazhdey *prep.* نژد nigh

nazhdey *a.* نژد proximate

nazhdey *a.* نژد near

nazhdey ashnatob *n.* نژداشناتوب
intimacy

nazhdey keydal *v.t.* نژدکدل
approach

nazhdey keydal *v.i.* نژدکدل near

nazhdey leedana *n.* نژدلیدنه
myopia

nazhdey leeday *a.* نژدلیدی myopic

nazhdey malgaray *n.* نژدملری
counterpart

nazhdeywalay *n.* نژدوالی
proximity

nazhdeywalay *n.* نژدوالی vicinity

nazhdeywalay; las raseyda *n.*
نژدوالی؛لاس رسدا approach

nazir *n.* ناظر controller

nazir *n.* ناظر supervisor

nazir; peyra dar *n* ناظر؛پرهدار
chamberlain

nazir; qanoonee wakeel *n.* ناظر؛
قانوني وکیل proctor

nazm; qayda *n* نظم،قاعده
discipline

nazowana *n.* نازوونه endearment

nazuk *a.* نازک fragile

nazuk *a.* نازک slim

**neekana; da plar neeka pa
arwand** *a.* نیکانه،دپلارنیکهپه
اوند ancestral

neekoona aw plaroona *n.* نیکونهاو
پلرونه predecessor

neel *n* نیل blue

neem *a* نیم half

neem kakha *adv.* نیم که ajar

neema shpa *n.* نیمهشپه midnight

neemawal *v. t* نیمول bisect

neemayee *n.* نیمایي half

neemayee kawal *v.t.* نیمایي کول
halve

neemayee wraz *n.* ور نیمایي
midday

neemgaray *a.* نیمی sketchy

neemgartya *n* نیمتیا deficit

neemgartya *n.* نیمتیا imperfection

neewa *v. t.* نیول catch

neewaka *n.* نیوکه objection

neewaka kawal *v. t.* نیوکهکول
castigate

neewaka kawal *v. t* نیوکهکول
criticize

neewal *v.t.* نیول arrest

neewal *v.t.* نیول nab

neewal; taskheerawal *v. t.* نیول،
تسخیرول capture

neewana *n.* نیونه capture

neewana *n.* نیونه catch

neewana *n.* نیوونه seizure

neewana; tawqeef *n.* نیونه،توقیف
arrest

neewani sakha eystal *v.t.* نیونخه
ایستل decontrol

neewoonkay *n.* نیوونکی occupant

neewoonkay *n.* نیوونکی occupier

neygh *a.* نغ straight

neygh pa neygha *a* نغپهنغه direct

neygh; sam *a.* نغ؛سم right

neygh; walar *a.* نغ؛ولا upright

neykee *n* نکي good

neykh laroonkay *a.* نلرونکی
stingy

neykhtar *n.* نتر lancet

neykmargha *a.* نکمرغه fortunate

neykmargha *a.* نکمرغه lucky

neyza *n* نزه bayonet

neyza *n.* نزه lance

neyza *n.* نزه spear

neyza wahoonkay *n.* نزهوهونکی lancer

nghota kawal *v.i.* نغوته‌کول allude

nghota; ishara *n* نغوته،اشاره allusion

nijat *n.* نجات emancipation

nijat warkawal *v.t.* نجات‌ورکول rescue

nijat; khlasoon *n* نجات،خلاصون rescue

nika *n.* نکاح wedlock

nisab *n.* نصاب quorum

nisbat; sharah *n.* نسبت،شرح ratio

nisbatan loy *a.* نسبتاًلوی sizable

nishasta *n.* نشاسته starch

nizamee dalgay *n.* نظامی‌ډله squad

nizamee zwak *n.* نظامی‌واک militia

nkhalawal *v.t.* نلول ally

nobat; halat *n* نوبت،حالت bout

nobatee bad wa baran *n.* نوبتی‌باد وباران monsoon

nobatee taba *n.* نوبتی‌تبه malaria

nobatee; beylgayeez *a.* نوبتي،بلهييز typical

nook *n.* نوک nail

noolas *n.* نولس nineteen

noolasam *a.* نولسم nineteenth

noom *n.* نوم name

noom lar *n.* نوم‌لار nomenclature

noom leekana *n.* نوملیکنه registration

noom leekana kawal *v. t* نوملیکنه کول enlist

noom leekana kawal *v. t* نوملیکنه کول enrol

noom pri eekhodal *v.t.* نوم‌پرایودل term

noom warakay *n.* نوم‌ورکي anonymity

noom warkawal *v.t.* نوم‌ورکول name

noomand *n.* نوماند candidate

noomand *n* نوماند nominee

noomand kawal *v.t.* نوماندکول nominate

noomawana *n.* نومونه nomination

noomawaray *n* نوموی celebrity

noomeez *a.* نومیز nominal

noomleek *n.* نوملیک list

noomoona leekal *v.t.* نومونه‌لیکل list

noompohana *n.* نوم‌پوهنه terminology

noompohaneez *a.* نوم‌پوهنیز terminological

noomyalay *a* نومیالی famous

noomyaleetob *n.* نومیالیتوب prominence

noomzaray *n.* نومزری pronoun

nooranee *a.* نوراني radiant

nooranee kawal *v.t.* نوراني‌کول transfigure

nooranee shpol *n.* نوراني‌شپول nimbus

nooraneeyat *n.* نورانیت radiance

noorlas kalan zwan *n. pl.* نورلس کلن‌وان teens

nor *a.* نور more

noro sakha jala kawal *v.t.* نوروخه
جلاكول segregate
notaka; nyal; sooka *n* نوتكه،نيال،
وكه sprout
numayanda *n.* نماينده
representative
numayinda *n.* نماينده proxy
numayinda *n* نمائنده deputy
numayindagee kawoonkay *a.*
نماينلي كوونكى representative
numayish *n* نمايش display
numayish *n.* نمايش manifestation
numayishee *a.* نمايشي gaudy
nuqs *n* نقص defect
nuqsan *n.* نقصان damage
nuqsan *n.* نقصان decrement
nuqtey eekhodana *n.* نقطايودنه
punctuation
nuqz *n* نقض breach
nuqzee *adj.* نقضي deficient
nuskha *n.* نسخه prescription
nuskha warkawal *v.t.* نسخهوركول
prescribe
nuskha; formool *n.* نسخه،فورمول
recipe
nuskha; naqal *n.* نسخه،نقل replica
nuskha; riwayat *n.* نسخه،روايت
version
nutfa *n.* نطفه sperm
nutfa; tukham *n.* نطفه،تخم semen
nutfawee *a.* نطفوي seminal
nyabatee *a.* نيابتي vicarious
nyal; qalma *n.* نيال،قلمه sapling
nyat baday *a.* نيت بدى jealous
nyat badee *n.* نيت بدي jealousy
nyaw *n.* نياو justice

nyawgar *a.* نياور just

oba *n.* اوبه water
oba kawal *v.* *t* اوبه كول drench
oba malham *n.* اوبه ملهم balsam
oba na akheestoonkay *a.* اوبه نه
اخيستونكى watertight
oba warkawal *v.t.* اوبه وركول
water
obawal *v.t.* اوبول irrigate
obawana *n.* اوبوونه irrigation
obdal *v.t.* اوبدل knit
obdal shaway *a.* اوبدل شوى textile
obdal shaway khazeena jakat *n.*
اوبدل شوى خينه جاك jersey
obdana; tanasta *n.* اوبدنه،تنسته
texture
obgarzanay *n.* اوبرنى whirlpool
oblan *a* اوبلن dilute
oblan *a.* اوبلن watery
oblan kawal *v.* *t* اوبلن كول dilute
oblan khorak *n.* اوبلن خوراك
mash
obo ki ghopa keydal *v.i.* اوبو كغوپه
كدل duck
obo ki lahoo keydal *v.i* اوبو كلاهو
كدل drown
obzad garzawal *v.t.* اوبضدرول
waterproof
obzad; na loondeydoonkay *a.*
اوبضد،نه لوندىدونكى waterproof
odal *v.t.* اول arrange

odal *v.t.* اول array

odoon *n.* اوون arrangement

ofqee karkha *n.* افقي کره horizon

oj *n.* اوج climax

oj ta raseydal *v.i.* اوجته‌رسدل culminate

oj; ghwara wakht *n.* اوج؛غوره وخت prime

oj; teyra sooka *n.* اوج؛ترموکه pinnacle

omeed *n* امید hope

omeed laroonkay *a.* امیدلرونکی optimistic

ooga *n.* اوه garlic

ooga warkawal *v. t* اوهورکول encourage

ooga; walay *n.* اوه؛ولی shoulder

oogad *a.* اود verbose

oogad *a.* اود lengthy

oogad aw azad kamees *n.* اوداو ازادکمیس robe

oogad aw azad kamees aghostal *v.t.* اوداوازادکمیس‌اغوستل robe

oogad aw dangar *a.* اوداونر lank

oogad aw teyra ghakh *n.* اوداوتره غا tusk

oogad dastkash *n.* اوددستکش gauntlet

oogad mahala *a.* اودمهاله chronic

oogad sadar *n.* اودادر toga

oogad zhwand *n.* اودژوند longevity

oogadwalay *n.* اودوالی length

oogadwalay *n.* اودوالی prolongation

oogda *a.* اود long

oogda *a.* اود oblong

oogda aw la qahra daka wayna *n.* اودهاولهقهره‌کهونا tirade

oogda mukhtalif rangoona laroonki patay *n.* اودهمختلف رنونهلرونکپ stripe

oogda sawkay *n* اودموک bench

oogda zhawara dara *n.* اودهژوره دره ravine

oogdawal *v. t* اودول extend

oogdawal *v.t.* اودول lengthen

oogdawal *v.t.* اودول prolong

oogdey khazeena jorabey *n.* اود ینه‌جوراب stocking

oogey porta khozawal *v.t.* اوپورته خوول shrug

oogey spakawal *v.t.* اوسپکول parry

ookh *n.* او camel

ookhka *n.* اوکه tear

oomar *n.* عمر age

oomar khwaralay *a.* عمرخولی old

oomar khwaralay insan *a.* عمر خولیانسان senile

oonay *n.* اوونز week

ooneez *a.* اوونیز weekly

ooray; sareykh *n.* اور؛سر gum

oqab *n* عقاب eagle

or *n* اور fire

or akheystoonkay *a.* اوراخیستونکی inflammable

or balawal *v.t.* اوربلول kindle

or lagawal *v.t* اورلول fire

or wazhal *v.t* اوروژل extinguish

ora *n* اوه flour

ora dawla *a.* اوهوله mealy

orakht *n* اورت rain
orakht wareydal *v.i.* اورتوریدل rain
orbal *n* اوربل forelock
orgaday *n.* اورای rail
orgaday *n.* اورای train
orlageet *n.* اورلیت match
orlageet balowal *v.i.* اورلیتبلوول match
ornay *adj* اونی aestival
orsheenday *a.* اورشیندی volcanic
orsheenday ghar *n.* اورشیندیغر volcano
ortak *n.* اورک lighter
os *adv.* اوس now
os mahal *adv.* اوسمهال presently
oseydal *v.i* اوسدل abide
oseydoonkay *n* اوسدونکی resident
ospana *n.* اوسپنه iron
oto kawal *v.t.* اوتوکول iron
oto kawal *v.t.* اوتوکول mangle
owa *n.* اووه seven
owallas *n., a* اولس seventeen
owallasam *a.* اوولسم seventeenth
owam *a.* اووم seventh
owama *a* اوومه seven


```
P
```

pa ... ki; pa ... manz ki *prep.* په
ك؛په_ـمنځ ك among
pa ... manz ki; la ... dali sakha
prep. په_ـمنځ ك؛له_ـلخه
amongst

pa adab sara *a.* پهادبسره
mannerly
pa adat sara *adv.* پهعادتسره
ordinarily
pa adilana toga *adv.* پهعادلانهتوه
justly
pa akhira ki *adv.* پهآخرهک
ultimately
pa ala natoona pranistal;
rashkawal *v.t.* پهآلهنونه
پرانستل؛راشکول wrench
pa amoomee rayo sara sharal
v.t. پهعمومیرایوسرهشل
ostracize
pa ara reybal *v.t.* پهارهربل saw
pa aram sara *adv.* پهآرامسره
leisurely
pa asal ki *adv.* پهاصلک mainly
pa asantya sara *adv.* پهآسانتیاسره
readily
pa azabawal *v.t.* پهعذابول agonize
pa badnyatay sara *a.* پهبدنیتهسره
niggardly
pa badraga malgartya kawal *v. t*
پهبدرهملرتیاکول escort
pa bal nama *adv.* پهبلنامه alias
pa bala akhta kawal *v.t.* پهبلااخته
کول plague
pa bala panra *adv.* پهبلهپاه
overleaf
pa balakht sar eekhodal *v.t.* په
بالتسرایودل pillow
pa barkho weyshal *v.t.* پهبرخو
وشل portion
pa barkho weyshal *v.t.* پهبرخو
وشل segment

pa bashpar dawl *adv.* پهبشپول
altogether

pa bashpar dawl *adv.* پهبشپول
fully

pa bashpar dawl *adv.* پهبشپول
stark

pa bata gota soolawal *v.t.* پهبهوته
سولول thumb

pa beera leekal *v.t.* پهبیهلیکل
scrawl

pa beera leekal *v.t.* پهبیهلیکل
scribble

pa beeri sara takhteydal *v.i* پهبی
سرهتتدل scamper

pa bey khabray sara *adv.* پهبخبر
سره unawares

**pa bey rahmay sara jinsee
khwand akheystoonkay** *n.* په
برحمسرهجنسيخوندهاخستونکی
sadist

pa beydya ki *adv.* پهبدياک afield

pa beykh ki prot *a.* پهبخ کپروت
terminal

pa beylchey sara arawal *v.t.* په
بلجسرهاول spade

pa bistar ki *adv.* پهبسترکی abed

pa bukhar alwatal *v.* i پهبخارالوتل
evaporate

pa bukhar arawal *v.t.* پهبخاراول
vaporize

pa campyootar tasneefawal *v. t*
په کمپیورتصنیفول compose

pa chatak harakat leyri kawal
v.t. پهچکحرکتلرکول whisk

pa chatakay *adv* پهچک early

pa chatakay sara *adv* پهچکسره
fast

pa chatakay sara *adv.* پهچکسره
speedily

pa chatakay sara zghaleydal *v.i.*
پهچکسرمغلدل speed

pa chatkay sara *adv.* پهچکسره
apace

pa cheekaro nanawistal *v.t.* په
چیکوننوستل mire

pa cheygho faryad kawal *n.i.* په
چغوفریادکول bawl

pa chrap chrap sara khwaral
v.t. پهچپچپسرهخول smack

pa dabaro pokhal *v.t.* پهبروپول
pave

pa dabaro weeshtal ya mokhal
v.t. پهبروویشتلیامول stone

pa dadman dawl *adv.* پهامنول
surely

pa daftar ki sabtawal *v.t.* پهدفترک
ثبتول register

**pa daftaro ki da istiqbal oogad
meyz** *n.* پهدفتروکداستقبالاودمز
counter

pa daga wayal *v.t.* پهاهویل profess

pa dakhil pori arwand *adv.* په
داخلپوراوند inside

pa dal sara zhghoral *v.t.* پهالسره
ژغورل shield

pa dala ki harakat kawal *v.i* پهله
کحرکتکول troop

pa dala tlal *v. t* پهلهتلل delegate

pa dalayalo walar *a.* پهدلایلولا
rational

pa dalo weyshal *v.t.* پهلووشل
group

**pa danda da ghondaski wahalo
loba kawal** *v.* i پهنهدغونسک
وهلولوبهکول bat

pa danda ghondaska wahoonkay lobgharay *n.* پەنه غونسکەوهونکیلوبغای batsman

pa dang peyalee *a.* پەانپیلی straightforward

pa daqeeqa toga *adv.* پەدقیقەتوه minutely

pa dar zarawona *n.* پەدارونه. gallows

pa darawano da peyso wasooltya *n* پەارونودیسو وصولتیا blackmail

pa dard khwarana *n.* پەدردخونه subservience

pa dard rawastal; rag awakhtal *v.t.* پەدردراوستل؛راوتل sprain

pa daro daro weyshal *v.t.* پەدودو وشل plank

pa daw talbana dawl *adv.* پەداو طلبانەول voluntarily

pa dawat rabalal *v.t.* پەدعوترابلل convoke

pa dayrawee lori bandi harakat kawal *n.i.* پەدایرویلورباند حرکتکول whirl

pa dey barkha ki *adv* پەدبرخەک over

pa dey dawl *adv.* پەدول thus

pa dey dawran *adv.* پەددوران meanwhile

pa dey shawkhwa ki *adv.* پەد شاوخواک hereabouts

pa dey wakhtoono ki *adv.* پەد وختونوک today

pa difaee toga *adv.* پەدفاعیتوه defensive

pa diqat sara palatal *v.i.* پەدقت سرەپلل pry

pa doodeez deen bawar laroonkay *n.* پەدودیزدینباور لرونکی orthodoxy

pa doodeez deen bawaree *a.* پە دودیزدینباوري orthodox

pa eesaeeyat ki asqaf *n* پەعیسائیت کاسقف bishop

pa eesaeeyat ki da tameed ghosal *n.* پەعیسائیت کدتعمید غسل baptism

pa eesaeeyat ki yaw mazhabee mashar *n.* پەعیسائیت کیومذهبی مشر cardinal

pa faaleeyat rawastal *v.t.* پەفعالیت راوستل prompt

pa fikree taraw bawaree *n.* پە فکريتاوباوري telepathist

pa fishar sara jorawal *v.t.* پەفشار سرەجوول imprint

pa fuzla shayano da yaw zai laral *v.t.* پەفاضلەشیانو دیوایلل litter

pa gada kar kawal *v.* *i* پەهکارکول collaborate

pa gada sara *adv.* پەهسره jointly

pa gada sara *adv.* پەهسره together

pa gada zhwand kawal *v.* *t* پەه ژوندکول cohabit

pa gadwad dawl *adv.* پەول pell-mell

pa gadwaday sara *adv.* پەوسره chaotic

pa gamoono sara andaza neewana *n* پەامونوسرەاندازه نیونه stride

pa ganro khudayano bawar *n.* پە وخدایانوباور polytheism

pa ganro khudayano bawar laroonkay *n.* پهوخدايانوباور لرونکی polytheist

pa ganro khudayano pori arwand *a.* پهوخدايانوپوراوند polytheistic

pa garandee dawl; nasapa *adv.* پهنديول،ناپه suddenly

pa ghakho shkawal *v.t.* پهغلو شکول nibble

pa ghalata ghag kawal *v.t.* پهغلطه غکول miscall

pa ghaleez dawl *adv.* پهغليظول thick

pa ghaltay sara *adv.* پهغلطسره wrong

pa ghamyo khkulay kawal *v.t.* په غميوکلی کول jewel

pa ghazab kawal *v.t.* پهغضب کول outrage

pa ghla ghla katal *v.i.* پهغلاغلاکتل peep

pa ghla ghla tlal *v.i.* پهغلاغلاتلل sneak

pa ghla katana *n* پهغلاکتنه peep

pa ghosa kawal *v.t.* پهغصه کول aggravate

pa ghosa kawal *v. t* پهغصه کول enrage

pa ghrap ghrap skhal *v.t.* پهغپ غپل sip

pa ghusa keydal *v.i.* پهغصه کدل rave

pa ghwara dawl *adv.* پهغوره ول better

pa godam ki satal *v.t* پهمودام کساتل warehouse

pa got nastay *n.* پهوناستی retirement

pa gul meykho seengarawal *v.t.* پهملمخوسينارول stud

pa hagha shawkhwa ki *adv.* پههغه شاوخواک thereabouts

nakhleydal; *v. t.* پهحلبيلوي کاچول can

pa haqeeqat ki *adv.* پهحقيقت ک substantially

pa har hal *adv.* پههرحال anyhow

pa har sa poh *a.* پههرهپوه omniscient

pa harakat rawastal *v.t.* پهحرکت راوستل propel

pa hawa arawal *v.t.* پههواول aerify

pa hayjan rapaseydal *v.i.* پههجان راپاډل rouse

pa heela mana toga *adv* پههيلهمنه توه avidly

pa hodman dawl *adv.* پههومنول purposely

pa hor wreetawal *v.t.* پههورريتول toast

pa ibtidayee toga *adv.* پهابتدايي توه primarily

pa ida leek sara makh torawona *n.* پهادعاليک سرهمخ تورنونه indictment

pa ilahee charo pori arwand *a.* پهالهيچاروپوراوند theological

pa infiradee toga *adv.* پهانفرادي توه solo

pa ishara sara har kar ta chamtoo keydal *n.* پهاشارهسره هرکارتهچمتوکدل beck

pa isharo pohawal *v.t.* پهاشارو پوهول signal

pa iztirab akhta *n* پهاضطراباخته agonist

pa jak sara *v.t.* پهجکسرهپورته کول jack

pa jal ki rageyrawal; akhta kawal *v.t.* پهجالکراول؛اخته کول tangle

pa jama pori arwand *n.* پهجمعپور اوند plurality

pa janjal oreydal *v. t* پهجنجالاوډل bustle

pa jaryan rawastal *v.t.* پهجريان راوستل mobilize

pa jazar aw mad pori arwand *a.* پهجذراومدپوراوند tidal

pa jibran pori arwand *a.* پهجبران پوراوند remunerative

pa jinayat kakartya *n.* پهجنايت کڅتيا implication

pa jinayat ki las laral *v.t.* پهجنايت کلاسلرل implicate

pa jinsee toga kamzoray *a.* په جنسيتوه کمزوری impotent

pa kakhtay ki *adv* په کڅکی aboard

pa kakhtay ki leygdawal *v.t.* په کڅ کالدول ship

pa kakhtay ki safar *n.* په کڅکسفر sail

pa kakhtay ki tafree ta tlal *v.i.* په کڅکتفريحتهتلل cruise

pa kakhtay ki wral *v. t* په کڅکول embark

pa kalee sara khlasawal *v.t* په کلي سرهخلاصول key

pa kaleesa ki saroodee dalgay *n* په کليساکسرودیډا choir

pa kam miqdar *adv.* په کممقدار less

pa kamila toga *adv* په کاملهتوه entirely

pa kanda ki achawal *v.t.* په کنده کاچول pit

pa kar achawal *v.t.* په کاراچول install

pa kar achawal *v.t.* په کاراچول use

pa kar achawona *n.* په کاراچوونه installation

pa kar achowana *v.t.* په کاراچول operate

pa karaw akhta kawal *v. t.* په کاو اختهکول encumber

pa kashak taral *v.t.* په کشکتل zip

pa kashoga sara khwaral *v.t.* په کاشوغهسرهخول spoon

pa kha andaz *adv.* پهخهانداز pretty

pa khabaro ataro ki land *a.* په خبرواترو کلڅ laconic

pa khanjar wahal *v.t.* پهخنجروهل stab

pa khatar ke achaval *v.t.* پهخطر کاچول imperil

pa khatar ki achawal *v.t.* پهخطر کاچول peril

pa khato ki raghreydal *v.i.* پهخو کرغدل wallow

pa khato laral *v.t.* پهخول silt

pa khawra bandi poza mokhal *v.* پهخاورهباندپوزهمول nuzzle

pa khkara dawl *adv.* پهکارهول openly

pa khob ki garzeydana *n.* پهخوب کرڅدنه somnambulism

pa khob ki garzeydoonkay *n.* somnambulist

pa khpal gooman *a.* پەخپلوومان would-be

pa khpal zay *adv* پەخپلءای duly

pa khuday bawar *n.* پەخدایءباور theism

pa khuday bawar laroonkay *n.* پەخدایءباورلرونکی theist

pa khwakhay cheygha wahal *v. t.* پەخوچغەوهل cheer

pa ki *prep.* پە ک in

pa kodo hazirawal *v.t.* پەکو حاضرول conjure

pa kom kar gumaral *v.t.* پەکوم کار مارل task

pa konato khwayeydal *v.i.* پە کوناووېدل backslide

pa kor danana *adv.* پەکوردننه indoors

pa lakara wahal *v. t.* پەلکەوهل cane

pa landa toga *adv.* پەلنەتوه short

pa landa toga *adv.* پەلنەتوه shortly

pa landa toga *adv.* پەلنەتوه summarily

pa landa toga bayanawal *v.t.* پەلنه توەبیانول summarize

pa lando *prep.* پەلنو across

pa langar zay ki da kakhtay darawalo lagakht *n.* پەلنرای ک دکتەدرولولت wharfage

pa lar ki *adv.* پەلا ک within

pa largee ki zhwand kawoonkay *a.* پەلرۍ کژوندکوونکی xylophilous

pa largee ya lakari pori taral *v.t.* پەلرییالکپورتل stake

pa larghono eetalweeyano pori arwand *a.* پەلرغونوایالویانوپور اوند italic

pa las ki neewal *v.t.* پەلاس کنیول grip

pa las ki neewana *n* پەلاس کنیونه grip

pa las ki takhtawal *v.t.* پەلاس ک تتول grab

pa las rawral *v. t* پەلاسراول earn

pa las samawal *v.t* پەلاسسمول handle

pa las sara samawal *v.t.* پەلاسسره سمول manipulate

pa laso aw pkho porta tlal *v. i* پە لاسواوپخوپورتەتلل clamber

pa laso aw pkho tlana *n* پەلاسواو پوتلنه scramble

pa leed pori arwand *a.* پەلیدپور اوند optic

pa leeka darawal *v.t.* پەلیکەدرول line

pa leeka ki shamilawal *v.t.* پەلیکه کشاملول deploy

pa leeka tlal *v.i.* پەلیکەتلل file

pa leekalee shakal ki rawastal *v.t.* پەلیکلیشکل کراوستل transcribe

pa lifafa ki achwal *v. t* کپەلفافه اچول envelop

pa lokhee ki achawal *v.t.* پەلوي ک اچول pot

pa looma ki geyrawal *v. t.* پەلومه ک رول entrap

pa looma ki geyrawal *v.t.* پەلومه ک رول noose

pa looma ki rageyrawal *v.t.* پهلومه
كرارول snare

pa loomi sara neewal *v.t* پهلومسره
نيول mesh

pa lor sara reybal *v.t.* پهلورسرهربل
scythe

pa lostana palatal *n* پهلوستنهپلل
browse

pa loy kach *adv.* پهلوىكچ highly

pa lwar ghag *adv.* پهلوغ aloud

pa lwar ghag aylanawal *v.i.* پهلوغ
اعلانول trumpet

**pa lwar ghag maloomat
warkawal** *v.t.* پهلوغمعلومات
وركول page

pa lwar ghag sara ralwaydal *v.t*
پهلوغسرهرالودل stump

pa lwar ghag wayal *v.i.* پهلوغويل
rattle

pa lwara *adv* پهلوه above

pa magwee razwarandawal *v.t.*
پهمويرراوندول peg

pa maharat bashparawal *v. t* په
مهارتبشپول elaborate

pa maharat sara karawal *v.t.* په
مهارتسرهكارول wield

pa makha di kha *interj.* پهمخهده
farewell

pa makhooka wahal *v.i.* پهموكه
وهل peck

pa manda warandi keydal *v.t.* په
مندهواندكدل outrun

pa manz ke *a.* پهمنكى inmost

pa manz ki *prep.* پهمنك amid

pa manz ki *prep* پهمنك between

pa maqtaee dawl khodal *v.t.* په
مقطعيولودل profile

pa maree pasi khayrat *n.* پهميپس
خرات pittance

**pa marpeychee dawl harakat
kawal** *v.i.* پهماريچيولحركت
كول snake

pa maskharo sara ghageydal *v.i*
پهمسخروسرهغدل sneer

**pa masnooee dawl da weeda
kawalo amal aw ilam** *n.* په
مصنوعيولدويدهكولوعملاوعلم
hypnotism

pa masnooee dawl weeda kawal
v.t. پهمصنوعيولويدهكول
hypnotize

pa masooleeyat takal *v.t.* په
مسؤليتاكل post

pa matrooka wahal *v.t.* پهمتروكه
وهل lambaste

pa mawzoon qadam tlal *v.i* په
موزونقدمتلل march

**pa meena aw shor mashor sara
lobeydal** *v.i.* پهمينهاوشورماشور
سرهلوبدل romp

pa meena majzoobawal *v. t* پهمينه
مجذوبول enamour

pa meeras rawral *v.t.* پهميراثراول
inherit

pa mehrabanay sara *adv* پهمهرباز
سره benignly

pa mehrabanay sara *adv.* پهمهرباز
سره kindly

pa mehwar taweydal *v.t.* پهمحور
تاودل pivot

pa merda barach wahal *a.* پرميه
بچوهل henpeck

pa meylmastya rabalal *v.i* په
ملمستيارابلل feast

pa miqdar ya peymayish ki barabareydal *v.* پەمقداريا پمائش کبرابردل amount

pa miqnateesee khob weedawal *v.t.* پەمقناطیسیخوبویدول mesmerize

pa mityazo pori arwand *a.* په متیازوپوراوند urinary

pa mukhtalifo tabqo bandi jala kawal *v.t.* پەمختلفوطبقوباندجلا کول laminate

pa munasib dawl *adv* پەمناسبول appositely

pa munasib dawl *adv.* پەمناسبول fairly

pa munasib dawl *a.* پەمناسبول seemly

pa munasiba toga *adv* پەمناسبەتوه pat

pa munazzama toga *a.* پەمنظمەتوه orderly

pa mushkil sara *adv.* پەمشکلسره scarcely

pa mustaqeem dawl *adv.* پەمستقیم ول straight

pa muzayda ki warandey kawoonkay *n* پەمزایدەکواندز کوونکی bidder

pa muzayda ki warandeyz *n* په مزایدەکواندز bid

pa muzayda ki warandeyz warkawal *v.t* پەمزایدەکواندز ورکول bid

pa nakha kawal; daghee kawal *v.t.* پەنەکول،داغيکول spot

pa nakho alamo khkara kawana *n.* پەنوعلامونکارەکوونه symbolism

pa nakho nakhano sara pohawal *v.t.* پەنونانوسرەپوهول sign

pa nakhro katal *v.t.* پەنخروکتل ogle

pa nama kawal *v. t* پەنامەکول betroth

pa nareentob sara *a.* پەنارينتوب سره manly

pa nasam zay ki karawal *v.t.* په ناسمایکیککارول misplace

pa nawara dawl *adv.* پەناوەول badly

pa nawara toga *adv* پەناوەتوه malafide

pa naz nakhro tlal *v.i.* پەنازنخرو تلل strut

pa naz palal *v.t.* پەنازپالل pamper

pa nazar ratlal *v.i.* پەنظرراتلل seem

pa nazaree ilam poh *n.* پەنظريعلم پوه theorist

pa neyza ghosawal *v.t.* پەنزەغوول spear

pa neyza ghosawal *v.t.* پەنزەغوول spike

pa neyza wahal *v.t.* پەنزەوهل lance

pa nika pori arwand *a.* پەنکاحپور اوند nuptial

pa nishasta klakawal *v.t.* پەنشاسته کلکول starch

pa nookano nakhlawal *v.t.* په نوکانونلول nail

pa noom kawal *v. t.* پەنومکول entitle

pa noom lar ki zayawal *v.t.* پەنومل کایول tabulate

pa obo ki ghopa keydal *v.i.* پهاوبو
کغوپه کدل submerge

pa obo weenzal *v.t.* پهاوبوينل
rinse

**pa obo ya sheydo ki eysheydalee
da joowaro ora** *n.* پهاوبوياشدو
کاشدلي دجوارواوه mush

pa oogadwalee *adv* پهاودوالي long

pa oogey sara zor kawal *v.t.* پهاو
سره زور کول shoulder

pa or teyl achawal *v.t.* پهاورتل
اچول stoke

pa owa wrazo ki *adv.* پهاوه ورو ک
weekly

pa pam ki neewal *v. t* پهپام کنیول
consider

pa pam war kach *prep.* پهپام و کچ
considering

pa pana matawal *v.t.* پهپانه ماتول
wedge

pa panra ray warkawal *v.i.* پهپله
رای ور کول ballot

pa parakha kacha *adv.* پهپراخه
کچه wholesale

pa parchoon dawl ploral *v.t.* په
پرچون ول پلورل retail

pa pardey sara pokhal *v.t.* پهپرد
سره پول screen

pa paree taral *v.t.* پهپيتل rope

pa pat dawl *adv* پهپول under

pa pata sara *adv.* پهپه سره
stealthily

pa patay sara taral *v.t* پهپسره تل
tape

pa pay ki *adv.* پهپای ک eventually

pa payla ki *adv.* پهپایله ک last

pa payla ki waqay keydal *v.i* په
پایله کواقع کدل ensue

pa pensal jorawal ya leekal *v.t.*
پهپنسل جوول یالیکل pencil

pa peych nakhlawal *v.t.* پهپچنلول
screw

pa planwalee sara *adv.* پهپلنوالي
سره wide

pa pokh ki achawal *v. t* پهپو ک
اچول encase

pa poza kash kawana *n* پهپوزه کش
کوونه sniff

pa poza pori arwand *a.* پهپوزهپور
اوند nasal

pa pranistani pori arwand *a.* په
پرانستنیپور اوند inaugural

pa preymanay *adv.* پهپرماز galore

**pa pyaz pori arwand yaw dawl
sabzee** *n.* پهپیازپوراوندیوول
سبزي leek

pa qalee sara pokhal *v.t.* پهقلعي
سره پول tin

pa qamcheena wahal *v.t.* په
قمچینه وهل whip

pa qanoonee palwa taqeebawal
v.t. پهقانونيپلوه تعقيیول
prosecute

pa qarara *adv.* پهقراره slowly

pa qaraval *v.t.* پهقارول irritate

pa qasdee dawl orbalawona *n* په
قصديول اوربلوونه arson

pa qeero laral; tarkol lagawal
v.t. پهقيرولل؛تار کول لول tar

pa qismoono ki weyshal *v.t* په
قسمونو کوشل sort

pa qulf bandawal *v.t.* پهقلف بندول
interlock

pa radeeyo khparawal *v.t.* پەرايو خپرول radio

pa rakhteenee dawl *adv.* پەرتيني ول quite

pa rakhteenee dawl *adv.* پەرتيني ول really

pa rasmee toga *adv.* پەرسمي‌توه officially

pa ratloonkee pori arwand *a.* پە راتلونكي‌پوراوند prospective

pa reekhteenee dawl *adv.* پەريتيني ول indeed

pa reekhtya sara *adv.* پەريتياسره actually

pa reeyakaray zan baryalay kawona *n.* پەرياكاران‌بريالى كوونه hypocrisy

pa roghtya pori arwand *a.* پە روغتياپوراوند hygienic

pa rohaneeyoono pori arwand *a* پەروحانيونوپوراوند clerical

pa sa dawl; sanga *adv.* پەهول،بنه how

pa sahil bandi *adv.* پەساحل‌باند ashore

pa sakani sara prey kawal *v. t.* پە سكذسره‌پركول chisel

pa sakhtay sara *adv.* پەسختسره hardly

pa sakhtay sara wahal *v.t.* پەسختى سره‌وهل ram

pa salor gotee pori arwand *a. & n.* پەلوروي‌پوراوند quadrilateral

pa saloro barkho weyshal *v.t.* پە لوروبرخووشل quarter

pa sama toga *adv* پەسمەتوه right

pa samandaryoonee toghondee weeshtal *v.t.* پەسمندريوني توغوندي‌ويشتل torpedo

pa sandan bandi takawal *v.t* پە سندان‌باندكول forge

pa sangal wahal *v.t.* پەنل‌وهل nudge

pa sapeyra wahal *v.t.* پەپەوهل whack

pa sar chapa dawl *adv* پەسرچپەول topsy turvy

pa sar khwali eekhodal *v. t.* پەسر خولايودل cap

pa sargand dawl *adv* پەرندول clearly

pa sarka ki eekhodal *v.t* پەسركەكى ايودل pickle

pa sarsaree dawl *a* پەسرسري‌ول cursory

pa sat *n* پە abaction

pa sat *a.* پە backward

pa sat keydana *v.t.* پەكدل reverse

pa sat keydana; shakast *n*, پەكدنه، شكست reverse

pa sat keydoonkay *a.* پەكدونكى reversible

pa sat tloonkay *n* پەتلونكى abactor

pa sata swazawal *v.t.* پەسطح‌سوول scorch

pa satak wahal *v.t* پەسك‌وهل maul

pa seemee paree taral *v. t.* پەسيمي پي‌تل cable

pa seeyasat ki azad khwakhay shakhs *n* پەسياست‌كآزادخوى شخص leftist

pa seher majzoobawal *v. t.* پهسحر مجذوبول charm2

pa seyr; yaw shan *a.* پهر؛يوشان similar

pa sfanj pakawal *v.t.* پهسفنجپاكول sponge

pa sha *adv* پهشا behind

pa sha keydal *v.i.* پهشاكدل recede

pa sha tambawal *v.t.* پهشاتمبول repel

pa sha tambawal *v.t.* پهشاتمبول repress

pa sha tlal; munakkis keydal *v.i.* پهشاتلل؛منعكسكدل recoil

pa sha tlana *n.* پهشاتلنه recession

pa shampoo weykhta weenzal *v.t.* پهشامپووتهوينل shampoo

pa shatag *adv.* پهشات recoil

pa shatranj ki mat aw mabhoot *n.* پهشطرنجكماتاومبهوت stalemate

pa shaw khwa ki *adv* پهشاوخواك around

pa shaw khwa ki *prep.* پهشاوخواك within

pa shidat wahal *v. i.* پهشدتوهل dash

pa shoghlo *adv.* پهشغلو aflame

pa shoghlo rokhan *adv.* پهشغلو روان aglow

pa shomal ki *a.* پهشمالك northerly

pa shumalee qotab pori arwand *n* پهشماليقطبپوراوند Arctic

pa simanto jorawal *v. t.* پهسمنو جوول cement

pa skarwato pakhawal *v.t.* په سكرووپخول bake

pa skarwato pakhowoonkay; nanway *n.* پهسكرووپخوونكى؛ نانواى baker

pa so so zala *adv.* پهوولمه retail

pa so zhabo poh *n.* پهوژبوپوه polyglot1

pa so zhabo poheydana *a.* پهوژبو پوهدنه polyglot2

pa sook wahal *v.t.* پهسوكوهل punch

pa sotee wahal *v. t* پهسويوهل belabour

pa speeno zaro pokhal *v.t.* پهسپينو زروپول silver

pa swayl ki prot *a.* پهسولكپروت southerly

pa sweylee qotab pori arwand *a.* پهسوليقطبپوراوند antarctic

pa syoree ki satal *v.t.* پهسيوريك ساتل shade

pa tabiee dawl *adv.* پهطبيعيول naturally

pa tadbeer sara kar akheystal *v.i.* پهتدبيرسرهكاراخستل manoeuvre

pa tadbeer sara kar akheystana *n.* پهتدبيرسرهكاراخستنه manoeuvre

pa takabbur tlal *v.i.* پهتكبرتلل swagger

pa takalee wakht dama kawal *v.t.* پماكليوختدمهكول relay

pa takan sara ghosawal *v.t.* پمكان سرهغوول slash

pa talgaraf khabrawal *v.t.* پهلراف خبرول telegraph

pa taloo pori arwand *a.* پهتالوپور اوند palatal

pa talweezyon khparawal *v.t.* په لويزيونخپرول televise

pa tama kawal *v.t.* په طمع کول allure

pa tambal sara *a.* پهمبلسره slatternly

pa tangsa ki achawal *v.t.* پهتنسه کې اچول straiten

pa tasmey sara taral *v.t.* پهتسمه سرهتل strap

pa tawdo obo weenzal *v.t* پهتودو اوبووينل foment

pa taylafoon ghageydal *v.t.* په تلفونغدل telephone

pa teengar sara zhmana kawal *v.t.* پهينارسرهژمنهکول vow

pa teylo ghwarawal *v.t* پهتلوغوول oil

pa teylu ghwarawal *v.t.* پهتلوغوول anoint

pa teyra shee sooray kawal *v.t.* په ترهشيسوريکول pierce

pa teyzay sara harakat kawal *v.t* پهتزسرهحرکتکول flog

pa tol takano ki da ray warkawalo haq *n.* پهولټاکنوکې درایورکولوحق suffrage

pa tol wazhna las pori kawal *v.t.* پهولوژنهلاسپورکول slaughter

pa tolaneez dawl *adv.* پهولنيزول throughout

pa toleez dawl *adv.* پهوليزول generally

pa tonday palatal *v.t.* پهونډپلل rifle

pa toora wahal *v.t.* پهتورهوهل sabre

pa toto weyshal *v.t.* پهوووشل parcel

pa wajad rawastal *v. t* پهوجد راوستل enrapture

pa wak ki laral *v.t* پهواککلرل hold

pa wak ki laral *v.t.* پهواککلرل possess

pa wak ki rawastal *v.t.* پهواککې راوستل subject

pa wakseen warkawalo mamoor *n.* پهواکسينورکولومامور vaccinator

pa warta dawl *prep* پهورتهول like

pa waseela *prep.* پهوسيله per

pa weeno laralay *a* پهوينولرى bloody

pa wilayat arawana *n.* پهولايت اوونه provincialism

pa wrandi *prep.* پهواند versus

pa wrandi; porta la *adv.* پهواند، پورتهله up

pa wro wro tlal *v.i.* پهورووروتلل slow

pa wrostyo wakhtoono ki *adv.* په وروستيووختونوکې lately

pa yad rawastal *v.t.* پهيادراوستل remember

pa yad rawastana *n.* پهيادراوستنه recall

pa yad rawastana *n.* پهيادراوستنه recollection

pa yad rawastoonkay *n.* پهياد راوستونکی reminder

pa yakh khwayeydal *v.t.* پهيخويدل skate

pa yaw dawl *adv.* پەيوەول
somehow

pa yaw khas andaza tlal *v.i.* پەيو
خاص‌اندازەتلل pace

pa yaw khwandee zay kkheynastal *v.i.* پەيوخوندي‌ای
كنستل perch

pa yaw shee warghorzeydal *v.i.*
پەيوشي‌ورغوردل pounce

pa yaw zay deyr bachyan zeygoonkay *a.* پەيوای‌ربچيان
زونكی multiparous

pa yaw zay ki darawal *v.t.* پەيوای
كدرول park

pa yawa dam *a* پەيوەدم outright

pa yawa dam nareydal *v.i.* پەيوه
دمندل slump

pa yawa karkha ki darawal *v.t.*
پەيوه‌كرەكدرول align

pa yawa khula *a.* پەيوەخوله
unanimous

pa yawa lori ki *adv.* پەيوەلورک
aside

pa yawa nazar *adv.* پەيوەنظر
prima facie

pa yawa wakht *a.* پەيوەوخت
simultaneous

pa yawa zangaree wuzeeyat ki anzor eystal *v.i.* پەيوهاني
وضعيت‌كانوراستل pose

pa yawazi *adv.* پەيواز only

pa yawazi sara *adv.* پەيوازسره
singularly

pa zamanat khlasawal *v. t.* په
ضمانت‌خلاصول bail

pa zamanat preykhwal *v.t.* په
ضمانت‌پرول parole

pa zan pak wachawal *v.t.* پمان
پاک‌وچول towel

pa zanee toga; bey ikhtyara *a.* په
 زاني‌توه؛باختياره spontaneous

pa zarawartob *adv.* پەزەورتوب
heartily

pa zat bandi khabeestob *n.* پەذات
باندخبيشتوب proclivity

pa zawab masool; zawabday *a.*
پەواب‌مسؤول؛بوابده answerable

pa zay *conj.* پمای for

pa zay kawal *v.t.* پمای‌کول place

pa zeegzag dawl *a.* پەزيزاول
zigzag

pa zeegzag dawl harakat kawal
v.i. پەزيزاول‌حركت‌كول zigzag

pa zehmat sara par makh tlal
v.i. پەزحمت‌سره‌پرمخ‌تلل
scramble

pa zhaba satal *v.t.* پەژبمل lick

pa zhabanee dawl *adv.* پەژبني‌ول
orally

pa zhabanee toga *adv.* پەژبني‌توه
verbally

pa zhabi sara *adv.* پەژبسره
viva-voce

pa zmaka da sarkh nakha *n.* په
مكەدرخنه rut

pa zmaka kkheynastal *v.i.* پەمكه
كناستل land

pa zmaka prot *a.* پەمكەپروت
prostrate

pa zmaka wahal *v.t* پەمكەوهل
floor

pa zolam wazhal *v. t* پەظلم‌وژل
butcher

pa zor akheestana *n.* پهزوراخیستنه usurpation

pa zor aw lwar ghag sara bandawal *v.t.* پهزوراولوغسره بندول slam

pa zor sara idara kawal *v.t.* پهزور سرهادارهکول manhandle

pa zor sara mandal *v.t.* پهزورسره منل thrust

pa zor sara par makh beywal *v.t.* پهزورسرهپرمخبيول shove

pa zor zana kawal *v.t.* پهزورزنا کول rape

pa zora dakawal 2 *v.t.* پهزورهکول stuff

pa zora drazawana *n* پهزورهدرزونه pop

pa zora kashawal *v.t.* پهزورهکشول tug

pa zora trapawal *v.i.* پهزورهتپول pop

pa zra pori *a* پهزهپور desirable

pa zra pori *a.* پهزهپور interesting

pa zra pori *a.* پهزهپور pleasant

pa zra pori *a.* پهزهپور remarkable

pa zra pori arwand *adjs* پهزهپور اوند cardiacal

pa zra pory *n* پهزهپوری favourite

pa zyadtar miqdar sara *adv* په زیادترمقدارسره more

pa zyarat ki eekhodal *v. t* پهزیارت کایودل enshrine

pa zyaree akhta kawal *v.t.* پهزیي اختهکول jaundice

pacha *n.* پاچا king

pacha *n* پچه lot

pacha *n.* پاچا sovereign

pacha achowana *n* پچهاچوونه draw

pacha ahowana *n.* پچهاچونه lottery

pacha kawal *v. t* پاچاکول enthrone

pacha kawal *v.t.* پاچاکول throne

pacha wazhoonkay *n.* پاچاوژونکی regicide

pachahee *a.* پاچاهي imperial

pachahee *n.* پاچاهي sovereignty

pachahee *n.* پاچاهي kingdom

pachahee *n.* پاچاهي royalty

pachahee *a.* پاچاهي regal

pachahee dawra *n* پاچاهيدوره reign

padree *n.* پادري priest

paf; da khuley da hawa awaz *n.* پف،دخولدهواواز puff

pak *a.* پاک chaste

pak پاک clean

pak *a.* پاک neat

pak; ganjay *a.* پک،ګنجی bald

pakawal *v. t* پاکول efface

pakawal *v. t* پاکول clean

pakawal *v.t.* پاکول purify

pakawal; imala kawal *v.t.* پاکول، امالهکول purge

pakawana *n.* پاکوونه wipe

pakbazee *n.* پاکبازي chastity

pakh *n* پ blacksmith

pakhawal *v. t* پخول cook

pakheydal *v.i* پخدل mature

pakheydal *v.i.* پخدل ripen

pakhlanzay *n.* پخلنای kitchen

pakhlay *n* پخلی cook

pakhleegar *n* ر پخلي cooker

pakht *n.* پت lineage
pakhwa *adv.* پخوا once
pakhwa; da makha *adv* پخوا؛د مخه formerly
pakhwanay *a.* پخواني previous
pakhwanay useydoonkay *n.pl* پخواني او سيدونکي aborigines
pakhwanay; makhkanay *a.* پخواني؛مخکني antecedent
paki nafooz kawal *v.t.* پکنفوذکول penetrate
pakowana *n.* پاکوونه lotion
pakowana *n.* پاکوونه obliteration
pakwalay; chanrawana *n* پاکوالی؛ چاونه clearance
pal *n.* پال omen
pal; gam *n.* پل،ګام step
pal; naray chara *n.* پل؛نرچاه razor
palal *v.t.* پالل nurture
palal; rozal *v.t.* پالل؛روزل mother
palana *n.* پالنه nurture
palana *n.* پالنه patronage
palang *n* پالنګ bed
palatal *v.t.* پلل search
palatal aw saral *v.t.* پلل او ارل audit
palatana *n.* پلنه audit
palatana *n.* پلنه inspection
palatana kawal *v.t.* پلنه کول inspect
palatoonkay *n.* پلونکي inspector
palaway *n.* پلوی partisan
palaweetob *n.* پلويتوب partiality
palee garzeydal; gam akheystal *v.i.* پلي ګرځيدل؛ګام اخستل step
paleed *a* پليد malign

paleedgee *n.* پليدي malignancy
pali lara *n.* لاره پلا pedestrian
pali safar kawal *v.t.* پلي سفرکول pad
palistar; leyw *n.* پلستر؛لو plaster
palistarawal *v.t.* پلسترول plaster
palmagar *a.* پلمهر shrewd
palmagar; daqeeq *n.* پلمهر؛دقيق subtle
pam *n* پام consideration
pam *n.* پام care
pam kawal *v.i.* پام کول care
pam kawal; fikar kawal *v.t.* پام کول؛فکر کول mind
pam larana *n.* پام لرنه observation
pam warta kawal; nazar warkawal *v.t.* پام ورته کول؛نظر ورکول remark
pam; yadawana *n.* پام؛يادوونه remark
pana ghokhtoonkay *n.* پناه غوتونکي refugee
pana warkawal *v.t* پناه ورکول harbour
pana warkawal *v.t.* پناه ورکول shelter
pana warwaral *v.i.* پناه ورورل resort
pana warwral *v.t.* پناه ورورل seek
pana; kadwaltob *n.* پناه؛کواالتوب refuge
panahzay *n* پناهای asylum
panazay *n.* پناهای haven
panazay *n.* پناهای shelter
pand *n.* پند moral
pandee *n* پني coolie
pandee *n.* پني porter

pandghalay *n.* پنغالی camp

pandukay *n.* پنکی parcel

paneer *n.* پنر cheese

panga *n.* پانه asset

panga achowana *n.* پانه‌اچوونه investment

pangawal *n.* پانوال capitalist

pangawal *n* پانوال financier

panjshamba; da zyarat wraz *n.* پنجشنبه؛دزيارت‌ور Thursday

panra *n.* پاه leaf

panra *n.* پاه page

pansmanawal *v.t.* پانسمانول invest

panzeydalay *a.* پندلی nascent

panzoon pal *n.* پنون‌پال naturalist

panzos *n.* پنوس fifty

panzowoonkay *adj.* پنوونکی creative

par ... bar seyra *adv* پر---برسره besides

par deenee aqeedi arwand *a* پر دينی‌عقيداوند dogmatic

par izafee aydato maleeya *n.* پر اضافی‌عايداتوماليه supertax

par khorak mayan *n.* پرخوراک مين glutton

par khpal wakht *a.* پرخپل‌وخت timely

par makh beywal *v.t.* پرمخ‌بيول promote

par makh tlal *v.i.* پرمخ‌تلل proceed

par makh tlal; rasawal *v.t* پرمخ تلل؛رسول forward

par makh tlalay *a.* پرمخ‌تللی forward

par makh waral *v. t* پرمخ‌ول boost

par makh warana *n* پرمخ‌ونه boost

par makh wral *v.t* پرمخ‌ول further

par makhtag *n.* پرمخته development

par seena khwayeydal *v.* پرسينه‌ایويدل creep

par sha tag *n.* پرشات withdrawal

par sha tagay; mukhalif *a.* پرشا تی؛مخالف reactionary

par sha tlal *v.i.* پرشاتلل retreat

par shatag; beyrta garzeydana *n.* پرشات؛برتهرزدنه rebound

par wakht; da wakht paband *a.* پروخت؛دوخت‌پابند punctual

par zay *a.* پرای apposite

par zay *a.* پرای opportune

par zay chaland *n* پرای‌چلند decorum

par zay; pa munasib wakht *a.* پر ای،په‌مناسب‌وخت well-timed

par; bandi *prep.* پر،باند on

par; da pasa *prep* پر،دپاسه upon

parakh *a.* پراخ large

parakhawal *v.t.* پراخول amplify

parakhtya *n.* پراختيا expansion

parakhtya *n.* پراختيا magnitude

parakhtya warkawal *v. t* پراختيا ورکول enlarge

parakhtya warkawal *v.t.* پراختيا ورکول expand

parakhtya warkawal *v.t.* پراختيا ورکول span

parakhtya warkawoonkay *n.* پراختياورکوونکی prompter

parakhtya; intishar *n.* پراختيا، انتشار spread

parakhtya; pyawartya *n* پراختيا؛ پياوتيا amplification

parakhwalay *n* پراخوالی breadth

parastish *n.* پرستش adoration

parawal *v.t* پارول acerbate

parawal *v. t.* پارول entice

parawal *v.t.* پارول inflame

parawal *v* پاروول motivate

parawal *v.t.* پارول stimulate

parawana *n.* پاروَنه irritation

parawoonkay *n.* پاروونکی stimulant

paray *n.* پی rope

paray *n.* پی tether

parayshan *a.* پرشان pensive

parayshan *a.* پرشان uneasy

parayshana *a.* پرشانه moody

parayshana kawal *v. t* پرشانه کول disturb

parayshana kawal *v.t.* پرشانه کول vex

parayshana kawal *v.t.* پرشانه کول upset

parayshana keydal *v.i.* پرشانه کدل mope

parayshana keydal *v.i.* پرشانه کدل worry

parayshanee *n* پرشانی vexation

parayshanee *n.* پرشانی worry

parayshanee *n.* پرشانی stumble

parayshanee; zyat diqat *n.* پرشانی؛زياتدقت solicitude

parchoon plorana *n.* پرچونپلورنه retail

parchoon ploroonkay *a* پرچون پلورونکی retail

parda *n* پرده curtain

parda *n.* پرده lobe

parda kawal *v.t.* پرده کول veil

parda; burqa *n.* پرده؛برقع veil

pareyshana kawal *v.t.* پرشانه کول nonplus

parganpal *n,a* پرنپال socialist

parganpalee *n* پرنپالي socialism

parhayzgar *a.* پرهزار pious

parhayzgar *a.* پرهزار righteous

parheyz *n.* پرهز spare

parheyz; taqdees *n.* پرهز؛تقديس taboo

parheyzgar saray *a.* پرهزارسی smug

parheyzgaree *n.* پرهزاري sanctity

park *n.* پک twinkle

park wahal *v.t* پکوهل flash

park; zaleydana *n* پک؛بلدنه shine

parkand *a.* پرکند refulgent

parkeydal *v.i.* پکدل twinkle

parkeydal *v.i.* پکدل shine

parkeydana *n.* پکدنه lightening

parkha *n.* پرخه dew

parkha *n.* پرخه frost

parla pasey *adv* پرلهپسې consecutively

parla pasey wrandeyz *a.* پرلهپسې واندیز alternative

parla pasi ~*a.* پرلهپس ceaseless

parla pasi *a.* پرلهپس successive

parla pasi dazi kawal *v.t* پرلهپسز کول volley

parla pasi goozaroona warkawal *v.t.* پرلهپسوزارونه ورکول pound

parla pasitob *n.* پرله‌پستوب succession

parmakhtyayee *a.* پرمختيايي progressive

parnara *n.* پرناه chimney

paro *n.* پارو manure

paroon *n.* پرون yesterday

paroonay; obash *n.* پوني؛اوباش hood

parora; boos *n* پروه؛بوس fodder

parowana *n.* پاروونه motivation

parowoonkay *n.* پاروونکی irritant

parozha *n.* پروژه project

parozha jorawal *v.t.* پروژه‌جوول project

parqeydal *v.i.* پقدل glitter

parqeydana *n* پقدنه glitter

parsob *n* پسوب swell

parsob; sokalee *n.* پسوب؛سوكالي weal

parta *adv.* پرته asunder

parta la *prep.* پرته‌له beside

parta la dey chi *adv.* پرته‌له‌دچ without

partalaeez *a* پرتله‌ييز comparative

parwazgah *n* پروازگاه aerodrome

parzawal *v.t* پرول fell

parzawoonkay *n.* پروونکی wrestler

pas *a* پ blunt

pas aw ghabee saray *n* پاوغبي‌سی dunce

pas la dey *adv.* پس‌له‌د henceforth

pas la dey *adv.* پس‌له‌د henceforward

pas laronki *a.* پاس‌لرونکی reverent

pas pas kawal *v.t.* پس‌پس‌كول mouth

pas pas kawal *v.t.* پس‌پس‌كول whisper

pas pasay; pati khabari *n* پس پسی؛پخبر whisper

pasarlanay; taza aw tand *a.* پسرلنی؛تازه‌اوتاند vernal

pasey *prep.* پس after

pasey *adv.* پس afterwards

pasi keydal *v.t.* پس‌کدل pursue

pasi keydana *n.* پس‌کدنه pursuance

pasi keydana *n.* پس‌کدنه pursuit

pasoon *n.* پاون uprising

pasoon *n.* پاون revolution

pasoon *n.* پاون revolt

pasoon aw balwa *n.* پاون‌اوبلوا outburst

pasoon kawal *v.i.* پاون‌کول revolt

pasra kawoonkay *a.* پاسره‌کوونکی thrifty

pasra shawi shtamanee *n.* پاسره شوشتمني thrift

past *a.* پست menial

past; lag *n.* پست؛ل slight

pat aw ghalay *a.* پاوغلی subterranean

pat harakat *n* پحرکت sneak

pat kar *n.* پکار undercurrent

pata eejaza *n.* په‌اجازه connivance

pata keydal *v.i.* پاته‌کدل remain

pata shaway *n.* پاته‌شوی remainder

pata shaway *a.* پاته‌شوی residual

pata shaway barkha *n.* پاته‌شوبرخه residue

pata shawee; maree n. ،پاتهشوي مي remains

pata shoonay; izafee n. ،پاتهشوني اضافي surplus

pata; katara n. ،په؛کاره bar

patang n. پتنگ butterfly

patanzay; morchal n. پناى؛مورچل stronghold

patasa n. پتاسه candy

patawal v. t. پول conceal

patawal v.t پول hide

patawana n. پونه hide

patay pri lagawal v.t. پپرلول tag

patay trina chapeyra kawal v.t. پ ترنهچاپرهکول gird

patay; karay n. پ،ک band

patay; naray tasma n. پ،نرتسمه strip

patay; tar n. پ،تار tape

patay; taranga n. پ،تانه ribbon

pati keydal; meysht keydal v.i. پاتکدل؛مشتکدل stay

pati ratlal v.i پاتراتلل fail

patkay n. پک turban

patloon n. پتلون pantaloon

patloon n.pl پتلون trousers

patnoos n. پتنوس tray

patokay tri arawal v.t پوکىتراول skin

pawlad n. پولاد steel

pawz a. پو military

pawzee n. پوي military

pay n. پاى end

pay ta rasawal v. t پاىتهرسول end

pay ta rasawal v.t پاىتهرسول finish

pay ta rasawal n پاىتهرسونه completion

pay ta rasawal a. پاىتهرسدونى terminable

pay; akhar n پاى،آخر extreme

pay; intiha n پاى،انتها finish

pay; khatmeyda n. پاى،ختمدا termination

paya; ospaneeza geera n. ،پايه، اوسپنيزهرا staple

paya; satoon n. پايه؛ستون pedestal

payakht laroonkay a. پايتلرونکى perennial

paydar a پايدار abiding

paydar a پايدار binding

paydar a پايدار durable

paydar a. پايدار interminable

paydawar; bar n پداوار؛بار yield

paydayshee a. پدايشي natal

payey aw stani ta warta a. پاياو ستنتهورته stellar

payey warkawal v.i. پايورکول skid

paygham n پغام errand

paygham n. پغام message

paygham laroonki leekana n. پغام لرونکليکنه missive

paygham wroonkay n. پغاموونکى messenger

payl n پيل commencement

payl n پيل start

payl kawal n پيلکول begin

payl kawal v.t. پيلکول start

payl; sar n. پيل،سر beginning

payla n پايله consequence

payla n. پايله outcome

payleydal v. t پيلدل commence

payleydana *n.* پيلدنه outbreak

payli ta raseydal *v. t* پايلتهرسدل conclude

paylot; jalawan *n.* پيلو؛جالهوان pilot

paylotee kawal; rehnumayee kawal *v.t.* پيلويكول؛رهنمايي كول pilot

paymalawal *v.t.* پايمالول trample

paymalawal *v.t.* پايمالول suppress

paymalawana *n.* پايمالوونه suppression

paymayish *n.* پمائش measure

paymayish *n.* پمائش measurement

paymayish kawal *v.t* پمائشكول measure

payshnihad *n* پشنهاد offer

paysoor *n.* پايو appendage

paysoor *n.* پايو appendix

peeka *a* پيكه pale

peeka banafsh rang *n.* پيكهبنفشرن lilac

peeka keydal *v.i.* پيكهكدل pale

peeka rang *n.* پيكهرن tint

peeka rang warkawal *v.t.* پيكهرن وركول tint

peeka zyar rang *n* پيكهزيرن buff

peelama; sareeza *n.* پيلامه؛سريزه overture

peenza *n* پنه five

peenza gotay *n.* پنهوى pentagon

peenzalas *n* پنلس fifteen

peesho *n.* پيشو cat

peeska *n* پيكه edge

peghor *a.* پغور ironical

peghor *n.* پغور irony

pensal tarashay *n.* پنسلتراشى sharper

pensal; da naqashay burs *n.* پنسل؛دنقاشبرس pencil

peych *n.* پچ screw

peych kash *n.* پچكش spanner

peychal *v.t.* پچل muffle

peychalay *a* پچل complex

peychalay *a.* پچلى intricate

peychalay kawal *v. t* پچلكول complicate

peychalay kawal *v.t.* پچلىكول intrigue

peychaltya *n.* پچلتيا complication

peychaltya *n* پچلتيا intrigue

peychaltya *n.* پچلتيا perplexity

peychowoonkay *n.* پچوونكى winder

peydayakht *n* پدايت creation

peyghambaree kawal *v.t.* پغمبري كول prophesy

peyghla *n.* پغله damsel

peyghla *n.* پغله maiden

peyghla *n.* پغله miss

peyghla; pak lamana *n.* پغله؛پاك لمنه virgin

peyghor *n.* پغور sarcasm

peyghor *n.* پغور skit

peyghor *n.* پغور jest

peyghor warkawal *v.i.* پغوروركول jeer

peyghor warkawal *v.i.* پغوروركول jest

peyghor wazma *a.* پغوروزمه sardonic

peykh lar; tareekhcha *n.pl.* پلۍ تاریخچه annals

peykh leekana *n.* پلیکنه chronology

peykh leekana *n.* پلیکنه journalism

peykh leekoonkay *n.* پلیکونکی journalist

peykha *n* په accident

peykha *n.* په occurrence

peykha; mreena *n.* په،مینه casualty

peykha; waqia *n* په،واقعه event

peykhey kawal *n.* پخکول mockery

peykheydal *v. t* پدل befall

peykheydal *v.t.* پدل happen

peykheydal *v.i.* پدل occur

peykheydana *n.* پدنه happening

peykhi kawal *v.t* پکول mimic

peykhi kawona *n.* پکونه mimesis

peyraway *n* پروی cream

peyrawee *n* پروی buttermilk

peyrawee kawal; naqal kawal *v.t.* پروي کول،نقل کول imitate

peyrawee; taqleed *n.* پروي،تقلید imitation

peyray *n* پری elf

peyray; saleeza *n.* په،سلیزه century

peyrodal *v.t.* پرودل purchase

peyrodana *n.* پرودنه purchase

peyrodoonkay *n.* پرودونکی buyer

peyrodoonkay *n..* پرودونکی client

peyrodoonkay *n* پرودونکی customer

peysey *n.* پسه money

peysey astawana *n.* پساستوونه remittance

peysey naghdawal *v. t.* پسنغدول cash

peysey tar lasa kawoonkay *n.* په ترلاسه کوونکی payee

peysh band *n.* پشبند apron

peyso lapara zana kawal *v.t.* پسو لپاره زناکول prostitute

peytawee ta kkheynastal *v.i.* پتاويته کناستل bask

peytay *n* پ carton

peywand *n.* پوند graft

peywand lagawal *v.t* پوندلول graft

peywand lagawal *v.t.* پوندلول patch

peywandawal *v.t.* پوندول join

peywandawal *v.t.* پوندول transplant

peywandawal; gandal *v.t.* پوندول،گندل stitch

peywandee bootay ya fasal *n* پوندي بوي يافصل hybrid

peywandee; dwa ragay *a.* پوندي، دوه رګی hybrid

peywasteydal *v. i.* پوستدل cling

peywasteydal *v.i.* پوستدل copulate

peywastoon *n.* پوستون alliance

peywastoon *n.* پوستون association

peywastoon; yaw keyda *n.* پوستون؛يو کدا incorporation

peyzhandana *n.* پژندپاه passport

peyzhandana *n.* پژندنه presentation

peyzhandana *n.* پژندنه recognition

peyzhandgalwee *n.* پژنلوي acquaintance

peyzhandgalwee *n.* پژندلوي introduction

peyzhandgalwee; shanakht *n.* پژندلوي؛شناخت indentification

peyzwan *n* پزوان bridle

peyzwan *n.* پزوان harness

peyzwanawal *v.t* پزوانول moor

peyzwanawal *v.t.* پزوانول picket

peyzwanee kawal *v.t.* پزواني‌کول tether

pkha *n.* په leg

pkhey pri eekhodal *v.t.* پپرايودل tread

pkheymanee *n.* پماني repentance

pkheymaneydal *v.i.* پماندل repent

plan *a* پلن flat

plan jorawal *v.t.* پلان‌جوول plot

plana panra *n.* پلنه‌پاه sheet

plana takhta *n* تخته پلنه paddle

planawal *v.t.* پلنول widen

planwalay *n.* پلنوالی width

plar *n* پلار father

plar neekoona *n.* پلارنيکونه ancestor

plaranay *a.* پلرنی paternal

plaranay meeras *n.* پلرنی‌ميراث patrimony

plaranay; koranay *n.* پلرنۀ؛کورنۀ ancestry

plarneeka *n* پلارنيکه forefather

plaway *n* پلاوی committee

plaway *n* پلاوی corps

plazmayna *n.* پلازمنه metropolis

plazmeyna; panga *n.* پلازمنه؛پانه capital

ploral *v.i.* پلورل shop

plorana *n.* پلورنه sale

ploranzay *n.* پلورنی shop

ploroonkay *n.* پلورونکی salesman

ploroonkay *n.* پلورونکی seller

podeena *n* پودينه mint

poh; aqil *a.* پوه؛عاقل quaint

poha *n* پوهه comprehension

poha *n.* پوهه knowledge

pohand *n.* پوهاند professor

pohaneez sayr *n.* پوهنيزسر excursion

pohaneez; andeykhman *a.* پوهنيز؛ اندمن apprehensive

pohaneeza baghwanee *n.* پوهنيزه باغواني horticulture

pohaneeza sanga *n* پوهنيزمانه faculty

pohanghond *n.* پوهنغوز encyclopaedia

pohanleek *n.* پوهنليک thesis

pohantoon *n.* پوهنتون university

pohanzay *n* پوهنی college

pohawal *v.t.* پوهول grasp

pohaway *n* پوهاوی grasp

pohaway; darak *n.* پوهاوی؛درک apprehension

poheydal *v. t* پوهدل comprehend

poheydal *v.t.* پوهدل know

poheydal *v.t.* پوهدل understand

poheydal; darakawal *v.t.* پوهدل؛ دَرَکول apprehend

pokh *a.* پوخ ingrained

pokh *a* پوخ ripe

pokh bawar *n.* پوخباور certainty

pokh shaway *a.* پوخشوی mature

pokh warkawal v. t پوورکول cushion
pokh; jild n. پو؛جلد cover
pokh; teykay n. پو؛تکی pod
pokhakh n. پو casing
pokhakh n پو coating
pokhal v. t. پول cover
pokhal; sadar pri ghwarawal v.t. پول؛بادرپرغوول sheet
pokhal; shanal v. t پول؛شنل bestrew
pokhowoonkay; lang n. پووونکی؛ لﻨ wrapper
pokhtal v.t. پوتل ask
pokhtal v.t. پوتل inquire
pokhtal v.t. پوتل question
pokhtana n. پوتنه inquisition
pokhtani garweygni n. پوتنروﻥ query
pokhtanleek n. پوتنليک questionnaire
pokhtawargay n. پوتوری kidney
pokhtay n. پوة rib
pokhtoonkay a. پوتونکی interrogative
pol n پل bridge
polee a. پولي monetary
pooch; bey adaba a. پوچ؛بادبه vulgar
poochtob n پوچتوب absurdity
pookanra n پوکله bubble
poola n پوله border
poola n پوله boundary
poola laral v.t پولهلرل border
poomba n په foot
poonba n. پنبه cotton

poonda n. پونده heel
poora a پوره absolute
poora a پوره entire
poora kawal; bashparawal v.t. پوره کول؛بشپول perfect
poora walay; kamal n. پورهوالی؛ کمال perfection
poora; mutlaq a پوره؛مطلق thorough
poora; zabardast a. پوره؛زبردست perfect
poozay n. پوز mat
popanak wahalay a. پوپنک وهلی musty
por n پور debit
por n پور debt
por n. پور loan
por akheystal v. t پوراخستل borrow
por akhistoonkay n پوراخستونکی creditor
por kawal v. t پورکول debit
por kawal v.t. پورکول loan
por waray n پوروی debtor
por waray keydal v.t پوروی کدل owe
por warkawal v.t. پورورکول lend
poray n. پو ladder
poray; martaba n. پو؛مرتبه stair
pori adv. پور across
pori watal v.i. پوروتل pass
pori watal; ghosawal v. t پوروتل؛ غوول cross
pori watana n پوروتنه pass
porta prep. پورته above
porta prep. پورته up

porta *a.* پورته upward

porta kawal *v.t.* پورته کول hoist

porta kawal *v.t.* پورته کول lever

porta kawal *v.t.* پورته کول raise

porta kawal *v.t.* پورته کول lift

porta kawona *n.* پورته کوونه hold

porta kawona *n.* پورته کوونه lift

porta keydal *v.i.* پورته کدل arise

porta tlal *v.t.* پورته تلل ascend

porta wral *v.t.* پورته ول uplift

porta; bar seyra *adv.* پورته؛برسره aloft

portanay *a.* پورتنی upper

portanay zama *n.* پورتنزامه maxilla

portanay; ghwara *a.* پورتنی؛غوره superior

portawalay *n.* پورته والی superiority

poshta *n* پشته embankment

postakay *n.* پوستکی husk

postakay *n.* پوستکی peel

postakay achawal *v.i.* پوستکی اچول moult

postakay achawal *v.t.* پوستکی اچول peel

postawal *v. t. & i* پوستول blanch

poz; lakhkar *n.* پو؛لکر army

poza *n.* پوزه nose

poza mokhal *v.t* پوزه مول nose

pozay; meyzaray *n.* پوزی؛مزری straw

pozband *n.* پوزبند muzzle

pozband *n.* پوزبند gag

pozband taral *v.t.* پوزبندتل gag

pozband warachawal *v.t* پوزبند وراچول muzzle

praday *a.* پردی alien

praday *a.* پردی outlandish

praday *n.* پردی outsider

praday *n.* پردی stranger

prakh *a* پراخ broad

prakh *a.* پراخ capacious

prakh *a.* پراخ vast

prakhtya *n.* پراختیا capacity

praneydal *v. t* پردل clot

prang *n.* پاز leopard

prang *n.* پاز panther

prang *n.* پاز tiger

pranistal *v.t.* پرانستل open

pranistal *v.t.* پرانستل loosen

pranistal *v.t.* پرانستل sever

pranistana *n.* پرانستنه inauguration

pranistana *n* پرانیستنه adjuration

pranistana kawal *v.t.* پرانستنه کول auspicate

pranistana; sooray *n.* پرانستنه؛ سوری opening

pranistay *a.* پرانستی open

pranistay *a.* پرانستی widespread

pranj *n* پرنج sneeze

pranjeydal *v.i.* پرنجدل sneeze

prata la dey *adv* پرته له دی else

prey kawal *v. t* پرکول cut

preykanda *a.* پرکنده categorical

preykanda izhar kawal *v.t.* پرکنده اظهار کول assert

preykanda; akheyree *a* پرکنده؛ آخري final

preykawal *v.t.* پرکول slice

preykhodal *v.t,* پريودل abdicate
preykhodal *v. t* پريودل discard
preykhodal *v.t.* پريودل leave
preykhodal *v.t.* پريودل release
preykhodana *n* پريودنه release
preykhowal *v.t.* پريوول abandon
preykhowana; las tri akheystana *n.* پريوونه؛لاستر اخستنه renunciation
preykoon *n.* پريکون interruption
preykra *n* پريکه decision
preykra kawal *v. t* پريکه‌کول decide
preymana; mufsal *a.* پرمانه؛مفصل ample
preymanee *n* پريماني abundance
preyshana kawal *v. t* پرشانه‌کول commove
pri akhta kawal *v. t* پراخته‌کول entangle
pri bawar na kawal *v.t.* پرباورنه کول mistrust
pri breed kawal *v.t* پربريدکول overrun
pri draneydal *v.t.* پردرندل out-balance
pri khatal *v.t.* پرختل mount
pri makhki keydal *v.t.* پرمخکېدل transcend
pri makhtaray zyatawal *v.t.* پرمختاریزیاتول prefix
pri musallat kawal *v.t.* پرمسلط کول overrule
pri toki kawal *v.t.* پروکول banter
pri zyateydal *v.t.* پرزیاتدل surmount
prora *n.* پروه hay

prot; bey parwa *a.* پروت؛بېپروا slipshod
proteen *n.* پروتین protein
psa *n.* پسه sheep
pukhla kawal *v.t.* پخلاکول conciliate
pukhlayana *n.* پخلاینه reconciliation
pukhlayana; sola *n.* پخلاینه؛سوله peace
pur ahang *a.* پرآهنّ melodious
pur mana *a.* مانا پر meaningful
pur omeed *n.* پراميد optimism
purasrar *a.* پراسرار mysterious
puraysh *a.* پرعيش mirthful
purfehem *a* پرفهم comprehensive
purjosh *a* پرجوش fervent
purtameen *a.* پرتمين glorious
purtameena nandara *n.* پرتمينه ندداره pageantry
pust *n.* پُست mail
pust leygal *v.t.* پُستلل mail
pust rasan *n.* پُسترسان postman
pust; da pust idara *n.* پُست؛د پُستاداره post
pustee *a.* پُستي postal
pustee tikat *n.* پُستيکټ postage
pyada *adv.* پياده afoot
pyada pawz *n.* پيادهپو infantry
pyala *n.* پياله cup
pyala; geelas *n.* پياله؛بيلاس tumbler
pyawaray *a.* پياوى potent
pyawaray azam *n.* پياوىعظم steadiness

pyawaray kawoonkay; zwakmanawoonkay *n* پياوى کوونکى،واکمنوونکى amplifier

pyawaray; loy *a.* پياوى،لوى huge

pyawaray; zorlaroonkay *a.* پياوى،زورلرونکى potential

pyawartya *n.* پياوتيا pontentiality

pyaz *n.* پياز onion

Q

qabar *n.* قبر grave

qabar *n.* قبر tomb

qabeela *n.* قبيله horde

qabeela *n.* قبيله tribe

qabeelawee *a.* قبيلوي tribal

qabil *n.* قابل genius

qabil khalk *n.* قابل خلک intelligentsia

qabil salakar *n.* قابل سلاکار mentor

qabileeyat *n* قابليت ability

qabili zamanat *a.* قابل ضمانت bailable

qablawal *n* قبلول acceptance

qablawal *v.t.* قبلول adhibit

qabrasee khwaga sharab *n.* قبرسي خواه شراب malmsey

qabz *n.* قبض constipation

qabz narmowoonkay *n.* قبض نرموونکى laxative

qabzeeyat zid *a* قبضيت ضد laxative

qachaq kawoonkay *n.* قاچاق کوونکى smuggler

qachaqawal *v.t.* قاچاقول smuggle

qachaqchee *n.* قاچاقچي jobber

qad; badanee banra *n.* قد،بدني به stature

qadar *n* قدر estimation

qadar kawal *v.t.* قدرکول admire

qadar kawal *v.t.* قدرکول adore

qadar; mafhoom; ahmeeyat *n.* قدر،مفهوم،اهميت significance

qadardanee *n.* قدرداني appreciation

qadardanee kawal *v.t.* قدرداني کول appreciate

qadari mutlaq *a.* قادرمطلق almighty

qafeeya *n.* قافيه rhyme

qafeeya jorawal *v.i.* قافيه جورول rhyme

qafeeya sazee *n.* قافيه سازي rhymester

qafila *n.* قافله caravan

qahar *n.* قهر indignation

qahar; tap *n.* قهر،پ tear

qaharmanee *a.* قهرماني heroic

qahraman *n.* قهرمان knight

qahramanee kawal *v.t.* قهرماني کول knight

qahrawal *v.t.* قهرول infuriate

qahreydalay *a.* قهردلى indignant

qahwa *n* قهوه coffee

qahwa khana *n.* قهوه خانه cafe

qahwayee; qahwayee rang *n., a.* قهويي،قهويي رن tan

qalam *n.* قلم pen

qalamraw *n* قلمرو domain

qalbee *a* قلبي cordial

qalee n. قلعي tin

qalib n. قالب mould

qalib; chawkat n چوكا،قالب frame

qalibawal v.t. قالبول frame

qalibawal v.t. قالبول mould

qam n. قام nation

qam pal n. قامپال nationalist

qam palana n. قامپالنه nationalism

qamcheena; shalakha n. ،قمچينه شلاخه whip

qamee a. قام national

qamoos n قاموس dictionary

qamoos n. قاموس lexicon

qanaat; marakht n. مت،قناعت satiety

qanay kawal v. t قانعكول convince

qanay kawal v.t. قانعكول satiate

qanay keydoonkay a. قانعكدونكى satiable

qanay; rizayee a. رضايي،قانع satisfactory

qand laroonkay a. قندلرونكى saccharine

qanoni haq n. قانونىحق franchise

qanoon n. قانون law

qanoon n. قانون statute

qanoon landi rawastal v.t. قانون لاندراوستل normalize

qanoon pohana n. قانونپوهنه jurisprudence

qanoon waza kawal v.i. قانونوضع كول legislate

qanoon waza kawona n. قانون وضعكوونه legislation

qanoonee a. قانوني legal

qanoonee a. قانوني legislative

qanoonee kawal v.t. قانونيكول legalize

qanoonee layha; bil n قانونيلايحه، بل bill

qanoonee taqeeb n. قانونيتعقيب prosecution

qanoonee wak n. قانونيواک jurisdiction

qanoonee wakeel n. قانونيوكيل prosecutor

qanooneetob n. قانونيتوب legitimacy

qanooneeyat n. قانونيت legality

qanoonpoh n. قانونپوه jurist

qanoonpoh n. قانونپوه lawyer

qanoonsaz n. قانون ساز legislator

qar qar kawal n. قرقركول croak

qarabat n قرابت affinity

qarardad kawal v. t قراردادكول contract

qarshavi a. قارشوى irate

qarzdar a. قرضدار indebted

qasab n قصاب butcher

qasad n. قصد determination

qasad n. قصد intention

qasam khwaral v.t. قسمخول swear

qasar n. قصر mansion

qasdee a. قصدي intentional

qasdee kawal v. i قصديكول deliberate

qaseeda n. قصيده ode

qash n. قاش slice

qashar tri speenawal v.t. قشرتر سپينول shell

qashar; postakay *n.* قشر؛پوستکی shell

qasid *n.* قاصد courier

qasoor; deywaleeya *n.* قصور؛دوالیه default

qata kawal *v.t.* قطع‌کول interrupt

qata kawal *v.t.* قطع‌کول intersect

qata kawal; ghosawal *v.t.* قطع کول؛غوول hew

qatal; wazhana *n* قتل؛وژنه assassination

qatil *n.* قاتل assassin

qatilana *a.* قاتلانه murderous

qatlawal *v.t.* قتلول assassinate

qatlawal *v.t.* قتلول massacre

qavi *a* قوی forceful

qawee *a* قوي energetic

qawee keydal; qawee kawal *v.t.* قوي کدل؛قوي کول strengthen

qayas; partalana *n.* قیاس؛پرتلنه analogy

qayda; farmool *n* قاعده؛فارمول formula

qayda; nizam *n.* قاعده؛نظام system

qayda; tanzeem *n.* قاعده؛تنظیم regularity

qaz (nar) *n.* قاز (نر) gander

qaza pori arwand *a.* قضاپوراوند judicious

qazawat *n.* قضاوت judgement

qazawat *n.* قضاوت advocacy

qazawat kawal *v.t.* قضاوت‌کول adjudge

qazawat kawal; manzgartob *v.t.* قضاوت کول؛منتوب کول arbitrate

qazayee *a.* قضای judicial

qazayee dalgay *n.* قضایی ډله jury

qazayee faysala kawal *v.i.* قضایي فصله‌کول judge

qazayee hukam *n.* قضایي‌حکم judge

qazayee wayna *n* قضایي‌وینا dictum

qazayee zwak *n.* قضایي‌ږواک judiciary

qazayee; salisana *a.* قضائي؛ثالثانه arbitrary

qazee *n.* قاضي magistrate

qazee *n.* قاضي arbiter

qeechee *n.* قیچي scissors

qeemat; arzakht *n.* قیمت؛ارزت worth

qeematee *a.* قیمتي costly

qeematee *a.* قیمتي precious

qeematee *a.* قیمتي valuable

qeematee kanray *n.* قیمتي کانی jewel

qeer; tarkol *n.* قیر؛تارکول tar

qeerat *n.* قیراط carat

qeeyafa *n.* قیافه semblance

qilat *n.* قلت scarcity

qisam *n.* قسم kind

qisam; dawl *n.* قسم؛ول type

qisam; kheyl *n.* قسم؛خل variety

qismat *n.* قسمت fortune

qist *n.* قسط instalment

qita *n.* قطعه nugget

qomandan *n* قومندان commandant

qomandan *n.* قوماندان prefect

qomar baz *n.* قمارباز gambler

qomar bazee *n* قماربازي gamble

qomar kawal *v.i.* قمار‌کول gamble

qoowat; payakht *n.* پايت،قوت strength

qorban zay *n.* قربانای altar

qos *n.* قوس arc

qudrat *n.* قدرت nature

qufal chi la dwaro khwaw sakha pranistal shee *n.* قفلچلهدواو خواوخهپرانستلشي latch

qurbanawal *v.t.* قربانول sacrifice

qurbanee *n.* قرباني sacrifice

qutab; stan *n.* قطب،ستن pole

qutbee storay *n.* قطبيستورى loadstar

qyamat *n* قيامت doom

R

rabalal *v. t.* رابلل call

rabalowoonkay *n* رابلوونکی caller

rabarseyra kawal *v. t* رابرسرهکول expose

rabita *n.* رابطه communication

rabita *n.* رابطه contact

rabita *n.* رابطه liaison

rabita kawal *v. t* رابطهکول contact

rabita shandawal *v.t.* رابطهشنول intercept

rabra *n.* ربه hardship

rabrawal *v.t.* ربول trouble

rabrawana *n.* ربوونه trouble

rabrawoonkay *a.* ربوونکی troublesome

rach; larz *n.* چ،لز thrill

rachapeyrawal *v.t* راچاپرول engulf

rachawal *v.t.* چول thrill

racheydal *v.t.* چدل jolt

rad rad katana; waranga *n.* رر کتنه،وانه stare

rad; inkar *n.* رد،انکار refuse

radawal *v.t.* ردول confute

radawal *v. t* ردول disapprove

radawal *v.t.* ردول negative

radawal *v.t.* ردول refuse

radawal *v.t.* ردول refute

radawal *v.t.* ردول reject

radawal; pa laghata wahal *v.t.* ردول،پهلغتهوهل spurn

radawana *n.* ردوونه rejection

radeeyo *n.* رايو radio

radyoyee ya talweezyonee parogram khparawal *v.t.* رايويیيالويزيونيپرورامخپرول telecast

raftar *n.* رفتار speed

rag awukhtal *n* راوتل wrick

rag; wareed *n.* ر،وريد vein

ragarzeydana; badla *n.* رارڅدنه، بدله return

rageyrawal *v. t.* رارول encircle

rageyrawal; jeyb wahal *v.t.* رارول،جبوهل purse

raghawal *v.i.* رغول heal

raghawal *v.t.* رغول mend

raghawal; samawal *v.t.* رغول، سمول amend

raghawana *n.* رغوونه repair

ragheydoonkay *a* رغدونکی curable

raghokhtal *v.t.* راغوتل muster
raghond *a.* راغوﻧ thick
raghondawal *v.t.* راغونول amass
raghondawal *v. t* راغونول collect
raghondawana *n* راغونونه collection
raghondawana *n.* راغونونه convocation
raghondawana *n* راغونونه muster
raghondawoonkay *n* راغونونکی collector
raghorzeydal *v.i.* راغورﺪﻟ fall
raghreydal *v.i.* رغدل wriggle
raghreydal *v.i.* رغدل slide
raghreydana *n* رغدنه wriggle
raghreydana *n.* رغدنه tumble
raghreydana; bey laritob *n.* رغدنه،بلارتوب slip
raghyanra *n.* رغیاﻧه oasis
rahat *n.* راحت convenience
rahbaree kawal *v.t* رهبريکول head
rahib *n.* راهب monk
rahib; rahiba *n.* راهب،راهبه votary
rahiba khaza *n.* راهبه nun
rakab *n.* رکاب stirrup
rakab *n.* رکاب pedal
rakad keydal; bey harakata keydal *v.i.* راکدکدل،بحرکته کدل stagnate
rakashawal *v. t* راکشول drag
rakashawana *n* راکشوﻧه drag
rakhatal *v.* راختل rise
rakhatal; rakhkareydal *v. i* راختل،راﮔاﺮﺪﻟ emerge
rakhatana *n.* راختنه rise

rakhchina *n* رخچینه coif
rakhna *n* رخنه gap
rakhna *n.* رخنه leak
rakhna *n.* رخنه leakage
rakhna payda kawal *v.i.* رخنهﭘﺪا کول gape
rakhteenay *a.* رتینه actual
rakhteenay *a.* رتینی veritable
rakhtoonay *a.* رتوﻧی true
rakhtoonay *a.* رتوﻧی truthful
rakhtya *n.* رتیا truth
rakhtya wayana *n.* رتیاوینه veracity
rakhtyapal *n.* رتیاﭘال realist
rakhtyapala *n.* رتیاﭘاله realism
rakkhata keydoonkay aw ospaneeza war *n.* راکته کدونکیاوسﭘنیزهور shutter
rakra warkra *n.* راکهورکه bargain
rakra warkra kawal *v.t.* راکهورکه کول bargain
rakra warkra; danda *n* راکهورکه، دنده business
ralwaydana *n* راﻟوﺪﻧه downfall
ram kawal *v.t.* رامکول subjugate
rama *n.* رﻣه herd
rama; gala *n* رﻣه،ﮔله flock
ramatowana; rakagawana *n* راﻣاﺗووﻧه،راکوﻧه fold
ramawal *v.t* راﻣول harness
rambari wahal *v. i* رﻣباوهل bellow
ramzee toray *n.* رﻣزيﺗوری cipher, cipher
ranaqlawal *v.t.* راﻧقﻟول quote
randa *n.* رﻧﺪه grate
randa kawal *v.t* رﻧﺪهکول grate

rang *n* رنگ colour
rang *n.* رنگ paint
rang alwatay; dangar *a.* رنگالوتی؛ دنگر wan
rang warkowana *n* رنگ ورکونه dye
rang; sayqal *n* رنگ؛صقل polish
ranga anzor *n.* رنگه انور pastel
ranga rang *a.* رنگارنگ varied
ranga rang *a.* رنگارنگ various
ranga rang khwara; makoolat *n.* رنگ رنگ خواره؛ماکولات *pl* victuals
ranga rang; beyla beyl *a.* رنگارنگ؛بیلا بیل sundry
ranga rangtob *n.* رنگ رنگتوب versatility
rangarang *a.* رنگارنگ motley
rangarang *a.* رنگارنگ multifarious
rangarang *a* رنگارنگ diverse
rangawal *v. t* رنگول colour
rangawal *v. t* رنگول dye
rangawal *v.t.* رنگول paint
rangawal *v. t.* نول demolish
rangawal *v.t.* رنگول tincture
rangawoonkay *n.* رنگونکی painter
rangharal *v.t.* رانغال wrap
ranra *n.* رڼا light
ranrawal *v.t.* رول light
ranrookay *n* رونکی temple
ranz *n* رنز disease
ranzara; nanzara *n.* رانزه؛ننزه turpentine
ranzoor *a.* رنزور ill
ranzoor pal *n.* رنزورپال nurse
rapor *n.* راپور inkling
rapor warkawal *v.t.* راپور ورکول report

rapor; khabar *n.* راپور؛خبر report
rapor; mufassil bayan *n.* راپور؛مفصل بیان recital
raqabat *n.* رقابت rivalry
raqabat kawal *v.t.* رقابت کول rival
raqeeb *n.* رقیب rival
raraseydal *v.i.* رارسدل arrive
raraseydana *n.* رارسدنه arrival
rasam gasht *n.* رسم ګشت parade
rasam gasht kawal *v.t.* رسم ګشت کول parade
rasam palana *n.* رسم پالنه observance
rasaseydal *v.i.* رسدل seep
rasawal *v. t* رسول deliver
rasawal *v.t.* رسول supply
rasawana *n* رسونه delivery
rasawoonkay; da tadarikato masool *n.* رسوونکی؛دتدارکاتو مسؤل supplier
rasay *n* رسی cord
raseed *n.* رسید receipt
raseydal *v.t.* رسدل reach
rasha darsha *n.* راشه درشه visit
rasha darsha kawal *v.t.* راشه درشه کول visit
rashpeyl wahal *v.i.* راشپل وهل paddle
rashpeyl wahoonkay *n.* راشپل وهونکی oarsman
rasman warandi kawal *v.t.* رسماً واندکول present
rasmawal *v. t.* رسمول depict
rasmee *a* رسمی formal
rasmee bayan warkawal *v.t.* رسمي بیان ورکول opine

rasmee eejazat laral;
tazmeenawal *v.t.* رسمی‌اجازت
لرل؛تضمینول warrant
rasmee haq *n.* رسمی‌حق
prerogative
rasmee maqam neewal *v.i.* رسمی
مقام‌نیول officiate
rasmee ya roohanee kalee *n.*
رسمی‌یاروحانی‌کالی vestment
ratal *v.t.* رتل reprimand
ratal *v.t.* رتل taunt
ratal; nakhwakhee kawal *v.t* رتل؛
ناخوی‌کول upbraid
ratal; radawal *v.t.* رتل؛ردول snub
ratana *n.* رتنه reprimand
ratana *n* رتنه taunt
ratana; radawana *n.* رتنه؛ردوونه
snub
ratawowal; ramatawal *v.t*
راتاوول؛راماتول fold
ratlal *v. i.* راتلل come
ratloonkay *a.* راتلونکی
forthcoming
ratloonkay *a.* راتلونکی future
ratloonkay *a.* راتلونکی next
ratloonki peykhey; afsana *n.*
راتلونکۍپ؛افسانه sequel
ratolawal *v.t.* راټولول gather
ratoobat *n.* رطوبت humidity
rawa *a.* روا admissible
rawa *a.* روا lawful
rawa *a.* روا legitimate
rawan *a* روان fluent
rawral *v.t.* راول adduce
rawral *v. t* راول bring
rawral *v.t* راول fetch

ray warkawal *v. i* رای‌ورکول comment
ray; intiqad *n* رای؛انتقاد comment
raya *n.* رایه vote
raya *n.* رایه opinion
raya *n.* رایه poll
raya warkawal *v.t.* رایه‌ورکول poll
raya warkawal *v.i.* رایه‌ورکول vote
raya warkawoonkay *n.* رایه
ورکوونکی voter
rayees *n* رئیس boss
rayees *n* رئیس chairman
rayees; aslee *a* رئیس؛اصلی arch
rayi ghokhtal *v. t.* رای‌غوتل canvass
raz *n.* راز mystery
raz *n.* راز secret
raz satal *v.t.* رازساتل secrete
raz satana *n.* رازساتنه secrecy
raz satana *n.* رازساتنه secretion
raz sparal *v. i* رازسپارل confide
raza *n.* رضا willingness
razalat *n.* رذالت roguery
razdar *n* رازدار confidant
razee *adj.* راضی complacent
razee *a.* راضی content
razee *a.* راضی willing
razee kawal *v.t.* راضی‌کول
consent3
razee kawal *v. t* راضی‌کول content
razee kawal *v.t.* راضی‌کول satisfy
razee kawal *v.t.* راضی‌کول suit
razee keydal *v. i* راضی‌کدل
consent
razee keydana *n.* راضی‌کدنه
consent
razeel saray *n.* رذیل‌سی rogue

razmee shair ya shairee *n* رزمي شاعرياشاعري epic

reekha; tana *n.* ره،تنه stem

reekhteenwalee *n* ريتينولي fidelity

reetara; patay *n.* رياته،پ tag

reetara; tasma *n.* رياته،تسمه strap

reeya kawal *v.t* رياكول feign

reeyakar saray *n.* رياكارسى hypocrite

reeyakar; bey mukhlis *a.* رياكار،بي * مخلص insincere

reeyakarana aw dwa makhee *a.* رياكارانهاودومخي hypocritical

reeyasatee *a.* رياستي presidential

reeyazat *n* رضايت contentment

reeyazat kawoonkay *n.* رياضت كوونكى ascetic

reeyazee *n* رياضي mathematics

reeyazee poh *n.* رياضي پوه mathematician

rehbaneeyat *n* رهبانيت monasticism

rehbaree kawal *v.t.* رهبري كول lead

rehbaree kawal *v.t.* رهبري كول pioneer

rehem; taqwa *n.* رحم،تقوا piety

rehen *n.* رهن mortgage

rehen kawal *v.t.* رهن كول mortgage

rehnumayee kawal *v.t.* رهنمايكول usher

reybal *v.t.* ربل reap

reyband *a.* ربند oblique

reyband kawal; kog aw pa dada tlal *v.t.* ربندكول،كواوپهدهتلل slant

reybanda zmaka *n.* ربندهممكه slope

reybandtob payda kawal *v.i.* ربند توبپداكول slope

reybaz *n.* رب sweep

reybaz wahoonkay *n.* ربوهونكى sweeper

reybazawal *v.i.* ربول sweep

reygdeyda *n.* رددا pulsation

reygdeyda *n* رددا pulse

reygdeydal *v.i.* رددل oscillate

reygdeydal *v.i.* رددل tremble

reygdeydal *v.i.* رددل vibrate

reygdeydana *n.* رددنه oscillation

reygdeydana *n.* رددنه vibration

reygdeydana *n.* رددنه tremor

reykha *n.* ريه root

reykha peyzhandana *n.* ريهپژندنه etymology

reykhanda kaga toree *n.* رنده كاه توري italics

reykhi ghazawal *v.i.* ريغول root

reykht; tarkeeb *n* رخت،تركيب form

reykhta garee; qalib ki achawana *n* ريختهري،قالب كه اچونه casting

reypat *n.* رپ rivet

riayat *n.* رعايت conformity

riayat kawal; ehtiram kawal *v.t.* رعايت كول،احترام كول regard

riayat; ehtiram *n.* رعايت،احترام regard

rifat *n.* رفعت sublimity

rifat; sar lwaree *n* رفعت،سرلوي uplift

risala *n* رساله brochure

risala *n.* رساله pamphlet

risala leekoonkay *n.* رسالهليكونکی pamphleteer

risalat; khidmat ta leywaltya *n.* رسالت؛خدمتتهلوالتيا vocation

riwajee *a* رواجي customary

riwayatee *a.* روايتي traditional

rizayat *n.* رضايت satisfaction

rodal; tay rodal *v.t.* رودل؛تىرودل suck

rodana *n.* رودنه suck

rogdawal *v.t.* رودول accustom

rogdawal *v.t.* رودول addict

rogday *a.* رودى accustomed

rogday *a.* رودى wont

rogday kawal *v. t.* رودىکول habituate

rogdeez *a* رودیز routine

rogdeez *a.* رودیز wonted

rogdtya *n.* رودتيا rote

rogdwalay *n.* رودوال addiction

rogh *a.* روغ sound

rogh ramat *a* روغرمه maiden

rogh ramat *a.* روغرمه sane

rogh ramat *a.* روغرمه wholesome

rogha jora *n* روغهجوه compromise

rogha jora kawal *v. t* روغهجوهکول compromise

roghtoon *n.* روغتون hospital

roghtya *n.* روغتيا health

roghtya *n.* روغتيا sanity

roghtya pohana *n.* روغتياپوهنه hygiene

roghtyayee *a.* روغتياي sanitary

rohaneeyoon *n* روحانيون clergy

rokhan fikra kawal *v. t.* روانفکره کول enlighten

rokhan fikray *n.* روانفکري liberalism

rokhana *a.* روانه luminous

rokhana jisam *n.* روانهجسم luminary

rokhana kawal *v. t* روانهکول elucidate

rokhanawal *v.i.* روانول alight

rokhanawal *v. t* روانول brighten

rokhanawal; pakawal *v. t* روانول؛ پاکول clear

rokhandan *n.* روندان loop-hole

rokhantya *n.* روانتيا illumination

roman; da meeni keesa *n.* رومان؛د مینکیسه romance

rond walay *n.* رووالى lustre

rooh *n.* روح soul

rooh; arwa *n.* روح؛اروا wraith

rooh; asal *n* روح؛اصل essence

roohanee *a* روحاني divine

roohanee *a.* روحاني spiritual

roohanee larkhod *a.* روحانيلارود pastoral

roohanee pal *n.* روحانيپال spiritualist

roohaneeyat *n.* روحانيت spirituality

roohee *a.* روحي psychic

roohee tadawee *n.* روحيتداوي psychotherapy

roond *a* روند blind

roonr *a.* رو transparent

roonr anday *a.* روآندى liberal

roonrtya *n.* روتيا lucidity

rostaray *n.* روستای suffix

rostaray jorawal *v.t.* روستای‌جوول suffix

rozal *v.t* روزل breed

rozal; tarbeeya warkawal *v.t.* روزل؛تربیه‌ورکول rear

rozana *a* روزانه daily

rozana *n.* روزنه nourishment

rozantoon *n.* روزنتون nursery

rozha *n* روژه fast

rozha neewal *v.i* روژه‌نیول fast

rujoo kawal *v.i.* رجوع‌کول revert

rukhsat *n.* رخصت discharge

rukhsat *n.* رخصت leave

rukhsatawal *v.t.* رخصتول assoil

rukhsatawal *v. t* رخصتول discharge

ruman; ishqeeya keesa *n* زمان؛ عشقیه‌کیسه novel

ruswa kawal *v.t.* رسواکول scandalize

ruswayee *n* رسوایی scandal

rutba warkawal *v. i* رتبه‌ورکول distinguish

rutba warkawal *v. t.* رتبه‌ورکول ennoble

S

sa *n* ساه breath

sa *interj.* ﻪ what

sa akeystal *v.i.* ساه‌اخستل respire

sa akheystal *v. i.* ساه‌اخستل breathe

sa akheystana *n.* ساه‌اخستنه aspiration

sa kakhana *n.* ساه‌کنه respiration

sa shay; sa *pron.* ﻪ،ﺶی what

sa wakht; kala *adv.* ﻪوخت؛کله when

sa warbandawana *n.* ساه‌وربندوونه suffocation

sa yi warbandawal *v.t* ساه‌یوربندول suffocate

saada *n.* ساده gull

saat; da zang awaz *n.* ساعت؛دزنگ آواز dial

saba *n.* سابه spinach

saba *n.* سبا tomorrow

saba ta *adv.* سباته tomorrow

sabab *n.* سبب cause

sabab *n.* سبب inducement

sabab; daleel *n.* سبب؛دلیل reason

sababee *adj.* سببی causal

sabandaval *v. t* سابندول belch

sabar *n.* صبر patience

sabar kawoonkay *a.* صبرکوونکی patient

sabit qadam *a.* ثابت‌قدم steadfast

sabit qadam satal *v.t.* ثابت‌قدم‌ساتل steady

sabit qadam satal *v.t.* ثابت‌قدم‌ساتل poise

sabit tamzay *n.* ثابت‌تمای standpoint

sabitawal *v.t.* ثابتول prove

saboon *n.* صابون soap

saboon pri mokhal *v.t.* صابون‌پر مول soap

saboonee *a.* صابونی soapy

saboot *n* ثبوت evidence

sabt; yadakht *n.* ثبت،ياد‌ت record

sabtawal; pa tarteeb sara eekhodal *v.t* ثبتول؛به‌ترتيب‌سره ايودل file

sabtawal; pa yad rawastal *v.t.* ثبتول؛به‌يادراوستل record

sabtawoonkay *n.* ثبتوونکی recorder

sabtawoonkay *n.* ثبتوونکی registrar

sabzee *n.* سبزي vegetable

sabzee khor *n.* خور سبزي vegetarian

sabzee khor *a* سبزي‌خور vegetarian

sabzee ploranzay *n.* سبزي‌پلورناى grocery

sabzee ploroonkay *n.* سبزي پلورونکی grocer

sada *a.* ساده frugal

sada *n.* ساده moron

sada *a.* ساده naive

sada *a.* ساده sheepish

sada kawal *v.t.* ساده‌کول simplify

sada kawang *n.* ساده‌کوز simplification

sada nakhcha jorawal *v.t.* ساده نخچه‌جوول sketch

sada nakhcha; tarha *n.* ساده‌نخچه، طرحه sketch

sada; asan *a.* ساده،آسان simple

sada; asana *a.* ساده،آسانه cozy

sada; khandoonay *a.* ساده؛خندونی rustic

sada; mutlaq *a* ساده،مطلق slick

sada; pak *a* ساده،پاک blank

sada; wazeh *a.* ساده،واضح explicit

sadar *n.* ‌ادر mantel

sadatob *n.* ساده‌توب naivete

sadatob *n.* ساده‌توب simplicity

sadiq *a* صادق downright

sadirat *n* صادرات export

sadirawal *v.i.* صادرول issue

sadma; goozar *n* صدمه،بوزار. shock

saf; katar *n.* صف،کتار tier

safa kawal *v.t.* صفاکول mop

safa kawoonkay tokar *n.* صفا کوونکی‌وکر mop

safar *n.* سفر journey

safar *n.* سفر trip

safar *n* سفر travel

safar kawal *v.i.* سفرکول journey

safar kawal *v.i.* سفرکول tour

safar kawal *v.i.* سفرکول travel

safarat *n* سفارت embassy

safarat kar *n* سفارت‌کار diplomat

safarat karee *n* سفارت‌کاري diplomacy

safaratee *a* سفارتي diplomatic

safayee *n* صفائي cleanliness

safeer sara arwand charwakay *n.* سفير‌سره‌اوندچاروا‌کی attache

safeer; seeyasee zaray *n.* سفير، سياسي‌ری ambassador

safra *n* صفرا bile

sagak *n* سک buckle

sagay *n* سی lung

sahar sark *n* سهارو‌ک twilight

saharanay *n* سهارز breakfast

sahee *a.* صحیح authentic

sahil *n* ساحل coast

sahil n. ساحل shore

sahilee adj. ساحلي costal

sahilee oba n. ساحلي‌اوبه offing

sahoolat n سهولت facility

sahoolat warkawal; tahweelawal v.t. سهولت‌ورکول؛تحویلول render

sajeeda kawal v.t. سجده‌کول prostrate

sajeeda; farmanbardaree n. سجده؛فرمانبرداري prostration

sakana n سکنه chisel

sakhawat n سخاوت benevolence

sakhawat n. سخاوت generosity

sakhawat n. سخاوت profusion

sakhawat kawal v. t سخاوت‌کول benevolent

sakhee a سخي benevolent

sakhee a. سخي generous

sakht a. سخت hard

sakht a. سخت rigid

sakht a. سخت rigorous

sakht a. سخت strict

sakht a. سخت onerous

sakht aw shadeed a. سخت‌اوشدید impetuous

sakht baran n. سخت‌باران shower

sakht goozar khwaral v.t. سخت وزارخول shock

sakht kar n. سخت‌کار perspiration

sakht kar kawal v.i. سخت‌کار کول perspire

sakht shay n سخت‌شی solid

sakht zaray a. سخت‌زی callous

sakht zaray a. سخت‌زی relentless

sakht; kanjoos a. سخت؛کنجوس stringent

sakht; khatarnak a. سخت؛ خطرناک grave

sakht; nawara a سخت؛ناوه burdensome

sakht; treekh a. سخت؛تریخ austere

sakhta azmoyana n. سخته‌آزموینه tribulation

sakhta hamla n. سخته‌حمله onslaught

sakhta neewaka n. سخته‌نیوکه censure

sakhta neewaka kawal v. t. سخته نیوکه‌کول censure

sakhtawal v.t. سختول harden

sakhtee aw shiddat n. سختي‌او شدت impetuosity

sakhtgeer n. سختیر martinet

sakhtgeer a. سختیر stern

sakhtgeer insan n. سختیرانسان stern

sakhtgeeree n. سختیري stringency

sakin n. ساکن static

sakin a. ساکن stationary

sakoon n. سکون tranquility

sakoon; dareydana n. سکون؛درډنه standstill

sal n. سل hundred

sal kaleeza adj. سل‌کلیزه centennial

salaheeyat; taleem n. صلاحیت؛ تعلیم qualification

salakar n. سلاکار counsellor

salakaree kawal v. t. سلاکاري‌کول counsel

salakaree; salakar *n.* سلاكاري؛ سلاكار counsel

salam achawal *v.t* سلام اچول hail

salam achawal *v.t.* سلام اچول salute

salam dua *n.* سلام دعا salutation

salam kawal *v.t.* سلام کول greet

salam; dranaway *n* سلام؛درناوى salute

salam; rogh ramat *a.* سالم؛روغ رمت whole

salama *n* سلمه cent

salama kaleeza *n* سلمه کلیزه centenarian

salamat *a.* سلامت healthy

salana; feesadee *adv.* سلنه؛فیصدي per cent

salanday *n.* ساهلنى asthma

salata *n.* سلاته salad

salb *n.* صلب loin

saleeb *n.* صلیب rood

saleebee jihad *n* صلیبي جهاد crusade

salees; hawar *a.* سلیس؛هوار smooth

salfar laroonkay *a.* سلفرلرونکى sulphuric

salgay *n.* سل hiccup

salgay *n* سل sob

salim *a.* سالم intact

salor *n.* لور four

salor barkheez *a.* لوربرخیز quadruple

salor ghbarga kawal *v.t.* لورغبره کول quadruple

salor gooteeza banra warkawal; jor jaray kawal *v.t.* لورویزه بنرورکول؛جوجاى کول square

salor gotay *n.* لوروى quadrangle

salor gotay *n.* لوروى square

salor goteez *a.* لورویز quadrangular

salor goteez *a* لورویز square

salor myashtanay *a.* لورمیاشتنى quarterly

salorama *n.* لورمه quarter

saltanat *n* سلطنت empire

saltanat *a.* سلطنت realm

salweykht *n.* لوت forty

sam aw jadee *a* سم او جدي bonafide

sam kar na kawal *v.i.* سم کارنه کول misfire

saman *n.* سامان luggage

samandar *n.* سمندر sea

samandar landi pawzee beyray *n.* سمندرلاندپوى،ب submarine

samandaree *a.* سمندري marine

samandaree *a.* سمندري maritime

samandaree *a.* سمندري nautical

samandaree *a.* سمندري naval

samandaree *a.* سمندري oceanic

samandaree changakh *n.* سمندري چنا lobster

samandaree feel *n.* سمندري فیل walrus

samandaree hoora *n.* سمندري حوره mermaid

samandaree khapeyray *n.* سمندري پر nymph

samandaree khoog *n.* سمندري خو seal

samandaree nareena makhlooq *n.* سمندريناارينهمخلوق merman

samandaree sragh *n* سمندريراغ beacon

samandaree toopan *n.* سمندري توپان typhoon

samandaree zwak *n.* سمندريواک navy

samandaryoon *n.* سمندريون navigation

samandaryoonay toghonday *n.* سمندريونيتوغوندی torpedo

samawal *v.t.* سمول adapt

samawal *v.t.* سمول adjust

samawal *v.t.* سمول ameliorate

samawal; samsorawal *v.t.* سمول، سمسورول improve

samawana *n.* سمونه renovation

samawana; jorakht *n.* سمونه، جوت amelioration

samawona *n* سمونه correction

sambalawal *v.i.* سمبالول minister

samdalasa *adv.* سمدلاسه just

sameemana *a.* صميمانه whole-hearted

sameydal *v.t.* سمدل right

samlastal *v.t.* سملاستل lay

samlastal *v.i.* سملاستل rest

samoon; islah *n.* سمون، اصلا ح amendment

samoonpal *n.* سمونپال reformer

samoontya *n.* سمونتيا reform

samoontya ramanz ta kawal *v.t.* سمونتيارامنته کول reform

samsa *n.* سمه ladle

samsar *n* سمسار broker

samsara *n.* سمساره lizard

samsortya *n.* سمسورتيا improvement

san *n.* سان muslin

sanad *n.* سند muniment

sanad; daraja *n* سند، درجه degree

sanat *n.* صنعت industry

sanatee *a.* صنعتي industrial

sanatgar *n.* صنعتر artisan

sanatoree *a.* سناتوري senatorial

sanay gharoonkay; taw warkawoonkay *n.* سنغونکی، ورکوونکی تاو spinner

sand *n.* سند jute

sanda *n* سه brim

sanda *n.* سه verge

sandan *n.* سندان anvil

sandara *n* سندره chant

sandara *n.* سندره song

sandara wayal *v.i.* سندرهويل sing

sandarbol *n.* سندربول songster

sandarbol; sandar gharay *n.* سندربول، سندرغای vocalist

sandargharay *n.* سندرغای singer

sandooq *n* صندوق box

saneeya *n* ثانيه second

sanf; tolay *n.* صنف، ولی guild

sang par sang *adv* پرسنګ abreast

sanga *n* ائه bough

sanga *n* ائه branch

sanga *adv.* نه wherein

sangal *n* نل elbow

sangal *n* نل ancon

sangar; morchal *n.* سنر، مورچل fortress

sangaroona jorawal *v.t.* سنرونه جوول fortify

sangeen; jiddee *a.* سنین؛جدي solemn

sangfarshee *n.* سنفرشي pavement

sangi sara mrasta *n.* سانسرهمرسته adjunct

sanjawana; churt *n* سنجوونه؛چرت deliberation

sanjawona *n* سنجوونه comparison

sanwee; da dwayami darajey *a.* ثانوي؛ددويمدرج secondary

saood *n* صعود mount

saood kawal; miqdar laral; zyateydal *v.i* صعودکول؛مقدار لرل؛زیاتدل amount

sapa *n.* په ripple

sapa *n.* په surf

sapa *n.* په wave

sapa payda kawal *v.t.* پهپداکول ripple

sapand keydal; takan khwaral *v.t.* پاندکدل؛ټکانخول wave

sapandwalay *n.* پاندوالی undulation

sapara *n* پره booth

sapara *n* پره bower

sapayeez kawal *v.i.* پهییزکول undulate

sapayeez; da mawjoono pa arwand *a.* پهییز؛دموجونوپهاوند sinuous

sapeedar *n.* سپدار poplar

sapey jorawal; sapand keydal *v.i.* پجوول؛پاندکدل surge

sapey wahal *v.i* پوهل billow

sapeyra *n.* په slap

sapeyra porta kawal *v.t.* پهپورته کول slap

sapray *n.* پر canopy

sar *n.* سر cape

sar *n.* سر head

sar badala *a.* سربداله giddy

sar beyra *adv.* سربره on

sar beyra par dey *prep.* سربرهپرد over

sar chapa *a.* سرچپه topsy turvy

sar chapa kawal *v. i.* سرچپهکول capsize

sar chapa kawal *v. t* سرچپهکول convert

sar chapa kawana *n* سرچپهکونه conversion

sar chapa par hookoomat bandi *n.* سرچپهپرحکومتباند coup

sar cheena *n.* سرچینه rudiment

sar cheena *n.* سرچینه source

sar cheena *n.* چینه سر originator

sar cheena akheysta; top wahal *v.i.* سرچینهاخستل؛ټوپوهل spring

sar cheena keydal *v.t.* سرچینهکدل originate

sar danga *n.* سردنه protagonist

sar ghandaway; sar laray *n.* سرغندوی؛سرلاری van

sar gharand *a.* سرغاند unruly

sar gharawana *n* سرغونه deviation

sar gharaway *n.* سرغاوی obstinacy

sar gharaway *n.* سرغاوی transgression

sar gharaway *n.* سرغاوی rebel

sar gharaway kawal *v.i.* سرغاوی کول rebel

sar gharaway; teyray *n.* سرغاوی، تری violation

sar ghosawal *v. t.* سرغوول behead

sar jama *n.* سرجمع overall

sar kakh *a.* سرکخ mettlesome

sar kashee *n* سرکشي defiance

sar khoogay *n.* سرخوی migraine

sar khozawal *v.i.* سرخوول nod

sar khozawana *n.* سرخوونه node

sar khreyana *n.* سرخرینه tonsure

sar koozay *n.* سرکوزی swine

sar lakhkar *n* سرلکر commander

sar lakhkar *n* سرلکر marshal

sar lobsaray *n.* سرلوباری umpire

sar lobsaree kawal *v.t.,* سرلوباري کول umpire

sar parast *n.* سرپرست overseer

sar parast *n.* سرپرست warden

sar parastee *n.* سرپرستي wardship

sar patoonay *n.* سرپونی wimple

sar pokh *n.* سرپو lid

sar sharee; tawleedee wartya *n.* سرشاري،تولیديوتیا productivity

sar shmeyrana *n.* سرشمرنه census

sar shmeyrana *a.* سرشمرنه statistical

sar ta rasawana; ijra *n.* سرته رسونه،اجرا performance

sar tamba *a.* سرمبه sturdy

sar tamba *a.* سرتمبه obstinate

sar tar sara *prep.* سرترسره throughout

sar tar sara; la payla tar paya *adv.* سرترسره،لهپیلهترپایه through

sar teyray *n.* سرتری trooper

sar zay *n.* سرای observatory

sar zay *n.* سرای pasture

sara *n* ساه cold

sara *n* سره fertilizer

sara areeki khatmawal *v. t.* سره ایکختمول boycott

sara gadawal *v. t* سرهول combine

sara gandal *v.t.* سرهنل rivet

sara na joreydal *v.t.* سرهنهجودل mismatch

sara nakhlawal *v.t.* سرهنلول table

sara peywandawal *v.t.* سرهپوندول weld

sara pukhla kawal *v.t.* سرهپخلا کول reconcile

sara sanjawal *v. t* سرهسنجول compare

sara tawawal *v.i.* سرهتاوول rove

sara; warsara *prep.* سره،ورسره with

sarab *n.* سراب mirage

sarak *n.* سک road

saral *v. t.* ارل chase1

saral *v.t.* ارل oversee

saral *v.t.* ارل invigilate

saral; pa naz nakhro tlal *v.i.* ارل، پهنازنخروتلل stalk

saran *n.* ارن invigilator

sarana *n.* ارنه invigilation

sarana kawoonkay *a.* ارنهکوونکی monitory

sarana; taqeeb *n.* تعقیب،ارنه chase2

saranay; wahshee *a.* ساراني؛وحشي wild

sarandoy sarteyray *n.* سارندوی ترى sentinel

saranga chi *conj.* رنه چ as

sarani lapara weekh pati keydana *n.* سارنلپاره ویباتکدنه vigil

sarawal *v.i.* رول graze

sarawal *v.t.* رول pasture

sarawal *v. i.* سول cool

sarawana *n* روونه graze

saray *n* سارى example

saray *n* سى male

sarayee orbasha *n.* سارايى اوربشه oat

sardar *n.* سردار chieftain

sareeza *n* سريزه foreword

sareeza *n.* سريزه prologue

sareeza *n.* سريزه preface

sareeza leekal *v.t.* سريزه ليكل preface

sareeza; ibtidayee *a.* سريز ه؛ابتدايي introductory

sareykh سر glue

sareykh *n.* سريـ adhesive

sarf kawal *v.t. & i.* صرف کول conjugate

sargand *a.* رند apparent

sargand *a.* رند manifest

sargand topeer *n* رندتوپير contrast

sargand topeer larl *v. t* رندتوپير لرل contrast

sarganda *a.* رنده evident

sargandawal *v.t.* رندول unsheathe

sargandawal; dalalat kawal *v.t.* رندول؛دلالت کول indicate

sargandeydal *v.i.* رندل appear

sargar *n.* ارو spy

sargaray *n* ارى scout

sargardan garzeydal *v.i.* سردان ردل wander

sargardan kawal *v.t.* سردان کول ramble

sargardan; koosa dabay *a* سردان؛کوهبى stray

sargardanee *n.* سردانى quandary

sargardanee *n* سردانى ramble

sargardanee *n* سردانى stray

sargaree kawal *v.i* ارويکول scout

sargaree kawal *v.i.* ارويکول spy

sargharawana kawal *v. t* سرغونه کول disobey

sarhadee sawkay *n.* سرحديوکه outpost

sarka *n.* سرکه vinegar

sarka keydal *v.* سرکهکدل acetify

sarkas *n.* سرکس circus

sarkh *n.* رخ axle

sarkh *n.* رخ pulley

sarkh; da akasay da feelam sarkh *n.* رخ؛دعکاسدفیلمرخ reel

sarkh; paya *a.* رخ؛پایه wheel

sarkhanay *n.* رخنى whirligig

sarkhandoy *n.* رخندوى revolver

sarkhawal *v.t.* رخول wheel

sarkhawal; tawawal *v.i.* رخول؛تاوول spin

sarkhay *n.* رخى clew

sarkheydal *v.i.* رخدل lurch
sarkheydal *v.i.* رخدل reel
sarkheydoonkay masheen *n.*
رخدونکیماشین turbine
sarkondai *n.* سرکوز somersault
sarleek *n.* سرلیک heading
sarmakhkay *n.* رمخ reptile
sarman *n.* رمن leather
sarman *n.* رمن skin
sarmaya *n.* سرمایه fund
sarnawakht *n.* سرنوت
predestination
sarokha *n.* سوخه chill
sarood; choonrar *n* سرود؛چوهار
warble
sarood; naghma *n* سرود؛نغمه carol
sarowoonkay *n* سوونکی cooler
sarparast *n.* سرپرست
superintendent
sarparastee kawal *v.t.* سرپرستي
کول superintend
sarpee *a.* سرپی leaden
sarsaree jangeydal *v.t.* سرسري
جندل skirmish
sarsaree; kam zhawar *a.* سرسري؛
کمژور shallow
sarshar *a.* سرشار profuse
sartambagee *n.* سرتمبهی obduracy
sartanee ghota *n.* سرطانيغوه
tumour
sarwa *n.* سرو cedar
sarway; salor pkhey laroonkay
n. ساروی؛بلورپلرونکی quadruped
sas *n.* ساس sauce
sasawal; wro wro wahal *v.t.* ول؛
ورورورووهل tap

saseydal *v. i* لد drip
saseydal *v.i.* لد leak
saseydal; la lasa ghorzeydal *v. i*
لد؛لهلاسهغورلد drop
saseydana *n* لدنه drip
saskay *n* لکی drop
sast *a.* سست loose
sastawal *v.t.* سستول loose
sastee *a.* سستي slack
sastee *n.* سستي slowness
sata *n.* سطح level
satak *n.* ک hammer
satal *v.t.* ساتل keep
satal ta warta lokhay *n.* سطلته
ورتهلوی peck
satal; palal *v.t.* ساتل؛پالل patronize
satana *n.* ساتنه maintenance
satana *n* نه lick
satana *n.* ساتنه retention
satana ki akheystal *v* ساتنهکاخستل
custody
satandoy *n.* ساتندوی bodyguard
satandoy *n.* ساتندوی patron
satandoy *n.* ساتندوی safeguard
satandoy *n.* ساتندوی warder
satanzay *n* ساتنای cache
sathee maloomat *n.* سطحيمالومات
smack
satoonkay *n* ساتونکی custodian
satoonkay *n.* ساتونکی keeper
satoonkay *a.* ساتونکی retentive
sawal; pokhtana *n.* سوال؛پوتنه
question
sawda *n.* سودا obsession
sawda *n.* سودا mart
sawdagar *n.* سودار trader

sawdagar *n.* سوداگر tradesman

sawdagar *n.* سوداگر merchant

sawdagaree kawal *v.t* سوداري کول market

sawdagaree saman *n.* سوداري سامان merchandise

sawdagareeza moassisa *n.* سوداريزهمؤسسه firm

sawdagareeza rakra warkra *n.* سوداريزهراکهورکه dealing

sawka kawal *v.t.* سوکهکول retard

sawka kawal; sastawal *v.t.* سوکه کول؛سستول slacken

sawka; pasawana *n.* سوکه؛پوونه retardation

sawkeedar *n.* وکیدار sentry

sayhat man; qawee *a.* صحتمن؛ قوي robust

sayins poh *n.* ساينسپوه scientist

sayinsee *a.* ساينسي scientific

sayl; jaryan *n* سل؛جريان current

saylab *n.* سلاب torrent

saylabee *a.* سلابي torrential

sayqalee kawal *v.t.* صقلي کول polish

saza *n.* سزا punishment

saza warkawal *v.t.* سزاورکول inflict

saza warkawal *v.t.* سزاورکول punish

sazayee *a.* سزايي punitive

seekhak; teyra rawataltya *n.* سيخک؛ترهراوتلتيا spur

seelanee *n.* سيلاني tourist

seelay *n.* سيل gust

seem *n.* سيم wire

seem aw mazee ghazawal *v.t.* سيم اومزيغول wire

seem ghazawana *n.* سيمغوونه wiring

seem ya mazay warachawal; kash kawal *v.t.* سيميامزى وراچول؛کش کول string

seema *n.* سيمه locale

seema *n.* سيمه territory

seemab *n.* سيماب quicksilver

seemab *n.* سيماب mercury

seemabee *a.* سيمابي mercurial

seemayeez *a.* سيمهييز local

seemayeez *a.* سيمهييز regional

seemayeez *a.* سيمهييز territorial

seemayeez kawal *v.t.* سيمهييز کول localize

seemayeez padree *n.* سيمهييزپادري parson

seemayeez; mahalee *a.* سيمهييز؛ محلي vernacular

seemayeeza lahja aw wayang *n.* سيمهييزهلهجهاوويﻨ vernacular

seemee paray *n.* سيميپى cable

seena *n* سينه bosom

seena band *n* سينهبند bodice

seenama *n.* سينما cinema

seend *n.* سيند river

seend kakhana *n.* سيندکنه lexicography

seengar *n.* سينار cosmetic

seengar *n* سينار decoration

seengar pori arwand *a.* سينارپور اوﻨﺪ ornamental

seengar; samawana *n* سينار؛ سموونه trim

seengarawal v.t. سينارول adorn
seengarawal v.t. سينارول attire
seengarawal v. t سينارول decorate
seengarawal v.t. سينارول ornament
seengarawal v.t. سينارول prune
seengarowoonkay a. سينروونكى cosmetic
seengarpal a سينارپال fashionable
seerat n. سيرت character
seeri kawal v.t. يركول rupture
seeri weeri kawal v.t يرويركول tatter
seeri weeri shay n. يرويرشى tatter
seeriwalay n. يروالى rupture
seeyahee n. سياهي ink
seeyara n. سياره planet
seeyarawee a. سياروي planetary
seeyasat pohana n. سياست‌پوهنه politics
seeyasatdaree n. سياست‌داري polity
seeyasatwal n. سياست‌وال politician
seeyasatwal n. سياستوال statesman
seeyasee a. سياسي political
seher; khkula n. سحر،ښكلا charm1
selai n. سيل gale
seyl n. سل spate
seyra n. ره aspect
seyra peyzhandana n. ره‌پژندنه physiognomy
seyra; qeeyafa n. ره،قيافه countenance
seyra; shakal n ره،شكل feature
seyra; zahiree banra n. ره،ظاهري به visage

seyral aw sparal v.i. لاوسپل rummage
seyrana aw sparana n نهاوسپنه rummage
seyray wuna n. ونه oak
sfanj n. سفنج sponge
sha; mla n. شا،ملا back
shaar n. شعار motto
shaar n. شعار watchword
shaayar n شعائر doctrine
shabahat laral a. شباهت‌لرل akin
shabaka n. شبكه lattice
shabasay warkawal v.t شاباسى وركول felicitate
shabasay; neykmarghee n شاباسى،نكمرغي felicity
shabash; da khoshalay yaw awaz interj. شاباش،دخوشاليو آواز hurrah
shadab a. شاداب lush
shadab a. شاداب youthful
shadal saray n شلسى boor
shadeed a. شديد intense
shadeed a. شديد intensive
shadeed a. شديد severe
shadeed a. شديد tense
shadeed a. شديد harsh
shadeed gham aw weer n. شديد غماووير woe
shadeed; tond a. شديد،توند vehement
shado n شادو ape
shafa warbakhal v.t شفاوربخل remedy
shafaf a. شفاف lucent

shafahee azmoyana *n* شفاهي آزموينه viva-voce

shafqat *n.* شفقت pathos

shaftaloo *n.* شفتالو peach

shaga *n.* شه pebble

shaga *n.* شه sand

shagardee *n.* شاردي apprentice

shaghal *n.* شغال jackal

shaglana *a.* شلنه sandy

shahadat *n.* شهادت martyrdom

shahadat nama *n.* شهادت‌نامه certificate

shahadat nama *n.* شهادت‌نامه testimonial

shahana *a.* شاهانه majestic

shahay *n.* شه paramour

shahee *a.* شاهي royal

shahee taj *n.* شاهي‌تاج tiara

shaheed *n.* شهيد martyr

shaheen *n* شاهين hawk

shahid keydal; shahidee warkawal *v.i.* شاهدكدل، شاهدي‌وركول witness

shahidee leekoonkay *n.* شاهدي ليكونكى deponent

shahkar *n.* شاهكار masterpiece

shahkar kartab *n* شهكاركرتب stunt

shahwanee *a.* شهواني lascivious

shahwanee *a.* شهواني lustful

shahwanee *a.* شهواني sensual

shahwanee *a.* شهواني sensuous

shahwanee *a.* شهواني sexual

shahwanee *a.* شهواني voluptuous

shahwaneeyat *n.* شهوانيت sexuality

shahwat *n* شهوت cupidity

shahwat *n.* شهوت lust

shahwat parast *a.* شهوت‌پرست lewd

shahwat parast *n.* شهوت‌پرست sensualist

shahwat parastee *n.* شهوت‌پرستي sensuality

shahwat paray *n.* شهوت‌پارى sexy

shahwat parowoonkay *a.* شهوت پاروونكى lusty

shahwatee *a.* شهوتي licentious

shahwatran *n.* شهوتران voluptuary

shahzada *n.* شاهزاده prince

shahzadgay *n.* شاهزاد princess

shair *n.* شاعر bard

shair *n.* شاعر poet

shair gotay *n.* شاعروى poetaster

shaira khaza *n.* ه شاعره poetess

shairana *a.* شاعرانه poetic

shairana khkula *n.* شاعرانهكلا poetics

shairay ki hagha kaleema chi qafeeya yi da bali haghi qafeeyi sara jora wee *n.* شاعر كى هغه كليمه‌چقافيه‌يدبلهغله‌قافيسره جوه‌وي crambo

shairee *n.* شاعري poetry

shairee; deewan *n.* شاعري؛ديوان poesy

shak *n* شك doubt

shak *n.* شك suspicion

shak laral *v. i* شكـلرل doubt

shakal *n.* شكل shape

shakal bandee *n.* شكل‌بندي outline

shakal warkawal *v.t* شکل‌ورکول shape

shakh; neygh *n.* شخ؛نغ stiff

shakhsee *a.* شخصي personal

shakhseeyat na warkawal *v.t.* شخصیت‌نه‌ورکول impersonate

shakhwalay *n.* شخوالی rigour

shakman *a.* شکمن sceptical

shakman *n* شکمن suspect

shakman *a.* شکمن suspicious

shakman *a.* شکمن uncertain

shakmanee *n.* شکمني scepticism

shal *n.* شال shawl

shal *a.* شل lax

shal *n* شل twenty

shal shoot *n* شل‌شو cripple

shalag *a* شل coarse

shalag shalag *a.* شل شل threadbare

shalam *a.* شلم twentieth

shalam *a.* شلم twenty

shalama barkha *n* برخه شلمه twentieth

shama *n.* شمع candle

shamil *a.* شامل inclusive

shamilawal *v.t.* شاملول include

shamilawal *v.t.* شاملول merge

shamilawoonkay *n.* شاملوونکی merger

shamileydal *v. i* شاملدل consist

shamooltya *n.* شمولتیا inclusion

shamshatay *n.* شمشتۍ turtle

shan; shawkat *n.* شان؛شوکت pomposity

shanakht *n.* شناخت identity

shanakht kawal *v.t.* شناخت‌کول identify

shanal aw sparal *v.i.* شنل‌او‌سپرل research

shanana aw sparana *n* شننه‌او‌سپنه research

shanawoonkay; tajzeeyatee *a* شننوونکی؛تجزیاتي analytical

shand; bey hasila *a.* شند؛بې‌حاصله sterile

shandar *a.* شاندار pompous

shandar *a* شاندار fine

shandar *a.* شاندار tremendous

shandar; waswasee *a* شاندار؛وسواسي fantastic

shandtob *n.* شنتوب sterility

shanshob *n.* شنشوب sediment

shaoor *n* شعور conscience

shaoor *n.* شعور wit

shaqol *n.* شاقول perpendicular

shar *n* شا barren

sharab *n* شراب alcohol

sharabkhana *n.* شرابخانه tavern

sharal shaway *n.* شل‌شوی outcast

sharal shaway kas *n.* شل‌شوی‌کس outlaw

sharal; eystal *v.t.* شل؛استل hurl

sharam *n.* شرم shame

sharamnak *a.* شرمناک shameful

shararat *n.* شرارت prank

sharay *n* شری measles

sharay *n* ش blanket

sharay *n* ش wrap

sharbal; kuch jorawal *v. t. & i.* شاربل؛کوچ‌جوول churn

shareef *a.* شریف noble

shareef saray *n.* شریف‌سی noble

shareef saray *n.* شريف‌سى nobleman

shareek *a.* شريک mutual

shareek; mrastandoy *a.* شريک؛ مرستندوى associate

shareekeydal *v.i.* شريکدل partake

shareer *a.* شرير mischievous

shareer *a.* شرير naughty

shareer; khabees *a.* شرير؛خبيث vicious

sharha kawal *v.t.* شرحه‌کول illustrate

sharha kawal; azada leekal *v.t.* شرحه‌کول؛آزادليکل paraphrase

sharha; tawzee *n.* شرحه؛توضيح illustration

sharmandookay *a.* شرمندوکى bashful

sharmawal *v.t.* شرمول abash

sharmawal *v. t* شرمول embarrass

sharmawal *v.t.* شرمول shame

sharmawal; ruswa kawal *v.t.* شرمول؛رسواکول reproach

sharmeendookay *a.* شرميندوکى timorous

sharmeydal *v.i.* شرمدل shy

sharmeydalay *a.* شرمدلى ashamed

sharminda *adv* شرمنده ablush

sharmindookay *n.* شرمندوکى shy

sharoonkay *n* شونکى repellent

shart *n* شرط bet

shart *n.* شرط proviso

shart taral *v.i.* شرطتل bet

shart taral *v.i.* شرطتل wager

shart tarana *n.* شرطتنه wager

shart; artya *n.* شرط؛اتيا requirement

sharteeya *a* شرطيه conditional

shat; sheera *n* شات؛شيره molasses

shata pati keydal *v.i.* شاته‌پاتۍ‌کدل lag

shata pati shakhs *n.* شاته‌پاتۍ‌شخص laggard

shatag *n.* شا ‌ ت retread

shateer *n.* شاه‌تير girder

shatranj *n.* شطرنج chess

shaw khwa *prep* شاوخوا about

shawq *n* شوق craze

shawq *n.* شوق zeal

shawqeen *a* شوقين fond

shawqeen *n.* شوقين zealot

shawqeen; leywal *a.* شوقين؛لوال ardent

shay *n.* شى item

shay *n.* شى object

shay; seez *n.* شى؛يز thing

shayan teet aw park eekhowal *v.* شيان‌تيت‌اوپرک‌ايوول *t* clutter

shayr *n.* شعر poem

shayree band *n.* شعري‌بند stanza

shaytan *n.* شطان satan

shazalmay *n.* شالمى bridegroom

shazalmay *n.* شالمى groom

sheen rang *n* شين‌رنگ green

sheen yaqoot *n.* شين‌ياقوت sapphire

sheendal *v.t.* شيندل sift

sheendal; da hasharato zaharjan darmal pashal *v.t.* شيندل؛دحشراتوزهرجن‌درمل‌پاشل spray sheenkay *n.* شينکی greenery

sheera tri eystal *v.t.* شيرهتراستل sap

sheerdan; sooray; nalka *n.* شيردان،سوری،نلکه tap

sheereen *a.* شيرين luscious

sheereenee raneewal *v. t.* شيريني رانيول candy

shehed *n.* شهد honey

sheyba *n.* شبه moment

sheyba *n.* شيبه minute

sheydatob *n.* شداتوب frenzy

sheydey *n.* شد milk

sheydey warkawal *v.t.* شدورکول foster

sheydey warkawal *v.i.* شدورکول lactate

sheydey warkawal *v.t.* شدورکول milk

sheydey warkawal *v.t.* شدورکول suckle

sheydey warkowoonkay *a.* شد ورکوونکی milch

sheyr khat *n* شرخط toss

sheyr khat *v.t.* شرخطکول toss

sheytan *n* شطان devil

shidat *n.* شدت severity

shiddat zyatawal *v.t.* شدتزياتول intensify

shiddat; da fayl zamana *n.* شدت، دفعلزمانه tense

shiddat; pyawartya *n.* شدت، پياوتيا vehemence

shikayat *n.* شکايت protest

shikayat kawal *v.i.* شکايتکول protest

shikayat; sarganda nakhwakhee *n.* شکايت،برندهناخوي protestation

shirakat *n.* شراکت partnership

shirkat *n.* شرکت company

shirkat *n.* شرکت participation

shirkat kawoonkay *n.* شرکت کوونکی participant

shirkat laral *v.i.* شرکتلرل participate

shkanja *n.* شکنجه persecution

shkanja kawal *v.t.* شکنجهکول persecute

shkanja kawal *v.t.* شکنجهکولrack

shkanja kawal *v.t.* شکنجهکول torture

shkanja; rabrawana *n.* شکنجه، ربورنه torture

shkeydal *v.t.* شکدل lacerate

shkhara *n* شخه dispute

shkhara *n.* شخه encounter

shkhara *n* شخه fight

shkhara *n.* شخه quarrel

shkhara *n.* شخه wrangle

shkhara kawal *v. t* شخهکول bicker

shkhara kawal *v. i* شخهکول dispute

shkhara kawal *v. t* شخهکول encounter

shkhara kawal *v.t* شخهکول fight

shkhara kawal *v.i.* شخهکول wrangle

shkhara; lanja *n.* شخه،لانجه tussle

shkhara; mobahisa *n.* شخه،مباحثه altercation

shkhwand wahal *v.i.* شخوندوهل
ruminate

shkhwand wahana *n.* شخوندوهنه
rumination

shkhwand wahoonkay *n.* شخوند
وهونکی rodent

shkhwand wahoonkay *a.* شخوند
وهونکی ruminant

shkhwand wahoonkay sarway *n.*
شخوندوهونکی‌اروی ruminant

shlakha *a.* شلاخه lash

shlawal; shkawal *v.t.* شلول،شکول
tear

shmeyr *n.* شمر calculation

shmeyr *n.* شمر number

shmeyr pohana *n.* شمرپوهنه
arithmetic

shmeyr pohaneez *a.* شمرپوهنیز
arithmetical

shmeyra *n.* شمره count

shmeyra kawal *v. t.* شمره‌کول
count

shmeyra; karkha *n.* شمره،کرخه
score

shmeyral *v. t.* شمرل calculate

shmeyral *v.t.* شمرل number

shmeyral *v.t.* شمرل score

shmeyral; andaza lagawal *v.t.*
شمرل،اندازه‌لول reckon

shmeyroonkay *n.* شمرونکی
numerator

shmeyroonkay *n.* شمرونکی scorer

shmeyroonkay masheen *n*
شمرونکی‌ماشین calculator

shobal *n* شوبل hurt

shobda baz *n.* شعبده‌باز juggler

shobda bazee kawal *v.t.* شعبده
بازي‌کول juggle

shoghal; danda *n* شغل،دنده
employment

shoghla *n* شوغله blaze

shohrat *n.* شهرت renown

shoja *a.* شجاع gallant

shomal *n.* شمال north

shomalee *a* شمالی north

shomalee *a.* شمالی northern

shooka *n.* شوکه robbery

shookawana; takhtawana *n.*
شوکونه،تتوونه snatch

shookmar *n.* شوکمار robber

shool pool *a* شول‌پول flabby

shoonay *a.* شونی obtainable

shoonay *a.* شونی probable

shoonda *n.* شونه lip

shoondak; poz *n.* شونک،پوز snout

shoontya *n.* شونتیا likelihood

shoora *n.* شورا council

shoorayee *a.* شورایی parliamentary

shor mashor *n.* شورماشور fuss

shor mashor jorawal *v.i* شورماشور
جوول fuss

shormashor *n.* شورماشور ado

shoro kawal *v.t* شروع‌کول initial

shpa *n.* شپه night

shpa teyrawal; zay warkawal
v.i. شپه‌ترول،ځای‌ورکول roost

shpag; shpagam *n., a* شپ،شپم six

shpagam *a.* شپم sixth

shparas; shparasam *n., a.* شپاس،
شپاسم sixteen

shparasam *a.* شپاسم sixteenth

shpeylak *n* شپلک whistle

shpeylak wahal *v.i.* شپلک‌وهل whistle

shpeylay *n* شپل bugle

shpeylay *n* شپل flute

shpeylay wahal *v.i* شپلوهل flute

shpeyta *n., a.* شپته sixty

shpeytam *a.* شپتم sixtieth

shpoon *n.* شپون herdsman

shpoon *n.* شپون shepherd

shranga *n.* شرنا clink

shrangeydal *v.i.* شرندل jingle

shranghar *n.* شرنهار jingle

shtaman *a.* شتمن opulent

shtaman kawal *v. t* شتمن‌کول enrich

shtamanee *n.* شتمني mammon

shtamanee *n.* شتمني riches

shtamanee *a.* شتمني richness

shtoon; wajood *n* شتون،وجود being

shuhrat *n.* شهرت popularity

shuja *a.* شجاع stout

shukawal; tolawal *v.t.* شکول،ټولول pluck

shumalee ya sweylee qutab *n.* شمالي‌یاسولي‌قطب polar

shuro *n.* شروع outset

shutar murgh *n.* شترمرغ ostrich

sifat *n.* صفت adjective

sigrat *n.* سر cigar

sika *n* سکه coin

sika jorawal *n* سکه‌جوړ coinage

sika jorawal *v.t.* سکه‌جوړ mint

silool; koochnay zandan; hajra *n.* سلول؛کوچنی‌زندان؛حجره cell

siloolee *adj* سلولي cellular

silsila; so barkheeza feelam ya keesa *n.* سلسله؛وبرخیزه‌فیلم‌یا‌کیسه serial

simant *n.* سمنت cement

sinama *n.* سینما movies

siraf *conj.* صرف only

sirinj *n.* سرنج syringe

sirinj wahal *v.t.* سرنج‌وهل syringe

skala; payshnihad *n.* سکاله،پیشنهاد proposition

skarwata *n.* سکروه spark

skatlandee wagaray *n.* اسکالندي‌وی Scot

skhak *n* اک drink

skhak *n* اک beverage

skhak jorawal *v. t.* brew

skhak jorawana *n* اک‌جوړونه brewery

skhal *v. t* اڅل drink

skoondal *v.t* سکونل goad

skoondal; chokhawal *v.t.* سکونل؛ چوخول prick

smas *n.* سمه cave

so arkheez *a.* واخیز multilateral

so arkheez *a.* واخیز versatile

so chanda *a.* وچنده manifold

so chi *prep.* وچ until

so goonay *a.* ووني multiple

so shaklay *n.* وشکلی multiform

so zaya mat aw munkasir khat *n.* وایه‌مات‌اومنکسرخط zigzag

so; so goonay *a* و؛ووڼ several

soba; kamyabee *n.* سوبه؛کامیابي victory

sodagareez mal *n.* سوداریزمال commodity

sofiana au zahidana jwand *n* صوفيانه‌اوزاهدانه‌ژوند benefice
sohan *n* سوهان file
sohanawal *v.t* سوهانول file
sok; kom yaw *pron.* وک؛کوميو some
sok; kom yaw *pron.* وک؛کومیو who
sok; yaw kas *pron.* وک؛يوکس one
solayeez *a.* سوله‌ييز peaceful
somia *n* صومعه convent
somrawalay *n.* ومره‌والی quantity
somrayeez *a.* ومره‌ييز quantitative
sond *n.* سوند ginger
sonreydal *v.i* سودل hiss
sonreydana *n* سودنه hiss
soocha *a* سوچه pure
soocha *n* سوچه virgin
soocha gata las ta rawral *v.t.* سوچه‌لاس‌ته‌راول net
soochawalay *n.* سوچه‌والی purity
soochawalay ghokhtoonkay *n.* سوچه‌والی‌غوتونکی purist
sood khor *n.* سودخور usurer
sood khwarana *n.* سودخونه usury
soofee *n* صوفي mystic
soofyana *a.* صوفیانه mystic
sooka *n.* سوکه tip
sooka; da zaweeyi ras *n.* وکه؛د زاويرأس apex
sooka; makhooka *n.* وکه؛موکه peak
sooka; oj *n.* وکه؛اوج top
soolawal *v.t.* سولول rub
soolawana *n* سولوونه rub

sooleydana *n* سولدنه erosion
soon *n* سون burn
soor *a.* سور red
soor banjan *n.* سوربانجان tomato
soor garanday *n* سورندی cockroach
soor kawal *v.t.* سورکول redden
soor rag *n.* سورور artery
soor rang *n.* سوررن red
soor ranga hashrat *n.* سوررنه حشرات vermillion
sooray *n.* سوری aperture
sooray *n* سوری hole
sooray *n.* سوری hollow
sooray kawal *v.* *t* سوری‌کول bore
sooray kawal *v.t* سوری‌کول hole
sooray kawal *v.t.* سوری‌کول perforate
sooray kawal *v.t.* سوری‌کول slit
sooray keydal; shleydal *v.t.* سوری کدل؛شلدل puncture
sooray; shleydalay *n.* سوری؛شلدلی puncture
soorbakhan *a.* سوربخن reddish
soorbakhan khurmayee rang *a* سوربخن‌خرمایي‌رن maroon
soorbakhan qahwayee rang *n.* سوربخن‌قهوه‌یي‌رن mahogany
sooreydana *n* سوردنه crimson
sor *a* سو cold
sor *a* سو cool
sorb saray *n* ورب‌سی fat
sotak khwaroonkay *a.* سوک خوونکی malleable
sotay *n* سوی cudgel
soya *n.* سویه hare

soya *n.* سويه rabbit

sozanda; khoonee *a* سوزنده،خوني fiery

sozawal *v.t.* سوزول singe

sozawal aw eerey kawal *v. t* سوول‌اواير‌كول cremate

sozawoonkay *a.* سوزوونكى caustic

sozeydal aw loogay kawal *v.i.* سوزدل‌اولوى‌كول smoulder

sozeydana *n* سوزدنه singe

spaga *n.* سپه louse

spak aw bey tarbeeyey saray *n* سپك‌اوبتربيسى cad

spak ganral *v.t.* سپك‌ل scorn

spak khob *n.* سپك‌خوب slumber

spak khob kawal *v. i* سپك‌خوب كول doze

spak khob kawal *v.i.* سپك‌خوب كول slumber

spak nazar kawal *v.t.* سپك‌نظر كول slight

spak shakhs *n* سپك‌شخص churl

spak tia *n* سپك‌تيا disrepute

spak; nakas *a.* سپك،ناكس base

spaka lasee nayza *n.* سپكه‌لاسي‌نزه javelin

spakawal *n* سپكول affront

spakawal *v. t.* سپكول debase

spakaway *v.t.* سپكاوى affront

spakaway *n.* سپكاوى insult

spaki saplay *n.* سپكپل sandal

spakwalay *n* سپكوالى abasement

spakwalay *n.* سپكوالى levity

spara askar *n.* سپاره‌عسكر cavalry

sparakhtana warta kawal *v.t.* سپارتنه‌ورته‌كول recommend

sparakhtana; tawseeya *n.* سپارتنه، توصيه recommendation

sparal *v.t.* سپارل assign

sparal *v.t.* سپارل vest

sparana *n* سپارنه surrender

sparana; tohmat *n.* سپارنه،تهمت charge

spareydal *v.t.* سپردل ride

sparghay badawal *v.i.* سپرغبادول scintillate

sparlay *n* سپرل ride

spay *n* سپ bitch

spay *n* سپى dog

spayee *n.* سپايي soldier

spayee joreydal *v.i.* سپايجودل soldier

speen *a.* سپين white

speen geeray *n* سپين‌يرى elder

speen goya *a.* سپين‌ويه frank

speen goyee *n.* سپين‌ويي candour

speen rang *n* سپين‌رن white

speen rang warkawal *v.t.* سپين‌رن وركول whiten

speen sandal *n.* سپين‌صندل sandalwood

speen wazma *a.* سپين‌وزمه whitish

speen zar *n.* سپين‌زر silver

speena wayna kawoonkay *a.* سپينه‌وناكوونكى outspoken

speenawal *v.t.* سپينول justify

speenawal; weenzal *v. t* سپينول،وينل bleach

speenawana *n.* سپينونه justification

speyda dagh *n* سپيده‌دا غ aurora

spogmakay *n.* سپومك sputnik

spogmakay; pleewanay n. سپومک؛ پليونی satellite

spogmay n. سپوم moon

spogmeez a. سپوميز lunar

sra kari ghwakha n سره کغوه fry

sra sharab n. سره شراب wine

sra zar n. سره زر gold

sragh n. راغ lamp

sragh n. راغ torch

srak kawal v.i. رک کول spark

srakeydal v.i. رکدل sparkle

srakeydana n. رکدنه sparkle

srangeez a. رنيز qualitative

srangwalay; mayar n. رنوالی؛معيار quality

sreeka n. يکه pang

sreykhawal v.t. سرول paste

sreykheydoonkay kaghaz n. سرډونکی کاغذ sticker

sreykhnak a. سريناک adhesive

sreykhnak n. سرناک sticky

sreykhnak a. سرناک slimy

sreykhnaka adj سرناکه cohesive

stan n. ستن needle

stana wahal v.t. ستنه وهل inject

stana; mlataray n. ستنه،ملاتی prop

stana; paya n. ستنه،پايه pillar

staneydal v.i. ستندل recur

staneydal v.i. ستندل return

staneydana n. ستندنه recurrence

staneydoonkay a. ستندونکی recurrent

star a. ستر grand

star kar n سترکار exploit

star ploranzay n. سترپلورنی store

staray kawal v.t ستی کول fatigue

staray keydal; staray kawal v.t. ستی کدل،ستی کول tire

staray; beyzara a. ستی؛بزاره weary

starga n ستره eye

starga patawal v.i. سترهپول nap

starga patawana n. سترهپوونه nap

stargak n سترک wink

stargak wahal v. t. & i سترک وهل blink

stargak wahal v.i. سترک وهل wink

stargey pri patawal v.t. سترپرپول ignore

stargi breykheydal v. t. سترپردل dazzle

stargi patawana n سترپوونه elusion

stargi pri patawal v. t سترپرپول evade

stargi taral v. t سترتل blindfold

stari byatee n. pl. سترپياتي shears

stariwalay n ستوالی fatigue

stayal v. t ستايل commend

stayalay a. ستايلی commendable

stayana n ستاينه commendation

stomana a. ستومانه lethargic

stomana n. ستوماني tedium

stomana kawal v. t. ستومانه کول exhaust

stomana kawal; beyzara keydal v.t. & i ستومانه کول؛بزاره کدل weary

stomana kawoonkay a. ستومانه کوونکی irksome

stomana kawoonkay *a.* ستومانه کوونکی mawkish

stomana kawoonkay *a.* ستومانه کوونکی tedious

stomana kawoonkay *a.* ستومانه کوونکی tiresome

stomana kawoonkay safar kawal *n.* ستومانه کوونکی سفر کول trek

stomana keydal *v.i.* ستومانه کدل moil

stomana safar *v.i.* ستومانه سفر trek

stomanee *n.* ستوماني laziness

stomanee *n.* ستوماني lethargy

stoonay *n.* مر ستونی، throat

stoonay wartakhta kawal *v.t.* ستونی ورتخته کول throttle

stoonay; ghara *n.* ستونی، غاه throttle

stoonez *a.* ستونیز guttural

stoonza *n* ستونزه difficulty

stoonza *n.* ستونزه problem

stoonzman *a.* ستونزمن inexplicable

stoonzman *a.* ستونزمن problematic

stoonzmanawal *v.i.* ستونزمنول snarl

stor peyzhand *n.* ستورپژاند astronomer

stor pohana *n.* ستورپوهنه astrology

stor pohand *n.* ستورپوهاند astrologer

stor ween poh *n.* ستوروین پوه astronomy

stor yoonay *n.* ستوریونی astronaut

storay *n.* ستوری star

storgay (da nakha *) *n.* ستوری(دا نه*) asterisk

storsaray larween *n.* ستورساری لروین telescope

storsaray larweenee *a.* ستورساری لروینی telescopic

suroor *n.* سرور glee

swa; korma *n.* سوه، کومه hoof

swarlas *n.* وارلس fourteen

swayl *n.* سویل south

swaylee *n.* سولی south

swaylee *a.* سولی southern

swazawal *v.* *t* سوزول burn

sweesee *a* سویسی swiss

sweesee wagaray ya zhaba *n.* سویسی وی یاژبه swiss

swich; tanray *n.* سوچ، switch

syal shay *a.* سیال شی liquid

syal; jora *n.* سیال، جوه peer

syal; maya *a* سیال، مایع fluid

syalee *n* سیالي competence

syalee kawal *v* سیالکول envy

syalee kawal *v.* *i* سیالي کول compete

syalee kawal *v.* *i* سیالي کول contend

syalee; da mandi musabiqa *n.* سیالي، دمنمسابقه race

syalee; raqabat *v.i.* سیالي، رقابت vie

syoray *n.* سیوری shade

syoray *n.* سیوری shadow

syoray laroonkay *a.* سیوری لرونکی shadowy

syoray laroonkay *a.* سیوری لرونکی sombre

syoray pri achawal *v.t* سیوری پر اچول shadow

T

ta pakhula kedonkay *a.* تهپخلا كيدونكى irreconcilable

taahud kawal *v.t.* تعهدكول pledge

taahud; zhmana *n.* تعهد،ژمنه pledge

taajjub *n* تعجب wonder

taayyun *n.* تعيين specification

taayyun kawal *v.t.* تعيينكول specify

taba *n* تبه fever

taba kawal *v.t.* تباهكول mortify

taba kawal *v.t.* تباهكول wreck

taba kun *a* تباهكن disastrous

taba; wagaray; mada; jisam *n.* تبعه،وى،ماده،جسم subject

tabah kar *a.* تباهكار maleficent

tabahee *n.* تباهى wreckage

tabar *n.* تبر axe

tabay *a* تابع dependent

tabay *a.* تابع obedient

tabay *a.* تابع subordinate

tabayeeyat; inhisar *n* تابعيت، انحصار dependence

tabdeel *n.* تبديل substitution

tabeeb *n.* طبيب medico

tabeed; daktar *n* طبيب،اكر doctor

tabiee kawal *v.t.* طبيعيكول naturalize

tabieeyat *n.* تابعيت allegiance

tabieeyat; madanee haqoona aw dandi *n* تابعيت،مدنيحقونهاودند citizenship

tableeghat *n.* تبليغات propaganda

tableeghat *n.* تبليغات publicity

tableeghatee plaway *n.* تبليغاتي پلاوى missionary

tableeghawal *v.t.* تبليغول propagate

taboot *n* تابوت coffin

tabqa; por *n.* طبقه،پو storey

tabqa; qashar *n.* طبقه،قشر stratum

tabyat *n.* طبيعت temperance

tadarikat; jins *n* تداركات،جنس supply

tadawee kawal *v.t.* تداويكول redress

tadawee; talafee *n* تداوي،تلافي redress

tadbeer *n.* تدبير plan

tadbeer jorawal *v.i.* تدبيرجورول scheme

tadbeer kawal *v.t.* تدبيركول plan

tadbeer; tarha *n.* تدبير،طرحه scheme

tadbeeree *a.* تدبيري strategic

tadeel *n.* تعديل adjustment

tadeelawal *v.t.* تعديلول modulate

tadreejee talqeen kawal *v.t.* تدريجيتلقينكول instil

tadweenawal *v. t* تدوينول compile

tafakur *n* تفكر contemplation

tafakurree *a.* تفكري meditative

tafree *n.* تفريح recreation

tafreehee chakar *n* تفريحيچكر canter

tafreehee chakar *n.* تفريحيچكر outing

tafreehee kakhtay *n.* تفريحيكت yacht

tafreehee kakhtay ki samandaryoon kawal *v.i* تفریحي کۀ کسمندریون کول yacht

tafreeq *n.* تفریق subtraction

tafreeqawal *v.t.* تفریقول subtract

tafseel *n* تفصیل detail

tafseel warkawal *v. t* تفصیل ورکول detail

tafseer *n* تفسیر commentary

tafteesh kawal *v.t.* تفتیش کول interrogate

tafteesh; palatana *n.* تفتیش؛ پلنه search

tafteeshee *a* تفتیشي detective

tafzeelee *n.* تفضیلي superlative

tag kawal *v.t* ذکول ambulate

tag loray; madar *n.* تلوری؛مَدار orbit

tag ratag *n* تراتگ haunt

tag ratag kawal *v.t* تراتگ کول ferry

tag ratag kawal *v.t.* تراتگ کول haunt

tag ratag kawal *v.i.* تراتگ کول traffic

tagay *adj.* تی athirst

tagay *a.* تی thirsty

tagay keydal *v.i.* تی کدل thirst

taghara *n.* تغاره kit

taghara *n.* طغرا monogram

taghayyur *n.* تغییر variation

tagloray *n.* تلوری route

tagloray; lar *n.* تلوری؛لار path

tahdeed *n* تهدید menace

tahdeedawal *v. t.* تهدیدول bully

tahleel wayana *n.* تهلیل وینه antiphony

tahreef; gholawana *n.* تحریف؛ غولوونه sophistication

tahreekawal *v.t.* تحریکول provoke

tahreekawal *v.t.* تحریکول tempt

tahseel *n.* تحصیل acquirement

tahseelawal *v.t.* تحصیلول acquire

tahseelee *a* تحصیلي academic

tahweelkhana *n* تحویلخانه bunker

tahweelkhana *n* تحویلخانه depot

taj *n* تاج crown

taj eekhodana *n* تاجاودنه coronation

taj poshee kawal *v. t* تاج پوشي کول crown

taj; jogha *n* تاج؛جوغه crest

tajaddud; tazotob *n.* تجدد؛تازه توب modernity

tajamul *n.* تجمل luxury

tajamulee *a.* تجملا luxurious

tajaray *n.* تجر safe

tajassum *n.* تجسم substantiation

tajasum *n* تجسم embodiment

tajir *n* تاجر businessman

tajleel *n.* تجلیل glorification

tajleelawal *v.t.* تجلیلول glorify

tajroba *n* تجربه experience

tajroba kar *a* تجربه کار expert

tajroba kawal *v. t.* تجربه کول experience

tajruba kar *a.* تجربه کار veteran

tajrubawee *a.* تجربوي tentative

tajweez *n.* تجویز proposal

tajweez warkawal *v.t.* تجویز ورکول propose

tajweez; tasweeb *n.* تجویز؛تصویب approval

tajzeeya *n.* تجزیه decomposition

tajzeeya kawal *v.t.* تجزیه کول analyse

tajzeeya kawal *v. t.* تجزیه کول decompose

tajzeeya kawal *v. t* تجزیه کول disperse

tajzeeya nigar; zeyrowoonkay *n* تجزیه نار،بروونکی analyst

tajzeeya; shanana *n.* تجزیه،شننه analysis

tak *n.* ټ gait

tak sheen *a.* تک شین verdant

tak soor *a.* تک سور vermillion

takal *v. t* ټاکل elect

takal *v.i.* ټاکل opt

takal; gomaral *v.t.* ټاکل،ګمارل appoint

takan; jatka *n.* ټکان،جکه hitch

takana; da mulaqat zhmana *n.* ټاکنه،دملاقات ژمنه appointment

takar *n* ټکر collision

takar *n.* ټکر clash

takar kawal *v. i.* ټکر کول collide

takar kawal *v.t.* ټکر کول hit

takar wahal *v. t.* ټکر وهل clash

takar; mayda shawi tota *n* ټکر، مده شووه smash

takar; tasadof *n* ټکر،تصادف hit

takawal *v.t.* ټکول knock

takawal; kotra kawal *v.t.* ټکول، کوټره کول thresh

takay *n* ټک ace

takay *n* ټکی dot

takay lagawal *v. t* ټکی لول dot

takay lagawal; ishara kawal *v.t.* ټکی لول،اشاره کول point

takay pa takay *a.* ټکی په ټکی verbatim

takay; sooka *n.* ټکی،سوکه point

takay; zay *n.* ټکی،ځای spot

takee aw nuqtey eekhodal *v.t.* ټکي او نقطایو ډل punctuate

takeeya kawal *v.i.* تکیه کول lean

takeeya kawona *n.* تکیه کوونه lean

takeydalay *a.* ټکېدلی jerky

takhallus *n.* تخلص pseudonym

takhcha *n.* تاخچه niche

takhcha *n.* تاخچه shelf

takhcha jorawal *v.t.* تاخچه جوړول shelve

takheer *n.* تاخیر postponement

takhfeef *n* تخفیف discount

takhfeefawal *v.t.* تخفیفول mitigate

takhmeenawal; arzawal *v.t.* تخمینول،ارزول appraise

takhneek pori arwand *a.* تخنیک پوراوند technological

takhneekee *n.* تخنیکي technical

takhneekee garana *n.* تخنیکي نه technicality

takhneekee karpoh *n.* تخنیکي کارپوه technician

takhneekee karpoh *n.* تخنیکي کارپوه technologist

takhneekee peyzhandana *n.* تخنیک پژندنه technology

takhnrawal *v.t.* تخول tickle

takhreeb *n.* تخریب sabotage

takhreebawal *v.t.* تخریبول sabotage

takhsees warkawal; pa arwand ganral *v.t.* تخصیص ورکول،په اوندل attribute

takht; istirahat zay *n.* تخت، استراحتهای couch

takhta kawal *v. t.* تخته کول compress

takhtawal *v.t.* تتول abduct

takhtawal *v.t.* تتول kidnap

takhtawana *n* تتونه abduction

takhteydal *v.i* تتدل abscond

takhteydal *v.i* تتدل escape

takhteydal *v.i* تتدل flee

takhteydoonkay *n.* تتدونکی fugitive

taklees kawal *v. t* تکلیس کول coke

takmeel *n.* تکمیل fullness

takmeel kawal *v.t.* تکمیل کول supplement

takmeel; zameema *n.* تکمیل، ضمیمه supplement

takra *a.* تکه agile

takra *a.* تکه adept

takrar *n.* تکرار repetition

takrar; tamreen *n.* تکرار،تمرین rehearsal

takratob *n.* تکهتوب agility

takya kawal *v* تکیه کول abut

takzeeb *n* تکذیب contradiction

tal *n.* تال abeyance

tal *n.* تال procrastination

tal pati *a.* تل پاتی everlasting

tal sheen *n* تل شین evergreen

tal zhwanday *a.* تل ژوندی immortal

tal; beykh *n* تل،بیخ bottom

tal; hameysha *adv* تل،همشه always

tal; heeskala *adv* تل،هیڅکله ever

tala; heesab *n.* تله،حساب balance

tala; paymana *n.* تله،پیمانه scale

tala; qaharmana *n.* تله،قهرمانه heroine

talafee *n.* تلافی recovery

talafee; jibran *n.pl.* تلافی،جبران amends

talaffuz *n.* تلفظ pronunciation

talaffuz kawal *v.t.* تلفظ کول pronounce

talaq *n* طلاق divorce

talaqawal *v. t* طلاق ول divorce

talasum; zra rakkhana *n.* طلسم، زهراکنه glamour

taleem; khowana *n.* تعلیم،پوونه tuition

taleemee *a* تعلیمی didactic

taleemee sanad *n* تعلیمی سند diploma

taleeq; darawana *n.* تعلیق،درونه suspension

taleydal *v.i.* الدل procrastinate

talf kawal *v.i.* تلف کول perish

talf kawal *v.t.* تلف کول squander

talf kawal *v.t.* تلف کول waste

talf kawana *n.* تلف کونه wastage

talgaraf *n.* لمراف telegraph

talgaraf karpoh *n.* لمراف کارپوه telegraphist

talgarafee *a.* لمرافی telegraphic

talim yafta khalak au da tarbiye sakhtanan *n.* تعلیم یافته خلك اودتربیتنان gentry

taloo *n.* تالو palate

talpati *a.* تلپاتی imperishable

talpati kawal *v.t.* تلپاتوکول immortalize

talpatitob *n.* تلپاتوب immortality

talqeen kawal *v.t.* تلقین کول inculcate

talweezyon *n.* لویزیون television

tamancha *n.* تمانچه pistol

tamas *n.* تماس engagement

tambakoo *n.* تنباکو tobacco

tambal *n.* مبل lazy

tambal saray *n.* مبل سی slattern

tambalee kawal *v.i.* مبلي کول laze

tambawana *n.* تمبوونه repulse

tambawana *n.* تمبوونه repulsion

tambawoonkay *a.* تمبوونکی repulsive

tambeeya *n.* تنبه admonition

tambeydal *v.i* تمبدل falter

tameel *n* تعمیل execution

tameelawal *v. t* تعمیلول execute

tameerawal *v. t* تعمیرول build

tameerawal *v.t.* تعمیرول repair

tamreen kawal *v.t.* تمرین کول rehearse

tamzay; markaz *n.* تمای؛مرکز station

tan pa tan jagara *n* تن په تن جه duel

tan pa tan jagara *n.* تن په تن جه melee

tan pa tan jangeydal *v. i* تن په تن جندل duel

tana payda kawal *v.i.* تنه پداکول stem

tana; da wani kanda *n.* تنه؛دوني کنده trunk

tanab aw paray gharal *n.* طناب او پری غل marl

tanasub *n.* تناسب proportion

tanda *n.* تنده thirst

tandar *n.* تندر thunder

tandar ta warta *a.* تندرته ورته thunderous

tanday *n* تندی forehead

tandi wari *n.* تندی وری lambkin

tang *a.* تن narrow

tangawal *v.t.* تنول constrict

tangawal *v.t.* تنول narrow

tangsa *n.* تنسه poverty

tanha *a.* تنها lone

tanha *a* تنها sole

tanha *a.* تنها solitary

tanhayee *n.* تنهايي celibacy

tanhayee *n.* تنهايي loneliness

tanhdeedawal *v.t* تهدیدول menace

tankha *n.* تنخوا stipend

tankha; ajoora *n.* تنخوا؛اجوره salary

tanoor *n.* تنور furnace

tanoor *n.* تنور oven

tanraka *n* تاکه blister

tanray *n* ز button

tanray bandawal *v. t.* تبندول button

tanz *n.* طنز scoff

tanz kawal *v.i.* طنز کول scoff

tanzeem *n.* تنظیم orderly

tanzeem *n.* تنظیم regulation

tanzeem kawal *v.t.* تنظیم کول model

tanzeemawal *v.t* تنظیمول marshal

tanzeemawal *v.t.* تنظيمول straighten

tanzeeya *a.* طنزيه satirical

taoon zad amil *n.* طاعون‌ضدعامل pesticide

tap *n.* پ wound

tap jorawal; ghosawal *v.t.* پ جوول؛غوول hack

tap zay pa patay taral *v.t* پ‌ای‌په‌پ تل bandage

tapa *n* اپه cachet

tapa *n.* اپه label

tapa lagawal *v.t.* اپه‌لول label

tapana *n.* تپنه daub

tapay *n.* اپی speck

tapee kawal *v.t.* پی‌کول injure

tapee kawal *v.t.* پی‌کول wound

tapoo *n.* اپو island

tapoo wazma *n.* اپووزمه isle

taq *a.* طاق odd

taqat *n.* طاقت power

taqato *n.* تقاطع intersection

taqatwar *a.* طاقتور powerful

taqaza *n* تقاضا request

taqaza kawal *v.t.* تقاضاکول petition

taqaza kawal *v.t.* تقاضاکول request

taqaza kawal; zaray kawal *v.t.* تقاضاکول؛زارکول solicit

taqcha *n.* طاقچه rack

taqdeer *n* تقدیر destiny

taqdees *n.* تقدیس sanctification

taqdeesawal *v.t.* تقدیسول consecrate

taqdeesawal *v.t.* تقدیسول hallow

taqdeesawal *v.t.* تقدیسول sanctify

taqeebawal *v. t* تعقیبول dog

taqeebawal *v.t.* تعقیبول trace

taqeebawal *v.t.* تعقیبول track

taqeebawal *v.t.* تعقیبول sue

taqleed kawal *v.t.* تقلیدکول ape

taqleed kawal *v. t* تقلیدکول emulate

taqleed kawoonkay *n.* تقلید کوونکی imitator

taqleed shaway *a.* تقلیدشوی stereotyped

taqleedee *a.* تقلیدي mimic

taqreeban *adv* تقریباً about

taqreeban *adv.* تقریبا almost

taqreeban *adv.* تقریبا near

taqreeban *adv.* تقریبا nearly

taqreeban *adv.* تقریبا nigh

taqteer *n* تقطیر distillery

tar *n* تار fibre

tar *n.* تار thread

tar ... landi *adv* تر___لاند below

tar akhira awreydal *v.t.* ترآخره اورلدل overhear

tar aw taza *a.* تراوتازه sprightly

tar azmayakht landi karmand ya zandanee *n.* ترآزمایت‌لاند کارمندیازندانی probationer

tar cha da makha keydal *v.t.* تر چادمخه‌کدل outwit

tar chat landi zay *n.* ترچت‌لاندای loft

tar dey chi *conj* تردچ until

tar dey chi *n. conj.* تردچ till

tar dey wrosta *adv.* تردوروسته hereafter

tar fishar landi rawastal *v.t* تر فشارلاندراوستل stress

tar goona warteyridana *n.* ترناه ورترېدنه condonation

tar hagha mahala *prep.* ترهغه‌مهاله till

tar har sa da makha *adv* ترهرهۀد مخه first

tar jagh landi rawastal *v.t.* ترجغ لاندراوستل yoke

tar jamo landi achowoonkay kamees *n* ترجامولانداچوونکی کمیس chemise

tar khpal agheyz landi seemo ta da pacha garzand astazay *n.* ترخپل‌اغزلاندسیموته‌دپاچارند استازی missis, missus

tar lag miqdar *prep.* ترلمقدار less

tar lasa kawal *v.t.* ترلاسه‌کول gain

tar lasa kawal *v.t.* ترلاسه‌کول receive

tar lasa kawoonkay *n.* ترلاسه کوونکی receiver

tar mreeni wrusta *a.* ترمینوروسته post-mortem

tar mreeni wrusta moayna *n.* تر معاینه وروسته مېن post-mortem

tar osa *adv.* تراوسه hitherto

tar osa *conj.* تراوسه yet

tar paki achawal *v.t* تارپکاچول thread

tar pokhtani landi neewal *v.t* تر پوتهلاندنیول query

tar samandar landi *a* ترسمندرلاند submarine

tar sara kawal *v.t.* ترسره‌کول fulfil

tar sara kawona *n.* ترسره‌کوونه fulfilment

tar sha *adv.* ترشا back

tar sifar kam *prep.* ترصفرکم minus

tar syooree landi *a.* ترسیوري‌لاند overcast

tar takalee wakht zyat *adv.* تر اکلي‌وخت‌زیات overtime

tar tolo akheyr *adv.* ترولوآخر lastly

tar tolo bad wuzeeyat ta beywal *v.t.* ترولوبدوضعیت‌ته‌بیول worst

tar tolo deyr *a* ترولوډیر further

tar tolo deyr *a.* ترولوډیر utmost

tar tolo ghwara *a* ترولوغوره foremost

tar tolo ghwara *a.* ترولوغوره pre-eminent

tar tolo hask maqam *n.* ترولو هسک‌مقام zenith

tar tolo kam kach ta rasawal *v.t.* ترولوکم‌کچ‌ته‌رسول minimize

tar tolo kam miqdar *n.* ترولوکم مقدار minimum

tar tolo kha *a.* ه‌ولو تر superlative

tar tolo khwakh *a* ترولوخو favourite

tar tolo koochnay *n.* ترولوکوچنی minim

tar tolo lag *a.* ترولولړ minimal

tar tolo loy miqdar *n* ترولولوی مقدار most

tar tolo lwar ghag *n* ترولولوغ alto

tar tolo lwar zay moondal *v.t.* تر ولولوای‌موندل top

tar tolo nawara *a* ترولولوناوه worst

tar yawa hada *adv.* تريوه‌حده somewhat

tar yawey andazey *adv.* تريواندازي something

tar zand wrosta *adv.* ترنزوروسته late

tar zangana pori land patloon *n.* ترزنانه‌پورلندپتلون breeches

tar zeyrmo dak *a.* ترزرموک replete

tar zmakay landi soora *n* ترزمکه لاندسوه burrow

tarafdar *a.* طرفدار partisan

tarafdaree *n.* طرفداري adherence

tarafdaree kawal *v.t.* طرفداري‌کول advocate

tarah kawal *v. t.* طرح‌کول design

tarah; khaka *n.* طرح؛خاکه design

taral *v.t* تل bind

taral *v. t* تل close

taral *v.t* تل fasten

taral; bandawal *v.t.* تل؛بندول seal

taral; mamnoo garzawal *v.t* تل؛ ممنوع‌ئزول bar

taralay zay *n.* تلي‌اي close

taranga *a.* تانه littoral

taranga *n* تانه brace

taraqee *n.* ترقي advancement

taraqee kawal *v.t.* ترقه‌کول meliorate

taraqee warkawal *v. t.* ترقي‌ورکول develop

taraqee yafta *n.* ترقي‌يافته advance

taraw *n.* تاو attachment

taraw *n* تاو connection

taraw laral; zyatawal *v.t.* تاولرل؛ زياتول append

tarbeeya warkawal *v. t* تربيه ورکول educate

tarbeeya warkawal *v.t.* تربيه ورکول train

tareef *n* تعريف definition

tareefawal *v. t* تعريفول define

tareekawal *v. t* تاريكول blear

tareekh leekoonkay *n.* تاريخ ليكونکي annalist

tareekh leekoonkay *n.* تاريخ ليكونکي historian

tareekh sakha makhkeenay *a.* تاريخ‌سخه‌مخكيني prehistoric

tareekh; peykh lar *n.* تاريخ؛پل history

tareekhee *a.* تاريخي historic

tareekhee *a.* تاريخي historical

tareekhee yadgar *n.* تاريخي‌يادګار monument

tareeqa *n.* طريقه manner

tareeqa *n.* طريقه procedure

tareeqa *n.* طريقه method

tareeqa kar *n.* طريقه‌کار mechanism

tareeqa laroonkay *a.* طريقه‌لرونکي methodical

tarha *n.* ترهه scare

tarha *n.* ترهه horror

tarha *n.* ترهه intimidation

tarha jorawana *n.* طرحه‌جوونه projection

tarha kawal *v.t.* طرح‌کول outline

tarha kawal *v. t* طرحه‌کول draft

tarha; namoona *n.* طرحه؛نمونه pattern

tarhagar *n.* ترهر terrorist
tarhagaree *n.* ترهري terrorism
tarhawal *v.t.* ترهول horrify
tarhawal *v.t.* ترهول intimidate
tarhawal *v.t.* ترهول scare
tarhawal *v.t.* ترهول terrify
tarhawal *v.t.* ترهول terrorize
tarhowoonkay *n.* ترهوونكی breakneck
tarhowoonkay *a* ترهوونكی dread
tarjee *n.* ترجيح priority
tarjee warkawal *v.t.* ترجيحوركول prefer
tark kawal *v.t.* تركـكول forsake
tarkanr *n.* تركا carpenter
tarkanr *n.* تركا joiner
tarkanree *n.* تركاۍ carpentry
tarkeeb *n* تركيب composition
tarkeeb *n* تركيب compost
tarkeeb *n* تركيب mould
tarkeeb; yaw zayakht *n.* تركيب،يو ايت synthesis
tarkeebawal *v.* i تركيبول compound
tarkeebawal *v.t.* تركيبول mingle
tarkeebawal *v.t.* تركيبول symbolize
tarkeebawal; seyra warkawal *v.t.* تركيبول،برهوركول form
tarkeebawal; weeli kawal *v.t.* تركيبول،ويلىكول fuse
tarkeebee joz *n.* تركيبىجز ingredient
tarman *a.* تمن lukewarm
taroon *n.* تون affiliation
taroon *n.* تون agreement

taroon kawoonkay *n* تونكوونكی contractor
taroon lasleekawal *v.t.* تون لاسليكول stipulate
taroon; beyt *n.* تون،بيعت plight
taroona sara gandal *v.t.* تارونهسره ـل weave
tarteeb *n.* ترتيب array
tarteebawal *v.t.* ترتيبول organize
tarteebawal *v.t.* ترتيبول range
tarteebawoonkay; satandoy *n.* ترتيبوونكی،ساتندوی ranger
tarz *n.* طرز style
tarz; dood *n.* طرز؛دود mode
tasadofee *a.* تصادفي casual
tasadufee *a* تصادفي accidental
tasalsul *n* تسلسل continuity
tasano *n* تصنع affectation
tasarruf kawal *v.t.* تصرفكول preoccupy
tasarruf; da loomreetob haq *n.* تصرف،دلوميتوبحق preoccupation
tasawee *n* تساوي equation
tasawor kawal *v.* t تصوركول conceive
tasawwuf *n.* تصوف mysticism
tasawwur kawal *v.t.* تصوركول suppose
tasawwur; farz; khyal *n.* ؛تصور، فرض؛خيال supposition
tasawwur; gholawoonkay zahir *n.* تصور،؛غولوونكیظاهر phantom
tasawwur; gooman *n.* تصور،بومان imagination

tasawwur; khyal *n.* تصور،خيال imagery

tasawwuree *a.* تصوري imaginative

tasawwuree; khyalee *a.* تصوري، خيالي visionary

tasbee *n.* تسبيح rosary

tasbeet shaway *a.* تثبيت شوى stable

tasdeeq *v.* تصديق acknowledge

tasdeeq *n* تصديق confirmation

tasdeeq *n.* تصديق verification

tasdeeq *n.* تصديق testimony

tasdeeq kawal *v.t.* تصديق كول recognize

tasdeeqawal *v. t.* تصديقول certify

tasdeeqawal *v.i.* تصديقول testify

tasdeeqawal *v.t.* تصديقول verify

tasees *n* تأسيس establishment

taseesawal *v. t.* تأسيسول establish

tasfeeya kawal *v.t.* تصفيه كول sublimate

tasfeeya kawoonkay *a.* تصفيه كوونكى sublime

tash *a* تش empty

tash lasay *n.* تش لاسى pauper

tash lasay *a.* تش لاسى penniless

tash zay *n.* تش ،اى vacancy

tash zay; naleekali panra *n* تش ،اى،ناليكلپله blank

tash; khalee *a* تش،خالي devoid

tash; khalee *a.* تش،خالي vacant

tashannuj wahalay shakhs *a.* تشنج وهلى شخص hysterical

tashannujee *a.* تشنجي spasmodic

tashawal *v* تشول empty

tashawal *v. t* تشول evacuate

tashawal *v.i.* تشول teem

tashawal; bey kara kawal *v.t.* تشول،بكاره كول vacate

tashawal; khalee kawal *v.t* تشول، خالي كول hollow

tashawana *n* تشونه evacuation

tashbee *n.* تشبيه simile

tashkhees *n* تشخيص diagnosis

tashkheesawal *v.t.* تشخيصول assess

tashreefat *n* تشريفات complement

tashreefatee *a.* تشريفاتي ceremonial

tashreefatee meylmastaya *n.* تشريفاتي ملمستيا banquet

tasht *n.* تشت basin

tashweesh *n* تشويش concern

tashweesh laral *v. t* تشويش لرل concern

tashyal; khala *n.* تشيال،خلا vacuum

taskeen *n.* تسكين solace

taskeenawal *v.t.* تسكينول solace

taskeenawal; khamoshawal *v.t.* تسكينول،خاموشول appease

tasleem keydal *v.t.* تسليم كدل submit

tasleemawal *v.t.* تسليمول concede

tasleemeydal *v. t* تسليمدل capitulate

tasleemeydal *v.t.* تسليمدل surrender

tasma; chingak *n* تسمه،چنک clasp

tasmeemawal *v. t* تصميمول determine

tasneefawoonkay *n* تصنيفوونکی compositor

tasob *n* تعصب bias

tasob *n* تعصب bigotry

tasob kawal *v. t* تعصب کول bias

taspod payda keydal *v.i.* تسپودپدا کدل swell

tasweeb *n.* تصویب approbation

tasweebawal *v.t* تصویبول approbate

tasweebawal *v. t.* تصویبول endorse

tasweebawal *v.t.* تصویبول subscribe

tasweebawal *v.t.* تصویبول ratify

tasweebawal; muwafiqat kawal *v.t.* تصویبول؛موافقت کول approve

tasweer *n* تصویر photo

tasweer; shakal *n.* تصویر؛شکل image

tat *a* تت dim

tat *n.* ١ canvas

tat *a.* تت opaque

tat; nasargand *a* تت؛نارنند dark

tatabuq *n.* تطابق symmetry

tatar *n* ر chest

tatar *n.* ١ار tinker

tatawal *v. t* تتول dim

tatawal *v.t.* تتول obscure

tatay *n.* toilet

tatbeeqawal *v.t.* تطبیقول tally

tateydana *n* تتدنه blur

tatmee; bramta *n* تطمیع؛برامتا allurement

tatwalay *n.* تتوالی opacity

taw khwaral *v.i.* تاوخول swing

taw khwaralay *a.* تاوخولی wry

taw khwarana *n.* تاوخونه spin

taw rataw *a* تاوراتاو crisp

taw rataw *a.* تاوراتاو spiral

taw rataw zeena *n.* تاوراتاوزینه maze

taw shaway seez *n.* تاوشوی یز roll

taw; da faaleeyat dawra *n* تاو؛د فعالیت دوره swing

tawafuq *n.* توافق adaptation

tawafuq *n.* توافق concord

tawafuq sara peykheydal *v. i* توافق سره پدل coincide

tawajo *n.* توجه attention

tawajo *n.* توجه concentration

tawajo *n* توجه focus

tawajo *n.* توجه tendency

tawajo *n* توجه heed

tawajo kawal *v.t* توجه کول focus

tawajo kawal *v.t.* توجه کول heed

tawajo satal *v. t* توجه ساتل concentrate

tawan *n.* تاوان harm

tawan akheystal *v.t.* تاوان اخستل ransom

tawan arowoonkay *a.* تاوان اوونکی noxious

tawan rasawal *v.t* تاوان رسول harm

tawan warkawal *v. t.* تاوان ورکول damage

tawan warkawal *v.t.* تاوان ورکول remunerate

tawan warkawal *v.i.* تاوان ورکول retaliate

tawan warkawana *n.* تاوان ورکونه remuneration

tawan warkawana *n.* تاوان ورکوونه
retaliation

tawan; awaz *n.* تاوان؛عوض
recompense

tawan; jareema *n* تاوان؛جريمه
forfeit

tawan; jibran *n.* تاوان؛جبران
indemnity

tawan; zarar *n* تاوان؛ضرر
disadvantage

tawaquf *n* توقف stoppage

tawas *n.* طاوس peacock

tawazo *n* تواضع deference

tawda; deyr garam *a.* توده؛ډېرګرم
torrid

tawdawal *v.t* تودول heat

tawdokha *n.* تودوخه heat

tawdokha *n.* تودوخه warmth

tawdokhee *n.* تودوخي temperature

tawdokhmeych *n.* تودوخمچ
thermometer

taweydal; sarkheydal *v.i.* تاودل؛
رخدل turn

tawheed *n.* توحيد monotheism

tawheen *n* توهين disdain

tawheen *n.* توهين humiliation

tawheen kawal *v. t.* توهين کول
disdain

tawheenawal *v.t.* توهينول
humiliate

tawkal *n.* توکل reliance

tawleed shaway mawad *n.* تولید
شوی مواد production

tawleed; hasil *n.* تولید؛حاصل
produce

tawleedawal *v. t* تولیدول create

tawleedawal *v.t.* تولیدول generate

tawleedawal *v.t.* تولیدول
manufacture

tawleedawal *v. t* تولیدول beget

tawleedawal *v.t.* تولیدول produce

tawleedawana *n* تولیدوونه
manufacture

tawleedawoonkay *n.* تولیدوونکی
generator

tawleedawoonkay *n* تولیدوونکی
manufacturer

tawleedee *a.* تولیدي productive

tawowal *v.t.* تاوول convolve

tawpeer *n* توپیر difference

tawpeer laral *v. i* توپیرلرل differ

tawpeer laral *v.t.* توپیرلرل vary

tawpeer moondana *n* توپیرموندنه
discrimination

tawpeerawal *v. t.* توپیرول
discriminate

tawqeef *n* توقیف curb

tawqeef kawal *v.t.* توقیف کول
intern

tawzee *n.* توضیح demonstration

tawzee *n.* توضیح gloss

tawzee kawal *v. t.* توضیح کول
explain

tawzee warkawal *v. t* توضیح
ورکول demonstrate

tawzee; daleel *n* توضیح؛دلیل
explanation

tay *n.* تی mamma

tay laroonkay *n.* تی لرونکی
mammal

tayarawal *v.t.* تیارول prepare

tayaray *n.* تیاری preparation

tayaree; muqarrarat takal *n.*
تیاری؛مقررات اکل provision

tayeed; afwa *n.* تایید،عفوه grace
tayeedawal *v. t* تائیدول confirm
tayeedawal *v. t.* تائیدول consign
taylafoon *n.* تلفون phone
taylafoon *n.* تلفون telephone
taylafoonee aw da rabitey areeki
n. تلفوني او د رابطایک
telecommunications
tayzab *n* تیزاب acid
tayzabee *a* تیزابي acid
tayzabeeyat *n.* تیزابیت acidity
taza *a.* تازه fresh
taza *a.* تازه up-to-date
taza intikhabawal *v.t.* تازه انتخابول
recruit
taza kawal *v.t.* تازه کول refresh
taza kawal *v.t.* تازه کول renew
taza kawana *n.* تازه کوونه
refreshment
taza kawana *n.* تازه کوونه renewal
taza; naway *a.* تازه،نوی recent
taza; naway *a.* تازه،نوی modern
tazad *n.* تضاد antithesis
tazad khwakhay *n* تضادخوی
antitheist
tazahar kawal *v.t.* تظاهر کول
prtend
tazahar; bahana *n.* تظاهر،بهانه
pretension
tazahur kawal *v.i.* تظاهر کول sham
tazatob; mastee *n.* تازه توب،مستي
vivacity
tazee spay *n.* تازي سپی greyhound
tazkeer aw tanees *n.* تذکیر او تأنیث
gender
tazkeeya *n.* تزکیه refinement

tazkeeya kawal *v.t.* تزکیه کول
refine
tazkira kawal *v. t* تذکره کول cite
tazkiree *a.* تذکري reminiscent
tee *n* تي breast
teekala *n.* ټیکله loaf
teekalay; disc *n.* ټیکلی،ډسک disc
teekat *n.* ټکټ ticket
teekaw *n.* ټیکاو perseverance
teekaw *n.* ټیکاو stability
teekaw warbakhal *v.t.* ټیکاوور بخل
stabilize
teeng azama; sar pa las *a.* ټینعزمه،
سر په لاس resolute
teengakht *n.* ټینت tenacity
teengakht *n.* ټینت stabilization
teengar *n* ټینار emphasis
teengar *n* ټینار urge
teengar kawal *v. t* ټینار کول
emphasize
teengar sara ghokhtal *v.t* ټینار سره
غوتل urge
teengar warkawal *v.t.* ټینارور کول
stable
teengawal *v. t.* ټینول consolidate
teengeydoonkay *a.* ټیندونکی
persistent
teengwalay *n* ټینوالی consolidation
teer *n* تیر beam
teet park *a.* تیت پرک sparse
teet; kog *n* کو یت؛ bow
teetakay *n.* ټیکی pigmy
teetawal *v.t.* ټول abase
teetawal; shanal *v.t.* ټیتول؛شنل
strew
teeteydal *v. t* ټیدل bow

tehqeeq *n.* تحقیق inquiry
tehqeeq *n.* تحقیق investigation
tehqeeq kawal *v.t.* تحقیق کول investigate
tehqeeqee; tafteeshee *a.* تحقیقي، تفتیشي inquisitive
tehqeer *n.* تحقیر scorn
tehreefawal *v.t.* تحریفول invert
tehreekawal *v. t* تحریکول excite
tehseen *n.* تحسین admiration
tehseen *n.* تحسین praise
tehseen; stayana *n.* تحسین،ستاینه applause
teredal *v.t* تیریدل forgo
teygh *n.* تغ blade
teykhta *n* تخته escape
teyl *n.* تل oil
teyla kawal *v.t.* له کول push
teyla; kokhakh *n.* له،کو push
teynas *n.* نس racket
teypar *n.* پر turnip
teyr *a.* تر past
teyr eystal *v. t* تراستل bluff
teyr eystal *v. t* تراستل dodge
teyr eystal *v.t.* تراستل sophisticate
teyr eystana *n* تراستنه bluff
teyr eystana *n.* تراستنه sophism
teyr mahal *n.* ترمهال past
teyr mahal ta nazar achawana *n.* ترمهال ته نظر اچوونه retrospection
teyr mahal ta staneyda *n.* ترمهال ستندا ته retrospect
teyr watal *v.t.* تروتل mistake
teyr watal *v.i.* تروتل stumble

teyr watana *n* وتنه تر misapprehension
teyr watana *n.* تروتنه mistake
teyra *a.* تره sharp
teyra kawal *v.t.* تره کول sharpen
teyra kawal; parawal *v.t.* تره کول، پارول whet
teyra kawoonkay *n.* تره کوونکی sharpener
teyra sooka *n.* ترموکه nib
teyra wraz *adv.* ترهور yesterday
teyrawalay *n.* ترهوال acumen
teyray *n* تری aggression
teyray *n.* تری intrusion
teyray kawal *v.t.* تری کول intrude
teyray kawal *n.* تری کول trespass
teyray kawal; tawheen kawal *v.t.* تری کول،توهین کول violate
teyray kawoonkay *a.* تیری کوونکی aggressive
teyreydana *n.* تردنه transit
teyreydana; da watalo lar; mukhalifat *n.* تردنه،دوتلولار،مخالفت crossing
teyro peykho pori arwand *a.* ترو پویوراوند retrospective
teysha; kawdar *n.* تشه،کور hatchet
teyz *a.* تیز acute
teyz *a.* تز rapid
teyz asmanee rang *n.* تز آسماني رنز indigo
teyz khwazeydal *v.t.* تزخودل wallop
teyz; faryadee *a.* تز،فریادي shrill
teyza aw stargi wroonki ranra *n* تزهاوسترووونکی را flare

teyza sa akheystal *v.i* تزه‌ساه‌اخستل
gasp

teyza sa akheystana *n.* تزه‌ساه
اخستنه gasp

teyzee; shiddat *n.* تزي؛شدت
intensity

teyzwalay *n.* تزوالی velocity

tib; fizeek *n.* طب؛فزیک physic

tibbee *a.* طبيی innate

tibee *a.* طبي medical

tibee botay *n.* طبي‌بوی herb

tibee ghwagay *n.* طبي‌غو
stethoscope

tibee katanzay *n.* طبي‌کتنای clinic

tijarat *n* تجارت commerce

tijarat *n.* تجارت trade

tijarat kawal *v.i* تجارت‌کول trade

tijaratee *a* تجارتي commercial

tijaratee *a.* تجارتي mercantile

tijaratee nakha *n* تجارتي‌نه brand

tiksee *n.* کسي taxi

tiksee ki tlal *v.i.* کسي‌کتلل taxi

tilayee *a.* طلايي golden

timsal *n* تمثال effigy

tlal *v.i.* تلل go

toba kawal *v.t.* توبه‌کول forswear

tobagar *a.* توبګار repentant

tod; garam *a.* تود؛ برم warm1

todawal; garmawal *v.t.* تودول؛
رمول warm

togal; trashal *v. t.* تول؛تراشل carve

toghanday *n.* توغندی rocket

toghanday *n.* توغوندی missile

toghawal *v.t.* توغول launch

toghawal keydoonkay jisam *n.*
توغول‌کدونکی‌جسم projectile

toghawal shaway *a* توغول‌شوی
projectile

toghawal; weeshtal *v.t.* توغول؛
ویشتل shoot

toghawana *n.* توغوونه launch

tok *n* توک episode

toka *n.* وکه hoax

toka *n.* وکه joke

toka *n.* وکه witticism

toka kawal *v.t* وکه‌کول hoax

tokal *v.t.* وکل contuse

tokampalana *n.* توکمپالنه
racialism

tokar *n* وکر cloth

tokar ploroonkay *n* وکرپلوروونکی
draper

tokar; kalbad *n* وکر؛کالبد fabric

tokham; rozana *n* تخم؛روزنه breed

tokhay *n.* وخی cough

tokheydal *v. i.* وخدل cough

tokhmar kawal *v.t* تخمر‌کول
ferment

tokhmar; hayjan *n* تخمر؛هجان
fermentation

toki *n.* وکی fun

toki *a.* وکی humorous

toki kawal *v.i.* وکی‌کول joke

toki kawal *v.i* وکی‌کول mime

tokmar *n.* وکمار banter

tokmar *n.* وکمار humorist

tokmar *n* وکمار mimic

tokmar *n* وکمار wag

tokmar *a.* وکمار witty

tokmaree *n* وکماري mimicry

tokmeez; nazhadee *a.* توکمیز؛
نژادي racial

tokray n. وکر basket
tol n ول all
tol a. ول total
tol n ول whole
tol takana n ولاکنه election
tol umree a. ولعمري lifelong
tol wazhana n ول وژنه carnage
tol wazhana n. ولوژنه massacre
tol wazhna n. ولوژنه slaughter
tol; bashpar a. ول؛بشپ all
tolana n. ولنه community
tolana n. ولنه society
tolaneez a ولنيز collective
tolaneez n. ولنيز social
tolaneez parmakhtag n. ولنيز پرمخته civilization
tolaneeza khayr kheygara n. ولنيزه خره commonwealth
tolanpohana n. ولنپوهنه sociology
tolawana n ولونه pluck
tolay n. ولى mass
toley peysey; majmooa n. ولپسې، مجموعه sum
tolga n وله set
tolo barkho ki badloonoona rawastal v.t. ولوبرخوکبدلونونه راوستل overhaul
tolpokhtana n. ولپوتنه referendum
tolwak n ولواک emperor
tolwak n. ولواک monarch
tolwakee n. ولواكي monarchy
tolwakpal n. ولواکپال royalist
tomatee a. تومتي slanderous
tomna n تومنه ferment
tomna n. تومنه yeast
tond a. توند poignant

tond aw teyz awaz n. تونداوتزباد hurricane
tond khooya a. خويه توند sullen
tond khooyee; mukhalifat n. توند خويي؛مخالفت frown
tond; teyz; chalak a. توند،تز، چالاک smart
tondee n. توندي poignacy
tondee n توندي hurry
tondee kawal v.t. توندي کول hurry
tookanri n توکا spittle
tookanri n. توکا spittoon
tookanri tookal v.i. توکاتوکل spit
tookanri; lari n توکا،لا spit
tookeydal; notaki kawal v.i. توکدل؛نوتکاکول sprout
toolul balad n. طول البلد longitude
toomaree harakat n. طوماري حرکت scroll
toonal keendal v.i. تونل کيندل tunnel
toonal; da eystani bahanz n. تونل؛داستبهنه tunnel
toopan n. توپان tempest
toopan; sooran n. توپان؛سوران storm
toopanee a. توپاني tempestuous
toopanee a. توپاني windy
toopanee; hayjanee a. توپاني؛ هجاني stormy
toopoona wahal v.i. توپونهوهل skip
toora n. توره sword
tooryalay a توريالى brave
toot n. توت mulberry
top i. وپ bound
top n. وپ jump

top v.i. وپ leap
top n. وپ vault
top wahal v.i. وپ‌وهل jump
top wahal n وپ‌وهل leap
top wahal v.i. وپ‌وهل vault
top wahoonkay n. وپ‌وهونکی skipper
topak n. وپک gun
topak n وپک rifle
topak wal n. وپکوال musketeer
topkhana n. توپخانه artillery
topkhana n. توپخانه ordnance
topoona wahal v. i وپونه‌وهل hop
tor a تور black
tor kargha n. تور‌کارغه raven
tor kargha n. تور‌کارغه rook
tor lagawal v.t. تورلول accuse
tor lagawal v. t. تورلول calumniate
tor lagawana n تورلونه accusation
tor postakay n. تورپوستکی nigger
tor postay ghulam n. تورپوستی‌غلام maroon
tor postay saray n. تورپوستی‌سی negro
tor posti khaza n. تورپوسته negress
tor rangay a. توررنی swarthy
tor ya badgoomanee leyri kawal v.t. توریابدگومانی‌لرکول vindicate
tora kahruba n. توره‌کهربا jet
tora khawra n. توره‌خاوره muck
toran n. تورن accused
toran; ghal n تورن؛غل culprit
toranawal v. t تورنول denounce
toranawal v.t. تورنول impeach
toranawal v.t. تورنول incriminate

toranawal v.t. تورنول vilify
torawal v. t. تورول blacken
torawona; taqeeb n. تورونه؛تعقیب impeachment
toray; tahal n. توری؛طحال spleen
torsh adj ترش acerb
toshaka n. توشکه mattress
toshakcha n. توشکچه pad
tota n. وه piece
tota kawal v. t وه‌کول chop
tota tota kawal v. t وموه‌کول dissect
tota tota kawal v.t. وموه‌کول splinter
tota tota keydal v. i وموه‌کدل crash
tota; barkha n. وه؛برخه fragment
tota; peena n وه؛پینه patch
totee n. طوطي parrot
totla keydal v.i. توتله‌کدل stammer
totlatob n توب‌توتله stammer
toy shaway seez n توی‌شوی‌یز spill
toyawal; narawal v.i. تویول؛نول spill
tra; kaka n. تره؛کاکا uncle
trakeydal v.t. ‌تکدل crackle
trashal v.t. تراشل whittle
trashal; hajamat jorawal v.t. تراشل؛حجامت‌جول shave
trashal; tarteebawal v.t. تراشل؛ترتیبول trim
trawa tanda n. ده‌تروه scowl
trawa tanda neewal v.i. تروهنديول scowl
trawey oba n تراوبه brine
treekh a تریخ bitter

treekh *a.* تريخ pungent
treekh aw khwandawar *a.* تريخاو خوندور piquant
treekhawal *v. t* تريخول embitter
treekhawal *v.t.* تريخول pepper
treekhwalay *n* تريخوالى acrimony
treekhwalay *n.* تريخوالى pungency
treew *adj* تريو acescent
treew *a.* تريو sour
treewwalay *n.* تريووالى salinity
tri ... landi *adv* تر___لاند beneath
tri gata akheystal *v.t.* ترىﻪاخستل avail
tri teyray kawal *v.t.* ترترىكول transgress
tri warandi keydal *v.t.* ترواندكدل antecede
tri wrandi keydal *v.i* ترواندكدل excel
trom; shpeylay *n.* تروم،شپل trumpet
tror *n.* ترور aunt
troshawal; naraza kawal *v.t.* تروشول،ناراضﻪكول sour
tuhmat *n* تهمت defamation
tuhmat *n.* تهمت libel
tuhmat lagawal *v. t.* تهمتلول defame
tuhmat lagawal *v.t.* تهمتلول libel
tukham shanal *v.t.* تخمشنل sow
tukhamdan *n.* تخمدان core
tukhamdan *n* تخمدان matrix
tukhamdan *n.* تخمدان ovary
tukhamdan *n.* تخمدان uterus
tukhmi badyan *n* تخمبادىان aniseed

twan *n.* توان energy
twan *n* توان main
twan *n.* توان might
twan; zhwand zwak *n.* توان،ژوند واک stamina
twan; zor *n* توان،زور force
twaneydal *v.* تواندل can
twaneydal *v* تواندل may
twanmand *a.* توانمند tough
tyara *n* تىاره dark
tyara *a.* تىاره gloomy
tyara kawal *v.t.* تىارهكول overshadow
tyara ki pateydal *v.i.* تىارهكپدل darkle
tyatar *n.* تىاتر theatre
tyatar pori arwand *a.* تىاترپوراوند theatrical
tyoob *n* تىوب cylinder

umeed bakhoonkay *a.* امىدبونکى promising
umeedwara *a.* امىدواره pregnant
unsar *n* عنصر element
usmanee turkeeya *n.* عثمانىترکىه ottoman
usool *n.* اصول principle
usooleeyat; aqlaneeyat *n.* اصولىت،عقلانىت rationality
ustad *n.* استاد master
ustadana *a.* استادانه masterly
ustadana *a.* استادانه scholastic

ustadee *n.* أستادي artifice
ustadee kawal *v.t.* أستادي کول master
ustawayee *a.* استوايِ tropical
uzlatee *a.* عضلاتي muscular
uzwee *a.* عضوي organic

W

waaz *n.* وعظ sermon
waaz kawal *v.i.* کول وعظ preach
waaz kawal *v.i.* کول وعظ sermonize
waaza (qalach) *n* وازه(قلاچ) fathom
waba *n.* وبا pest
waba; taoon *a.* وبا،طاعون plague
wabayee n وبايي epidemic
wach *adj.* وچ arid
wach *a* وچ dry
wach klak; tanha *n.* وچ کلک،تنها stark
wach; dad awaz *a.* وچ؛آواز husky
wacha pakha lara n وچهپخهلاره causeway
wachawal *v. t* وچول drain
wachawana *n* وچونه drainage
wacheydal *v. i.* وچدل dry
wachi ta watana *n.* وچتهوتنه landing
wachkakhpak *n.* وچکپاک rubber
wachkalee *n* وچکالي famine
wachtya *n* وچتيا draught
wachtya *n* وچتيا drought

wada *n.* واده marriage
wada *n.* واده matrimony
wada *n.* وده promotion
wada *n.* واده spousal
wada *n.* وده germination
wada *n* وعده promise
wada *n.* واده wedding
wada kawal *v.t.* وادهکول marry
wada kawal *v.i* ودهکول flourish
wada kawal *v.i.* ودهکول germinate
wada kawal *v.t.* ودهکول grow
wada kawal *v.t* وعدهکول promise
wada kawal *v.t.* وادهکول wed
wada kawoonkay; amalee *a.* وده عملي کوونکي؛ viable
wada na makhki da halak aw najlay tar manz meena naki khabari *n.* وادهنهمخکدهلک‍او نجلاتر منمینهناکخبر courtship
wada warkawoonkay; paloonkay *n.* ودهورکوونکی؛ پالونکی grower
wada; karhanra *n.* وده؛کرهه growth
wadanawal *v.t.* ودانول piece
wadanay *n* ودانز building
wadanee jorawal *n* ودانيجوول construction
wafadar *n.* دار وفا loyalist
wafadar; sabit qadam *a.* وفادار؛ ثابتقدم staunch
wafadaree *n.* وفاداري loyalty
wagay *n* وی bunch
wagay *a.* وی hungry
wagi *n.* وا rein
wagma *n* ومه breeze

wagma *n.* ومه whiff
wagon; bar leygdawoonki waseela *n.* واون؛بارلدوونكوسيله wagon
wahal *v. t.* وهل beat
wahal dabawal; kar bandeyz *n* وهل‌بول؛كاربدنز strike
wahoonkay *n.* وهونكى striker
wahshat *n.* وحشت savagery
wahshatnak *a.* وحشتناك terrible
wahshee *a.* وحشي savage
wahshee khoog *n* وحشي‌خو boar
wahshee marghano khkari *n.* وحشى‌مارغانوكارى fowler
wahshee zanawar *n* وحشي‌ناور brute
wahshee zanawar ya insan *n* وحشي‌ناوريا‌انسان savage
wahsheetob; bayaban *n.* وحشيتوب؛بيابان wilderness
waiz *n.* واعظ preacher
wajad *n.* وجد rapture
wajeeba; danda *n* وجيبه؛دنده duty
wajib *a.* واجب obligatory
wajood *n* وجود؛شتون existence
wajood laral *v.i* وجودلرل exist
wajood warkowana *n.* وجود وركونه incarnation
wak warkawal *v.t.* واك‌وركول authorize
wak warkawal *v. t* واك‌وركول empower
wak; hookoomat *n.* واك؛حكومت rule
wak; preykhla *n.* واك؛پرله authority

wakalat kawoonkay; mahir *n.* وكالت‌كوونكى؛ماهر practitioner
wakeel *n.* وكيل attorney
wakeel *n.* وكيل barrister
wakha *n* واه cockle
wakha *n* واه grass
wakhay *n* وى bracelet
wakht barabarawal *v.t.* وخت برابرول؛وخت‌اكل time
wakht peyzhandana *n.* وخت‌پژندنه punctuality
wakht teyrawal *v.t.* وخت‌ترول while
wakht yi poora keydal *v.i.* وخت‌يې پوره‌كدل expire
wakht zandawal *v.i.* وخت‌نول linger
wakht zaya kawal *v.i.* وخت‌ضائع كول loaf
wakht; dawran *n.* وخت؛دوران period
wakman *a.* واكمن authoritative
wakman *n.* واكمن ruler
wakman; hakim *n* واكمن؛حاكم despot
wakmanee *n* واكمني dominion
wakseen *n.* واكسين vaccine
wakseen warkawal *v.t.* واكسين وركول vaccinate
wakseen warkawana *n.* واكسين وركونه vaccination
wal *n.* وَل loop
walar *a.* ولا perpendicular
walee *n.* والي governor
walee *n.* ولي guardian
walee; buzurg *n.* ولي؛بزر saint

wali; da sa lapara *adv.* ول،دهلپاره why

walja *n* ولجه booty

walja; ghaneemat *n* ولجه،غنیمت plunder

walwala; leywaltya *n.* ولوله،لوالتیا ardour

wana *n.* ونه tree

wand; skakht *n.* ونډ،سکت share

wanda *n* ونه contribution

wanda *n.* ونه lot

wanda akheystal *v.i* ونهاخستل mass

wanda wal *n* ونهوال co-partner

wanda wal; shareek *n.* ونهوال، شریک associate

wanda wanda kawal *v. t* ونهونه کول distribute

wanda warkawal *v. t* ونهورکول contribute

wanda warkawal *v.t.* ونهورکول involve

wanda warkawal; gata pa barkha kawal *v.t.* ونهورکول،به پهبرخهکول impart

wanda; tol lagakhtoona *n.* ونه،ټول لتونه input

wandawal *n.* ونهوال partner

waqaf *n* وقف dedication

waqaf kawal *v. t* وقفکول devote

waqaf kawal *v. t* وقفکول endow

waqaf kawoonkay *n* وقفکوونکی devotee

waqar; tashreefat *n.* وقار،تشریفات solemnity

waqfa *n.* وقفه pause

waqfa *n.* وقفه recess

waqfa kawal *v.i.* وقفه کول pause

waqiee *a.* واقعي objective

waqiee; muwassaq *a.* واقعي،موثق substantial

war *n* ور door

war *a* و able

war *a.* و capable

war garzawal *v. t* ور ول enable

war garzeydal; rutba moondal *v.i.* ورډل،رتبهموندل qualify

war khatayee *n* وار خطایي confusion

war; kaman laroonkay war *n.* ور،کمانلرونکیور portal

wara man *a* من واره favourable

wara tota *n* وه وه nibble

waraktoon *n.* وکتون kindergarten ;

waral; bar waral *v. t.* ول،بارول carry

warandeenay *prep.* واندیني afore

warandeyz kawal *v.t.* واندزکول offer

warandwayana *n* واندوینه forecast

warandwayana *n.* واندوینه anticipation

warandwayana *n* واندوینه foresight

warandwayana kawal *v.t.* واندوینه کول anticipate

warandwayana kawal *v.t* واندوینه کول forecast

warandwayana kawal *v.t* واندوینه کول foresee

warandwayana kawal *v.t* واندوینه کول foretell

warang achawal; teer achawal *v. i* واناچول;تيراچول beam

waranga *n.* وانه ray

waranga achawal *v.i.* وانهاچول irradiate

warastawal; muntaqilee *n.* وراستول;منتقلي transfer

waray *n* و fleece

waray *n.* و wool

waray shookawal *v.t* وشوكول fleece

waraz *n* ور day

warazpanra *n.* ورپه daily

warbakhal *v.t.* وربل grant

warbakhal *v.t.* وربل spare

warbandi beyrta tlal *v.t.* ورباند برتهتلل retrace

warbashi *n.* وربش barley

wareen *a.* وين woollen

wareen astar *n* ويناستر nap

wareen tokar *n.* وينوكر serge

wareen tokar *n* وينوكر woollen

wareena gharal shawi sanay *n.* وينهغلشوسنه worsted

wareez *n.* وريز cloud

wareezan *a* ورين cloudy

wareezhi *n.* وريژ rice

wareydal *v.i.* ورلل pour

wareydana *n.* ورلنه affluence

warghaway katana *n.* ورغوىكتنه palmistry

warghaway katoonkay *n.* ورغوى كتونكى palmist

waridat *n.* واردات import

waridawal *v.t.* واردول import

waris *n.* وارث heir

warkawal *v.t.* وركول give

warkh *n.* ورخ valve

warkh; patam *n.* ورخ;پم sluice

warkhatal *v.i* ورختل climb

warkhatana *n.* ورختنه climb1

warookay kheekhayee botal *n.* وركىيهيىبوتل phial

warookay shay ya insan *n* وركى شىياانسان small

warooktya *adv.* وركتيا smallness

warpasey *conj.* ورپس after

warpasey *a.* ورپس subsequent

warpayadawal *v.t.* ورپهيادول remind

warpori khandal *v.t.* ورپورخندل ridicule

warrasawal *v. t.* وررسول convey

warsakha draneydal *v.t.* ورخه درندل outweigh

warsakha gokha keydal *v.i.* ورخه وهكدل secede

warsakha khabrawal *v.t.* ورخه خبرول portend

warsakha makhki keydal *v.t.* ورخهمخككدل surpass

warsara barabaray kawal *v.t.* ورسرهبرابرىكول offset

warsara makhamakheydal *v. i* ورسرهمخامخدل cope

warsara malgartya kawal *v. t.* ورسرهملرتياكول befriend

warta *a.* ورته like

warta aw mushabay kawal *v.t* ورتهاومشابهكول fabricate

warta barabarawal *v.i.* ورته برابرول provide

warta darmal warkawal *v.t.* ورته درملورکول physic

warta ghag laroonkee toree sara da parla pasey kalmo peyleydana *n.* ورته‌غلرونکي توريسره‌دپرله‌پسکلموپيلدنه alliteration

warta heela laral *v.t.* ورته‌هيله‌لرل hope

warta kawal *v.t.* ورته‌کول liken

warta makh kawal *v.t* ورته‌مخ‌کول front

warta shakhseeyat warkawal *v.t.* ورته‌شخصيت‌ورکول personify

warta walay *n.* ورته‌والی conformity

warta walay *n.* ورته‌والی like

wartatob *n.* ورته‌توب likeness

wartawalay *n.* ورته‌والی similarity

wartlana *n.* ورتلنه reference

wartya *n.* وتيا capability

wartya *n.* وتيا talent

warya *adv.* ويا gratis

warzash ta zan chamtoo kawal *v.t.* ورزش‌تمان‌چمتوکول limber

warzashee *a.* ورزشي sportive

warzda kawal *v.t.* ورزده‌کول teach

warzish *n.* ورزش exercise

warzish kar *n.* ورزش‌کار athlete

warzish kawal *v.t* ورزش‌کول exercise

warzishee syalee *n.* ورزشيسيالي tournament

wasayil *n* وسايل equipment

wasayil *n* وسايل means

wasayil pa las warkawal *v.t* وسايل‌په‌لاس‌ورکول outfit

waseela *n.* وسيله resource

waseeyat kawal *v.t.* وصيت‌کول will

washarmeyga *! interj* اوشرمه! fie

waskat *n.* واسک vest

wasl kawal *v.t.* وصل‌کول connect

wasla *n.* وسله armament

wasla *n.* وسله weapon

wasla toon *n.* وسله‌تون armoury

wasla wal kawal *v.t.* وسله‌وال‌کول arm

waslatoon *n.* وسله‌تون arsenal

wasleen *n.* واسلين vaseline

wasley *n.* وسلي munitions

wast *a.* وسط middling

wastee *a.* وسطي median

waswas *n.* وسواس caprice

waswas *n.* وسواس melancholia

waswas *n.* وسواس melancholy

waswasee *a.* وسواسي capricious

waswasee *a.* وسواسي melancholic

waswasee *adj* وسواسي melancholy

watalay aw barjasta *a.* وتلیاو برجسته prominent

watalay; ramzee *a.* وتلي؛رمزي signal

watan *n* وان distance

watanee *n* وطني native

wawra *n.* واوره ice

wawra *n.* واوره snow

wawra wareydal *v.i.* واوره‌وريدل snow

wawreen *a.* واورين icy

wawreen *a.* واورين snowy

wayal *v.t.* ويل say

wayal *v.t.* ويل tell

wayand *n.* وياند spokesman

wayand; shmeyroonkay *n.* وياند، شمرونکی teller

wayay pa wayay *adv.* ويیپهويی verbatim

wayay; lughat *n.* ويی،لغت word

wayee panga; qamoos *n.* ويیپانه، قاموس vocabulary

waylon *n* وايلون fiddle

waylon ghagawal; apalti wayal *v.i* وايلونغول،اپلتويل fiddle

wayloon ghagoonkay *n.* ويلون غوونکی violinist

wayna *n.* ونا locution

wayna *n.* ونا oration

wayna kawana *n.* وناکوونه speech

wayna; bayan *n.* ونا،بيان parlance

wayna; khabara *n.* ونا،خبره say

waynawal *n.* وناوال orator

wayroos; da fasad tomna *n.* ويروس،دفسادتومنه virus

waza kawal; rol lobawal *v. t* وضع کول،رول لوبول enact

wazahat *n* وضاحت clarification

wazahat kawal *v. t* وضاحت کول clarify

wazan *n.* وزن gravity

wazan *n.* وزن weight

wazan kawal *v.t.* وزن کول weigh

wazan larana *n.* لرنه وزن weightage

wazan laroonkay *a* وزنلرونکی bulky

wazar *n.* وزر wing

wazar; banraka *n* وزر،بکه feather

wazarat *n.* وزارت ministry

wazay *a.* واضح obvious

wazda weeli kawana aw ghwarawana *n.* وازدهويلکوونه اوغووونه tallow

wazeefa; rol *n.* وظيفه،رول role

wazeer *n.* وزير minister

wazeh *a.* واضح intelligible

wazeh *a.* واضح patent

wazgar wakht teyrawal *v.i.* وزار وختترول loiter

wazhal *v.t.* وژل kill

wazhal *v.t.* وژل murder

wazhana *n.* وژنه homicide

wazhana *n.* وژنه kill

wazhana *n.* وژنه murder

wazhghona *n* وژغونه bristle

wazhoonkay *a.* وژونکی lethal

wazhoonkay *n.* وژونکی murderer

weeda *adv.* ويده asleep

weeda keydal *v.i.* ويدهکدل sleep

weejarawal *v. t* ويجاول destroy

weejarawal *v.t.* ويجاول raze

weejarawal *v.t.* ويجاول scourge

weejarawal *v.t.* ويجاول ruin

weejarawana *n* ويجاونه annihilation

weejaree *n* ويجاي destruction

weejaree *n.* ويجاي ruin

weekh *a.* ويخ alert

weekh *a* ويخ awake

weekhawal *v.t.* ويول arouse

weekhawal; weekheydal *v.t.* ويول،ويدل wake

weekheydal; weekhawal *v.t.* ويدل،ويول awake

weekhtob; sarani ta weekh pati keydana *n.* ويتوب،بارنتهوپياؤ كدنه vigilance

weekhwalay *n.* ويوالى alertness

weekhwalay *n* ويوالى wake

weeli keydal *v.i.* ويلكدل melt

weeli keydal *v.i* ويلكدل thaw

weeli keydana *n.* ويلكدنه fusion

weeli keydoonkay; halawoonkay *a.* ويلكدونكى؛حلوونكى solvent

weeli shaway *a.* ويليشوى molten

weena *n* وينه blood

weena lagay *n* وينهلي anaemia

weena toyawana *n* وينهتويونه bloodshed

weenayeez *a.* وينهييز sanguine

weeney ta nanawatalay chark *n.* وينتهننوتلىچرک sepsis

weeni keydal *v. i* وينكدل bleed

weenzal *v. t* وينل cleanse

weenzal *v.t.* وينل launder

weenzal *v.t.* وينل wash

weenzana *n.* وينه purification

weenzana *n* ويننه wash

weer *n* وير lament

weer *n* وير wail

weer kawal *v.i.* ويركول lament

weer kawal *v.i.* ويركول wail

weer laralay *a.* ويرللى wistful

weer laralay *a.* ويرللى tragic

weer larali peykha *n.* په ويرلل tragedy

weerawal; ghwarawal *v.i.* ويول، غوول spread

weerjan *a.* ويرجن woebegone

weeshtana; da booto rawataltya *n* ويشتنه؛دبووراوتلتيا shoot

weetameen *n.* ويامين vitamin

weeyareydal *v. i* ويلدل exult

wehem; khyal *n* وهم؛خيال fancy

wehem; khyal *n* وهم؛خيال figment

wehshee *a.* وحشي barbarous

wehshee insan *n.* وحشيانسان barbarian

wehsheetob *n.* وحشيتوب barbarism

wehsheeyana *a.* وحشيانه barbarian

wehsheeyana amal *n* وحشيانهعمل barbarity

werawonki *a.* ويروونكى ghastly

weykhta *n* وته hair

weyra *n* وره dread

weyra *n* وره fear

weyrawal *v.t* ورول dread

weyreydal *v.i* ورېدل fear

weyreydal *a.* ويريدل afraid

weyrowoonkay *a.* وروونكى fearful

weysh *n* وش distribution

weysh *n* وش division

weysh *n.* وش partition

weysh; takhsees *n.* وش؛تخصيص allotment

weyshal *v.t.* وشل apportion

weyshal *v.t.* وشل partition

weyshnal; zay pa zay kawal *v.t.* وشنل،ىپهماىكول scatter

weystana *n* وستنه elimination

wilayat *n.* ولايت province

wilayatee *a.* ولايتي provincial

woolas *n.* ولس public

woolas mashr *n.* ولس‌مشر president

woolaspal *n* ولسپال republican

woolaspala *a.* ولسپاله republican

woolaswakee *n* ولسواکي democracy

woolaswalee *n* ولسوالي district

wraga *n.* وره flea

wrakeydal *v. i* ورکدل disappear

wrakeydal *v.i.* ورکدل vanish

wraktob *n* ورکتوب disappearance

wrana rawrana; tag ratag *n.* ونه راونه،تراتگ traffic

wranawoonkay *n.* ورانوونکی wrecker

wranay; kharabay *n.* ورانی؛خرابی wrack

wrandeenay *a.* واندینی prior

wrandi *n.* واند precedent

wrandi sakha gooman *n.* واندسخه ومان presupposition

wrandi sakha gooman kawal *v.t.* واندسخه‌ومان‌کول presuppose

wranditob *n.* واندتوب precedence

wrankaray *a.* ورانکاری untoward

wrara *n.* وراره nephew

wray *n.* وری lamb

wrazanay *adv* ورځ adays

wrazanay *a.* ورځی workaday

wrazanay chari *n.* ورځچار routine

wreen *a.* ورین nice

wreentob *n.* ورینتوب nicety

wreet shaway *a* وریت‌شوی roast

wreeta shawi ghwakha *n* وریته‌شو غوه roast

wreetawal *v.t.* وریتول fry

wreetawal *v.t.* وریتول parch

wreetawal *v.t.* وریتول roast

wreez *n* وریز brow

wreykham *n.* ورم silk

wreykhmeen *a.* ورمین silken

wreykhmeen *a.* ورمین silky

wreyra *n.* وریره niece

wro wro chakar wahal *v.i.* ورو وروچکروهل stroll

wro wro eyshawal *v.t.* ورو ورو اشول stew

wro wro kamzoray kawal *v.t.* ورووورو کمزوری‌کول undermine

wro; sast *a* ورو؛سست slow

wroon; panday *n.* ورون؛پ thigh

wror *n* ورور brother

wror wazhana *n.* وژنه ورور fratricide

wrorwalee *n* ورورولي brotherhood

wrost *adj* وروست addle

wrosta *adv* وروسته after

wrosta la *adv.* وروسته‌له next

wrostanay *n* وروستنی last

wrostanay barkha *n.* وروستنی‌برخه rear

wrostay *a.* وروستی last1

wrusta la *prep.* وروسته‌له since

wrusta la *adv.* وروسته‌له thereafter

wrusta; badan *adv.* وروسته،بعد post

wrustanay tamzay *n.* وروستنی‌تمای terminus

wrustawal; kharabawal *v.t.* ورستول؛خرابول spoil

wurmeyg *n.* ورم nape

wuzeeyat; waqar *n* وضعيت،وقار poise

wuzgartob; rukhsatee *n.* وزارتوب،رخصتي vacation

wyala *n.* وياله brook

wyala *n.* وياله canal

wyala *n.* وياله stream

wyala *n.* وياله rivulet

wyareydal *v. t* ويامل cocker

wza *n.* وزه goat

yadakht *n.* يادت notation

yadakht *n.* يادت memoir

yadakht *n* يادت memorandum

yadakhtawal *v.t.* يادتول note

yadawaree *n* يادآوري anamnesis

yadgar *n.* يادار keepsake

yadgar *n.* يادار souvenir

yadgar *n.* يادار memorial

yadgaree *a.* يادارې monumental

yadgaree *a.* يادارې memorable

yadgaree dabar leek *a* يادارۍبر ليک memorial

yadgaree dabara *n.* يادارۍبره megalith

yadowana *n.* يادوونه mention

yag *n* يه bear

yahoodee *n.* يهودي Jew

yak shamba; yoonay *n.* يک‌شنبه، يوڼ Sunday

yakh *a* يخ chilly

yakh aw taza satana *n.* تازه او يخ ساتنه refrigeration

yakh satal *v.t.* يخ ساتل refrigerate

yakhchal *n.* يخچال fridge

yakhchal *n.* يخچال glacier

yakhchal *n.* يخچال refrigerator

yam (loomray kas; laka: za yam) يم(لومړی‌کس،لکه:زه‌يم) am

yana *n.* ينه liver

yaq dol salor araba beza bagai *n.* يوول‌لورارابه‌بيزه‌ب barouche

yaqeenan *adv.* يقيناً certainly

yaqeenee *a* يقيني certain

yaqoot *n.* ياقوت ruby

yar; shareek *n.* يار،شريک pal

yarghal *n.* يرغل raid

yarghal gar *n.* يرغل‌ر aggressor

yarghal kawal *v.t.* يرغل‌کول raid

yarghal rawral *v.t.* يرغل‌راول attack

yarghalgar *n* يرغلر offensive

yarghmal *n.* يرغمل hostage

yateem *n.* يتيم orphan

yateem kawal; yateem keydal *v.t* يتيم‌کول،يتيم‌کدل orphan

yateemano da astogni zay *n.* يتيمانو‌داستونای orphanage

yaw *a.* يو a

yaw *a.* يو one

yaw (laka yaw kas; yaw keetab) *art* يو(لکه‌يوکس،يوکتاب) an

yaw arkheez *a* يواخيز ex-parte

yaw aroopayee koochnay gharsa *n.* يواروپايي‌کوچنغره roe

yaw awaz larana *n* يوآوازلرنه monotony

yaw awazay *a.* يوآوازى
monotonous

yaw bal *a* يوبل another

yaw botal chi pa labratwar ki kareygee *n* يوبوتلچپهلابراتوارکه
کاري flask

yaw cheyri; pa kom zay ki *adv.*
يوچر،پهکومهایکه somewhere

yaw dandi sakha arzee bali dandi ta arawal *v.t.* يودندخه
عارضيبلادندتهاول second

yaw dawal; warta *a.* يوول؛ورته
alike

yaw dawl amreekayee gharsanay *v.i* يوولامريكاييغرۀ
mouse

yaw dawl bootay *n.* يوولبوی sage

yaw dawl bootay *n.* يوولبوی
mistletoe

yaw dawl bootay; parta la juftgeeray zeygeydalay *n* يو
ولبوی؛پرتهلهجفتيرزدلا agamist

yaw dawl chanrey *n.* يوولچ pea

yaw dawl chogha *n.* يوولچوغه
cloak

yaw dawl da dabaro skara *n.* يو
ولدبروسکاره lignite

yaw dawl da kheekhey botal *n.*
يوولديبوتل jar

yaw dawl darmal *n.* يوولدرمل
tincture

yaw dawl dastkash *n.* يوولدستکش
mitten

yaw dawl gaya chi zyar gulan laree *n.* يوولياچزيلانلري
dandelion

yaw dawl gharanay aw wehshee bakam laroonkay ghwayay *n*
يوولغرنياووحشيبكاملرونكی
غوايی bison

yaw dawl ghat mosh khurma *n.*
يوولغموشخرما mink

yaw dawl ghwakheen sas *n.* يوول
غوينساس pudding

yaw dawl gopee *n.* يوولوپی
broccoli

yaw dawl heelay *n.* يوولهيل
marionette

yaw dawl jakat *n.* يوولجاک
pullover

yaw dawl kab chi da kakhtay beykh pori nakhalee *n* يوول
کبچدکتبخپورنلي barnacles

yaw dawl keymyayee mada *n* يو
ولکمياييماده chlorine

yaw dawl khkulay koochnay khkaree spay *n.* يوولکلی
کوچنيکاريسپی terrier

yaw dawl khwaga *n.* يوولخواه
comfit

yaw dawl khwaga khwara *n.* يو
ولخواهخواه jelly

yaw dawl khwali *n* يوولخولا
bonnet

yaw dawl khwaranzay *n.* يوول
خونای canteen

yaw dawl koochnay goongata *n.*
يوولکوچنونه weevil

yawdawlkoochnaykhorakeekab *v.t.* يوولکوچنيخوراکيکب
smelt

yaw dawl koranay toora aw speena kawtara *n.* يوولکورۀ
تورهاوسپينهکوتره magpie

yaw dawl manra *n.* یوولمه
nonpareil

yaw dawl margha *n.* یوولمارغه
leghorn

yaw dawl naray spaka toora *n.*
یوولنرسپکهتوره rapier

yaw dawl pasta doday *n.* یوول
پستهو toast

yaw dawl patloon *n.* یوولپتلون
jean

yaw dawl qaseeda *n.* یوولقصیده
ballad

yaw dawl sandar bola marghay
n. یوولسندربولهمرغ warbler

yaw dawl saranay bootay *n.* یوول
سارانیبوی weed

yaw dawl sharab *n* یوولشراب
brandy

yaw dawl sharab *n.* یوولشراب
whisky

yaw dawl spay *n* یوولسپیbulldog

yaw dawl stara ghombasa *n.* یو
ولسترهغومبسه hornet

yaw dawl teyl *n.* یوولتل castor oil

yaw dawl treekh bootay *n.* یوول
تریخبوی wormwood

yaw dawl wana *n.* یوولونه birch

yaw dawl wana *n* یوولونه rush

yaw dawl wana *n.* یوولونه teak

yaw dawl wareen kalee *n.* یوول
وینکالي masquerade

yawdawlzalawarkawoonkimada
n. یووللاورکوونکماده varnish

yaw deyr star badanay kab *n.* ر یو
کب بدنی ستر whale

yaw dol botay che tal sheen we *n*
یوولبویچهتلشینوی ivy

yaw dol kab *n.* یوولکب herring

yaw hija *n.* یوهجا monosyllable

yaw hijayee kalma *a.* یوهجایيکلمه
monosyllabic

yaw kam miqdar *n* یوکممقدارless

yaw kar takrarawal *v.t.* یوکار
تکرارول reiterate

yaw kaseez wayna *n.* یوکسیزونا
monologue

yaw kaseeza sandara *n* یوکسیزه
سندره solo

yaw kawal *v.t.* یوکول incorporate

yaw kawal *v.t* یوکول link

yaw kawal *v.t.* یوکول unite

yaw kawana *n* یوکوونه weld

yaw kawang *n.* یوکوز unification

yaw keydana *n* کدنه یو coalition

yaw khas kaleeza *n.* یوخاصکلیزه
jubilee

yaw khas tarz ki sandara wayal
v.i. یوخاصطرزکسندرهویل
warble

yaw khyalee haywad *n.* یوخیالي
هواد utopia

**yaw lar nabatee aw heywanee
meykroboona** *n.* یولنباتياو
حوانيمکروبوونه bacteria

yaw loy samandaree kab *n.* یولوی
سمندريکب shark

yaw margha *n.* مارغه یو swan

yaw misree eenzar *n.* یومصرياینر
sycamore

yaw nawakht; dadman *a.*
یونواخت،امن steady

**yaw oogdey pkhey laroonkay
margha** *n.* یواودپلرونکيمارغه
stilt

yaw pa bal bandi takia *n.* يوپهبل باندتكيه interdependence

yaw pa bal bandi takia *a.* يوپهبل باندتكيه interdependent

yaw pa bal pasey ratlal *v.t.* يوپهبل پسراتلل alternate

yaw pa manz ki; motanawab *a.* يوپهمنز كي،متناوب alternate

yaw qeematee kanray *n.* يوقيمتي كانئ jade

yaw radyoekteef aw tashashee unsar *n.* يورايواكتيفاوتشعشعي عنصر radium

yaw rangarang khkulee rangoona laroonki mada chi ghamee tri joreygee *n.* يو رنارنكليرنونهلرونكمادهچغميتر جوي opal

yaw sa mooda *adv.* يوهموده awhile

yaw saat *n.* يوساعت hour

yaw samandaree sadaf *n.* يو سمندريصدف oyster

yaw seez; yaw shay *pron.* يويز،يو شی something

yaw shan *a* يوشان equitable

yaw shan *adv* يوشان alike

yaw shan. *a.* شان يو same

yaw shan kawal; jazab kawal *v.* يوشان كول؛جذب كول assimilate

yaw shaway *adj.* يوشوى corporate

yaw shaway *a.* يوشوى incorporate

yaw so *a* يو و few

yaw sok *n.* يووك somebody

yaw star topak *n.* يوستروپك cannon

yaw stargeez *a.* ستريز يو monocular

yaw stargeeza aynak *n.* يوستريزه عينك monocle

yaw unsar *n.* يوعنصر manganese

yaw unsar *n.* يوعنصر neon

yaw wahshee as *n.* يووحشيآس mustang

yaw walay *n.* يووالى unity

yaw warta ghag laroonkee toree sara da parla pasi kalmo peyleydal *v.* يوورتهغلرونكي توريسرهدپرلهپسكلموپيلدل alliterate

yaw zaharjana mada *n.* يوزهرجنه ماده nicotine

yaw zghastee syalee *n.* يوغاستي سيالي marathon

yaw zyat miqdar *n.* يوزياتمقدار multitude

yaw; tanha *n.* يو،تنها single

yawa dabareena panra *n.* يوهبرينه پله slate

yawa karkha ya lika ki darawana *n.* يوه كرهياليكهك درونه alignment

yawa khaza laroonkay *a.* يوهه لرونكى monogynous

yawa lor ta meelan laral *v.i.* يوه لورتهميلانلرل trespass

yawa mom dawla mada *n.* يوهموم ولهماده paraffin

yawa paysa; da amreeka sika *n.* يوهپسه؛دامريكاسكه penny

yawa qandee mada *n.* يوهقنديماده saccharin

yawa salor konja tota *n.* يوهلور كونجهوه pane

yawa sandarghari wara marghay *n.* يوهسندرغاوهمرغ wren

yawa sreykhnaka khoshbooya mada *n.* يوهسرناكهخوشبويهماده myrrh

yawa tal shna wana *n.* يوهتلشنهونه laurel

yawa tota *n.* يوموه monolith

yawa tota; laga barkha *n* يوموه،له برخه bit

yawazeenay; infiradee *a.* يوازينى؛ انفرادي solo

yawazey *a.* يواز alone

yawazeytob *n.* يوازتوب singularity

yawazi *a.* يواز lonely

yawazi *a.* يواز only

yawazi insan *n.* انسان يواز recluse

yawazi preykhodal *v.i.* يوازپرودل strand

yawazi tlal; yaw keydal *v.t.* يواز تلل؛يوكدل single

yawazi; tanha *a* يوازى؛تنها exclusive

yawazi; yaw kaseez *a.* يواز؛يوكسيز single

yawazitob *n.* يوازتوب celibacy

yawazitob *n.* يوازتوب individualism

yawazitob *n.* يوازتوب isolation

yawey khwa ta tlal *v.i.* يوخواتهتلل side

yawolas *n* يوولس eleven

yawoon *n.* يوون unit

yawrangwalay *n.* يورنوالى resemblance

yawrangwalay laral *v.t.* يورنوالى لرل resemble

yawshantob *n.* يوشانتوب parallelism

yawshanwalay *n.* يوشانوالى par

yawtob *n.* يوتوب oneness

yeywi *n.* ييو plough

yeywi shawi zmaka *n* ييوشومكه fallow

yeywi shawi zmaka *n.* ييوشومكه furrow

yoon; safar *n.* يون؛سفر tour

yoonanee *a* يونانى Greek

Z

za *pron.* زه I

zaboor *n.* زبور psalm

zabtawana *n* ضبطونه forfeiture

zaeef *a.* ضعيف infirm

zaeef kawal *v.t.* ضعيفكول depauperate

zafran *n.* زعفران saffron

zag kawal *v.t* كول foam

zag; kaf *n* ؛ كف foam

zagh zagh *n.* غزغ sizzle

zahar *n.* زهر poison

zahar *n.* زهر venom

zahar warkawal *v.t.* زهرورکول poison

zahar zad *n.* زهرضد mithridate

zaharjan *a.* زهرجن poisonous

zaharjan *a.* زهرجن venomous

zaharjan *a.* زهرجن virulent

zaharjantob; wayrooseetob *n.*
زهرجنتوب؛وىروسيتوب
virulence

zahid *a.* زاهد ascetic

zahid *a.* زاهد piteous

zahir; shakal *n.* ظاهر،شكل guise

zahiree banra *n* ظاهري به format

zahireydal *v.t* ظاهرلدل evolve

zahoor; banra *n* ظهور،به
appearance

zaka *conj.* كه because

zaka *conj.* كه so

zakha *n.* زخه wart

zakham *n.* زخم injury

zakham *n* زخم sore

zakheem kawal *v.i.* ضخيم كول
thicken

zakheera *n.* ذخيره stock

zakheera kawal *v.t.* ذخيره كول
stock

zala *n.* ‌اله nest

zala *n.* ‌لا glare

zala *n.* ‌لا radiation

zala jorawal *v.t.* ‌اله جوول nest

zala jorawal *v.i.* جوول ‌اله nestle

zala warkawal *v.t.* ‌لاوركول
varnish

zala; sapara *n.* ‌اله،پره cot

zaland *adv.* ‌لاند ablaze

zaland *a* ‌لاند bright

zaland *a.* ‌لاند candid

zaland *a.* ‌لاند glossy

zaland *a.* ‌لاند lustrous

zaland *a.* ‌لاند resplendent

zalanda *a* ‌لانده clear

zalanda kawal *v.t.* ‌لانده كول
illuminate

zalandtob *n* ‌لاندتوب clarity

zalaval *v.t.* ‌لول glaze

zaleydal *v.i* ‌لدل glare

zaleydal *v.t.* ‌لدل radiate

zaleydal; shuhrat payda kawal
v.t. ‌لدل؛شهرت پدا كول star

zaleydana *n* ‌لدنه flash

zalim *a* ظالم cruel

zalim *n.* ظالم oppressor

zalim jabir *n.* ظالم جابر tyrant

zalimana *a.* ظالمانه oppressive

zalmotay *n.* زلموى youngster

zalzala *n* زلزله earthquake

zama *pron.* زما mine

zama *a.* زما my

zaman mafhoom *v.t.* ضمن مفهوم
imply

zamanat *n.* ضمانت bail

zamanat *n.* ضمانت guarantee

zamanat *n.* ضمانت parole

zamanat *n.* ضمانت warrantee

zamanat *n.* ضمانت warranty

zamanat leek *n.* ضمانت ليك
voucher

zamanat warkawal *v.t* ضمانت
وركول guarantee

zamanat warkawal *v.i.* ضمانت
وركول vouch

zambeydal *v.i.* ‌مبدل lounge

zambeydal; rang rang tlal *v.i.*
نزتلل ‌مبدل؛ stagger

zambeydana *n.* ‌مبدنه stagger

zambeydana; ngokheydana *n.*
‌مبدنه؛نوldنه shuffle

zameema *n.* ضميمه appendix

zameema kawal; nakhlawal *v.t.* ضميمه کول،ننلول annex

zameena *n.* زمينه basis

zameena *n.* زمينه conspectus

zameena *n* زمينه context

zameena; da zmaki yawa tota *n.* زمينه،دمکيوهوه plot

zamin *n.* ضامن warrantor

zamoong *pron.* زموږ our

zamrod *n* زمرد emerald

zan dabalshakhseeyatpaseyra ganral *n.* ان دبل شخصيت پهرمل impersonation

zan ghokhtana *n* ان غوتنه egotism

zan khodana *n.* ان ودنه pretence

zan khodani pori arwand *a.* ان ودنپوراوند pretentious

zan larzawal *v.i.* ان لزول wince

zan leedana *n.* ان ليدنه arrogance

zan pak *n.* ان پاک towel

zan pasi kagal *v.t.* ان پسکال trail

zan raghondawal *v. i.* ان راغونول cringe

zan sara khwandee satal; zeyrga kawal *v.t.* ان سره خوندي ساتل؛ زرمه کول reserve

zan sara khwandee satana *n.* ان سره خوندي ساتنه reservation

zansarasatal *v.t.* ان سره ساتل retain

zan sara satal *v.t.* ان سره ساتل withhold

zan seyral *v.i.* ان سيرل introspect

zan seyrana *n.* ان سيرنه introspection

zanshatakawal *v.t.* ان شاته کول resign

zanshatakawal *v.t.* ان شاته کول retread

zan stayana *n.* ان ستاينه narcissism

zan ta rakkhal; mutasira kawal *v.t* ان ته راکل؛ متاثره کول fancy

zan tri satal *v.t.* ان تر ساتل shun

zan wazhna *n.* ان وژنه suicide

zan wazhnee *a.* ان وژني suicidal

zan zanee; fardee *n.* ان زاني؛ فردي individuality

zan; nafas *n.* ان؛ نفس self

zana *n.* زنه chin

zana *n.* زنا adulteration

zana karee *n.* زنا کاري adultery

zana kawal *v.t.* زنا کول adulterate

zanawar *n.* ناور animal

zanawar ya kaban neewalo lapara pa dam ki da khwaro mawad *n* ناور يا کبان نيولو لپاره په دام کد خورو مواد bait

zandan *n.* زندان cage

zandanee kawal *v.t.* زنداني کول imprison

zandaneetob *n.* زندانيتوب captivity

zandawal *v.t.* نول postpone

zandawal *v.t.* نول prorogue

zandawal; zandeydal *v.t. & i.* نول؛ ندل delay

zandaykawal *v. t.* زند کول choke

zanday kawal; khamoshawal *v.t.* زند کول؛ خاموشول stifle

zanday kawana *n.* زند کونه strangulation

zanday shaway *a.* زندشوى stuffy

zandeydalay *adj.* ندلى belated

zandeydalay *a.* ندلى late

zandeydalee poroona *n.pl.* ندلي پورونه arrears

zandeydaly *a.* ندل overdue

zanee; yawazi zan *a.* اني؛يوازان individual

zang *n* زن bell

zang *n.* زن rust

zang na akheystoonkay *a.* زننه اخستونکی stainless

zang wahal *v.t.* زنوهل ring

zang wahal *v.i* زنوهل rust

zang wahalay *a.* زنوهلی rusty

zang wahana *n.* زنوهنه rusticity

zangal *n* نل forest

zangal *n.* نل jungle

zangal *n.* نل woods

zangal jorawal *v.t.* نلجوول afforest

zangal meyshtay *a.* نلمشتی sylvan

zangal poha *n* نلپوهه forestry

zangal wan *n* وان نل forester

zangalee seema *n.* نليسيمه woodland

zangarana; takana *n.* اننه؛باکنه allocation

zangaray kawal *v.t.* انیکول allocate

zangaray kawal *v.t.* انیکول allot

zangaray sifat *n.* انیصفت attribute

zangari honaree zhaba *n.* انرهنري ژبه jargon

zangari jamey *n.* انجامه livery

zangari zhaba *n.* انژبه lingo

zanghwaray *a.* انغوای selfish

zango *n* زانو cradle

zankhkaray; batoo *a.* انکاری؛بلو vainglorious

zankhoday *a.* انودی proud

zanta kawal *v. t* انتهکول detach

zanza *n.* اهmillipede

zanza *n.* زنزه centipede

zanzeer *n* زنير chain

zaqoom *n.* زاقوم cactus

zar *n.* زر thousand

zar bawara *adj.* زرباوره credulity

zar kala *n.* زرکاله millennium

zar; beeranay *a* زر؛بینی early

zara *n* ذره mite

zara *n.* ذره molecule

zara *a.* ذره particle

zara *n.* ذره modicum

zarab *n.* ضرب multiplication

zarab kawal *v.t.* ضربکول multiply

zarabkhana *n.* ضرابخانه mint

zarafa *n.* زرافه giraffe

zarafat *n* ظرافت elegance

zarafat; da kanjkaway his *n* ظرافت؛دکنجکاوحس curiosity

zarakht *n* زت fray

zarakht *n.* زت senility

zarar *n* ضرر mischief

zararnak *a.* ضررناک baleful

zaratee *a.* زراعتي agrarian

zarawal; la moda lweydal *v.t.* زول؛لهموهلویدل stale

zarawee *a.* ذروي molecular

zaray *n.* زی seed

zaray kawal *v.t.* زارکول implore

zarb; wahana *n* ضرب،وهنه beat

zarba; goozar *n.* ضربه،بوزار stroke

zard aloo *n.* زردآلو apricot

zaree dozee *n.* زري‌دوزي fret

zaree dozee kawal *v.t.* زري‌دوزي كول fret

zaree kawal *v. t.* زاري‌كول entreat

zaree sheendal *v.t.* زي‌شيندل seed

zareeya *n* ذريعه medium

zarfeeyat *n* ظرفيت content

zargar *n.* زرر goldsmith

zargar *n.* زرر jeweller

zarghon; taza *a.* زرغون،تازه green

zarobay *n.* وبى cascade

zarobay *n.* وبى waterfall

zarooree *a* ضروري essential

zaroorere *a.* ضروري indispensable

zaroorere *a.* ضروري integral

zaroorere *a.* ضروري major

zaroorere *a* ضروري necessary

zaroorere shay *n.* ضروري‌شى necessary

zartoray kawoonkay *a.* زتورى كوونكى weary

zatee leywaltya *n.* ذاتي‌لوالتيا appetite

zawab *n* واب answer

zawab *n.* واب response

zawab warkawal *v.t* واب‌وركول answer

zawab warkawal *v.i.* وركول واب reply

zawab warkawal *v.i.* واب‌وركول respond

zawab warkawoonkay *n.* واب وركوونكى respondent

zawab; difa *n* واب،دفاع reply

zawabee tuhmat *n.* وابي‌تهمت counttercharge

zawal زوال decay

zawal *n* زوال decline

zawal moondal *v. t.* زوال‌موندل decline

zaweeya *n.* زاويه angle

zaweeya laroonkay *a.* زاويه‌لرونكى angular

zaweeyadar kawal *v.t.* زاويه‌دار كول crankle

zawqee kar *n* ذوقي‌كار fad

zay badlawal *v.t.* اى‌بدلول move

zay badlawal *v.t.* اى‌بدلول shift

zay laroonkay *a.* اى‌لرونكى spacious

zay laroonkay; hawadar *a.* اى لرونكى،هوادار roomy

zay nastay kawal *v.i.* اى‌ناستى‌كول sojourn

zay neewal *v.t.* اى‌نيول contain

zay neewal *v.t.* اى‌نيول replace

zay neewana; taweez *n.* اى‌نيوونه، تعويض replacement

zay takal *v.t.* اى‌كل locate

zay; iwaz *n.* اى،عوض lieu

zaya kawana *n.* ضايع‌كوونه waste

zaya; shar *a.* ضايع،شا waste

zayawal *v.t* ايول accommodate

zaybayish *n.* زبائش ornamentation

zaynastay *n.* ايناستى substitute

zaynastay *n.* ايناستى successor

zayqa *n.* ذايقه savour

zayqa *n.* ذايقه taste

zayqa laral *v.t.* ذايقه‌لرل taste

zaytoon n. زيتون olive

zaywar n. زور ornament

zda kawal v.i. زده‌كول learn

zda kawoonkay n. زده‌كوونكى learner

zda kawoonkay n. زده‌كوونكى pupil

zda kawoonkay n. زده‌كوونكى trainee

zdakra n. زده‌كه learning

zdakra kawal; lostal v.i. زده‌كه كول،لوستل study

zdakra; tarbeeyat n. زده‌كه،تربيت training

zdakro lapara malee mrasta; tehseel n. زده‌كولپاره‌مالى‌مرسته، تحصيل scholarship

zdakrotay; leesansa n. زدكوتى، ليسانسه graduate

zdakryal n. زدكيال student

zeen n. زين saddle

zeen ya kata eekhodal v.t. زين‌يا كته‌ايودل saddle

zeeni wakhtoona adv. ينى‌وختونه sometimes

zeeni; yaw shmeyr a. ين؛يوشمر some

zeep; kashak n. زيپ؛كشک zip

zeeyanman a. زيانمن inimical

zeeyar n زيار endeavour

zeeyar basal v.i زيارباسل endeavour

zeeyar kakh a زيار ك diligent

zeeyar kakh a. زيار ک industrious

zeg a. زِ hoarse

zehen; khyal n. ذهن؛خيال mind

zeher zid n. زهرضد antidote

zehmatawal v. t زحمتول bother

zehnee a. ذهنى mental

zehnee tawajo n. ذهنى‌توجه aptitude

zer kedal v.t. يركيدل gaze

zer zer katana n يريركتنه gaze

zeygantoon n. زنتون maternity

zeyganzay n. زناى womb

zeygeydal v. زييدل born

zeygeydalay adj. زدلى borne

zeygeydana n. زدنه birth

zeygeydana n. زدنه nativity

zeygowoonkay a. زوونكى reproductive

zeyr a ر careful

zeyr a. يِ yellow

zeyr khana n زرخانه cellar

zeyr rang n زِرنگ yellow

zeyr yaqoot n. زياقوت topaz

zeyr zeyr katal v.i. يريركتل stare

zeyramtoon n. زرمتون repository

zeyrawal v.t. زيول yellow

zeyray warkawal v.t زرى‌ور كول herald

zeyrbakhan a. زيبخن yellowish

zeyrmatoon n. زرمتون godown

zgeyrway; faryad n. زيروى،فرياد moan

zgeyrwee kawal v.i. زروي‌كول groan

zgeyrwee kawal v.i. زيروي‌كول moan

zghageydal v.i. غدل sizzle

zghaland nazar n. غلندنظر glance

zghaland nazar n. غلندنظر glimpse

zghaland nazar kawal *v.i.* غلندنظر كول glance

zghalawana *n.* غلوونه shove

zgham *n.* زغم tolerance

zghamal *v.t.* زغمل afford

zghamal *v.t.* زغمل tolerate

zghamal *v.t.* زغمل stomach

zghamal *v.t.* زغمل undergo

zghamoonkay *a.* زغمونكى tolerant

zghara *n.* زغره armour

zghara *n* زغره mail

zghara; wasla *n.* زغره،وسله armature

zghastoonkay *n.* غاستونكى runner

zhaba *n.* ژبه language

zhaba *n.* ژبه tongue

zhaba kawal; zhmana kawal *v.t.* ژبه كول،ژمنه كول undertake

zhabanay *a.* ژبنى lingual

zhabanay *a.* ژبنى oral

zhabanay *a* ژبنى viva-voce

zhabanay *a.* ژبنى wordy

zhabawar *a.* ژبئور articulate

zhabdood *n.* ژبدود grammar

zhabgharand *a.* ژبغاند talkative

zhabkhod *n.* ژبود grammarian

zhabpoh *n.* ژبپوه linguist

zhabpohan *n.* ژبپوهنه linguistics

zhabpohana *n.* ژبپوهنه philology

zhabpohand *n.* ژبپوهاند philologist

zhabpohaneez *a.* ژبپوهنيز linguistic

zhabpohani pori arwand *a.* ژبپوهنى اوند پور philological

zhama *n.* ژامه jaw

zhamanay *a.* ژمنى wintry

zhamay *n.* ژمى winter

zhamay teyrawal *v.i* ترول ژمى winter

zhanrkay *n.* ژكى youth

zhar stareydoonkay *a* ژر ستريدونكى rank

zhar tar zhara *adv.* ژره تر ژر instantly

zhar teyreydoonkay *a.* ژرتريدونكى fugitive

zhar teyreydoonkay *a.* ژرتريدونكى momentary

zhar teyreydoonkay; mutadee fayl *n.* ژرتريدونكى؛متعديفعل transitive

zharal *v.i.* ژل weep

zharghonay *a.* ژغونى tearful

zhawar *a.* ژور deep

zhawar *a.* ژور steep

zhawar dand *n* ژور نـ abyss

zhawar fikra; roonr anda *a.* ژور فكره،رو آنده profound

zhawara *n.* ژوره snail

zhawarghalay; kasa *n.* ژورغالى، كاسه socket

zhawartya *n* ژورتيا depth

zhawlan *a* ژاولن elastic

zhay *n.* ژ brink

zhay *n.* ژ rim

zhbara *n.* ژباه translation

zhbaral *v.t.* ژبال translate

zhbaran *n.* ژبان interpreter

zhbarana kawal *v.t.* ژبانه كول interpret

zheyrwee *n* زروى ژروى groan

zghamal *v.t.* زغمل endure

zghoral *v.i.* ژغورل guard

zghoral *v.t.* ژغورل protect

zghoral *v.t.* ژغورل save

zghorana *n.* ژغورنه protection

zghorandoy *n.* ژغورندوی saviour

zghorandoy *a.* ژغورندوی protective

zghoroonkay *n.* ژغورونکی protector

zghoroonkay; satoonkay *n.* ژغورونکی،ساتونکی guard

zhman plar ya mor *n.* ژمنپلاریا مور sponsor

zhmana *n.* ژمنه onus

zhmana matawal *v.i.* ژمنهماتول perjure

zhmana matawana *n.* ژمنهماتوونه perjury

zhmana matawana *n.* ژمنهماتوونه treason

zhmana; moahida *n.* ژمنه،معاهده compact

zhmna; taroon *n.* ژمنه،تون covenant

zhobanr *n.* ژوب zoo

zhoblawal *v.t.* ژوبلول hurt

zhopoh *n.* ژوپوه zoologist

zhopohana *n.* ژوپوهنه zoology

zhopohani pori arwand *a.* ژوپوهـ پوراوند zoological

zhowal *v. t* ژوول chew

zhowali khabari *v.i.* ژوولخبر mutter

zhowali khabari kawal *v.i.* ژولاخبر کول mumble

zhranda *n.* ژرنده mill

zhranda kawal *v.t.* ژرندهکول mill

zhrandagaray *n.* ژرندی miller

zhwand *n* ژوند life

zhwand *n.* ژوند subsistence

zhwand kawal *v. i* ژوندکول dwell

zhwand kawal *v.i.* ژوندکول live

zhwand kawal *v.i.* ژوندکولsubsist

zhwand leek *n* ژوندلیک biography

zhwand leek leekoonkay *n* ژوند لیکلیکونکی biographer

zhwand pohana *n* ژوندپوهنه biology

zhwand pohand *n* ژوندپوهاند biologist

zhwand warbakhal *v. t.* ژوندوربل enliven

zhwand warkawal; zhwand warbakhal *v.t.* ژوندورکول، ژوندوربخل animate

zhwanday *a.* ژوندی animate

zhwanday *a.* ژوندی live

zhwanday *a.* ژوندی living

zhwanday kawal *v.t.* ژوندیکول vitalize

zhwanday mawjood *n.* ژوندی موجود wight

zhwanday pati keydal *v.i.* ژوندی پاتکدل survive

zhwanday satal *v. t* ژوندیساتل conserve

zhwanday wajood *n.* ژوندیوجود organism

zhwanday; sarshar *a* ژوندی، سرشار alive

zhwandoon *n* ژوندون living

zid aw naqeez *n.* ضداونقيض antonym

zid; makoos *a.* ضد؛معكوس reverse

ziddi hamoozat *adj.* ضدحموضت antacid

zikar *n.* ذكر mediation

zikar kawal *v.t.* ذكركول meditate

zikar kawal *v.t.* ذكركول mention

zima war *a.* ذمهوار responsible

zima waree *n.* واري ذمه responsibility

zimnee qanoon; seemayeez qanoon *n.* ضمني‌قانون؛سيمه‌ييز قانون bylaw, bye-law

zimnee; arkheez *a.* ضمني؛اخيز tacit

zmaka *n* مكه earth

zmaka *n.* مكه land

zmaka da kakht lapara tayarawal *v.t.* مكه‌دكت‌لپاره تيارول till

zmaka yeywi kawal *v.i* مكه‌ييوكول plough

zmakmeyshtay hashra khor *n.* مكمشتى‌حشره‌خور toad

zmakmeyshtay shamshatay *n.* مكمشته‌شمشته tortoise

zmakpeyzhand *n.* مكپژاند geologist

zmakpeyzhandana *n.* مكپژندنه geology

zmakpoh *n.* مكپوه geographer

zmakpohana *n.* مكپوهنه geography

zmaray *n.* زمر lioness

zmaray *n* زمرى lion

zof *n.* ضعف infirmity

zolana *n* زولنه fetter

zolanay *n* زولانى anklet

zolanay warachawal *v.t* زولا وراچول fetter

zoq; khwand *n* ذوق؛خوند relish

zor *n* زور compulsion

zor *a.* زو aged

zor achawal *v.t* زوراچول accentuate

zor azmoyal *v.i.* زورآزمويل wrestle

zor halat ta staneydal *v.i.* زوحالت تهستندل relapse

zor karawal *v.t* زوركارول force

zortokarpeywandawal *v.t.* زووكر پوندول rag

zor warkawal; takhta kawal *v.t.* زورورکول؛تخته‌كول press

zor zyatay *n.* زورزياتى tyranny

zor zyatay *n.* زورزياتى stricture

zor zyatay *n.* زورزياتى violence

zor; istaydad *n.* زور؛استعداد potential

zor; khwa badowana *n.* ؛ور، خوابدوونه nuisance

zor; matbooat *n* زور؛مطبوعات press

zor; pata shaway *a.* زو؛پاته‌شوى stale

zorandawal *v. t* وندول dangle

zorawal *v.t.* ورول annoy

zorawal *v. t* ورول bedevil

zorawana *n.* ورونه annoyance

zorawar *adj.* زورور mighty

zorawar *a.* زورور strong

zordar *a* زوردار emphatic

zoreydal; zghamal *v.t.* وردل؛ زغمل suffer

zoreydalay shakhs *n.* وردلیشخص nag

zorowoonkay *a.* ووروونکی injurious

zorwaka *a* زورواکه autocratic

zoy *n.* زوی son

zra *n.* زه heart

zra keydal *v.t.* زهکدل aspire

zra keydal *v.i.* زهکدل yearn

zra khoogee *n.* زهخوي pity

zra matawal *v. t* زهماتول dishearten

zra na zra keydal *v.i.* زهنازهکدل hesitate

zra na zratob *n.* زهنازهتوب hesitation

zra nazra keydal *v.i.* زهنازهکدل waver

zra nazra keydal *v.i.* زهنازهکدل vacillate

zra nazratob kawal *v.i.* زهنازهتوب کول shilly-shally

zra rahaskeydana *n.* زهراهسکدنه nausea

zra rakhkoonay *a.* زهراکونی winsome

zra rakkhal *v.t.* زهراکل attract

zra rakkhana *n.* زهراکنه attraction

zra rakkhowoonkay; jalabowoonkay *a.* زه راکوونکی؛جلبوونکی attractive

zra saway kawal *v. t* زهسویکول commiserate

zra saway; rehem *n.* زهسوی؛رحم mercy

zra seyzal *v.t.* زهسزل pity

zra swanday *n* زهسواندي compassion

zra swanday *a.* زهسواندی pitiful

zra ta nazhdey *a* زهتهنژد darling

zra torowoonkay *a.* زهتوروونکی loathsome

zra tri wral *v. t* زهترول enchant

zra war *a.* ور زه bold

zra war *a.* ور زه courageous

zra wartob *n.* زهورتوب courage

zra wartya *n* زهورتیا boldness

zra wartya warkawal *v. t.* ورتیا زه ورکول embolden

zra wral *v.t* زهول fascinate

zra wrana *n.* زهونه fascination

zraswand *a.* زسواند sympathetic

zratoray *a.* زتوری reluctant

zrawar *a.* زهور chivalrous

zrawar sarteyray *n* زهورسرتری chevalier

zrawar; garam *n* زور؛رم stalwart

zrawartob *n.* زهورتوب chivalry

zubanee yadawal *v. t* زبانيیادول cram

zukam *n.* زکام influenza

zulam *n.* ظلم oppression

zulam kawal *v.t.* ظلمکول molest

zulam kawal *v.t.* ظلمکول oppress

zulam zyatay *n.* ظلمزیاتی molestation

zulm *n* ظلم cruelty

zwag *n* و clamour

zwag *n.* و noise

zwag jorawal *v. i.* زوگجوجوول clamour

zwag kawal *v.t.* وکول murmur

zwak warbakhal *v.t.* واکوربل reinforce

zwak warbakhana *n.* واکوربنه reinforcement

zwakman *a* واکمن sovereign

zwan *a.* وان young

zwan halak *n.* وانهلک lad

zwana najlay *n.* نجلوانه lass

zwanaka *n* وانکه acne

zwanaka *n.* وانکه chit

zwar ghwagay babar spay *n.* و غوىببرسپى spaniel

zwaranda kangal shawi wawra *n.* ونده کنل شوى واوره icicle

zwarandawal *v.t.* وندول hang

zyadakht *n.* زيادت augmentation

zyadakht *n* زيادت increase

zyadakht *n.* زيادت superfluity

zyan *n.* زيان loss

zyan arowoonkay *a.* زياناوونکى pernicious

zyanawal *v.i* زيانول abort

zyar *n* زيار struggle

zyar *n.* زير pale

zyar kakh *a.* زيارک trying

zyar kakhal *v.i.* زيارکل strive

zyar kakhal *v.i.* زيارکل struggle

zyarat; haj *n.* زيارت؛حج pilgrim

zyarat; haj *n.* زيارت؛حج pilgrimage

zyaratzay *n.* زيارتاى shrine

zyat *a* زيات abundant

zyat *n* زيات accessory

zyat *a* زيات excess

zyat *n.* مقدار زيات heap

zyat *a* زيات much

zyat bar *n* زيات بار overload

zyat barawal *v.t.* زيات بارول overburden

zyat barawal *v.t.* زيات بارول overload

zyat darmal khwaral *n.* زيات درمل خول overdose

zyat darmal khwaral *v.t.* زيات درمل خول overdose

zyat diqat *n.* زيات دقت subtlety

zyat ghageydal *v.i.* غدل زيات prattle

zyat kach *n.* زيات کچ plenty

zyat kar *n.* زيات کار overwork

zyat kar kawal *v.t.* زيات کار کول outdo

zyat kar kawal *v.t.* زيات کار کول overact

zyat kar kawal *v.t.* زيات کار کول overdo

zyat khalk *n.* زيات خلک throng

zyat khorak khwarana *n.* زيات خوراک خونه gluttony

zyat khorak; marakht *n* زيات خوراک؛مت glut

zyat khoshala *a* زيات خوشاله overjoyed

zyat lagakht *n* زيات لت overcharge

zyat lagakht kawoonkay *n.* زيات لت کوونکى spendthrift

zyat lagakht rawastal *v.t.* زيات لت راوستل overcharge

zyat miqdar warkawal *v.t* زيات مقدار ورکول heap

zyat na zyat *n* زيات نه زيات maximum

zyat peychal *v.t.* زيات پچل overlap

zyat sara nakhleydalay *n* زيات سره نندلی overlap

zyat shmeyr *n.* زياتشمر multiplicity

zyat tar *a.* زياتتر most

zyat warakht *n* زياتورت downpour

zyat zaleydal *v.t.* زياتزلدلoutshine

zyata gata kawal *v.i.* زياته کول profiteer

zyata parakhtya moondal *v.t.* زياتهپراختياموندل outgrow

zyata stayana kawal *v. t.* زياته ستاينه کول extol

zyatawal *v.t.* زياتول add

zyatawal *v.t.* زياتول augment

zyatawal *v.t.* زياتول increase

zyatee kawal *v.t* زياتی کول exceed

zyateyda *n.* زياتدا proliferation

zyateydal *v.i.* زياتدل abound

zyateydal *v.i.* زياتدل preponderate

zyateydal *v.i.* زياتدل proliferate

zyattara *adv.* زياتره most

zyattara *adv* زياتره much

zyatwalay *n.* زياتوالی preponderance

zyatwalay *n.* زياتونه addition

10 x 3

30